Why Do You Need This New Edition?

If you're wondering why you should buy this new edition of *Community Psychology*, here are six good reasons!

1. Inclusion of newly derived "principles to guide" community research and action (from the Society for Community Research and Action).
2. Major updating of all chapters. New findings and reports provide constructive critique and new directions for community interventions.
3. New chapter on Stress, Coping, Social Support, and Resilience.
4. More ecological and preventive orientation throughout the text.
5. Examination of community psychology perspectives in various systems (mental health, physical health, youth settings and schools, law, work settings, social services, and public health).
6. Vastly increased coverage of racial, ethnic, and global issues facing today's communities.

PEARSON

FOURTH EDITION

COMMUNITY PSYCHOLOGY

JOHN MORITSUGU
Pacific Lutheran University

FRANK Y. WONG
Georgetown University

KAREN GROVER DUFFY
State University of New York, Geneseo

Allyn & Bacon

Boston ■ New York ■ San Francisco
Mexico City ■ Montreal ■ Toronto ■ London ■ Madrid ■ Munich ■ Paris
Hong Kong ■ Singapore ■ Tokyo ■ Cape Town ■ Sydney

Acquisitions Editor: *Michelle Limoges*
Editorial Assistant: *Paige Clunie*
Marketing Manager: *Nicole Kunzmann*
Production Editor: *Pat Torelli*
Editorial Production Service: *TexTech International*
Manufacturing Buyer: *JoAnne Sweeney*
Electronic Composition: *TexTech International*
Cover Administrator: *Kristina Mose-Libon*

Copyright © 2010, 2003, 2000, 1996 Pearson Education, Inc., publishing as Allyn & Bacon, 75 Arlington Street, Suite 300, Boston, MA 02116.

All rights reserved. Manufactured in the United States of America. No part of the material protected by this copyright notice may be reproduced or utilized in any form or by any means, electronic or mechanical, including photocopying, recording, or by any information storage and retrieval system, without written permission from the copyright owner.

To obtain permission(s) to use material from this work, please submit a written request to Pearson Higher Education, Rights and Contracts Department, 501 Boylston Street, Suite 900, Boston, MA 02116, or fax your request to 617-671-3447.

Library of Congress Cataloging-in-Publication Data

Moritsugu, John.
   Community psychology / John Moritsugu, Frank Y. Wong, Karen Grover Duffy.—4th ed.
     p. cm.
   Rev. ed. of: Community psychology / Karen Grover Duffy, Frank Y. Wong. 3rd ed. c2003.
   Includes bibliographical references and index.
   ISBN-13: 978-0-205-62771-4 (alk. paper)
   ISBN-10: 0-205-62771-4 (alk. paper)
   1. Community psychology.   I. Wong, Frank Y.   II. Duffy, Karen Grover.
III. Duffy, Karen Grover. Community psychology.   IV. Title.
RA790.55.D84 2010
362.2'2—dc22   2008053690

10 9 8 7 6 5 4 3 2 1   HAM   13 12 11 10 09

Allyn & Bacon
is an imprint of

PEARSON

www.pearsonhighered.com

ISBN-10: 0-205-62771-4
ISBN-13: 978-0-205-62771-4

CONTENTS

Preface   xv
About the Authors   xix

PART I   INTRODUCTORY CONCEPTS

CHAPTER ONE
Introduction   1

HISTORICAL BACKGROUND   3

WHAT IS COMMUNITY PSYCHOLOGY? WHAT IS A COMMUNITY PSYCHOLOGIST?   7

FUNDAMENTAL PRINCIPLES   8
- Respect for Diversity   8
- The Importance of Context and Environment   10
- Empowerment   11
- The Ecological Perspective/Multiple Levels of Intervention   12
  - CASE IN POINT 1.1   Clinical Psychology, Community Psychology: What's the Difference?   15

OTHER CENTRAL CONCEPTS   16
- Prevention Rather Than Treatment   16
- Emphasis on Strengths and Competencies   18
  - CASE IN POINT 1.2   Does Primary Prevention Work?   19
- Social Change and Action Research   20
- Interdisciplinary Perspectives   21
  - CASE IN POINT 1.3   Social Psychology, Community Psychology, and Homelessness   22
- A Psychological Sense of Community   23

COMMUNITY PSYCHOLOGY TODAY   25

RESEARCH   25

WHAT'S IN IT FOR YOU?   26
- Undergraduate Education   26
- Advanced Training in Community Psychology   28

PLAN OF THE BOOK   30

SUMMARY   30

CHAPTER TWO
Scientific Research Methods 31

THE ESSENCE OF SCIENTIFIC RESEARCH   32
    Why Do Scientific Research?   33
    What Is Scientific Research?   34
        Theory   34
        Models and Paradigms   35
        Falsifiability   36
        Example   36
        Scientific Revolutions   36
        CASE IN POINT 2.1   A Theory of Substance Abuse and HIV/STDs That Incorporates the Principles of Community Psychology   37
    The Fidelity of Scientific Research   39

TRADITIONAL SCIENTIFIC RESEARCH METHODS   41
    Population and Sampling   41
    Correlational Research   42
    Experimental Research   42
    Quasi-Experimental Research   44

OTHER RESEARCH METHODS USED IN COMMUNITY PSYCHOLOGY   44
    Ethnography   44
    Network Analysis   46
        CASE IN POINT 2.2   Case Study of a Consumer Run Agency   46
        CASE IN POINT 2.3   Cracking the Network   47
    Epidemiology   47
    Needs Assessment and Program Evaluation   48
    Participatory Research   51

THE URGENCY OF RESEARCH IN COMMUNITY PSYCHOLOGY AND RELATED PITFALLS   52
    The Politics of Science and the Science of Politics   52
    Ethics: Cultural Relativism or Universal Human Rights?   53
    The Continuum of Research: The Value of Multiple Measures   55
    The Importance of Cultural Sensitivity   55
    Community Researchers as Consultants   56

SUMMARY   58

CHAPTER THREE
Stress and Resilience   59

THE STRESS MODEL AND THE DEFINITION OF COMMUNITY PSYCHOLOGY   60

STRESS   61
- The Stress Reaction   61
- Stressor Events   62
    - *Acute versus Chronic Stress*   62
    - *Racism and Minority Status: An Example of Stressful Social Contexts*   63
- Stress as a Process   63
    - **CASE IN POINT 3.1**   Contemporary Racism   64
- Coping   65
    - *Emotion-Focused and Problem Solving–Focused Coping*   65
    - *Active and Avoidant Coping*   65
    - *Emotional Approach Coping*   66
    - *Three Dimensions of Coping*   66
    - *Collectivist Coping*   66
    - *A Schema for Coping*   66
- Social Support   67
    - *Types of Social Support*   68
    - *Buffering and Additive Effects*   68
    - **CASE IN POINT 3.2**   Mexican American College Student Acculturation Stress, Social Support, and Coping   69

RESILIENCE   70
- At-Risk to Resilient   70
- The Kauai Longitudinal Studies   71
- A Useful Model   71
- The Fourth Wave   72

SUMMARY   73

PART II   SOCIAL CHANGE AND INTERVENTION STRATEGIES

CHAPTER FOUR
The Importance of Social Change   75

REASONS FOR SOCIAL CHANGE   77
- Diverse Populations   77
- The Perception of Declining or Scarce Resources   78
    - **CASE IN POINT 4.1**   Funding Dilemmas for Nonprofit Organizations   79

Accountability 80
Knowledge-Based and Technological Change 81
Community Conflict 82
Dissatisfaction with Traditional Services 82
 CASE IN POINT 4.2 Community Conflict: Adversity Turns to Opportunity 83
Desire for Diversity of Solutions 83

TYPES OF SOCIAL CHANGE 85

Spontaneous or Unplanned Social Change 85
Planned Social Change 88
Issues Related to Planned Change 88

DIFFICULTIES BRINGING ABOUT CHANGE 90

SUMMARY 93

CHAPTER FIVE
Community Intervention Strategies 95

CREATING PLANNED CHANGE 96

CITIZEN PARTICIPATION 97

 CASE IN POINT 5.1 The Community Development Society 97
Who Participates? 99
Advantages and Disadvantages of Citizen Participation 101

NETWORKING 103

 CASE IN POINT 5.2 Online Networks for Ethnic Minority Issues 104
Issues Related to Networks 105
Advantages and Disadvantages of Networks 105

CONSULTATION 106

Issues Related to Consultants 107
Advantages and Disadvantages of Consultants 107

EDUCATION AND INFORMATION DISSEMINATION 109

Issues Related to Information Dissemination 109
Advantages and Disadvantages of Educational Change 111

PUBLIC POLICY 112

 CASE IN POINT 5.3 Rape Crisis Centers: A National Examination 113
Issues Related to the Use of Public Policy 114
Advantages and Disadvantages of Public Policy Changes 116
A Skill Set for Practice 117

SUMMARY 118

PART III COMMUNITY PSYCHOLOGY APPLIED TO VARIOUS SETTINGS

CHAPTER SIX
The Mental Health System   119

EPIDEMIOLOGICAL ESTIMATES OF MENTAL ILLNESS   120

MODELS OF MENTAL HEALTH AND MENTAL DISORDER   121
- The Medical Model   121
- The Psychoanalytic Model   122
    - *Freud*   122
    - *Adler*   123
- The Behavioral Model: The Social-Learning Approach   123
- The Humanistic Model   124
    - **CASE IN POINT 6.1**   Mental Health Care Professionals   125

THE EVOLUTION OF THE MENTAL HEALTH SYSTEM   126
- Brief History of Mental Health Care   126
    - **CASE IN POINT 6.2**   Rosenhan's Study of Hospital Patients' Stigmatization   129
- Deinstitutionalization   130
- The Social Context to Deinstitutionalization   131
- Early Alternatives to Institutionalization   135
- Measuring "Success" of Deinstitutionalized Persons   135

BEYOND DEINSTITUTIONALIZATION   137
- Model Programs for Individuals with Mental Disorders   137
    - *Lodge Society*   138
- Intensive Case Management   138
    - *Assertive Community Treatment*   138
    - *Wraparound Milwaukee*   140

THE BATTLE CONTINUES: WHERE DO WE GO FROM HERE?   141

SUMMARY   143

CHAPTER SEVEN
Social and Human Services in the Community   145

HISTORICAL NOTES ABOUT SOCIAL WELFARE IN WESTERN SOCIETY   147
- **CASE IN POINT 7.1**   Poverty in America   147
- **CASE IN POINT 7.2**   The Grameen Bank   150

SPECIFIC SOCIAL ISSUES AND SOCIAL SERVICES   151

 Child Maltreatment   151
  Scope of the Issue   *152*
  Causes of Maltreatment   *154*
  Prevention Programs   *155*
 Teen Pregnancy   157
  Scope of the Issue   *157*
  Causes of Teen Pregnancy   *157*
  Prevention Programs   *158*
  Secondary Prevention: Working with Pregnant Teens   *162*
 The Elderly   163
  Scope of the Issue   *163*
  Prevention Programs   *164*
 Homelessness   166
  Scope of the Issue   *166*
  CASE IN POINT 7.3   How Do Cultures Differ on the Issue of Homelessness?   168
  Causes of Homelessness   *169*
  Prevention Programs   *170*

SUMMARY   172

CHAPTER EIGHT
Schools, Children, and the Community   174

THE EARLY CHILDHOOD ENVIRONMENT   175

 Child Care   176
  Necessity for Child Care   *177*
  Effects of Child Care   *177*
  Plans for the Child Care Dilemma   *179*
 Enrichment Education and Early Intervention   180

THE PUBLIC SCHOOLS   184

 Desegregation, Ethnicity, and Prejudice in the Schools   184
  The Historical Context   *184*
  Prejudice and Its Companions   *185*
  Fostering Acceptance of Diversity in the Classroom   *186*
  Effects of Desegregation   *189*
 The Schools and Adolescents   190
  The School Climate   *190*
  CASE IN POINT 8.1   Students' Memories of Public School   192
  Other Factors Related to School Success or Failure   *193*

Dropping Out of School   194
School Violence   196
    CASE IN POINT 8.2   Children of Divorce   199

SUMMARY   200

CHAPTER NINE
Law, Crime, and the Community   202

THE TRADITIONAL JUSTICE SYSTEM   204
    Introduction   204
    Crime and Criminals   205
        CASE IN POINT 9.1   Neighborhood Youth Services   207
    The Prisons   208
    Victims and Fear of Being Victimized   210
    Enforcement Agencies   212

ADDRESSING JUSTICE SYSTEM ISSUES WITH COMMUNITY PSYCHOLOGY   213
    Primary Prevention   214
        Prevention with At-Risk Individuals   214
        CASE IN POINT 9.2   Working with At-Risk Youth   215
        Designing the Environment to Prevent Crime   217
    Secondary Prevention   219
        Early Assistance for Crime Victims   219
        Crisis Intervention for Victims   220
        Restorative Justice Programs   221
        Reintegration Programs for Incarcerated Individuals   223

SUMMARY   226

CHAPTER TEN
The Health Care System   228

THE AMERICAN HEALTH CARE SYSTEM   229
    National Health Indicators   229
    Observations on the System   231
        Cost and Access   232
        Adherence and Compliance   233

COMMUNITY PSYCHOLOGY AND THE HEALTH CARE SYSTEM   234
    Prevention over Remediation   235
    Shifting Focus from Individuals to Groups, Neighborhoods, and Systems   235

Building Systems   236
Increasing Accessibility   237
   Timely Interventions   237
   CASE IN POINT 10.1   Teen Pregnancy Prevention   238
   Dealing with Diverse Communities   239
   Rural Health   240
Social Support and Health   240

SUMMARY   241

CHAPTER ELEVEN
Community Health and Preventive Medicine   242

TOBACCO   244
   Extent of the Problem   244
   Antitobacco Efforts   246
   Community-Based Approaches   248

ALCOHOL   249
   Extent of the Problem   249
   Alcohol Safety Laws   250
   A Community Psychology Approach   251

ILLICIT DRUGS   252
   Extent of the Problem   252
   Possible Solutions and Challenges   253
      CASE IN POINT 11.1   Prescription Drug Misuse: Risk Factors for Problem Users   254

SEXUALLY TRANSMITTED DISEASES   255
   Extent of the Problem   255
   Possible Solutions and Challenges   257

HIV AND AIDS   259
   Overview   259
   Extent of the Problem   260
   Complexities and Controversies   263
   Possible Solutions: Community-Based Approaches   264
      CASE IN POINT 11.2   Evaluation and Implementation of STD/HIV Community Intervention Program in Lima, Peru   265
      CASE IN POINT 11.3   The Bilingual Peer Advocate (BPA) Program   266

SUMMARY   266

CHAPTER TWELVE
Community/Organizational Psychology   269

WHAT DO ORGANIZATIONAL AND COMMUNITY PSYCHOLOGY SHARE?   271
    CASE IN POINT 12.1   Smart Car Sales Personnel   272

EVERYDAY ORGANIZATIONAL ISSUES   273
    Stress   274
    Burnout   274
    Organizational Culture   275
    Other Ecological Conditions   278
        CASE IN POINT 12.2   Dealing with a Diverse Workforce   278

TRADITIONAL TECHNIQUES FOR MANAGING ORGANIZATIONS   279
    Compensation Packages   279
    Rules and Regulations   280

OVERVIEW OF ORGANIZATIONAL CHANGE   281
    Reasons for Change   281
    Issues Related to Organizational Change   281

CHANGING THE ORGANIZATION   282
    Leadership   282
    Reorganization   283
    Quality of Work Life Programs   284
    Team Building   286

HELPING INDIVIDUALS CHANGE WITHIN THE ORGANIZATION   287
    Burnout and Stress   287
    Health Maintenance Issues: Smoking Cessation Example   289

SUMMARY   289

PART IV   WHERE TO FROM HERE?

CHAPTER THIRTEEN
The Future of Community Psychology   291

THE ESTABLISHMENT OF INSTITUTIONAL MARKERS   292

GROWING BEYOND NATIONAL BOUNDARIES   293

COMMENTARIES   294

ANSWERING THE PRESENT AND FUTURE NEEDS OF SOCIETY   297
    Appreciation for Differences and the Search for Compassion   298
    Environmental Concerns   298
    Disparities in Opportunity for Health, Education, and Economic Success   299
    Aging and End of Life   300

SUMMARY   301

FINAL REFLECTIONS   301

References   303
Name Index   363
Subject Index   379

PREFACE

Community psychology deals with the very best of our human tendencies—to care for and nurture each other through life's adversities, bond with others, and value our linkages to one another. As community psychologists, we are interested in how our collective efforts and the social contexts that we construct aid in protecting us from negative events and promoting our well-being (Cowen, 2000; Shinn & Toohey, 2003). We present what the field is doing presently, how it has been formed, and its potential for creating what could be. We feel that we have summarized the work in community psychology in a manner that is both understandable and engaging, telling a tale of theory development and research and providing examples of its use to better the community. Community interventions in a variety of settings are reviewed, and the research on these interventions elaborated.

One reason to study psychology is because one is curious about one's self and other human beings. We have tried to build on this basic curiosity by providing an opening story to each chapter. This story presents a theme or issue that is realized through the explanation of community concepts or interventions. There are also examples of applications within the chapters, called "Cases in Point," so that readers might see how the research or theory brings about action in the real world. At its core, community psychology wants to bring about a better world. Though guided by science and research, the community psychologist is a person who is in the field, using what has been discovered about communities and how they function. The curiosity we have about our social world is put to good use.

The text is divided into four sections. The first provides the historical, theoretical, and research framework for the field. We present the political, historical, and psychological research context that contributed to the start of community psychology in America as well as its guiding principles. We describe the scientific foundations for the field in terms of the classic experimental designs and the more recently adapted qualitative techniques. Also described is the participatory action research model, which engages the community in definition of the problems and issues, derivation of possible solutions, and the methods by which the intervention can be evaluated. In such a manner, ecological relevance is addressed. We describe the stress and resilience models that have provided a framework for many of our studies and intervention strategies. Beyond these models, in the second part, the issue of social change is elaborated, that is, how change comes to us and how we can use it constructively. The final chapter to the second section explores the typical ways community interventions have occurred. We review a representative sample of methods by which community psychologists positively influence social or systems change.

The third section presents the variety of ways community psychology might help in the specific social systems that influence our well-being. The most obvious of these systems is in mental health, but others include social services, the schools and youth organizations, work settings, the justice system, public health, and health care. These are a broad set of topics, and in all of them we find community psychology theories or applications involved. The good news is that change is occurring in these systems. The challenge is that there is more to do.

The fourth and final section explores community psychology addressing the future. Though there have been successes, there are also problems with the sustainability and integrity of the field. More specifically, how do we continue as a community psychology? How do we maintain our ideals and vitality? And of course, there are new areas to develop and new concerns to address.

Every chapter contains special interest features that we believe will engage our student readers. The Cases in Point are designed to make the issue or topic practical and to stimulate critical thinking. In the typical Case in Point, a topic such as homelessness or community conflict is discussed in at least one of two ways: The issues related to the topic are examined and/or the relevant research is reviewed.

The chapters also contain several pedagogical aids. For example, each chapter begins with a chapter outline to forecast the structure of the chapter. Similarly, each chapter commences with an opening vignette. The vignettes are alluded to throughout the chapters and are used to crystallize the material at various points in the reading. We have done something with these vignettes that might be controversial for some professors. The vignettes start with a case history—sometimes a clinical one, sometimes a community one. We did this in recognition of the fact that many graduate programs in psychology are clinical-community programs. For professors trained in this tradition, the opening vignettes will assist them in moving their students from a clinical point of reference to a community or more ecological perspective by the end of the chapter. For those professors oriented exclusively to community psychology (and not clinical psychology), the Cases in Point are constructed to be more purely based on community psychology.

In addition to these tools, key terms that are important to the field of community psychology but that might be new to the students' vocabularies are boldfaced in all chapters. Each chapter concludes with a summary as well. Students are advised to read this summary after they first peruse the outline so as to direct their attention to primary issues in each chapter and to better organize their studying.

We hope that you find both information and a way of thinking emerging from reading this text. Community psychology is a body of knowledge, a theoretical framework, and a practice of psychology that relates to how our best tendencies—to fellowship and caring, to compassion and support, to coping and resilience—are brought to bear on the stresses and crises we all face. Community psychology is also a way of conceptualizing the world and ourselves in it. You will see how thinking contextually and transactionally might shift your construction of problems and solutions. There is also the challenge to take longitudinal and systemic perspectives on community and personal issues and their solutions. From these ways of thinking and the information presented, your curiosity may be satisfied and possibly new questions raised.

As the new coauthor on this text, I thank the original authors, Karen Duffy and Frank Wong, for their kind invitation to join them in this writing effort. We have worked together well as a trio with much support, encouragement, and tolerance. The advantage of three authors has been the contribution of diverse perspectives and different areas of expertise. This has made for a richer text. It somehow seems fitting that a community psychology text has been written collectively.

We would like to thank the editorial staff at Pearson, Michelle Limoges and her assistant, Paige Clunie, for their patience and understanding, help, and advice. We also thank our reviewers, whose critical appraisals of the book often helped us reframe issues and add material that resulted in a better product. The reviewers of this edition include Annie Flynn, DePaul University; Dale Fryxell, Chaminade University; Fernando Padro, Monmouth University; and Cheryl Ramos, University of Hawaii, Hilo. In addition, I thank my wife and fellow psychologist, Jane Harmon Jacobs, who read and encouraged my portion of the rewrites, and my son, Michael Moritsugu, who provided his own form of help and support in this process.

We are the product of our own intellectual and emotional communities. Among my early advisors and teachers have been Ralph Barocas and Emory Cowen from my graduate school days at the University of Rochester. I thank them for their support and challenges during my time in the snow country of upstate New York and throughout my career. Among the many colleagues I found in graduate school, three in particular have remained helpful in continuing to engage me in discussions about the field of community psychology. I thank Leonard Jason, David Glenwick, and Robert Felner for their fellowship and connection over the years. Finally, to you the reader, thank you for considering and reflecting on what we have produced.

J.M.

ABOUT THE AUTHORS

John Moritsugu received his Ph.D. in clinical psychology from the University of Rochester, New York. He is Professor of Psychology at Pacific Lutheran University in Tacoma, Washington. A coeditor of the text *Preventive Psychology,* he has also been on the editorial boards of the *American Journal of Community Psychology,* the *Journal of Community Psychology,* and *Cultural Diversity and Ethnic Minority Psychology.* He is a Fellow of the American Psychological Association in Divisions 1 (General Psychology), 27 (Society for Community Research and Action), and 45 (Society for the Psychological Study of Ethnic Minority Issues).

Frank Y. Wong, Ph.D., a social psychologist, is Associate Research Professor in the Department of International Health at the Georgetown University School of Nursing and Health Studies with expertise in community-based research on HIV-related risk behaviors and alcohol, tobacco, and other drugs (ATOD) use/abuse among racial/ethnic and underserved populations. He currently has multiple grants supporting his research programs. His NIH-funded research focuses on social epidemiology as well as prevention of ATOD and HIV targeting migrant and/or nonindigenous populations and sexual minorities and the effects of migration on ATOD use/abuse and HIV-related knowledge, attitudes, beliefs, and behaviors in the United States and China. He has also conducted and published research in South Africa.

Karen Grover Duffy holds a Ph.D. in psychology from Michigan State University. She is a Distinguished Service Professor-Emerita from the State University of New York at Geneseo. She taught community psychology for many years as well as social psychology and psychology of personality. She instituted and directed the service learning program at her college. She won two Fulbright Fellowships to St. Petersburg State University in Russia, where she taught both community psychology and community mediation. She still teaches in Russia and continues her award-winning community service projects in the United States, Russia, and other countries—most recently Mongolia.

CHAPTER 1

INTRODUCTION

HISTORICAL BACKGROUND

WHAT IS COMMUNITY PSYCHOLOGY?
WHAT IS A COMMUNITY PSYCHOLOGIST?

FUNDAMENTAL PRINCIPLES
　Respect for Diversity
　The Importance of Context and Environment
　Empowerment
　The Ecological Perspective/Multiple Levels of Intervention
　■ CASE IN POINT 1.1　Clinical Psychology, Community Psychology: What's the Difference?

OTHER CENTRAL CONCEPTS
　Prevention Rather than Treatment
　■ CASE IN POINT 1.2　Does Primary Prevention Work?
　Emphasis on Strengths and Competencies
　Social Change and Action Research
　Interdisciplinary Perspectives
　■ CASE IN POINT 1.3　Social Psychology, Community Psychology, and Homelessness
　A Psychological Sense of Community

COMMUNITY PSYCHOLOGY TODAY

RESEARCH

WHAT'S IN IT FOR YOU?
　Undergraduate Education
　Advanced Training in Community Psychology

PLAN OF THE BOOK

SUMMARY

It was the best of times, it was the worst of times, it was the age of wisdom, it was the age of foolishness, it was the epoch of belief, it was the epoch of incredulity, it was the season of Light, it was the season of Darkness, it was the spring of hope, it was the winter of despair, we had everything before us, we had nothing before us, we were all going direct to heaven, we were all going direct the other way—in short, the period was so far like the present period, that some of its noisiest authorities insisted on its being received, for good or for evil, in the superlative degree of comparison only.
—Charles Dickens, *A Tale of Two Cities*

　　The pictures or video are all very familiar to those who have stood in grocery store lines or have watched entertainment-oriented news shows. The young women are sleek and dressed in high fashion, and the young men are impeccably tailored or fashionably grungy. The people seem to be trying to shield themselves from flashbulbs or klieg lights. They are coming out of jail, drug or alcohol rehabilitation programs, or trying to explain why they are in the predicament they find themselves in with the law, their neighbors, their friends. . . . The usual analysis is that they are somehow flawed and morally destitute, spoiled, pampered, overprivileged, and therefore doomed. We watch this spectacle and wonder what is going on. They go off to treatment and return rehabilitated, only this improvement does not last. They are found all too soon again under scrutiny for some other misdeed.

What is going on? From a traditional clinical perspective, these people are displaying symptoms of disorder. The treatment is individual-focused and very personal. What of their choices? What of their sense of self-worth? What of their family background? Is there an imbalance they are dealing with, or a need they are trying to fill? We have seen or heard of it for many years.

What is insightful and provocative is to place these scenarios under a community psychology lens. What would be focused on, seen, hypothesized? In turn, what would intervention consist of? How might outcomes be measured? The language and perspective would be very different from what we have heard before. The problems would be defined in terms of stress, social settings, normative behaviors, prevention, developmental issues, and the skills needed to contend with them, significant others, mentors, peer groups, and support. The intervention framework would be larger scale, epidemiologically driven, considering risk factors, multiple determinants, and the teachable moments/situations. There would be consideration of long-term effects and changes in the systems that create and sustain maladaptive and adaptive behaviors. This is the language of community psychology. It is not pathology-driven but wellness-driven. It looks not for flaws but for strengths. It calls for not only individual change but also social change.

If you are surprised to find references to privileged people in this opening, then we have accomplished what we intended. The community psychology principles and the programs that arise from these principles are for everyone. Community is not just the concern of the downtrodden and the destitute, but of all people. All are influenced by surroundings, social settings, and the press of the environment. We all desire to be connected, to belong, to have some sense of direction and purpose to our lives, to have a sense of our social realities, and to make contributions to our communities. Whether we are among the socially advantaged and wealthy or the destitute or somewhere in the middle, we all search for community, we derive strength from those around us, struggle with adapting to our surroundings, or contend with differences between what we have learned and what we must do to be valued in our society. All of these things are the purview of a community psychology.

By the end this book you will be familiar with this language and the way of thinking about the issues and problems that we face. The topics that are addressed by community psychology range from drug and alcohol abuse by young adults, to the concerns and crises that we face in each of our developmental epochs (relationships, independence, adult maturity, work, vocation, meaning in life), to dealing with HIV/AIDS, to teen pregnancy and sexuality, to crime and living in a civil society and in an institutionalized setting. The "beautiful people" described in the opening scenario are examples of all that we face, possibly exaggerated by the media to fit its/our entertainment needs. A community psychology will study and intervene, working to provide the best opportunities for fulfillment of the individual and advancement of the society. It is an ambitious goal, and one that we all share. Ahead, we will investigate what has been done in an effort to achieve it.

This chapter examines the history and growth, philosophy and goals, and current status of community psychology. This background provides the historical and theoretical context from which community psychology emerged. You will be introduced to the fundamental principles of the field, the concepts that have helped guide it as well as theories that have emerged from the study of a community psychology. The chapter concludes with an examination of educational opportunities at the undergraduate and graduate levels.

HISTORICAL BACKGROUND

In colonial times, the United States was not without social problems. However, the close-knit, agrarian communities that existed often cared for needy individuals, and such care was generally provided without special places to house these individuals (Rappaport, 1977). As cities grew and became industrialized, a trend developed to institutionalize various populations: those who were mentally ill, indigent, and otherwise powerless. Perhaps from an abnormal psychology or other class, you know what these early institutions were like. They were often dank, crowded places where treatment ranged from restraint to cruel punishment.

It was not until the 1700s that Philip Pinel, followed somewhat later by Dorothea Dix and others, attempted to reform institutions by removing the restraints and establishing more positive attempts at changing behavior. However, these more "moral" treatments were sometimes limited to people of financial means (Rappaport, 1977). Nonetheless, institutions, especially public ones, continued to grow and house lower-class as well as powerless and other less privileged members of society. As waves of early immigrants entered the United States, many were often mistakenly diagnosed as mentally incompetent and found themselves in the same overpopulated institutions.

In the late 1800s, Sigmund Freud developed a keen interest in mental illness and its then current treatment. You are probably already familiar with his method of treatment, **psychoanalysis,** and his other contributions to psychology and psychiatry. Freud's basic premise was that emotional disturbance was due to intrapsychic forces within the individual caused by past experiences. These disturbances could be treated by individual therapy and by attention to the unconscious. Freud gave us a legacy of intervention aimed at the individual (rather than the societal) level. Likewise, he conferred on the profession the strong tendency to divest individuals of the power to heal themselves; the physician, or expert, knew more about psychic healing than did the patient. Freud also oriented professional healers to examine an individual's past rather than current circumstances as the cause of disturbance and to view anxiety and underlying disturbance as endemic to everyday life. Freud certainly concentrated on an individual's weaknesses rather than strengths.

At about the same time as Freud's death, President Franklin D. Roosevelt proclaimed his New Deal era. Specifically, heeding the lessons of the Great Depression of the 1920s and 1930s, he proposed a two-pronged approach for attacking poverty: income transfers and employment programs. Both led to the development of the Social Security system, unemployment and disability benefits, and a variety of work relief programs. Roosevelt's programs seemed more employment-based than anything; at the time, there were no broad-based programs to attack poverty (Gottschalk & Gottschalk, 1988). For example, many women did not work. They could not benefit from these programs, however, even though they may have been living in poverty. On the other hand, the idea that poverty (as caused by unemployment) could be rectified with social programs had been planted in the American psyche.

Another important point in the history of the development of community psychology occurred in 1946 when Congress passed the National Mental Health Act. This act gave the U.S. Public Health Service broad authority to combat mental illness and promote mental health. With the passage of this act and the interest in mental illness generated by World War II, clinical psychology began to thrive. Shortly thereafter, the National Institute of Mental Health (NIMH) was established. This organization made significant federal funds available for research and training in mental health issues (Strother, 1987).

At the time, clinical psychologists were battling with psychiatrists to expand their domain from testing, which had been their primary thrust, to psychotherapy (Walsh, 1987). Today, **clinical psychology** is the field within psychology that deals with the diagnosis, measurement, and treatment of mental illness. It differs from **psychiatry,** in part, in that psychiatrists have a medical degree and can prescribe medication. On the other hand, clinical psychologists hold doctorates (Ph.D.s) in psychology, which are considered to be research degrees, or Psy.D.'s, which are practitioner-scholar degrees focused on assessment and psychological interventions. The battle between the fields of psychiatry and psychology continues today, as some psychologists seek the right to prescribe medications and obtain practice privileges at the balance of the hospitals that do not recognize them (Sammons, Gorny, Zinner, & Allen, 2000).

Another aspect of history related to both world wars is that when formerly healthy veterans of the wars returned home, some came back as psychiatric casualties (Rappaport, 1977; Strother, 1987). What had intervened to change the soldiers' mental status? The wars themselves. The terror of war forced psychologists to recognize the role the environment plays in an individual's mental health.

In 1949, the U.S. Public Health Service sponsored a conference in Boulder, Colorado. The participants fashioned a model for the training of clinical psychologists that guided training for years to come (Rappaport, 1977). The model emphasized education in science *and* the practice of testing and therapy. Psychologists sometimes credit this event with the ability of psychology to further divorce itself from psychiatry or the field of human medicine.

Of social significance, during World War II, the need for labor pressed women into nontraditional work settings. "Rosie the Riveter" was the archetypal woman working in a skilled blue-collar position, doing the dangerous, heavy duties previously reserved for men in industrial America. Following the war, it was difficult to argue that women could not work outside the home, because they had contributed directly to the winning war effort. Besides this revolution in women's work places, returning soldiers were given new educational opportunities with the support of the G.I. Bill. College, once the preserve of an elite social class, was made accessible through scholarships and grants. Then there was the baby boom. Add thousands of young men returning home from the war to thousands of young women, and in time there are babies. According to the population statistics, there were lots of babies. The baby boom started in 1946–47 and continued into the early 1950s. Eighteen years later, these boomers were reaching adulthood and feeling the power of their numbers. We note the effect of this boom on the social context of the 1960s later.

The 1950s brought significant change to the treatment of mental illness. One of the most influential developments was the discovery of pharmacologic agents that could be used to treat psychosis and other forms of mental illness. Various antipsychotics, tranquilizers, antidepressants, and other medications created extensive change in the institutions, the major change being that patients became more tractable, or docile. The use of these drugs proliferated despite major side effects. It was suggested that with appropriate medication, patients would not require the very expensive institutional care they received, and they could proceed with learning how to cope and adjust to the larger communities to which they might return. Given adequate resources, the decision seemed more humane. There was also a financial argument for deinstitutionalization, given that the costs of hospitalization were high. There was potential for savings in the care and management of psychiatric patients. The focus for dealing with the mentally ill shifted from the hospital to the community. Unfortunately, what was forgotten was the need for adequate resources to successfully do this.

In 1952, a pioneering article was published. Hans Eysenck Sr., a renowned British scientist, launched an attack on the practice of psychotherapy (Eysenck, 1952, 1961). By reviewing the literature on psychotherapy, Eysenck was able to demonstrate that no treatment worked. In fact, the mere passage of time was often as effective as professional treatment. Other mental health professionals followed suit and leveled criticisms at psychological practices, such as psychological testing (Meehl, 1954, 1960), and the whole concept of mental illness (Elvin, 2000; Szasz, 1961). These criticisms, of course, have not gone unrebutted; we review these issues further in the chapters on mental illness. If intervention were not useful, as Eysenck maintained, mentally ill individuals would be left to roam the streets because they would be given little hope by the helping professions, especially if communities and helping systems remained uncaring.

In the early 1950s, the Supreme Court decision in **Brown v. Board of Education of Topeka, Kansas** declared that educating groups separately based on race was not considered equal treatment. School systems that had segregated African Americans away from Whites were determined to be in violation of the U.S. Constitution. Children were to be considered equal and had the right to the same education. This was a part of a larger movement by African Americans to seek equality under the law. Later actions included a tired and defiant Rosa Parks, in 1955, refusing to give up her bus seat to a White passenger, merely because the rules at the time required her to defer to the White; nine African American students seeking entry into an all-White school in Little Rock, Arkansas, because of its opportunities for a better education; African Americans seeking the right to eat at the same restaurants as Whites, and trying to register to vote. These actions were all a part of the civil rights movement.

The 1960s witnessed further, sometimes sweeping reforms. The civil rights movement of the 1950s carried over to the 1960s. Minorities, women, and other less privileged members of society cried out for equal rights. Notably, the baby boomers, born in the 1940s were starting to come of age, making the U.S. demographics look particularly young. With the onset of the 1960s came the election of a young president, a member of the generation who had gone to war in the 1940s and had helped win it. John F. Kennedy was considered by some to be too young and too inexperienced. He brought with him a willingness to take on challenges. His first inaugural speech proclaimed, "ask not what your country can do for you, ask what you can do for your country." It was a clear call for service. During his tenure, the Peace Corps was created to send Americans out into the world to help nations develop and communities thrive. Psychologists were also encouraged to "do something to participate in society as psychologists" (Walsh, 1987, p. 524). Those issues, coupled with the increasing moral outrage over the Vietnam War, fueled excitement about citizen involvement in social reform and generated understanding about the interdependence of social movements (Kelly, 1990).

Kennedy's own sister had special needs, and this may have contributed to his interest in mental health issues. He was elected on a platform of social change. Social conditions and poverty, he reasoned, were responsible in large part for negative psychological conditions (Heller, Price, Reinharz, Riger, & Wandersman, 1984). Mental health issues were given ample consideration. Why were mental health services usually reserved for the privileged few and institutionalization for mental health issues predominantly for the lower social class (Hollingshead & Redlich, 1958)? In a bold move, mental health for communities was proposed. Kennedy helped secure the passage of the Community Mental Health Centers Act of 1963, which authorized funds for *local* mental health centers. The centers were to provide outpatient, emergency, and educational services, among others. Although not without problems and not necessarily revolutionary, this act recognized the need for immediate, local intervention in the form of emergency services as well as the need for prevention through education.

After Kennedy's assassination, President Lyndon B. Johnson appeared to be moving the country toward "the Great Society." For the first time, a president issued a blueprint for the War on Poverty in his State of the Union address. The 1964 annual report of the President's Council of Economic Advisors stated:

> Conquest of poverty is well within our power. About $11 billion a year would bring all poor families up to the $3,000 income level we have taken to be the minimum for a decent life. The majority of the Nation could simply tax themselves enough to provide the necessary income supplements to their less fortunate citizens. But this "solution" would not have touched most of the roots of poverty. Americans want to earn the American standard of living by their own efforts and contributions. It will be far better, even if more difficult, to equip and to permit the poor of the Nation to produce and to earn the additional $11 billion, and more.

These statements strongly indicate that Johnson and his advisors wanted to find ways or mechanisms that could empower people who were less fortunate and help them become productive citizens. Programs such as **Head Start** (addressed in Chapter 8) and other federally funded early childhood enhancement programs for the disadvantaged were conceived within this ideology. Also, many of the prototypes of social and human services were developed around this time.

Important to the history of community psychology was a conference held in **Swampscott,** Massachusetts, in May 1965. This conference is usually cited as the official birthdate of community psychology in the United States (Heller et al., 1984; Hersch, 1969; Rappaport, 1977). This conference was attended by clinical psychologists concerned with the inadequacies of their field and oriented to creating social and political change. As a result of their small-group discussions, the Swampscott participants agreed to move from treatment to prevention and the inclusion of an ecological perspective (loosely, a person–environment fit) in their work (Bennett et al., 1966). The Swampscott attendees noted the work of social psychologist Kurt Lewin (http://www.ntl.org/about-history.html) and his National Training Laboratories (NTL). Lewin's work emphasized the importance of the context in understanding people's behaviors and emphasized the interactions of person and environment. The NTL model worked on learning about groups from direct experience and feedback and espoused the value "that science should be used to integrate democratic values in society" (http://www.ntl.org/about-history.html).

The Swampscott Conference was followed by other conferences. Today, the Society for Community Research and Action (Division 27) holds conferences every other year. Community psychology is a recognized division of the American Psychological Association (APA) (Division 27). Several journals (*Journal of Community Psychology, American Journal of Community Psychology, Journal of Rural Community Psychology, Journal of Community and Applied Social Psychology, Journal of Primary Prevention,* and *Journal of Prevention and Intervention in the Community*) represent the field, along with many other related journals on social change, community mental health, and other relevant areas (Kelly, 1990).

WHAT IS COMMUNITY PSYCHOLOGY?
WHAT IS A COMMUNITY PSYCHOLOGIST?

Community psychology focuses on social issues, social institutions, and other settings that influence groups and organizations (and therefore the individuals in them). The goal is to optimize the well-being of communities and individuals with innovative and alternate interventions designed in collaboration with affected community members and with other related disciplines inside and outside of psychology. Donald Klein (1987) recalled the adoption of the term for a 1963 grant proposal to the National Institute of Mental Health (NIMH). He also credits William Rhodes, a consultant in child mental health at NIMH, for writing of a "community psychology" prior to Swampscott. The critical mass for the creation of a community psychology field seems to have been achieved at the Swampscott Conference (Bennett et al., 1966).

Iscoe (1987) made a distinction between "community psychology" and a "community psychologist." He believed the field of community psychology studied communities and the factors that made them healthy or at risk. In turn, a **community psychologist** used

TABLE 1.1 Four Broad Principles Guiding Community Research and Action

1. Community research and action requires explicit attention to and **respect for diversity** among peoples and settings.
2. Human competencies and problems are best understood by viewing people within their social, cultural, economic, geographic, and historical **contexts**.
3. Community research and action is an **active collaboration** among researchers, practitioners, and community members that uses multiple methodologies. Such research and action must be undertaken to serve those community members directly concerned, and should be guided by their needs and preferences, as well as by their active **participation**.
4. Change strategies are needed at **multiple levels** to foster settings that promote competence and well-being.

Source: From www.scra27.org/about.html, July 4, 2008

these factors to intervene for the betterment of the community and the individuals within it. The distinction is interesting, given that the Division of Community Psychology was renamed the Society for Community Research and Action (Division 27 of the APA) in the 1980s, so as to better emphasize the dual nature of the field.

In the beginning years of the 21st century, following work on a vision and a mission statement, which included surveying the membership, Division 27 defined four basic principles for a community psychology (see Table 1.1). These principles may be summarized as: a respect for diversity, a recognition of the power of context, an appreciation of a community's right to empowerment, and an understanding of the complexity of ecologically relevant interventions.

FUNDAMENTAL PRINCIPLES

The Society for Community Research and Action, previously known as the Division of Community Psychology of the APA, proposed a set of fundamental principles to define the field. (As noted in the *Compact Oxford Dictionary, principles* are here defined as "a fundamental truth or proposition serving as the foundation for belief or action. Or 2. a rule or belief governing one's personal behaviour" (http://www.askoxford.com/concise_oed/principle?view=uk). The framers of these principles hoped to portray what they believed to be the fundamental beliefs to which all community psychologists could agree. We might think of these points as aspirations for all work in the field.

Respect for Diversity

There is an appreciation for diversity in community psychology. People have the right to be different, and *different* does not mean *inferior*. If difference is accepted as a fact of life, then resources ought to be equitably distributed to all of these different people. These beliefs are not just noble rhetoric. From a belief in the diversity of people also comes a recognition of the distinctive styles of living, worldviews, and social arrangements that are not part of mainstream society but that characterize our society's diversity. Moreover, a recognition of these distinctions results in the ability to avoid comparing diverse populations with mainstream cultural standards and therefore labeling these different others as "deficient" or "deviant" (Snowden, 1987), as well as the ability to design interventions that are culturally appropriate (e.g., Dumas, Rollock, Prinz, Hops, & Blechman, 1999; Marin, 1993).

Sue (1977), early in the community mental health movement, pointed out the differential treatment and outcomes for ethnic minority group clients in the system. He called for provision of responsive services to these populations. More recently, Sue (2003) has continued his defense of the need for cultural competency in treatments, emphasizing the importance of understanding relationships and context in our interventions. He believes these variables to be just as important, if not *more* important, than specific techniques. Padilla, Ruiz, and Alvarez (1975) also called attention to the barriers of geography, class, language, and culture that led to the scarcity of Spanish-speaking and -surnamed populations in mental health systems. Their recommendations of barrio- (neighborhood) and family-focused services have been models of what community-based services should be. In particular, they placed an emphasis on respect for cultural context in devising treatments. When interventions fail, it is not necessarily the fault of the client or patient. The system and its assumptions must also be examined.

In the early community psychology literature, reviewers found that about 11 percent of the articles in community psychology journals pertain to people from ethnic minorities. The authors concluded that progress toward understanding the diverse population was being made but that more needed to be done (Loo, Fong, & Iwamasa, 1988). Martin, Lounsbury, and Davidson (2004) found this rate to more than double in the time period from 1993 to 1998, with approximately 25 percent of the articles in the *American Journal of Community Psychology* addressing diversity issues.

Some authors have decried the fact that there is no general framework for relating significant social-psychological markers such as gender and race to theory, research, and action in community psychology. However, such a framework could be seen to be emerging (Watts, 1992). O'Donnell (2006) described a "cultural-community" model, where all community considerations are framed in terms of their specific cultural context. As he said, all phenomena and interventions should be preceded by the phrase "it depends." His comments build on the work of Trickett (1996), who described the importance of both culture and context in understanding and working in diverse communities.

Suarez-Balcazar, Durlak, and Smith (1994) surveyed directors of 56 community psychology graduate programs to assess multicultural training practices and attitudes. Although most program directors agreed that cultural diversity was a major goal for training community psychologists, fewer than half of the programs required students to take any such coursework. Moreover, only half of the programs surveyed had any faculty who were members of an ethnic minority group. However, five years later Cherniss (1999) found that many graduate programs in community psychology were working with multiple avenues for introducing their students to diversity—for example, via the formal curriculum, research projects in minority communities, workshops on diversity, and committees that develop ways to infuse the graduate program with diversity experiences. Toro (2005) pointed out that 23 percent of the membership of the Society for Community Action and Research self-identifies as ethnic minority. This is in comparison with approximately 6 percent of the entire APA membership identifying as ethnic minority. Though the progress may have been slow, the direction is positive.

Some in the field of community psychology still believe that certain marginalized groups continue to be ignored or underserved—for example, homosexuals, individuals with disabilities, and women (Bond, Hill, Mulvey, & Terenzio, 2000). Bond and Harrell (2006) caution that there is little work on the subtleties, contradictions, and dilemmas that arise from working with the many diversities that exist within our communities. As well as the obvious issues of competing ethnic groups, there are the intersections of gender and ethnicity, the combinations of sexual orientation and class, or all of these considerations together creating practical challenges to the practice of community psychology. Although diversity has a history of recognition within the field, its implications are still being worked out and understood.

The Importance of Context and Environment

Our behaviors are governed by the expectations and demands of given situations. For example, student behaviors in lectures are different from behaviors in a seminar. When watching people greet each other, we can note a variety of symbolic gestures that are displayed. Many in our culture shake hands. Many in other cultures bow. Some people hug. These behavior sequences are learned, and they are governed by the situation. We don't usually shake hands in the middle of a conversation. That would seem strange.

Kurt Lewin (1936) formulated that behavior is a function of the interaction between the person and the environment ($B = f(P \times E)$). A social-Gestalt psychologist, Lewin intended to capture the importance of both the individual and his or her context. To consider the individual alone would provide an incomplete and weak description of the factors influencing action. It would be like a figure without a ground. Therefore, any study of behavior must include an understanding of the personal dispositions *and* of the situation in which the person finds him- or herself.

Roger Barker (1965), a student of Lewin, studied the power of behavior settings to guide sets of activities for their inhabitants. People in a given setting would display prescribed rituals. Violation of these environmentally signaled patterns were negatively viewed, so these patterns persisted over time. Barker observed and analyzed the social and psychological nature of these settings. Among the various phenomena was the observation that a given setting required a certain amount of people to maintain it. For example, the production of a school paper required the accomplishment of particular tasks. Without all of these tasks being completed, the setting could not accomplish its tasks. Each setting had an optimal level of staffing. When there were too many people, a surplus of individuals in relation to the work that needed completion would make it likely that the setting would be more selective in whom it chose to perform the tasks. If two or three people wanted to do a task requiring one person, there was competition to fill that position. This is considered a case of **overmanning**. Then newcomers are less likely to be welcome, because they would add to the competitive pool. On the other hand, if there were insufficient numbers of people to complete a task, there would be more environmental demand to use every available individual. In this case, one person might be available to fill a two-person task, or there might be no one to fill a position. There is no competition in this situation and therefore more willingness to take on new individuals, who could help fill the roles. If there are insufficient numbers to fill all the necessary positions, **undermanning** occurs. In this case, the environment is open and positively inclined to newcomers. It might be noted that in economically difficult times, the sentiment toward newcomers, immigrants to a community, is less positive. When there is a clear need for more task performers, the social attitudes are more open. Many times this can be manipulated by perceptions of overmanning or undermanning. For example, the attitudes toward new workers can be manipulated so as to generate a belief of too many people, even though newcomers might be performing tasks that others would not do.

Barker's and Lewin's works have underscored the importance of environmental factors in behavioral tendencies. Regularities of behavior are not determined solely by personality and genetics. These behaviors are also the result of environmental signals and pressures on the individual. Different environments bring different behaviors. Change the environment, change the behavior.

Bogat and Jason's (2000) discussion of behavioral community perspectives is a reminder that the importance of context can also be interpreted from a learning theory perspective. **Discriminative stimulus** and **setting control** (under specific stimulus or setting conditions the person acts) are contextual terms. In behavioral terminology, the "context" can be construed as the stimulus setting that an individual or a population has learned to discriminate as the appropriate place to display certain behaviors. The reward or reinforcement for those behaviors is the basis of the community learning. Learning that certain behaviors will be rewarded or reinforced in a given setting increases the probability of those behaviors in those settings. This is a Skinnerian (1974) explanation of setting control. Beyond this strict behavioral interpretation of context, Mischel (1968) argued for the importance of looking at setting as well as personality and at the interactions of setting and personality, that is, certain behavioral tendencies might appear stronger in particular settings and much weaker in others. For example, we might not see drinking behaviors in one setting, but in another setting, differences in drinking would appear. Behavioral community programs have been a part of the community psychology tradition for many years, contributing to the understanding of context and the power of learning theory in devising interventions (Bogat & Jason, 1997, 2000; Fawcett, 1990; Glenwick & Jason, 1980).

No matter what the theoretical framework, the importance of context or setting is clearly a part of a community psychology. Whether the context is defined as a system or a set of discriminative stimuli, it is a significant factor in determining the life of a community.

Empowerment

If people recognize that everyone is unique and individuals differ from one another, it would be presumptuous to think that one individual is more expert at designing environments for others. A crucial concept in community psychology is **empowerment**, the process of enhancing the possibility that people can more actively control their own lives (Rappaport, 1981). Empowerment is a process by which individuals gain control and mastery not only over their own lives but over the democratic processes in their community as well (Zimmerman & Rappaport, 1988). Julian Rappaport (1987), a leading proponent of empowerment, wrote that empowerment conveys a sense of personal control or influence and involves an individual's determination over his or her own life. Zimmerman (1995) described it this way: "Empowerment is a construct that links individual strength and competencies, natural helping systems, and proactive behaviors to social policy and social changes. Empowerment theory, research, and intervention link individual well-being with the larger social and political environment" (p. 569).

Foster-Fishman, Salem, Chibnall, Legler, and Yapchai (1998), using interviews and observations, found that there are multiple pathways to empowerment in community organizations. One is through job autonomy, where employees have control and influence on their jobs. A second pathway is through gaining job-relevant knowledge; the greater an employee's knowledge, the more influence that organizational member can have on the job. Other pathways to empowerment include feeling trusted and respected in the organization and having the freedom to be creative on the job. A fifth way is the perception of job fulfillment or job satisfaction. Satisfied employees discern that they have more influence and control than do dissatisfied employees. Of course, the converse is true, too; employees who have authority and direction over their jobs feel more satisfied with them. One final pathway to empowerment is participatory decision making in the organization.

Empowerment, then, means *doing* (Swift & Levin, 1987); however, it does not mean that community psychologists do things for others. Rather, community psychologists, in the roles of researchers-reporters, collaborators-educators, or advocates-activists, empower others so that they can *do* for themselves.

The concept of empowerment has not gone without criticism. Riger (1993) argued that empowerment often leads to individualism and therefore competition and conflict. Similarly, she criticized the construct for being traditionally masculine, in that it involves power and control, rather than feminine, which concerns communion and cooperation. Riger issued a challenge to community psychologists to develop a vision that incorporates both empowerment and community, despite what she construed as the paradoxical nature of the two phenomena. Sprague and Hayes (2000) agreed that the notion of empowerment can indeed backfire, and Porter (2001) added that the construct is vague and lacking in concrete ways to implement it.

There is a growing interest in empowerment as a research topic. From 1974 to 1986, there were 94 articles on the topic of empowerment. From 1987 to 1993, the number increased to 686 articles and 283 book chapters. Other disciplines have also recognized the importance of empowerment. For example, the number of articles on the topic in the educational literature rose from 66 between 1966 and 1981 to 2,261 from 1982 to early 1994 (Perkins & Zimmerman, 1995). In just seven short years between 1995 and 2001, over 1,000 other citations were added, an indication that interest in the concept of empowerment certainly is not waning (PsychInfo, 2002).

The Ecological Perspective/Multiple Levels of Intervention

Urie Bronfenbrenner (1977) described four layers of ecological systems that can influence the development of a child. At the center of the schema is the individual and "immediate system," which contains the person. It is composed of particular physical features, activities, and roles. For example, there is the home situation in which one might be engaged in cleaning activities and playing the role of daughter. This is called a **microsystem.** Other examples of microsystems would include a neighborhood, or a school. These microsystems directly influence the individual, and the system can be directly acted on by the individual.

At the next level are the **mesosystems** where the microsystems interact. These are where the major settings interact. Examples of this would be places where school and family come together. A mesosystem is a "system of microsystems" (Bronfenbrenner, 1977, p. 515). Research has shown the advantages of clear and demonstrated linkages between the school and the family on the child's school adaptation and academic performance. In turn, there are also findings that schools seen as a part of their community are more likely to be supported and less likely to be the target of vandalism. Children who feel connected to family, school, and neighborhood may feel the responsibilities of membership and the supportiveness of their wholistically integrated social and psychological environment.

The **exosystem** is an extension of the mesosystem that does not immediately contain the child or individual. The exosystem influences the mesosystem. An example would be government agencies or the work situation for family members.

The **macrosystem** does not contain specific settings. The macrosystem contains the laws, culture, values, or religious beliefs that govern or direct the lower systems. Bronfenbrenner's argument was that any conceptualization of a child's development needed such a comprehensive examination to adequately understand the processes that enriched or deprived the child's progress. Devising interventions to address this progress deserve a comprehensive and conceptual basis addressing multiple levels.

Bronfenbrenner believed that consideration of all of these systems was important to determining the validity or reality of a phenomenon. Anything less provides us with an artificial perspective on what really happens in the life of an individual or group.

In a similar vein, James Kelly argued that communities may be best understood from an ecological model. He suggested an attention to the ecological processes. Toward this end, he advocated awareness of interdependence, cycling of resources, adaptive capacity, and succession (Kelly, 1968).

Kelly (2006) emphasized the centrality of **interdependence** to this model. The idea is that various elements of an ecosystem are dependent on each other. Change in one element can bring about changes throughout the system. Using quotes from Billy Martin, then the New York Yankees baseball manager, Kelly (1980) once likened the ecological model to Billy Martin's description of a baseball game (Angell, 1980). Every game is different. Each pitch of the ball requires shifts in personnel and changes in both strategy and tactics. The basemen might align themselves differently, the outfielders might shift their positions, the batter might change his disposition to swing or not swing, and if he swings, where to place the ball. All of this also takes into account the stadium they are in, the wind conditions, the time of day, the position of the sun, and the players on each team. Who are defending? Who is next up in the batting order? Everything is interdependent on the other. Kelly likened it to a controlled exercise in community psychology analysis and practice.

The second principle of Kelly's ecological model is the **cycling of resources,** a variation on the First Law of Thermodynamics, that energy is conserved, or rather, the amount of energy in a system remains constant. If there is an expenditure of energy in one area, it is the result of transfer of energy from another area. For resources to be dedicated to one area, they must come from another area.

The third ecological principle deals with an organism's breadth of **adaptive capacity** given environmental demands. Those with better abilities to deal with their environment are more likely to survive, and those with greater ability to deal with a broader range of environments should find wider distribution across settings. And so it is not just adaptation to one environment but also the adaptive range enabling the organism to survive across more situations. One might figure that the argument for flexibility and openness to social and cultural variation would allow a person to do well in more social situations.

The final ecological point is that of **succession**. This calls for a time perspective, which acknowledges changes that occur in the individual and in the systems in which the individual resides. Social organizations and their inhabitants are not static but dynamic. Just as a high school student moves from freshman to senior, the high school changes as well, growing more or less diverse, more or less academically minded, more or less interested in sports. There is a direction to this change, and there are elements of the community that are shifting as a function of this change. Succession requires the community psychologist to pay attention to these changes. Kelly believed these ecological dimensions to be helpful in understanding the person and environment issues that arise in studying communities.

Moos added to the considerations of **person and environment fit** by devising a method to assess a person's perception of the environment (Social Climate Scales) (Moos, 1973, 2003). These scales could be used to assess both real and ideal environments, so that discrepancies between them could be noted. This set of questions focused on the environment and how the person fit into it. In contrast to this, most psychological evaluations focus on the person and the temporal and situational regularities of the individual's behaviors and feelings. Of course, this purely trait-type focus has been critiqued by Mischel and Bandura, so that some personality theories have taken an interactionist or transactionalist turn. It could be argued that current personality theory has come to acknowledge the ecological model.

Ecological settings can be altered; for this and other reasons, settings are important to community psychology. More correctly stated, **person–environment fit** (Pargament, 1986) is important in community psychology. Exactly what does this mean? Rappaport (1977) explained this term well. The **ecological perspective** means an examination of the relationship between persons and their environments (both social and physical) and establishment of the optimal match between the person and the setting. Labeling the person who does not fit the setting as a "misfit" is not productive. Rather, the ecological perspective recognizes the transactional nature that people and environments have. Individuals influence the settings in which they find themselves; settings influence the individuals in them (Kuo, Sullivan, Coley, & Brunson, 1998; Peterson, 1998; Seidman, 1990). If something is awry with the individual or the environment, *both* can be examined and perhaps changed.

Given the ecological framework, community psychology research and action of necessity must consider more than the individual and the environment that contains the individual. There are other factors at play, whether it be at the mesosystem or exosystem level. These should be considered in any attempt to understand the phenomena under study or under intervention. The more completely the ecology is understood, the more thoroughly the intervention may be devised and the more effective it can be. Communities are not simple systems; they are complex and reciprocal in nature and must be dealt with as such.

Applying these principles to our opening story of celebrity misbehaviors, we might see alternative interpretations of what is happening and the causes for the problems. The principle of diversity would instruct us to be aware of where a person is developmentally as well as socially. Are some of these behaviors better understood as the first attempts at adult behavior as defined by their social group? Contextually, peer pressure and normative behaviors may suggest that some "deviant behaviors" are expected or permitted. Given the possible setting of sycophantic followers and the access to seemingly unlimited resources, the usual constraints of social propriety or economic limitations may allow for living out of what would be fantasy for others. Although this would seem to provide them with power, their sense of empowerment may in fact be limited by their sense of entrapment in their own images and all that goes with maintaining those images. It would be very difficult to have normal relationships and normal encounters or to appreciate the world around them when their every move is tracked and documented. There is little room for failure or being wrong, because this can be amplified by the press and the public. What would a world be like where there can be no mistakes? Empowerment might in fact be the ability to make mistakes without the pressure of having them amplified and broadcast to millions. Finally, the principle of multiple levels and ecological considerations would point to the layers of influences at work on these people. There are industry values and economics at play. There are social settings that allow for or normatively require certain behaviors. There are peer groups and follower groups who may reinforce certain lifestyles. Then there are the family, school, and neighborhood settings to contend with, which include all the normal demands of adult development and intimacy. The description here should be notable in that there is no use of pathological language and no blaming of the individual. Responsibility is there, of course, but with an understanding of the other forces at play, influencing the behaviors and settings under scrutiny. Responsibility is a value that is either supported or not supported by one's social setting. Community psychology provides an alternative way to look at ourselves and those around us. Through this new lens we devise innovative interventions for promoting our communities. We think systemically, ecologically, and with appreciation for the differences we bring to our social milieu. Beyond the principles outlined here, several concepts have high currency within the field. We examine them next.

CASE IN POINT 1.1
CLINICAL PSYCHOLOGY, COMMUNITY PSYCHOLOGY: WHAT'S THE DIFFERENCE?

Clinical psychology and community psychology both grow out of the same motivation to help other individuals using the science of psychology. Clinical psychology's orientation has traditionally been on the individual and the internal variables that influence their lives. Among those internal variables are emotions, cognitions, neural structures, and behavioral tendencies. Clinicians tend to speak of personality and what has influenced personal qualities. Given the assumption that a clinician is called into service when there is an identified personal problem, clinical skills include testing and assessment, diagnosis, and psychotherapy. A clinician is trained to deal with psychopathology. A quick survey of the chapters in two clinical psychology texts (Plante, 2005; Trull, 2004) reinforce our impression of these foci.

Among the clinical psychologist's work settings may be a hospital, a health clinic, a group or private practice office, a university, or a research setting. You may note the medical nature of many of

(continued)

CASE IN POINT 1.1 CONTINUED

these sites. Lightner Witmer is credited by many as the father of American clinical psychology. His work focused on schoolchildren and their treatment, learning, and behavioral problems in the psychological clinic. American clinical psychology traces its origins back to the late 1800s.

In contrast to clinical psychology, community psychology is oriented on groups of people and the external social and physical environments' effects on them, that is, communities. External variables include consideration of social support, peer and familial environments, neighborhoods, and formal and informal social systems that may influence individuals or groups. There is interest in social ecology and public policy. The orientation is toward prevention of problems and promotion of wellness. Skill sets would include community research skills; the ability to understand community problems from a holistic perspective; the ability to relate to community members in a meaningful and respectful manner; skill in noting the existing systems of establishing norms, maintenance, and change; an appreciation for the many ways in which context/environment influences behaviors; being able to assemble and focus resources toward the solution of a community problem; and being able to think outside the established normative world. A review of two community psychology texts support these descriptions. Rappaport (1977) dedicates much of his early text to social interventions and systems interventions. Kofkin-Radkin's (2003) chapters include Beyond the Individual, Embracing Social Change, Prevention, Empowerment, and Stress. Neither of the community texts has any chapters on psychopathology, assessment, or psychotherapy.

Community psychologists might be working for urban planners, government offices, departments of public health, community centers, schools, and private program evaluation agencies, as well as universities and research centers. They are not usually found in medical settings doing therapy but might work there examining delivery systems and community accessibility programs. The American community psychology area traces its origins to the Swampscott Conference of the 1960s. However, some have noted the work of Lightner Witmer for community psychology.

This overlapping history underscores that although there are clear differences between clinical and community psychology topics, there are common interests in providing effective interventions for the human good. One could also note that some community psychologists are trained as clinical psychologists. Of course, the Swampscott Conference was made up of clinicians. In turn, clinical psychology has taken on the themes of pathology prevention and health promotion in a significant way. Clinical or community, or clinical and community, the areas are distinctive enough to be clearly different and yet have the potential to inform one another.

OTHER CENTRAL CONCEPTS

Besides the principles that have been identified as foundational to a community psychology, several concepts are central. These ideas have informed the field and aided in its work. Among them are the ideas of prevention, a strength focus, social change and action research, a sense of community, and an interdisciplinary perspective.

Prevention Rather Than Treatment

Prevention rather than treatment was inspired at the Swampscott Conference by the public health movement (Heller et al., 1984; Kelly, 1990) and work in child psychiatry (Caplan, 1964). Prevention is an important, pivotal concept in the field. The underlying theme is that treatment comes too late in the intervention process; it is usually provided long after the individual has developed the problem, so is often ineffective. Noted psychologist Emory Cowen (1980) stated, "We became increasingly, indeed alarmingly, aware of (a) the frustration and pessimism of trying to undo psychological damage once it had passed a certain critical point; (b) the costly, time-consuming, culture-bound nature of mental health's basic approaches, and their unavailability to, and effectiveness with, large segments of society in great need" (p. 259).

On the other hand, prevention might counter any trauma before it begins, thus saving the individual and perhaps the whole community from developing a problem. In this regard, as stated earlier, community psychology takes a proactive rather than reactive role. For example, community psychologists believe it is possible that sex education *before* adolescence, teamed with new social policy, can reduce the teenage pregnancy rate. Kirby (2007) provides clear research-based guidelines on pregnancy prevention programs. In the following chapters, you will read about a variety of techniques in prevention: education, altering the environment, development of alternate interventions, and public policy changes.

Distinctions are made between levels of preventive intervention. **Primary prevention** attempts to prevent a problem from occurring altogether (Heller, Wyman, & Allen, 2000). Levine (1998) likened primary prevention to an inoculation. Just as a vaccination protects against a targeted disease, so, too, can other primary preventive strategies help an individual fend off other problems. *Primary prevention* refers most generally to activities that can be undertaken with a healthy population to maintain or enhance its health, physical and emotional (Bloom & Hodges, 1988), in other words "keeping healthy people healthy" (Scileppi, Teed, & Torres, 2000, p. 58). Primary prevention can also mean working with populations who are at risk for developing dysfunction and preventing the dysfunction from ever occurring (Cowen, 1997a, 1997b). Which preventive strategies are best (or whether they are equally efficacious) is part of the current debate in community psychology (Albee, 1998).

Cowen (1996) argued that the following criteria must be met for a program to be considered truly *primary* preventive:

- The program must be mass- or group-oriented.
- It must occur *before* the maladjustment.
- It must be intentional in the sense of having a primary focus on strengthening adjustment of the as yet unaffected.

Levine (1998, 1999) added further characteristics. Primary prevention interventions should do the following:

- Evaluate and promote synergistic effects and consider how to modify countervailing forces.
- Be structured to affect complex social structures, including redundant messages. They should be continued over time.
- Examine institutional and societal issues, not just individual factors.
- Recognize that whatever the program, it is just one part of a much larger cultural effort.
- Acknowledge that because high-risk behaviors tend to co-occur, several behaviors should be targeted.

Later, once there are some signs of problems beginning to arise, **secondary prevention** attempts to treat a problem at the earliest possible moment before it becomes severe or persistent. In other words, at-risk individuals are already manifesting some symptoms or problems. For example, youths at a particular high school might already have experimented with drugs and alcohol. Secondary preventive efforts would be directed at keeping them from becoming habitual users.

Tertiary prevention attempts to reduce the severity of an established problem and prevent it from having lasting negative effects on the individual. It is seen as similar to therapy, in that it attempts to help the afflicted person adjust to their situation (Heller, Wyman, & Allen, 2000). In other words, the at-risk individuals are already manifesting some symptoms or problematic behaviors. An example of tertiary prevention would be designing a program to help hospitalized persons with mental disorders return to the community as soon as possible (Scileppi, Teed, & Torres, 2000). Many argue that this is not really a form of prevention.

A second method for defining prevention is provided by Mrazek and Haggerty's (1994) Institute of Medicine (IOM) report. They describe three types of prevention based on the target populations involved. The first is a **universal** prevention program, which addresses the general public. Here the effort is to help the total population. The second is a **selective** program, aimed at those considered at risk for future development of problems. These risk factors may be biological, social, or psychological in nature. Last, there are **indicated** prevention programs for those who are starting to show symptoms of disorder. They also make a distinction between illness prevention programs and health promotion programs. The authors point to the difference between the nondevelopment of pathologies and the development of personal potential and sense of well-being. The first is successful when a phenomenon does not appear, and the second is successful when a phenomenon does appear. Cowen (2000) and Weissberg, Kumpfer, and Seligman (2003) argue for a synthesis of the prevention and promotion components. They point out that promotion of well-being does have a positive effect on the prevention of disorder.

Case in Point 1.2 discusses two different reviews of the literature that examined the efficacy of primary prevention programs. Both came to the same conclusion: primary prevention works.

Throughout this book, you will read about the uses of preventive programs in various settings in which psychologists work, whether they are industrial settings, law enforcement agencies, mental health agencies, or sports programs in communities. It is incumbent on psychologists, no matter where they work, to be knowledgeable about appropriate healing interventions and prevention techniques (Price, Cowen, Lorion, & Ramos-McKay, 1988). As Felner (2000) cautions, the true preventive program is one that is intentional with regard to its theoretical basis, its understanding of causal pathways, and purposeful planning and execution of programs to intercept those pathways to gainful ends.

Emphasis on Strengths and Competencies

Related closely to the idea of prevention is the notion of competence and strength. The field of psychology has historically focused on individuals' weaknesses and problems. Freud planted the seed that was cultivated by later clinicians. However, in 1959, Robert White

CASE IN POINT 1.2
DOES PRIMARY PREVENTION WORK?

Community psychologists respect prevention efforts, especially those aimed at primary prevention. Can one demonstrate, however, that primary prevention works? Primary prevention programs have been around a long time. Some have been individually evaluated, but not until the 1990s did researchers set out to determine whether, overall, primary prevention works. Fortunately, two major statistical reviews of the literature, called **meta-analyses,** were performed. Each set of researchers came to the same conclusion. Primary prevention *does* work. It is helpful to understand why the converging conclusions of both studies are rather astonishing.

In the early 1990s, at the request of the U.S. Congress, the Institute of Medicine (Mrazek & Haggerty, 1994) performed a statistical review of the mental health literature. Using "reduction of new cases of mental disorder" (p. 9) as its definition of *primary prevention,* the Institute of Medicine generated 1,900 journal citations on primary prevention of mental health problems. Overall, the institute found that primary prevention, as previously defined, does work. A quote from the final report divulges their conclusions: "With regard to preventive intervention research . . . the past decade has brought encouraging progress. At present there are many intervention programs that rest on sound conceptual and empirical foundations, and a substantial number are rigorously designed and evaluated" (p. 215).

Shortly thereafter, Durlak and Wells (1997) also completed a statistical review of the literature on primary prevention of mental health disorders. In this instance, the researchers examined programs only for children and adolescents. Using 177 programs designed to prevent behavioral and social problems, such as depressive reaction to parental divorce, they, too, found empirical support for primary prevention. For example, the average participant in the primary prevention programs surpassed the performance of between 59 and 82 percent of children in control groups, depending on the study. A quote from their journal article summarizing their findings again lends support to the notion that primary prevention, at least of mental disorders, is effective: "Outcome data indicate that most categories of primary prevention programs for most categories of primary prevention programs for children and adolescents produce significant effects. These findings provide empirical support for further research and practice in primary prevention" (p. 142).

Psychologist Emory Cowen (1997a) compared both of these statistical literature reviews and concluded that although there was amazingly little overlap in the citations each set of researchers used, the concept of primary prevention is sound. One other point he made is that each meta-analysis used a different definition of *primary prevention.* Recall that the Institute of Medicine's study definition was "reduction of new cases of mental disorder." Durlak and Wells defined *primary prevention* as reducing potential for mental health problems (like the Institute of Medicine) *as well as* increasing the competencies (or well-being) of the prevention program participants. After his comparison, Cowen concluded that research on primary prevention programs is both positive and encouraging for the future.

---

wrote about **competence,** by which he meant a sense of mastery when interacting with the environment. White's notion offered a conceptual change for psychologists concerned that clinical psychology was mired in negative human behavior.

As individuals, none of us likes to feel incompetent; instead, we like to feel a sense of strength that comes from mastering some part of our environment. Perhaps you recall the joy you felt when you passed your driver's test or exhilaration when speaking a newly learned foreign language for the first time to a native speaker. The joy of mastery is the result of competence.

Ryan (1971) claimed that our usual response to problems was to "blame the victim." It might be blatant, such as claims of laziness, lack of intelligence, incorrect priorities, or "asking for it." It could also be more subtle, such as claims of inferior cultural opportunities, lack of adequate mentoring, or the need for more services. These all place the individual victim in a place of inferiority. What if the individual was not seen as the result of "deprivation, deficits, or weakness"? What if these populations had strengths within them and had the resources to make the break from their confines? Ryan argued that the cause of many social issues is the *lack* of power.

The concept of competence was quickly embraced by early community psychologists. First, it had ecological, or environmental, implications. Ecological settings could be altered to maximize an individual's competence in them. Second, environmental competence aligned nicely with the concept of prevention. If coping was learned and strengths were enhanced early in life, problems might be avoided more easily in the future. This approach fits well with the research on resilience, which will be presented in Chapter 3. The emphasis on promoting protective factors has been found to work very well in prevention programs.

Social Change and Action Research

Community psychology has called for **social change** from its beginnings (Bennett et al., 1966; Rappaport, 1977; Seidman, 1988) and continues to incorporate it within its operational frameworks (Revenson et al., 2002; Tseng & Seidman, 2007). Social change may be defined as efforts to shift community values and attitudes and expectations as well as "opportunity structures" to help in the realization of the inherent strengths of all within a population. Keeping in mind that there have been historical advantages to some within society, efforts may be focused on ways to bring equality in these advantages and the opportunities they offer (Seidman & Rappaport, 1974).

If a variety of services are necessary for both individual and community well-being and the fit between the individual and the service is crucial, then the best way to ascertain which services and which individuals match is by means of science. Science can help community psychologists evaluate which preventive efforts work best for whom, when, and why. Research grounded in theory and directed toward resolving social problems is called **action research.**

A strong, explicit value in community psychology is that research should promote social change (Hill, Bond, Mulvey, & Terenzio, 2000). In community psychology, most action research is *participatory*; affected individuals are not merely "subjects" in a study but are active participants in shaping the research agenda (Nelson, Ochocka, Griffin, & Lord, 1998; Rappaport, 2000). An active partnership between researcher and participants is therefore the norm (Hill et al., 2000). In other words, where research is concerned, community psychologists embrace the philosophy of "nothing about me, without me" (Nelson et al., 1990).

The next chapter discusses how action research is conducted. At this point, it is important to remember that social problems are difficult to resolve, and research in community settings is complex. For instance, if one wanted to change a human services agency so that it better addresses community needs, one would probably have to research the whole agency and the people involved, including clients and staff as well as all of their interrelationships and processes within the agency. A special issue of the *American Community Psychologist* presented articles reviewing the state of the science-practice synthesis reached in community action research. Although community psychology has successfully influenced a variety of fields within the larger psychology discipline, there continue to be creative tensions between the search for empirical validation and the need to be relevant to the context. Linney (2005) pointed to four themes arising from the science-practice issue:

1. Effective strategies to bridge science and practice, so as to strengthen the capacity to do both within the community.
2. Changing who determines what is important, that is, giving the community power in determining what is important and useful, the direction of the decision making changing from a science directing practice, to a model where the community is a full partner in decision making.
3. A broadening of the definition of good science beyond the "narrow" laboratory-based experimental designs.
4. Dealing with the difficulty of implementing the values and ideals given the contingencies under which many psychologists work, for example, publish or perish, the valuing of true experimental designs and the devaluing of quasi- or nonexperimental designs.

Action research is a strong allied concept. It relates to community psychology's emphasis on research and on its valuing of empowerment.

Interdisciplinary Perspectives

Creating social change is a monumental task. Community psychologists would have to be quite audacious to suggest that they can create change by themselves. Collaboration with sister disciplines is a means of producing more sweeping and well-reasoned change (Maton, 2000; Strother, 1987). Contemporary community psychologists have long enjoyed intellectual and research exchanges with colleagues in other academic disciplines, such as political science, anthropology, and sociology, as well as other areas of psychology, such as social psychology (Altman, 1987; Jason, Hess, Felner, & Moritsugu, 1987). Some are calling for renewed interdisciplinary efforts (Linney, 1990; Wardlaw, 2000) with other community professionals, such as substance-abuse counselors, law enforcement personnel, school psychologists, and human services professionals, among others.

Kelly (1990) suggested that **collaboration** with others gives new awareness of how other disciplines experience a phenomenon. A benefit of consultation with others such as historians, economists, environmentalists, biologists, sociologists, anthropologists, and policy scientists is that perspectives can be expanded and new perspectives adopted. Case in Point 1.3 demonstrates integration of social and community psychology theories.

CASE IN POINT 1.3
SOCIAL PSYCHOLOGY, COMMUNITY PSYCHOLOGY, AND HOMELESSNESS

You have learned in this chapter that community psychologists have issued a call for collaboration with other disciplines both within and outside of psychology. In response to that, we agree that community psychologists and social psychologists have much that they can learn from each other (Serrano-Garcia, Lopez, & Rivera-Medena, 1987).

Social psychologists study social phenomena as they affect an individual. They may have the answer as to why the media, the public, and other psychologists blame a person's homelessness on the person. Social psychologists have developed an explanation using **attribution theory,** which explains how people infer causes of or make attributions about others' behaviors (Kelly, 1973). Research on attribution has demonstrated that people are likely to place explanatory emphasis on the characteristics of the individual or use trait explanations for another's shortcomings (Jones & Nisbett, 1971). That is, when explaining the behavior of others—especially others' problems—people are less likely to attend to the situation and more likely to blame the person for what is happening.

Does this theory apply to homelessness? Can this theory explain why the media and the public often blame the victim, the homeless person, for his or her problem? *Victim blaming* (Ryan, 1971) is a phrase that describes the tendency to attribute the cause of an individual's problems to that individual rather than to the situation the person is in. In other words, the victim is blamed for what happened to him or her. Social psychologists believe that blaming the victim is a means of self-defense (e.g., if a bad thing can happen to her by chance, then it can happen to me; on the other hand if the person was to blame for what happened, then it won't happen to me because I am not that way). In the case of the homeless, did their personality create their homeless situations? Did something in their environment contribute to it? The average person who blames the victim would blame the person for contributing to their homelessness.

Shinn, a prominent community psychologist, reviewed research on homelessness and conducted a monumental and well-designed study on the issue (Shinn & Gillespie, 1993). She concluded that person-centered explanations of homelessness, although popular, are not as valid as situational and structural explanations of homelessness. Specifically, Shinn suggested that the researched explanations for homelessness are twofold—that is, person-centered and environmental. She reviewed the literature on each and concluded that person-centered or deficit explanations for homelessness were less appropriate than environmental or situational explanations.

Shinn found studies that suggest that structural problems offer some of the most plausible explanations of homelessness. For example, Rossi (1989) found that between 1969 and 1987, the number of single adults (some with children) with incomes under $4,000 a year increased from 3.1 to 7.2 million. Similarly, Leonard, Dolbeare, and Lazere (1989) found that for the 5.4 million low-income renters, there were only 2.1 million units of affordable housing, according to the U.S. Department of Housing and Urban Development standards. Poverty and lack of affordable housing seem to be far better explanations for today's phenomenon of homelessness than person-centered explanations. Solarz and Bogat (1990) would add to these environmental explanations of homelessness the lack of social support by friends and family of the homeless.

What is important about Shinn's review is not so much that it illustrates that the public and the media may indeed suffer from **fundamental attribution error**—the tendency to blame the person and not the situation—but rather that Shinn offers these data so community psychologists can act on them. Public policy makers need to understand that situations and structural problems produce homelessness. Psychologists and community leaders need to be convinced that providing temporary solutions, such as soup kitchens, are merely bandages on the gaping wound of the homeless. Furthermore, shelter managers and others have to understand that moving the homeless from one shelter to another does little for them. Families and children, not just the stereotypical old alcoholic men, are part of today's homeless (Rossi, 1990). Being in different shelters and therefore different school systems has negative effects on children's academic performance and self-esteem (Rafferty & Shinn, 1991); homeless children lose their childhoods to homelessness (Landers, 1989).

Something must be done about the permanent housing situation in this country. On this point, both community and social psychologists would agree.

A Psychological Sense of Community

The sense of community is one of the most important concepts emerging from community psychology (Sarason, 1974). It is a way to bridge the seeming contraction between the group-oriented term *community* and the individual-oriented focus of psychology. The psychological sense of community (PSC) is an individual's perception of group membership.

If environments and individuals are well matched, a community with a sense of spirit and a sense of "we-ness" can be created. Research has demonstrated that a sense of community, or what is sometimes called *community spirit* or sense of belonging in the community, is positively related to a subjective sense of well-being (Davidson & Cotter, 1991). In an optimal community, members probably will be more open to changes that will further improve their community.

On the other hand, social disintegration of a community or neighborhood often results in high fear of crime and vandalism (Ross & Jang, 2000) as well as declines in children's mental health (Caspi, Taylor, Moffitt, & Plomin, 2000) and increases in school problems (Hadley-Ives, Stiffman, Elze, Johnson, & Dore, 2000), loneliness (Prezza, Amici, Tiziana, & Tedeschi, 2001), and myriad other problems. Community disorder may intensify both the benefits of personal resources (such as connections to neighbors) and the detrimental effects of personal risk factors (Cutrona, Russell, Hessling, Brown, & Murry, 2000).

Interestingly, research has demonstrated that happiness and the sense of satisfaction with one's community is not found exclusively in the suburbs. People living in the suburbs are no more likely to express satisfaction with their neighborhoods than people living in the city (Adams, 1992) or small towns (Prezza et al., 2001). Many laypeople and psychologists believe that residents of the inner city are at risk for myriad problems. However, research has found that some very resilient individuals are located in the most stressful parts of our cities (Work, Cowen, Parker, & Wyman, 1990).

Community has traditionally meant a locality or place such as a neighborhood. It has also come to mean a relational interaction or social ties that draw people together (Heller, 1989b). To these definitions could be added the one of community as a collective political power.

If those are the definitions for *community*, what is the sense of community? **Sense of community** is the feeling of the relationship an individual holds for his or her community (Heller et al., 1984) or the personal knowledge that one has about belonging to a collective of others (Newbrough & Chavis, 1986). More specifically, it is "the perception of similarity to others, an acknowledged interdependence with others, a willingness to maintain this interdependence by giving to or doing for others what one expects from them, the feeling that one is part of a larger dependable and stable structure" (Sarason, 1974, p. 157). If people sense community in their neighborhood, they feel that they belong to or fit into the neighborhood. Community members sense that they can influence what happens in the community, share the values of the neighborhood, and feel emotionally connected to it (Heller et al., 1984).

A sense of community is specifically thought to include four elements: membership, influence, integration, and a sense of emotional connection (McMillan & Chavis, 1986).

1. *Membership* means that people experience feelings of belonging in their community.
2. *Influence* signifies that people feel they can make a difference in their community.
3. *Integration,* or fulfillment of needs, suggests that members of the community believe that their needs will be met by resources available in the community.
4. *Emotional connection* implies that community members have and will share history, time, places, and experiences.

Although there have been a variety of criticisms and alternatives to this conceptualization of psychological sense of community (Long & Perkins, 2003; Tartaglia, 2006), the operational definition of this sense by McMillan and Chavis (1986) remains the definitive model for this concept. Long and Perkins (2003) found a three-factor structure for their data: social connections, mutual concerns, and community values. Tartaglia (2006), using an Italian sample, produced a three-factor measure that included attachment to place, needs fulfillment and influence, and social bonds. In its newest evolution, Peterson, Speer, and McMillan (2008) have produced an eight-item Brief Sense of Community Scale, which produces all four of the McMillan and Chavis (1986) elements with significant statistical validity.

A concept related to sense of community is **neighboring,** which is a person's emotional, cognitive, and social attachment to a neighborhood that makes him or her more likely to participate in neighborhood organizations (Unger & Wandersman, 1985) and is therefore a different or distinct concept from sense of community (Prezza et al., 2001). **Neighborhoods** might be defined as local communities that are bounded together spatially where residents feel a sense of social cohesion and interaction, homogeneity, as well as place identity (Coulton, Korbin, & Su, 1996). Research has demonstrated the utility of conceptualizing "sense of community" separately from "neighborhoods" (Prezza et al., 2001). A sense of community need not be experienced only in a whole community. People can develop a sense of community in a group, an organization, or for almost any aggregate of individuals. A promising scale has been developed to measure the sense of community

FIGURE 1.1 Sample Items from the Brief Sense of Community Scale

1. I think my neighborhood is a good place to live.
2. I can recognize most of the people who live in my neighborhood.
3. I expect to live in this neighborhood a long time.
4. If there is a problem in the neighborhood, people who live here can get it solved.

Source: From Peterson, Speer, and Hughey (2006).

(Buckner, 1988). This scale, which is designed to measure neighborhood cohesion or fellowship, seems psychometrically sound. Wilkinson (2007) found in a Canadian sample, validation of the Buckner conceptualization of neighborhood cohesion, and also discovered a three-factor structure to his findings. For his data cohesion was based on a psychological sense of community, neighboring, and attraction.

COMMUNITY PSYCHOLOGY TODAY

Where is the field of community psychology today? Has it achieved some of its lofty goals? Fortunately, there is research assessing historical changes in the field to determine whether community psychology is making any progress.

Some in the field feel the ardor, zeal, optimism, and commitment that once characterized community psychology have faded (Linney, 1990). Kelly (2002) recalls the spirit with which community psychology started. There was enthusiasm for the new field and excitement over the promise of what could be made of it. He cautions that this "spirit" could be lost, given the demands of universities and professional organizations. Do the data bear out that community psychology is progressing or backsliding? We hope to provide a lengthy answer throughout this book.

RESEARCH

One way to answer this question is to examine the earlier research with the newer research. Speer et al. (1992) examined the topics, the populations studied, and the sophistication of the measures and methodologies used in community psychology research. Fortunately for them, previous research conducted by Lounsbury, Leader, Meares, and Cook (1980) from approximately a decade earlier was available for comparison purposes. Speer and colleagues reviewed 235 empirical studies (defined as reporting the results of research investigations) in the top two journals of community psychology from 1984 to 1988 and compared their findings to those of Lounsbury and associates. Here is what they found.

In community psychology, the number of **experiments** where variables were actively manipulated decreased over the decade, whereas the number of **field studies,** where no variables were actively manipulated, increased. The use of **control groups** or comparison groups also decreased, as one might expect because experimental manipulations had decreased. Hence, there is a recognition today that experiments may not be feasible or appropriate for community research (Casswell, 2000).

Participants with identified psychological problems were less likely to appear in the more recent studies than the older studies. Over the years, the reporting of participant gender and ethnic origin increased. Articles categorized as dealing with mental health services decreased with time, but the number of articles categorized by the authors as problem-specific increased, particularly in the areas of social support and prevention.

Martin et al. (2004) completed the latest of these research reviews. Looking at over half of the 244 articles published in the *American Journal of Community Psychology* between 1993 and 1998, they found a continuing decline in use of mental health setting participants (6 percent, down from 12 percent), a continued use of individual-level dependent variables, and a decline in the use of experimental design. The research design of choice was the quasi-experimental with 60 percent of the examined studies in this category. The authors believed that these research trends exemplified a continuing shift into research more relevant to the study of communities and the real world. The laboratory study is an anomaly. There was a growing use of mixed and quasi-experimental designs as well as qualitative methods to help discern the complexities of community phenomena and the diverse groups studied.

Notably, there are now fewer studies of people who are chronically mentally ill. Instead, examination of larger portions of participants from the community at large demonstrates that research is being conducted in settings *as* and *where* social problems occur.

The disappointing news is that many of the dependent measures in these studies continue to focus on the individual level of analysis. Although it is true that today there are more studies on person–environment variables, such as **social support** (where individuals assist one another with coping), the literature still very much retains an individual-based, adjustment orientation.

Of note is Toro's (2005) comment on how the field has become so diverse. This diversity extends to the many theories, approaches to problems, issues addressed, and populations served. Although some may call this unfocused, Toro believes this to be an indication of health and vitality as the field expands its boundaries and takes on new challenges.

WHAT'S IN IT FOR YOU?

Undergraduate Education

Many psychology departments now offer community psychology courses. Others offer classes in community mental health or clinical psychology, where the professor prefers to adopt a community orientation. However, the training offered to undergraduates may only be a course or two. Carmony et al. (2000) found 77 undergraduate community psychology classes in an Internet search. They reviewed 24 of the course syllabi, finding that a majority of classes included the topics of prevention, historical context, social change and action, ecology, empowerment, research methods, social support, and stress. We cover all of these topics in this text.

Another way undergraduates can learn more about the community is to become involved in the local college community or the students' hometowns. Thousands of community agencies solicit volunteers, but of course, many of these agencies do not adopt a community psychology orientation. For example, many supply treatment and therefore do not focus on prevention. Volunteers are the lifeblood of many community agencies that run on limited budgets. College personnel may be able to give you the names and phone numbers of local agencies. If you choose to volunteer, try to determine whether the agency promotes the goals of community psychology and if not, why not.

Students often volunteer in the community as part of their course experience, and many continue the experience after the community psychology course ends. Volunteers are indeed special people in terms of their commitment and identification with the organizations for which they work (Clary & Snyder, 1999). Likewise, by working for someone else's benefit rather than for self-interest, volunteers show selflessness. Research on volunteerism demonstrates that volunteers report significantly greater satisfaction than stress from volunteering, despite whether their volunteer work is mandatory or fully voluntary (Ferrari, Billows, Jason, & Grill, 1997; Ferrari & Jason, 1996). Research also confirms that volunteering gives coursework more meaning and students more awareness of social issues as well as increased appreciation for diversity (Primavera, 1999). However, there is research that demonstrates *requiring* service can actually reduce intentions to volunteer in the future. The most important aspect of volunteering appears to be the match between the motives of the volunteer and the actual volunteer situation (Clary & Snyder, 1999). Here are comments from some student volunteers:

> When I began volunteering I wasn't sure how much of an impact I would have, if any. I have come to realize that it is not the impact of me on members at [my volunteer site] but their combined effect on me. Each time I give my time for them, they truly appreciate it. My "problems" seem so superficial when I am at [my volunteer site]. I can compare myself to them and realize how fortunate I am for the life I live. Volunteering is one way that I can show how thankful I am for all I have. I plan to continue my volunteering through graduation. I know that the time I sacrifice is going to a good cause. —Sue Strom, class of 1999

> Admittedly, people lead very busy lives. However, when we say we do not have time, we often mean that we do not have time for others, not realizing the personal fulfillment that volunteering can bring. To volunteer is to not only make time for others but to make time for yourself and your community. . . . As I was getting ready to leave [my volunteer site at a developmental center for clients with mental disabilities] to go to class one morning, I made a point of walking over to Stephen to say goodbye. He and I had spent some time together that morning stenciling a rose and coloring it in. When I walked over to him and told him I was leaving, he gently grabbed my hand. He then reached for my other hand and held them both firmly. I smiled, and after a few seconds gradually pulled my hands loose. Stephen then raised his arms and reached for my neck. Although [he] is a very passive man, I do not know if he has mood swings or if there is a more aggressive side to his personality. Therefore, I was taken aback at first and pulled away. However, when I did so, Stephen looked a little puzzled and tried to pull me closer. Reluctantly, I decided to give him the benefit of the doubt and allowed him to put his hands around my neck. When he did so, he pulled me toward him and gave me a kiss on the cheek. He then gently let go and smiled.
>
> I left that morning with a greater sense of personal satisfaction than I have felt in a long time. Stephen told me that he appreciated the time I spent with him. He taught me that a little time and patience go a long way. —Susan Ehrhard, class of 2000

Figure 1.2 provides some interesting facts about volunteering.

FIGURE 1.2 Facts about Volunteering

- 61.2 million people volunteered in the United States during 2006
- 18.1 billion hours were donated
- 26.7 percent of Americans volunteered
- Utah and Vermont were ranked first and second for youth volunteer rates

Source: 2007 Volunteering in America: State Trends and Rankings in Civic Life (www.independentsector.org).

The growth of the service learning movement in college has brought the college student into the community (Chapman & Ferrari, 1999; Wilczenski & Coomey, 2007). Service learning is not restricted to psychology but is offered throughout many liberal arts curriculum departments. Its effects have been measured in quasi-experimental designs and suggest that giving time to the community can make an impact on student perceptions of the community (less distant) and themselves (more connected) (Howard, 2003).

Advanced Training in Community Psychology

Concentrated training programs in community psychology tend to be master's or doctorate programs. The discipline is still rather new compared to other areas of psychology, but some research does exist on graduate training in community psychology. Sandler and Keller (1984), in a review of graduate programs in community psychology, found that most programs use a *scientific practitioner* model. The students are trained to conduct research but also to act on the research or practice the discipline based on its scientific foundations. Some community psychology programs are freestanding; others are clinical-community programs (combinations of clinical and community psychology).

Clinical-community programs emphasize intellectual ability in selecting student applicants and are more likely to place students at child-family services, hospitals, and community mental health centers. On the other hand, freestanding community psychology programs emphasize a commitment to action in student applicants and place students at human services and advocacy organizations (Maton, Meissen, & O'Conner, 1993). Courses at the graduate level generally include program evaluation, a community psychology seminar, and interdisciplinary courses. The content relates to several areas of community psychology, including (but not limited to) systems change, individual change, prevention, and the psychology of particular settings.

Walfish, Polifka, and Stenmark (1986) conducted a survey of job-search outcomes for recent doctoral students in community psychology. The students had little difficulty finding positions; in fact, 84 percent reported that it was easy or very easy to find a job. Some 83 percent reported obtaining the job at their first-choice agency. The major employment settings for the doctoral graduates were universities, community mental health centers, medical schools, research and consulting firms, and health care facilities. O'Donnell and Ferrari (2000) provide a collection of essays from around the world considering the many areas in which community psychologists have found employment. Over 20 years after the Walfish et al. study, we find graduate programs in community psychology to be quite diverse. Figure 1.3 lists some of the universities with doctoral programs in community

FIGURE 1.3 Sample of Graduate Programs in Community Psychology

PH.D. PROGRAMS IN COMMUNITY PSYCHOLOGY
Curtin University, Australia
DePaul University
Edith Cowan University, Australia
Georgia State University

University of Hawaii
University of Illinois—Chicago
Université Laval, Canada
Michigan State University
University of Maryland—Baltimore County
Portland State University
University of Québec in Montréal
Vanderbilt University, Peabody College
University of Virginia
University of Waikato, New Zealand
Wichita State University
Wilfrid Laurier University, Canada
Instituto Superior de Psicologia Aplicada, Portugal

PH.D. CLINICAL-COMMUNITY PSYCHOLOGY
University of Alaska
Arizona State University
Bowling Green State University
California School of Professional Psychology—L.A.
University of Connecticut
George Washington University
Georgia State University
University of Illinois—Urbana-Champaign
University of La Verne
University of Maryland—Baltimore County
Michigan State University
Rutgers University, GSAPP
University of South Carolina
Wayne State University
Wichita State University

MASTER'S PROGRAMS IN COMMUNITY PSYCHOLOGY
Central Connecticut State University
London School of Economics
Manchester Metropolitan University
University of Massachusetts—Lowell
Pennsylvania State University—Harrisburg
The Sage Colleges
Victoria University of Technology, Australia

Source: Society for the Community Research and Action (Division 27 of the American Psychological Association) (www.scra27.org/resources/educationc/academicpr) December 1, 2008.

psychology, clinical-community psychology and master's programs of community psychology. Of note is the inclusion of at least a few foreign universities. Our sense is that there are in fact several more foreign programs that have not made these lists. We discuss this more in the final chapter.

PLAN OF THE BOOK

Now that you are on your way to understanding community psychology, you probably would like to know what the rest of your journey through this book will be like. The remainder of Part I, which is the introductory portion of the book, will introduce you to its research processes (Chapter 2) and the stress and resilience models (Chapter 3) from which the work in community settings takes direction. Researchers in community psychology employ some of the venerated methods used by other psychologists as well as techniques that are fairly unique and innovative. You then explore the stress and resilience models for understanding adaptation and adjustment to the social environment.

Part II consists of two chapters on social change (Chapter 4) and intervention (Chapter 5). The first chapter outlines why social change is important and yet so difficult. The second chapter discusses strategies for community interventions.

Part III (Chapters 6–12) examines settings into which community psychology have come to be applied. From mental health settings and issues, community psychologists easily moved into social and human services, school systems, criminal justice, health care, and community organizational settings and issues. Part IV, the final chapter of the book, looks ahead at what the future holds for the field of community psychology.

Each chapter provides one or more Cases in Point to engage you more actively with the material or to exemplify or elucidate a particular point. Unlike the chapter opening vignettes, which may be somewhat clinical in nature, as explained in the Preface, the Cases in Point will be more purely oriented to community psychology.

SUMMARY

Community psychology evolves from social science attempts to understand the human condition and effectively improve it. Lewin's legacy is apparent in the themes of social change and community research. With a belief in the power of diversity, an understanding of the influence of context on individual actions, a realization of the advantages of a multilayered ecological perspective on behavior patterns and how they can be effectively changed, and a conviction that empowered individuals can be healthier individuals, community psychology addresses the prevention of pathology and the promotion of health. Embedded in these principles is the assumption that we all seek and need community. Without it, we are alone and alienated. With it, we are grounded and secure. The area has grown from a set of ideas to an organized and developing approach to psychological interventions. Graduate programs are now identified with the field. The reader is invited to explore the possibilities of a community psychology.

CHAPTER 2

SCIENTIFIC RESEARCH METHODS

THE ESSENCE OF SCIENTIFIC RESEARCH
   Why Do Scientific Research?
   What Is Scientific Research?
      Theory
      Models and Paradigms
      Falsifiability
      Example
      Scientific Revolutions
   ■ CASE IN POINT 2.1 A Theory of Substance Abuse and HIV/STDs that Incorporates the Principles of Community Psychology
   The Fidelity of Scientific Research

TRADITIONAL SCIENTIFIC RESEARCH METHODS
   Population and Sampling
   Correlational Research
   Experimental Research
   Quasi-Experimental Research

OTHER RESEARCH METHODS USED IN COMMUNITY PSYCHOLOGY
   Ethnography
   Network Analysis

■ CASE IN POINT 2.2 Case Study of a Consumer Run Agency
■ CASE IN POINT 2.3 Cracking the Network
   Epidemiology
   Needs Assessment and Program Evaluation
   Participatory Research

THE URGENCY OF RESEARCH IN COMMUNITY PSYCHOLOGY AND RELATED PITFALLS
   The Politics of Science and the Science of Politics
   Ethics: Cultural Relativism or Universal Human Rights?
   The Continuum of Research: The Value of Multiple Measures
   The Importance of Cultural Sensitivity
   Community Researchers as Consultants

SUMMARY

> *The connection between cause and effect has no beginning and can have no end.*
> —Leo Tolstoy, *War and Peace*

Edisak, his wife, and their two young sons came to the United States as refugees in the early 1990s from a war-torn Southeast Asian country. Their immigration application was sponsored by Catholic Charities. Soon after their arrival, there were signs of domestic problems. His wife and children moved into a shelter for a brief period of time. The family was subsequently reunited. Edisak started working as a full-time clerk in a grocery store, and his wife worked part-time as part of a cleaning crew in a local hospital. Caseworkers continued to work with the family in their adjustment to the new culture and environment, among other psychosocial issues.

In the mid-1990s, Edisak took one of his frequent trips back to his home country. The purpose of these trips was unclear; his wife did not question his motives. Edisak came back from the latest trip seriously ill. Subsequently, he tested positive for HIV. His wife also tested positive; she was pregnant with their third child. Edisak insisted he did not know how he contracted the virus; he denied any extramarital activities and drug abuse.

Without a vaccine, prevention is the only weapon for halting the spread of the disease. There are many strategies of HIV prevention. A highly controversial prevention strategy is the use of legal means (i.e., health-related policy as prevention) to gauge the pandemic. The U.S. government requires all potential immigrants and refugees to undergo HIV testing before settling in the United States. Only those who test HIV-negative are allowed to enter the country; a waiver is available for refugees requiring them to be seen and have follow-up visits by medical and health professionals once they are admitted into the United States. But this legal mechanism has little recourse in preventing people (including those born in the United States) who are already HIV-positive or living with AIDS in the United States from traveling back and forth overseas. In the case of Edisak, he was probably infected during one of his trips to Asia. Because HIV and AIDS carry tremendous social stigma, verbal inquiry of people's HIV status may not be an effective prevention strategy. Meanwhile, testing as a prevention strategy is only effective when people are willing to be tested and understand the consequences and responsibilities of testing positive. What strategies or scientific methods should be used with a mobile population? What strategies should be used with HIV-positive pregnant women?

THE ESSENCE OF SCIENTIFIC RESEARCH

The preceding vignette presents a scenario that is all too familiar to community psychologists. The two scientific research techniques (HIV blood testing and self-report measures) *have not produced the same results.* Furthermore, some scientific research techniques are insensitive or inappropriate to investigate certain issues, especially those that may jeopardize the well-being of the participants. It should come as no surprise that many people do not disclose their HIV status because of its stigma as well as the general AIDS phobia and homophobia (despite the fact that it is not a disease afflicting only homosexuals) of the general U.S. public. Although the U.S. Supreme Court ruled that HIV falls within the general purview of the Americans with Disabilities Act, disclosure is about more than legal rights and protection—it's about being socially ostracized.

This example also intimates that research in community psychology is often conducted with a sense of urgency not seen in other fields of psychology. That is, the issues examined by community psychologists are often important, pressing social issues of the day. Before discussing some of the issues (e.g., confidentiality and cultural sensitivity) related to this urgency, we present some definitions and the reasons for engaging in scientific research. The discussion follows with a review of the various types of scientific research methods used by community psychologists—both traditional and nontraditional psychological research methods.

Why Do Scientific Research?

We have come to assume that our experiences in life help us determine what is true and real. This assumption that experience is our window on reality is called *empiricism*. The tradition of examining the world around us for evidence of what to believe goes back to the Greek philosophers and later to the observational studies of the Renaissance. We have come to accept this tradition as the science on which our modern world is built. How do we know about the world around us? We observe it, note its regularities and patterns, test its possibilities, and determine the likelihood of particular events predicting or causing other events.

A major intervention strategy in the field of community psychology is to create or engage in some form of social change so that individuals and communities may benefit. To distinguish the effective from the less effective changes, psychologists need a way to help understand and assess these changes. Scientific research provides that mechanism and so has been an essential part of community psychology from its conception and throughout its development (Anderson et al., 1966; Cohen, 1966; Lorian, 1983; Price, 1983; Tolan, Keys, Chertak, & Jason, 1990).

For example, how can researchers be sure that decreases in risky behaviors, such as unprotected sex or sharing needles when injecting drugs, are solely due to people's participation in some form of prevention programs? If Edisak and his wife had the opportunity to participate in such a program, how could someone determine whether their participation reduced their likelihood of unprotected sex rather than other factors, such as sharing needles when injecting drugs? Although one might find that women who enroll in such programs (a social change) are less likely to engage in unprotected sex compared with those who do not, a further analysis of the data might indicate that women with spouses who are willing to use condoms are the ones who benefit from the programs. That is, for many women, such as Edisak's wife, enrollment in a prevention program is not sufficient to reduce unprotected sex *unless* they can go back to a home environment or community with some support (the ecological perspective)—the differential power between the genders often work to the disadvantage of the women in negotiating safer sex. However, the validity of this assumption can be verified using some form of scientific research.

Price (1983) pointed to areas in which the community psychologist would need research. First, problems or areas of concern need to be identified and described. Second, the factors related to these problems and concerns would need to be articulated. From this articulation, possible interventions or solutions may be constructed and tested. Once a program has been found to be effective, there is still the need to examine whether the intervention can be successfully implemented in given community contexts. If the implementation succeeds, then the issue of successful launching of programs on a broader scale needs to be studied. If these programs are successful, the researcher is left to reexamine the community status and see what other needs may exist. The research cycle provides guidance from identification of community problems to community-wide dissemination of answers to the problems. This process is an integral part to a community psychology.

What Is Scientific Research?

On a daily basis, people observe and make attributions about many things. For example, you might have some hunches as to why men do or do not use condoms or why people abuse alcohol and drugs. However, to scientists, research is more than hunches. In other words, when scientists conduct research, they use a set of related assumptions and activities. Figure 2.1 depicts the process of scientific research.

Theory and theory-based research are an integral part of all scientific disciplines (Kuhn, 1962, 1996), and the field of community psychology is no exception. Before discussing theory, however, we explain three theoretical terms that often confuse scientists and laypersons alike.

Theory. At one time or another, you probably have heard some people use the terms *theory, model,* and *paradigm.* The words are often used interchangeably, but they are not quite synonymous. A **theory** is a systematic attempt to explain observable or measurable events relating to an issue such as homelessness or alcoholism. More exactly, a theory is a "set of interrelated constructs (concepts), definitions, and propositions that present a systematic view of phenomena by specifying relations among variables, with the purpose of explaining or predicting the phenomena" (Kerlinger, 1973, p. 9). The goal of a theory is to

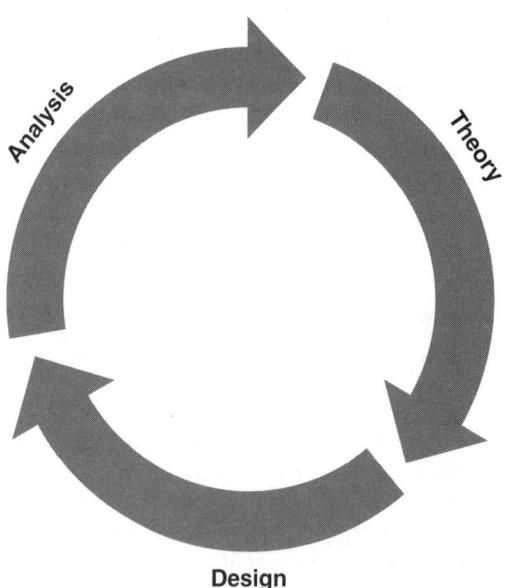

FIGURE 2.1 The Process of Scientific Research

allow researchers to describe, predict, and control for *why* and *how* a variable or variables relate to observable or measurable events pertaining to an issue. For example, did Edisak's numerous trips to Asia predict his HIV status? During one of his trips, did he engage in risky behaviors promoting the contraction of HIV—injecting drugs (sharing needles) or having unprotected sex with someone other than his wife?

Bear in mind that social science theories best serve as guideposts for studying observable or measurable events. In other words, description and prediction of as well as control for these events are based on suggested *rules* rather than *absolute laws* such as what is more often found in the physical sciences (Kuhn, 1970).

Models and Paradigms. On the other hand, a **model** is a working blueprint of a theory. A **paradigm** is a smaller framework that guides researchers to conceptualize events in a consistent fashion. Figure 2.2 depicts these relationships. In his classic but controversial essay on science and scientific revolutions, Kuhn (1962/1996) uses the term *paradigm* with two meanings. The first is to describe a set or collection of ideas, values, and theories that are commonly agreed on in a sociological way to guide the direction and conduction of scientific inquiry. The second sense is as the "concrete puzzle solution" to a given problem. Our definition here emphasizes the second sense of the term. However, we note that when speaking of paradigm shifts in psychology, that reference is to the first sense, that is, the sociologically based collective and group-oriented definition of the term paradigm. Initial reactions to Kuhn criticized his mixing of definitions, which did make for confusion. He tried to clarify and correct this in an apologetic postscript in the later edition of his book.

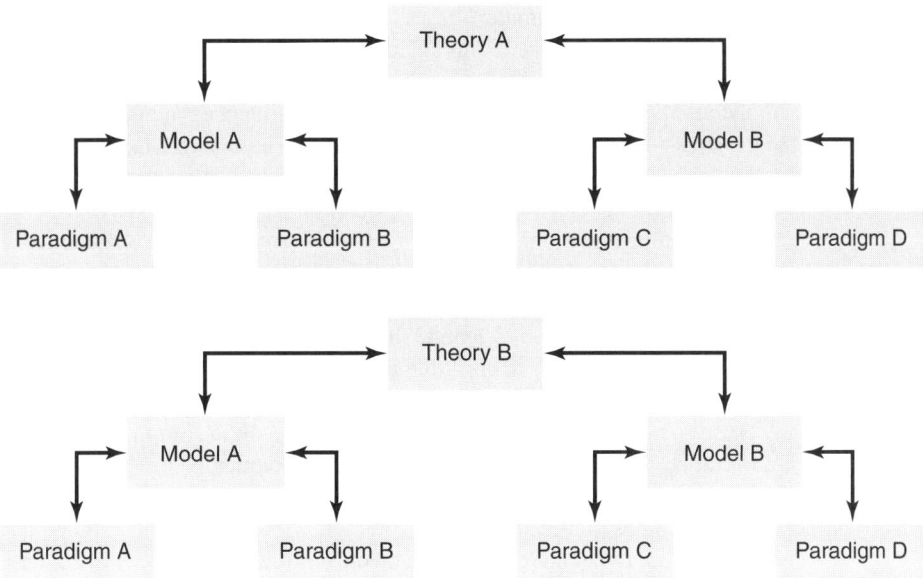

FIGURE 2.2 The Relationship among Theories, Models, and Paradigms

A theory may consist of more than one model or blueprint. These models guide the understanding of the different observable events pertaining to an issue. A well-developed theory is likely to be made up of two or more compatible models, which are likely to be conceptualized using similar concrete paradigms or frameworks. In the case of an undeveloped theory, different paradigms may lead to the formulation of different models. It is plausible, then, for observable or measurable events relating to an issue to be explained by more than one theory.

Falsifiability. The hallmark of a science according to Popper (1957/1990) is the continuous testing of the proposition or theory at hand. The testing assumes that there is always the possibility of the proposition or theory being false. This *falsifiability* calls for a reliance on observable events to help support any given concept.

Example. A more concrete example will help you understand these terms. For decades, researchers investigating alcoholism or alcohol abuse (the issue) have conceptualized excessive drinking (the observable or measurable event) as a consequence of a genetic predisposition—a medical explanation of alcoholism as a disease (the theoretical perspective). This theory helped shape the development of various models about alcohol abuse. For example, one model promoted the identification of the gene(s) responsible for alcoholism. Another model allowed for the comparison of alcohol use in identical twins versus genetically unrelated individuals.

In recent years, some researchers have begun to challenge the genetic disease theory of alcoholism. Instead, they argue that some aspects of excessive alcohol use (again, the observable or measurable event) may be a consequence of something in the environment, such as stress from losing one's home, a difficult life on the streets, prolonged unemployment, or some other traumatic life event. Thus, a new theory emerges—the distress or disorder theory of alcoholism. This sociological *paradigm shift* or refocusing of thinking or conceptualizing from genetics to environment again leads to the development of models. One model specifies that socioeconomic status influences alcoholism. Another suggests that the stress of minority ethnic status plays a role in alcoholism. In other words, this theory allows for the description and prediction of differential alcohol use for individuals with different environmental stressors. On the other hand, the first theory—the disease theory—offers description and prediction of individual differences based on genetics.

Scientific Revolutions. These two examples illustrate the dynamic nature or ever-evolving aspect of the development of scientific theories. Kuhn (1962/1996) argued that major scientific development is not linear, not a step-by-step accumulation of fact. Such is the case of theory and research in the field of community psychology. Within a scientific discipline, a crisis may cause a shift in thinking; such a sociological paradigm shift may shape the development of a new theory. Recall that just such a crisis (discouragement with traditional methods of treatment of mental illness) gave birth to the field of community psychology, which developed new methods and theories about community problems. Kuhn argued that a paradigm serves as a *guide* rather than an absolute theoretical standard for scientific interpretation.

Theories, models, and paradigms in the field of community psychology serve this function as guides. When a theory does not work, it needs either fine-tuning or abandonment. You will read about many of the current theories, models, and paradigms in the field of community psychology in other chapters of this book. You will also be introduced to the research related to each theory; through research, one makes judgments about theories. Case in Point 2.1 introduces an integrated theory of drug abuse.

CASE IN POINT 2.1
A THEORY OF SUBSTANCE ABUSE AND HIV/STDS THAT INCORPORATES THE PRINCIPLES OF COMMUNITY PSYCHOLOGY

There are over 40 theories for studying drug abuse (see Lettieri, Sayers, & Pearson, 1984). Some of these theories are person-centered, such as the medical or genetic theory of alcoholism; other theories are environmental, such as the stress or disorder theory.

Flay and Petraitis (1991) identified a number of determinants of drug abuse on the basis of 24 studies. They concluded that the determinants of abuse are some combination of the social environment; social bonding of the individual to the family, peers, and community organizations such as schools; social learning and learning from others; intrapsychic factors such as self-esteem; and the individual's own knowledge of, attitudes toward, and behaviors related to alcohol and drugs. Flay and Petraitis argued that a majority of these theories address only one of these domains. For the field to advance, an effort needs to be made to integrate more of these domains into one coherent theory. Community psychologists would heartily agree.

Responding to this challenge, Wong and Bouey (2001) proposed an integrated theory for studying substance abuse as well as HIV/STDs (sexually transmitted diseases) among American Indian/Alaska Natives (AI/ANs). This population was singled out because, compared to other racial/ethnic groups in the United States, many AI/ANs have a more serious substance abuse problem (National Household Survey on Drug Abuse, 1999 in Substance Abuse and Mental Health Services Administration, 2000), which places them at risk for STDs, including HIV (CDC/IHS National Epidemiology Program, 2001; Howard, Bouey, Greenwood, & Duran, 2001).

Most substance abuse and HIV prevention and intervention programs have enlisted psychosocial models of individual behavior. These models, however, tend to isolate individuals and assume all individuals follow regular and rational decision-making processes (e.g., DiClemente & Peterson, 1994; Leviton, 1989; Valdiserri, West, Moore, Darrow, & Hinman, 1992), a position consistent with the reasoning of the dominant medical model in health-related programs (Singer, Flores, Davison, et al., 1990). Though individuals are undeniably the key component of such programs, individual behavior occurs in a complex social and cultural context, and analysis that removes that behavior from its broader setting ignores essential determinants (Auerbach, Wypijewska, & Brodie, 1994). Individuals may, in fact, behave rationally, but they do so within the confines of their own sociocultural milieus. Attempts to address this breadth of factors result in the recognition that responses to typical knowledge, attitude, and behavior measures are constructions by individual actors situated within the interplay of (a) political, (b) economic, (c) social, and (d) cultural realms (Bouey, Duran, Hendrickson, et al., 1997; Nemoto et al., 1998; see Figure 2.3). These forces create opportunities and obstacles for individuals and define the parameters within which they function (Conners & McGrath, 1997). Bouey and others (1997) and Nemoto and others (1998) asserted that it is also necessary to recognize that although these domains are frequently isolated as conceptually distinct entities, these realms possess multiple dimensions and overlap each other. If one is to understand and address solutions to drug–HIV risks, one has to perceive clients as participants in these systemic contexts. These contexts, too, are anything but static. They and their constituent elements are very dynamic, evolving rapidly within

(continued)

CASE IN POINT 2.1 CONTINUED

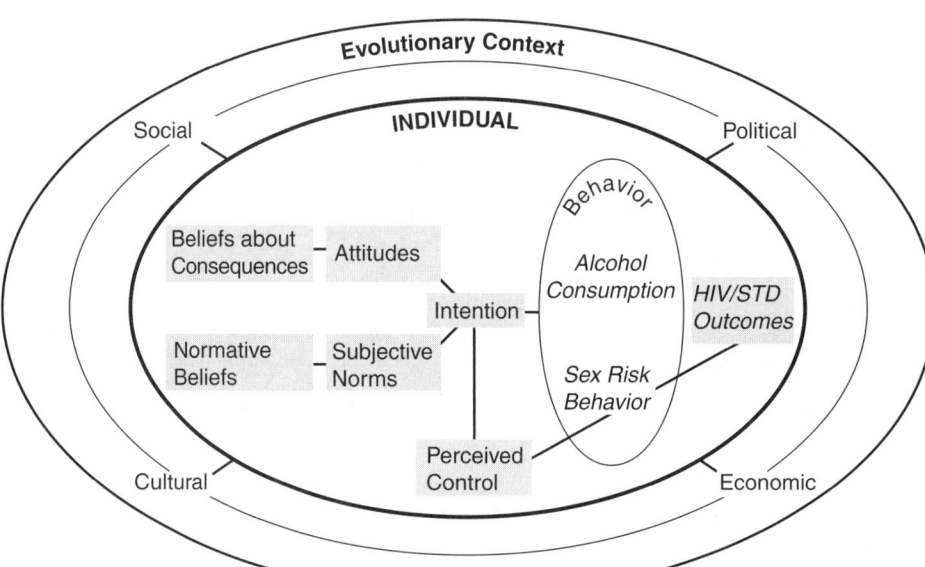

FIGURE 2.3 A Conceptual Model on HIV/STD Prevention

themselves and within their encompassing milieus. Historical processes, consequently, are of great significance if one is to comprehend choices made by individuals. In brief, it is useful to understand substance use/abuse, sexual risk practices, and HIV/STDs among AI/ANs as outputs of a *process* that involves or moves through at least *five domains*.

Within this theoretical setting, all populations are subject to factors associated with the distribution of power and resources (Conners & McGrath, 1997). This applies to all individuals in the larger scale of political-economic systems, as well as to those same persons in smaller-scale personal relationships (Conners & McGrath, 1997). Marginalized, inner-city populations provide the extreme examples of these relationships. Unemployment, homelessness, substandard nutrition, violence, substance abuse, health care access, stress, class, race, gender relations, family, community organization, support networks, sex-partner networks, and culture among other features of inner-city life contribute to this imbalance (Conners & McGrath, 1997; Singer, 1994a; Singer et al., 1990; Weeks, Schensul, Williams, Singer, & Grier, 1995).

As a consequence of these extremes, inner-city conditions represent one example of international manifestation of AIDS as a disease of poverty, wherein AIDS is just one of a host of community problems (Singer & Weeks, 1996). These circumstances also exhibit tremendous structural variability, supporting the notion that the AIDS pandemic is more adequately described as thousands of separate epidemics (Mann, Tarantola, & Netter, 1992). Exploratory models need to address individuals and communities through these unique circumstances, and these models have to possess the capacity to adjust to each "micro-epidemic and its particular route(s) of transmission, sub-population at risk, and socio-behavioral context" (Singer & Weeks, 1996, p. 490; also see Singer, 1994b).

Inner-city populations also constitute one class of "hidden populations" (Lambert, 1990; Watters & Biernacki, 1989), groups that are out of the mainstream and little known to those outside its boundaries. These communities are a particular challenge for research and program development, because they can be hard to define, difficult to understand, and especially complex. The initial step toward project goals is to engage the communities in the process, opening a dialogue to define their needs and priorities (Wallerstein & Bernstein, 1998; Weeks, Singer, Grier, Hunte-Marrow, & Haughton, 1991). Through this form of participation, for example, we can delineate how people assign meaning to their encompassing networks and communities, how they perceive risk and vulnerability, how they behave in particular ways, and how they are most likely to respond to prevention and intervention efforts. These models also must reflect the "micro-epidemics" and must be culturally competent in the manner by which they use cultural information (Singer & Borrero, 1984; Trotter, 1995; Weeks, 1990).

Although it is clear that context has a tremendous influence on each individual, context alone does not account for all relevant aspects of the model. *Individuals* themselves play an important role, not only in the perpetuation of risky behaviors but also in constructing the parameters of those behaviors as well as their resolutions. Various psychosocial learning and behavior theories apply to these circumstances, and although their specific labels and categories might differ, they share the same basic components. For example, the health belief model (e.g., Becker, 1974; Becker & Maiman, 1980; Janz & Becker, 1984) and the theory of planned behavior (e.g., Ajzen, 1985, 1991; Ajzen & Fishbein, 1980) both incorporate aspects of an individual perspective, of a societal or normative perspective, of an individual's desire to behave in a particular manner, and of an individual's actual behavior. Versions of both models also integrate self-efficacy (Bandura, 1986, 1994) or "perceived control" (Ajzen, 1985; also see Jemmott & Jemmott, 1994) as key elements, and both identify nonspecific external factors as having some influence on any segment of the central, "individual" section of the model.

These learning/behavior models have been successfully used for decades and continue to be instrumental in contemporary efforts to describe, explain, and alter health-related behaviors. Wong and Bouey (2001) incorporated the theory of planned behavior into a more inclusive political-economic model with the intent of obtaining an improved understanding of substance use/abuse, sexual risk practices, and HIV/STDs (see Figure 2.3). The theory of planned behavior holds that HIV/STD infections are determined by behavior, which in turn is predicted by intentions. The latter are a product of individual attitudes and subjective norms, both results of more inclusive individual perceptions of social group expectations and of behavioral consequences. This particular model has been selected because of its long history of development and because of its successful use in prevention and intervention efforts pertaining to general health, sexual risk behaviors, and substance abuse. For interventions focusing on individuals, this model directs attention to specific attitudinal and normative components that are salient to certain behaviors. Simultaneously, with the expanded scope of our political-economic model, one can isolate those contextual and structural factors that predict beliefs/attitudes and norms related to behaviors. Individuals integrate these inputs, in addition to those they carry with their personal histories, and construct their perceptions of behavior and norms. Attitudes and subjective norms are derived from these exchanges, ultimately defining intentions with commensurate behavioral correlates. This framework is directly applicable to substance use/abuse, sexual risk practices, and HIV/STDs, facilitating the identification of linkages surrounding and coupling those behaviors and HIV/STDs.

The Fidelity of Scientific Research

Reliability, internal validity, and external validity are the three sets of related issues that speak to the fidelity of research. Each of these needs to be examined in more detail.

Reliability refers to the extent that concrete or measurable features, or both, of a theory are replicable. For example, using Wong and Bouey's (2001) theory of drug abuse, pregnancy status (an individual characteristic or the independent variable) is said to be reliable if it consistently predicts the number of days of sobriety and the number of Alcoholics

Anonymous meetings attended (the results or dependent variable) of women participating in primary and secondary substance-abuse prevention or treatment programs.

Internal validity refers to the degree to which an independent variable is responsible for any observed changes in a dependent variable. In other words, research is said to have high internal validity when confounding effects are at a minimum. **Confounding effects,** or variables, are extraneous variables that influence the dependent variable or results and invalidate the conclusions drawn from the research. For example, using Wong and Bouey's (2001) theory of drug abuse, pregnancy status (an individual characteristic) is said to have high internal validity if it is related to the number of days of sobriety (the results) of women participating in primary and secondary substance-abuse prevention or treatment programs. On the other hand, pregnancy status might not be related to sobriety because some other factor (e.g., brain size or the presence of friends who use drugs) is related. Researchers would then acknowledge that pregnancy status is not internally valid.

External validity refers to the generalizability of results from one study to other studies or to settings other than the researched one. Can we generalize the findings to normal people living in the real world? Do the results apply to larger community settings? Sue (1999) argues that the consideration of external validity is not a high enough priority in research studies that do not account for the diversity of group perspectives found in the larger population. Many psychology studies are done with first-year college students. They may not be representative of the larger population of the United States, much less the population of the world. The need for adequate and representative samples is pointed out for description of the characteristics of the sample taken, as well as the need for replication of studies. Again, using Wong and Bouey's (2001) theory of drug abuse, one may find that women in New York City (urban dwelling) who enroll in primary and secondary substance-abuse prevention or treatment programs are less likely to abuse drugs during pregnancy compared to those in Long Island (suburban or rural dwelling) who do not. Until these results are replicated with similar samples in other cities or settings, the results must be interpreted as norms only for New York City women.

A number of factors may also influence the fidelity of research. If it is important for a study to have a random sample, one must be certain that there is no **selection bias.** That is, all potential participants should have a statistically equal opportunity to be selected into a study. For example, using Wong and Bouey (2001), one could investigate people's reactions to two different primary and secondary substance-abuse prevention and treatment programs, although those who are not selected to participate in the program that they desire may work harder, or **compensate,** for their participation in the program where they belong. Even when compensation (not to be confused with a monetary reward) is at a minimum, it is possible that those who enroll in different programs communicate with each other.

A consequence is **diffusion of treatment,** meaning that it would be difficult to draw definitive conclusions about the respective efficiency and effectiveness of each program because neither program is now pure. The effects of one treatment have spilled over into the other. Participants of such programs are also likely to have other problems (e.g., homelessness) in addition to substance abuse, which make them vulnerable to discontinued participation. When participants drop out, this is known as **experimental mortality.** Enrollment in such programs is no guarantee that participants' subsequent abstinence or recovery is solely due to some components of the programs. Possibly certain client characteristics (e.g., less physical tolerance of the drug) lead to abstinence or recovery naturally over time. In other words, it is due to some form of **maturation.** Certain historical events might also influence results (e.g., a terrorist attack influencing people's attitudes toward the right to privacy).

TRADITIONAL SCIENTIFIC RESEARCH METHODS

There are traditional group research strategies that all psychologists, including community psychologists, utilize. The usual first step in devising these studies is to conduct a review of the scientific literature. The researcher then draws what appears to be the logical conclusion from reading the past work. The statement of what might be expected is called a **hypothesis.** (More formally, it is a tentative statement made to test out its empirical consequences. Adopted from Merriam-Webster Online Dictionary, http://www.merriam-webster.com/dictionary/hypothesis, on July 8, 2008.) A choice is made as to which of two research designs to use in the study to examine the hypothesis, the correlational or experimental design. The **design** is the systematic plan to test this hypothesis.

The researchers use these designs to guide what kind of data and how data are gathered from groups of people. There are assumptions regarding what this group data represent. This takes us into definitions of population and sampling.

We look at these definitions, explore the two traditional research designs, and then look at a third category called the quasi-experimental design, which attempts to gain the advantages of the experimental design in its explanatory capabilities and yet deal with the situational limitations that are sometimes presented to the researcher. We follow the descriptions of these designs with an exploration of other research methods likely to be used by community psychologists.

Population and Sampling

Social research attempts to understand human behavior. A **population** is defined as that group of people that the research is attempting to understand. If we want to know how people in New Zealand think and behave, the population is "all the people in New Zealand." If we are interested in males in Seattle, the population is "all the males in Seattle." Psychology's ambition is to understand all human beings, in which case the population is all human beings. That is the ambition, but getting data on an entire population is difficult. We therefore use a sample of those in whom we are interested.

A **sample** is a subset of the population that is supposed to represent that population. A **random sample** is a sample in which every member of a population has an equal chance of being selected. On the other hand, a **convenience sample** is chosen for no other reason than it is available. College students often represent a convenience sample in much psychological research, because the students are readily available to participate in research conducted in psychology departments in colleges and universities. A **stratified sample** tries to match the known characteristics of the population; for example, if we know that 40 percent of the population is male, we would try to get a sample that is 40 percent male. A **purposive sample** is one chosen for a specific reason. In a test of drug use among pregnant women, only pregnant women would be chosen to be assessed; they represent a purposive sample. Random samples are the revered form of sampling in psychology.

Correlational Research

Correlational methods include a class of designs (e.g., surveys) and measurement procedures, as well as techniques (e.g., self-report), that allow one to examine the *associations or relationships* between two or more variables in their natural environments. In other words, correlational methods do not contain active manipulations of the variables under study; rather, they are usually descriptive in nature. For example, using Wong and Bouey's (2001) theory of drug abuse, one might want to investigate the relationship between the number of months pregnant and the severity of substance abuse; these variables are not manipulated. The fact that one has no control over them means that the distinction of independent from dependent variables may be arbitrary, albeit dictated by a theory.

Also, causation cannot be determined, because intervening or other unstudied variables could easily have produced the effects noted. Associations are said to be **spurious,** (false while giving the appearance of being correct) when intervening or confounding variables are thought to be responsible for the relationships. In experimental research, intervening variables are controlled for through randomly assigning participants to groups, holding conditions constant, and manipulating the independent variable. In correlational research, these criteria are seldom (if ever) met.

In its simple form, the associations between two or more variables are quantified using a statistic known as the **Pearson correlation coefficient,** which ranges from +1.00 to –1.00. The sign (+ or –) indicates the direction of the association. For example, if the sign is positive (+), both variables move in the same direction, or as one gets smaller, so does the other. A positive correlation can also mean that as one variable increases, so does the other. A negative or inverse correlation means that the variables move in opposite directions. For example, as one variable increases, the other decreases. The number (e.g., .35) indicates the magnitude or intensity of the relationship, with 1.00 being the largest correlation and 0.00 indicating little or no relationship.

Using Wong and Bouey's (2001) theory of drug abuse, a Pearson correlation coefficient of –.80 between the number of months pregnant and substance abuse means that women who are at more advanced stages of pregnancy are less likely to abuse drugs (a strong negative association). However, one *cannot* conclude that advanced stages of pregnancy *cause* decreases in substance abuse. Also, this association may be spurious when there is reason to suspect that pregnant women's perceived support from their spouses later in pregnancy is largely responsible for decreases in substance abuse rather than due to the pregnancy itself.

Experimental Research

The **experimental method** includes a class of designs (e.g., between-groups designs where no two groups receive the same treatment) and measurement procedures that allow one to manipulate independent and dependent variables. An **independent variable (IV)** is the condition that is varied between groups (e.g., person in need who is known to the subject versus person in need who is unknown to the subject). The **dependent variable** is what the scientist measures to see the effects of the independent variable (e.g, willingness to help, as measured by the amount of money offered in aid). A common design is the **pretest-posttest control group design** (Campbell & Stanley, 1963; Cook, Shadish, & Campbell, 2002), which involves the assessment of an effect or effects both prior to and following an experimental manipulation in one group (the experimental group) but not in another (no-manipulation group or control group). That is, one group of participants is exposed to an independent variable and another group is not.

In addition to this manipulation of the independent variable, assignment to the experimental or control group is **random**—participants have an equal chance of being assigned to either the experimental or control group. Given these conditions, there can be an assumption of the two groups, experimental and control, being similar to each other, or rather equivalent. If there are any differences between the groups at the end of the process, it is believed that the independent variable is what has brought about the change. The independent variable is seen to cause the differences in the dependent variable, because the only difference between the groups is the independent variable's presence or absence.

If the experimental manipulation is functioning as predicted by a theory, the dependent variable ideally should be observable as a change from premanipulation to postmanipulation scores within the experimental but not the control group. In other words, the

TABLE 2.1 Characteristics of Three Scientific Research Designs

	CORRELATION	QUASI-EXPERIMENTAL	EXPERIMENTAL
Type of question	Are the variables of interest related to each other?	Does an independent variable that the researcher does not completely control affect the dependent variable or the research result?	Is there a relationship between independent and dependent variables that addresses the cause?
When used	Researcher is unable to manipulate an independent variable. Sometimes used in explanatory research.	Researcher wants to assess the impact of real-life intervention in the community or elsewhere.	Researcher has control over the independent variable and can minimize the number of confounding variables in the research.
Advantages	Convenience of data collection. May avoid certain ethical and/or practical problems.	Provides some information about cause–effect relationships. Permits assessment of more real-world interventions.	Ability to demonstrate cause–effect relationship. Permits control over confounding variables and the ruling of alternative explanations.
Disadvantages	Cannot establish a cause–effect relationship.	Lack of control over confunding variable. Strong causal inference cannot be made.	Some questions cannot be studied experimentally for either practical or ethical reasons. May lead to artificial procedures.

Source: Adapted from Wong, Blakely, & Worsham (1991). Copyright 1991 by Guilford Press. Used by permission.

pretest-posttest observations of participants in the control group should remain relatively constant over time, unless some natural maturation occurs or the initial pretest sensitizes all participants to the nature of the assessment being conducted. For example, using Wong and Bouey (2001), pregnant substance abusers who participate in primary and secondary prevention or treatment programs should report an increase in days of sobriety from pretreatment to posttreatment compared to those who do not.

Quasi-Experimental Research

Many variables (e.g., school climate or minors being exposed to alcohol or cigarettes) studied in the field of community psychology cannot be experimentally manipulated for practical and ethical reasons. Similarly, subjects cannot always be randomly assigned to groups. For example, if a participant is pregnant, it is not possible to randomly assign her to the nonpregnant group. In studies of pregnancy, one would probably end up using intact groups. Thus, a compromise is the use of the **quasi-experimental method,** which approximates experimental conditions and random assignment but is not quite able to get all of the necessary conditions for a true experimental design (Campbell & Stanley, 1963; Cook et al., 2002). A common quasi-experimental design is the **nonequivalent pretest-posttest control design,** which involves the comparison of a group before and after some experimental manipulation with another group that has not been exposed to the manipulation or treatment. As mentioned earlier, this design differs from the pretest-posttest design previously discussed in that participants are not randomly assigned to experimental or control conditions.

Although the quasi-experimental design allows for more natural or realistic research, initial differences between experimental and comparison groups may not be balanced. For example, using Wong and Bouey's (2001) theory of drug abuse, pregnant women who voluntarily participate in primary and secondary prevention or treatment programs may be more educated than those in the comparison group, which may include women who are high school dropouts. Thus, differences already exist between the two groups before the study begins. Care must be taken in drawing conclusions about causal differences between the two groups, as they already differ at the onset of the research, and other explanations for the data cannot be ruled out.

We now examine several research methodologies used by community psychologists but not by laboratory-based psychologists.

OTHER RESEARCH METHODS USED IN COMMUNITY PSYCHOLOGY

Ethnography

Due to the urgency of the issues in the field of community psychology, diverse methods or approaches are often employed. One such research method is **ethnography,** which refers to a broad class of designs (e.g., semi-structured interviews) and measurement procedures and techniques (e.g., behavioral ratings) that allow one to conduct social interactions with participants of the study. The primary purpose of ethnography is to allow one to gain an understanding of how people view their own experiences.

Ethnography should allow an individual to describe his or her own experiences without having to translate them into the words of the researchers. In other words, the informants or participants should use their own language to describe their own experiences. An ethnographic interviewer should probably also provide an explanation of why he or she is asking particular questions so as to be more fully understood by the informants. Similarly, in contrast to the more traditional scientific definitions of objectivity or neutrality, in ethnography, the value systems of the researcher may influence the social interactions between the researcher and the informants and thus influence the course of the research. Hence, a researcher is better off taking a stance of ignorance about the experiences of the informants than making predetermined judgments (Heller et al., 1984). Of course, no scientific research method is truly objective, because how one conceptualizes an issue logically dictates the course of its action.

Compared to cultural anthropologists and sociologists who first developed this technique, community psychologists use ethnography at a lower rate. However, as research issues become more socially oriented, these methods are more likely to be employed than experimental methods (Speer et al., 1992). Ethnography is perhaps most informative when research questions asked do not have a strong theoretical framework. Thus, **qualitative information** that is likely to be gleaned from ethnographic studies can inform the researcher about future directions of study, some of which may include field experiments where variables are actively manipulated. Qualitative information is more subjective and anecdotal in nature, where the research looks for ideas and themes that are apparent in the verbal responses of the subjects. This is opposed to **quantitative data,** which is usually considered objective in nature and can be expressed in numerical terms.

The use of a combination of qualitative and quantitative techniques (mixed-method) for studying community phenomena is seen by Cauce (1990) to have the potential to strengthen community research. The qualitative information may inform the direction in which the quantitative study may go and then later inform the meaning of that quantitative data (Banyard & Miller, 1998). It is a way to both empower and transform those being studied and, in a manner of speaking, is an intervention in itself (Stein & Mankowski, 2004). The qualitative methods require more awareness of the relationship between researcher and participant and the potential impact of one on the other (Brodsky et al., 2004). The qualitative data assumes a more interactive role between the researcher and participants. There are indications that qualitative studies may be increasingly more accepted as a model of research in selected journals, especially as a part of mixed-method research (Marchel & Owens, 2007). Some feminist psychology perspectives believe qualitative data allow for capturing richer and more meaningful descriptions of social phenomena (Brodsky et al., 2004; Campbell & Wasco, 2000; Hill et al., 2000;).

Participant observation is a popular and special type of ethnographic technique. Although the researcher often assumes the role of an observer (i.e., systematic observation with neutrality) in participant observation and ethnography, a prototypical study using participant observation often involves ongoing dialogues between the researcher and participants. For example, a researcher who is interested in the study of teenage gangs often needs to "hang out" with the gangs for a period of time. Also, the researcher needs to acquire the language used by the gangs to facilitate his or her investigation of the gangs' social network characteristics as well as establish trust. Meanwhile, the constant social interactions between the researcher and gang members may affect their perceptions of and relationships with each other. A consequence can be role ambiguity, where it becomes unclear to gang members what role the researcher is adopting. Is the researcher a member of the gang, a researcher, or both?

Network Analysis

With difficult-to-reach or hidden populations, or when working with limited empirical databases, **network analysis** as a methodology has the advantage of informing researchers about key issues pertaining to these populations (i.e., formative research), thus allowing preparation for subsequent large-scale or population-based studies. Friedman and colleagues (1997) argued, "Social networks are relationships that can influence ideas, norms, and behaviors. Risk networks are behaviors and materials . . . that can transmit HIV from person to person. Social and risk networks often overlap. Recent evidence indicates that both kinds of networks have major consequences for HIV epidemiology and behavior" (p. 95). Case in Point 2.3 shows the utility of network analysis.

A *New York Times* article reported on the potential uses of computer links to identify social and informational networks in the age of the Internet (Lohr, 2006). With the rise of

---

CASE IN POINT 2.2
CASE STUDY OF A CONSUMER RUN AGENCY

Felton (2005) studied a consumer run agency working on mental health services. She wanted to find the characteristics of that work community. Using a variety of methods, including participant observations, ad hoc interviews, behavioral observations, and the standardized Work Environment Scale (Moos, 1994), she spent two years on site, interacting for periods of time and then retreating to analyze the data.

A content analysis of her qualitative interview data yielded a variety of staff-generated themes: pride in the agency, an understanding and compassionate place, and the feeling like it was family. The quantitative scale measures verified these general themes, yielding comparatively high scores (2 standard deviations higher) on worker involvement, task orientation, and Cohesion. The scale suggested high "relationship" orientation. There was also a very high score on clarity of work mission. These scores **triangulated** well with the qualitative data. The agency understudy seems to be doing well in providing a service setting with which workers feel engaged and to which they are committed.

The idea behind triangulation is a referent to anthropological terminology, which likens social sciences efforts to obtain an understanding of phenomena to geological mapping. To locate a site, one takes two readings from different perspectives/sites, focusing on the site to be defined. The two sites *triangulate* with the one point under examination, yielding a better understanding of the one point. It is a kind of social geometry. In a similar way, the qualitative data, the interviews, yield one "siting" on the social phenomena being examined. The quantitative data, the scale scores, yield the second "siting" on what the agency is really like. The ensuing picture is more comprehensive, sensitive to personal nuance, and yet also more verifiable, given the two sets of data.

CASE IN POINT 2.3
CRACKING THE NETWORK

Gillespie and Murty (1994) used network analysis to determine potential cracks in a postdisaster service delivery system. Network analysis allows a community consultant to partition community organizations into equivalent, peripheral, isolated, or central organizations. In this manner, interrelationships among organizations can be examined to determine where the weak linkages, or cracks, are in a service system.

To avoid the problem of having to wait for an actual disaster to occur, Gillespie and Murty used a vignette with participants from various organizations (e.g., the American Red Cross) that respond to large-scale community disasters. The participants were asked to respond as if it were 18 hours after the initial impact of an earthquake. In their research, Gillespie and Murty identified nine groups or clusters of organizations in the postdisaster network. One group had no interorganizational relations to the rest of the network. In other words, this group represented a serious crack in the network because it had not established any way to coordinate its services with organizations outside its origin. The researchers suggested that community planning councils, after using network analysis, target peripheral and isolated organizations and encourage them to initiate contacts with more central organizations such that service delivery could be improved.

sites like MySpace and Facebook, and the capabilities of Skype and text-messaging, we have opportunities to establish and sustain personal relationships that are rich in information and not limited to geography.

The two major types of network methodology are egocentric and sociometric. **Egocentric** methodology refers to the relationships and shared behaviors *between* an individual and his or her peers. **Sociometric** methodology refers to relationships and shared behaviors *among* individuals. In both types, the objective is to identify and delineate patterns of relationships and shared behaviors. Other methodological criteria (e.g., definitions for types of relationships and shared behaviors) are contingent on theoretical framework(s) or research question(s). For example, one variant of the sociometric network study on injection drug use and HIV is to ask participants to provide information about up to 10 individuals with whom they have injected drugs and had unprotected sex during the past 30 days. Analytic procedures for both types of network methodology can be quite elaborate and involved, as well as technical.

Conceptually, network analysis as a methodology should appeal to community-based researchers. However, the use of the methodology is not immune from cultural barriers or other social obstacles. Thus, to reap the benefit of this type of methodology, researchers must have a good grasp of the targeted populations. Trust is the foundation for the methodology.

Epidemiology

Another set of methods used more by community psychologists than other psychologists is **epidemiology.** This research entails "the study of the occurrence and distribution of diseases and other health-related conditions in populations" (Kelsey, Thompson, & Evans, 1986, p. 3). This includes a broad class of designs (e.g., prospective or, loosely, "futuristic" studies and retrospective or, loosely, "historical" studies) and measurement procedures and techniques (e.g., random telephone dialing, neighborhood surveys).

There are two measures of the rate of illness in the community: prevalence and incidence. The **prevalence** of a disease or health-related condition is the total number of people within a given population who have the disorder. **Incidence** refers to the number of people within a given population who have acquired the condition within a specific time period, usually a year.

Incidence rates can be established using a **prospective design** or investigation of new cases. Here, all new cases for the given time frame are counted, yielding a rate of onset for the disease. If the incidence rates are rising, it tells us that the problem is increasing. If the incidence rates are declining, it suggests that the problem is lessening. We might think about flu season, when the cases of flu rise. The epidemiologist continues to measure the rate of onset to see when the flu season is over.

Prevalence rates can be established using a **retrospective design** or investigation of known cases. So we would count all old cases and all new cases. In the case of depression, we would count all old cases, take away all cases that have been cured, and then add all the new cases. This tells us the number of all cases in the population at one time.

Prevalence rate is a more inclusive measure than incidence rate and is easier to calculate. However, the disadvantage of prevalence rates is that they are difficult to interpret, as they must take into account both the incidence and duration of a disorder.

Depending on the objectives of the epidemiological investigation, measurement procedures as well as techniques used in the design can range from household interviews to random telephone digit dialing. Others include the use of birth certificates, death certificates, census records, or all of these.

Having defined these concepts, an example is in order to show how epidemiology is used. HIV is responsible for AIDS, one of the deadliest incurable diseases of our time. Epidemiological surveys (mostly retrospective studies) conducted by the Centers for Disease Control and Prevention (CDC) in the early 1980s called attention to the onset of this epidemic in the United States. Over 1 million HIV or AIDS cases were reported to the CDC by 2004 (CDC, 2004). Following the 1980s onset, the report of incidences (new cases) of AIDS reached a high point in 1992 (78,000). As of 1998, the incidence rate has stabilized at about 40,000 per year. Although most of the cases are male, the number of female cases has increased from the 1990s into 2004. Male-to-male sexual contact accounted for 44 percent of new cases, with heterosexual contact second at 34 percent and intravenous drug use accounting for 17 percent.

Once the prevalence and/or incidence rates for a disorder have been determined, epidemiologists can attempt to isolate variables that seem to have caused the disorder. For example, once the CDC had an understanding of who was at risk for HIV, they could search for the cause of the disease. For HIV, the exchange of blood or other body fluids from an infected individual to another spreads the virus.

Needs Assessment and Program Evaluation

Needs assessment refers to a set of methods to determine if a program or intervention can be of use to a given population. From our example at the beginning of the chapter, the incubation period of AIDS is about 10 years. What are the needs for Edisak, who may be at various stages of HIV? Individuals who are newly diagnosed may need social support, whereas those who are in the late stages of AIDS may need intensive medical and hospice care. Needs assessment could also examine where prevention programs or other interventions might decrease the risk of contracting HIV. The promotion of safe sex practices, such as condom use, could address risky sexual behaviors. Needle exchange programs could decrease risk of transmission through intravenous drug use.

Needs assessments can be conducted via ethnographic interviews, surveys, and other observational or descriptive techniques, each of which has advantages and disadvantages. For example, in ethnographic face-to-face interviews, individuals might be reluctant to reveal that they are unmarried and pregnant or are HIV-positive. They might be more likely to disclose this information in an anonymous survey. On the other hand, during an interview, the interviewer (or the informant, for that matter) can change the direction of the interview and thus reveal information not discovered on written surveys, which are less easily modified on the spot.

Having developed or refined a program to address needs related to a particular issue, whether it be AIDS or teen pregnancy or illiteracy, the effectiveness or efficiency of the program should be evaluated. This process is called program evaluation. **Program evaluation** refers to a broad class of designs, methodologies, and measurement procedures and techniques (e.g., examining birth certificates, counting the number of clients, observing behaviors in a given setting, taking surveys on attitudes or knowledge) that allow one to examine "social programs . . . and the policies that spawn and justify them, [and] aim to improve the welfare of individuals, organizations, and society" (Shadish, Cook, & Leviton, 1991, p. 19). Given unstable economies worldwide, there is an increasing trend to hold social programs accountable for their performance, so program evaluation is becoming more important.

It is beyond the scope of this chapter to conduct an extensive discussion of the processes involved in the evaluation of a typical social program. We do note that besides needs assessment, there are generally two kinds of evaluations: process and outcome. *Process evaluation* examines what a program is doing. Are things going as planned, with interventions occurring in a timely fashion? What are the day-to-day operations like? Where are the problems of implementation and execution? A good process evaluation should report on what a program is doing well and what it is not doing well. The adjustments to the process can then be made based on the process evaluation findings.

An *outcome evaluation,* on the other hand, looks at the effects of a program. At the end of the intervention, what has been accomplished? Does the program do what it intended to do? Most program evaluations look at immediate outcomes, but community programs may require extended outcome evaluations. Many treatment evaluations now look at outcomes one to two years following conclusion of the intervention. This tries to answer the question of whether the outcomes endure beyond the period of intensive attention or if the natural contingencies within the environment are sufficient to sustain the benefits that accumulated.

A good evaluation usually consists of four related components: (1) the goals, (2) the objectives, (3) the activities, and (4) the milestones. The **goal** refers to the aim of the evaluation. A good evaluation is likely to be driven by theory. That is, the concept of goal addresses the question, What does the evaluation hope to achieve? (or *why* should an evaluation be conducted?). The construct of an **objective** refers to the plan. That is, objectives address the question, *How* does one go about achieving the goal? The concept of **activity** refers to the specific task. That is, activity addresses the question, *What* does the plan consists of? **Milestone** refers to the outcome; that is, does the evaluation *achieve* its intended goal?

Using Wong and Bouey's (2001) theory of drug abuse, one might want to investigate the differential effectiveness of mainstream versus native-focused prevention and treatment programs for American Indian/Alaska Native adults (the *goal*). Therefore, one reviews records and interviews clients and staff of the two types of programs (the *objective* or design). Given the voluminous records and possible number of informants or interviewees, only a randomized stratified sample will be used (the *activity,* including analysis). It might be reasonable to hypothesize that a higher enrollment rate will be observed in the native-focused programs than programs in the mainstream because of cultural competent services. However, the two types of programs may not differ in dropout rates, because, as you know by now, intervention outcomes are often contingent on a host of factors other than program type (the *milestones*).

This example certainly is a very simplistic picture of program evaluation. Although program evaluation may seem more objective, role ambiguity is still possible. Role ambiguity is most likely to occur with internal evaluation. That is, an evaluator who is also on the staff of the agency assumes not only the role of evaluator but also is someone interested in using data derived from the evaluation for future program development or refinement. To guard against this problem, agencies usually establish an advisory panel so that program development or refinement is executed by the group rather than a single, internal evaluator. Another solution is to employ an external evaluator, such as a community consultant.

Social dynamics are crucial in evaluating any social program. People do not like to be judged, especially when potentially negative consequences exist. Many not-for-profit social programs are more sensitive to funding issues and public scrutiny. If these programs are shown to be less than effective, they are likely to be eliminated. If they are effective but less efficient (i.e., more expensive to maintain), they may still be eliminated. The potential for bias in favor of maintaining the program is obvious.

The tensions between program evaluators and practitioners often exist when only "objective" assessment or feedback is used with no active or direct engagement of program staff. Wandersman and colleagues (1998) argued that "there has been a growing discussion of new and evolving roles for evaluators. . . . Unlike traditional evaluation approaches, empowerment evaluators collaborate with community members . . . to determine program goals and implementation strategies, serve as facilitators . . . not outside experts . . . in ongoing program improvement" (p. 4). Ultimately, it is about program accountability. To that end, eight questions (along with their corresponding strategies for addressing them) serve as guides for program accountability. They are as follows:

1. Are there needs for a program? (needs assessment)
2. What is the scientific knowledge or best practices bases for a program? (consult scientific literature and promising practice programs)

3. How do new program(s) integrate with existing programs? (feedback on comprehensiveness and fit of program)
4. How can a program best be implemented? (planning)
5. How effective is implementation? (process evaluation)
6. How effective is a program? (outcome and impact evaluation)
7. How can a program be improved? (lessons learned)
8. How can effective programs be institutionalized? (replication or spin-off)

Obviously, this process is much more elaborate. Wandersman et al. (1998) pose the evaluation process as an integral part of programming. Program evaluation may be seen as a form of intervention (Kaufman, Ross, Quan, O'Reilly, & Crusto, 2004; Patton, 1997). Evaluation is not a passive process, because the evaluator helps the organization define and objectify the goals and direction of the program under scrutiny. Beyond the definition of tasks, the evaluator defines which data are important, which are attended to, who is given a voice (administrators, staff, clients, community), and how that voice may be heard (surveys, interviews, focus groups, numeric or personal testament). The evaluator engages in interpretation, weighting, and summation of the data. This is a lot of power and can have a significant effect on the direction and functioning of the targeted system.

Kaufman et al. (2006) present an excellent example of the evaluation process and its potential for community change. They work to increase the likelihood of evaluation findings being used by developing a clear logic and strategy for the program need; having all relevant parties actively engaged in the process of planning, implementation, and evaluation; using a variety of both qualitative and quantitative data from a variety of sources so all felt they were being respected and heard; working to be as scientifically rigorous as possible in the generation of data; working to increase the community's ability to do its own evaluations; and being sure to share findings with all involved once they had the opportunity to comment on first drafts (which increased the ownership of the data and made for no surprises). Among their efforts to have the evaluation accepted by the community was a conscious decision to become regulars within the community, or as Kelly (1988) called it, "showing up" in the neighborhoods. The evaluators were also open and willing to provide help when needed, even when it was above and beyond what was contracted. One gets the impression the evaluators became a part of the community. Thus, the comments were not from a distant and uninvolved team who examined things without knowing in detail who and what they were examining. The evaluation in turn helped in bringing about a variety of changes within the community and the service systems it served. We move now to a type of research that closely resembles the process described here. Whereas the focus of Kaufman et al. was evaluation, their goals were community change. The incorporation of community participants in the research and intervention planning process is made even more explicitly in participatory research.

Participatory Research

The action research tradition (Lewin, 1946) has always incorporated the inclusion of the targets of any study in the research process. Participatory research is a continuation of this tradition. In this model, the studied community helps to define the areas to study, the methods for studying and the use of the study results. Kidd and Kral (2005) define participatory research as a sharing of power with the participants themselves, and emphasize that it is an attitudinal change more than it is a specific methodology. It can include both qualitative-anecdotal and quantitative-numeric data. Participant research "involves the development of human relationships and friendships with participants as opposed to the supposedly objective disinterest of traditional paradigms. It can be a genuine connection, an 'authentic participation' that is motivational, contributes to personal growth and reduces the barriers between peoples" (p. 192). Jason, Keyes, Suarex-Balcazar, Davis, and Taylor (2004) elaborate at length on the participatory research tradition and its place within community psychology. The partnership between researcher and participants creates a structure of respect and the research process can be conceived as the intervention.

Kelly et al. (2004) provided an example of a 10-year relationship with an African American community on Chicago's South Side, in which community leadership was both studied and developed. The Developing Communities Project (DCP) wanted to take a community organization approach to preventing substance abuse. In close collaboration with the DCP, researchers and community developed relationships and group mechanisms to define and describe African American church-based organizing and leadership. Admitting to the lack of relevant literature on the topic, the researchers built on the information from the citizen-leader panelists. The reliance on community knowledge and feedback in devising appropriate data-gathering procedures was an integral part of the process. Clearly, the development of personal relationships (common interests in jazz) and community-based metaphors (such as "leadership as making a soup; there being many ingredients needed in its making") was essential to the project. Data were collected and reported to the community and then refined so as to be more useful (the use of oral history videotapes to communicate the findings).

Although participatory research is acknowledged to be complex and time-consuming, as well as not as respectable in mainstream academia, nonetheless its potential for contribution to our understanding of meanings within the communities we study seems great (Kidd & Kral, 2005). As well, a second powerful recommendation for its use is the potential for participatory research to empower the communities it studies (Kelly et al., 2004; Jason et al., 2005)

THE URGENCY OF RESEARCH IN COMMUNITY PSYCHOLOGY AND RELATED PITFALLS

As mentioned earlier, research in the field of community psychology is often conducted with a sense of urgency not often seen in other areas of psychology. Some aspects of this urgency were demonstrated by using the example of drug abuse among pregnant women. Other related issues deserve some brief comment.

The Politics of Science and the Science of Politics

Up to this point, you have been implicitly introduced to the idea that sound policy (e.g., substance-abuse prevention targeting pregnant women) should be based and grounded in scientific evidence. That is, systematic and vigorous examination of an issue using scientific principles would result in the most desirable outcome(s) or impact(s). A close examination reveals that the impact of science on policy and the distinction between science and politics may be less than ideal and clear-cut.

Ethics: Cultural Relativism or Universal Human Rights?

A major principle of scientific research is that the well-being of research participants must be ensured (American Psychological Association, 1985). In other words, participation in research should not endanger people in any physical, psychological, or social way. All participants must be informed about the purpose of the research as much as possible (without jeopardizing the integrity of the research), and the use of deception must be minimized. It is **ethically** undesirable to do otherwise (see Christensen, 1988). In many research institutions and universities, before research can be initiated, approval from an **institutional review** board must first be secured, demonstrating that all ethical guidelines (e.g., participants must be fully debriefed about the purpose of the study) have been met.

These general principles and premises seem straightforward and objective (i.e., research is neutral). To the 399 African American men in the Tuskegee Syphilis Study (conducted by the U.S. government from 1932 to 1972) who were deliberately denied effective treatment for syphilis to document its natural history, the study at best reeked of racist overtones and at worst demonstrated genocide. Decades later, President Bill Clinton expressed his regrets on May 16, 1997: "The legacy of the study at Tuskegee has reached far and deep, in ways that hurt our progress and divide our nation. We cannot be one America when a whole segment of our nation has no trust in America." However, to many African Americans, as well as other racial and ethnic minorities, such injustices (e.g., forced sterilization of the so-called mentally feeble) continue to prevail—they have just become more covert (in the name of science). These outrages and debates have also assumed new dimensions, guises, and significance in the AIDS pandemic (see *American Journal of Public Health,* 88, 1998)—extending the boundaries to international scientific research. These are extremely complex issues, so two related sets of ideas will be examined: informed consent and experimental-control (placebo) design.

Informed consent, a major principle of scientific research, is ensuring that a clear and articulated procedure and process is in place so that participants understand the nature of the research, including the right to refuse participation without any repercussions. In other words, the process of informed consent has two key components: comprehension of materials and voluntary participation. In an HIV testing study conducted in a South African hospital, Karim, Karim, Coovadia, and Susser (1998) found that although participants understood the process of informed consent (i.e., comprehension of materials), many felt that they had little choice in refusing enrollment in the study (i.e., voluntary participation) due to the fact that participation was the only opportunity for receiving needed medical care or services. Karim and colleagues concluded that "subtle and unexpected elements of coercion can reside in the perceptions (real or imagined) held by patients being recruited into a research project in a medical care setting. . . . Ethicists and institutional review boards should certainly explore the issue further" (p. 640).

Once participants consent to enroll in a study, they may be assigned to an experimental or control (or comparison) group. A true control group (most scientifically rigorous) is one that does not receive any intervention or treatment (or receives a placebo). Without any other known efficacious intervention or treatment, a true experimental design is the preferred way to ascertain the efficacy of an intervention or treatment. However, what should researchers do when they know that without any intervention or treatment the participants in the control group will likely be in jeopardy? Alternatively, should researchers provide a known efficacious intervention or treatment (e.g., condoms) simultaneously when testing an intervention or treatment with unknown efficacy (i.e., vaginal microbicides)? This procedure might compromise the integrity of the scientific conclusions.

Based on findings of a trial in Thailand, the CDC, together with the National Institutes of Health (NIH) and the Joint United Nations Program on Acquired Immunodeficiency Syndrome (UNAIDS), announced that placebos should not be used in vertical HIV transmission clinical trials (maternal–fetal transmission, or the 076 Study). The Thailand study found that vertical HIV transmission was reduced by half, even in an abbreviated treatment (10 percent of the standard U.S. regimen). These issues have quickly prompted some researchers to advocate the use of *equivalency trials* (i.e., a new treatment versus a standard treatment). However, the CDC acknowledged that the efficacy of the newly found treatment could not have been achieved without the use of a placebo. Thus, Dr. Varmus (then director of NIH) and Dr. Satcher (then director of CDC) continued to favor placebo-controlled trials. Subsequently, the CDC and NIH, together with several European governments, funded a series of trials in Africa. Both Varmus and Satcher justified their position by quoting the chair of the AIDS Research Committee of the Uganda Cancer Institute: "These are Ugandan studies conducted by Ugandan investigators on Ugandans. . . . It is not NIH conducting the studies in Uganda, but Ugandans conducting their study on their people for the good of their people" (Varmus & Satcher, 1997). Nonetheless, it is not difficult to appreciate the controversy of the issue.

For some researchers, such as George Annas and Michael Grodin (cofounders of the Global Lawyers and Physicians), as well as the late Jonathan Mann (former director of WHO Global Programme on AIDS and a well-known advocate for human rights in the context of public health practice), the issue is about universal human rights. Annas and Grodin (1998) argued that "unless the interventions being tested will actually be made available to the improvised populations that are being used as subjects, developed countries are simply exploiting them in order to quickly use the knowledge gained from the clinical trials for the developed trials" (p. 561). In addition, they raised similar concerns as Karim and associates (1998) did on informed consent. It is virtually certain that for many of the participants in these developing countries, enrollment in such trials guarantees access to minimal medical or health care. The argument of cultural sovereignty may be nebulous at best—for example, those authorities making the decision in the developing countries are unlikely to be the ones to be enrolled in the trials or subjected to the experimentation. Moreover, many of these policy makers have economic ties to an increasing global economy (e.g., the pharmaceutical industry).

Does this mean we should not conduct any studies in such countries? There are no easy answers. These debates demonstrate the interdependence between the integrity of scientific research and societal forces (e.g., cultural norms, economy, racism, sexism, classism, etc.). Bayer (1998) stated:

> The tragedy of the recent trials is that they bear a profound moral taint, not of a malevolent research design but, rather, of a world economic order that makes effective prophylaxis for the interruption of maternal-fetal HIV transmission available but unaffordable for many—this is true, as well, for a host of treatment for AIDS and other diseases. In a just world, this would not be the case and the research under attack would be unnecessary. It is the social context of maldistribution of wealth and resources that both mandates these studies, and at the same time, renders them so troubling. (p. 570)

The Continuum of Research: The Value of Multiple Measures

Speer and associates (1992) indicated that there has been a shift in the field of community psychology. This shift has been toward the use of correlational designs and away from experimentation, because topics of investigation often relate to major social issues. Even in those cases where quasi-experimental or experimental designs can be used, one may have to face a multitude of methodological issues or dilemmas. One class of issues or dilemmas concerns the logistics of implementing a research program. For example, how do researchers locate drug-using pregnant women to investigate drug use? Not only are they hard to access, especially if they do not seek medical attention, but they may also be homeless or change addresses often.

Also, how do researchers increase the probability that pregnant teens will tell the truth when using self-report measures? Another way to further validate self-reported alcohol use would be to count the number of empty alcohol beverage containers that pregnant women have discarded. A nonreactive measure like this, where people are not contacted face to face, is called an **unobtrusive measure.** Unobtrusive measures are ethically questionable, because participant consent is often not obtained. Likewise, unobtrusive measures do not speak to why a certain behavior occurs, only that it does occur.

When working with complex social issues such as teen pregnancy, one should always make an attempt to use **multiple methods.** For example, self-reports, nonreactive or unobtrusive measures, as well as umbilical cord blood samples could be obtained to determine whether pregnant women are using drugs or alcohol. However, multiple methods take more time than single methods and may generate different conclusions for the same issue. Although it is hoped that a theory is solid enough to guide the interpretation of results, one would need to reexamine the theory and research if different methods produce different outcomes.

The Importance of Cultural Sensitivity

Another class of methodological issues or dilemmas concerns **cultural sensitivity,** or awareness and appreciation of intragroup and intergroup differences. The authors have chosen to define cultural sensitivity in a very *liberal* sense. People belong to many categories and have multiple expectations or identities. For example, a person can be an African American (racial or ethnic identity) and also a college graduate (educational background) and a white-collar worker (socioeconomic status). This individual may have more in common with White college graduates (of similar educational background) who are also white-collar workers (similar socioeconomic status) than other African Americans who are high school dropouts (different educational background) or living on welfare (different socioeconomic status).

In other words, cultural sensitivity underscores the importance of the issue of person–environment fit. For example, White researchers and consultants might encounter resistance from African American research participants or program clients. Similarly, male researchers who study pregnant women in drug treatment may encounter resistance not only from the women but also from the program staff. Neither the women nor the staff share the same goal or vision as the male researcher (i.e., effective treatment based on scientific knowledge). Rather, the women and staff perceive the researcher as intrusive. In other words, there is a poor person–environment fit between the researcher and the pregnant women as well as between the researcher and staff. Ecologically valid research hinges on cultural sensitivity. The methodology used needs to enhance or at least take into account the person–environment fit.

Even when one is able to deal with the preceding classes of methodological dilemmas, there may be ethical dilemmas with which to contend. For example, when drug abuse among pregnant women is investigated, not only does one need to maintain the integrity of the study (including confidentiality), one must also have a clear sense of ethical and legal responsibility. In other words, should one report to a legal authority those pregnant women one thinks are endangering themselves, their unborn children, and perhaps their other children? There are no simple answers. Although research in community psychology is crucial to a better society, conducting it is not easy.

Community Researchers as Consultants

When community psychologists conduct research, they often do so in the role of consultant. A **consultant** is someone who engages in collaborative problem solving with one or more persons (the **consultees**) who are often responsible for providing some form of assistance to another third individual (the **client**; Mowbray, 1979). Because consultants *collaborate with* the consultees, those who participate in the research, including the consultees and their clients, are not called *subjects,* as they are in other psychological research, but *participants.*

Consultants work in a variety of community settings: educational, industrial, human services (especially related to mental health), governmental, and others. Some consultants conduct research for the government. A number of universities have developed or are developing public policy research laboratories to assist in public and private sector research. Other consultants evaluate programs or conduct needs assessments, and still others lend their expertise to solving social problems by designing preventive education programs or by helping change aspects of agencies and communities. In other words, consultants appear in many different settings and work on a variety of problems, most of them related to research.

Many of you may perhaps dream of being a highly paid consultant, but the life of a consultant is not always easy. A variety of complex issues face most community consultants.

Consultants often enter a situation not knowing what the real problem is that they are being asked to help solve. In a business setting, for instance, a consultant might be hired by management because productivity is low. However, the real underlying problem might be that the management style is so unwelcomed that employee productivity has declined. Would you want to be the consultant who delivers the news to the management team who hired you that management is the problem? Given the nature of the problems for which they are asked to intervene, community psychologists acting as consultants need to weigh the ethical considerations of to whom they are responsible and for what (O'Neill, 1989).

A consultant is also faced with what methods of investigation and change to use (Heller, 1990). For instance, the consultant might recommend educational or research services. Similarly, he or she might choose some mix of outcome or process measures. **Outcome measures** address what happens *after* the change occurred (i.e., did the change work?). **Process measures** address the transactions or processes that took place *during* the change (Kazden, 1980). Processes often underlie outcome. An example of an outcome measure might be that there are fewer pregnant drug users in a community after instituting a prevention program for them. Higher self-esteem and satisfaction with their pregnancies would be processes that underlie the success of the prevention program.

Consultants also need to ask, Are the methods and research affordable, workable, and understandable for this set of clients? Furthermore, ethical consultants work *with* not *for* those who hire them (Benviente, 1989; Christensen & Robinson, 1989). In fact, all consultants need to ensure **constituent validity,** which means that those participating in the research or change are not considered subjects to be acted on but participants whose perspectives *must* be taken into account in planning and other related activities for the activities to be valid (Keys & Frank, 1987). Consultants need to *empower* the population with whom they are working to create and sustain the change initiated by the presence of the consultant. This means that the consultant needs to find a good way to "wean" the clients or participants, lest they become too dependent on the expert.

Professional change agents or consultants also need to assess the prevailing culture as well as the trust and the respect held for them in a particular setting. Such assessment will help consultants determine how visible they should be. Consultants also need to evaluate their own personal values and communicate them openly *before* the consultation or research begins to avoid ethical dilemmas after the collaboration process has commenced (Heller, 1989a). Finally, consultants must evaluate their work with their clients; they need to ask the question, Did I improve the community by my presence? Through research, this question can best be answered. Without evaluation, how would a change agent know if the change worked and whether it ought to be repeated?

Kaufman et al.'s (2006) work, cited in the previous section, and Kelly et al.'s (2004) discussion of an ongoing consultative-research relationship, as described earlier, seem especially pertinent here. The consultative process is one in which the personal aspects of systems engagement are important. What is becoming clearer in the consultative process is the need to be aware of the larger system with its own agendas and concerns for survival and change. Both Kaufman's and Kelly's work speaks to the establishment of a working relationship, where the client/agency/community comes to understand itself as a partner in the research/consultative process. Whether this requires just being there at significant events, on a regular and longer term basis, or contributing resources and time above and beyond normal expectations, the perception of consultant as engaged community member or ally versus detached and disinterested party places the research, data, and conclusions or recommendations in an entirely different light. Brodsky et al. (2004) highlight the role of such relationships in the community research context. The skill set that the community psychologist brings to the consultative process is a knowledge of what makes for good science but also an understanding of what makes for usable science.

SUMMARY

Community psychology is interested in identifying and understanding the social contexts that contribute to the creation of healthy populations and help prevent the development of pathology. Community psychologists are also interested in the "creation of settings" that bring about positive changes in our society. In both instances, research plays a crucial role in providing an empirical basis for the building of theory and interventions.

The community psychologist uses correlational, experimental, and quasi-esperimental designs to conduct their studies. There is growing awareness of the breadth of other data gathering possibilities. In particular, the potential contributions of qualitative information and ethnographic methodologies have gained favor. Needs assessment and program evaluation are valuable skills as well, providing feedback mechanisms as well as methods for intervention.

There is a growing awareness of the participatory action research model, where the population under study is engaged in determining what is to be studied as well as how it is to be studied. This empowering collaborative process has potential to yield more complete and useful data on the lives of those being researched.

Other considerations in the scientific endeavor are the ethics of any study. Cultural issues are especially important as we venture into the broader and more diverse community. The importance of scientific inquiry within this field is conveyed by the name of the APA division for community psychology, the Society for Community Research and Action.

CHAPTER 3

STRESS AND RESILIENCE

THE STRESS MODEL AND THE DEFINITION
OF COMMUNITY PSYCHOLOGY

STRESS
  Stress Reaction
  Stressor Events
    Acute versus Chronic Stress
    Racism and Minority Status: An Example
      of Stressful Social Contexts
  Stress as a Process
■ **CASE IN POINT 3.1**   Contemporary Racism
Coping
    Emotion-Focused and Problem
      Solving–Focused Coping
    Active and Avoidant Coping
    Emotional Approach Coping
    Three Dimensions of Coping

    Collectivist Coping
    A Schema for Coping
  Social Support
    Types of Social Support
    Buffering and Additive Effect
■ **CASE IN POINT 3.2**   Mexican American
    College Student Acculturation Stress,
    Social Support, and Coping

RESILIENCE
  At-Risk to Resilient
  The Kauai Longitudinal Studies
  A Useful Model
  The Fourth Wave

SUMMARY

There is an art to facing difficulties in ways that lead to effective solutions.
—John Kabat Zinn

Linda was the first in her family to go to college. She had done well in high school, getting mostly A's and an occasional B. At the encouragement of her school counselor, she applied to several universities, getting scholarships to many of them.

    Once at college, she felt lost. The students were different. The classes were different. The dorms seemed very strange. She slept next to a complete stranger in a double room. The other woman came complete with Nordstrom college accessories, whatever that was. They all dressed a particular way. It was like they had called each other up and talked about what to bring and what to wear. Everyone knew, except her. The rest of the hall seemed comfortable with the setting. Their parents had talked to them about college life. They seemed to know the acceptable language and speech cadence, which signaled that they were on the inside. Everyone seemed to know what to do and when to do it. But for Linda, even the food was strange. The dilemma was what to do.

A community psychology would analyze this example, look to the systems at work for Linda and others like her in the college setting, and make particular recommendations, which could be based on a stress model and a resilience model. We will pursue what goes into these related models and see what might help Linda and those in her situation.

THE STRESS MODEL AND THE DEFINITION OF COMMUNITY PSYCHOLOGY

Barbara Dohrenwend's presidential address to the Division of Community Psychology in 1977 (Dohrenwend, 1978) described a model that she believed would coalesce the many and varied activities of a new community psychology. She proposed a stress model that described a psychosocial process leading to the development of psychopathology in given populations. In this model, a particular event or set of events could produce stress reactions. However, the stress event itself was just one of several factors that influenced the individual's reaction. In the model, there were **personal psychological characteristics** to be calculated into the process, for example, the person's information, skills or intelligence would make a difference in how they might react. There were also **situational characteristics** defining the setting in which the event occurred, such as the time of day, the physical setting, the social groups present. Then there were intervening factors placed between the event and the reaction that mediated the impact of the event on the individual. There were **situational mediators,** such as social support or material support, and **psychological mediators** like coping skills or personal values. The outcome of the stressful event on the individual was determined by the combination of stress events, present characteristics, and the mediators. She noted that the experience could lead to either negative or positive consequences, depending on the combination of factors. With this model in mind, Dohrenwend saw community psychologists intervening at the characteristics level (education for changing the psychological characteristics, political action to change the situation characteristics) or at the level of mediators (community organization to strengthen situational mediators or skills training to positively influence psychological mediators). This stress model could be used to direct community intervention efforts. Finally, she distinguished the form and timing of community psychologists' interventions from that of clinical psychologists' in that the clinician focused exclusively on the individual and on later in the process, after pathological reactions had developed. The community psychologist dealt with both the individual and the situation and intervened early in the process before the displays of severe and chronic problems.

In a later article on community psychology, George Albee (1982) made liberal use of the stress model and its elements. Using stress as a conceptual basis, he proposed programs to prevent the development of psychopathology and promote human potential. He believed the incidence of mental disorder took into account organic factors, stress, coping skills, support, and self-esteem. Decreasing stress or increasing coping skills and support lowered disorders and increased health. Increasing stress or decreasing coping skills and support heightened disorders and decreased health. Stressors could come from a variety of sources—economic, social, or psychological—but the process remained the same. We need to decrease stress and increase coping and social support.

As we can see from these two examples, the stress model has historically been an integral part of community psychology used by some of its earliest theorists and researchers. However, it has not been without controversy. Rappaport (1977, 1981) believed stress considerations were too person-focused and clinical in nature. Calling it "old wine in new bottles," he advocated a broader, more group, system, or policy focus for interventions. Why should we use the old ways of doing things when they appear to have failed and new ones hold such promise?

Yet Cowen (1985) argued that an understanding of the stress process and the circumstances that influence the process provided valuable information for those working on community person-centered interventions. "A significant portion of what we call psychological wellness derives from people's abilities to adapt . . . effectively with stressful events and circumstances" (pp. 32–33). **Situation-focused approaches** look at specific stressful events and intervene in those situations. **Competency enhancement approaches** look to the individual's skills in coping with stress in general and work to increase these skills. In both of these approaches, an understanding of the stress model was central and included those factors that served to protect an individual in risky circumstances and promote general well-being.

This chapter presents the development of stress concepts, explores coping styles in dealing with stress, and reviews some of the work on social support as a mediating factor. We then examine the work on resilience, where at-risk individuals thrive. Although resilience takes stress and its components into account, it does more. Both the stress model and the resilience model have informed community psychology research and community psychologists' interventions. In Chapters 4 and 5 we look at social change and community interventions. Here, we examine two models that have helped in the conceptualization of community psychology's studies and community psychologists' interventions.

STRESS

The term *stress* has been used to indicate the occurrence of three things: a stimulus event, a process, and a reaction. This ambiguity is confusing, so for our purposes, we talk of the stimulus event as a **stressor,** the process as a **stress process,** and the reaction as the **stress reaction.**

Stress Reaction

Hans Selye (1936) was the first to note a particular set of physiological reactions to a variety of harmful or noxious stimuli. He came to describe this reaction process as the General Adaptation Syndrome (GAS). This involved an initial alarm reaction, followed by resistance, and if this fails, exhaustion. His definition and elaboration of the stress process became the focus of his life work (Selye, 1956). His approach was physiological, documenting the shifts in the organism when the balanced, "homeostatic state" was disrupted. Selye believed this syndrome was activated by any generalized upset to the physical system. Since then, the stress reaction has been measured in both physiological terms, such as illness in various forms, or in psychological terms, such as depression, anxiety, or other measures of multiple symptoms, like the Symptom Check List (Derogatis & Coons, 1993).

Stressor Events

Stress as a stimulus event has also been called the *stressor,* to distinguish it from the process. In the 1960s, a list of life change events was devised called the Schedule of Recent Experience (Rahe, Meyer, Smith, Kjaer, & Holmes, 1964) and a weighted scoring system by which to measure the level of stress (Holmes & Rahe, 1967). These 42 life events ranged from "death of a spouse" to "getting fired at work" to a "minor legal violation." The list of events with their weighting scores is called the Social Readjustment Rating Scale (SRRS). The SRRS is one of the most widely used measures of stressors today. The scale scores have been shown to be related to the variety of measures of stress reactions (Scully, Tosi, & Banning, 2000).

Although the events from the SRRS are typically considered major life changes, a second way of looking at stressful events was proposed by Kanner, Coyne, Shaefer, and Lazarus (1981) and Derogatis, Coyne, Dakof, Folkman, and Lazarus (1982). In their research, the smaller, everyday hassles were found to be a better indicator of stress than the major life changes. Hassles could include things like worrying about one's weight, having too much work with too little time, forgetting things, and concerns about home repair needs.

Wagner, Compas, and Howell (1988) found first-year college students undergoing major life changes had an increase in hassles. In turn, this increase in hassles related to physical symptoms of distress. In this model, major life changes led to hassles which predicted physical stress symptoms, neatly tying the three concepts together.

Acute versus Chronic Stress. There is a distinction made in the stressful event literature between acute, time-limited problems that can arise and chronic, persistent demands on an individual (Gottlieb, 1997; Wheaton, 1997). One issue is the precise definition of what is chronic and what is acute. Wheaton (1997) defines the **acute stressor** as a "discrete, observable event . . . possessing a clear onset and offset" (pp. 52–53). He defines **chronic stressors** as "less self-limiting in nature, . . . typically open ended, using up our resources in coping but not promising resolution" (p. 53). These persistent problems are seen to be "located in the structure of the social environment" (p. 57). There is clear acknowledgment that these classes of stressors can and do lead to different processes and coping strategies (Gottlieb, 1997). These stressors result in differing physiological results. An acute stressor brings activation of the neuroendocrine system and the resultant heightened levels of adrenaline and cortisol. The acute stressor raises an individual's attention and makes him or her ready to act. The physical system is ready for "fight or flight." With prolonged stress, studies find eventual neurological breakdown (Compas, 2006; Romeo & McEwan, 2006). Chronic stress has been demonstrated to have destructive effects on DNA and contribute to aging (Epel et al., 2004). The differences between acute and chronic stressors therefore are more than a mere timeframe. Chronic stressors may directly contribute to the physical and mental deterioration of the individuals or groups affected. Notably, the work on African American psychosocial stress models supports the contention that the presence of a chronic socially based stressor like racism could be a significant contributor to heightened levels of physical disorders (Clark, Anderson, Clark, & Williams, 1999). Similar claims may be made for those affected by other forms of chronic stress.

Racism and Minority Status: An Example of Stressful Social Contexts. Moritsugu and Sue (1983) described some of the negative impacts of minority status. From self-esteem to social support, those with numeric minority status may be placed at risk. This minority status effect was found in modest form when examining patterns of psychiatric complaint in ethnic groups in Great Britain by Halpern and Nazroo (2000). Kaufman, Gregory, and Stephan (1990) found that statistical minority children showed some indications of adjustment disorder in a classroom setting. Mays, Cochran, and Barnes's (2007) review confirmed the risk of health issues for African Americans. Clark et al. (1999) proposed a biopsychosocial stress model to explain these persistent negative outcomes for African American populations. Mays et al. (2007) reported physiological measures of stress supported the contention that perception of racism serves as a chronic social stressor for ethnic minorities. This stress, resulting from a culture of racism (Jones, 1997), may serve as a credible explanation for some of the health issues of African Americans and other ethnic minority groups in America.

Dovidio and Gaertner (2004) find that subtler, more covert forms of racism or prejudice continue to persist today. As opposed to outright racist statements, there may be unconscious, nonverbal behaviors displayed that send conflicting messages. What people are saying is nonracist, but what people do is. Although this can be corrected, many people don't know they are exhibiting these contradictory signals and the topic of racism is so repugnant that no one wants to talk about it.

Sue, Bucceri, Lin, Nadal, and Torino (2007) describe Asian American experiences with what are called **microaggressions.** These are "brief, commonplace, daily ... indignities ... that communicate negative or derogatory slights" (p. 271). They note that the type of microaggressions may vary among the ethnic minority groups. These microaggressions may be both unconscious and unintentional. Three kinds of microaggressions are identified: **microassault** (explicit racial belittling remark or action, e.g., displaying a swastika or telling a racial joke), **microinsult** (racial insult or belittling, e.g., saying the best qualified should get the job when a person of color does not get the job), and **microinvalidation** (excluding or denying one's experiences, e.g., "I do not believe racism exists today"—saying that someone's report of racism is *not* true). These examples need further research, yet they provide an illustration of social contextual stressors for particular populations in our community.

Stress as a Process

Lazarus and Folkman (1984) defined psychological stress as "a particular relationship between the person and the environment that is appraised by the person as taxing or exceeding his or her resources and endangering his or her well-being" (p. 19). They saw stress as a process that was influenced by multiple variables and emphasized that the

CASE IN POINT 3.1
CONTEMPORARY RACISM

Implicit and Explicit Prejudice

In today's world, racial prejudice and discriminatory action are not approved. Most people speak explicitly of their lack of racism, and this is encouraged socially. Unfortunately, we are products of our past learning. Historically, one culture is valued over another. This difference in how groups and cultures are valued results in less favorable associations with particular racial groups. These associations of which we may not be aware and that appear to come "instantly" lead to differences in how we feel about members of different groups (Devine, 1989). Research has found that how people *talked* to each other in an interracial situation could be predicted by their explicit, stated attitudes on prejudice—that is, the less prejudiced, the more they interacted favorably. However, the way people *acted* was predicted by a measure of their implicit associations regarding the racial group. In the same interracial situation, the less favorable associations lead to less friendly nonverbal behaviors. These unfavorable nonverbal behaviors are noted by the the interracial partner and by an independent observer (Dovidio, Gaertner, & Kawakami, 2002).

The problem for many racial minorities is then dealing with the double message. At the same time that there are nonfriendly nonverbal behaviors being exhibited, there is friendly verbal behavior and denial of any prejudicial behavior, because at an explicit and conscious level many believe they are not racist.

---

appraisal of a given situation was the first step in this process. **Primary appraisal** determined whether the event before a person can mean trouble for them. The **secondary appraisal** looked to the person's expectations of handling the potential for trouble. In the secondary appraisal stage, the individual's coping skills and other resources were evaluated and determined to be either helpful or not helpful in contending with the situation. Stress was related to the person's ability to deal with the environmental demands. How successful we were in responding and using the available resources determined the level of stress experienced. The consideration of ecological fit in social/community contexts would seem a reasonable consideration for understanding a socially stressful situation. These early formulations regarding a model of stress guided research for many years (Lazarus, 1999).

Dandeneau, Baldwin, Baccus, Sakellaropoulo, and Pruessner (2007) found that diverting attention away from a social stressor led to a reduction in a physiological measure of stress (cortisol) and self-report of stress. This finding reinforces Dickerson and Kemeny's (2001) review of 280 laboratory studies on threats to self tending to activation of physiological reactions in subjects. An intervention of note used a resource-activating stress training program to reduce both report of stress and physical stress measures over time (Storch, Gaab, Kuttel, Stüssi, & Fend, 2007). This intervention matches the Lazarus and Folkman (1984) emphasis on resource activation factors in the stress process. It is especially interesting in that it uses the language of primary prevention and psychoeducation; that it is targeted to healthy individuals in business systems; and that it originates in Switzerland. But in a way, we are getting ahead of ourselves because this resource-activating stress management program is based on an understanding of the coping and resource factors presented next.

Coping

Compas (2006) defines two specific processes involved in the response to stressors. The first is automatic and for the most part not consciously controlled. The second is a voluntary response to the stressors at hand, which includes "regulation of emotion, cognition, behavior, physiology and the environment in response to stressful events or circumstances" (Compas, Connor-Smith, Saltzman, Thomsen, & Wadsworth, 2001, p. 89). As conceptualized by Compas et al. (2001), coping is a part of the self-regulatory process in dealing with environmental demands. Studies of coping have found a variety of ways of describing the ways in which we respond. We now examine some of those many ways.

Emotion-Focused and Problem Solving–Focused Coping. Lazarus and Folkman (1984) point to two different types of coping emerging from the research literature: emotion-focused and problem solving–focused. **Emotion-focused** styles work on lessening or strengthening the emotional impact of an event. These include cognitive activities like distancing, selective attention, reinterpretation, or intensifying one's attention on emotional reactions. **Problem solving–focused** coping seeks to change the environment. Individuals try to deal with what is bothering them by examining the given situation and what troubles them about it, then weigh options as to possible changes to make within one's self (alternative choices, alternative ambitions, alternative behaviors) and within the environment (alternatives for the specific setting, possible moves, what needs to be changed, and how it can be changed).

Lazarus and Folkman (1984) reported that these two styles of coping related to how individuals felt they could control the elements in their environment. They believed the emotion-focused styles typically are used when there is a feeling that nothing could be done to modify the environment. The problem-solving strategies are more to be expected when a person believes things are changeable.

Active Coping and Avoidant Coping. Carver, Scheier, and Weintraub (1989) presented a second system for distinguishing coping styles. They constructed a broad, theoretically based measure that presented aspects of **active coping,** where the individual does something to try to solve the stressful situation, and avoidant coping, "where responses potentially impede or interfered with active coping," (p. 280). Examples of active coping include planning, seeking social support, turning to religion, restraining oneself, and acceptance of reality. Avoidant coping is typified by denial, use of alcohol, and withdrawing from the situation.

Much research has focused on these distinctions and pointed to their varying effectiveness. The majority of findings suggest that active or problem-solving coping leads to better results over avoiding/passive coping (Ayers, Sandler, West, & Roosa, 1996; Compas et al., 2001; Ebata & Moos, 1991). Nonetheless, Lazarus (1999) and Sandler, Braver, and Gensheimer (2000) caution that coping is best understood under specific situational conditions. Holahan, Moos, and Bonin (1997) pointed out that the appropriate coping strategy is best matched with the problem at hand. At times where there is a controllable situation, approach styles are best applied. However, in cases where stressors are uncontrollable, avoidance strategies may be appropriate. Vitaliano, DeWolfe, Mauiuro, Russo, and Katon (1990) found that problem-solving styles favored over emotion-focused styles were associated with less depression only when the situation was appraised as controllable.

Different problems require different solutions. There is criticism of the artificial distinctions made in these breakdowns. Such criticism is elaborated in the discussions of a "Schema for Coping" later in this chapter.

Emotional Approach Coping. A study of **emotional approach** coping suggests there are healthy and productive roles for emotion in the stress process (Stanton, Kirk, Cameron, & Danoff-Burg, 2000). They report the acknowledgment of and attempts to understand one's emotions and the expressing of one's emotions are related to better adjustment. These emotional styles help the person identify his or her feelings and communicate them to those around him or her. This can be useful information for the resolution of problem situations. They note that the appropriateness of emotional approach behaviors are dependent on the actor, the situation, and the receptivity of the listener to such emotional behaviors. We are again reminded by Lazarus and Folkman's (1984) earlier admonition that coping is best understood as an individual's attempt to adapt to a given context. Feelings are an important part of that adaptation.

Three Dimensions of Coping. Other variations on coping of particular note come from Hobfoll's (1998) proposal of a coping scheme that takes into account the **active-passive, prosocial-antisocial,** and **direct** and **indirect** ways that coping could be divided. He argues that such a multidimensional consideration could account for cultural variations in coping. He emphasizes the need to take the context of the problem and the response into account. His system gives prominence to the cultural and community/social contributions to coping and the research literature on active versus avoidant and problem-solving versus emotional styles researched by others.

Collectivist Coping. Based on research conducted in Taiwan, Heppner et al. (2006) report a five-factor instrument representing **collectivist coping** activities not usually found in coping inventories. Examples of these collectivist styles are: I tried to accept the trauma for what it offered me; I believed that I would grow from surviving; Shared my feelings with my family; Saved face by not telling anyone. An adolescent coping style that taps Chinese values has been derived by Hamid, Yue, and Leung (2003). This instrument reflects concepts such as "as shui-chi tzu-an (let nature take its course), I pu-pien ying wan-pien (coping with shifting events by sticking to one unchangeable way), and k'an-k'ai (to see a thing through)," which were derivatives of a Taoist philosophy where, for example, nonaction is not seen as avoidance but rather the understanding and acknowledgment of the nature of things.

Coping is diverse. It is one category of resources available to an individual dealing with stressful events in life. Another resource is social support. We explore its definition and its effects on the stress process next.

A Schema for Coping. Skinner, Edge, Altman, and Sherwood (2003) reviewed the literature on coping measures and reported problems with the typical ways of organizing coping behaviors. From this review they identified 13 ways of coping (see Table 3.1). Taking these basic categories and organizing them into types of coping proved more difficult. They

TABLE 3.1   Coping Families

1. Problem solving
2. Support seeking
3. Avoidance
4. Distraction
5. Positive cognitive restructuring
6. Rumination
7. Helplessness
8. Social withdrawal
9. Emotional regulation
10. Information seeking
11. Negotiation
12. Opposition
13. Delegation

From Skinner et al. (2003, pp. 240–241)

believed a functional definition, that is, problem-solving versus emotional-focused coping style, was not workable because behaviors could perform more than one function. A behavior may be both emotional and problem focused as we can see in the "positive emotional focus approaches" described earlier. A topological definition based on what is done, for example, the approach versus avoidance distinction, is confusing because behaviors have multiple dimensions. A coping response may require both avoidance for a time, to gain perspective, and then approach to directly contend with the problem.

Skinner et al. (2003) argue that the method for organizing the specific coping response families might be better conceptualized from an adaptive process viewpoint. They believe the three adaptive processes to be: 1. coordination of **action and contingencies** within an environment; 2. coordination of **social and personal resources,** and 3. coordination of **preferences and options.** Note that the emphasis is on coordination, or rather, the efforts of the individual to understand the environment and themselves so as to better fit into the presenting context. Skinner et al. propose that these three processes might best describe the coping processes in general. Further studies of coping might be guided by these distinctions.

Social Support

The concept of social support would seem to be a natural area of investigation for community psychology. Those around us are a resource. Seeking social support is listed among Lazarus and Folkman's coping styles. It assumes there is a social support system from which to receive assistance.

> Social support might be usefully re-conceptualized as coping assistance, or the active participation of significant others in an individual's stress management efforts. Thus social support might work like coping by assisting the person to change the situation, to change the meaning

of the situation, to change the emotional reaction to the situation, or to change all three. (Thoits, 1986, p. 417)

Research has demonstrated the advantages of a good social support system to one's health (Barerra, 2000; House, Landis, & Umberson, 1988; Thoits, 1984, 1985; Uchino, Cacioppo, & Kiecolt-Glaser, 1996). Some early research found that social support was even more powerful than stressor measures in explaining the variations in psychopathology in a community sample (Lin, Simonre, Ensel, & Kuo, 1979). This relationship continues to be found in a variety of populations dealing with different kinds of problems. The relationships are not always direct or self-evident (Barrera, 2000) and there are distinctions found between perceived and received support (Haber, Cohen, Lucas, & Baltes, 2007). Keinan (1997) points to several intervening variables that figure into the translation of supportive behavior to the appraisal of support. She finds that for low anxious mothers who have had experience in birthing (not a first birth), the presence of a supportive husband during the birth process led to higher levels of mother tension. For first birth experience mothers, the presence of a husband was helpful. Keinan believes the situational and personality variables influenced the effects of social support.

Nonetheless, the generally positive impact on adaptation continues to be demonstrated using more and more sophisticated physiological measures of stress reactions (Gallagher, Phillips, Ferraro, Drayson, & Carroll, 2008).

Types of Social Support. Supportive behaviors are typically divided into three areas: emotional, informational, and instrumental (Helgeson & Cohen, 1996; Thoits, 1985). Emotional support comes in the form of expressing compassion for the person. The support is directed at making the person feel loved and cared for. In the informational dimension, the person being supported is provided with helpful facts or instruction. The knowledge imparted may help the person gain some mastery of the tasks required of him or her. The third form of support is instrumental, where the person is provided with materials, transportation, or physical assistance.

Holahan et al. (1997) and Valentiner, Holahan, and Moos (1994) note that the role of initial family support (Are they critical or disapproving? Do they understand you?) on later psychological adjustment of a college student sample was dependent on the assessment of controllability of the stressor. In cases where the stressor was believed to be controllable, support was related to adaptive coping, which in turn related to adjustment. In uncontrollable conditions, adaptive coping strategies were not related to adjustment. Family support was related to adjustment directly. When one can't do anything to resolve a problem, it is nice to believe someone is there for you.

Buffering and Additive Effect. One issue that has arisen is the manner in which support brings about the well-being of a person. Some believed that support raised one's positives regardless of the stressors in the environment (Thoits, 1984, 1985). We are happier because we have friends. The other explanation is the "buffering" theory (Dean & Lin, 1977; Wilcox, 1981). Social support helps us deal with stressors that arise. When facing a problem, it is good to have people to help, so the burden of the problem can be shared and a better solution devised. When in trouble, we have a little help from our friends. In later considerations of this debate, it appears that both explanations are valid. Cohen and Wills (1985) found that the *quality* of one's social support network relates to the buffering capacities. Alternatively, the structure of social support, such as size, relates to the overall sense of well-being.

Hobfoil and Vaux's (1993) review of the literature on social support led them to believe the best explanatory model to be one where social resources were fitted to the needs of the situation. The individual played an active role in fitting the resources to the demands at hand, and so the person's characteristics influenced the capabilities to deploy resources.

Social support continues to prove a powerful factor in predicting health outcomes (Richmond, Ross, & Egeland, 2007). In a national Canadian sample of indigenous people, women reporting high levels of positive interaction, emotional support, and tangible support were more likely to report thriving health. For men, emotional support was the only social support variable related to thriving health. Though gender differences appeared with regard to which specific social support components mattered, the overall trends were clear.

Brissette, Scheier, and Carver (2002) studied the reasons optimism was associated with good psychological adjustment. They examined the experiences of first-year college students, measuring optimism, social support systems, number of friends, stress, and depression. They found that the correlation between optimism and well-being (low depression and low stress) was in fact mediated by coping and social support. Optimism was associated with more problem solving and positive reinterpretation coping. Optimism was also associated with perception of a good quality social support system and the number of friends within one's network. These coping styles and perceptions of social support are what relate to better overall adjustment. Optimism works through these two mediating mechanisms, coping and social support, to bring about positive results for the individual. The present example illustrates the importance of coping and social support in helping mediate the effects of personality on depression.

CASE IN POINT 3.2
MEXICAN AMERICAN COLLEGE STUDENT ACCULTURATION STRESS, SOCIAL SUPPORT, AND COPING

There is a 75 percent increase in the number of Latino students entering college. Unfortunately, their rate of graduation has not kept pace with this increase of entrants. A meta-analysis attributed these problems in retention rate to the higher levels of financial and academic preparedness and acculturative stress (Quintana, Vogel, & Ybarra, 1991). Crockett et al. (2007) studied the acculturative stress in one group of Latino college students, Mexican Americans. Using data from a university in Texas and two universities in California, Crockett et al. (2007) studied the relationship of acculturative stress, parent and peer social support, coping (active or avoidant styles), and psychological distress. Among those with low levels of social support, higher levels of acculturative stress were related to higher levels of anxiety and depression. For those with high levels of social support, acculturative stress was not important to the development of psychological symptoms. There were also significant interactive effects with avoidant and approach coping styles. The authors believe this to be the first time acculturative stress and the buffering effect of social support and of coping styles were demonstrated with Latino college students. The stress model and its components provide a clear framework for the study of this at-risk population.

Examining our chapter's example of Linda, the first-year college student, we see high stressor scores for life changes in coming to college. We would expect more hassles as a result of these changes. Her social support would depend on her relationship with her parents, family, and friends and her ability to find new friends and mentors in the college setting. If these support systems are good, she could receive good advice and material support when needed or a "shoulder to cry on" when things get frustrating. As for her coping with the stressors, current research would recommend active and engaged styles of dealing with her environment when the problems are workable. Other styles of coping may be called for if the problems are not so workable. If she finds effective ways to deal with her life changes, for example, meeting new people, finding constructive advice, and building a socially supportive support group, then Linda may find her changes less stressful and more like manageable challenges.

The research of resilience examines how people at risk survive and thrive. Resilience is what we will study next.

The stress model is central to much of the work on resilience. We reference a number of stress concepts in the following section.

RESILIENCE

Why do some succeed and others do not in difficult times? There are children born into high-risk situations who seem to thrive and succeed, despite their circumstances. Not everyone goes the way of pathology and failure in these contexts. As opposed to focusing on the problems, resiliency researchers have delved into who does well and why.

At-Risk to Resilient

One of the interesting facts about resilience is that researchers initially looked at factors placing people at risk of failure and pathology (Garmezy, 1974; Garmezy & Streitman, 1974; Rutter, 1981). Garmezy was studying families that had at least one schizophrenic parent. Rutter was looking at children from poor urban neighborhoods in comparison to children from a rural setting. From this initial focus came the insight that there were many who did well despite their circumstances (Garmezy, Masten, & Tellegen, 1984; Rutter, 1985, 1987). Rutter (1987) emphasized that resilience is a process, not a single static variable. He pointed to the impact of gender (expectations and ways in which upsets are expressed), temperament (likable versus unlikable), marital support in child-rearing, the ability to plan, and school successes and their effects on a child's resilience or vulnerability. Rutter also noted the importance of "turning points" in the lives of at-risk children. There were important junctures in life's pathways. The direction taken at these critical points had long-lasting influence on the life of the individual. Garmezy and the Project Competence group explored what it meant to positively adapt to the environment, what was effective across multiple tasks, and developmental phases (Masten & Obradovic, 2006).

Among the early studies of at-risk populations was one by Sandler (1980). He found strong social support to be related to lower levels of maladjustment in at-risk inner-city children. It was a good example of the use of the earlier described stress model for examining the resilience process.

The Kauai Longitudinal Studies

Resiliency researchers embarked on longitudinal studies that allowed them to look at the characteristics of children who eventually did well despite their placement in "risky circumstances." An excellent example of these longitudinal studies was that conducted by Werner and Smith over several decades on the island of Kauai in the state of Hawaii. Werner and Smith (2001) reported on this longitudinal study of individuals who appeared to be at risk based on a history of family psychopathology, poverty, lack of education, and/or family alcoholism. Following these at-risk subjects into their middle age (50s), Werner and Smith found resilience to be linked to the individual's capability to accomplish age-appropriate developmental challenges. Because the study was situated on an island, the population was relatively stable, and the influence of off-island factors somewhat controlled. Starting in 1955, the researchers looked at the developmental progression of the identified group of at-risk infants as they matured into full adulthood. They found that about two thirds of this at-risk population developed problems. The third that did not were characterized by their ability to engage the environment in an age/developmental stage–appropriate way. They were nurtured by a parent or parent substitute, who served as a positive role model for them. The "vulnerable but invincible" children also found support outside their families in a variety of community settings: school, neighborhood, informal friend networks, churches, or youth organizations. By late adolescence, these children had developed the internalized resources that aided in mastering their environment (high self-esteem, internal locus of control, a feeling that life made sense, and an effective support system). The more risk factors there were, the more protective factors were needed to deal with the risks raised. Family protective factors related to the parents' ability to be nurturing at critical times. The most important community factor was the presence of caring adults, who served as teachers and mentors or later as a friends, co-workers, or bosses. Among the protective factors in the environment were emotional support throughout the life cycle and a lower number of stressful life events. By age 30, the resilient men and women were more accomplished in both education and careers and were more likely to be married than their nonresilient counterparts or the national norm. By age 40, they were more likely to be settled and contributing members in their communities. Such studies as these serve as a blueprint for community interventions, because they pointed out those aspects of the children's experience that were predictive of later life success.

A Useful Model

Masten and Coatsworth (1998) pointed to the usefulness of these naturalistic studies on resilience and competence in at-risk populations. From the Kauai studies and the work of Garmezy and Rutter, important protective factors in the developmental life process were identified. These were later used in devising interventions. In particular, prevention program emphases on parent competence, early child preparation for school success, the acquisition of specific child skills, and expanded opportunities for community mentoring were directly in line with resilience findings. Masten (2001) stated, "Resilience does not come from rare and special qualities, but from the everyday magic of ordinary, normative human resources in . . . children, in their families and relationships, and in their communities." The natural capacity to build competencies and strengths and their importance in the coping process have shifted community prevention interventions from prevention to promotion efforts.

Rutter (2006) reminded us that resilience was more than the development of social competence or positive mental health. Resilience occurred when individuals thrived *despite* their risky circumstances. He cautioned that there were differences in how well people fare. Some thrived, but a significant number did poorly and succumbed to the negative environment. Nonetheless, for some the experience of successfully contending with stressful situations made them stronger. Elder's (1974) study of the children of the Great Depression found that those who successfully overcame the adversity of those times appeared to be made all the more capable of contending with later challenges.

The Fourth Wave

Masten and Obradovic (2006) described four waves of resilience research. The first started with the study of the causes of psychopathology and the discovery of children who were healthy and successful emerging from risky circumstances. The research focused on what was associated with such failure and illness or success and health. The second wave of work examined the processes in developing resiliently. The third wave attempted to apply what had been learned from the descriptive studies. Interventions were attempted and evaluated. These first three waves have provided focal points for the study of resilience. Emerging from these first three waves have come the "discovery" of the important adaptive systems—family, school, community relationships, spiritual practices—and the important skills—self-control, goal-directed behavior, dealing with affect, motivation to succeed, and dealing with stress. The fourth wave of resiliency work has started to look at the integration of multiple levels (neurological, personality, social, community) and disciplines (psychology, sociology, biology, neurology). Resilience resulted from interconnected systems performing in coordination.

For example, Davis and Cummings (2006) found that parental conflict was associated with heightened risk of childhood adjustment problems. Hypothesizing the wear-down of the neurobiological system in children faced with such conflict, Davis, Sturge-Apple, Cicchetti, and Cummings (2007) examined the level of stress reaction in children of conflicted families. They discovered the children with high-conflict parents had less adrenocortical reactions when exposed to a parental conflict incident. Adrenocortical reaction had earlier been linked to typical physiological reactions to stressors as a part of the hypothalamic-pituitary-adrenocortical system linked to stress. This dampened reaction was also found to be related to heightened tendencies for acting out and aggressive behaviors. The neurophysiological reactivity findings and their link to this class of problem behaviors were first steps in understanding a child's risk for acting out. Have these children learned not to get excited when witnessing conflict? Did this in turn make them less sensitive to the effects of aggression? Or did it mean that they required more aggression in their world to be stimulated? Future studies are needed on these lowered adrenocortical reaction–aggressive behavior links. Future findings would help direct the creation of possible early interventions to decrease the likelihood of aggression in children.

A second example of the multilevel analysis of stress and resiliency was provided by Greenberg, Riggs, and Blair (2007) who provided a multilayer analysis of the plasticity (openness to being shaped, the ability to be altered) of the brain, and the impact of childhood and adolescent experiences on neural development. Greenberg et al. elaborated on the neurological context for the Promoting Alternative Thinking Strategies (PATHS) program, which focused on social and emotional learning. There was clear evidence that neural development was the product of the interactions of genetics and environment. Neuron generation, synaptic formation, pruning, and density were all neurological developments that over time formed the basis of frontal cortex maturation and the increasing power of thoughtful control of behaviors. In addition, the growing complexity of right and left hemisphere communications and the use of language in determining action were well-documented neurological trends.

Greenberg et al. (2007) found Moffitt's (1993) distinction between life course persistent and adolescent limited (AL) antisocial behaviors provocative to their program development. Life course persistent patterns started at a young age, were frequently found throughout the life of the individual, and were severe deviations from acceptable behaviors. The AL behaviors did not appear until the onset of puberty, were infrequent, and were not as grave a violation of social rules. The AL behaviors tended to stop after adolescence and might, in fact, be normative to the developmental period. Think of "teenage rebellion" versus criminal tendencies. Given this distinction, the importance of early intervention in problem behavior seemed clear.

The research with Greenberg et al.'s PATHS program suggested that the intervention could have a significant impact on young children's (first- and second-graders') ability to inhibit incorrect responses and to sequence relevant information. In turn, these capabilities have been shown to relate to teacher- and parent-reported problems. The ability to control one's behavior and hold back from acting inappropriately was very important. We might think of how impulsive behaviors have been viewed as immature. The children who received the PATHS intervention were better able to control themselves. In turn, being able to talk things through and work out a problem verbally was important. This skill at verbal problem solving was positively affected by the PATHS program, and in turn, this skill related to fewer problem behaviors.

An awareness of the multiple levels at which the processes exist and of the interactions among these various processes informs the derivation of new theory and interventions. From this holistic perspective, the resilience literature provides direction for community-based programs. The incorporation of the biological to the sociological is in keeping with community psychology's multidisciplinary traditions as well as to the biopsychosocial models that are gaining currency in psychology.

SUMMARY

The stress, coping, social support, and resilience literature has contributed to a theory and research base for community programs. The models propose that people face a changing and demanding world. This world presents a set of challenges with which the individual must cope. The existence of social supports and the ability to access these supports is an important resource to the individual's coping process. Examination of those who have succeeded in threatening and risky contexts, that is, resilient people, highlight the importance of personal and social resources to those successes.

We have come to understand that humans can deal with a variety of adversities. Our example of Linda dealing with the stress of the first year of college helps point out that in high-risk populations (e.g., those in transition), some fail and some succeed. The resilience research suggests that the qualities needed for success are specific to the developmental tasks. It is not a smooth, continuous process from one point in life to another, but a series of challenges. The difference between those who succeed and those who fail is the ability to self-regulate and meet the challenges placed before us. Toward this end, it is helpful to have the support of mentors. This support comes from the interaction of personal qualities and contextual qualities helping the individual "construct" the opportunities needed. Ask most college students and they will tell you their world is daunting. One college graduate likened it to "entering a dark tunnel" (Candice Hughes, 2008). What you find there and how you cope with your discoveries in the tunnel is dependent on your resources, including your ability to bring aid when needed. This is a normative process, or rather the result of "ordinary magic," within the community (Masten, 2001).

CHAPTER 4

THE IMPORTANCE OF SOCIAL CHANGE

REASONS FOR SOCIAL CHANGE
   Diverse Populations
   The Perception of Declining or Scarce Resources
   ■ CASE IN POINT 4.1   Funding Dilemmas for Nonprofit Organizations
   Accountability
   Knowledge-Based and Technological Change
   Community Conflict
   Dissatisfaction with Traditional Services

■ CASE IN POINT 4.2   Community Conflict: Adversity Turns to Opportunity
   Desire for Diversity of Solutions

TYPES OF SOCIAL CHANGE
   Spontaneous or Unplanned Social Change
   Planned Social Change
   Issues Related to Planned Change

DIFFICULTIES BRINGING ABOUT CHANGE

SUMMARY

We are the ones we have been waiting for.
—June Jordan
—Alice Walker
—Barack Obama

A noted African American psychologist once told a story of traveling with her family as a child (Wyatt, G., personal communication, August, 1987). When going on a long car trip, they would pack all their necessities and carefully map out their route. There needed to be sufficient food and water. They needed to plot where they could stop for bathroom breaks and gas. Every detail of the trip needed to be planned. The reason for this detailed planning was that they could not stop just anywhere. If they did not have enough to drink, they could not just go and buy what they needed. They could not use just any lavatory facilities, nor could they go just anywhere to eat. During those times, there were clearly marked places designated "For Whites" and "For Blacks," and they were not free to cross those lines. This story was told by a friend, who is still living and is working at one of the nation's premier research universities.

"Separate but equal" had been set as U.S. law by the Supreme Court decision in the late 1800s. The case of *Plessy v. Ferguson* established that a Louisiana law mandating different facilities for blacks and for whites was fair, because these facilities would be equal to each other. The Supreme Court at that time believed that this law did not make one group inferior to the other. This interpretation allowed for separate schools, separate bathrooms, separate entrances, and the basis for a clearly segregated society. In 1954, the Supreme Court decided in the case of *Brown v. the Board of Education of Topeka, Kansas* that segregated schools led to inherently inferior facilities for a targeted group. This decision paved the way for the desegregated society in which we live today. The idea of separate entrances, toilets, or schools is so foreign to us that this story is sometimes met with disbelief that these times ever happened. This landmark Supreme Court case brought about changes in our society that are still being resolved today. We now consider the idea of separate entrances, or separate restaurants, or separate facilities to be absurd. Social change does occur. In this case of *Brown v. Board of Education,* psychology had a hand in influencing the verdict. The testimony and work of psychologists Kenneth Clark and Mamie Phipps Clark played significant roles in this decision, changing American society and American psychology as we know it (Benjamin & Crouse, 2002; Keppel, 2002; Lal, 2002; Pickren & Tomes, 2002). Social change in its best sense moves us to reconsider our present circumstances and imagine the improvements and aspirations toward our overall betterment.

In 1971, psychologist Leigh Marlowe wrote that the rate of social change was accelerating. Change, some planned and some unplanned, continues today at a breakneck pace. In fact, change seems to be a pervasive condition of modern times (Christensen & Robinson, 1989). Actively participating in and fashioning social change is a fundamental value of community psychology (Jason, 1991; Maton, 2000).

Watzlawick, Weakland, and Fisch (1974) believed there to be two types of change: "one that occurs within a given system which itself remains unchanged and one whose occurrence changes the system itself" (p. 10). These have been called **first order change** and **second order change,** respectively. First order change seems to address change *directly* but essentially defeats its purpose. For example, an excellent first order solution would be to tell someone, "Be spontaneous!" This is difficult, don't you agree? A second order solution is one that *truly brings changes* to the system itself. As Watzlawick et al. (1974) noted, second order change requires the innovator to step outside his or her basic assumptive world and think and act creatively. Second order change requires the change agent to have sufficient "outside" perspective to perceive the existing problem in its entirety and to come to a solution.

An example of second order thinking is the solution to the nine-dot grid problem found in Figure 4.1. Try the problem to determine whether you can devise a second order solution.

We find reference to the "revolutionary" nature of community psychology in Rappaport's 1977 text and many subsequent definitional articles on community psychology (Goodstein & Sandler, 1978). The shift in paradigm from reactionary to preventive mental

FIGURE 4.1 **The Nine Dot Problem.** Instructions: Connect the nine dots in the following grid, using four straight lines, without lifting your pencil. The solution to this problem may be found at the end of the chapter, in Figure 4.3.

health, from person-centered to system-centered interventions, and from pathology-focused to wellness-focused work is found throughout the community psychology literature. Social change is an integral part of this shift.

Questions regarding social change for community psychologists are complex and interrelated. Social scientists want to know what causes change; how to predict change; how best to cope with change; and, most of all, how to fashion or direct change that improves the living conditions of community members.

This chapter looks at what creates social change—planned or not—especially in today's complex world. The discussion draws from all areas within psychology, as well as anthropology, medicine, public health, political science, sociology, and other disciplines (Maton et al., 2006; Wandersman, Hallman, & Berman, 1989). In fact, a multidisciplinary approach for examining and intervening in social change is often desirable (Maton, 2000; Seidman, 1983), especially if the diversity (U.S. Department of Labor, 2006) and challenges of our vast population are to be appreciated (Freedman, 1989; Maton, 2000; Salazar, 1988).

What are some of the phenomena that induce change in society? Factors such as diverse populations, declining resources, demands for accountability, expanding knowledge or changing technologies (Kettner, Daley, & Nichols, 1985), economic changes, community conflict (Christensen & Robinson, 1989), dissatisfaction with traditional approaches to social problems, the desire for choices and the need for diversity of solutions to social problems (Heller et al., 1984), and other issues lead the list of reasons for social change. Although the list is not exhaustive, some of these forces need to be considered in more detail to help you comprehend their roles in shaping social change.

REASONS FOR SOCIAL CHANGE

Diverse Populations

During the Middle Ages, no one expected a long life. Today, life expectancies in the United States are increasing. The growing elderly population, as well as pregnant teens, victims of violence, the bereaved, the disabled, the unemployed, and other groups create dramatic social changes and the need for new community interventions.

For example, some Americans do not vote. The homeless are often denied the right to vote because they do not have fixed street addresses. Many with disabilities also do not vote due to transportation costs and other factors (Schur & Kruse, 2000). This situation creates the added problem that those individuals who ought to voice their political opinions on nutrition, health care, housing, and other programs do not go to the polls. Finding a means for the disabled to have transportation to the polls on election day or furnishing them with alternate means of voting may provide them with a greater voice in issues directly concerning them. Taking the service to the people who most need it empowers them to participate in social change.

Special populations (Fairweather & Davidson, 1986) cause changes in society and, in turn, create more social change by virtue of either their swelling ranks or special situations. One should never underestimate the importance of population trends in social change (Duffy & Atwater, 2008; Light & Keller, 1985). If formal, established institutions are insensitive to the special issues of diverse populations, these groups themselves can and will create change (Kettner et al., 1985; Maton, 2000). Grassroots efforts to create or deal with social change will be discussed in the next chapter.

The social change described at the opening of this chapter was the result of work across several decades. The lawsuit resulting in the *Brown v. Board of Education* decision had been brought by the National Association for the Advancement of Colored People (NAACP). As pointed out before, the court finding for *Brown* was pivotal in opening opportunities for many groups who had previously been excluded from mainstream society.

The Perception of Declining or Scarce Resources

Because few community service programs are self-supporting, most are highly dependent on external funding sources (Kettner et al., 1985), and most attempts to create social change are limited by lack of funding and other resources (Maton, 2000). External funding for community services generally comes in the form of government-sponsored legislation, as well as grants from public or private endowments or foundations. Both types of funds are likely to be awarded for experimental programs or services, which must seek other sources of funding after some specified period. New programs therefore compete with older programs for limited pools of money (Levine, Perkins, & Perkins, 2004; Sarason, 1972). Likewise, these "demonstration" programs are deemed insufficient because the time lag for them to be documented and disseminated to other communities is too long (Chavis, Florin, & Felix, 1992). Also, both the federal government and local governments have provided less funding for human services than in the past, thereby creating a sort of "Robin Hood in reverse" effect (Delgado, 1986).

Because government funding for community services is decreasing, there is more pressure on other granting institutions, such as private foundations. Examples of such granting foundations for community services include the Ford Foundation, the Charles Stewart Mott Foundation, the Henry J. Kaiser Foundation, the Robert Wood Johnson Foundation, the MacArthur Foundation, the Carnegie Foundation (Chavis et al., 1992), and more recently the Bill and Melinda Gates Foundation. More programs and human services agencies are applying for these limited funds; hence, the competition for both government and foundation monies is often fierce.

Although some agencies charge fees to clients for services, many are reluctant to become dependent on client fees, because such fees also fluctuate depending on caseload and other factors. Even agencies that charge clients on a **sliding scale** (where fees are tied to income and/or number of dependents) are reluctant to increase charges to their most financially needy clients. The trend towards allocating resources away from the poor (Delgado, 1986) contributes to the perception of declining resources. When funding issues become severe (and even when they are not so severe), clients and service administrators demand reform or social change. However, taxpayers question tax increases to fund changes.

One other source of funding for community service agencies is voluntary or charitable contributions from the public. Such contributions also vary as a function of the economy and other uncontrollable factors. Community service directors are therefore reluctant to become too dependent on charitable contributions. Funding issues for community services have been and will continue to be delicate and volatile (Frumkin, 2000).

Case in Point 4.1 discusses in more detail some of the funding dilemmas faced by nonprofit agencies.

When resources are in decline, there is a perception of comparative scarcity. What has been established as a baseline for funding is lessening. Scarcity results in changing social dynamics, with increasing competition for these resources (Foundation Center, 2008; Smart Growth, 2008).

CASE IN POINT 4.1
FUNDING DILEMMAS FOR NONPROFIT ORGANIZATIONS

The number of nonprofit or charitable organizations and the number of foundations willing to make philanthropic donations to them have grown in the past few decades (Foundation Center, 2008; Smart Growth, 2008). But are they keeping pace with each other? In other words, are funding opportunities shrinking while the number of organizations seeking funding is growing? Or are they growing in tandem?

In the 1950s, foundation start-ups grew by approximately 195 new funders a year. By the 1980s, the average number of new funders had increased to 348 per year. Between 1980 and 1995, the number of foundations in the United States nearly doubled, from 22,088 to 40,140 (Siska, 1998). Today, there are over 57,000 such foundations and corporate givers that offer 246,000 different grants (Smart Growth, 2008). These grants are available in the areas of social services, arts and sciences, protection of democracy, support for vulnerable and needy populations, care for victims of natural disasters, health care, and education (Independent Sector, 2006). In recent years, the leading issue in terms of growth is peace and international affairs, which grew by a whopping 72.5 percent (Foundation Center, 2008).

What about the number of nonprofit organizations that tap into or are dependent on grants from these foundations? Have their ranks grown, too? Yes. There are now more than 1.9 million groups recognized by the Internal Revenue Service as nonprofit organizations (Independent Sector, 2006) and vying for funding. Some are small and have receipts under $5,000; others have receipts of millions of dollars. On the surface, then, it appears there should be fierce competition for charitable funding despite the growth in number of grant makers.

These statistics can be deceptive, though because of economic and other changes, for example, natural disasters such as the hurricanes that hit the Louisiana coast (Foundation Center, 2008; Center on Philanthropy, 2001). Closer examination shows that money is not evenly distributed among all nonprofit organizations. Some organizations receive very large grants of millions of dollars; in fact, the number of grants over $5 million to non-profits has grown enormously. Do you think that a

(continued)

CASE IN POINT 4.1 CONTINUED

small human service organization (such as a church's nonprofit child daycare center) can compete against a large national organization (e.g., the American Cancer Society) for such large amounts of money? Indeed, DeVita's (1997) study showed that although most nonprofit groups are quite small, the largest organizations obtain the bulk of the finances. More specifically, small organizations with expenses of less than $100,000 accounted for 42 percent of the organizations, whereas organizations with total expenses of over $10 million accounted for only 4 percent of charities. The smaller charities received only 3 percent of the support dollars, whereas the larger organizations received half of all support dollars. This same study demonstrated that a disproportionate share of monies ends up in nonprofit organizations related to educational or health issues. Additionally, organizations in northeastern United States receive the lion's share of support dollars. One-fourth of U.S. charities are located in the Northeast, yet they devour one third of the support dollars.

The answer to the opening question, then—Are funding opportunities shrinking?—is likely to be both *yes* and *no;* yes in that the number of foundations pouring dollars into nonprofit agencies is growing (but not fast enough), and no in that the support dollars are probably not distributed equitably.

Accountability

Accountability and its sister term, *cost effectiveness,* seem to be the buzzwords of today. **Accountability** is the obligation to account for or be responsible for various transactions, monetary or otherwise. In times of scarce funding, it is especially fair and reasonable to ask for accountability of both new and continuing community programs (Wandersman et al., 1998). Table 4.1 provides a list of questions important to planning and evaluation as they relate to accountability.

Cost effectiveness means that money should be spent wisely; that is, there should be some return or profit on money expended. Cost effectiveness often refers to money; accountability can refer to such matters as time expended and quality of decisions made.

Spending has always been an important issue, but it is more likely to be historically in the forefront of the minds of today's citizens than it was in the past. Who requests

TABLE 4.1 Planning and Evaluation Strategies That Address Accountability

1. *Why* is the intervention needed?
2. *How* does the program include science and "best practices"?
3. *How* will this new program fit with other existing programs?
4. *How* will the program be carried out?
5. *How* well was the program carried out?
6. *How* well does the program work?
7. *How* can the program be improved?
8. *What* can be done to "spin off" or institutionalize the program?

Source: Adapted from Wandersman et al., "Comprehensive quality programming and accountability: Eight essential strategies for implementing successful prevention programs," *The Journal of Primary Prevention* (1998) vol. 19, pp. 3–30. With kind permission of Springer Science and Business Media.

accountability? Almost anyone today: clients, staff, administrators, taxpayers, elected officials, licensing boards, and others. Any of these constituencies is likely to want to know the answers to such questions as: Where was my money spent? Did the targeted population benefit? Were goals accomplished, and if not, why not?

When answers to these questions are not forthcoming or not the expected ones, the parties leveling the query are likely to demand change. Some individuals may want new administrators; others might want new spending guidelines. The list of demanded changes can be so exhaustive that the end result is the demise of any organization not readily accountable to its constituents. Again, the final outcome is likely to be some kind of ongoing change.

Knowledge-Based and Technological Change

Do you recall the first time you sat at a computer? You probably experienced trepidation and later felt embarrassment caused by thinking a machine could get the better of you. **Technological changes** in the form of computer services and speedier communication systems have, in turn, created new demands on workforces in business as well as in human services. Some organizations and individuals adapt well to technological advances. Others—for a multitude of reasons such as reluctance to use new technologies or lack of funds—do not adapt well or quickly.

People today may think that they are undergoing rapid and extreme technological changes more than ever before. Technological changes, whenever they occur, obligate further changes (Frank, 1983; Kling, 2000). Consider, for example, how your first experience with a computer changed you. Today, you probably complete your term papers, balance your checkbook, keep track of appointments, and perhaps pass your idle time browsing the Internet. The computer has therefore changed your methods of conducting business, completing your work, and socializing.

If these "galloping technological changes" (Frank, 1983) are not enough, mainstream U.S. society is also experiencing a knowledge explosion. New methods for practicing anything from psychotherapy to landscape architecture, new guidelines for human resources management, additional legislation controlling all parts of people's lives, as well as other innovations and applications all requiring new understanding and new skills can overwhelm society's members, create additional change, and perhaps at the same time stimulate anxiety.

Despite the fact that technology is ubiquitous in our occupational, educational, and leisure lives (Brosnan & Thorpe, 2006), many people remain afraid of it. The general fear of technology has been called **technophobia** in the psychological literature (Brosnan & Thorpe, 2006). A specific fear of computers has also been identified and is known as **computerphobia** (Hudiburg, 1990) or, more recently, as **computer anxiety** (Thorpe & Brosnan, 2007). In fact, some claim that this phobia or fear is so strong that it might well be diagnosable (Thorpe & Brosnan, 2007) and in need of treatment (Brosnan & Thorpe, 2006) for success in the modern world.

This so-called digital divide extends to many different people and across international borders (Cooper, 2006). Research has found computer anxiety in older adults (Laguna & Babcock, 1997). Marginalized individuals who are not well educated, are poor or elderly or disabled, and some minority groups remain more technophobic than the majority population (Duffy & Atwater, 2008; Karavidas, Lim, & Katsikas, 2005; National

Science Foundation, 2003). There remains a dispute in the literature, however, as to whether there are true gender differences in computer anxiety and technophobia (e.g. Cooper, 2006; Popovich, Gullekson, Morris, & Morse, 2008). Perhaps as technological changes advance, the more these same individuals will continue to fear it. Few traditional community systems (such as the Department of Health) provide help in coping with technical disasters (Webb, 1989)—a situation that does not help allay fears. One possible way to address these concerns is via education and information dissemination. These strategies are discussed in the next chapter on creating social change.

On the upside, Wittig and Schmitz (1996) and Kreisler, Snider, and Kiernan (1997) found that community organizing can now be done electronically. Such technological organizing seems to obscure social boundaries, alter perceptions regarding stigmatized groups, enhance participation of previous nonparticipants in civil life, and empower activism.

Community Conflict

Some communities experience the strife of conflict, for example, in the demonstrations and riots of the 1960s, some of which were triggered when Whites clashed with Blacks. Conflict, however, does not always produce negative changes (Worchel & Lundgren, 1991). Sometimes a positive outcome of community conflict is social change. **Community conflict** involves two or more parties with incompatible goals that usually have specific values (positive and negative) attached to them. Because of the strongly held values, power struggles, and varying interest levels of the parties, conflict in the community can be difficult to resolve or manage (Christensen & Robinson, 1989). However, such conflict, whether resolved or unresolved, often results in social change because goodwill alone does not always resolve or dissipate conflict (Fairweather & Tornatzky, 1977).

Dissatisfaction with Traditional Services

Probably no other cause has fostered social change more than consumer dissatisfaction with existing community services, especially external expert–dominated approaches (Maton, 2000). In fact, you will recall from Chapter 1 that such dissatisfaction with traditional mental health services spawned the birth and growth of community psychology itself when psychologists at the Swampscott Conference expressed dismay with traditional forms of mental health treatment.

One example of dissatisfaction creating community change relates to this chapter's opening vignette. The African American community was well aware of the prejudices and discrimination present in society. The disadvantages were systemically rooted and pervasive in their social world.

Closer to the issue of psychological interventions, it is important to look at another example of how dissatisfaction with services leads to change. As you may already know from your training in psychology and related disciplines, one of the earliest forms of psychotherapy (or "the talking cure") was psychoanalysis as developed by Sigmund Freud. Freud's own protégés, such as Carl Jung and Alfred Adler, became disenchanted with Freud's approach to therapy and modified psychoanalysis as they knew it (Phares & Chaplin, 1997). Contemporary therapists, disgruntled with such concepts as pansexuality and the unconscious from Freudian

CASE IN POINT 4.2
COMMUNITY CONFLICT: ADVERSITY TURNS TO OPPORTUNITY

In the 1960s, an unfortunate but interesting instance of community conflict occurred in Rochester, New York. Surprisingly, from this adversity grew opportunity. An African American neighborhood decided to hold a neighborhood party. The party occurred on a hot summer night, and many young adults showed up for the festivities. Halfway through the night, a group of White youths came to the party and were seen as intruders. One brusque remark led to another, which eventually erupted in violence. Rochester, like many other cities, quickly exploded in racial conflict.

Several community groups, concerned that such violence not repeat itself, came together in an attempt to find a solution to the city's problems. As a result, the American Arbitration Association was asked to consult on the design of a community program for handling many types of conflict. The **community mediation** program was born. This program manages community disputes between individuals or groups in a peaceful fashion by assigning a neutral third party—a **mediator**—to facilitate discussion and problem solving between the disputants (Duffy, Grosch, & Olczak, 1991). The program also monitors community agency elections as well as urban renewal housing lotteries, "lemon law" (automobile owner/manufacturer) arbitration, and other community projects where a neutral party is needed. The initial community conflict, racial tension, was probably part of the larger national civil rights movement—a movement that created sweeping social changes, which are not yet complete.

From the Rochester conflict, however, came more social change in the form of the Community Dispute Resolutions Centers Act (Christian, 1986). This legislation established in every county in New York a mediation center modeled after the one in Rochester. With New York as the pioneer, other states followed. Today, there are hundreds of functioning mediation or neighborhood justice centers in the United States. Some are adjuncts to the courts; others are run by religious and other charities (McGillis, 1997). All hope to inspire the peaceful resolution of conflict. Community conflict, then, creates snowballing social reform and social change, of which the Rochester experience is only one example. You will read more about community mediation in Chapter 9.

theory, have also developed an array of therapies exemplified by behavior modification, cognitive-behavioral therapy, and existential-humanistic counseling, to name a few. Today, the mental health client has a long menu of therapies from which to choose.

Desire for Diversity of Solutions

Walk into any store in the United States and the display of available goods is overwhelming. Americans are used to choices between brands X, Y, and Z. Americans do not just want diversity in goods, however. They also expect diversity and choice among services. Individuals seeking psychotherapy want to know that they have options in the training of the therapist, the type of therapy, the payment plan, and the length of treatment. Similarly, Americans want to be able to choose between private and public educational institutions for their children and between law firms and lawyers when they want to recover damages or close a real estate deal. Americans have come a long way since the 1800s, when families had one doctor, one school, and one pharmacy in their towns. When individuals find that agencies are insensitive or that there are few options from which to choose, and sometimes this is coupled with dissatisfaction with those existing options, they often demand and create change.

Here is an example from the justice system of how the desire for more options creates change. Anyone who has watched one of the several televised courtroom judges hand down a verdict knows that the courts often leave both complainants and defendants disgruntled. Sometimes even the "winner" does not feel as if he or she has won. One answer to handling this dissatisfaction and to providing more diversity for users of the court system is to develop a **multidoor approach,** as is found in Washington, DC (Ostermeyer, 1991). This is a *coordinated* system of assisting citizens involved in the justice system to find the most appropriate option for them: various courts (small claims, city, state, and federal); mediation and arbitration programs; legal aid offices; public, private, and volunteer attorneys; and other agencies, such as those assisting with mental health. The multidoor approach helps citizens and agencies avoid the frustration of multiple and overlapping referrals and lessens the perception that the justice system is a confusing maze of bureaucracies (Ostermeyer, 1991).

The preceding catalog of reasons for social change, which is not exhaustive, is summarized in Table 4.2. It will familiarize you with some of the causes for social changes. The *Brown v. Board of Education* example presented at the beginning of this chapter has multiple causes and multiple solutions. America's history of social and economic development has provided it with a pluralistic society. We believe in equality and freedom of opportunity as basic rights for all people, yet we struggle with how to honor these rights for both in-group and out-group members of our society (Gaertner & Dovidio, 2005). Though we want to be fair, the common perception is that there are limited resources. Our natural and sometimes unconscious tendencies to categorize or group people can work against this

TABLE 4.2   Reasons for and Examples of Social Change

REASON FOR CHANGE	EXAMPLE OF SOCIAL CHANGE
Special population	AIDS patients desire emotional support from a group of other AIDS patients, and their families get together and form a support group.
Declining resources	The national economy is depressed; less grant money is available from private foundations.
Accountability	A taxpayer group attends a public hearing and demands to know how a tax increase will improve community services.
Technological advances	A corporation buys new software for midlevel managers who now require training.
Community conflict	An agency seeks a halfway house in a residential neighborhood not zoned for multiple-family dwellings; two residents groups, one in support and one against, conflict at a public meeting.
Dissatisfaction with traditional services	An area's private practice psychologists charge high fees not covered by insurance, so citizens inquire about funding possibilities for a mental health clinic that will charge on a sliding scale.
Desire for diversity of solutions	A multidoor courthouse program offers a variety of options for solutions to neighbors fighting in the neighborhood.

desire for equality and freedom for all (Devine, 1989, 2005). The reasons for our groupings have historic, economic, political, sociological, and psychological roots (Jones, 2003). The solutions to our grouping and prejudgment tendencies and their discriminatory outcomes are also multiple. Political and legal solutions go back to the framing of the U.S. Constitution, the U.S. Civil War, and the 14th Amendment to the constitution (Equal Protection under the Law) to name but a few. The *Brown v. Board of Education* case was just one of many court decisions to help further equal treatment for all in the United States. In the *Brown* case, it had to do with education, but in fact, it opened the door for many more solutions to the issues of fairness. Through these many legal, social, institutional, and personal solutions have come increased opportunities for contact, interactions, mutual dependencies, and other contexts that we know can psychologically build empathy and change the out-group members into in-group members (Allport, 1954/1979; Dovidio, Glick, & Budman, 2005). We now understand race to be a politically derived category and that differences of skin color or facial configuration have nothing to do with intelligence, social skill, and ambition. Thus, the reasoning for separation of individuals due to this arbitrary categorization does not hold true. The Supreme Court decision helped in the *integration* of groups. This has led to our society as we know it today. There has been significant progress in providing access to opportunities for all, including African Americans, other ethnic minorities, women, those with mental health issues, the economically challenged, the disabled, and many others members of groups categorized as outside.

Next we examine some ways in which change occurs, whether planned or unplanned.

TYPES OF SOCIAL CHANGE

Forecasting social trends and social changes can be tricky but also very useful in designing prevention programs. For example, the U.S. Census Bureau expected the 2000 census to show demographic changes as well as population increases. The Census Bureau is able to forecast some changes. Projected changes, though, do not always come true and are sometimes more or less dramatic than anticipated. If the 2000 census figures are correct, the population growth of 32.7 million people represents the largest census growth in U.S. history. For example, educators riding the tide of the baby boom built schools and school annexes in the suburbs until the number of schools had soared. Today, these same schools are witnessing a wave of violence from alienated youth. Community activists have much that they can learn from demographers and other forecasters about where change will occur next, particularly spontaneous or unplanned change.

Spontaneous or Unplanned Social Change

Naturally occurring change is called **unplanned** or **spontaneous change.** Most disasters are not planned. For instance, no one planned the Great Chicago Fire in 1871, and, more recently, few predicted the epidemic of school violence.

Natural disasters result in much distress as well as social change (Ginexi, Weihs, Simmens, & Hoyt, 2000). Droughts, earthquakes, floods, fires, and other natural events displace community members from their homes and jobs. Although these disasters are not necessarily always distressing (Bravo, Rubio-Stipec, Canino, Woodbury, & Ribera, 1990; Prince-Embury & Rooney, 1995), they typically result in some large-scale change.

Unplanned major shifts in the population also cause social change (Rosenberg, 2006) and, in fact, much social dissatisfaction and divisiveness (Katz, 1983). For example, as the swell of baby boomers moves through time, their needs change. Baby boomers are now middle-aged or older (Rosenberg, 2006), and many are caring for their elderly parents (Carbonell, 2003; Naisbett & Aburdene, 1990). They often find a dearth of community services that provide elder care, and this creates much stress in the boomers' lives (Duffy & Atwater, 2008). Some baby boomers also have young children who require day care, which can be in short supply. The stress of caring for both the younger and older generations in their lives has resulted in such adults being labeled the **sandwich generation** (Spillman & Pezzin, 2000). The boomers may also soon deplete the funds for Social Security and Medicare, adding to further social changes.

Similarly, other demographic shifts create further social changes. Historically, for instance, there has been an increase in the number of dual-career families (Cromartie, 2007; see Figure 4.2) that need day care for their young children (Naisbett & Aburdene, 1990). As you can readily see, one social change invariably creates another.

Behavioral changes in the population over time are often unplanned. A realistic example of these changes would be historic increases in crime, especially violent crimes. Although high crime rates do not always result in fear (Taylor & Shumaker, 1990), individuals who live in areas where they fear the high crime rate may desire special community

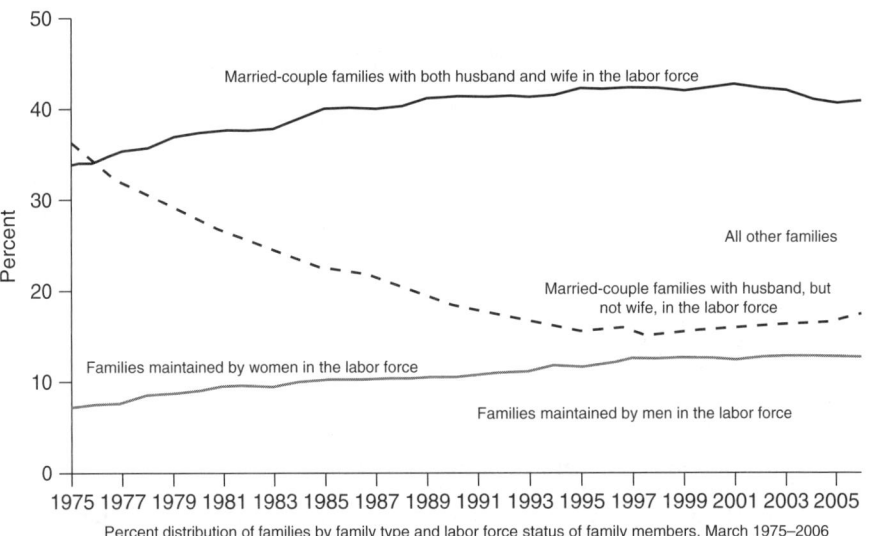

FIGURE 4.2 **Work Patterns of Families Have Changed Over Time**

Source: Cromartie, S. P. (July/August 2007). Labor force status of families. A visual essay. *Monthly Labor Review,* 35–41.

programs, such as neighborhood watches or escort services for the elderly. One interesting study established that those who have been crime victims are not always the most afraid of crime. Rather, this research demonstrated that those most fearful of crime live in neighborhoods with abandoned buildings, vandalism, idle teens, and other signs of deterioration that indicate concomitant declines in social control within the community (Baba & Austin, 1989; Kruger, Reischl, & Gee, 2007; Ross & Jang, 2000).

What makes unplanned or unintentional change stressful is that, although it is rare, it is often uncontrollable and unpredictable. Research (Rodin, Timko, & Harris, 1986) has shown that uncontrollable events are quite stressful. In other words, when individuals feel they control their fates, they experience less stress; when they feel they have lost control, they experience distress (Boggiano & Katz, 1991; Duffy & Atwater, 2008; Taylor, Helgeson, Reed, & Skokan, 1991). African Americans in the civil rights movement may have felt that their lives were not under their own control but under the control of the White majority. Studies performed several years after the *Brown v. Board of Education* decision show African Americans to have a tendency toward an external locus of control (Bruce & Thornton, 2004). However, the study of locus of control suggests that with a more mature, sophisticated, and positive racial identity, an African American sample shifted their locus of control from external to more internal, or self-controlled (Martin & Hall, 1992). Ruggiero and Taylor (1997), though, still find the perception of discrimination to be a threat to self-concept and to perception of self-control. Through organization and planned action, elements of the African American community have moved from a feeling of uncontrolled to controlled change.

Unplanned change is often confined to particular ecological situations in which individuals may unwittingly be placed. For example, crime and natural disasters are generally confined to particular environments (Taylor & Shumaker, 1990), so when individuals find themselves in those environments, they may experience stress. In line with this thinking, individuals walking at night in a neighborhood rife with signs of social disintegration (e.g., graffiti, litter, etc.) may well feel distressed.

Besides assisting in the design and development of community services, community psychologists can also assist with coping for unplanned change by playing a role in *forecasting* it. Remember that one of the tenets of community psychology is *prevention*. This does not mean that community psychologists can prevent these changes—obviously psychologists cannot prevent floods—but learning how to predict unplanned changes can enable the community to prepare for the changes as they occur or even before. Such preparation can prevent the change from being as severe and distressing as it otherwise might be.

The science of prediction is complex, and there are scientists who specialize in prediction and forecasting. Census data, for example, can help forecast population changes. By way of example, as the baby boomers age, they will represent the largest group of elderly the United States has ever had, so if elder care is in short supply now, it may be in even shorter supply in two decades if no one prepares for it. **Social indicators** are measures of some aspect of society based on combined, corrected, and refined social statistics (Johnston, 1980) and can be used in social forecasting. By using techniques such as extrapolative forecasting, network analysis, latent curve analysis, environmental prediction, and others, social trends can be forecasted and preventive measures can be prepared (Kellam, Koretz, & Moscicki, 1999a, 1999b). Indeed, the use of "future studies" can do much for prevention in communities (Sundberg, 1985), but not without some limitations. Lorion (1991), for example, raised the issue of the **base rate problem.** This issue pertains to the fact that although many individuals seem to have the antecedents of diagnosable disorders, for example, few may really actually develop the disorder.

Planned Social Change

Suppose people do not want to wait for change to happen, as in unplanned or unintended change (McGrath, 1983); instead, they want intentionally to create change, called planned change or induced change (Glidewell, 1976). How could people go about this seemingly monumental task? There are some venerated strategies suggested in the community psychology literature: self-help, including grassroots activism; networking of services and social support; the use of external change agents or consultants; educational and informational programs; and involvement in public policy processes. All of these issues are detailed in the next chapter. None of these approaches is easy, and each has advantages and disadvantages. With planned change, however, the desired effects are more likely to be obtained than with unplanned or spontaneous change.

Exactly what is planned change? Kettner and associates (1985) wrote a good working definition. **Planned change** is an intentional or deliberate intervention to change a situation—or, for the present discussion, a part of or a whole community. Planned change is distinguished from unplanned change by four characteristics. First, planned change is *limited in scope;* that is, what is to be changed is targeted or earmarked in advance. Second, planned change is directed toward *enhancing the quality of life* of the community members. This is the primary purpose of planned change in communities. Planned change should enhance (not inhibit) community life. Third, planned change usually *provides a role* for those affected by change. Community psychologists should not impose change on community members. Rather, their role is to inform citizens of the viable options, assist them in the selection of appropriate options, and then participate with them in the design and implementation of change. Finally, planned change is often (but not always) *guided by a person who acts as a change agent.* **Change agents** (Lippett, Watson, & Westley, 1958; Oskamp, 1984) are often trained professionals but can also be advocates for or from client groups, political activists, educational experts, or others interested in inducing change (Ford, Ford, & D'Amelio, 2008). Psychologists often act as consultants or change agents. The role of consultants is detailed in the next chapter. The role of the NAACP and the Clarks in the opening story is a very good example of planned change. They targeted the specific school district to bring about intended changes in the law of the land, the quality of life was most certainly improved with increased educational opportunities, and the African American community was clearly leading in determining the goals and intervention.

Issues Related to Planned Change

A major issue regarding planned change is *who* decides change will occur and *when, how,* and *what* changes will take place. Before the civil rights movement, Whites had pretty much decided what would change in society. Blacks first (and later other less powerful groups) wanted and were eventually provided with equal opportunity to create planned changes in our society. Ask yourself, though, for any planned change, just *who* should decide *what* to do? Any citizen regardless of age? Residents only? All affected voters? Only taxpayers? Elected officials?

Some change experts argue that government officials, administrators, and managers are responsible for initiating change; others argue that the bottom of the organization (e.g., staff, clients, citizens, or members of the community) should create change (Bauman, 2000; Kettner et al., 1985). Many in the field of community development agree that almost anyone and everyone involved in the changes is the appropriate person (Christensen & Robinson, 1989; Heller et al., 1984; Kettner et al., 1985; Levine & Perkins, 1987).

In community psychology, the concept of *collaboration* is embraced (Bond, 1990; Fawcett, 1990; Maton, 2000; Oskamp, 1984; Rappaport, 1990; Rappaport et al., 1985; Serrano-Garcia, 1990). The idea of collaboration—of social scientists and clients coming together to examine and create solutions for social problems—is a major tradition in community psychology (Rappaport, 1990). Collaboration is also called **participatory decision making** or **collaborative problem solving** (Chavis et al., 1992; Kelly, 1986a). As Christensen and Robinson (1989) suggested, self-determination has practical problem-solving utility in that those who live with the problem can best solve it. Acceptance is therefore higher than in imposed changes. Moreover, collaborative decision making helps build a stronger sense of community and avoids client–consultant conflict and duplication of effort because collaboration is a mutual influence process. The key to collaboration is empowerment, which enhances the possibility of self-determination.

Anyone embarking on planned social change needs to prepare carefully for the changes (Maton, 2000). Ongoing, carefully planned change requires hard work and a substantial investment of time, talent, money, and other resources that might otherwise be useful elsewhere (Kettner et al., 1985). The change agents should also prepare participants for change to take a long time (Fairweather & Davidson, 1986; Seidman, 1990), as it is likely to be resisted (Ford, Ford, & D'Amelio, 2008). Likewise, the more important the problem, the more difficult it will probably be to solve (Shadish, 1990), and the more numerous the necessary levels of intervention (Maton, 2000).

Planners also need to consider whether change is really possible (e.g., Will all involved parties cooperate? Are funds available? etc.) and whether, in the end, the desired results can be realistically achieved. For example, although thousands of community programs and organizations exist across the country, many fail (Florin, 1989). Prestby and Wandersman (1985) found that 50 percent of voluntary neighborhood associations, many of which are designed to create and support social change, become inactive after only one year. Such organizations, therefore, seem particularly vulnerable to demise or failure (Chavis et al., 1992).

Fairweather and Davidson (1986) have explained that a single attack on a social problem will not create substantial change. A multipronged and continual approach is generally more successful. A once-and-for-all solution probably will not be effective, either (Levine & Perkins, 1987). Fairweather and Davidson have also cautioned that although some old practices might work well, any useless approaches should be discarded. It is worthwhile to remember, too, that *complete* change might not always be necessary.

Besides the preceding dimensions, planners also need to consider the other parameters of beneficial change (Fairweather & Davidson, 1986). Change must be humane—that is, it must be socially responsible and represent humanitarian values that emphasize enhancing human potential. Change techniques should also be problem-oriented—in other words, they should be aimed at solutions of problems rather than merely be idealistic. Similarly, change strategies should focus on multiple social levels rather than on specific individuals. The techniques may need to be creative and innovative. Old, stale methods may not work; creativity is the constant companion of community activists. The change plans also need to be feasible in terms of dissemination to other groups or situations. Not all techniques fit all groups, but there are some communities that can adopt tried methods from other communities.

Context or *environment* is a concept important to the ecological tradition of community psychology. For example, implementation of planned changes can be influenced by the *social* climate of the settings. In one study, individual school contexts predicted the level of lesson plan presentation of an antiviolence program (Gregory, Henry, & Schoeny, 2007). Administrative leadership (e.g., "at this school, information flows smoothly through channels") and a supportive climate (e.g., "in this school, even low-achieving students are respected" and "teachers in this school are proud to be teachers") were found to result in better program implementation over a three-year period.

Change agents also need to value social experimentation and action research. In this regard, planners cannot be timid about innovation—neither can they be afraid to evaluate their innovations. Social experimentation and evaluation go hand in hand (Fairweather & Davidson, 1986). Any interventions and programs developed to create community change need to be honestly evaluated, modified based on the evaluation, evaluated again, and so on. Then and only then do change agents and communities know that they have the best possible ideas in place.

Finally, planners or change agents need to be realists, particularly with regard to the prevailing political climate (Light & Keller, 1985). Change always makes something different that otherwise would not be changed (Benviente, 1989). Some individuals will like the change; others will not. Hence, the power struggles related to change are likely to commence as soon as change is suggested.

DIFFICULTIES BRINGING ABOUT CHANGE

Why do programs that are designed to create social change or provide alternative services fail? Why do the most well-intentioned efforts sometimes go awry? What if citizens are divided as to what they should do? A multitude of reasons exist, but only a few will be mentioned here.

One of the most important reasons for failure of planned change is *resistance* (Ford, Ford, & D'Amelio, 2008; Glidewell, 1976; Levine & Perkins, 1987), which can come from a variety of sources, including administrators, practitioners, clients, or any other community member. Why does resistance occur? Societies tend to have built-in resistance to change (Bagby, 1981; Ford, Ford, & D'Amelio, 2008); members of groups seem trained to follow their own ways—the old ways—which they regard as safe or superior (Glidewell, 1976). Groups feel their existence is threatened by new groups or new ideas. Ellam and Shamir (2005) believed the acceptance of change is related to the change's concordance with the organizational members' self-concepts. If the change is felt to be self-determined, to be in agreement with their sense of self-distinctiveness, to be self-enhancing, and to have some continuity with existing self-concepts, changes are much easier to accomplish. In the end, change agents themselves may do something to alienate the community or create resistance to change (Ford, Ford, & D'Amelio, 2008).

There are still other reasons for the failure of social change efforts. Psychologists have long documented the effects of in-groups and out-groups in which people favor their own groups (the **in-group**) and stereotype or denigrate outsiders (the **out-group**) (Allport, 1954/1979). In the community, for instance, for-profit businesses, especially big private sector corporations, often resist social change instituted by small nonprofit businesses or by new government policies because the for-profit enterprises think their revenues will be affected. The assumptions of in-group advantages and out-group disadvantages help maintain in-group cohesion but also add to the reluctance to accept any out-group information or characteristics. The inability to empathize and therefore understand the situation of the out-group members can hamper in-group members' ability to accept information and make changes based on that information (Batson et al., 1995). Helping for the sake of "the other" is very difficult, though not impossible, to find (Strumer, Snyder, & Omoto, 2005).

Sometimes change is resisted by those who would benefit from it because they have been socialized to think change is not possible and the status quo is all that is available to them. The South American liberation educator Paulo Freire (1970) argued that the oppressed are many times unaware of the constraints they live under. As a function of the social structure conditioning in which they have grown, they do not see any hope of change. **Conscientization** occurs when the oppressed come to awareness of their oppression. Freire (1994) believed that this occurs when individuals come to a realization of their self-determination and the "unveiling of opportunities for hope" (p. 9). He argued for the value of "the unity in diversity" to create a power base, and of shifting the blame for dysfunction from the "oppressed" individual to the "oppressive" structures (pp. 157–158). These ideas are prescient to (seem to anticipate) the psychological research and theory related to Bandura's "collective self-efficacy" discussed later and Rappaport's "empowerment" efforts identified in Chapter 1.

Change is often seen as unwelcome, not just by groups but by individuals as well (Kettner et al., 1985). Social psychologists working with community psychologists know that individuals are also resistant to change, one of the causes of which is mere cognitive laziness or the desire not to have to think too hard. Most humans are **cognitive misers** who take the path of least effort in terms of decision making and thinking. Other individuals are also closed-minded or **dogmatic** (Rokeach, 1960); they conserve their old ways and shun new ideas because of rigidity in thinking. Individuals resist change for the same reasons as groups—because they feel that change threatens their reputation, job security, or well-being. Furthermore, Kuhn's (1962/1996) argument regarding the difficulty of paradigm shifts—or ways of seeing the world—suggests social change, as with scientific ways of conceptualizing the world, requires people to overthrow that which they have learned to be "real" and to think of things in new ways. Although this can and does occur, a critical mass of evidence needs to accumulate before such change can occur, and the shift in viewpoints is dramatic, and therefore is not taken lightly. Watzlawick et al. (1974) support this notion of difficulty in finding change. As Foster-Fishman and Behrens (2007) suggest, change requires more than shifts in skill sets, it requires shifts in *mindsets* as well. In addition,

Vygotsky's concept of proximal development suggests that new learning beyond one level above how we presently conceptualize the world is extremely difficult and fraught with resistance (Hedegaard, 1996). So we understand that any social change can be difficult to conceptualize, much less execute and find acceptable to the establishment.

Other factors also create the failure of planned change. When a social movement is seen as promoting only a single cause or a cause alien to a large number of people, change is often slow or does not occur at all. Had the civil rights movement, as discussed in the opening scenario, not inspired groups other than African Americans (e.g., women, other minorities), perhaps the momentum it developed would have dwindled; fortunately, it did not. By way of another example, had the March of Dimes stuck with the single issue of the defeat of polio, the organization would have ensured its own demise because polio has been abated in much of the world. Refocusing on the elimination of *all* birth defects has ensured the health of the March of Dimes organization for a long time.

Often, agents of change and their programs fail (Ford, Ford, & D'Amelio, 2008) because their tactics are uncomfortably confrontational and may be seen to violate "politeness norms." Alinsky (1971), Kettner and associates (1985), and Wolff (1987) see risk taking, including the risk that change will be unwelcome, as part and parcel of all change. However, the reality is that if those people planning change receive only negative exposure (by the media, for example) or fail to suggest their own solutions to the problems they are protesting, their protests are perceived as hollow or disruptive rather than productive. Agitation, protest, and confrontation do not always work, and published research supports this contention (Oskamp, 1984). If a community activist chooses a radical or confrontational route to change, Alinsky's work will be of interest. Alinsky noted that no power change ever occurred without some struggle. Notably, those involved in creative power struggles can use existing rules to bring about pressure on the status quo. Table 4.3 summarizes some of Alinsky's sometimes radical approaches.

Collective planning for change is construed as good, but this is only true within limits. If the organization or individuals planning change are too loosely structured, if solid leadership does not exist, or if the decision makers show no discipline in their plans, then

TABLE 4.3 Ten Rules for Radicals*

1. Use whatever you've got to get attention.
2. Don't go outside the experience of your people.
3. Whenever possible, go outside the experience of the enemy.
4. Make the enemy live up to its own rules.
5. Ridicule is a potent weapon, and it makes the opposition react to your advantage.
6. A good tactic is one that your people enjoy—if they don't enjoy it, there is something wrong.
7. A tactic that drags on too long becomes a drag.
8. The threat is usually more terrifying than the thing itself.
9. Power is what you have and what the enemy thinks you have.
10. Keep the pressure on.

*These are general guidelines. According to Saul Alinsky, they should be adapted to the uniquenesses of each situation.
Source: Adapted from Alinsky (1971).

they can fail. Often, as the planners begin to fail, conflict breaks out in the ranks (Levine & Perkins, 1987). Delgado (1986) reviewed several organizations that had good intent but evaporated because of the inadequacy of their own organizational infrastructures. Maton (1988) found that groups with higher role differentiation, greater order and organization, and capable leaders reported more positive well-being and more positive group appraisal. Chapter 12 takes a closer look at community psychology and organizational psychology.

Foster-Fishman and Behrens (2007) caution that too often the conceptualization of social systems changes is too simplistic. When one particular change is targeted without consideration of the multiple levels it can impact, the change efforts can fail or fail to be sustained. Change agents should plan globally or holistically so as to see the *whole* picture rather than disjointed pieces of problems. Pluralistic (Freedman, 1989) or multilevel planning (Maton, 2000) is likely to ensure success because the context or environment within which the change will occur will be more likely to have been considered.

One of the best solutions to *prevent* failure—and, after all, prevention *is* a critical part of all of community psychology—is to lay a good foundation for change by gaining community endorsement for such change and establishing an empirical justification for the need to change. Community psychologists regard research and practice as interdependent on one another (Kelly, 1986b). Action research, as you have already read, is scientific work grounded in theory, accounting for community input to the research and intervention process, and directed toward resolving problems (Deutsch & Hornstein, 1975; Lewin, 1948; Oskamp, 1984). Community psychology sees this as one of its principal methods of action and research (Jason, Keys, et al., 2004; Primavera & Brodsky, 2004). Action research in the community is not without its problems, though (Price, 1990; Tolan et al., 1990). Problems include the lack of trust in the researcher by community members, breakdowns in negotiating with program and community administrators, the inability to randomly assign subjects to conditions, the selection of appropriate and adequate measures, and so on (Fairweather & Davidson, 1986). Despite all these reservations, "through the collaborative enterprises, we have seen many examples of community members who have gained self-awareness, established important network connections, and achieved social change" (Jason, Davis, et al., 2004, p. 241).

SUMMARY

Social change is a pervasive condition of today's world. There are many reasons change occurs. Diverse populations, such as the growing number of elderly, have issues that must be addressed but for which society may not be prepared. Another reason for change is declining resources, which include money, space, and commodities such as food. On the other hand, galloping technological advances also necessitate change on the part of individuals as well as society. One technology that has caused all sorts of modification in our daily lives and in methods of conducting business is the addition of computers. On the other hand, many people fear the advance of technology (technophobia), and traditional community services do little to help individuals cope with the fear.

Demands for accountability also create change. People expect that funds will be expended wisely, and they grow concerned when spending is not accounted for. Related to

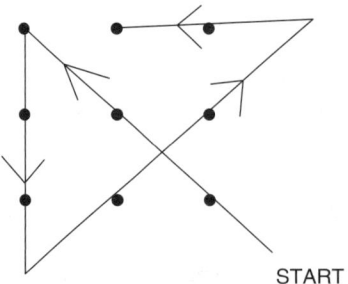

FIGURE 4.3 The Nine Dot Problem Solution. The solution requires you to think *beyond* the dots. By going outside the grid of dots, the solution *is* possible. If you were able to solve this problem, you were engaging in second order thinking.

accountability is cost effectiveness, which refers to how wisely money is spent (i.e., whether there is a profit).

Community conflict is yet another reason for change. Groups in communities experience ethnic strife, conflict over resources such as land use, and so on to create change. A growing sentiment against traditional methods for dealing with today's problems—for instance, the treatment of the mentally ill—as well as a desire for choices or diversity among solutions to problems also prompt change.

There are two types of change: planned (or induced) change and unplanned (or spontaneous) change. Planned change occurs when changes are intentional or deliberate. Planned change is limited by its scope, usually enhances the quality of life for community members, provides for a role for affected groups, and is often guided by a professional change agent or consultant. In unplanned or spontaneous change, change is unexpected, sometimes disastrous (as in a natural disaster such as a flood) and often of a large magnitude (such as when a segment of the population experiences growth, as in the baby boom generation).

Community psychologists are interested in both studying *and* implementing social change for the betterment of the communities served. Some of the tools they bring to this process are discussed in the next chapter. Whether the change is planned or unplanned, the resources of the community can be brought to bear on the problems or issues at hand.

CHAPTER 5

COMMUNITY INTERVENTION STRATEGIES

CREATING PLANNED CHANGE

CITIZEN PARTICIPATION
- **CASE IN POINT 5.1**   The Community Development Society
- Who Participates?
- Advantages and Disadvantages of Citizen Participation

NETWORKING
- **CASE IN POINT 5.2**   Online Networks for Ethnic Minority Issues
- Issues Related to Networks
- Advantages and Disadvantages of Networks

CONSULTATION
- Issues Related to Consultants
- Advantages and Disadvantages of Consultants

EDUCATION AND INFORMATION DISSEMINATION
- Issues Related to Information Dissemination
- Advantages and Disadvantages of Educational Change

PUBLIC POLICY
- **CASE IN POINT 5.3**   Rape Crisis Centers: A National Examination
- Issues Related to the Use of Public Policy
- Advantages and Disadvantages of Public Policy Changes
- A Skill Set for Practice

SUMMARY

I am in Birmingham because injustice is here . . .
I am cognizant of the interrelatedness of all communities and states . . .
Injustice anywhere is a threat to justice everywhere.
—Martin Luther King Jr., Letter from a Birmingham Jail

The neighborhood had gotten progressively worse over the previous decade. Crime rates had risen, and residential transiency had increased. Neighbors no longer knew neighbors, out of habit, lack of interest, time pressures, or fear. Then the drug dealers moved in. The area became known for crack houses, methamphetamine production, and the attendant violence that comes with their sale and use. It was a neighborhood that commanded sweeping views of the water in places. But no one wanted to move in.

Yet it was an old neighborhood. There were residents who had lived through the decline or had chosen to move in because of affordability, or old loyalties, or the vision of its potential. There were businesses there, there was a hospital there, there was all one would hope for in area conveniences and services. These had been there for a long while. Despite several transitions in economic circumstances, they remained. Yet most talked about the difficulties and risks of business in the area.

Then it happened. A very violent incident in the neighborhood made statewide news. Reporters spoke of the plight of those law-abiding residents, now caught in their homes with little hope of selling and moving. Few wanted to buy and live there. In response to all of these negatives, a group of citizens came together. Some say it started with a block party/barbecue. The neighbors banded together and identified problems and the advantages of working together. They organized block watches and surveillance of the known drug houses. They traded phone numbers and agreed to help each other out. They called on the police, who were encouraged by this and happy to help where possible.

The drugs moved out of the neighborhood, since drug operations require secrecy. The neighbors found common ground and connectedness in the process. They saved their homes and their neighborhood. This was the beginning of Safe Streets and later, the National Night Out, where neighbors come together, talk, have dinner together and get to know each other.

This chapter reviews some of the ways social change is brought about by community psychologists. These are planned efforts. They have been studied at the descriptive and predictive levels. From a community psychology, we might better understand the processes. From this understanding, we might better devise interventions to aid in bringing these transformations.

CREATING PLANNED CHANGE

Sarason (1972/1988) considers at length the importance of "creating settings" and the implications of these creations. Some would argue that society has never needed change more than it does today. Multiple reports and commissions have concluded that we are a nation at risk with regard to many social indicators, such as alcohol abuse, drug use, teen pregnancy, and violence (Wandersman et al., 1998). Creating and sustaining social change is not an easy task, but community psychologists are at the forefront of researching the best ways to create and maintain positive societal change. Cook and Shadish (1994) suggest that there are three ways by which social change can occur; the first (which they believe is the most successful) is by increments bringing gradual changes to the system. The second is to test innovative programs and then offer them for acceptance. The third and most dramatic is to change the structure of the system in question.

Participating in social change is a fundamental value in community psychology (Jason, 1991; Maton, 2000) as well as a basic property of social reality (Keys & Frank,

1987). This chapter examines established methods for fashioning both small- and large-scale social change. For each technique, its use, its advantages and disadvantages, and related research will be discussed. When change is intentional and considered in advance, it is called **planned change.**

CITIZEN PARTICIPATION

The Safe Streets Project, described in the opening vignette, engaged neighborhood residents in the solution. They understood the problem with all of its details, because they were daily observers of the environment and its residents. They knew where the drug houses were and the pattern of comings and goings. They could identify the drug makers and drug dealers as well as their customers. In turn, they were the ones who constantly inhabited the environment. It did not take time to respond to things, because they were already there. By reporting what they saw, they could gain better police intervention. The citizens were the critical variable that changed the course of things in the neighborhood.

Perhaps no other method of creating social change has received as much attention as participant-induced change, and interest in this type of change is mounting (Linney, 1990). Various authors have given different labels to this type of change, including *citizen participation* (Levi & Litwin, 1986; Wandersman & Florin, 2000), *empowerment* (Rappaport, Swift, & Hess, 1984), *grassroots activism* (Alinsky, 1971), and *self-help* (Christensen & Robinson, 1989). **Citizen participation** can be broadly defined as involvement in any organized activity in which unpaid individuals participate in order to achieve a common goal (Zimmerman & Rappaport, 1988). At the root of this method of change is the belief that people can and should collaborate to solve common problems (Joseph & Ogletree, 1998). In fact, some hold self-help as the most promising mechanism for changing society (Florin & Wandersman, 1990). An example of citizen participation is **grassroots activism,** which occurs when individuals define their own issues and press for social change to address these issues and work in a bottom-up fashion (rather than top-down). For example, when citizens who are tired of lives being senselessly taken on our highways urge policy makers to pass laws with stiffer penalties against drunk driving, the citizens are practicing grassroots activism. Case in Point 5.1 discusses further citizen involvement in community change by introducing the Community Development Society.

CASE IN POINT 5.1
THE COMMUNITY DEVELOPMENT SOCIETY

Community change and citizen participation have become an accepted—in fact, expected—part of daily life in the United States. For this reason and others, the Community Development Society (CDS) was established. CDS recognizes citizens' capacity to build and take democratic action as keys to success in a complex and ever-changing world. Community development is a process designed to create conditions of economic and social progress with the active participation of the whole community and with

(continued)

CASE IN POINT 5.1   CONTINUED

the fullest possible reliance on the community's initiatives (Bradshaw, 1999; Levine, Perkins, & Perkins, 2004; Rothman, 1974).

CDS members are multidisciplinary and come from the fields of education, health care, social services, government, and citizen groups (to mention just a few) and believe that community is the basic building block of society (Bradshaw, 1999). In addition, members realize that communities can be complex, growth and development are part of the human condition, and development of each community can be promoted through improvement of the individual, organizational skills, and problem-solving knowledge. CDS members fervently believe that good practice can lead to sound community development and social change.

In response to these beliefs, CDS has developed several principles of good practice for community development specialists, whether they be citizens or professionals:

- Citizen participation needs to be promoted so that community members can influence the decisions that affect their lives.
- Citizens should be engaged in problem diagnosis so that affected individuals can understand the causes of the situation.
- Community leaders need to understand the economic, social, political, and psychological impact associated with various solutions related to community problems and issues.
- Community members should design and implement their own plans to solve consensually agreed-on problems (even though some expert assistance might be needed). Furthermore, shared leadership and active participation are necessary to this process.
- Finally, community leaders need the skills, confidence, and motivation to be influential in the community.

According to Maton (2000), these strategies for good practice result in *capacity-building* or *assets-based* change. Do these various principles sound familiar? Many of them are embraced by community psychologists. The significant point here is that there are many community citizens and leaders who adopt community psychology principles and goals without ever having studied community psychology.

Another example of this type of change but at a more personal level is **self-help groups** (Levy, 2000), such as Alcoholics Anonymous, where individuals with common issues come together to assist and emotionally support one another. Because self-help groups are often overseen by professionals, some psychologists prefer the term **mutual assistance groups** for groups comprised solely of laypeople (Levine, 1988). Shepherd and associates (1999) pointed out, however, that the dichotomy between professionally led and peer-led groups is artificial because the extent of professional involvement in such groups varies on a continuum of minimal to extensive. Often, individuals in these groups learn coping strategies from each other. At a personal level, community members—such as friends, family, and neighbors—can assist in supporting each other through difficult times by providing **social support** (Barrera, 2000). Social support is an exchange of resources (such as emotional comfort or material goods) between two individuals where the provider intends the resources to enhance the well-being of the recipient (Shumaker & Brownell, 1984, 1985). Social support can be another means by which social change occurs.

The usual settings for citizen participation are work settings, health care programs, architectural environments, neighborhood associations, public policy arenas, education

TABLE 5.1   Examples of Citizen Participation

Voting
Signing a petition
Donating money or time to a cause
Reading media articles on community needs or change
Boycotting environmentally unsound products
Being interviewed for a community survey
Joining a self-help group
Participating in a question-answer session or a debate
Serving on an ad hoc committee or task force
Participating in sit-ins and marches
Leading a grassroots activist group in the community
Doing volunteer work in the community
Conducting fund-raising for a community service
Offering consultation services
Serving in public office or supporting a particular candidate

programs, and situations applying science (especially social science) and technology. This type of participation can occur by electoral participation (voting or working for a particular candidate or issue), grassroots efforts (when citizens start a group and define its goals and methods), or government-mandated citizen participation in which citizens are appointed to watchdog committees or attend public hearings. Table 5.1 provides more examples of mechanisms for citizen participation, which vary in terms of effort expended and commitment.

Who Participates?

Not everyone wants to participate in social change nor believes that he or she can be effective in fashioning social change, which is known as **helplessness** (Zimmerman, Ram'rez-Valles, & Maton, 1999). Research by O'Neill, Duffy, Enman, Blackman, and Goodwin (1988) examined what types of individuals are active in trying to produce social change. The researchers administered a modified I-E Scale and an Injustice Scale to introductory psychology students and single mothers (both of whom were considered nonactivist groups), board members of a day-care center (a moderately activist group), and board members of a transition house for victims of domestic violence (the high activist group). The I-E Scale (Rotter, 1966) measures **internal** versus **external locus of control.** Individuals with an internal locus of control believe that they control their own reinforcers; individuals with an external locus of control believe that other people or perhaps fate (something external to the individual) controls reinforcers. The researchers modified the scale to measure personal power or the sense that a person is in control of his or her fate. The Injustice Scale measures individuals' perceptions about whether the world is just (for example, do the courts let the guilty go free and convict innocent people?). O'Neill and associates found that neither personal power nor a sense of injustice alone is sufficient to predict who will be a social activist. Both a sense of personal power *and* a belief in the injustices of society combine to produce social activism. Figure 5.1 reproduces these results in graphic form.

Participation appears to be related to people's sense of rootedness in their neighborhood, that is, the length of time in the area, plans to stay in the area, and having children

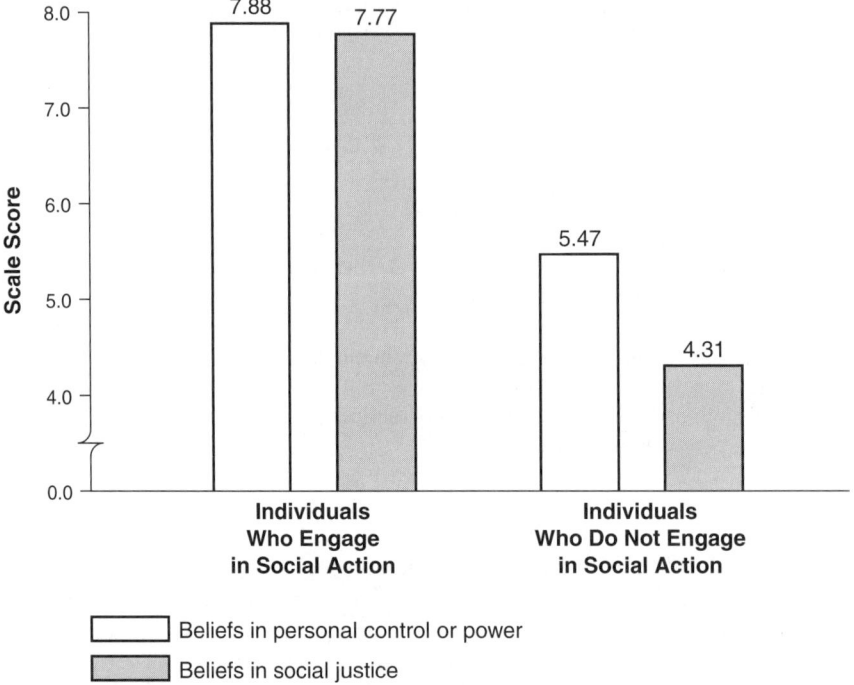

FIGURE 5.1 Results of Research on Social Activism

Note: Citizens who believe in personal control (or power) and social injustice are likely to be social activists.
Source: Data compiled from O'Neill et al. (1988).

(Wandersman, Florin, Friedman, & Meier, 1987). Not surprising is a finding by Chavis and Wandersman (1990) that a sense of community seems important to participation in block associations. Perkins, Florin, Rich, Wandersman, and Chavis (1990) proposed an ecological framework for understanding participation. There needs to be a perceived need for coming together and then a set of "enabling conditions," such as neighborly behaviors, that allow the group to do that. Research by Sampson (1999) points to the negative relationship between strong social cohesion and crime. It seems that the residents in the Safe Streets story, which opened this chapter, were correct in assuming that by coming together as neighbors, they would change the climate for crime in their area. Strong neighborhoods equaled less crime.

Kelly and Breinlinger (1996) suggested that community activists identify with the group with which they are associated. They also proposed that individuals need a self-image of themselves as activists to engage in social change projects. Finally, Perkins, Brown, and Taylor (1996) found that community-focused cognitions (such as a sense of civic responsibility or a perception of community attachments) as well as relevant behaviors (such as volunteer work in the community) were consistently and positively predictive of participation in social activism. Finally, Zimmerman et al. (1999) found that for African American youths, high levels of sociopolitical control limited the negative consequences of helplessness (feelings of no or low control) on mental health. **Sociopolitical control** may be defined as beliefs that actions in social and political realms can lead to desired outcomes. Zimmerman and associates believe that sociopolitical control contributes to self-esteem and self-confidence, making it more likely that individuals with such control will take action against challenges in other spheres of their lives.

Measuring the impact of citizen participation is difficult but necessary if one is to understand the process and to determine whether it works (Kelly, 1986b). The citizens—the stakeholders, so to speak—might want hard evidence that their efforts were worthwhile, but such direct evidence is often difficult to obtain. Involved individuals might also disagree about what is solid evidence: cost savings, increased profits, higher client satisfaction, less stress, improved community relations, and so forth.

Some citizens may want to participate but lack the appropriate skills; few laypeople, for example, know how to lobby for policy change or how to conduct meaningful scientific research. Chavis et al. (1992) and Levi and Litwin (1986) noted that citizen groups might also need group dynamics skills sharpened. Their leaders might need leadership development in the form of training in negotiations or incentive management (Prestby, Wandersman, Florin, Rich, & Chavis, 1990) or in strategic planning.

Speer and Hughey (1995) have identified the importance of the reciprocal relationship between development of power for community organizations and individual empowerment for organization members. In other words, the organization and its members both need to be empowered to change but in a transactional or dynamic way. Specifically, Speer and Hughey identified four interrelated phases for community organizing or change. First is the process of *assessment,* through which crucial issues affecting the community are identified by its members and its organizations. This allows the organization, community, and its members to focus on the other three phases.

A second phase is labeled *research.* In this phase, participants examine causes and correlates of issues identified in the assessment phase. In other words, information about the nature of the issues and their potential influences and solutions is gathered. One important piece of information that needs to be gathered in the research phase is the ways in which community resources are allocated and how key players exercise social power around a particular issue.

A third stage, *action,* represents a collective attempt to exercise social power. Actions include public events that demonstrate organizational or citizen power and perhaps attract attention from outside the organization or community. Finally, *reflection* from community or organizational members is important. Effectiveness of action strategies, discussion of lessons learned, consideration of how power was demonstrated, and development of future plans are explored. The process can then start over again with assessment of other related critical issues for the community. Notably, this process mirrors the action research described by Lewin (1946) and the prevention research cycle espoused by Price (1983). The process of community engagement is a part of the intervention and the research.

Advantages and Disadvantages of Citizen Participation

Active participation in change efforts usually is highly motivational (Chavis et al., 1992; Yates & Youniss, 1998). That is, people are more likely to accept change that they themselves have generated (Duffy, 1991). Involved individuals are also likely to know the problems that need addressing because they have lived with the problems. For that same reason, this type of community participation often helps build a sense of community (Levi & Litwin, 1986) or social consensus and cohesiveness (Heller et al., 1984). Conversely, feeling a sense of community also increases participation in grassroots efforts (Chavis & Wandersman, 1990).

Another advantage of citizen participation is that the average citizen often participates in change efforts for little pay but with enthusiasm and a sense of responsibility (Selznick, 2000). For example, it is no secret that many community organizations are dependent on volunteers. The Beacon Hill Institute for Public Policy Research (1997) conducted a survey of executive directors of private charitable organizations and found the following results:

- Ninety percent of the directors say that volunteers are crucial to efficiency because they save the organization money.
- Seventy-three percent said that the time and money spent on training volunteers was well worth the effort.
- Seventy-seven percent said they can depend on their volunteers.

As desirable as this type of participation is, it is not without its pitfalls (Barrera, 2000; Oskamp, 1984). Christensen and Robinson (1989) reported that not every citizen wants to participate. Although it is easy to level a charge of apathy against nonparticipants, the rights of those who prefer not to be involved need to be respected.

With this type of social change, results can be long in coming. The delay may cause some early inspired individuals to run out of steam before their efforts show results. Studies in human services settings suggest that burnout is high (Maslach & Jackson, 1981; Ross, Altmaier, & Russell, 1989) and that those with the highest dedication often burn out first (Schultz & Schultz, 1990).

Finally, because they often are not comprised of all members of a community but rather comprised of a select few, citizen groups can fail. If these individuals are not representative of the affected groups or the population at large, the solutions might not be viable or acceptable for everyone. Furthermore, if this small group of activists is not representative of the larger constituency, then the large group might distrust or reject the smaller group (Worchel, Cooper, & Goethals, 1991), which also causes failure. Participants in community intervention need to recognize the politics of the conflicting goals and interests

TABLE 5.2 Summary of Characteristics for Block Associations that Continue

1. Greater proportion of residents join
2. More activities and participation opportunities
3. More officers and committees
4. More methods of communication, more personalized outreach, more proactive in recruitment and leadership training, used consensus and formal decision making
5. Established ties with external resources
6. More incentives for membership

From Wandersman and Florin (2000, p. 259).

of the various involved parties (Riger, 1989). Similarly, if activity in the efforts costs more than any benefits that accrue, individuals are likely to become inactive (Prestby et al., 1990; Wandersman & Florin, 2000). Citizen participation occurs when the benefits of action are apparent and the costs of such action are outweighed by the perceived advantages of engagement.

NETWORKING

When those attempting to create change disregard others in the community or disregard other community problems, failure can also take place. A solution to avoiding isolated change is **networking.** A network is an interconnected and interactive social relationship among various individuals or organizations in which reciprocity of information, resources, and other support between individuals or organizations is maintained (Chavis et al., 1992).

Note that in the Safe Streets story, the neighbors were living next to each other. They knew of the problem. What they did not have was the knowledge and support of other like-minded citizens. Meeting each other at the block party gave them the needed connection to each other. They could be assured that they were not alone in their concerns. They would have support in their reporting of illegal behaviors. The party served as the critical networking opportunity.

One means for fostering community development or community change is to develop enabling systems (Chavis et al., 1992). **Enabling systems** are vehicles whereby multiple community initiatives can be simultaneously mobilized, supported, and sustained in an efficient and effective manner by developing specified links among the social actors (Chavis et al., 1992). Chavis (1993) has offered a good example of enabling. He empowered many community groups and organizations to conduct their own program evaluations by teaching them to design, conduct, and analyze research. He has therefore made them independent of the need for reliance on professionals in the future for their research needs.

Networks (Chavis et al., 1992; Fischer, Jackson, Stueve, Gerson, & McAllister-Jones, 1977; Sarason, Carroll, Maton, Cohen, & Lorentz, 1977) are confederations or alliances of related community organizations or individuals. Members of networks regularly share funding sources, information, and ideas with one another. Thus, their futures are more secure by networking their information and sometimes their clients. Another advantage is that clients are less likely to fall through the cracks in the service system. Granovetter (1973, 1983) believed these advantages accrued to those who were even weakly tied to a network. The advantages of strong networks were their durability and usefulness in providing resources to its members (they would share food and babysit for each other). However, the weak ties could serve as bridges to other networks and therefore extend the spread of information and influence beyond the usual strongly held relationships. If one of the functions of networks was the ability to access new information and wield influence beyond the usual circles, then the weak networks have their place in the creation of extended communities.

From the sociological literature comes the concept of **social capital** (resources made available to individuals as the result of their placement within a social structure). "Like other forms of capital, social capital is productive, making possible the accomplishment of certain ends that in its absence would not be possible" (Coleman, 1999, p. 16). Through relationships, the individual is able to do more. This concept is operationalized and used to demonstrate the importance of social ties/networks to the development of building and community organizations (Saegert & Winkel, 2004). Their data suggest that there are advantages of frequent face-to-face contact, even if the contacts are brief. Bonding is important, even if it is not at a high level. The concept of networks is a way of linking the individual to larger social systems. Therefore, the creation and understanding of networks would seem an especially relevant area for community psychologists.

At a higher systems level, **umbrella organizations** are created to achieve this networking among agencies or systems. This overarching organization oversees the health of member organizations. Again, they act as clearinghouses for information that members can share. A concrete example might prove useful. United Way of America is perhaps one of the best-known umbrella organizations in the United States. United Way, through charitable contributions, is known for its financial support of community agencies that might otherwise flounder. In addition, it provides community service agencies with office supplies, furniture, and other desperately needed tangible provisions. However, United Way also offers expert consultation on fund-raising, staff training, development of publications, and other issues crucial for community agency survival.

Community development corporations (Vidal, Howitt, & Foster, 1986) and **neighborhood associations** (Speigel, 1987) are citizens' groups that have come together to conquer a social problem or to ensure that the community develops in a healthy, planned fashion, much as did the neighbors of Safe Streets.

CASE IN POINT 5.2
ONLINE NETWORKS FOR ETHNIC MINORITY ISSUES

A complaint of many ethnic minority psychologists is that there are not very many of them and they are widely dispersed geographically. Outside of large urban centers like New York, Chicago, San Francisco, and Los Angeles, there are small numbers of psychologists of color. If there is a question regarding a particular research or clinical issue relating to race or racism, the likelihood of finding someone within a day's drive is small for many parts of the United States. It could feel lonely at times and certainly isolated.

With the development of ethnic minority psychological associations (Asian American Psychological Association, Association of Black Psychologists, National Latina/o Psychological Association, Society of Indian Psychologists) and the Society for the Psychological Study of Ethnic Minority Issues (Division 45 of the APA), psychologists who are interested in these kinds of issues can join online discussion groups and connect with each other. Once on one of these association groups, the access to the network of psychologists and graduate students is no more than a Web site away. These networks are active in sending out information on events, funding opportunities, personal victories, and occasions for sadness. Job announcements that targeted those interested in ethnic minority issues can be sent out to the entire network with no delay. In turn, questions are asked and answered on the discussions. Who knows a good speaker on covert racism? What would be a good reading on diversity issues in general? What do people think of a particular psychological test? It is like having access to all who are in the network. Typically, news travels fast. Although the geographic dispersion of psychologists of color continues, the linkage provided by the Internet has provided the kinds of advantages discussed within community psychology.

Issues Related to Networks

Networks and umbrella associations offer ongoing support to participants, reciprocally share ideas and resources, provide role modeling for each other, and offer accessible resources to participants (Sarason et al., 1977). For instance, these systems allow small community agencies to share information about grants, staff-training opportunities, and resource libraries; exchange successful publicity ideas; refer clients to each other's services; and build lobbying coalitions. Thus, the health and success of each smaller service is assisted or enabled. Research has documented the effectiveness of these networking systems for AIDS services (Madera, 1986) and unemployed and deinstitutionalized populations (Wolff, 1987).

A somewhat similar notion is that of a **clearinghouse.** Clearinghouses are typically umbrella organizations for individuals seeking self-help groups. Of course, the clearinghouse concept means that the self-help groups themselves are loosely networked. These clearinghouses are reported to result in high consumer satisfaction and good community receptivity (Maton, Levanthal, Madera, & Julien, 1989; Wollert, 1987).

Enabling systems and networks represent a form of social change because they build on existing resources and develop more productive and creative relationships between already existing services. In other words, such systems reweave the social fabric of what might otherwise be a more tattered and frayed community and its services and thus ensure survival and continued growth of the services.

Advantages and Disadvantages of Networks

Besides enhancing the viability of many services, networks are advantageous because they ensure that important systems come to know each other better, find effective ways to work together, and learn to plan or advocate for change in a collaborative rather than competitive manner (Wolff, 1987). Likewise, enabling systems better ensure that resources are equitably distributed (Biegel, 1984), help reduce community conflict (Christensen & Robinson, 1989), and focus collective pressure on public policy makers and other decision makers (Delgado, 1986; Seekins & Fawcett, 1987). Networks also enable related services to detect cracks in the service system. **Cracks** are defined as structural gaps in the service systems and are exemplified by missing or inaccessible services and missing information (Tausig, 1987). Granovetter (1973, 1983) described some of the problems of networks that are so strong that they do not structurally encourage linkages to others. If the networks are without connections to other networks, they exclude others and lose the information and access to resources that others might provide.

Few authors have addressed other disadvantages of umbrella organizations, even though several disadvantages exist. For one thing, private sector businesses might feel threatened by and perhaps launch a successful attack against the collective power of activist community organizations (Delgado, 1986). Similarly, when umbrella organizations grow large, they develop their own set of problems in terms of bureaucracy, conflict, and expense.

Another disadvantage is that when an umbrella organization becomes a controlling, parental organization, member agencies can become dissatisfied. The authors know, for instance, of one rural domestic violence program that broke from a strong countywide coalition of churches over staffing and funding issues, despite the program's already precarious existence. The bad feelings between the smaller domestic violence program and the larger parent organization resulted in the establishment of a second, redundant domestic violence program in the same geographic region.

Another possible disadvantage of community coalitions is that different community services as well as the whole community may be in different stages of development or readiness for change (Edwards, Jumper-Thurman, Plested, Oetting, & Swanson, 2001). The new ones need staff training; the older ones may be seeking to expand their client bases. Coordinating the different developmental needs of member organizations can be difficult for the parent organization. Finally, if the reach of the association grows beyond one particular community's boundaries because member organizations have satellites in other geographic areas, existing associations in neighboring communities may feel threatened and subvert each other's purpose. At a personal level, those who network are at a distinct advantage over those who do not. Given the work on social capital, established residents of the "neighborhood" are more likely to be participants and, by definition, may glean the benefits of the network.

CONSULTATION

In the opening scenario for this chapter, there was a neighborhood in crisis, with high crime rates, high transiency, and a general sense of alienation among its residents. An individual within the neighborhood or some small group of neighbors could have called on a consultant to help them in solving their problems. Some communities write grants, get funding, and hire community organizers or professionals to provide expertise in community functioning and interventions. Sarason (1976) believed one of the advantages a community psychologist had over others was access to information.

Professional change agents or expert consultants seek to create social change through modification, renewal, and improvement. A **consultant** or **professional change agent** is someone who engages in collaborative problem solving with one or more persons (the **consultees**) who are often responsible for providing some form of assistance to another third individual (the **client**) (Mowbray, 1979). Consultants are often professionals well versed in scientific research. They are typically called on to conduct program evaluations and needs assessments for community organizations.

Community psychologists seem uniquely qualified to be consultants because they possess skills in community needs assessment, community organizing, group problem solving, and action research. The community psychologist is also likely to focus on the social systems and institutions within a community rather than on individuals (Weed, 1990). Weed suggested that community psychologists offer a cohesive and uniting perspective, which is, of course, one of the values cherished by community development specialists. While the neighborhood mechanisms and the group phenomena already exist and the strengths and latent potential are already present, community psychologists bring a "more consciously and expertly applied" operation of these phenomena, given their familiarity with past research and former attempts to realize the possibilities of a better community (Sarason, 1976b, p. 328).

Issues Related to Consultants

An important issue related to the expense of consultants is whether they really do help the client. One general study of the use of consultants was conducted by Medway and Updyke (1985), who reviewed the literature on outcome of consultations. In the better designed studies, the researchers found that compared to control groups, both consultees and clients in the intervention groups (where consultants were utilized) made gains in solving their problems or promoting change as measured by such things as attitude scales, observed behaviors, and standardized scores. In the control groups (in which no consultants were used), there were fewer of these improvements. This literature review therefore offers clear statistical evidence for the value of consultants.

Weed (1990) identified several steps for community psychologists acting as consultants to primary prevention programs that are adaptable for almost all change agents—expert or not. The first step is *defining the goals* to be accomplished. The second step is to *raise the awareness* of the individuals in the setting under consultation and then to *introduce the new program* or research. At this point, other, related organizations or communities can be networked for collaboration, support, and learning about new techniques and funding sources. Consultants also need to collaborate on effective methods for *evaluating changes*. Favorable evaluation justifies the money, time, and effort expended. Evaluation also leads to modification and fine-tuning, should that be necessary. Unfortunately, evaluation is a step sometimes forgotten in many change situations. Without evaluation, how would people know if the change worked and whether it ought to be repeated?

Bishop and Drew (1998) stated that another issue related to consultation is that of *trust*. It takes time before the professional achieves the trust required to act in the role of consultant. The researchers discussed several projects for which years passed before consultants were let into the process and trusted.

Serrano-Garcia (1994) explained that there are often unequal power relationships between community members and outside professionals, with the professional having more power because of specialized knowledge and other resources. She issued a challenge to professionals who act as community consultants to "establish more equitable professional-client relationships" (p. 17) by means of collaboration and empowerment.

Advantages and Disadvantages of Consultants

There are several advantages to expert consultation. The first is obvious—the professional is an expert at what he or she does. The professional change agent has been specially trained and has the knowledge base on which to make wise decisions. One not so apparent advantage is that the consultant is a neutral person. Because the consultant is not embroiled in the presenting problems and should have no vested interest in the community or organization, he or she can make unencumbered, unbiased judgments and recommendations.

Consultants also generally take a long-term approach to problem solving. Individuals in the community or organization often focus on short-term issues because they are living with them day to day. For the continued health of the community or organization, a long-term approach might be best. As stated earlier, too many community groups fail quickly; fast, ineffective fixes may be one of the reasons.

Finally, if a consultant is experienced, she or he comes with a vast array of ideas, past successes, and relevant ideas because of experiences with past but similar situations. Consultants should neither betray nor create a conflict of interest with past clients, but previous experiences can help them find common ground that might be useful to similar communities or organizations.

Despite these somewhat apparent advantages, professional change agents are not without disadvantages (Maton, 2000); one is cost. Cost can be a major burden and can thwart the best-laid plans of any community or organization needing expert assistance. Ideally, some community psychologists acting as change agents would consider pro bono or voluntary consultations. The national psychological association, the American Psychological Association, encourages pro bono work by psychologists. Community psychologists may serve as consultants to the organization and write grants for independent funding of their work, offering awareness of the literature and knowledge of the research process (Suarez-Balcazar et al., 2004), or help in reframing the task or the question based on the expertise that they may bring to the process (Kelly et al., 2004). When the consultant and the community are viewed as equal and reciprocal partners in the process, the community and the consultant are better informed and the problem more effectively addressed.

However, developing cooperation from all involved in the consultation can be a problem. Outside consultants sometimes inspire fear (of job loss or criticism), defensiveness, and resistance to change. Consultants might want to consider using less direct or nondirective techniques to avoid these problems (Heller et al., 1984).

Consultants' contacts with their clients are often time-limited. They need to quickly assess the issues, assist in the development of solutions and their implementation, and foster maintenance strategies in a short period of time. Often, the issues on which they are asked to consult are complex compared to the amount of available resources, including time. For example, many communities and their organizations grew haphazardly rather than in a planned fashion. Redesign can be difficult, if not impossible. Some problems defy solutions; they are essentially insoluble (Sarason, 1978). Many of these issues can be avoided if consultants carefully match their skills and expertise to client situations.

Finally, clients sometimes hold high and unrealistic expectations of what a consultant can do. Other clients may use the consultant for their own misleading purposes, especially when there are conflicting views about what ought to be done. In these situations, the ethical consultant will probably leave clients feeling disappointed. Again, careful intake by a

TABLE 5.3   Bloom's Principles to Guide the Development of Community Programs

1. Regardless of where your paycheck comes from, think of yourself as working for the community.
2. If you want to know about a community's mental health needs, ask the community.
3. As you learn about community mental health needs, you have the responsibility to tell the community what you are learning.
4. Help the community establish its own priorities.
5. You can help the community decide among various courses of action in its efforts to solve its problems.
6. In the event that the community being served is so disorganized that representatives of various facets of the community cannot be found, you have the responsibility to help find such representatives.

From Bloom (1984, pp. 429–431).

consultant to ensure that his or her expertise fits the clients' issues can help. The consultant is wise to be aware of the purpose for being hired and whether there are multiple and competing interests at work. Bloom's principles, found in Table 5.3, provide useful points to community consolidation.

EDUCATION AND INFORMATION DISSEMINATION

The terrorized citizens of the neighborhood from the opening example would have benefited from information on police communication and response rules. They soon came to understand the frustration of law enforcement over the lack of willing witnesses or the protocols of effective evidence gathering. With the support of the police, the neighborhood learned what they needed to note and how to contact the police in a timely way. This and other information made for an effective neighborhood–police partnership.

Information dissemination remains a vital part of social change efforts. In fact, some community psychologists have challenged their colleagues to renew efforts to disseminate useful information and innovative programs as a method of addressing social problems (Linney, 1990).

Just what is meant by **information dissemination** (Mayer & Davidson, 2000) or **education** in community psychology? As you now know, community psychologists seek to prevent, intercede in, and treat (if necessary) community problems with what are typically innovative programs. If innovative or experimental programs are researched and found to be successful, but the results are never shared with other communities or adopted by others, the results are of limited use (Fairweather, 1986). Dissemination of information can save change agents and social activists working with similar populations or in similar settings much time, money, and effort. Thus, dissemination of innovation is crucial.

However, there has been much debate in the literature about how programs can be effectively transferred to other settings. Adopters of innovations from community psychology need to be careful in their translation efforts. Adopters should be faithful to the original change model, especially to the mechanism that caused change, but they may also need to do some reinventing, given that not all settings are the same (Blakely et al., 1987; Bowman, Stein, & Ireys, 1991).

Whenever information from community psychology is shared with community members, its main purpose should be to improve the community, promote prevention, and empower community members to shape their own destinies (Fairweather & Davidson, 1986). Information for educational purposes can also be used to shape ideology and to direct action in a community, as well as to inform those in a position of power (the **gatekeepers**) (Levine, Perkins, & Perkins, 2004). With advances in technology—for example, distance learning—diverse and geographically distant communities can be educated and empowered, and information can be disseminated more easily than in the past (Kreisler, Snider, & Kiernan, 1997).

Issues Related to Information Dissemination

Several important issues need to be carefully considered by community psychologists hoping to educate community members about research results or innovative programs

(Mayer & Davidson, 2000). First, it is important to remember that not all individuals will be receptive, nor will they be open to the information and ideas at the same time. Despite great enthusiasm, some individuals will be slow to accept what you wish to share, and some never adopt what you have to offer (Rogers, 1982). Fairweather and Davidson (1986) suggest that at least two phenomena could interfere with taking the information: the personal characteristics of adopters and the social context in which adopters find themselves. For instance, some individuals are close-minded or **dogmatic** (Rokeach, 1960). They will not accept new ideas readily; in fact, they might not accept the ideas at all. Other individuals may find themselves in a social situation or social context in which the suggested change is unacceptable, so they conform with the group's wishes and do not adopt an idea, no matter how good it is.

Second, measuring whether the information dissemination is useful will be problematic. A variety of measures could be used, including number of adoptions, replication of previous results in the imitative program, and so on. Selecting several measures will result in better understanding of whether the shared information was successfully adopted. For example, Seitz, Apfel, and Rosenbaum (1991) used several measures—such as dropping out of school, failing grades, enrolling in vocational or alternate school programs, and grade point average—to measure efficacy of an intervention program for pregnant teens. They found that on several different measures, the adolescents experiencing the special intervention were more likely to succeed in school. Had the researchers used only one measure, their results might have indicated otherwise.

Disseminators of information, especially those sharing information on new programs, should also be mindful that only some pieces of the program might be useful to adopters and that disseminators are collaborators rather than dictators about how the shared information should be used. Fairweather and Davidson (1986) suggested that anyone trying to diffuse innovation in a community needs to learn to be a graceful loser at times! As noted by Jason and Glenwick (2002) any information has to compete with the "high density" of competing messages. It is no small task to get the message across, given the distractions to the learner.

A final issue related to the use of education as a social change mechanism is that it must be culturally sensitive. What works for one ethnic group might not work in another. There is a *Handbook of Racial and Ethnic Minority Psychology* (Bernal, Trimble, Burlew, & Leong, 2003) and a sixth edition of *Counseling across Cultures* (Pedersen, Draguns, Lonner, & Trimble, 2008), to name just two of the many texts dealing with this issue. Although Pederson (2008) warns of the dangers of oversimplifying "multiculturalism," Sue, Bingham, Porché-Burke and Vasquez (1999) see the recognition of multiculturalism in psychology as a revolution in its own right. Even though innovations taking place are well intentioned and promising, equal benefits for minorities and equal avoidance of harm cannot be taken for granted.

For example, in considering mentoring relationships, Darling, Bogat, Cavell, Murphy, & Sánchez (2006) noted that culture and ethnicity played a significant role in determining the patterns of who was perceived as a mentor and the nature of these relationships. In some cases, parents and extended family members were important; in other cases, the family was on an equal par with nonfamily members; in still other cases, certain family members were the farthest thing from a perceived mentor. If we are to tap into the natural teaching mechanisms within communities, the mentoring process makes intuitive sense. However, variations in how this relationship works should be carefully considered in the derivation of these programs.

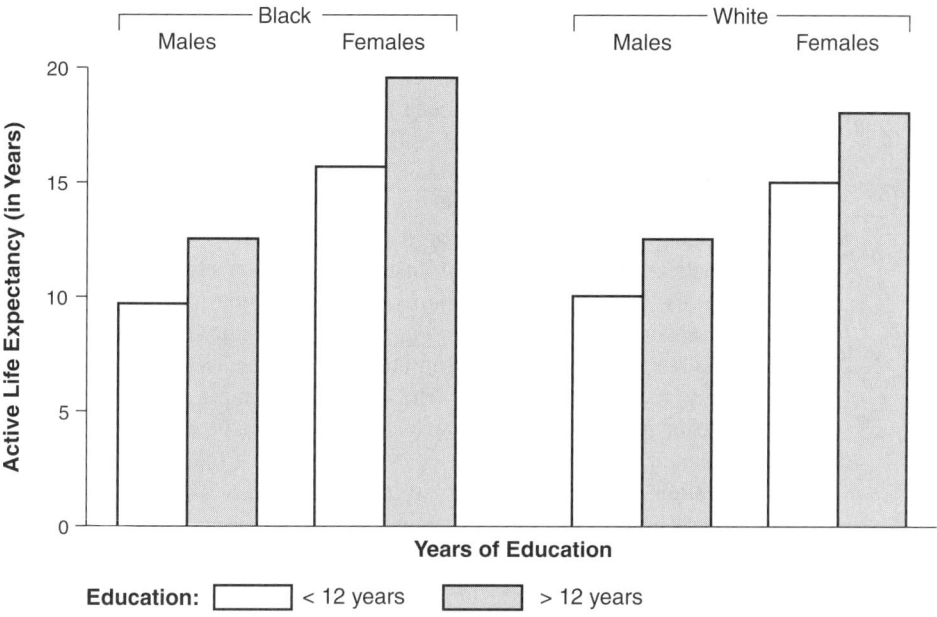

FIGURE 5.2 Active Life Expectancy at Age 65 by Education and Race
Source: From Kaplan (1994).

Figure 5.2 provides a second example. This figure demonstrates what education and information dissemination can perhaps accomplish for the population in the United States. The graph depicts life expectancy (at age 65) by education, race, and sex. The important thing to notice is that individuals with the least education have shorter life expectancies (regardless of race and sex) than those with more education.

Note also that there are other differences, for example between Blacks and Whites and between males and females. Sex differences might be accounted for by physiological differences between men and women or by occupational hazards faced by the types of jobs men and women stereotypically hold. The race differences might be accounted for by income level; those with higher incomes (the majority of whom are White) typically have better access to quality health care. In fact, income level and occupational status both correlate highly with education, so they, too, might account for the life expectancy differences between men and women and between Blacks and Whites. The secondary point here, then, is that education might not be the sole basis for life expectancy and other health differences.

Advantages and Disadvantages of Educational Change

Advantages of educational change are several. First, a wide audience can often be reached with these change efforts because a multiplex approach to disseminating ideas, especially by mass media such as television and newspapers, can be used (McAlister, 2000). Second, education as a whole is generally revered in the United States, so the average community citizen as well as those in power are likely to accept this pathway to change rather than more radical approaches. Finally, this may be one of the least expensive forms of social change for community activists to pursue if they use certain vehicles such as public media for dissemination. A picture may indeed be worth a thousand words. Similarly, a research report written in lay terminology can easily be distributed to many individuals at once.

There are disadvantages, however. Closed minds are not easily opened, no matter how much information is presented. Also, the vehicle for dissemination may have to be custom designed for the audience. For instance, consciousness-raising groups worked well to disseminate information about feminism in the women's movement (Levine, Perkins, & Perkins, 2004). For physicians' groups, professional journals may be the best vehicle. Another disadvantage, especially of using the mass media for large-scale intervention, is that media advertising sometimes promotes the very behavior the educational intervention is designed to reduce or prevent (Jason, 1998). An example would be televised advertisements for beer juxtaposed with an educational campaign designed to lessen or prevent drunk driving.

Education as an intervention strategy brings the advantages of impacting large groups in little time. The target of such educational programs is broad, from developmental preparation for school, to providing information relevant to adjustment concerns, to dealing with particular problems of personal health (the dangers of smoking, weight, stress, dealing with trauma) or of a social nature (littering, environmental concerns, conservation). Educational efforts bring the challenge of understanding one's audience or students and how to most effectively reach them and bring about the desired change. A community psychology may inform these efforts, thus making them more effective.

PUBLIC POLICY

If the besieged neighborhood had decided to get particular laws passed so as to make it easier to arrest the drug dealers in the neighborhood, or had programs implemented that would address the crime in the area, such social change would be sought through public policy changes. Though sometimes a lengthy effort, a shift in policies can bring about long-lived changes in the way people live. It is a direct intervention at the systems level.

Consider: Did you vote in the last election? It is often surprising how many citizens, college students in particular, do not vote. Voting, drafting legislation, and lobbying for particular interests comprise actions that change (often dramatically) our national and local social agendas. For citizens and community psychologists alike, participating in public policy endeavors opens a "window of opportunity" (Nikelly, 1990) for what can often be sweeping social changes.

Just what is **public policy**? The aim of public policy is to improve the quality of life for community members. Although the term is often used for government-mandated legislation, it can refer to policy at a specific agency or at the local community and state governmental levels. Public policy can also influence to what issues various resources are allocated (Levine & Perkins, 1997).

A concept relevant to public policy is **policy science,** which is the practice of making findings from science (and in the case of community psychology, findings from social science) relevant to governmental and organizational policy (Oskamp, 1984). A well-known example of this is the use of actual scientific studies on desegregation of schools and to shape policies on integration (Oskamp, 1984; Perkins, 1988). Given the Supreme Court ruling (*Meredith vs. Jefferson County, Kentucky and Parents Involved in Community Schools-PICS vs. Seattle School District*) in June 2007 stating that schools may no longer take a student's race into account in attempting to devise desegregation programs (Greenhouse, 2007), the challenges of integration continue.

Sarason (1984) pointed out the lack of effort of community psychology in areas of public policy. He believed this has been a missed opportunity. Public policy can bring system-wide change and, with that, governmental resources to bear on the change. Using a public policy strategy, we might better deal with problems such as divorce, deviance, education, and the structures that define and maintain our society.

At this point in your reading, you have learned about the variety of techniques that can be utilized to create social change. Any reliable change agent knows that a multifaceted approach is best. That is, a single change strategy by itself may be weak. Using several change techniques is more likely to result in the desired outcomes. Case in Point 5.3

CASE IN POINT 5.3
RAPE CRISIS CENTERS: A NATIONAL EXAMINATION

Campbell, Baker, and Mazurek (1998) hypothesized that many rape crisis centers have undergone significant changes since their beginnings during the feminist movement of the 1970s. The researchers used interviews with center directors to examine the current structure and functions of 168 randomly selected rape crisis centers across the nation.

First, the study demonstrated that there are many avenues to social change. An early goal of rape crisis services was the provision of services to survivors of sexual assault. Ancillary to this was the provision of 24-hour crisis intervention hotlines as well as counseling and assistance in negotiating the legal and medical systems. Many (but not all) centers also eventually sought to raise public awareness about sexual assault in the community. Some centers additionally became active in public demonstrations, such as Take Back the Night marches. Finally, some centers also sought to conduct large-scale change by lobbying state legislatures for reform. In response, most states did alter their rape statutes in the late 1970s and early 1980s.

Second, although the average center in the study was 16 years old, there were many that were older or younger than this. The older, freestanding, collective centers had larger budgets and staffs as well as a change orientation when interacting with other social services agencies. These centers used participatory decision making for deciding internal issues. Older centers were also more likely to participate in public demonstrations such as Take Back the Night marches and in prevention programming. The younger centers, especially those that were affiliated with larger service agencies and therefore followed a hierarchical organizational structure, were more likely to engage in political lobbying rather than preventive education and public demonstrations as their forms of social activism.

Both types of centers, then, engaged in social activism or social change, but the types of activities differed by organizational structure and age. In addition, this study also demonstrates that rape crisis organizations and perhaps other service-oriented organizations often need to adapt to the changing political climate to continue to provide quality services to their communities.

describes the evolution of rape crisis centers, which generally take this multifaceted strategy of social change. In a later chapter we describe at greater length the efforts to change the educational system in the United States. Among the more notable areas for change have been in the area of preschool education, such as Head Start (Zigler, 1994). The research evidence on resiliency shows a clear advantage to early child enrichment and parental education. Long-term outcome studies on Head Start are now coming on line. They support the positive effects of work with young children (Garces, Thomas, & Currie, 2000). You will read more about these issues in Chapter 8.

Issues Related to the Use of Public Policy

Politics and community psychology are deeply intertwined (Vogelman, 1990), although changing social policy is a relatively unexplored extension of community psychology (Phillips, 2000). There is general agreement among community psychologists that their science and politics are inseparable. However, community psychologists do not agree on how much science should impinge on policy and how much public policy should pervade science. Some argue that good policies are those based solely on scientific evidence. In other words, one should not attempt to influence any public policy until one has solid scientific evidence. Others argue that pressing social problems such as AIDS and homelessness do not afford the luxury of time for conducting research. Society is not likely to have solutions to this complex situation for some time to come.

Most community psychologists do agree that the development of public policy should be a collaborative effort between researchers, affected populations, and the decision or policy makers. The idea of collaboration leads psychologists to avoid "colonial" relationships with the affected community members (Chavis, Stucky, & Wandersman, 1983). In fact, collaboration with appropriate community members, particularly those affected by policy research or policy decisions, is not only strategically sound, it is good ethics (Robinson, 1990). The awareness of the university-based professional with access to the resources and status that higher education symbolizes automatically creates a power imbalance and barriers to collaborative work. These imbalances and barriers can be overcome through careful and conscientious work on the part of both psychologists and community members (Shpungin & Lyubansky, 2006), though they can potentially alienate those higher up in the social hierarchy. Striking the balance between advocacy and acknowledgment of the status quo reminded Shpungin and Lyubansky (2006) of the Paulo Freire admonition to be both patient and to act, when reading of the environment suggests the chance for change is there.

Americans like to think that the public policy that guides social change is predicated on science, humanism, and logical thinking, but often what happens in Washington, D.C., and elsewhere occurs whether or not rational thought enters the process (Johnson, 1991). The political climate, lobbying groups with cross-purposes, and other vicissitudes can often influence the end product in public policy as much or more than science and other logical factors. Phenomena such as a more sophisticated electorate than that of yesteryear (Greenberg, 1999) and shifting public concern (e.g., from national defense issues to social problems) (Johnson, 1991) can sway the direction of public policy. Likewise, funding created for various policy changes will remain a heated issue in the foreseeable future, and behavioral and social scientists unfortunately are often the underdogs for social change funding (American Psychological Society, 1991). The media also set an important emotional tone that shapes public policy in this country (Schmolling, Youkeles, & Burger, 1989) and influences what people think about. This is called **agenda setting.** Recently, scandals associated with government leaders have reduced public trust in the government (Chanley, Rudolph, & Rahn, 2000). In a January 2006 *USA Today* poll of 1009 people, only 15 percent gave U.S. senators high or very high marks for honesty and ethical standards (Koch, 2006). This is down from a high of 25 percent receiving these ratings in 2001. A May 2006 Zogby poll found that 75 percent of respondents reported trusting government less than they did five years ago (http://www.zogby.com/News/ReadNews.dbm?ID=1116).

Policy science serves several functions: instrumental, conceptual, and persuasive (Shadish, 1990). The authors personally feel that research can and should also serve a predictive purpose. When research shapes the direction of change or of public policy, it serves an **instrumental purpose.** Research can also be aimed at changing the way people think or conceptualize social problems and solutions. Research with this function serves a **conceptual purpose.** When research persuades policy makers to support a particular position or solution to a social problem, it then functions in the **persuasive** mode. Finally, when research is designed to forecast what change will occur in the future or predict whether change will be accepted, the function is **predictive.**

Is there any evidence that social science research influences legislators as they develop public policy? Yes, one can see the impact of researchers in part by what type of research is funded by the federal government. Except for economists, psychologists perhaps receive the largest amount of funding of all social scientists (Oskamp, 1984). Furthermore, public officials have reported using social science in drafting policies with psychological research cited as the most influential of all these sciences (Caplan, Morrison, & Stambaugh, 1975). While on the staff of the U.S. Senate, Trudy Vincent (1990) reported that the activities in which members of Congress engage are very similar to those of ecologically minded community psychologists. That is, legislators also need to pay careful attention to the people, settings, events, and history of their districts before establishing policy. Directly and indirectly, then, psychology can influence public policy.

No matter what the role of research in policy development or in the community, it should always be returned to the community for application (Chavis et al., 1983) and not kept solely in the scientific journals for consumption by scientists. Remember, though, that when research is given away to the community, it can also be used for political ammunition, manipulation, and self-serving purposes (Oskamp, 1984).

Research in the service of public policy is not the only way to address social change. Community psychologists and community members can also **lobby** to change policy. Lobbying means to direct pressure at public officials to promote the passage of a particular piece of legislation or policy. Individuals wishing to influence policy can also disseminate appropriate pieces of information, such as public opinion polls and results of field research, to policy makers in an attempt to educate them (Perkins, 1988). Education and information dissemination as a means of social change have already been discussed.

The average citizen hoping to influence legislation may find the process bewildering, whether it is at the local, state, or federal level. Fortunately, there are materials available to the average citizen that will take the mystery out of the legislative process (Alderson & Sentman, 1979; Ebert-Flattau, 1980; Zigler & Goodman, 1982). The American Psychological

Association (APA) has created a Public Interest Directorate, the mission of which is to advance the scientific and professional aspects of psychology as applied to human welfare. The directorate disseminates reports and other written materials to state and federal governments and legislators. Similarly, the APA also developed a guide to advocacy in the public interest that includes sections on the legislative process and on effective means of communications with congressional staff.

A community psychologist or community member could also seek an elected office, work on the campaign of a particular candidate, or vote for a particular candidate supporting a favored social change program. Holding an important elected office may seem alien to some, but it is often the ideal role for a scientist. Why? The community scientist's training places him or her in the position to be able to demand evidence for proposed programs. Scientists also best know the importance of evaluating change mechanisms, such as new or experimental programs (Fairweather & Davidson, 1986).

Another role for politically active scientists is to act as expert witnesses and **amicus curiae** (friend of the court). A case of the *amicus curiae* role for psychologists in the courts was the use of sex stereotyping research by Susan Fiske in the *Price Waterhouse v. Hopkins* case heard and cited in the local, appellate, and Supreme Courts. The APA also filed an *amicus curiae* brief in the case. The testimony about the psychology of stereotyping played a crucial role at each court level as well as in the eventual vindication of the wronged female employee (Fiske, Bersoff, Borgida, Deaux, & Heilman, 1991). Community psychologists in these endeavors play a role in shaping case law and setting precedents on which other cases may be based (Jacobs, 1980; Perkins, 1988).

Advantages and Disadvantages of Public Policy Changes

The advantage of using public policy efforts—including research, lobbying for or sponsoring a particular policy, and elections—is that sweeping social changes can often be induced, especially if the efforts of broad alliances are all aimed in the same direction. Another advantage is that the average U.S. citizen is known to have considerable respect for the law (Kohlberg, 1984; Lempert & Sanders, 1986), and some people may accept the change because it is the law.

Often, the real issues underlying social problems are economic and political rather than psychological, so the policy solution might be the most appropriate anyway (Nikelly, 1990). Finally, policy makers often (but not always) have a broad perspective on the community that elected or appointed them and are likely to understand the interrelationships between seemingly segregated groups and isolated social problems. Therefore, solutions in the form of policy can take a broad-brush and long-term approach rather than a narrow or short-term focus, which is more likely to fail.

No method of social change is without problems, however, and policy science and public policy are not without theirs. For instance, much social science research is completed by academics operating in a "publish or perish" mode (Phares, 1991) to impress colleagues; the research is often not returned to the community for social change. Similarly, community researchers are often perceived as agents of a traditional system that has historically been oppressive and are consequently not perceived as guests or collaborators in the community (Robinson, 1990). Therefore, research participation, results, and dissemination efforts are shunned, rendering the research useless.

Another serious problem with using public policy avenues to create social change is the electorate. Bond issues, school budgets, referenda, and other elections are participated in by a select few. Most voters are disproportionately well educated and older than the average citizen. Hence, the voices of the poor, young, and minorities are not heard via voting. This means that those who may most benefit from prosocial change are not participating in the direction of these changes (Hess, Markson, & Stein, 1991).

Perhaps the greatest disadvantage to using public policy efforts to create social change is that policy shaping can be a slow, cumbersome, politicized process. For instance, the average time span from initial writing to passage of a bill in Congress is about a year. However, less controversial policies pass more quickly. More complex or controversial issues take much longer. In the meantime, the needs of the affected groups may have changed; indeed, the group itself may have evaporated, or its needs may have become more severe so that the original policy solution is insufficient.

A Skill Set for Practice

Community psychologists can go a long way toward bettering communities. Many community members, however, do not know how to approach them or exactly what they do. To that end, the Society for Community Research and Action of the APA proposed some crucial changes. In a report titled "Finding Work as a New Community Psychologist," the SCRA Practice Task Force (2007) recommended that community psychologists not depend on their title and rather describe what they can do. By listing competencies, they do not have to deal with a definition and broaden their opportunities. These competencies could include political advocacy, assessment and evaluation, capacity building for organizations, collaboration and consultation skills, communication within organizations and to the public, report writing, an awareness and appreciation of cultural diversity, knowledge of group processes, the ability to apply scientific knowledge, the ability to organize and supervise, an understanding of how to build and maintain a positive environment, and research skills. A veteran community psychology practitioner and member of this task force, Alan Ratcliffe (personal communication, January, 2008) stated that he never looked at the job title of what people were looking for. He would describe what he could do for a system, a community, or an organization. He found there to be demand for the skills he brought.

As for a mind set for community interventions, Kofkin-Radkin (2003) has said it well. It is a matter of realizing the point between contradictions. Her admonitions regarding action in the community include:

- The situation is urgent, so take your time
- The outcome is critical, so don't worry about it
- The problems are huge, so think small
- Social change is complex, so keep it simple
- Social change is serious business, so have fun
- Social change requires staying on course, so relinquish control. (pp. 171–173)

SUMMARY

Many methods for creating and sustaining social change exist. Each has its own advantages and disadvantages. Activists hoping to fashion social change need to consider what strategies will work best for the issues they address. Some combination of strategies will probably work better than a single strategy, and what worked once might not work again or in a different community or for a different issue.

Planned change, such as grassroots activism and information dissemination, intentionally addresses and prepares the community for changes. The primary purpose of planned change should always be to improve the community. Each method of planned change has disadvantages and advantages. Methods available for induced change include citizen participation, networking with other community resources, the use of professional consultants, education or knowledge dissemination, and participation in public policy efforts by citizens and scientists.

In citizen participation, citizens produce the changes they desire by mechanisms such as grassroots activism, which is a type of bottom-up rather than top-down change. Such change results in empowerment, in which individuals feel they have control over their own lives.

When community agencies come together to aid one another, they are networking. Networking has been shown to directly assist in the longevity of community organizations. Sometimes umbrella organizations, such as the United Way, also provide services to community agencies or enhance their functioning, thus again ensuring their success.

Professional change agents or consultants can also help communities evolve. Community consultants need to be careful not to overtake the community but empower the community to create its own changes.

Education and information dissemination are still more means of producing social change. Although these methods sometimes produce vast changes, care must be taken to use the most appropriate information with sensitivity to the cultural diversity of the community.

Passing new legislation and policies or revamping existing laws and policies are other means of creating social change and are known collectively as public policy. Public policy changes can create sweeping social change, but often such policy is fraught with the politics of competing groups and can take time to fashion and implement.

Community practitioners find it useful to think of what skill sets they bring to social problems. The title of "community psychologist" may be unknown to many. This pragmatism and flexibility are good illustrations of what a community psychology should be.

CHAPTER 6

THE MENTAL HEALTH SYSTEM

EPIDEMIOLOGICAL ESTIMATES
OF MENTAL ILLNESS

MODELS OF MENTAL HEALTH AND
MENTAL DISORDER
    The Medical Model
    The Psychoanalytic Model
        Freud
        Adler
    The Behavioral Model: The Social-Learning
        Approach
    The Humanistic Model
    ■ CASE IN POINT 6.1   Mental Health Care
    Professionals

THE EVOLUTION OF THE MENTAL
HEALTH SYSTEM
    Brief History of Mental Health Care
    ■ CASE IN POINT 6.2   Rosenhan's Study
    of Hospital Patients' Stigmatization

    Deinstitutionalization
    The Social Context to Deinstitutionalization
    Early Alternatives to Institutionalization
    Measuring "Success" of Deinstitutionalized
        Persons

BEYOND DEINSTITUTIONALIZATION
    Model Programs for Individuals with
        Mental Disorders
        Lodge Society
    Intensive Case Management
        Assertive Community Treatment
        Wraparound Milwaukee

THE BATTLE CONTINUES: WHERE DO
WE GO FROM HERE?

SUMMARY

In individuals insanity is rare, but in groups, parties, nations and
epochs it is the rule.
—Friedrich Wilhelm Nietzsche, *Beyond Good and Evil*

Min, age 25, was of Chinese descent and lived in the United States. Not only was she convinced that her psychiatrists did not understand her illness, she was also convinced that they did not understand her Chinese values.

    Min had drifted in and out of a large state hospital because of what her doctors called schizophrenia. Each time she entered the hospital, she was given medication that eased her symptoms, particularly her hallucinations and the imaginary voices talking to her. When medicated, Min would develop better contact with those around her, take better care of her daily needs, and then be released from the hospital to her family's care. However, her two parents worked hard to support the family, which included Min's brother and sister. Her siblings were in school. Therefore, Min was alone much of the time. Because her family was not available to supervise her medications, she often forgot to take them. Eventually, she would become out of control, which would prompt the family to call the psychiatrist, who, after some pleading from the family for intervention, would tell them to return Min to the hospital.

Such was Min's state. She would leave the hospital only to return. She would take her medication and be briefly liberated from her symptoms only to forget the medication later. She is one of the country's chronically mentally ill who seem to be in desperate need of long-term, coordinated intervention but who are not necessarily receiving it.

This chapter examines the plight of Min and others like her. It will begin with some historical highlights and move to the issue of deinstitutionalizing the mentally ill. While examining deinstitutionalization, discussions focus on how to measure the success of moving individuals out of institutions as well as the common alternatives to institutionalization. Interestingly, many of the early alternatives have been tantamount to reinstitutionalization. Newer programs are coming into place. The question is whether they do what they have been intended to do. Can there be an effective tertiary prevention program, keeping patients out of institutions and reintegrating them successfully into the community? First we examine the question of how many people are like Min, that is, how many people in our community have to contend with mental health disorders.

EPIDEMIOLOGICAL ESTIMATES OF MENTAL ILLNESS

In the early 1980s, the National Institute of Mental Health (NIMH) surveyed the psychiatric status of more than 20,000 people in five cities. This study, known as the **Epidemiologic Catchment Area (ECA) Study,** attempted to estimate and describe the incidence and prevalence of psychiatric disorders meeting the criteria of the *Diagnostic and Statistical Manual of Mental Disorders,* 3rd edition (DSM-III). For example, in a comparison of three communities, Robins and colleagues (1984) estimated that lifetime prevalence rate of a given DSM-III disorder was 28.8 percent, 38.8 percent, and 31.0 percent, respectively, in New Haven, Baltimore, and St. Louis. Note that there are variations in numbers, as we would expect different cities to have different characteristics. The researchers' intention is to gather data from enough sites in the United States so as to get a representative sample of rates from across the nation and come to some estimate of problem rates in the United States as a whole. Findings suggest that men and women are equally likely to be afflicted with psychiatric disorders. This study leads us to estimates of one-year prevalence (having symptoms during the previous year) of anxiety disorders at 13 percent, of major depression at 6.5 percent, and schizophrenia at 1.3 percent. Nineteen percent of the sample is believed to have some psychiatric disorder. A second multiple site study sponsored by NIMH in the 1990s provides estimates based on the DSM-III Revised, a different set of criteria (Kessler et al., 1994). This study is called the National Comorbidity Study (NCS). The one-year prevalence estimates for this study are: anxiety disorder 18.7 percent, major depression 10 percent, any psychiatric disorder 23.4 percent. Lifetime prevalence for having a psychiatric disorder is 50 percent. However, 17 percent of the population has multiple diagnoses (comorbid), and the most severe cases have the highest concentration of disturbances. A third estimate of mental health epidemiology was conducted in 2000–2002. This study is called the National Comorbidity Study, Replication (NCS-R), and is based on the *Diagnostic Statistical Manual* IV criteria for psychiatric disorders. Results using these criteria yield an anxiety disorder percentage of 18 percent for one-year prevalence, major depression prevalence of 6.7 percent, and any psychiatric disorder prevalence of 26.2 percent (Kessler, Chiu, Demler, & Walters, 2005). Again, a small proportion of the population has the worst symptomatology and multiple disorders. In both NCS reports, less than half of those with diagnosable disorders are in treatment.

Findings from the ECA, NCS, and NCS-R are consistent with the **Midtown Manhattan Study,** a longitudinal study investigating the prevalence of psychopathology from 1952 to 1960. Across several decades, from multiple sites, using a variety of measurement criteria, the findings seem consistent that mental health issues are a part of our communities. They are not a trivial part, because mental health issues should affect half of us sometime during our lifetime.

Also notably consistent over time, the most recent epidemiological study (Kessler et al., 2005) finds that the general practitioner M.D. has seen the highest rise in treatment demands. This is reminiscent of the findings by Gurin, Verof, and Feld (1960), who found similar reports of medical doctors being the people most likely to be consulted regarding psychological problems.

MODELS OF MENTAL HEALTH AND MENTAL DISORDER

In answer to these mental health needs, psychology has traditionally responded by providing individual-focused clinical psychological services. As you may recall, the effectiveness of these services was called into question by Eysenck's (1952) meta-analytic study. We might make note of a more recent review of psychotherapy outcome studies that examined the variety of factors that affected outcome (Lambert & Barley, 2001). The specific therapeutic technique accounted for approximately 14 percent of the results, a small amount. What did seem to matter was the therapeutic relationship that developed between client and therapist. But we digress. The basic argument against the clinical orientation is that it is an inefficient and reactive model of treatment of well-entrenched psychological symptoms. This was discussed in Chapter 1. We elaborate on some of the treatment models here so as to better understand the traditional systems that are in place and the community applications that have, at times, evolved from them.

The Medical Model

The standard and traditional model for care is the medical model. Based on the practice of medicine, the assumption is that the patient's illness is based on internally based dysfunctions.

The patient is a passive recipient of knowledge from the expert physician, who provides the answer to the patient's problems. The patient obediently follows the advice and partakes of the medicine (a preparation or potion that will bring about a cure of the ailment or relief from the physical symptoms). The tradition has among its roots the Greek and Roman physicians who dealt with physical disorders. Both physical and mental health were the result of maintaining a balance. For the ancient Greek philosopher/physician Hippocrates, this was a balance among the four elements within us: phlegm, blood, black bile, and yellow bile. These traditions are believed to be traced to even older Egyptian and Mesopotamian beliefs.

Of course, modern medicine has come a long way from this elementary model. Yet the procedures are similar in some ways. The patient presents a set of symptoms. These are problems with their physical functioning. Based on the presenting symptoms, there is a diagnosis of what is malfunctioning or out of balance. We might come to understand the etiology or origins and development of the disorder. Once the correct diagnosis is made, there is a prescription of the appropriate medicine or therapy to cure the problem. The next time you go to the doctor, note how the procedure works. He or she will ask what is troubling you, that is, the set of symptoms; then, based on the fit of symptoms to a set of criteria for the various illnesses, he or she will decide what is wrong. He or she will then make a set of recommendations for therapy (bed rest and fluids, or maybe decrease sugar or salt intake) and may provide a prescription of certain medicines to be taken in a particular pattern so as to alleviate symptoms (e.g., fever, chills, low energy) or strengthen the system (increase level of antibiotics in the body) or cure the illness (correct the imbalance). The patient chooses when to come to the doctor. This is most likely when the patient has experienced enough disorder to make him or her believe that help is needed. Most clinical psychologists use this medical model of investigation of symptoms, diagnosis, and prescription of treatment and therapy.

Given the strength of the biological, or medical, model, two authoritative references about mental illness (*The Diagnostic and Statistical Manual of Mental Disorders* [DSM] and the *International Code of Diagnosis* [ICD]) have been developed. The medical model leaves at least two important legacies in traditional psychology. One is the reliance on diagnostic labels, as found in the DSM. The other legacy is the assumption of authority and power by the professional over the patient. Both of these legacies, though, are eschewed by community psychologists.

The Psychoanalytic Model

Freud. For those of you who are psychology majors or have taken a course in abnormal, child, or personality psychology (or are fans of Woody Allen movies), Sigmund Freud (1856–1939) will be no stranger. Freud is the father of psychoanalysis. Although many people today disagree with his theories, it cannot be denied that Freud's influence is felt in psychology as well as in psychiatry. Although Freud believed that biology played an important role in the development of psyches, he argued that most psychological disorders are treatable or curable with the use of free association or verbal therapy. Psychoanalytic treatment takes the form of individual verbal therapy up to five times a week over several years.

Somewhat later, the psychoanalytic approach began to split into two paths: traditional psychoanalytic individual verbal therapy versus biological psychiatry. A German contemporary of Freud, Adolf Meyer (1866–1950), argued for the importance of the interplay between biology, psychology, and environment, but many others preferred only biology as an explanation for mental disorders, after a strict biological-medical model. The traditional psychoanalytic individual verbal therapy model has consistently failed to show its effectiveness with the severely mentally ill (Wilson, O'Leary, & Nathan, 1992).

Adler. Among the alternatives to Freud coming out of the early 20th century is Alfred Adler. He emphasized the individual's concern about powerlessness, and the person's goal of seeking fulfillment in his or her life. Toward this end, Adler's work was directed at helping people gain this sense of empowerment over their situations. He is credited by some for the psychoeducational movement, which brought knowledge to the people so that they could use it for their lives.

His theory also included *gemeinschaftsgefuhl,* which translates into "community feeling" or what is typically called **social interest.** Social interest is the individual's sense of connection to the people around him. If there is high social interest, the individual feels a part of his family, his neighborhood, his community. If there is low social interest, the individual feels alienated from people and will act in his or her own self-interest without regard to the consequences for others.

Adler theorizes that these social feelings and our feelings about our selves are heavily influenced by childhood experiences, so his theory also focused on childhood education. The emphasis in the teacher–child relationship is on encouragement of the child and her or his curiosity about the world.

As is surely notable from this description, the emphasis is on development of a healthy individual. Pathology is averted through provision of positive social environments that both empower and set appropriate normative limits on the individual. This is reminiscent of community psychology practices.

The Behavioral Model: The Social-Learning Approach

As you may recall from an introductory psychology course, by using dogs as subjects, Russian physiologist Ivan Pavlov (1849–1936) was able to demonstrate that behavior could be formed as a result of **classical conditioning.** This is the process by which a response comes to be elicited by a stimulus, an object, or a situation other than what is the natural or normal stimulus. Pavlov repeatedly exposed his dogs to a **conditioned stimulus** in the form of a bell whenever the **unconditioned stimulus** in the form of meat powder was present. Although the **unconditioned response** or natural response for meat powder was salivation, eventually these dogs learned to display a **conditioned response** or learned response in the form of salivation *in the absence of* meat powder.

Dissatisfied with the psychoanalytic approach and rejecting the method of **introspection** or self-examination (a method advocated by Wilhelm Wundt, the father of experimental psychology), two U.S. psychologists, John B. Watson (1878–1985) and B. F. Skinner (1904–1990), further developed Pavlov's theory by using humans as subjects. Instead of pairing a conditioned stimulus with an unconditioned stimulus, Skinner developed and preferred the use of **operant conditioning,** in which behavior is more likely to be engaged in when it is **reinforced** or rewarded. Often, the reinforcers and the conditioned and unconditioned stimuli are provided by something external to the organism. Thus, in part, behavioral tradition provides one with a sense that ecology is important.

Extending the principles of learning theory, or the **behavioral model,** Martin Seligman (1975) argued that depression can be explained as a form of **learned helplessness,** or a lack of perceived control due to uncontrollable events in the environment. Other advocates of the social-learning approach, such as British psychiatrist Hans Eysenck Sr. and U.S. psychologist Joseph Wolpe, have developed techniques such as **desensitization** or step-by-step relaxation training to change phobic or fearful behavior.

Generally speaking, the social-learning model is an effective treatment with many forms of mental distress. However, it is labor-intensive because each behavioral treatment must be tailored to match the individual's needs. Moreover, to many critics, the social-learning approach appears to deal with the symptoms rather than the cause of mental distress. Finally, most community psychologists note that this model treats one individual at a time—not a very efficient way to manage change.

However, there have been several successful attempts at translating these learning principles into community analysis and action. Bogat and Jason (2000) review many of these programs, concluding that the behavioral principles provide added "technological tools" to a community psychologist's skill set. In particular, the use of behavioral techniques can provide the small successes on the path toward systems change.

The Humanistic Model

The 1960s witnessed the growth and emphasis of the movement of human rights, such as the introduction of the Civil Rights Act in 1964. The movement of human rights had a profound impact on how mental health and mental disorders were perceived or defined. That is, to some mental health care experts and professionals, such as U.S. psychologists Abraham Maslow (1908–1970) and British psychiatrist R. D. Laing, maladjustment had more to do with **labeling,** or an individual being told he or she is not healthy or is sick, than with innate determinants. In other words, people sometimes behave in accord with what they are told. Thus, treatments should be designed to help these people understand and reflect on their unique feelings. In conjunction with this notion, U.S. psychologist Carl Rogers (1902–1987) developed **client-centered therapy,** in which the role of the therapist is to facilitate the client's reflection on his or her experiences. Note the word **client** in the previous sentence. To humanistic psychologists, clients are not sick and thus are not labeled **patients.**

Similar to the psychoanalytic model, the **humanistic model** emphasizes the use of verbal therapy. Unlike the psychoanalytic model, both individual and group verbal therapy are common to the humanistic model. However, the humanistic model suffers from some of the same criticisms as does the psychoanalysis theory. Faith, Wong, and Carpenter (1995) found that the effectiveness of a sensitivity training group (a form of humanistic group therapy) is not so much due to the fact that people gain a sense of self-worth but due to improved mental health as a function of social skills learned during therapy.

There are, however, at least two more major ideas derived from humanistic psychology that have been transplanted to the field of community psychology. One is that all people are worthy individuals and have the right to fulfill and discover this worth. The second is that the individual best knows him- or herself and thus needs to provide input on solutions to problematic issues. This directly feeds into community psychology's principle of empowerment and the philosophical justifications for participatory action research.

These models of mental health serve to direct psychotherapy and the field of clinical psychology. Yet there are clear connections that can and have been made between aspects of these models and community psychology principles and practices. The shift in theory and action in community psychology is to the social and systems level focus for interventions as well as an appreciation of the wider ecological contexts that influence human behavior maintenance and change. The interplay of models fits well with community psychology's openness to multiple perspectives and the understanding of multiple levels required for change. It also belies the clinical and counseling psychology roots to some aspects of American community psychology. For example, the Swampscott meeting was a community mental health training conference. As well, there are clinical training backgrounds to many (but not all) of the founders of this area. Nonetheless, we should see the differences between the traditional hospital and office base of clinical psychology and the broader ranging community psychology.

CASE IN POINT 6.1
MENTAL HEALTH CARE PROFESSIONALS

Various professional services are available to help people cope with stress. Many of the mental health care services are delivered by individuals from four major professional disciplines. **Psychiatrists** are medical doctors (M.D.s) who specialize in psychiatry. They can be employed in either the public (governmental) or private sector (such as private practice). In addition to their training, psychiatrists must pass a licensing examination before they can practice the discipline. Within the field, there are subspecialties, such as biological psychiatry and community psychiatry. The role of psychiatry is usually medication maintenance, although mental health patients who are financially capable can often receive some form of therapy, such as psychoanalytic therapy, up to five times a week.

Many individuals who hold advanced degrees in any subfields of psychology consider themselves psychologists. **Clinical psychologists** are mental health care professionals who have advanced training (usually a doctoral degree) in clinical psychology, and their training includes exposure to more severe pathology and hospital settings. Similar to psychiatrists, clinical psychologists can be employed in either the public or private sector. Unlike psychiatrists, in most states clinical psychologists cannot prescribe medication. However, a pilot project in the U.S. military trained psychologists in limited use of medications directed at psychological disorders (Sammons & Brown, 1997). There is now a small number of psychologists trained to provide these services within the U.S. states and territories to whom limited prescription authority has been granted. This topic is not without controversy (Gutierrez & Silk, 1998; Lavoie & Barone, 2006; Sammons & Brown, 1997).

The long-standing professional conflict between the fields of psychiatry and clinical psychology has created many interesting twists as to who is qualified to be called a *psychologist*. One

(continued)

CASE IN POINT 6.1 CONTINUED

outcome is that in many instances, the government (state and federal) recognizes as psychologists only those individuals with advanced training in clinical psychology or related areas, such as counseling or industrial psychology, and who have passed some licensing examination.

Furthermore, these scenarios are complicated by several other factors. Sometimes, the term **therapist** is used interchangeably with the terms *clinician* and *psychologist,* although not all clinicians and therapists (such as those in social work and psychiatric nursing) have training in clinical psychology. Also, many doctoral-level psychologists receive their training in nonclinical areas, such as community psychology.

There are also disagreements within the subfield of clinical psychology. Traditionally, clinical psychologists were trained using the **scientist-practitioner model** or trained to be both scientists and practitioners. These psychologists hold a doctor of philosophy (Ph.D.), the highest degree in any scientific discipline. There is a growing trend in the subfield of clinical psychology to train people as clinicians or *practitioners* for which the degree doctor in psychology (Psy.D.) has been created. Here the emphasis is on clinical application and less on research skills.

A third group of mental health care professionals called **social workers** help clients find and access services in the community but also may provide treatment. They usually hold a degree called a master's of social work (M.S.W.). Unlike psychiatrists, they cannot prescribe medication. Similar to psychiatrists and clinical psychologists, social workers can be employed in either the public or private sector. The primary role of a social worker is as a practitioner.

What psychiatrists, clinical psychologists, and social workers have in common is that they treat *individuals* who are experiencing stress. Note that typically these three groups of mental health providers focus on individual functioning. Another common feature is that all of these caregivers operate from a position of authority regarding their clients.

A final and important issue related to these mental health care providers is the one of health insurance or third-party payments. Health insurance companies act as third parties who pay the mental health care provider, whether that professional is a psychiatrist or social worker, for the treatment of the client or person covered by the insurance. In most states within the United States, these three professional groups are licensed and may be covered by insurance. As of 2008, and the passage of the Mental Health Parity Act, levels of insurance coverage for physical and mental health are supposed to be equal. The details are just beginning to be worked out. There appears to be a somewhat disconcerting trend for insurance companies to reduce their payment costs such that those providers who charge less (for example, the psychiatric nurses and social workers) are the ones covered by insurance. Community activists need to stay on top of this issue—for example, by conducting research to ascertain whether there is a relationship between the success of treatment and the cost of the treatment. That still leaves the matter of the large number of people in the nation without insurance.

Community psychologists, who sit outside most of these professional boundary disputes, believe that an ounce of prevention is by far the most cost-effective intervention of all. Mental health education could go a long way toward preventing the need for treatment and health insurance coverage all together.

THE EVOLUTION OF THE MENTAL HEALTH SYSTEM

Brief History of Mental Health Care

Although the ancient world has always been portrayed as less than civilized, some older cultures gave more emphasis to the study of mental health than others. For example, to most Chinese (ancient and modern), physical and psychological well-being is thought to depend on a balance of two natural forces: **yin,** the female force, and **yang,** the male force. Furthermore, these two forces are thought to regulate the five elements—gold, wood, water, fire, and earth—that are responsible for people's daily health. Among other things, the concentration of each element is thought to vary with the type of food group. Thus, a proper diet and regular exercise are important to maintain a balance between these elements.

According to Chinese folklore, a wise king named Sun Lone Tse, whose name meant "to cultivate," in ancient times (circa 600–700 B.C.) was thought to be responsible for the first classification system of herbs used in medicine. Also, Chinese historical texts mention a doctor named Wah Torr as the father of Chinese medicine. On one occasion, he performed minor surgery on a general's arm using **acupuncture** as anesthetic. Needles were used to stick into the **meridians** (pressure points) to facilitate the release of **endorphins** (natural pain relievers) in the brain. Wah Torr wrote many medical texts. These concepts relating mind and body are important to the fields of clinical psychology and behavioral medicine, sister disciplines to the field of community psychology. If Min were in ancient China or even modern-day China, the treatments for her disorder might be different from what they are in the United States.

As one moves through history, one notices that the ancient Greeks are also important. Hippocrates (circa 460–377 B.C.), who was known as the father of Western medicine, spoke about four natural **humors,** or fluids, that were thought to regulate people's mental health. Specifically, great fluctuations in mood were thought to be caused by an excess of blood. Fatigue was considered to be caused by an excess of phlegm or thick mucus. Anxiety was thought to be caused by an excess of yellow bile or liver fluid, and depression by an excess of black bile.

Whatever medical and psychological advancements were achieved by the ancient Chinese and Greeks, the majority of their contemporaries relied on the supernatural to explain mental illness. After the collapse of the Roman Empire in Europe (in 476 A.D.), supernatural or religious beliefs became the norms for explaining mental illness in Western society. For example, according to the church and those in power in many Western societies, the mentally ill and other disenfranchised people were thought to be sinners. Religious zealotry reached its peak in the 1480s, when Pope Innocent VIII officially sanctioned the persecution of witches, some of whom were actually suffering from mental illness; many others were just dissenters of the mainstream cultures. This period of almost 900 years in Western societies has come to be associated with the infamous name, the Dark Ages.

In many Western societies during the Renaissance (revival) period (circa 1300–1600), the idea of **humanism** finally developed. Thus, the mentally ill gained indirect benefits from the notion that all people had certain inalienable rights and should be treated with dignity. Furthermore, some doctors began to challenge the concept that mental illness was a defect of moral character. By the middle of the 1600s, institutions known as **asylums,** or madhouses, were established to contain the mentally ill. Perhaps the most famous was London's Bethlehem Hospital, nicknamed "Bedlam," which is now a word meaning chaos and confusion. The first asylum in the United States was established in the late 1700s. Asylums were places where the socially undesirable or misfits were kept. More often than not, residents of the asylums were chained.

The further development of humanism during the American (1776) and French (1789) revolutions provided more incentives to the mental health care reform movement throughout the European continent and in the United States. For example, two pioneers were instrumental in the movement in this country. Benjamin Rush (1745–1813), known as the father of American psychiatry, wrote the first treatise on psychiatry and established its first academic course. The second person was Dorothea Dix (1802–1887), whose experience with mental health care was derived from her teaching of women inmates. During her day, it was not unusual for the mentally ill to be kept in prisons. Dix traveled extensively in the country to raise money to build mental hospitals.

The mental health care reform movement further benefited from the pioneer work of several doctors who devoted their lives to the development of scientific **nomenclatures,** or classifications, of mental illness. These classifications eventually led to the study of **etiology,** or the cause of mental illness. It was probably a French doctor named Philippe Pinel (1745–1826) who first used the term **dementia** to describe a form of psychosis that was characterized by deterioration of judgment, memory loss, and personality change. A German doctor, Emil Kraepelin (1956–1926), further studied this condition and described it using the term **dementia praecox** (premature dementia). Subsequently, Swiss doctor Eugen Bleuler (1857–1930) gave the same disorder the name **schizophrenia,** which has become a household term in today's psychiatric practice. Also, Bleuler extended previous work by describing several subtypes of this illness.

Meanwhile, the **germ theory,** as advocated by Frenchman Louis Pasteur, had gained unprecedented recognition in the medical and scientific community. That is, many illnesses were thought to be caused by germ infections. Thus, the development of psychiatry as a field was destined to take on a medical or biological tone. In other words, under the influence of germ theory, mental illness was conceptualized as a *disease* rather than a *disorder* or psychological dysfunction.

At about the same time, the American Psychiatric Association and the American Psychological Association were formed in 1844 and 1892, respectively. Although the original mission of the American Psychological Association was not specifically concerned with issues relating to mental health and mental illness, as the subdiscipline of clinical psychology became more dominant, these issues became a priority. This shift in emphasis no doubt does not sit well with the American Psychiatric Association, which has seen itself as the sole guide in the field of mental health and mental illness since its inception. Over the years, these professional conflicts have been further complicated by a number of other factors, including the emergence of social work as a professional field.

After the work of Rush and Dix, the mental health care reform in this country can be roughly divided into three more eras: 1875–1940, 1940–1970 (Grob, 1991), and 1970 to the present (Shadish, Lurigio, & Lewis, 1989). During the period from 1875 to 1940, the government assumed the major responsibility in caring for the mentally ill. Two-thirds of all the patients were living in state-run psychiatric hospitals. In many ways, this system was an extension of Dix's thesis of moral management. More often than not, these patients received little treatment.

Meanwhile, there were a small number of privately owned psychiatric hospitals, such as the Menninger Foundation and the Institute of Living, providing services or treatments to those who could afford them. Although these services or treatments may be crude by today's standards, they contributed to the development of **community psychiatry,** a subdiscipline of psychiatry that argues that mental patients should be treated using the least restrictive method in the least restrictive environment. Many of these private mental patients lived in small, comfortable units, and they were encouraged to take lessons in cooking, sewing, and other self-improvement skills.

However, the initial optimism associated with moral management began diminishing in society. In almost all instances, psychiatric hospitals were no more than human warehouses. If treatments were provided, they tended to be **electroconvulsive therapy,** or electric shock to the brain, and **lobotomy,** or brain surgery. Furthermore, the cost associated with these hospitals had become a major strain on society, especially during the Great Depression and World War II. There were concerns that hospitalization itself brought certain self-fulfilling expectations to bear on the patient. This stigmatization was demonstrated in the Rosenhan study of the 1970s (see Case in Point 6.2).

As noted in Chapter 1, beginning in the 1960s, the **zeitgeist,** or atmosphere, of the society began to change. For example, the introduction of **psychotropic drugs** (mood-altering drugs) such as Thorazine (chlorpromazine) rekindled the idea that the mentally ill could be treated with dignity. Coupled with the ideology of community psychiatry, the use of medication allowed for the discharge of many mentally ill people back into the community.

In this chapter's opening vignette, medications successfully allowed Min to return to her family. When she went off the medication, her problems resurfaced. A consequence was the development of **outpatient treatment,** or nonhospitalized treatment (e.g., community mental health centers), as opposed to **inpatient treatment,** or hospitalized treatment. Also, to accommodate these newly released inpatients, alternative housing such as

CASE IN POINT 6.2
ROSENHAN'S STUDY OF HOSPITAL PATIENTS' STIGMATIZATION

Researcher D. L. Rosenhan was especially interested in whether mental health professionals (particularly psychiatrists) could detect genuine mental disorders or problems from false ones. He decided to conduct a study. First, Rosenhan (1973) trained his graduate students and others in how to fake symptoms of psychiatric disorders. For example, he instructed the pseudo-patients to tell hospital staff that they heard a thudding sound or a voice saying "thud." Rosenhan then sent his pseudo-patients to a psychiatric emergency facility.

To Rosenhan's amazement, the students were admitted. Soon after their admission to the psychiatric ward, the pseudo-patients were each given diagnoses.

Not long after their admission, the pseudo-patients began to act "normal." Curiously, many of the other patients realized that the pseudo-patients were normal. The staff did not recognize this normalcy partly because they rarely saw it. According to Rosenhan's report, the staff did not spend much time with the patients.

The pseudo-patients began to request release from the psychiatric ward. However, the staff consistently told the students that they were not well enough to be released. Eventually, Rosenhan had to intervene so that some of the pseudo-patients could be released. However, on release, many were labeled *schizophrenia in remission.* The pseudo-patients were kept in the hospital from 7 to 52 days, with an average stay of 19 days.

Without minimizing the agony associated with mental disorders, Rosenhan demonstrated that many perceived disorders are due to the process of labeling. Although some mental health professionals might argue otherwise, Rosenhan demonstrated that once labeled, it is difficult to overcome the label and the expectations and behavioral interpretations that go with it.

community residences, or group homes, were established but not without controversy. We now examine the deinstitutionalization of the 1960s and 1970s and the efforts to deal with its implications.

Deinstitutionalization

Deinstitutionalization is usually defined as sending mental patients back into the community. Recall that Min was institutionalized and sent back to her community—in fact, she was repeatedly institutionalized and returned. This definition, however, is too simplistic. A casual review of the field of mental disorders indicates that there is a great deal of controversy about what exactly *deinstitutionalization* is (Grob, 1991; Shadish et al., 1989). A deeper examination of some of these definitions and related issues is in order.

John Talbott (1975), a renowned psychiatrist, argued that the term *deinstitutionalization* is a misnomer. Instead, a better term is **transinstitutionalization** to describe "the chronically mentally ill patient who has his or her locus of living and care transferred from a single lousy institution to multiple wretched ones" (p. 530). Min presents a picture of this phenomenon. She was in and out of institutions, living with her family between institutionalizations. On a related note, Mathew Dumont (1982), another psychiatrist, argued that "deinstitutionalization is nothing more or less than a polite term for the cutting of mental health budgets" (p. 368).

The popular literature, such as the *New York Times,* defined *deinstitutionalization* as "moving mental patients from enormous, remote hospitals into small community residences" ("Willowbrook Plan Worked," 1982). Another *New York Times* editorial stated that deinstitutionalization is "dumping mental patients out of state hospitals onto local communities, with promises of community treatment that never came true." Also, the *New York Times* claimed that *deinstitutionalization* is synonymous with *homelessness* ("Redeinstitutionalization," 1986, p. A24).

Indeed, these definitions illustrate the many different aspects of deinstitutionalization. Reconciling these differences, some mental health care experts (Bachrach, 1989; Rein & Schon, 1977; Shadish et al., 1989) proposed that the term *deinstitutionalization* be understood as a semantic mechanism to frame the complex, often conflicting, and seemingly unrelated sets of issues associated with ongoing mental health care reform. In other words, *deinstitutionalization,* like any term, has its concrete (explicit) and implied (implicit) meaning. More often than not, the concrete aspects of deinstitutionalization, such as budget constraints, are the impetus for the driving forces behind mental health care reform. Policy is likely to be the product of practical concern or ideology (Grob, 1991; Kiesler, 1992; Warner, 1989). However, a growing number of mental health care professionals are arguing that society must look beyond the immediate practical concern to develop plans that can anticipate *long-term* consequences. For example, one concern is the growing number of the homeless mentally ill who also have HIV or AIDS. According to a survey conducted in a New York City shelter that housed homeless men, Susser, Valencia, and Conover (1993) found that 12 out of 62 (19.4 percent) of the mentally ill men tested positive for HIV. These men need all three issues (mental disorder, homelessness, and AIDS) addressed over the long run.

What can a society do to anticipate some of these long-term mental health care consequences? To that end, Bachrach (1989) provided a more heuristic or meaningful definition of *deinstitutionalization* as

> the shunning or avoidance of traditional institutional settings, particularly state mental hospitals, for chronic mentally ill individuals, and the concurrent development of community-based alternatives for the care of this population. *This definition assumes three primary processes:* depopulation—*the shrinking of state hospital censuses through release, transfer, or death;* diversion—*the deflection of potential institutional admissions to community-based service settings;* and decentralization—*the broadening of responsibility for patient care from a single physically discrete service entity to multiple and diverse entities, with an attendant fragmentation of authority.* (p. 165)

According to Bachrach (1989), this definition of *deinstitutionalization* underscores three related elements: facts, process, and philosophy. That is, sound mental health care policy must be based on credible research or evidence (the facts). To plan for long-term goals, one must know the characteristics of the mentally ill and the resources or systems where they receive their services (process). Historical events and philosophical ideology often determine the direction of mental health care movements (philosophy).

The Social Context to Deinstitutionalization

What were some of the issues U.S. society (especially mental health care professionals and policy makers) did and did not anticipate about the watershed effect of deinstitutionalization beginning in the late 1960s? Although it is beyond the scope of this chapter to give a full account, these complex issues can be understood from several related perspectives: philosophical, biomedical, economic, sociological, and psychological.

If Sir Thomas More were alive in the 1960s, he probably would have felt the optimism in the United States that Americans were on their way to utopia. Indeed, President John F. Kennedy was asking middle-class Americans to give to the less fortunate. Programs such as Project Head Start (including free meals for schoolchildren from low-income families) and the Peace Corps (e.g., teaching people in developing countries about family planning, including the practice of prenatal care as well as abortion as an option of family planning) were established. The notion or philosophy of humanism appeared to reach its peak. The field of mental health benefited from these effects. Meanwhile, the advancement in medical technology also allowed people with mental disorders who were once unmanageable now to be controllable by using psychotropic drugs such as Elavil (amitriptyline chloride) and Thorazine. Thus, professionals had one more reason to treat the mentally ill using the least restrictive method.

This optimism was fused by both professional (Thomas Szasz's [1961] *The Myth of Mental Illness*) and popular writing (Ken Kesey's *One Flew Over the Cuckoo's Nest*). People in the legal profession also took up the cause—for example, the American Civil Liberties Union initiated the Mental Health Law Project, and the Church of Scientology initiated the Citizens Commission on Human Rights. A common theme in these legal efforts was an opposition to involuntary hospitalization (Torrey, 1997).

However, some mental health care experts (Kiernan, Toro, Rappaport, & Seidman, 1989; Warner, 1989) have argued that however admirable and persuasive the notion or philosophy of humanism, a more pragmatic explanation to account for the occurrence of deinstitutionalization is economics. Investigating deinstitutionalization in different Western countries in the past 30 years, Warner (1989) found that

> the process was stimulated by the opportunity for cost savings created by the introduction of disability pensions and, in some countries, by postwar demand for labor. Where labor was in short supply, genuinely rehabilitative programs were developed. Where cost saving was the principal motivation, community treatment efforts were weak. (p. 17)

Also, Kiernan and colleagues (1989) found that manufacturing employment was negatively related to both first admissions in state hospitals and case openings in community outpatient facilities. That is, when the economy was good, fewer people were admitted into state psychiatric hospitals.

Since World War II, the world economy had been relatively good until the 1970s. The argument that deinstitutionalization is associated with economic stability appears to be consistent with the number of psychiatric hospital beds per 10,000 individuals in the Western industrialized countries. As long as there was a demand for a labor force, more people were deinstitutionalized.

Whether or not one agrees with this interpretation, deinstitutionalization has significant economic impact. The federal budget for care of the mentally ill has continued to rise. States have little financial incentive to provide comparable assistance because significant sources of this care are in the form of Supplemental Security Income, food stamps, Medicaid, Medicare, and so on. This imbalance between federal and state resources directed to the care of the mentally ill has created havoc (Torrey, 1997). Indeed, in a critical analysis of factors associated with deinstitutionalization, Brooks, Zuniga, and Penn (1995) found that financial burden is the principal determinant in this process. These researchers argued that "faced with the increasing costs associated with replacing or upgrading an aging system . . . most changes in services have been the outcome of budget, not medical, decisions, with medical or legal rationalizations applied post hoc or in parallel" (pp. 55–56).

Although these findings appear to explain the reasoning behind deinstitutionalization, they do not adequately account for its falling short of its goal to enhance the quality of life of the mentally disordered. Community psychologists and mental health care experts (Cheung, 1988; Earls & Nelson, 1988; Lovell, 1990; Mowbray, 1990; Mowbray, Herman, & Hazel, 1992; Struening & Padgett, 1990) have argued that sociological factors (such as adequate housing) and psychological factors (such as stigmatization) often hinder the progress of deinstitutionalization. Case in Point 6.2 discussed interesting research on stigmatization—research in which institutionalized patients faked their disorders.

Use of mental health facilities is related to personal poverty. Banziger and Foos (1983) found that unemployment and welfare factors were strong predictors of utilization of mental health centers. Bruce, Takeuchi, and Leaf (1991) also demonstrated a causal link between mental disorder and poverty. They examined the patterns of new disorders that developed over a six-month period in an epidemiological study. Their sample included African Americans, Hispanics, and Whites. The researchers found that a significant proportion of new episodes of mental disorder could be attributed to poverty. In addition, Bruce and associates found that the risk for developing disorders was equal for men and women and for African Americans and Whites—in other words, poverty does not discriminate on the basis of race or gender.

In a case study, Cheung (1988) argued that the successful reintegration of the mentally disordered into the community to a large extent is dependent on public relations. Community members who are not familiar with mental illness are likely to be concerned with or resistant to having a halfway house built in their neighborhood. Earls and Nelson (1988) found that housing concern was positively correlated with negative affect. That is, former patients who had to worry about basic shelter were likely to have poor mental health. These two findings indicate the difficulty of balancing the seemingly incompatible forces of public good and private want.

Also, many people with mental disorders are discharged from hospitals into the community without adequate planning or support systems. For example, Mowbray (1990) argued that many of them do not have adequate living or social skills (e.g., cooking and paying bills) to survive in an unstructured environment. For deinstitutionalization to be effective, adequate and appropriate treatments must be in place. Struening and Padgett (1990) found that homeless adults in New York City had high rates of alcohol and drug abuse as well as mental illness. It is not unlikely that a large portion of these people were mental patients who were discharged from hospitals without adequate planning. Thus, they became homeless and had alcohol and drug-abuse problems (Levine & Huebner, 1991; Susser, Valencia, et al., 1993). Meanwhile, a majority of the mentally disordered are continuously being discharged from hospitals into nursing homes or board-and-care homes that are ill prepared to provide the services these patients need. Another consequence is a high burnout rate among staff at these agencies (Shadish et al., 1989).

Deinstitutionalization of people with mental disorders is also viewed as one of the major reasons (Pogrebin & Poole, 1987; Pogrebin & Regoli, 1985) for the increasing number of former mental health patients in prisons (Jemelka, Trupin, & Chiles, 1989). A 2006 U.S. Department of Justice report states that 56 percent of state prisoners, 45 percent of federal prisoners, and 64 percent of local jail prisoners have a history of mental disorder (James & Glaze, 2006). Those with mental disorder histories were more likely to be young, female, and White. They are more likely to be violent. In state courts, they are more likely to receive longer sentences. According to Harcourt (2007), within the United States over 2 million people are imprisoned. This is 5 times Great Britain's rate and 12 times Japan's rate, making for the highest number and rate of prisoners in the world. The point of this is that the idea that deinstitutionalization from hospitals has saved money is very incorrect. The mental patients have not been deinstitutionalized but rather reinstitutionalized in a different setting.

In an interesting study of what happens to the chronically mentally disordered, Diamond and Schnee (1990) tracked 21 men who were perceived to be most at risk for potential violence and were also high users of jails. The men were tracked for two and a half years through various service systems. The men used up to 11 different systems, including the mental health, criminal justice, health care, and social services systems. Criminal justice services were the most frequently used, and mental health services were usually only short-term, crisis care services, although some of the men had been hospitalized for long-term psychiatric care. Diamond and Schnee believe that their figure is an *underestimate* and calculated that the cost of care of the 21 men in all service systems totaled $694,291. That figure does not include costs to victims, nor property damaged in the men's violent episodes. The researchers called for a more coordinated effort of the various systems to better assist the men and to reduce costs.

Belcher (1988) suggested that when people with mental disorders are released from hospitals or institutions, they are often unable or unwilling to follow through on their own aftercare. This situation increases the likelihood of these individuals being involved in the criminal justice system. In addition, because the legal system and the mental health systems view mental disorders differently (Freeman & Roesch, 1989), the mentally disordered are not afforded the same level of therapeutic services for their disorder when they are incarcerated. The legal system narrowly deals with mental illness only as incompetence to testify in one's own behalf or as insanity, which is a defense against guilt.

The U.S. Department of Justice reports that about a third of state prisoners, a quarter of federal prisoners, and 17 percent of local jail prisoners receive some kind of mental health treatment while they are incarcerated (James & Glaze, 2006). Although hospitalization is very rare, use of medications is most popular.

The solution may be that mental health, criminal justice, and other professionals *need to collaborate in innovative and integrative ways* to prevent the mentally ill from being incarcerated in a correctional facility and to treat their disorders when they are incarcerated (Diamond & Schnee, 1990; Pogrebin & Regoli, 1985). Another alternative is to provide treatment and community support for these mentally ill individuals in sufficient strength, so as to forestall their ever getting involved in the criminal justice system. Heller, Jenkins, Steffen, and Swindle (2000) argue that the deinstitutionalization of the 1960s has come full circle. They believe the dream of community-based mental health treatment with community-based prevention programs has never been realized. Among the factors they cite for the problems in implementing the vision are a lack of understanding of what would be required for medication maintenance programs, a disregard of natural communities and neighborhoods in setting up program boundaries, and professional resistance to anything other than traditional treatment programs for patients. Heller et al. (2000) cite the reduction in community support program funding occurred at the same time the economy took a downturn, leaving many of the mentally ill to become homeless.

Seidman and Rappaport (1986) believe that in searching for solutions, we are hampered by a tendency to overgeneralize conclusions regarding a group of people based on extreme examples from that group. Social psychology would add that this tendency to overgeneralize regarding negative aspects of a group is related to our feeling distant from that group, that is, they are considered members of an out-group (Allport, 1954/1979; McConnell, Rydell, & Strain, 2008). For example, after finding one case of an ethnic minority mother on welfare driving a new Cadillac, people may tend to believe all welfare cases are ethnic minorities who abuse the system. In reality, most of those on welfare are not abusive and are White. Bloom (1985) believes our desire for simplicity leads us to look for the one factor that leads to problems, when in fact problems usually are the result of multiple factors whose arrival to the case may be quite varied and come at critical times to the development of the problem. The search for solutions is many times simplistic and based on incorrect conclusions.

Early Alternatives to Institutionalization

The ideal setting for the institutionalized individual would be one that enhances his or her well-being because of the optimal fit between his or her competencies and the support provided in the environment. However, this may be just a pipe dream. In reality, many community placements are based as much on what is available and on economics as on the individual's competencies.

If not in institutions, where are the people who have mental disorders? Ironically, today most chronic mental patients are still cared for either in institutions such as nursing homes or in other community settings often characterized by poverty, stigma, social isolation, and poor care that depict large psychiatric hospitals (Shadish et al., 1989). About 1.15 million mentally disordered individuals reside in nursing homes; in fact, the nursing home industry is the largest system of long-term care for the severely and persistently mentally disordered (Bootzin, Shadish, & McSweeney, 1989). Research suggests that nursing homes do not return patients to mental hospitals as often as other forms of mental health care that is provided to deinstitutionalized persons (Bootzin et al., 1989). The reason, however, is not that the patients improve. Research demonstrates that symptomatology does not change; in fact, it might become slightly worse. The reason that nursing homes do not return patients to mental hospitals might be related to economics. More mental health dollars go to nursing home care than to any other mental health program (Kiesler, 1980). It behooves nursing homes to keep their clients!

Another type of community placement is **board-and-care homes.** These are typically community-based shelter-care facilities that include group homes and family care homes. The Public Health Service (1980) estimated that 400,000 people with chronic mental disorders may reside in these settings. This particular industry, compared to nursing homes, is relatively unregulated and more decentralized. The individuals in these settings tend to be younger and need less intensive care than those in nursing homes. Their care is typically paid for by Supplemental Security Income (disability checks), which they turn over to the shelter owners (Shadish et al., 1989). As funding for these options dwindled, so did the space for these former clients (Heller et al., 2000).

This fragmentation of care and the supposed economization of services implies that society has essentially moved from a mental health system to a welfare system (Kennedy, 1989). It is time to look at the success (or failure) of these changes in care for the mentally disordered.

Measuring "Success" of Deinstitutionalized Persons

Many in the mental health field would quickly jump to the conclusion that deinstitutionalization has not been successful. We have reviewed some of the myriad problems that deinstitutionalization has created, including but not limited to transinstitutionalization, homelessness, and jail terms. How is successful integration into the community measured? The answer depends on whom you ask and what issues you discuss.

Society needs to take a closer look at the measurement of success of deinstitutionalization. Table 6.1 shows the names of famous people who at one time or another experienced mental impairment and were also able to integrate successfully into society.

TABLE 6.1 Famous Individuals with Some Form of Mental Disorder

PERSON	FIELD	MENTAL DISORDER
Kim Basinger	Actress	Anxiety disorder
Connie Francis	American 1950s singer	Bipolar disorder
Ernest Hemingway	American Nobel Prize–winning writer	Depression
Abraham Lincoln	16th American president	Depression
Vincent Van Gogh	Late nineteenth-century Dutch painter	Psychosis
Virginia Woolf	Early twentieth-century British writer	Depression

The typical measures of success are social integration and recidivism. **Social integration** was defined in the last chapter as people's involvement with community institutions as well as their participation in the community's informal social life (Gottlieb, 1981). **Recidivism** means relapse or return to the institution or care—in this case, return to the psychiatric hospital. However, both of these terms imply limited criteria. Recent efforts in the literature of the field of community psychology indicate that measurement of success is a more complex issue.

For example, Shadish, Thomas, and Bootzin (1982) found that different groups use different criteria for success. Residents, staff, and family members of community care facilities often express that the quality of life (e.g., a clean place to live and something to do) ought to serve as a measure of success. On the other hand, federal officials and academicians cite psychosocial functioning (e.g., social integration and reduction of symptomatology) as good measures of success of community placement.

Clinicians (psychologists and psychiatrists) also use different criteria for different groups. Stack, Lannon, and Miley (1983) queried clinicians about their prognostic judgments for 269 patients in a state community mental health center. Specifically, the clinicians were asked to judge their expectations that the patients would be readmitted within the next two years. Clinicians' judgments were biased in regard to the patients' ethnicity; that is, they judged African American patients as more likely to be rehospitalized than White patients. The same clinicians were unduly influenced by their perceptions of the severity of the patients' disorder instead of other favorable factors, such as lack of prior hospitalization, youthfulness, lack of severe impairment, and living in a residentially stable neighborhood.

Despite suspected clinician bias, do client characteristics help clinicians make accurate judgments about whether particular clients will be more successful once released from an institution? Mitchell's (1982) work seems to suggest this is so. Mitchell recruited 35 clients from outpatient psychiatric clinics, as well as their family members. The ability of the client to solve problems and be independent positively related to the number of intimates or friends and the degree of support received from peers that the clients reported.

A few in the field of community integration of the chronically mentally disordered feel that the criteria for judging community competence of people with mental disabilities are amorphous and ambiguous. These professionals feel that a psychometric scale should be used to optimize the fit between the client and the community placement. Searight, Oliver, and Grisso (1986) suggested using the Community Competence Scale, which is a multiscale instrument of an individual's problem-solving skills, appropriateness of social judgment, and other factors related to social competence. In their research, Searight and associates found that the scale discriminated effectively between client groups requiring differing levels of guidance in the community.

A very different but also very prominent measure of success for deinstitutionalization is the economic one (Brooks et al., 1995). Arguments for programs are still based on cost efficiencies. Unfortunately, these costs are frequently based on short-term budgeting and without regard to potential long-term savings.

BEYOND DEINSTITUTIONALIZATION

Certainly, the preceding scenarios do not reflect the optimism when deinstitutionalization began in the late 1960s. It was thought then that the introduction of the **Community Mental Health Act** could "reduce the census of state hospitals and . . . provide treatment to maintain psychiatric patients in the community" (Levine, Toro, & Perkins, 1993, p. 526). Now, with hindsight, it seems obvious that one reason for the existing "patchwork" system is the lack of systematic planning, or poor coordination. However, some mental health care experts (Rein & Schon, 1977) argued that "the villain . . . is not poor coordination but the poor quality of services" (p. 244). Responding to this challenge, NIMH and some state agencies have begun to collect data about the characteristics of the mentally disabled, including people who are not part of the mainstream population. That is, quality of services are dependent on professionals' knowledge about people who have mental disorders.

Model Programs for Individuals with Mental Disorders

Emerging from the deinstitutionalization movement are several model programs that may be examined for their community psychology properties. These programs range from empowering participatory communities for the severely mentally ill (SMI), to intensive and comprehensive focus on management of each individual case of community-based SMI, to a team effort to provide the multiple levels and multiple areas of services needed for adult SMI or for youth. These are all tertiary prevention efforts, which reflect some of the basic community psychology concepts of respect for the diversity of individuals who need services, the empowerment of individuals or their family systems to deal with problems, and the recognition of multiple levels of intervention required to adequately address the full ecology of the mental health needs. Last, for those who continue to require institutional care, we review an effort to shift the social and environmental contexts within the institutions. A program to "reduce the use of restraints" takes an approach to change the physical environments and the social and professional assumptions related to patients and their care, so as to shift the need for restraints in the institutional environment. We begin with an examination of one of the earlier studies of providing an alternative, community based environment to SMI, the Lodge Society.

Lodge Society. It is sad to note that community psychologists and mental health care experts know more about what does *not* work rather than what *does* work with people who are mentally disordered. However, coupled with the knowledge gained from pioneer programs such as the **Lodge Society** (Fairweather, 1980; Fairweather, Sanders,

Maynard, & Cressler, 1969) and epidemiological investigations, some innovative psychosocial rehabilitation models (Bond, Miller, & Krumweid, 1988; Bond, Witheridge, Dincin, & Wasmer, 1991; Bond et al., 1990; Olfson, 1990) have been developed for treating people with mental disorders. Fairweather's concept of lodge societies encompassed structured *halfway houses* or group homes for the mentally disabled that emphasized *skill building* and *shared responsibility* as well as *decision making*. The concept of empowerment was clearly a central part of his program (Fairweather & Fergus, 1993). The long-standing effectiveness of the model and its derivatives serves to demonstrate the workable nature of such community interventions. The Coalition for Community Living (downloaded on December 6, 2008 from the website, http://theccl.org) reported that as of the end of 2008, there were 90 Lodge programs sited across the United States. A study of 25 of these programs in 2007 showed residents' medication compliance rate (staying on their medications) to average 99% and rehospitalization rates to be at 60%.

Intensive Case Management

Common to the newer models is the use of **intensive case management (ICM),** or intensive case support, including instruction in daily living skills (e.g., cooking and paying bills). Service delivery linking both monitoring and brokering of delivery of a variety of services performed by the case manager is also advocated (Snowden, 1992). In other words, a case manager (usually a social worker) works *closely* with former mental patients, possibly being on call 24 hours a day for any emergency that might arise. Also, case management can easily be integrated into **residential** or outpatient treatments.

It is thought that intensive social support in the form of case management should mitigate recidivism or relapse. Compared to traditional treatments (e.g., outpatient), case management is labor-intensive. However, research indicates that case management "repeatedly has been shown to reduce both hospital use and costs across a number of different studies performed in different communities . . . although other desirable effects (e.g., symptom reduction, improved social relationships, . . .) have been less than robust" (Levine et al., 1993, p. 529). These findings are understandable, given the complex nature of mental disorder. As you may recall, even when housing is not a problem, improved social relationships are contingent on many different people—the patient being just one of the many.

Nelson, Aubrey, and Lafrance (2007) differentiate ICM from Assertive Community Treatment in that ICM does not employ a team approach. The case receives close supervision and help in accomplishing the tasks necessary to survive in normal life, but there is not the interdisciplinary perspective that the Assertive Community Treatment approach brings.

Assertive Community Treatment. One especially powerful variation on the case management model is **Assertive Community Treatment (ACT),** known variously as *mobile treatment teams* and *assertive case management.* It is designed "to improve the community functioning of clients with serious and persistent mental illness, thereby diminishing their dependence on inpatient care while improving the quality of life" (Bond et al., 1990, p. 866). ACT focuses on teaching practical living skills, such as how to shop for groceries and maintain finances. A multidisciplinary team of professionals provides group case management, lending their various expertise and resources to the conceptualization of the case needs and to the interventions called into play. ACT ensures attention to medications, service planning, and coordination, as well as assessment and evaluations. Assertive community treatment uses a low staff–client ratio—approximately 10:1. Moreover, clients do not visit staff offices but rather staff visit clients in vivo—that is, in their own environments.

Stein and Test (1985) developed one of the first ACT programs in the United States in Madison, Wisconsin. Wanting more research on ACT, Bond and colleagues (1990) compared ACT clients to clients at a drop-in center. Drop-in centers usually provide an informal meeting place for clients who typically are formerly institutionalized mental patients. These centers offer a range of social and recreational programs in a self-help atmosphere. In sharp contrast to ACT, drop-in centers have a central meeting place, a higher client–staff ratio, and no requirement for frequent staff contact.

Bond and associates (1990) found overall that after one year, 76 percent of the ACT clients were still involved in ACT, whereas only 7 percent of the drop-in clients were involved in their programs. The ACT staff team averaged only two home and community visits per week per client, but their clients averaged significantly fewer state hospital admissions and fewer days per hospital stay. The researchers estimated that ACT saved over $1,500 per client per year. ACT clients themselves reported greater satisfaction with their program, fewer contacts with the police, and more stable community housing than clients from the drop-in center.

Assertive community treatment takes an ecological approach to clients. The staff is assertive in offering assistance to clients and capitalizing on client strengths, the latter of which meets the tenets of community psychology. ACT prevents further client deterioration and provides a strong community alternative to hospitalization. Finally, ACT uses a holistic approach with each client as well as integration of services (Mowbray, 1990), all within the philosophies of the field of community psychology introduced at the beginning of this book.

These studies are, however, not without criticism, although other reviewers (Mowbray, 1990) have questioned why community psychologists have not been *more* involved in research on ACT and the seriously mentally disordered. Toro (1990), for example, suggested that the study had differential and therefore biasing drop-in ratios in the two groups. Toro also argued that such research indicates that even though ACT prevents rehospitalization, more research is needed on its impact in other domains, such as employment and social relationships. Salem (1990) concluded that a more thorough investigation of consumer- or client-run programs is needed, as well as more diversity among interventions for people with mental disabilities.

Nelson et al. (2007) reviewed comparison studies of ACT, ICM, and housing programs for SMI clients. They found that the provision of permanent housing for SMI clients led to reduced rates of institutional recidivism. In addition, the ACT programs resulted in better housing outcomes, with ICM the least successful of the newer models. Otherwise, those in ACT and ICM usually reported better community functioning and better feelings about themselves. One of the studies suggested the provision of ACT to be more expensive than standard treatment. Nelson et al. (2007) remark that ACT and ICM appear to reduce homelessness and hospitalization and improve community functioning. Though the intervention may be initially more costly, the reduction in institutionalization costs compensates for these temporary and superficial upfront expenditures (Rosenhack, Kasprow, Frisman, & Liu-Mares, 2003).

Wraparound Milwaukee. These types of comprehensive programs are not just limited to adult SMI populations. Wraparound Milwaukee is a multiyear program targeting youth with "serious emotional disorders," who are at risk for institutionalization in the mental health or legal system, and their families. The key characteristics of the program are (1) a strengths-based strategy to children and families, (2) family involvement in the treatment process, (3) a needs-based services planning and delivery (see Figure 6.1), (4) an individualized service plan, and (5) an outcome-focused approach. These approaches are structurally integrated into and implemented by four structural components: (1) care coordination, (2) the child and family team, (3) a mobile crisis team, and (4) a provider network. Over "80 mental health, social and support services" are provided within this plan.

The plan differs from others in that it focuses on the strengths of the child and the family systems, building on them so as to maintain the child in the community if possible. It points to the uniqueness of each case and honors it by providing choices and individualized programs for each client/family. It speaks of empowering families to work with their children. Toward that end, there are family social events, satisfaction surveys, and recruitment of families to serve on program committees and in program training. There is a 24-hour Mobile Urgent Treatment Team (MUTT), available to all clients and their families. The outcome focus of the program is to reduce the need for institutionalization.

The program "sustains itself by pooling dollars from its system partners and taking an integrated, multiservice approach . . . based on the Wraparound philosophy and the managed care model, offers care that is tailored to each youth" (Kamradt, 2000, p. 14). An innovative feature is the blending of funding (Medicaid, Supplemental Security Income, and other insurances) to maximize quality of care based on a case management model. It is estimated that "child welfare and juvenile justice systems fund Wraparound at $3,000 per

FIGURE 6.1 Services in the Wraparound Milwaukee Benefit Plan

Care coordination	Crisis home care
In-home therapy	Treatment foster care
Medication management	Residential treatment
Outpatient—individual family therapy	Foster care
Alcohol/substance abuse counseling	Day treatment/alternative school
Psychiatric assessment	Nursing assessment/management
Psychological evaluation	Job development/placement
Housing assistance	Kinship care
Mental health assessment/evaluation	Transportation services
Mentoring	Supervision/observation in home
Parent aide	After-school programming
Group home care	Recreation/child-oriented
Respite care	Discretionary funds/flexible funds
Child care for parent	Housekeeping/chore services
Tutor	Independent living support
Specialized camps	Psychiatric inpatient hospital
Emergency food pantry	

Source: Adapted from Kamradt (2000).

TABLE 6.2 Recidivism Rates of Delinquent Youth Enrolled in Wraparound Milwaukee (n = 134)

OFFENSE	1 YEAR PRIOR TO ENROLLMENT	1 YEAR POSTENROLLMENT*
Sex offense	11%	1%
Assaults	14%	7%
Weapons offenses	15%	4%
Property offenses	34%	17%
Drug offenses	6%	3%
Other offenses (primarily disorderly conduct without a weapon)	31%	15%

*Data collected and analyzed as of September 1999.
Source: Adapted from B. Kamradt (2000).

month per child. Prior to Wraparound, these funds were used entirely for residential treatment care systems [that] paid $5,000 or more per month per child" (Kamradt, 2000, p. 18).

Preliminary results of the program indicates that use of residential treatment has decreased by 60 percent (from an average daily census of 364 placements to fewer than 140 since the inception of Wraparound Milwaukee). Inpatient psychiatric hospitalization has dropped by 80 percent (see Table 6.2). These positive results have continued. In an annual report for 2005, Wraparound Milwaukee reported seeing over 1,000 youth (http://www.county.milwaukee.gov/WraparoundMilwaukee7851.htm). The program continues to demonstrate the targeted youth as having decreases in legal offenses, increases in school performance, and more positive parent evaluations. The president's New Freedom Commission on Mental Health named Wraparound Milwaukee as a model program in 2004.

THE BATTLE CONTINUES: WHERE DO WE GO FROM HERE?

Although having a mental disorder still incurs a stigma in society, the general public has become more familiar with mental health and mental illness. This awareness is responsible, in part, for the formation of the National Alliance for the Mentally Ill (NAMI). NAMI functions as more than a self-help group; it also operates as a political lobbying body. It is estimated that in 2008 NAMI has about 1,100 affiliates in the country with a membership of about 130,000. NAMI is a key player in the ongoing mental health care reform. At the local level, individual chapter members provide support to each other as well as educate the public via educational activities, including education about medication and rehabilitative services.

Some psychosocial models based on the concept of case management and political efforts such as those engaged by NAMI appear to be hopeful for the mentally disabled. Mental health care continues to struggle with stigma and stereotype, short- and long-term focus, responsibilities and cost, and the public will to address these issues. Although community psychologists and mental health care professionals can help empower the mentally ill using appropriate and culturally sensitive intervention models, mental health care reform must *not* be carried out in isolation from other health agendas. Mental health care needs to be framed within a *unified* health care agenda. Research (D'Ercole, Skodol, Struening, Curtis, & Millman, 1991; Levine & Huebner, 1991; Susser, Valencia, et al., 1993; U.S. Surgeon General, 1999) indicates that physical health and mental health are interdependent, such as the case of drug abuse among many homeless mentally disordered people. D'Ercole and colleagues found that physical illnesses among psychiatric patients tended to be underdiagnosed when using the traditional psychiatric diagnostic tools of the DSM-IV. This was especially true for older and female patients. These findings suggest that poor physical health is likely to exacerbate existing poor mental health, which can become a vicious circle.

Knowledge that community psychologists have gained in the past 30-plus years about health issues (mental health and mental illness in particular) strongly cautions us against the false optimism of the 1960s. No one should be denied mental health care services simply because she or he cannot afford to pay. The quality of services must *not* be contingent on amount of payment. The community as a whole must address these problems one way or another. Mental illness is addressed in our policies for the homeless, those in prison, the rehospitalized, or those within our communities.

Meanwhile, the demands on the system are rising. According to Torrey (1997), approximately 150,000 people with mental illness are homeless on a given day, and another 150,000 are in jails and prisons. The aging baby boomers pose another challenge for caring for the older or elderly mentally ill (Hatfield, 1997). Each of these scenarios demands a somewhat different response or strategy, although the populations are not mutually exclusive. Estimates were that 26% of the U.S. population has a diagnosable mental disorder (Kessler, et al., 2005). As of December, 2008, the estimated population for the United States has reached over 300,000,000 (as downloaded on December 6, 2008 from http://www.census.gov/population/www/popclockus.html). The number 78,000,000, which is 26% of the population, seems almost incomprehensible.

Proponents such as Breakey (1996) have argued that the pressure of managed care on psychiatry and clinical psychology is likely to limit the role of these clinicians. That is, the type of care that is not reimbursable is not allowed. Although evidence (e.g., ACT, Wraparound Milwaukee) reviewed in this chapter suggests that people with mental illness who receive *integrated services* tend to fare better than those who do not receive such services, integrated care comes with a bigger initial price tag (real dollar and other human capitals and resources) (Sharstein, 2000). Can we be farsighted enough to pay the bill? What role does community psychology play in communicating the advantages of tertiary prevention over traditional services?

On the other end of the continuum, influential psychiatrists such as Torrey (1997) have argued that recent discoveries in biological psychiatry indicate that "severe psychiatric disorders are no more linked to minor mental perturbations than are multiple sclerosis or Parkinson's disease. Their proper treatment demands expertise in brain physiology and pharmacology, rather than human relationships" (p. B5). Torrey argued for a formal separation or "divorce" of mental health (in this case, including community psychology) from psychiatry. Resources should be redirected to allow psychiatry to merge with neurology

> to produce researchers and clinicians who possess expertise on the full spectrum of brain diseases. This would place neuropsychiatry as a single entity exactly where it was 100 years ago, before the Freudian revolution and the mental-hygiene movement led it to focus on general mental health rather than the most severe mental disorders. (1997, p. B5)

This is both provocative and ominous! Given the rapid advancement in medical technology, it is all too easy to lose sight of the human side of feelings and behaviors. The atmosphere of managed care certainly aids in this process. These issues no doubt confuse the debate over whether clinical psychologists should have the right to prescribe psychotropic medications. Currently, a small number of clinical psychologists who have gone through a pilot training program are allowed to prescribe psychotropic medications. This issue is more than just identity politics—the reality is that being able to prescribe such medications translates to another revenue for reimbursable services.

In the foreseeable future, people in community psychiatry and community mental health have an unenviable task: to argue that integrated care (e.g., case management) is the norm. Meanwhile, the shift to an emphasis in biological psychiatry could hinder work already under study in areas such as social support and development of personal resources. Hopefully, the work being done on resilience (see Chapter 3), with its emphasis on multilevel interactive processes will bring better appreciation of the interplay between the biological, the personal, the social, and the institutional variables affecting well-being. The field of mental health services continues to increase in its utilization of the ecological model (Bronfenbrenner, 1977; Kelly, 1990, 2002) for understanding the human experience.

Heller, Jenkins, et al. (2000) mark the neglect of prevention programs in the traditional mental health care programs. Others have noted the problems of prevention programs, which may have detectable results a decade or two later, and the economic pressures to demonstrate present savings to the system (Felner, Jason, Moritsugu, & Riger, 1983). Nonetheless, prevention has been demonstrated to work, focusing on children and working with those systems that are important to the lives of those children, that is, families and schools (Albee & Gullotta, 1997; Durlak & Wells, 1997; Heller, 1990; Ialongo et al., 2006). The aim of these prevention programs is of course to divert the trajectory of the potential mental health client, providing personal and social resources that may aid in dealing with life stressors and in learning life tasks (see Chapter 3 regarding resilience and social support). The present chapter is very much aware of these programs and their potentials. However, the focus here is on tertiary prevention for cases within the mental health system. That system has a lack of prevention programs.

A second notable concern raised by Heller, Jenkins, et al. (2000) is the lack of natural communities in the first community mental health center formulations (Hunter & Riger, 1986). The concept of a *catchment area* (geographic region that the community mental health center served) used large areas based on street boundaries. There was no sense of naturally defined neighborhoods, whose strengths and existing networks could be brought to bear on problems. This shortcoming may now be addressed by the inclusion of communities in devising programs and research for themselves via the participatory action research models that are growing in use.

SUMMARY

The presence of mental health concerns in the U.S. population has been studied for several decades, and the results draw a sobering conclusion. The prevalence of mental illness is substantial, and the possibility of some disturbance within one's lifetime is nearly one in two.

Yet there is a concentration of disorders in a smaller segment of the population, usually with multiple problems co-occurring. For these few, the impact of mental illness is devastating.

Our traditional models of mental health are individual-focused and reactive in nature. The shortcomings of these models have led us to the community perspective with its preventive orientation and ecological perspective.

Although a historical overview of treatment for mental illness shows a progression toward more humanitarian and inclusive treatment, the deinstitutionalization of the mentally ill has not come without major problems. A casual review of the field of mental health and illness indicates that there is a great deal of controversy about exactly what deinstitutionalization is. Some have argued that a better term is *transinstitutionalization* to describe the dumping of patients from one setting to another. Also, the characteristics of the mentally disabled have changed in the past 30-plus years. Now, ethnic minorities constitute a sizable sample of the mentally disordered, and they are likely to be undetected by the existing systems.

The common placement for a deinstitutionalized individual is, interestingly, another institution—possibly jail or prison. Many of the deinstitutionalized end up among the homeless. We measure successful functioning of the mentally ill in their community in terms of social integration and recidivism, or rate of return to the psychiatric hospital, but the economic indicators of cost have remained important determinants to policy decisions. Most analyses of success focus on problems of the individual, but the environment plays a significant role in successes or failures. Depersonalization of services can also account for problems faced by deinstitutionalized individuals. Lack of adequate or integrated support can lead to problems, especially for those who have lost their natural social supports or who have care needs beyond the resources of those supports.

The ideal that led to the enactment of the Community Mental Health Act in the 1960s has not been fully realized. Now it seems obvious that one reason for the existing patchwork system is the lack of systematic planning or poor coordination.

Innovative psychosocial rehabilitation models have been developed for treating the mentally disordered. Common to these models are the provision of comprehensive, integrated, and personal programs for identified clients, which include forms of daily living skill training and empowerment of the support systems that help these clients. These may be the natural systems, such as families and friends, or might be the formal systems of agencies and programs that offer services. Individualized case management and smaller case loads that allow for that can be very helpful.

Although community psychologists and mental health care professionals can empower the mentally ill by using appropriate and culturally sensitive intervention models, mental health care reform must *not* be carried out in isolation from other health agendas. That is, mental health care needs to be framed within a *unified* health care agenda. A holistic approach with an understanding of the interactions of the mind and body, and transactions of ecological settings seems the prescription for treatments of the future, based on the extant research in our communities at present. There is a lot of promise yet to be realized.

CHAPTER 7

SOCIAL AND HUMAN SERVICES IN THE COMMUNITY

HISTORICAL NOTES ABOUT SOCIAL WELFARE IN WESTERN SOCIETY
- **CASE IN POINT 7.1**   Poverty In America
- **CASE IN POINT 7.2**   The Grameen Bank

SPECIFIC SOCIAL ISSUES AND SOCIAL SERVICES
Child Maltreatment
  Scope of the Issue
  Causes of Maltreatment
  Prevention Programs
Teen Pregnancy
  Scope of the Issue
  Causes of Teen Pregnancy
  Prevention Programs
  Secondary Prevention: Working with Pregnant Teens
The Elderly
  Scope of the Issue
  Prevention Programs
Homelessness
  Scope of the Issue
- **CASE IN POINT 7.3**   How Do Cultures Differ On The Issue Of Homelessness?
  Causes of Homelessness
  Prevention Programs

SUMMARY

> *Of all the people in the world, 852 million are chronically hungry; every day, almost 16,000 children die from hunger-related causes.*
> —MCC.org/food

> *An empty sack cannot stand up*
> —Haitian proverb

Rock was a high school senior. His girlfriend, Monique, was a sophomore in the same school. Both teenagers lived in middle-class suburban homes. Rock was bored with his humdrum life in the suburbs and liked to "live on the edge." He listened to the newest music, had many tattoos, smoked weed, and liked to thrill ride on his motorcycle. His unpredictability and careless living attracted Monique to Rock, although neither set of parents was thrilled with their child's choice of dating partner. Monique's parents were especially displeased because her mother thought several pieces of her gold jewelry were missing and might have found their way into Rock's pockets.

Both Rock and Monique had a history of cutting classes and occasionally not coming home for several days. Rock taught Monique to buy and smoke marijuana early in their relationship, and their use increased as the relationship progressed. They ultimately were caught smoking marijuana behind their school. Because both were minors, the judge ordered them to enroll in a drug-treatment program.

The treatment program was one of a dozen funded by a federal agency in collaboration with two state agencies. The goal of the program was to *prevent* (not intervene or treat) youths from using alcohol and other drugs. Past research has shown that youths who have various risk factors (e.g., cutting class and stealing) are more likely to use or abuse drugs than those who do not. Thus, youths who have certain risk factors were identified by the child and family welfare divisions of governmental sponsored social services and were referred to the drug-treatment programs at another state agency.

In the case of Rock, he was ordered by the court (rather than identified by the child and family welfare agency) to enroll in the drug-treatment program. After intake, he was immediately placed into one of the programs. He was to participate in both individual and group counseling. Family counseling with Rock's parents was provided on a limited basis because the program was mainly designed for drug treatment.

Monique's treatment placement was still pending because during her intake, it was discovered that she was pregnant. The state agency responsible for the drug-treatment programs did not accept pregnant clients. Thus, staff at both state agencies did not know what to do with Monique. Both agencies were also experiencing some difficulty in complying with all of the requirements of the federal agency that funded their drug-treatment programs.

Since the inception of the drug-treatment programs, several major political changes at the state level had led to a leadership vacuum at the state agencies. The two executive directors of the respective agencies resigned after the governor announced that she would not seek reelection. A consequence was the lack of coordination of the patient referral process.

Meanwhile, direct-care staff felt strongly that alcohol and other drug abuse in youths was likely to be symptomatic of other issues, including parent–child and school problems. Moreover, most of these youths were already using or abusing some form of drug; therefore, to talk about prevention was utter folly. However, since the government funding agency focused on prevention, the staff was obligated to comply by educating about prevention of use of drugs.

This true story illustrates that social problems often do not have a single cause and do not develop in isolation. In the case of Rock and Monique, direct-care staff appeared to be correct in that drug treatment for both teens was merely treating their symptom (marijuana use) but not the cause(s) (e.g., school alienation and generational conflicts between parents and children). Moreover, Monique needed a treatment program that specialized in drug rehabilitation for pregnant women. However, staff at the drug-treatment program was limited by resources and expertise. Here is a good example of the inappropriate depletion of limited and sometimes scarce social and human resources. As you can see from this case, effective social services delivery is contingent on good organizational infrastructure and management.

This chapter begins with a review of what poverty is and, because of it, how social services emerged in Western society. Poverty, although not the cause of Rock and Monique's situation, is one of the root causes of many societal problems and affects all of us, whether or not we are poor (Grogan-Kaylor, 2005; Rank, 2005). The chapter then reviews selected social and human services as well as affected groups.

HISTORICAL NOTES ABOUT SOCIAL WELFARE IN WESTERN SOCIETY

What is **poverty?** Does poverty merely mean the lack of sufficient money to acquire essential things to survive, such as food? Or does poverty mean being born and living in a ghetto or slum, which might lead to attending a substandard school and might further lead to a vicious circle of unemployment and subsequent homelessness (Hochschild, 2003)? Probably, the latter notion is what President Lyndon B. Johnson had in mind when he made his 1964 State of the Union address about the War on Poverty. Poverty is not just about lacking money; it is also about a sense of hopelessness and perhaps racial or ethnic discrimination (Yang & Barrett, 2006). For example, without a good education, an individual is unlikely to find a decent-paying job. Poorly educated people are less likely to be well-informed citizens—especially about their basic rights and entitlements—compared to those who are educated. Poverty affects all of us, not just the poor, in myriad ways and is not just about individual shortcomings but about economic structures and failed political policies (Rank, 2005).

With these thoughts in mind, we are ready to examine the effectiveness of public assistance, one objective of which is to lift people from poverty and from other social problems so that they can move on to a better life. First, Case in Point 7.1 provides some compelling and alarming statistics about poverty in the world and, in particular, the United States.

CASE IN POINT 7.1
POVERTY IN AMERICA

Community psychologists and other experts consider poverty the number one social problem in the United States as well as the root cause of many other social problems, such as delinquency, substance abuse, school problems, crime, and homelessness. Here are some startling statistics about poverty both in the United States and worldwide. As you sip your $4 mocha latte and read these statistics found at two Web sites dedicated to combatting poverty (solvingpoverty.com and ch08.org), you may have to try hard to imagine yourself living in poverty.

(continued)

CASE IN POINT 7.1 CONTINUED

- Worldwide, 25,000 people die each day of hunger; every 3.5 seconds, someone in the world dies of hunger.
- In the United States, one in eight or 36.5 million people live in poverty. The 2008 federal poverty guideline is that a family of two that lives on less than $14,000 a year lives in poverty.
- In the United States, 15.4 million Americans live in *extreme* poverty (that is, they live at less than half of the federal poverty guidelines).
- The United States leads all industrialized nations in child poverty.
- Poverty rates for African Americans, Latinos, and single mothers are the highest—in some cases, twice that of White men.
- Forty-seven million Americans are without health insurance; one in every five adults did not receive needed medical attention in 2006 due to lack of insurance or inability to pay.
- Food stamp programs provide only $1 per meal per person. Could you live on that?

According to Handel (1982), **social welfare** is "a set of ideas and a set of activities and organizations for carrying out those ideas, all of which have taken shape over many centuries, to provide people with income and other social benefits in ways that safeguard their dignity" (p. 31). Without sounding simplistic, this seemingly innocuous statement describes the complex nature of social welfare. Social welfare serves both ideological (e.g., political and religious) and practical (e.g., inability to provide for oneself) concerns.

Until modern times, one major form of social welfare was charity, otherwise known as philanthropy. **Charity/philanthropy** refers to social welfare in which a **donor** (voluntary giver) assists a **recipient** (beneficiary). An example of this is when an individual donates money to Habitat for Humanity so that this nonprofit organization can buy building materials to help a homeless family build a house. The nature of charity/philanthropy is largely a function of the ideology of the time period. For example, research indicates that during religious seasons (e.g., Christmas and Passover), people are more likely to be charitable than during nonreligious seasons. **Public welfare,** on the other hand, is where the government (rather than private donors) assumes responsibility for the poor or for recipients of aid who have not contributed to this particular system of aid.

Charity/philanthropy and public welfare are likely to create social stigmas whereby some individuals hold negative views of those who require such aid (Applebaum, Lennon, & Lawrence, 2006; Cadena, Danziger, & Seefeldt, 2006). Specifically, Handel (1982) succinctly argued that recipients of social welfare

> are widely believed to be lazy and immoral.... Although recipients must prove their need, their claims are often thought to be fraudulent.... These people receive less social honor than other members of society. Such methods of providing income are therefore regarded as demeaning, as impairing the dignity of the people who depend upon them. (pp. 8–9)

Even recipients of social welfare are likely to have a negative view of themselves (Chan, 2004; Sennett, 2003) or of other recipients (Coley, Kuta, & Chase-Lansdale, 2000).

Moving beyond these so-called traditional forms of social welfare, we now turn to two more modern forms of social welfare: social service and social insurance. **Social services** (*non*materialistic benefits) are an offshoot of charity/philanthropy. Derived from the

19th century, the government uses taxes to provide *services rather than direct monetary aid*. A major goal of social services is to ensure and maintain a productive workforce via prevention of or intervention in social problems. Rock and Monique, the two teenagers in the opening vignette, were the recipients of social services (e.g., treatment programs from the substance-abuse agency). It was hoped that these services could prevent (or intervene with) both youths from becoming more dependent on marijuana or other drugs in the years to come.

Social insurance (or **public assistance,** as it is otherwise known) has its origin in the 19th century, around the time of the Industrial Revolution. The basic premise of social insurance is that the government assumes responsibility for individuals *who may have contributed in some way to the assistance system*. The funds for these systems generally derive from taxes. In other words, the *difference* between public welfare and social insurance (i.e., public assistance) is that "the recipients of social insurance are receiving benefits that have been earned by work, either their own, or work by someone else on their behalf" (Handel, 1982, p. 15), whereas recipients of public welfare do not contribute to this process. Because Monique had never held a job, if she turned to the government for benefits for her baby, she would be deemed in the strictest sense to be on public welfare, not on public assistance. Some well-known programs of social insurance/public assistance in this country include Medicare (health care for the elderly), Social Security (unemployment and disability benefits or old-age pensions for the formerly employed), and veterans' benefits. Eligibility guidelines (e.g., the federal poverty guidelines, for example) are established by the government and can often be cumbersome and Byzantine.

Public welfare programs have changed under the Personal Responsibility and Work Opportunity Reconciliation Act of 1996. Public welfare recipients now have to transition to full- or part-time work and cannot remain indefinitely on government assistance except under certain stringent circumstances. Interestingly, research demonstrates that most welfare recipients would like to work (Allen, 2000; Bell, 2007; Scott, London, & Edin, 2000). Perhaps one reason for their motivation is that such assistance, as mentioned previously, creates a social stigma against the recipients as well as diminishing recipients' own sense of dignity.

This seemingly more enlightened view of public welfare is emerging in the United States among the public and some government officials. First, there is growing concern that people should be less dependent on public welfare. Such assistance is seen as degrading and stigmatizing. Second, recipients should be encouraged to work; that is, incentives to encourage work should be more available than incentives to encourage dependence on public assistance. This appears to be the underlying philosophy of the Personal Responsibility and Work Opportunity Reconciliation Act of 1996, already mentioned (Scott, London, & Edin, 2000). Third, there is growing recognition that if employment participation is mandatory, employment should make families better off by working rather than by not working. Some recent studies have found that movement into employment and away from public welfare is associated with increases in income and personal well-being but may have little effect on other aspects of family life, such as parenting skills or home environments (e.g., Coley, Lohman, Votruba-Drzal, Pittman, & Chase-Lansdale, 2007). At the time of this writing, results of other studies on welfare-to-work programs are mixed (e.g. Cadena et al., 2006), so more research is needed to sort out the effects of this new effort. Interestingly, other countries have instituted very different alternatives to welfare as a means of reducing poverty; for example, read Case in Point 7.2 on the award-winning program at the Grameen Bank.

CASE IN POINT 7.2
THE GRAMEEN BANK

Can a small loan (microcredit) of $25 to $50 "cure" poverty? An interesting experiment is under way worldwide. The experiment in microcredit is known as the Grameen Bank. Founder Muhammad Yunus was struck by the extreme poverty, especially of women, in Bangladesh. In 1976, with some difficulty, he took out a loan from a bank and distributed the money to poor women in Bangladesh. In fact, his loans went to the poorest of the poor. The small loans are generally used by the women to begin their own cottage-type industries, such as raising farm animals and producing or creating crafts to sell. Yunus views microcredit as a cost-effective weapon to fight poverty. He could not, however, convince any traditional banks to continue loaning money to the poor, so he started his own bank, the Grameen Bank, and continued his microcredit loan program.

The Grameen Bank uses principles that run counter to traditional banking wisdom. It seeks the poorest borrowers. No collateral is necessary for a loan. Instead, the system is based on trust, accountability, participation, and creativity. Borrowers are required to join the bank in groups of five; the group members provide each other with support and advice.

The Grameen Bank is now the largest rural financial institution in Bangladesh, with more than 7.34 million borrowers in over 80,000 villages. Furthermore, in line with community psychology, the bank brings the loans *to* the people, rather than the other way around. Of course, community problems cannot always be solved by merely throwing money at people, but in this instance, the amount of money is nominal, and the return is enormous.

A cogent question is this: Do the Grameen Bank and microcredit have a positive and long-term effect on these impoverished individuals? The answer is a resounding "yes." First, over 98 percent of the loans are repaid, indicating that people are not always looking for a free handout. Second, the bank has a positive effect on both the women and their children. Independent research demonstrates that the women's economic security and status within the family are elevated. The children of the women are better schooled and healthier than other children in the community. Best of all, extreme poverty (as defined by the United Nations) declines by more than 70 percent within five years of the borrowers joining the bank.

Elsewhere in this chapter, some information on how poverty is measured in the United States (e.g., annual household income for various size families) is provided. The Grameen Bank measures poverty level in completely different and more functional and practical ways. Staff members monitor borrowers to determine whether their quality of life is improving. For example, if a family successfully owns a house with a metal roof, has a sanitary latrine, drinks potable water, finally has adequate clothes for everyday use, eats three square meals a day, gains access to schooling for the children, and has reasonable access to health care, then that family is considered to have moved beyond poverty. Would such a program work in the United States? Yunus thinks not. Costs in the United States are such that the operations would be far more expensive. However, individuals from other nations have completed Grameen Bank training so as to create replication programs in dozens of different countries.

The Grameen Bank concept for addressing poverty has been so successful that in 2006 Muhammad Yunus and the Grameen Bank were awarded the Nobel Peace Prize. Muhammad Yunus, by the way, has a degree in economics, not in community psychology. He is living proof that professionals from many disciplines can come together to address serious community issues such as poverty.

Adapted from Yunus (1999, 2007) and www.grameen-info.org.

Because welfare-to-work programs appear to have mixed results (Geen, Fender, Leos-Urbel, & Markowitz, 2001), such programs are not without their critics. Piven and Cloward (1996) noted that proponents claim miraculous social and cultural transformations that are unrealistic, such as increased family cohesion and lower crime rates. Piven and Cloward viewed such welfare-to-work programs as nothing more than a class war between the haves and the have-nots. Opulente and Mattaini (1997) suggested that sanction-based programs (such as the Personal Responsibility and Work Opportunity Reconciliation Act) are likely to be ineffective and produce undesirable side effects, such as anger. Wilson, Ellwood, and Brooks-Gunn (1996) and also Cadena et al. (2006) have offered the criticism that the best research methods are not being used to examine the outcomes and processes of such programs. Finally, Aber, Brooks-Gunn, and Maynard (1995) as well as Coley et al. (2007) concluded that welfare-to-work programs do little to enhance children of poor parents. In fact, poor children continue to be exposed to more family turmoil, family separation, and instability; come from more polluted environments; live in more dangerous neighborhoods; and experience more cumulative risk factors than wealthier children (Evans, 2004).

SPECIFIC SOCIAL ISSUES AND SOCIAL SERVICES

Many groups access social and human services for a variety of reasons. To evaluate and judge the effectiveness or impact of these services, a consensus of standards is essential. According to Price et al. (1988), model programs possess one or more of five characteristics.

1. These programs have a specific target audience.
2. The goal of these programs is to make a long-term and significant impact on the target groups, thus enhancing their well-being.
3. The programs provide the necessary skills for the recipients to achieve their objectives.
4. The programs strengthen the natural support from family, community, or school settings.
5. The programs have evaluative mechanisms to document their success.

Using these criteria as standards, our attention turns to four groups to examine the problems, people, and interventions to the problems within social and human services systems. These groups have been selected for several reasons. First, these groups are large or growing in number. Second, some of these groups are currently receiving much media attention, including maltreated children and pregnant teens. Third, all four groups have received attention to some extent in the field of community psychology. The groups are maltreated and neglected children, pregnant teens (like Monique), the elderly, and homeless individuals.

Child Maltreatment

Child maltreatment is a complex and emotionally charged issue. Let's commence by defining the issue and then move to information on its scope. Defining child maltreatment is very difficult, so there is no universally agreed-on definition. One reason for definitional difficulties is that each culture sets its own generally accepted principles of child-rearing, child care, and discipline (Elliott & Urquiza, 2006; Runyan, Wattam, Ikeda, Hassan, & Ramiro, 2002). There is, however, general agreement across many cultures that child abuse should not be allowed and that harsh discipline and sexual abuse are not allowable at all (Runyan et al., 2002). Also making a clear definition difficult is the fact that some definitions take into account the impact or harm on the child, whereas others focus more on the behavior or actions of the perpetrators.

For now, let's use a broad definition as provided by the World Health Organization (WHO) (2004):

> Child abuse or maltreatment constitutes all forms of physical and/or emotional ill-treatment, sexual abuse, neglect or negligent treatment or commercial or other exploitation, resulting in actual or potential harm to the child's health, survival, development or dignity in the context of a relationship of responsibility, trust or power.

Scope of the Issue. The Centers for Disease Control and Prevention (CDC) (2007b) reported that in 2005 there were nearly 900,000 cases of verified child maltreatment and that almost 1,500 children died due to maltreatment in the United States. Worldwide, as many as 40 million children may be abused (WHO, 2004). Though these statistics are alarming, they need to be viewed with some qualifications because many authorities believe there is underreporting. Why? First, many child injuries and deaths are not routinely investigated, and postmortem examinations are not always carried out, which makes it difficult to establish the precise number of cases (CDC, 2006; Runyan et al., 2002). Furthermore, many cases of abuse and neglect are concealed from investigators, and there is great variation in how states review and report suspected cases. Medical personnel sometimes make inaccurate determinations of the manner and cause of injuries and death of children, too, for instance, blame a neglected child's death on sudden infant death syndrome. Additionally, investigations are often uncoordinated and not multidisciplinary in their approaches (CDC, 2006). Although these data are disheartening, recent trends indicate that child maltreatment may be declining. The exact causes for the decline and whether it is permanent or a fluke are still unknown (Finkelhor & Jones, 2006).

As shown in Figure 7.1, nearly 84 percent of victims were abused by a parent acting alone or in conjunction with another person. Approximately 40 percent of child victims were maltreated by their mothers; another 18.3 percent were maltreated by their fathers; and 17.3 percent were abused by both parents. Victims abused by nonparental perpetrators accounted for 10.7 percent. A nonparental perpetrator is defined as a caregiver who is not a parent and can include foster parents, child day-care staff, an unmarried partner of a parent, a legal guardian, or a residential facility staff member. Data for victims of specific maltreatment types can also be analyzed in terms of perpetrator relationship to the victim. Of the victims who experienced neglect, 86.6 percent were neglected by a parent. Of those who were sexually abused, 28.7 percent were abused by a relative other than a parent (Administration for Children and Families, 2005).

The toll of child abuse on the victim, family, community, and society are enormous and quite varied. Here are some of the consequences of maltreatment.

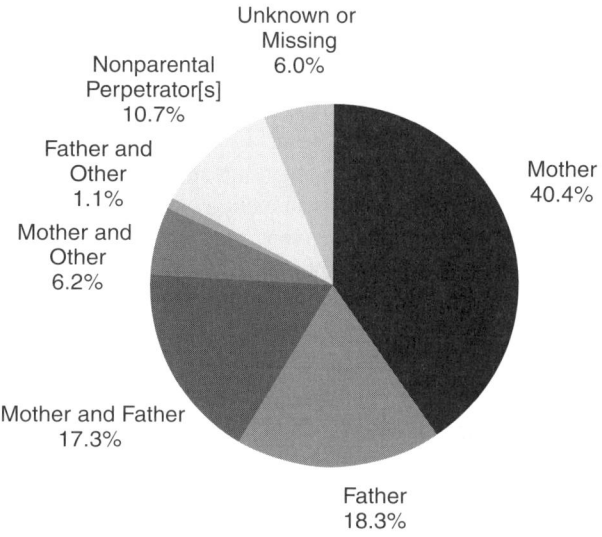

FIGURE 7.1 Victims by Perpetrator and Relationship, 2005

Source: Administration for Children and Famlies (2005). Child maltreatment. Washington, D.C. U.S. Department of Health and Human Services.

- Children who experience maltreatment are at increased risk for adverse health effects as adults, including smoking, alcoholism, drug abuse, eating disorders, severe obesity, depression, suicide, sexual promiscuity, and certain chronic diseases (Felitte et al., 1998; Runyan et al., 2002).
- Child abuse and neglect are associated with an increased risk of major depressive disorder in early adulthood (Widom, DuMont, & Czaja, 2007).
- Individuals with a history of child abuse and neglect are 1.5 times more likely to use illicit drugs, especially marijuana, in middle adulthood (Widom, Marmorstein, & White, 2006).
- Maltreatment during infancy or early childhood can cause important regions of the brain to form improperly, which can cause physical, mental, and emotional problems such as sleep disturbances, panic disorder, posttraumatic stress disorder, and attention deficit hyperactivity disorder (Cicchetti, 2007; Cicchetti & Valentino, 2006; U.S. Department of Health and Human Services, 2001a; Watts-English, Fortson, Gibler, Hooper, & De Bellis, 2006).
- Approximately 1,300 children experience severe or fatal head trauma as a result of abuse each year. Nonfatal consequences of abusive head trauma include varying degrees of visual impairment (e.g., blindness), motor impairment (e.g., cerebral palsy), and cognitive impairments (National Center on Shaken Baby Syndrome, 2005).
- Early child maltreatment can have a negative effect on the ability of both men and women to establish and maintain healthy intimate relationships in adulthood (Colman & Widom, 2004).
- Emotional and behavior dysregulation, school failure, and antisocial behaviors are consequences to the victims, too (Olds, Hill, & Rumsey, 1998).

The costs to society are monumental as well. Abused children in addition to the abusers, are typically the focus of intensive efforts from various social and human services specialists. Suspected cases of maltreatment are often investigated by the Department of Social Services and law enforcement. Abused children and their parents are often referred by judges and other professionals to mental health care providers for treatment. These direct costs are estimated at billions of dollars a year while indirect costs (such as long-term economic consequences) add additional billions annually.

Perhaps if we know the causes of maltreatment, we can better design prevention and intervention programs. We'll examine the complex causes next. From what you have learned already, try to determine if you think Monique and Rock might maltreat their expected child.

Causes of Maltreatment. There is widespread agreement among family violence experts that multiple factors are responsible for child maltreatment, such as stressors in the parents' lives, poverty, social isolation, and unrealistic expectations by parents of children. Studies have also identified poor prenatal care, dysfunctional caregiving, closely spaced unplanned pregnancies, dependence on welfare, community violence, and parental substance abuse among multiple causes. Researchers, therefore, need to look at several levels including (but not limited to) societal, institutional, and interpersonal factors as providing the explanatory framework for child maltreatment and other forms of family violence, such as partner violence. Societal factors, for example, can contribute to child maltreatment in the following ways. Poverty and economic downturn diminish the capacity for consistent and involved parenting. Parental job loss might produce pessimism and irritability in the parent. The parent might then become less nurturing and more arbitrary in interactions with the children.

Community psychologists would be quick to point out that other ecological factors contribute to child maltreatment. Indeed, child maltreatment may represent one of the greatest failures of the environment to offer opportunities for fostering wellness (Cicchetti, Toth, & Rogosch, 2000; Cicchetti & Valentino, 2006). Garbarino and Kostelny (1994; Garbarino & Kostelny, 1992;) investigated community dimensions in child maltreatment. They examined two predominantly African American and two predominantly Hispanic areas of Chicago. Some 60,000 child maltreatment cases were plotted for location for the years 1980, 1983, and 1986. Garbarino and Kostelny found significant location differences in maltreatment. As part of this same research, community leaders from social services agencies were also interviewed. The interviews revealed that high-risk locations were characterized by a lack of community identity, whereas low-risk areas were characterized by a sense of community or greater community cohesiveness. Garbarino concluded that abuse is not necessarily a sign of an individual or a family in trouble but a sign of a community in trouble. Other scientists agree that neighborhood factors, such as impoverishment (Coulton, Korbin, & Su, 1999) and community violence (Lynch, 2006) affect child maltreatment and child development as much as or more than individual risk factors. You'll read more about community disorder and disintegration in the chapter on crimes and communities.

Korbin and Coulton's (1996) research, in which they conducted in-depth interviews with residents in 13 high-, medium-, and low-risk census tracts in Cleveland, Ohio, also demonstrated that intervention efforts can be reoriented to the neighborhood level. They found that neighborhood conditions, such as distrust of neighbors and of social agencies as well as the dangers and incivilities of daily life, limit the abilities of neighbors to help one another act in the best interests of neighborhood children. Neighbors *do* feel that they should be able to help each other; in fact, many participants reported being optimistic that they could help prevent child maltreatment. However, neighborhood conditions often inhibited their willingness to do so. The researchers concluded that because economic and social conditions are inextricably bound together, child maltreatment prevention programs must be embedded within comprehensive efforts to strengthen communities.

Freisthler, Bruce, and Needell (2007) also examined how neighborhood characteristics were associated with rates of child maltreatment. Their study included 940 census tracts in California. Their results demonstrated that for Black children, higher rates of poverty and higher densities of off-premise alcohol outlets were positively associated with maltreatment rates. Percentage of female-headed families, poverty, and unemployment were positively related to maltreatment rates among Hispanic children. For White children, the percentage of elderly people, percentage of poverty, ratio of children to adults, and percentage of Hispanic residents were positively associated with neighborhood maltreatment rates. The researchers concluded that reducing neighborhood poverty may reduce rates of child maltreatment for all children, and efforts to prevent maltreatment at the neighborhood level may need to be tailored to specific neighborhood demographic characteristics to be most effective.

Just what efforts have been attempted to intercede in child maltreatment and neglect? Traditional efforts at intervention occur at the individual clinical level where maltreated children and their parents are given counseling to help overcome personal problems and understand the abuse. Although these methods may be laudable, they do little to prevent the abuse in the first place. This method of treatment is also difficult and expensive to implement on a wide scale. Moreover, these methods focus only on the individual or family and not on other ecological systems (e.g., poverty and community violence) that share responsibility.

Some people have argued that the best way to improve the situation for abusers and their victims is through national policies aimed at creating jobs, reducing unemployment and poverty, or providing income maintenance, such as welfare or public assistance. Prevention experts, like community psychologist, believe better and more realistic strategies can be aimed at high-risk groups *before* the maltreatment commences (Olds, 2005, 2006). Prevention of child maltreatment and neglect is certainly the more humane route to take.

Prevention Programs.   Perhaps one of the oldest, best known, and most highly acclaimed preventive programs is one designed by David Olds and his research team (Olds, Henderson, Chamberlin, & Tatelbaum, 1986; Olds et al., 1998). Their project, known in its earliest form as the Prenatal/Early Infancy Project and more recently as the Nurse-Family Partnership, provides nurse home visitation to prevent a wide range of maternal and child health problems associated with poverty, one of which is child abuse. Despite the usual criticisms of the program (see Chaffin, 2004; Olds, Eckenrode, & Kitzman, 2005), one of the aspects that makes it outstanding is that evaluation research typically is well designed, using randomly assigned experimental and control groups. Likewise, by recruiting a heterogeneous group of participants, these interventionists are better able to compare those who are not at risk for abuse with those who are.

Primiparous mothers (women having their first child) who are young, single parents, or from the lower socioeconomic class are welcomed into the program. The researchers want to avoid the appearance of being a program only for potential child abusers and on the other hand to ensure family engagement and avoid stigmatization. Olds and colleagues, therefore, have actively avoided labeling the program as one aimed at preventing maltreatment. Nevertheless, it was developed explicitly to reduce risk and at the same time promote protective factors associated with child abuse and neglect (Olds et al., 2005).

Nurses typically visit the participants' homes every other week during the prenatal (before birth) and the perinatal (after birth) periods. The mother's primary support person (perhaps her own mother, a friend, or the baby's father) is also invited to attend. Social support from the nurses and significant others is a vital component of this program. Even when abuse has already occurred, this type of social support is deemed important in preventing further maltreatment (secondary prevention).

The nurses carry out three major activities during their home visits: educating parents about fetal and infant development, promoting the involvement of family members and friends in support of the mother and care of the child, and developing linkages between family members and other formal health and human services in the community. In the education component, mothers and family members are encouraged to complete their own education and make decisions about employment and subsequent pregnancies. Before the baby's birth, the nurses concentrate on educating the prospective mothers to improve their diets and eliminate the use of cigarettes, drugs, and alcohol; recognize pregnancy complications; and prepare for labor, delivery, and care of the newborn. After the baby is born, the nurses concentrate on improving parents' understanding of the infants' temperaments and promoting the infants' socioemotional, cognitive, and physical development. The nurses also provide links to other formal services, such as health providers, mental health counselors, and nutritional supplement programs for mother and infants (Women, Infants, and Children [WIC] programs) (Olds, 2005, 2006).

One of the most important results of the program is on verified cases of child abuse and neglect. For women with all three risk characteristics (poor, unmarried, and adolescent) of abuse, there is usually a remarkable 80 percent difference in the incidence of verified cases of child abuse and neglect over the comparison (nonintervention) group. Remarkably, these differences persist at the 15-year follow-up. The mothers in the nurse-visited group also report that their infants are easier to care for. The interviewers of the mothers often observed less punishment and restriction of the mothers toward their children and a greater number of growth-promoting playthings in the homes of the nurse-visited mothers. The medical records of the nurse-visited families show fewer visits to emergency rooms for illnesses and fewer childhood accidents. This is true even for the women who report little sense of control over their lives when they first registered for the program. The results also hint at improved developmental life courses for the nurse-visited mothers, as well. For example, once these mothers become older and more employable, they work at their jobs longer than do their counterparts in the comparison group. Thus, program participants are less dependent on public welfare. The mothers also have fewer subsequent pregnancies, and both the mothers and their children are less likely to become entwined with the criminal justice system. Olds (1997, 2005; Olds et al., 1998) has replicated this program in several communities across the United States with equally impressive results. At present the program is being disseminated for public investment throughout the United States (Olds, 2007).

Research, however, has unveiled at least one limitation of the nurse home visit program. In homes where other forms of domestic violence are occurring, nurse home visitation is less effective at reducing child maltreatment (Eckenrode et al., 2000; Gomby, 2000). Further research has also shown that other, more long-term programs, such as ones based in schools where children are taught to identify abuse, especially sexual abuse, may be as effective as nurse home visitation programs (Davis & Gidycz, 2000).

The causes of child maltreatment are many. Cases of abuse keep large numbers of social workers and mental health professionals busy with the aftermath. However, Olds' and others' programs demonstrate that child maltreatment can be prevented. Expenditure of human and social service efforts at the outset may be more productive and humane, less destructive, and more cost effective than efforts after the fact.

Teen Pregnancy

Scope of the Issue. Adolescent pregnancy, like Monique's, has long been a concern, but the issue has recently become one of the most frequently cited examples of perceived social decay in the United States. Between 750,000 to 1 million teenagers become pregnant each year (McCave, 2007), with over 80 percent of the pregnancies unintended (National Campaign to Prevent Teen and Unwanted Pregnancy, 2008). Although the rate of teen pregnancy dropped in the mid-1990s, new data indicate that it is again on the rise (National Center for Health Statistics, 2007a). Adolescent birth rates in the United States still remain higher than those in other industrialized countries (CDC, 1999; Coley & Chase-Lansdale, 1998; National Campaign to Prevent Teen and Unwanted Pregnancy, 2008). Even though U.S. teenagers do not exhibit different patterns of sexual activity compared with teens from other countries, they use contraception less consistently and less effectively, thereby giving the United States a much higher birth rate (Coley & Chase-Landsdale, 1998).

Teen pregnancy is an important issue because these mothers' babies are often low in birth weight and have a disproportionately high mortality rate (McCave, 2007; National Campaign to Prevent Teen and Unwanted Pregnancy, 2008; Olds, 2005). The young mothers themselves have a high rate of dropout from school and often live in poverty and therefore are likely to end up on public assistance (McCave, 2007; National Campaign to Prevent Teen and Unwanted Pregnancy, 2008; U.S. Department of Health and Human Services, 2001b). Monique may be at risk for all of these problems. Teen mothers also have lower levels of marital stability and lower employment security compared to peers who postpone childbearing (Coley & Chase-Lansdale, 1998). Teen mothers and their children are more likely to end up in prison, and their daughters are more likely to become teen mothers themselves compared to other teens (National Campaign to Prevent Teen and Unwanted Pregnancy, 2008). Teen pregnancy can also be hard on teen fathers, such as Rock. The pregnancy can strain fathers' relationships with their girlfriends and their own parents. Teen fathers do not go as far in school and make less money when they go out on the job market than do teens who are not fathers (4parents.gov, 2007). Teen pregnancy costs the United States at least $9 billion annually in public assistance, medical care, and other expenses (National Campaign to Prevent Teen and Unwanted Pregnancy, 2008).

Causes of Teen Pregnancy. Some critics argue that the social welfare system in the United States may, in fact, be responsible for the nation's high pregnancy rate among teens. In particular, they believe that such assistance as a source of income actually promotes teen pregnancy and the growth of female-headed households. However, this assumption is not supported by research. Other industrialized countries, such as Sweden and the United Kingdom, that have more comprehensive welfare programs than the United States have *lower* teenage pregnancy rates (Alan Guttmacher Institute, 2004, 2006; CDC, 2007a; Kotch, Blakely, Brown, & Wong, 1992; Wilcox, Robbennolt, O'Keeffe, & Pynchon, 1996). Therefore, public assistance does not appear to cause young women to become or want to become pregnant.

Besides focusing mainly on females, mainstream psychological literature on adolescent pregnancy focuses on the individual and individual deficits as causes, something community psychologists would shun. Traditional reasons often cited for teen pregnancy include lack of self-esteem (Foster, Greene, & Smith, 1990), low expectancies (Scales, 1990), and psychopathology (Reppucci, 1987). Thus, a typical solution offered for lowering the pregnancy rate is counseling (Hofferth, 1991).

Community psychologists typically examine different causes—*contextual or ecological ones*—for adolescent pregnancy, for example, school alienation that produces low educational aspirations. Another contextual factor is living in poverty (Crosby & Holtgrave, 2005) as experienced by many minorities in America. It is not surprising, given the poverty of African Americans and Hispanics, that major disparities exist in pregnancy and birth rates by race and ethnicity. Hispanics and Blacks have the highest pregnancy and birth rates of all, nearly 3.5 times higher than White teens (CDC, 2007a). Other ecological reasons for teen pregnancy include perceptions of limited life options as well as exposure to the mass media or to peer pressure to engage in sex (Alan Guttmacher Institute, 2004; Schinke, 1998). These latter reasons help explain teen pregnancies such as that of Monique, a White, suburban teen who was not living in poverty. On the other hand, perhaps Rock, two years older and adored by Monique, put immense pressure on her to engage in sex. Also contributing to teen pregnancy are lack of a support system (parents or peers) and being the victim of sexual assault (Alan Guttmacher Institute, 2004). In addition, social capital, defined in Chapter 4 as resources made available to individuals as the result of their placement within a social structure, is beginning to emerge as another important ecological feature that can prevent teen pregnancy (Crosby & Holtgrave, 2005). In this case, **social capital** includes trust, reciprocity, cooperation, and supportive interaction within families, neighborhoods, and communities. Deficient social capital can contribute to teen pregnancy. Whatever the causes of adolescent pregnancy, the issue is better addressed on a large scale, rather than by individual counseling.

Prevention Programs. Although the majority of American teachers and parents agree that sex education is needed in our schools (Alan Guttmacher Institute, 2006), the overly rationalistic perspective that such efforts simply need to expose adolescents to more information or provide them with contraceptives is too narrow (SIECUS National Guidelines Task Force, 2004; Reppucci, 1987). Early in the teen pregnancy intervention movement, Reppucci (1987) reiterated, "The limited effects of these changes are evident in the [still] concomitant high rates of pregnancy, clinic dropouts, and contraceptive nonuse" (p. 7).

What is needed is less focus on individual education (Patterson, 1990) and more focus on an ecological or transactional approach to teen pregnancy (Allen-Meares & Shore, 1986). The ecological approach takes into account the environment surrounding the adolescent.

However, the ecological perspective is complicated. It is complex because the adolescent may be confronted by differing viewpoints on sexuality by peers, family members, the community, and the culture. Furthermore, the media to which the adolescent is exposed flagrantly exploit sexuality (Alan Guttmacher Institute, 2004) yet prohibit contraceptives from being advertised (Reppucci, 1987). Also unhelpful is that many celebrities admired by teens are bearing children at young ages or out of wedlock. The issue of the second-class status of women in the United States also needs to be acknowledged (Bond et al., 2000). Early motherhood may be an attractive alternative to low-paying, dead-end jobs available to young, uneducated, and impoverished women (Lawson & Rhode, 1993).

Adding to the conundrum of what to do about sex education, President George W. Bush intensified efforts to direct federal funding to abstinence-only sex education programs as well as to faith-based institutions (rather than schools) (Marx & Hopper, 2005; McCave, 2007). As of this writing, federal law establishes a stringent eight-point definition of abstinence-only education that requires programs to teach that sexual activity outside of marriage is wrong and harmful for people of any age. The law also prohibits programs from advocating contraceptive use or discussing contraceptive methods except to emphasize their failure rates (Alan Guttmacher Institute, 2006). Monique (but not Rock) was exposed to a little bit of sex education in her health class, but it clearly was not enough to prevent her pregnancy.

Let's first look at an abstinence-only program—Campaign for Our Children. This program is designed to promote abstinence among 9- to 14-year-olds, an age group not yet likely to have experienced sexual intercourse. In this way, the program practices primary prevention. Ecologically, the program engulfs the adolescent with information in many forms—print, television, radio, billboard, and even mass transit media. Other research-based, educational materials developed by Campaign for Our Children can be used in schools, by communities, or by parents and other individuals or groups. There is also an interactive Web site available where individuals can join chat groups, and teens, parents, public officials, health professionals, and others can look up relevant information. Teachers can access lesson plans there, and researchers can locate much data. The questions teens ask at the "Ask the Expert" portion of the site reveal their scanty understanding of human reproduction and their lack of access to health care providers as well as their mistrust in these providers. As an aside, such archival data can help inform sex education professionals and policy makers about what needs to be emphasized to help young people protect themselves from unwanted pregnancies and sexually transmitted diseases (Campaign for Our Children, 2001; Flowers-Coulson, Kushner, & Bankowski, 2000). Research on Campaign for Our Children in the state of Maryland, which was the first state to institute it, shows a dramatic decline in teen pregnancy rates. Maryland ranked 4th highest in the nation in 1987 but dropped to 30th by 1996. Campaign for Our Children has now spread in varying degrees to all 50 states (Campaign for Our Children, 2001).

Abstinence-only programs (which generally do not include information on contraception) may be helpful for younger children—in elementary and early middle school—who have not yet actively engaged in sex. However,

> Proponents of abstinence-only education believe they can instill important moral values through such programs, which will then affect adolescent behaviors. They also believe that

comprehensive sexuality education [actually] promotes sexual promiscuity. Those in favor of comprehensive sexuality education [on the other hand] assert that while postponing sexual activity is optimal, adolescents have the right to be educated on how to protect themselves if they choose to become sexually active. (McCave, 2007, p. 17)

Many adolescents *do* choose to become sexually active, so abstinence-only education for them is ineffective. By their 18th birthday, 6 in 10 teenage women and more than 5 in 10 teenage men have had sexual intercourse anyway (Alan Guttmacher Institute, 2006).

It therefore might be wise to turn our attention to comprehensive sexuality education. Comprehensive sexuality education should cover sexual development, reproductive health (including contraception and sexually transmitted diseases), interpersonal relationships, emotions, intimacy, body image, and gender roles, not just abstinence (SIECUS National Guidelines Task Force, 2004). Moreover, there are important issues related to these more comprehensive types of programs that speak to their significance over abstinence-only sex education. First, most teachers believe that topics such as birth control methods, sexual orientation, and other information *should* be taught alongside of abstinence. Second, 82 percent of American adults support comprehensive—not abstinence-only—sex education. Third, research demonstrates that the use of contraceptives explains 75 percent of the above-mentioned (early 1990s to mid-2000s) decline in teen pregnancies while abstinence explains only 25 percent (SIECUS National Guidelines Task Force, 2004).

We now focus on one well-known comprehensive program—the Carrera Program. In 1984, Dr. Carrera and The Children's Aid Society developed a comprehensive sex education/teen pregnancy prevention program that centers on the belief that success in school, meaningful employment, access to quality medical and health services, and interactions with high-caliber, adult role models have a potent "contraceptive" effect on teens. The program focuses on all the forces and factors affecting the life of a teen at an important time in his or her development and includes sexual issues within the context of an adolescent's *whole* life. In other words, the Carrera Program takes a holistic view of adolescents, which is a relatively new direction for the prevention of teen pregnancy (Allen, Seitz, & Apfel, 2007). The program incorporates parental participation and includes at least seven program components: educational support, a career awareness job club, lifetime sports, creative expression, comprehensive medical and dental services, mental health services, and family life/sex education (The Children's Aid Society, 2008). Specific program components include:

- **Education:** Individual academic plans for each participant, daily one-on-one or small group tutoring, PSAT and SAT preparation, college trips, and a college scholarship fund.
- **Employment:** Job Club is a full introduction to the world of work, including opening bank accounts, exploring career choices, and providing summer and part-time jobs. Participants are paid a stipend and make monthly deposits in their bank accounts.
- **Family Life and Sexuality Education (FLSE):** Weekly comprehensive sexuality education sessions taught in an age-appropriate fashion.
- **Self-Expression:** Weekly music, dance, writing and drama workshops led by theater and arts professionals, where children can discover talents and build self-esteem.

- **Lifetime Individual Sports:** A fitness program emphasizing sports that build self-discipline and can be played throughout life, including golf, squash, swimming, and surfing.
- **Full Medical and Dental Care:** Comprehensive physicals and medical services in partnership with the Adolescent Health Center of the Mt. Sinai Medical Center. Full dental services provided by The Children's Aid Society.
- **Mental Health Services:** Counseling and crisis intervention as needed, and weekly discussion groups led by certified social workers.
- **Parent Family Life and Sexuality Education:** A program that facilitates parents'/adults' ability to communicate more effectively with their [adolescent] children about important family life and sexuality issues (The Children's Aid Society, 2008).

These programs run five days a week during the school year. In the summer, young people receive assistance with employment, and maintenance meetings are held to reinforce sex education and academic skills. There are also occasional social, recreational, and cultural trips (Philliber, Kaye, & Herrling, 2001).

In a multisite program evaluation using random assignment of at-risk youths to either control or treatment groups, researchers (Philliber et al., 2001) determined that the program successfully reduced teen sexuality and teen pregnancy by 50 percent in the communities served. One way the program produced this latter result was to facilitate effective use of protection (contraception) among young women who became sexually active. The program also resulted in additional benefits, such as linking young people with medical care (private physicians rather than visits to the emergency room), encouraging them to participate in the workforce, enhancing participants' computer skills, promoting higher graduation rates, and increasing certain standardized test scores (Children's Aid Society, 2008).

Community psychologists would remind us that prevention programs need to be culturally sensitive, too—an important topic not yet addressed on the issue of teen pregnancy—because no one program or component holds all the solutions for all groups (Stoiber & McIntyre, 2006). Just as surely as culture and ethnicity influence child-rearing, they undoubtedly shape sexual practices and beliefs, such as when, where, and with whom to engage in sex.

To enlarge on the issue of culture, let's focus on Hispanic teen pregnancy, because the rates currently are highest for this group. Several authors have elaborated on values and themes in Hispanic cultures that may account for the higher rates of teen pregnancy in that population. Gilliam (2007) explains that Latina mothers rely on fear to dissuade their daughters from pregnancy; open communication about sexuality and contraception rarely occur. Fathers frequently echo these same threatening messages. Wilkinson-Lee and her colleagues (2006) identified other facets of Hispanic culture that may be important. One cultural value is **familismo,** which is a collective loyalty to the extended family that outranks the needs of the individual. For example, important decisions are made by the extended family, not the individual alone. **Personalismo,** translated as "formal friendliness," is another important value. Hispanic individuals expect to have formal but warm personal relationships with any authority figure, such as health care professionals or educators. Some of this formalness is also based on **respecto,** or respect. Wilkinson-Lee and her colleagues also remind us that cultural sensitivity includes understanding the variability among Hispanic subgroups—immigrant generation, country of origin (e.g., Puerto Rico versus Mexico), and social class. Likewise, they remind us that Hispanic teens often hear conflicting messages from their traditional culture and religion versus mainstream American culture. Clearly, cultural sensitivity is important to program design and effectiveness. Here we examine a sample program related to these issues.

Méndez-Negrete, Saldaña, and Vega (2006) preliminarily report on a culturally sensitive program in San Antonio, Texas, called Escuelitas for Mexican American girls who are at risk for pregnancy. San Antonio unfortunately leads the nation in pregnancy among girls age 15 and under. Escuelitas provide an after-school organizational and social structure that supplements the formal, social institutions of traditional schools and families. The Escuelitas (translated as "little schools") provide experiences and activities that support and encourage academic, personal, cultural, and social achievements designed to prevent teen pregnancy and delinquency as well as reduce school dropout rates.

Girls come from low-income families and are recruited from schools with high incidences of teen pregnancy, delinquency, and school dropout. In the Escuelitas, students meet after school for three 90-minute sessions each week. Activities consist of guest speakers, tutorials, group discussions, and relational workshops with their mothers or guardians (familismo). University students and adult Hispanic role models act as mentors and presenters (respecto and personalismo). Presentations by the Hispanic role models, for example, focus on the cultural assets of the students and on their cultural heritage, for example, Dia de los Muertos (the Day of the Dead).

Note that students are not randomly assigned to the Escuelitas and are not compared to a no-intervention group; these are important factors that should moderate enthusiasm for the following results. Presently, the preliminary results point to several successes. As of 2004, *none* of the participants had dropped out of school, and *none* had become pregnant. Though these results are encouraging, we certainly need more data and better designed research on Escuelitas before the program is adopted and disseminated elsewhere.

One of the major problems of teen pregnancy prevention is that although effective and scientifically based programs are available, they are not well known in local communities across the country. Stated another way, there is lack of dissemination of information about these programs from the scientific community to communities at large. Efforts are now under way to build prevention infrastructures in and guide large-scale prevention strategies for various communities, thanks to the efforts of certain community psychologists (Lesesne, Lewis, White, & Green, 2008).

Secondary Prevention: Working with Pregnant Teens. Because many prevention programs have failed, teenage pregnancy rates remain higher than desired. As mentioned earlier, the United States leads all industrialized countries in teenage pregnancy, abortion, and childbearing. Data also indicate that there is a trend for teens to become pregnant at younger ages (Coley & Chase-Landsdale, 1998; Thomas, Rickel, Butler, & Montgomery, 1990).

For those teens who do become pregnant, like Monique, primary prevention is too late. Programs are needed that will encourage them to continue their education, give them parenting skills, and prevent subsequent pregnancies. Let's examine a program designed to prevent further pregnancies, especially because the expected birth rate for teen mothers is 500 percent higher than for teen girls who have not already given birth (Corcoran & Pillai,

2007; Key, O'Rourke, Natalie, & McKinnon, 2005–2006). A second pregnancy and birth for a young mother compounds all of the health, social, and educational risks that the first pregnancy and birth did, so secondary prevention—preventing another pregnancy—is extremely important and quite difficult. Even the primary prevention program for child maltreatment that was presented before (the Nurse-Family Partnership) is not always successful in preventing repeat pregnancies in teen mothers (Gray, Sheeder, O'Brien, & Stevens-Simon, 2006).

Key et al. (2005–2006) researched the Second Chance Club, a peer education, school-based program to prevent second pregnancies among teen mothers. The program uses peer support at group meetings; health education on adolescence, parenting, and career issues; health care for the mothers and their babies (including contraception); and social services in the form of home visits, counseling, and other forms of case management. Archival data (public records of second births) were collected over three time periods (before, during, and after program implementation) in various catchment areas where the program was offered. The data in the catchment areas were also compared to state birth records for a similar population of teens during the same time periods. Results showed a decrease in repeat births in the program treatment areas from before to after program implementation. Similarly, comparison to the state birth rates for age- and race-mates over the specified time periods demonstrated less change in the treatment groups for secondary birth rates. Key and colleagues, while acknowledging the limitations of their type of study, confirm that such school-based, multidimensional, intensive programs can be successfully designed to reduce repeat pregnancies by teen mothers. It is unfortunate that Monique was not exposed to a teen pregnancy primary prevention program; perhaps a secondary prevention program will become available to her.

The Elderly

Scope of the Issue. The population of the United States is aging. As the swell of baby boomers moves through time, the ranks of the aged are increasing. Medical advances allow people to live longer, with most women outliving men. At the beginning of the 20th century, only 4.1 percent of the total U.S. population was elderly (Blakemore, Washington, & McNeely, 1995). Today, the percentage of Americans age 65 and older has tripled and the total number has increased almost 12-fold (from 3.1 million to 36.3 million). Figure 7.2 illustrates the dramatic increase in our elderly population and provides projections through 2050.

The elderly, unfortunately, have been largely ignored in the community psychology literature. Steffen (1996) reviewed articles in the *American Journal of Community Psychology* from 1988 to 1994 and found a weak emphasis on aging. Over the seven-year period, only 13 articles focused specifically on older adults. In our own search of this journal for the period 1995 to 2008, we found five or fewer articles (depending on our search terms) related to aging community members. Indeed, this is a neglected area of community psychology. Given that in 2005 many elderly lived at (3.6 million) or near (2.3 million) the poverty line, and given the demographics in Figure 7.2, the topic of aging Americans shouldn't be so ignored in the literature. Other professionals agree that as a society, we are way behind in our efforts to study and promote optimal aging (Chapman, 2007).

The stereotype of the elderly in the United States is that of a wrinkled, incoherent person rocking in a chair in a nursing home. Obviously, this negative stereotype, while

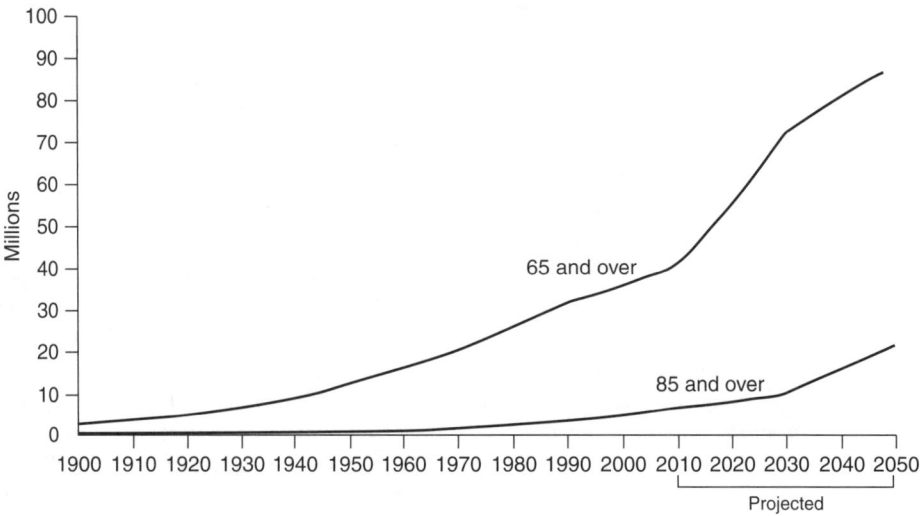

FIGURE 7.2 Number of People Age 65 and Over, by Age Group, for Selected Years 1900–2000 and Projected to 2010–2050

Source: U.S. Census Bureau (2000), Decennial Census and Projections. Washington, D.C.

incorrect, persists (Cuddy, Norton, & Fiske, 2005; Kite, Stockdale, Whitley, & Johnson, 2005). Most elderly, in fact, live and die in their own homes (Steffen, 1996) rather than in hospitals or nursing homes. Separation of the young and the old in American culture is one factor that leads to such stereotyping (Hagestad & Uhlenberg, 2005).

This is not to say that our aging population, as with any group, is entirely without problems. For example, two frequent and particularly important transitions of aging are loss of health and loss of spouse. Loss of spouse and significant others in an elderly person's life can cause depression and stress (Siegel & Kuykendall, 1990). In addition, declining health is exacerbated by perceived lack of control over health matters, personal barriers such as memory deficits, and societal barriers such as lack of transportation and high-cost health care (Chipperfield, 1993; Dapp, Anders, von Rentein-Kruse, & Meier-Baumgartner, 2005). Families of the elderly who provide caregiving can also find themselves under stress (Hardin & Khan-Hudson, 2005; Singleton, 2000), especially employed family members (Gignac, Kelloway, & Gottlieb, 1996; Hardin & Khan-Hudson, 2005). As you can see, the situation in which the elderly find themselves has a direct bearing on their well-being.

We concentrate here on two issues that have received much play in the prevention literature—personal control and social support. Both are postulated to enhance the well-being of the elderly. Note, however, that there are many other factors affecting the welfare of the elderly (Lehr, Seiler, & Thomae, 2000) that we cannot include here due to limited space.

Prevention Programs

Social Support Myriad programs exist for the elderly that focus on enhancing the quality of their lives, with only a few mentioned here. One well-examined approach to preserving the emotional well-being and sense of security of the elderly is to provide them with social support (Greenglass, Fiksenbaum, & Eaton, 2006). Social support by means of informal networks of family (Tice, 1991), confidants (Lowenthal & Haven, 1968), or others (Abrahams & Patterson, 1978–1979) has been reputed to increase morale, buffer the effects of loss of loved ones, and slow the deterioration of health (Choi & Wodarski, 1996; Greenglass et al., 2006).

In one of the first studies of its kind, Heller, Thompson, Trueba, Hogg, and Vlachos-Weber (1991) set up telephone dyads between an elderly person and another elderly phone companion. Interestingly, there were no significant differences in well-being between the phone dyads and a no-contact comparison group. There are several explanations as to why this was so. For one, the phone companion was not deemed as necessarily being available in a time of need (Willis, 1991) nor as an enduring source of support (Schiaffino, 1991). Another reason could have been that this was too new a relationship for the phone companion to be a true confidant (Vaux, 1991). Given some of these criticisms, perhaps phone dyads with family members would have been more successful (Roak, 1991).

More recently, creative researchers have made use of newer technology—the Internet— to provide social support to the elderly, especially those who might feel isolated due to age or disability. First, the Internet can be viewed as a preventive tool that might delay or avert age-associated physiological and behavioral changes restricting elderly functioning, for example, isolation. Second, the Internet might help compensate for age-related losses in strength and perceptual-motor functioning, such as slowed eye-hand coordination. Third, it might be a good communication tool for the frail elderly, those too frail or too hard of hearing to leave their homes or use their telephones for social interaction (Fozard & Kearns, 2007).

Shapira, Barak, and Gal (2007) compared older adults in day-care centers and nursing homes trained on Internet use with a comparison group of nontrained individuals. Both groups were administered interviews, health assessments, and life satisfaction, depression, loneliness, and other scales. On all measures (except physical functioning) the Internet group improved while the comparison group declined. The researchers concluded that indeed, Internet use can contribute to older adults' well-being and sense of empowerment by affecting their interpersonal interactions, promoting better cognitive functioning, and contributing to the sense of personal control and independence. This latter finding provides an interesting segue to our next topic.

Sense of Self-Control   As mentioned, self- or personal control is one issue relevant to the elderly. Every facet of aging, such as health and cognitive functioning, involves the issue of control (Baltes & Baltes, 1986). **Self-control** is the belief that we can influence events in our environment that affect our lives (Duffy & Atwater, 2008). Increasing the sense of self-control of the elderly is a technique that has proven to produce positive results (Shapira & Barak, 2007; Thompson & Spacespan, 1991; Zarit, Pearlin, & Schaie, 2003), such as better mental health (Reich & Zautra, 1991). An enhanced sense of control leads to feelings of empowerment, a coveted principle of community psychology.

In a very early test of this issue, Langer and Rodin (1976) matched two groups of elderly in a nursing home on age, health, and other important dimensions. One group was shown in detail how much control they had over their lives. They decided how to arrange their rooms, when to greet visitors, and how to spend spare time. Each of these residents was given a plant to care for. The second group was told that their lives were mainly under staff control. For example, these elderly were also given a plant but were told the staff would take care of it. Pre- and postintervention questionnaires about feelings of personal control, happiness, and activity level were administered to the elderly and completed by the care staff. Almost all before-and-after comparisons favored the intervention group—the one with a higher sense of self-control. Eighteen months later, Rodin and Langer (1977) conducted a follow-up. Half as many experimental participants had died as had control participants. This study demonstrates that the quality of life for the elderly can indeed be enhanced when they believe they have more control over it (Schultz & Heckhausen, 1996). Subsequent research has replicated the fact that a sense of self-regulation (e.g., Wrosch, Dunne, Scheier, & Schultz, 2006) or self-control (e.g., Zarit et al., 2003) has an enhancing effect on the quality of life and the health of older individuals.

Homelessness

Some Americans stereotype the homeless as drunk or mentally disabled old men who deserve what they get—a life of misery on the streets. Rock and Monique, for example, would taunt the homeless who lived near subway entrances of the city close to the suburbs where they lived. On the other hand, some people feel sorry for homeless individuals and hand them money. Research reported in 2006 revealed that young, female, liberal, and less wealthy individuals are more likely to be sympathetic to the homeless (Tompsett, Toro, Gizicki, Manrique, & Zatakia). Community psychologists are concerned with homelessness not just for humane reasons but because homelessness carries with it myriad problems for the individual. The issue of homelessness is discussed here for these reasons and because homeless individuals end up interfacing with a variety of social and human services.

Scope of the Issue. The extent of the problem of homelessness is difficult to determine, for one thing because homelessness is difficult to define (National Coalition for the Homeless, 2007b; Shinn et al., 2007; Tompsett et al., 2006). How long does a person need to be without shelter to be considered homeless? A night? Three months in a row? Depending on the method of study, the U.S. government estimates that the number of homeless people ranges anywhere from four to eight million (U.S. Department of Health and Human Services, 1998), whereas the National Coalition for the Homeless (2007a) estimates that over 3.5 million men, women, and children are homeless. Another reason for the difficulty in making accurate estimates is that the homeless are a heterogeneous group; the group includes people of all races, families with or without children, single individuals, individuals who move from temporary shelters to homelessness and back to some type of shelter, as well as others (National Coalition for the Homeless, 2007b). Furthermore, estimates vary depending on the motives of the groups doing the estimating. Dowell and Farmer (1992) contended that because the image of homelessness in a community is not good for business, community officials often underestimate or minimize the problem. Varying estimates of homelessness can cause public policy gridlock, too. If some community members view the problem as insignificant, they will view the problem as not necessitating immediate nor extensive attention. However, others—community psychologists included—urgently press for sweeping solutions to the issue of homelessness.

Who are today's homeless? The answer to this question is again difficult and varies, depending on which study one examines. Rossi (1990) devised an interesting way of classifying the homeless. He suggested that there are old homeless and new homeless. The **old homeless** are the individuals who are generally stereotyped as homeless. These are older, alcoholic men who sleep in cheap flophouses or skid-row hotels. They are "old" because they are the type of homeless who were seen on city streets after World War II. The **new homeless** are indeed truly homeless. They do not sleep in cheap hotels but on the streets or find public buildings to escape into during inclement weather.

The new homeless include more women and children than in the past, although the National Coalition for the Homeless (2007b) estimates that single men make up over half of all homeless adults (see also Shinn et al., 2007). Likewise, there are age differences between the new and old homeless, with the new homeless being much younger. The National Coalition for the Homeless (2007a) estimated that children under the age of 18 account for 1.35 million of the homeless population. Another difference is that the new homeless suffer a much more profound degree of economic destitution than the old homeless. One final difference between the old and the new homeless is that the ethnic and racial composition has changed over the years. Today's homeless are more likely to be from minority groups rather than White, as was true of the old homeless (American Psychological Association, 2005; National Coalition for the Homeless, 2007b).

As for families experiencing homelessness, homeless children suffer a number of compounding problems, largely due to their homelessness (Burt, Pearson, & Montgomery, 2007). Studies have consistently shown that homeless children have elevated levels of acute and chronic health problems compared to housed children (Gewirtz, 2007; Walsh & Jackson, 2005) as well as poorer nutrition (Molnar, Rath, & Klein, 1990). Homeless children are also more likely to experience developmental delays, such as short attention spans, speech delays, inappropriate social interactions (Molnar, 1988), and psychological problems such as anxiety, behavior disorders, and depression (Bassuk & Rosenberg, 1988). In addition, achievement scores on standardized tests for homeless children are well below those of housed children (Rafferty, 1990), primarily because homeless children frequently move from school to school—when they are lucky enough to be enrolled in school.

Zugazaga (2004) and Muñoz, Panadero, Santo, and Quiroga (2005) have also studied homelessness in relationship to stressful life experiences. The latter group of researchers has found that there are distinct groups of homeless based on analyses of stressful life events. Their results revealed the existence of three subgroups of homeless. Group A was characterized by economic problems, such as unemployment; this group functioned well and had few mental health or substance abuse problems. Group B was typified by substance abuse and health problems, resulting in longer durations of homelessness. Psychologists and health care professionals have long recognized that poor health and homelessness are intricately intertwined (Flick, 2007; O'Connell, 2007; Smith, Easterlow, Munro, & Turner, 2003). Group C was of lower average age and manifested multiple problems, many stemming from childhood (such as abuse or parental alcoholism). Note that this study was conducted in Spain, but the overarching conclusion is important—the existence of subgroups of homeless people emphasizes the importance of designing different interventions for each group, adapted to their diverse needs. Another stressful life event related to homelessness but not necessarily revealed in the cited research is exposure to trauma or traumatic life events, such as being the victim of violence (Kim & Ford, 2006). Preventing posttraumatic stress disorder and addressing its influence on people in the early stages of homelessness can go a long way toward intervening in homelessness.

Interest in understanding cross-national homelessness is also growing in the field of community psychology because there may be much we can learn from the experiences of other countries. Interest in the United States is mounting, especially in other developed countries and their programs designed to address homelessness. For example, in Great Britain and the countries of the European Union, men and minorities (those discriminated against) are overrepresented among the homeless ranks just as in the United States (Toro, 2007). Case in Point 7.3 provides more information on international perspectives on homelessness.

CASE IN POINT 7.3
HOW DO CULTURES DIFFER ON THE ISSUE OF HOMELESSNESS?

You have been reading the American perspective on homelessness. Because one of the goals of this text is to introduce you to multicultural aspects of community problems, we are well served by examining how other countries are researching and managing homelessness. As we turn our attention to other cultures to learn from them, be mindful that we "cannot transplant policies and programs from one country to another without considering the foreign soil in which the plants must take root" (Okamato, 2007, p. 525).

A recent edition of the *Journal of Social Issues* (2007) offered articles from authors and researchers from around the world. Understanding what produces homelessness and just who is homeless in other countries might provide lessons and insights for the American public as well as for community psychologists. Two particular authors from seemingly different cultures—the Czech Republic and Japan—offered interesting cultural perspectives on homelessness.

In Japan, there was no word for homelessness until after the destruction of World War II (Okamato, 2007). With a changing economy (i.e., movement toward a technological society) and government policy changes, there is now not only a phrase, "rough sleeping," but increased interest in homelessness. The term **rough sleepers** was essentially coined by the media for individuals who sleep in public places, such as parks. Many of the rough sleepers are minorities, just as they are in the United States. Koreans, for example, are minorities in Japan and are thus more likely to be homeless than are Japanese citizens. As in the United States, the majority of homeless are men—some are even employed—but they are likely to be older than homeless men in the United States. One major cause of homelessness in Japan is that housing was often tied to employment; that is, employers offered housing to employees as a perk, so when jobs were lost, housing was lost. Japanese companies today are less likely to offer the lifetime employment and housing security they offered in the past.

As in the United States and Japan, in the Czech Republic there are personal as well as structural reasons for homelessness. A personal reason might be divorce or loss of employment; a social or structural reason is the problem of runaway or homeless youth for whom there are no shelters. In both Japan and the Czech Republic (and some would argue, the United States) the government provides low budgets for social welfare spending (Shinn, 2007).

There are differences, however, between Japan and the Czech Republic. In the Czech Republic (Hladikova & Hradecky, 2007), rough sleepers are those who are literally roofless; they do not sleep under a roof, as in a shelter. Other nomenclature exists in the Czech Republic for the remainder of the homeless population, such as those in *insecure* housing (where the housing might be lost at any minute due to job loss) and those who have *inadequate* housing (where an apartment is too crowded or substandard with no heat or running water). To mention a few other differences, homelessness historically became an issue and a larger problem in the Czech Republic with the fall of communism. People today retain a right to work (just as they did under the communists), but continual corruption and bribery make the employment system much more competitive and difficult than in the past. The political break-up of Czechoslovakia also contributed to much social strife; no such massive political upheaval has occurred recently in Japan to contribute to the homeless problem. In the Czech Republic, rather than the government providing social services, nongovernmental organizations (NGOs) or private social services and charities have taken up the banner of helping the homeless. In Japan, the law states that all people shall have the right to maintain minimum standards of wholesome and cultured living. Furthermore, in all spheres of life, the state shall use its endeavors for the promotion and extension of social welfare and security, although this is not a common practice (e.g., low government spending) when it comes to housing. In reality, Japanese families, rather than NGOs and the government, have often taken over the burden of providing housing for those in need.

Causes of Homelessness. To prevent something from happening, one needs to know what causes it or have the ability to predict in advance when or to whom it will happen; this, of course, applies to homelessness (Burt et al., 2007). Studies show that homelessness is often episodic, or at least is not a chronic condition for all individuals (National Coalition for the Homeless, 1999; Shinn, 1997; Sosin, Piliavin, & Westerfelt, 1990), so focusing only on person-centered factors may not account for all cases of homelessness. Sometimes we need to focus on the settings individuals find themselves in as well. For instance, the rate of psychiatric hospitalization for today's homeless is as low as 4 percent when the whole family is homeless (Shinn & Weitzman, 1990; Weitzman, Knickman, & Shinn, 1990). As for those who are homeless with a mental disorder, a lack of housing may be more critical to the likelihood of their rehospitalization than is the quality of their psychiatric care (Rosenfeld, 1991). Adequate and effective discharge planning on release from the hospital can significantly prevent their homelessness (Backer, Howard, & Moran, 2007).

Let's turn our attention to some so-called person-centered causes of homelessness but with recognition of the fact that there are other contributors, especially the environments in which individuals find themselves. Person-centered approaches include but are not limited to such issues as mental disorders and life stressors, as previously mentioned. Unemployment is also another major consideration in homelessness (McBride, Calsyn, Morse, Klinkenberg, & Allen, 1998; Shaheen & Rio, 2007; Shinn et al., 2007). Interestingly, Koegel, Burnam, and Farr (1990) found that 33 percent of the homeless had been employed within the past month, and 59 percent had been employed in the past six months. Know, however, that a minimum wage worker typically needs to work 87 or more hours a week (two full-time jobs) to afford a two-bedroom apartment (National Coalition for the Homeless, 1999). Poverty, then, is probably a better explanation for homelessness than unemployment.

Person-centered explanations such as mental disorders, life stressors, and unemployment are only partially useful for explaining homelessness—regardless of how popular these explanations are in the mass media. We wisely turn our attention to ecological factors.

Shinn (1992) conducted research to expand the understanding of whether structural variables explain homelessness. In her study, a sample of 700 randomly selected homeless families requesting shelter were compared to 524 families selected randomly from the public assistance caseload. The first group represented "the homeless" and the second "the housed poor." Only 4 percent—a small percentage—of the homeless in the sample had been previously hospitalized for mental illness. Only 8 percent of the homeless and 2 percent of the housed poor had been in a detoxification center for substance abuse. Shinn concluded that individual deficits were relatively unimportant in differentiating the homeless from the housed poor.

Shinn also found that only 37 percent of the homeless, compared to 86 percent of the poor housed families, had broken into the housing market (i.e., had been primary tenants in a place they stayed for a long time). In addition, 45 percent of the homeless versus 26 percent of the housed poor reported having three or more persons per bedroom in the place they had stayed the longest. The researcher regards poor housing opportunities and crowding to be better explanations for homelessness than personal deficits or individual level explanations. (See also Shinn & Tsemberis, 1998.)

In a five-year follow-up on homelessness, Shinn, Weitzman, Strojanovic, Knickman, Jimenez, Duchon, James & Kranz (1998) stated that "subsidized housing is the only predictor of residential stability after shelter" (p. 1655). In other words, the research team found that once a family entered a shelter, five years later many were able to have their own residences but only with financial assistance. Zlotnick, Robertson, and Lahiff (1999), in a 15-month prospective study, also reported that subsidized housing is one of the most important factors associated with exiting homelessness. Thus, due to the newer welfare laws as well as fewer new units of subsidized housing, future homeless families may not fare so well (Western Regional Advocacy Project, 2006).

Other ecological and structural causes—outside of the person—have been identified. The National Coalition for the Homeless (2007b) identifies lack of affordable health care as a cause of homelessness. Individuals who are struggling to pay the rent and also have a serious illness or disability can start a downward spiral into homelessness when payment of medical bills results in lack of funds to pay rent (Burt et al., 2007). Domestic violence also results in homelessness (National Coalition for the Homeless, 2007b). Many women choose to become homeless rather than remain with an abuser. Recently, Shinn et al. (2007) also identified a paucity of social capital (defined earlier) as a major contributor to homelessness. Without social support and nearby family members or friends who can provide aid, many individuals find themselves homeless. These factors do not exhaust the list of causes but do help identify the myriad pathways by which individuals and families descend into homelessness. Because no social problem originates from a single cause, clearly, solutions to the problem of homelessness are not simple. Until prevention policies focus on a general strategy against *all* aspects of poverty (Firdion & Marpsat, 2007), focusing on keeping people in their homes or on person-centered factors such as unemployment are less likely to work. Poverty indeed is a primary contributor to nearly every major social problem in this chapter.

Prevention Programs. Several suggestions for addressing homelessness have already been reviewed—planning psychiatric hospital discharges better, addressing unemployment, increasing the amount of affordable housing, and subsidizing housing expenses, to mention a few. Given that these approaches take much time and money or are subject to the caprices of politicians, what else is available to address homelessness?

Many communities in the United States have programs in place to prevent or address homelessness. Some professionals, though, argue that these community programs have yet to provide strong evidence that their homelessness prevention efforts are effective (Burt et al., 2007). Others appear more optimistic and suggest that prevention efforts are promising (Moses, Kresky-Wollf, Bassuk, & Brounstein, 2007). Fortunately for us, Burt and colleagues (2007) have published fairly new, albeit sketchy evidence that community-wide strategies for preventing homelessness, especially among those being released from institutional care, can be successful. The researchers, with great difficulty, identified five possibly effective programs from a multitude of federal grant applications. Not surprisingly, they also found that many of the programs they reviewed but did not include in their analysis did not maintain adequate data on the efficacy or efficiency of their programs. Because the sample is small and because of other design factors, the following results must be balanced with some uncertainty while we await other such studies.

Burt and colleagues found five activities that are useful for preventing homelessness and may be used alone or in combination in community-wide prevention programs:

- Providing housing subsidies (money) for first-time homeless individuals and families.
- Coupling supportive social services with permanent housing.
- Utilizing housing-court mediation between tenants and landlords to prevent eviction.
- Cash assistance for rent or for mortgage arrears.
- For secondary prevention, rapid exiting from homeless shelters to housing.

Burt et al.—and the American Psychological Association (2005)—also emphasize that merely throwing money and services at high-risk populations will not work *unless* the following key elements are also present in the programs:

- At-risk populations need to be well targeted, using data from multiple agencies.
- The community must accept as important its obligation to assist at-risk populations.
- Relevant community agencies must collaborate with one another on prevention efforts.
- Someone or some agency needs to take the lead collecting data on progress, monitoring gaps in the system, knowing the needs of the population, and contacting agencies so as to establish collaboration.

The best solution to the homeless problem in the United States, though, may be a concerted and organized public policy program at the federal level. Charities and local governments alone cannot meet the growing needs of the homeless (Gore, 1990). One piece of legislation aimed at grappling with the homeless problem on a national level is the McKinney-Vento Homeless Assistance Act. It established an Interagency Council on Homelessness to coordinate, monitor, and improve the federal response to the problems of homelessness. The act established an Emergency Food Shelter Program National Board as well as local boards across the country to determine how program funds could best be used. Grants and demonstration programs—for example, for drug and alcohol-abuse treatment for addicted, homeless individuals—were authorized by the law, and the Temporary Emergency Food Assistance Program was reauthorized as well (Barak, 1991). A coherent policy of federal legislation needs to pursue increased low-income housing, treatments for mentally disabled and substance-abusing homeless, and education and job training for homeless individuals (American Psychological Association, 2005; Gore, 1990).

What have we learned by examining child maltreatment, teen pregnancy, the elderly, and the homeless? Messages for community psychologists and other prevention experts cut across these groups.

- The types of individuals affected by these problems are diverse.
- There are multiple causes for each of these social problems, few of which are created by the individuals affected by the problem.
- Single solutions for these problems will not work; *multifaceted* efforts will yield better results.
- When various social service agencies are involved in interventions—whether the interventions be primary or secondary in nature—their efforts need to be *coordinated* to be effective.
- Government officials, affected individuals, and social service agencies must come together or collaborate in order to address these issues.

SUMMARY

Social welfare or ideas and activities to promote social good have a long history in Western society. Until modern times, two major forms of social welfare were charity/philanthropy (private assistance) and public welfare (public assistance). During the 19th century (around the time of the Industrial Revolution), two other forms of social welfare were born: social insurance (public assistance derived from taxation) and social service (public nonmaterialistic human services derived from taxation). To receive social welfare, people must demonstrate their need, usually in the form of a low standard of living or poor economic means.

It is generally believed (i.e., stereotyped) that recipients of social welfare are lazy, despite the fact that they might genuinely need such assistance. On the other hand, donors to community services are perceived to be honorable people, although research indicates that willingness to help is often a function of environmental factors (e.g., people are more generous during religious seasons).

Four groups that interface regularly with human services in U.S. communities are maltreated children and their families, pregnant teens, the elderly, and the homeless.

Teen parents and others—such as people who themselves were abused children—are predicted to be at risk for maltreating a child. Providing social support, parenting and prenatal education, and links between the parents and services in the community can sometimes prevent child abuse. The Nurse-Family Partnership program has proven to be particularly successful in reducing child maltreatment among first-time, at-risk teen mothers and has been disseminated nationwide.

The problem of pregnant adolescents is major; the United States leads other industrialized countries in this statistic. The prevailing culture does not provide good role models;

thus, the problem persists. Programs to reach teenagers before they become sexually active include abstinence-only and comprehensive sex education. Comprehensive sex education (rather than abstinence-only education) provides teens with sex education that better ensures they will not be stuck in the welfare quagmire so frequently found in teen parenthood.

The elderly sometimes interface with services in the community, too, although the elderly are a rather neglected group in the community psychology literature. Declining health, loss of mobility, death of loved ones, and loss of control are problems for the elderly. As is true with other groups, not all community interventions are effective with the elderly. However, providing the elderly with social support and increasing their sense of control or sense of personal efficacy can maintain their self-esteem and health for longer periods.

Homelessness is an increasing problem in the United States. Stereotypically, the homeless are drunk or mentally disabled old men. The new homeless, however, include many children and women as well as previously employed and previously housed individuals. Providing more affordable housing and better and coordinated public policies and social services will go a long way toward solving this problem.

What has been learned from the examination of maltreated children, pregnant teens, the elderly, and the homeless? For one thing, not all interventions work equally well, and no single intervention works for all groups. Interventions need to be multifaceted; that is, they must address multiple issues and utilize multiple approaches. Efforts should take into account ecological factors, too, and not just focus on the individual level. Efforts by all affected individuals and groups need to be well coordinated to be effective and efficient.

CHAPTER 8

SCHOOLS, CHILDREN, AND THE COMMUNITY

THE EARLY CHILDHOOD ENVIRONMENT
  Child Care
   Necessity for Child Care
   Effects of Child Care
   Plans for the Child Care Dilemma
  Enrichment Education and Early Intervention

THE PUBLIC SCHOOLS
  Desegregation, Ethnicity, and Prejudice in the Schools
   The Historical Context
   Prejudice and Its Companions
   Fostering Acceptance of Diversity in the Classroom
   Effects of Desegregation
  The Schools and Adolescents
   The School Climate
  ■ **CASE IN POINT 8.1** Students' Memories of Public School
   Other Factors Related to School Success or Failure
   Dropping Out of School
   School Violence
  ■ **CASE IN POINT 8.2** Children of Divorce
SUMMARY

I touch the future. I teach.
—Christa McAuliffe (teacher, astronaut)

Mi nombre es Roberto. Nací en Mexico y me mude a los Estados Unidos cuando era un niño. En mi casa, solamente se hablaba español. Un día, cuando estaba en el séptimo grado, mi maestra me pidió que leyera en frente de la clase. Yo trate de leer, pero no pude reconocer algunas de las palabras en inglés. La maestra me interrumpió y me dijo que yo no sabía leer muy bien y que debía sentarme. Después, ella llamó a un niño Americano, quien leía mejor que yo. Yo me senti bastante avergonzado.

Could you read this passage? Imagine how frustrating textbooks, television programs, and public announcements are to individuals for whom English is a second or third language. We will restart, this time in English.

> My name is Roberto. I was born in Mexico, and I moved to the United States when I was a child. In my house, only Spanish was spoken. One day, when I was in the second grade, my teacher asked that I read in front of the class. I tried to read, but I was not able to recognize some of the English words. The teacher interrupted me and told me that I did not know how to read very well and to sit down. After that, she called on an American child who read better than I. I was quite embarrassed.
>
> Roberto's story continues: I had to repeat the second grade, but this time with a different teacher, Miss Martinez. She had experienced much the same embarrassment when she was a child, so she was sympathetic to my situation. Her extra help inspired me to do my best. In no time, I was speaking and reading English well, almost as well as my classmates. By high school, I was a very good student. My good grades and my ability to play soccer well had endeared me to my fellow classmates enough so that they liked me. Unlike some of the other Hispanic students, I was quite popular, which made my life easier than theirs.
>
> Today, I am in college; I am studying to be a lawyer. Actually, I don't want to be a lawyer; I want to be a legislator. I view law as the avenue to a political career. One of my goals as a legislator is to reform American schools so that all children will feel welcome and comfortable in them.

Consider for a moment how it feels to be a child whom others view as different, either because of a different skin color, a foreign-sounding name, an accent or language other than English, or the use of a wheelchair. This chapter explores the world of schools as it relates to children and families. In a special issue about human capital, the National Behavioral Science research agenda committee of the American Psychological Society (1992) remarked, "There is no better way to invest in human capital than to improve our schools" (p. 17). The schools themselves are small communities as well as integral parts of the communities they serve. Every school issue cannot possibly be covered here, but this chapter touches on some of the more salient ones: child care, diversity in the classroom, and stressful events such as school violence and parental divorce.

THE EARLY CHILDHOOD ENVIRONMENT

Urie Bronfenbrenner (1979, 1999) presented what he considered an unorthodox approach to child development. He formulated the ecological perspective of human development. **Development,** to Bronfenbrenner and other psychologists, usually means "a lasting change in the way in which the individual perceives and deals with the environment" (p. 3, 1979). The **ecological setting** refers to a set of nested structures, or settings, one inside the other. At the innermost level is the immediate setting in which the individual finds him- or herself, such as the home or a classroom. The next layer consists of the interrelationship between these settings, as in the links between the child's home and the school. The third level, interestingly, is the environment that the child or individual is not in but that has an effect anyway, such as the policies of the parents' places of employment that have an impact on the child (e.g., day care and health care). All levels are interconnected rather than independent. The way the individual transacts with these settings and perceives them is important in influencing the course of the individual's development. As you may already know, the ecological perspective and the transactional nature of the individual's encounters with various elements in the environment are of utmost importance in community psychology.

A concrete example might further your understanding. Suppose Johnnie is having trouble focusing his attention on his studies in the third grade. Using the individual level of analysis, his teacher might believe that Johnnie needs extra tutoring and additional assistance with his math and spelling or medication for his attention-deficit disorder. An ecological perspective would take into account other contexts, such as Johnnie's home and neighborhood or even the playground at the school. The reality might be that Johnnie's home life is distressing because his parents are divorcing. Furthermore, his father might be unemployed, which is contributing to his parents' discord and Johnnie's inattention. Johnnie is also being teased on the playground and thus finds concentrating in the classroom difficult when surrounded by the bullies. Perhaps what would most assist Johnnie is some social support from other children whose parents have divorced or an adult who watches over his safety on the playground—not extra tutoring from the teacher.

As Bronfenbrenner suggested, advances in understanding development require investigation in the actual environments, both immediate and remote, in which human beings live. This chapter examines settings in which children develop—especially educational ones such as day-care centers and schools. Although some of the topics presented will be discrete for the sake of parsimony, it is important to remember that children do not enter each situation in a vacuum; they bring connections and experiences from myriad other contexts, regardless of their stage of development. For example, immediately following this paragraph, the topic of day care will be discussed. Research has demonstrated that the tripod of family structure (one versus two parents), the day-care structure (in-home care or day-care center), and the day-care process (content of the activities) influence a child's language development in very complex ways (National Institute of Child and Human Development [NICHD], 2006). Research has demonstrated that other ecological factors such as the family environment and teacher perceptions of students predict future academic success (Seyfried, 1998). Studies generally show that in-school prevention programs have significant positive impacts on children (Durlak, 1995). Because the organization of this chapter is chronological (i.e., human developmental), early childhood care is discussed first.

Child Care

Child (day) care can be defined as all the ways children are cared for when they are not being cared for by the mother (NICHD, 2001) or primary caregiver. In the opening vignette, Roberto did not reveal whether his parents worked during his early childhood. However, if his parents worked and he was left with a neighbor, he would have been in child day care. Child-care or day-care providers can include licensed and unlicensed centers, family members or relatives other than the parents, neighbors, informal sitters, and even preschools. Some provide nothing more than babysitting services while others provide health care, educational materials, nutritious meals, field trips, and so on (Haskins, 2005). Indeed, we have a mixed system—a crazy quilt of sorts—of child care in the United

States (Lamb & Ahnert, 2006; Muenchow & Marsland, 2007), making this important issue difficult to research and to discuss.

Necessity for Child Care. The need for day care for children in the United States has grown historically such that today over 90 percent of all families have at least one parent in the labor force. In dual-parent families, 62 percent have both parents employed. In families maintained by women, 72 percent of the mothers are employed, and in families maintained by men, 93.5 percent of the fathers work. Among mothers with children under a year old, over 56 percent work. Because more and more parents are working today than ever before, there are more and more children at younger and younger ages in nonparental childcare (Belsky, 2006) as demonstrated in Figure 8.1. Notice that today, not only are higher percentages of children in child care, but child-care centers are used more frequently than any other type of care. This latter point is cogent to later discussions.

Day care in the United States is not without controversy. Some individuals believe that day care, which means separation in early life from the parents, can be harmful to young children. Others argue that it is not *whether* care is provided but *the type and quality of care* that make a difference in the children's lives. Still others comment that availability of *good* care at a reasonable cost is this nation's biggest problem. These and other issues are explored here in more detail.

Effects of Child Care. In the 1970s, as more mothers entered the workforce, a popular question asked by parents and researchers was: "How much damage is done to infants and young children by working mothers?" (Scarr & Eisenberg, 1993). What was really being asked was whether nonmaternal care was a threat to the child. For example, if Roberto was left with a neighbor, would that affect his development differently than if his mother cared

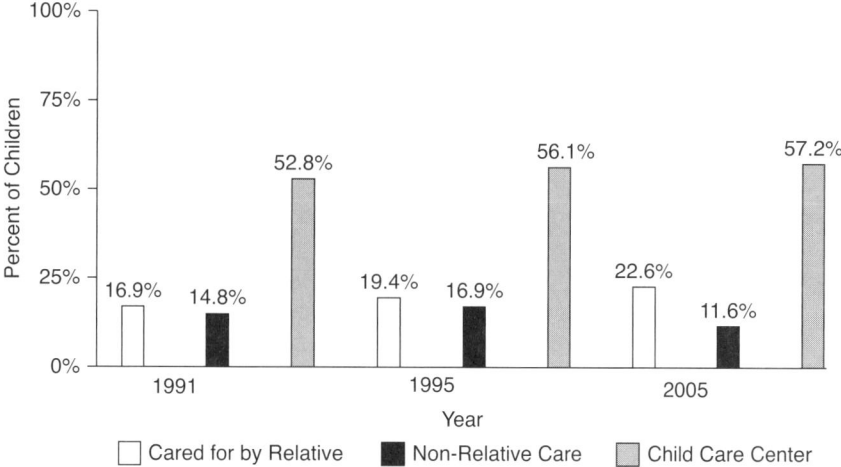

FIGURE 8.1 Child-care Arrangements of Preschool Children by Year and Type of Arrangements

Note: Columns do not add up to 100% because children were sometimes in mixed types of care or were cared for by parents.

Source: U.S. Census Bureau (2008). The 2008 statistical abstracts. Washington, D.C: author.

for him at home and did not work? A second related issue is what effect nonmaternal care has on the child's development: social, cognitive, language, and other abilities. Scarr and Eisenberg (1993) warned that there are no simple answers to these questions. Nonparental child care, for example, includes for-profit (such as the large national chains) and not-for-profit centers (such as church-sponsored centers) as well as family (relatives)-based care, and other permutations. Not only are there different types of care but also differences in the *quality* of care within the same category.

Because high-quality care, whether provided by parents or others, is the cornerstone of child development, we examine the issue of child care in more detail. Only well-designed, large-scale studies can tease out conclusions about the effects of early child care—parental or nonparental—on child development (NICHD, 2001). Fortunately for us, the recent, large, well-designed, and ongoing NICHD (2006) study is helping sort out some of the caregiving factors that enhance or hinder optimal child development. In longhand, the study is known as the NICHD Study of Early Child Care. In Phase I, this study followed the development of over 1,000 children from birth through age three at 10 different sites in the United States. Phase II followed their development through first grade, and Phase III studies their development in middle childhood (NICHD, 2006).

The primary purpose of the NICHD study is to examine how variations in nonmaternal care are related to children's social adjustment as well as cognitive and physical development. Family characteristics are also of concern. The life course approach of this study helps focus attention on not only the timing of events but also the transitions in the lives of the young children and their families. The network of researchers has attempted to obtain a sample of children that includes families from diverse geographic, economic, and ethnic backgrounds with parents who have diverse work-related issues. The parents, however, come from higher educational and income levels than census data indicate are typical, and Whites are overrepresented in the sample. However, on many other dimensions the sample is quite representative of the U.S. population (NICHD, 2001).

The study involves observations in the home and various measures of social-emotional as well as linguistic and cognitive development. Several indices of quality of day care, such as training of the staff and child-to-staff ratios, are also used. Because of the study's design, the psychologists are able to follow children through a wide range of child-care experiences and to assess combinations and changes in child-care arrangements over time. For example, some infants are cared for at home in the first few months of life, then are turned over to a relative (perhaps a grandmother or an aunt) until the parents decide the child can attend day care or preschool at the age of two. Some of the early results are in.

A critical first question is what constitutes high-quality child care? The NICHD (2006) identified the following specific and measurable guidelines as indicating high-quality care:

- Appropriate adult-to-child ratio (e.g., for infants, a maximum of six children to one adult).
- Small group size (e.g., for children one and a half to two years old, a maximum of eight children).
- Appropriate caregiver education (e.g., completed high school and better yet, completed college with a degree in early childhood education or child development).
- Accreditation by state and/or federal agencies.

Notably, quality of care has been linked to both good cognitive and social development (NICHD, 2006; Wasik, Ramey, Bryant, & Sparling, 1990; Zigler & Gilman, 1998), with high-quality care, of course, enhancing development no matter where it is provided. It is not surprising that NICHD researchers found that when these guidelines are followed (i.e., the standards are high), the more positive the child care and thus the better the children's outcomes. For example, the better the standards, the better the child's cognitive functioning and language development. Similarly, the higher the standards, the more cooperative and sociable the children are. The NICHD (2006) study, however, found that most child care in the United States rated only "fair," with a mere 10 percent of children receiving very high quality care and another 10 percent receiving very poor quality care. On some quality dimensions (such as child-to-adult ratio), only 20 percent of the caregiving arrangements met important criteria.

The NICHD study also made clear that beyond these guidelines there are *processes* that also contribute to high-quality care, such as the caregivers':

- positive attitudes, positive interactions, and warm physical contact (e.g., holding hands) with the children;
- communications to the child, such as asking questions, making comments, or providing answers;
- reading stories, singing songs, and other activities designed to help children learn;
- encouragement of the child's development, such as helping an infant walk;
- social behaviors, such as smiling and laughing.

Sadly, the NICHD (2006) study found that only a small percentage of children received a lot of these positive processes. The study also found that as the child grows older (and thus becomes more sociable), the less positive caregiving the child receives. We might conclude, then, that the child-care experience provides both risks and benefits in the United States (Belsky, 2006).

One other finding of the NICHD study is very important. In the end, despite these interesting results, child-care arrangements had less impact on social-emotional and cognitive development than did family characteristics. This finding has been documented by other researchers (de Schipper, Van Ijzendoorn, & Tavecchio, 2004). In fact, the NICHD researchers concluded that family characteristics overall were better predictors of child development than any other aspects of the child-care situation. Effective parenting may be the most protective factor a child can experience (Knitzer, 2007). Thus, it is clear that early child care cannot be adequately assessed without taking into account the children's experiences *in their own families*. All of these findings, as ever, hold important implications for public policy and for families making decisions about child care.

Plans for the Child Care Dilemma. Over a decade and a half ago, child-care expert Edward Zigler and his colleague Mary Lang (1991) asked how we could make our mixed system of child care effective for all families. The same holds today; how can we make quality, affordable child care available to the many who need it? The solutions are not simple, but the United States seems to have made some baby steps in the right direction, and more can be done (Muenchow & Marsland, 2007). Progress can be made on the family, employer, governmental, and societal levels.

At the most immediate ecological level—the parental or family level—parents can and should familiarize themselves with information about quality child care. Recent studies (for example, the NICHD study) have detailed characteristics of (and importance of) high-quality care. Many of those features were already detailed herein. Parents, however, might not know where to search for such information, so pediatricians, public schools, health departments, and other agencies need to help them find it. Families also need to understand the value of participating in and asking appropriate questions about their children's care. Additionally, many low-income families and single working parents may benefit from higher child tax credits or other subsidies for child care.

At the employer level, there is also much that can be done (Murphy & Halpern, 2006). Generous family leave time, flexible working hours, telecommuting, and in-house child-care centers would help ensure that the organizational climate is family-friendly. A menu of these workplace enhancements, rather than just one option, would also demonstrate to employees that they need not be afraid to utilize them. Working families are here to stay, and what happens to families and children in society should be everyone's concern (Murphy & Halpern, 2006).

Other experts call for sweeping policy changes and rethinking of current policies and funding at the state or federal level (Doherty, Forer, Lero, Goelman, & LaGrange, 2006; Haskins, 2005; Knitzer, 2007; Muenchow & Marsland, 2007; Scarr & Eisenberg, 1993) or increased funding for early childhood care and education (Ludwig & Phillips, 2007). Some of these professionals have called our federal policies downright antifamily (Murphy & Halpern, 2006). European countries, for example, often provide generous family leave time for the arrival of a new child. Sweden allows over 400 days *paid* leave combined for new mothers and fathers. Likewise, based on their research, Phillips, Howes, and Whitebook (1992) favor more federal intervention because state policies vary from good to nonexistent or unenforced regulations. There is much variety among states in their regulations (Riley, Roach, Admans, & Edie, 2005), and states with more demanding standards house fewer centers providing poor-quality care (Lamb & Ahnert, 2006). Rigorous standards, however, are no guarantee of high-quality care. Doherty and her team (2006) found that because appropriate education of child-care workers translates into better care, requiring people who have no interest in working with children (such as in the work-for-welfare programs mentioned in Chapter 7) to provide care to them is incompatible with providing quality care. Others suggest paying child-care workers higher salaries and requiring early childhood education for them (Doherty et al., 2006).

Certainly, although it is difficult, child-care research needs to continue. We know little, for example, about after-school care for older children or the effects of day care on children from various cultural backgrounds. Further research into the exact processes that contribute to high quality care is also needed, although the NICHD study is a good beginning. Among other research issues that are rather neglected are the effect of the child's attachment to the surrogate caregiver, his or her relationship to peers as affected by day care, and how to improve support among the public for high quality child care (Lamb & Ahnert, 2006). Furthermore, most research is center-based, but much care is provided informally or in family/home settings. More research is needed on this latter type of care, too (Raikes, Raikes, & Wilcox, 2005).

Enrichment Education and Early Intervention

Many professionals argue that child care alone is not enough for some children. Although its provision may offer relief to working parents, there are children who, if not provided enrichment education, preschool, or other early interventions, will continue to be behind educationally, socially, and developmentally. Most of these arguments center on economically disadvantaged children or children from various ethnic or racial groups, because such children are relatively less prepared for school (Administration for Children and Families, 2008; Magnuson & Waidfugel, 2005; Stipek & Hakuta, 2007) and are more at risk for later behavior problems (Caputo, 2003; Webster-Stratton & Reid, 2007), such as crime and school dropout. Programs designed to assist economically disadvantaged children and children of color—those believed to be more likely to live in poverty—first came to be known as **compensatory education** or **early intervention** programs. Today such programs are more likely to be known as **enrichment education.** Such programs are thought to form an "invisible safety net" (Currie, 2006) to prevent future problems of children at risk (Administration on Children and Families, 2008). With the growth of the Hispanic population, the increased role of technology in high-paying jobs, more mothers entering the workforce, and other societal changes, these programs are becoming more important yet more contentious.

The seminal debate is as follows. Are compensatory education programs really beneficial to these children, especially given their costs, most of which are carried by the taxpayers? For example, if Roberto had attended a preschool designed especially for Hispanic children about to enter mainstream public schools, would his early elementary education have been easier, better, and more successful? To address this question, we explore the best-known enrichment education program: **Head Start.**

The Economic Opportunity Act of 1964 established a variety of ways that children might benefit from social programs, one of which was Project Head Start (Ludwig & Phillips, 2007). By means of a national preschool program, the goal of Head Start is to reach children between the ages of three and five from low-income families. It is a total or comprehensive program in that it attempts to meet the children's mental, emotional, health, and educational needs (Haskins, 2005). The federal government picks up much of the cost, although under various administrations the program has fared better or worse (Ludwig & Phillips, 2007; Knitzer, 2007; Zigler, 1994; Zigler & Muenchow, 1992). Head Start is now the largest program providing comprehensive educational, health, and social services to young children and their families living in poverty; thus, it is an important player in the early childhood service delivery system. Here are some program statistics for 2006 (Office of Head Start, 2007), the latest available at the time of this writing:

- Over 900,000 children were enrolled (since its inception, Head Start has serviced 24 million children).
- Over 39 percent of the children were White, over 30 percent were Black, and 30 percent were Hispanic.
- 72 percent of Head Start teachers have at least an AA degree in early childhood education.
- 27 percent of Head Start program staff members were parents of current students or were former Head Start children.
- Nearly 925,000 parents volunteered in their local Head Start program.
- More than 211,000 Head Start fathers participated in organized, regularly scheduled activities designed to involve them in Head Start programs.
- 91 percent of Head Start children had health insurance.

Head Start historically has been somewhat unique among early childhood education programs. Because of some of its unique features, the program incorporates some of the principles of community psychology as outlined earlier in the book. First, although it is a nationwide program, Head Start programs can be tailored to each individual community. Second, it was one of the first programs to demonstrate that a single approach or a single intervention is insufficient. For example, Project Head Start is not just a preschool program. One of the revolutionary ideas of this program is to involve parents as decision makers and learners (Zigler & Muenchow, 1992). Many Head Start parents have become certified Head Start teachers. Although not meant to substitute for regular health care, Head Start was also designed to ensure that the children received health screening and follow-up treatment. Moreover, Project Head Start was not designed simply to enrich children's environments so as to enhance IQ. Rather, the program was developed so that children would be motivated to make the most of their lives (Zigler & Muenchow, 1992). An important question is, Has it done this?

Head Start has been in existence for over 40 years, so researchers should easily be able to assess both its short- and long-term effects. Right? Not exactly! Head Start research is extremely difficult to conduct for a number of reasons. First, the programs are rather variable across the country and do not use random assignment for enrolling children (Lamb & Ahnert, 2006). Moreover, Head Start programs have been evolving over time such that today's programs are not identical to the earlier ones; the few long-term evaluations that have been conducted do not take this into account (Ludwig & Phillips, 2007). Third, researchers do not agree on exactly what constitutes "progress" by the children. A large or small gain? In what? School readiness? Social skills? Cognitive skills? Better health? What if gains are so small that the program is not cost-effective? In addition, the larger ecological environment surrounding Head Start children is continually in flux, as, for example, when societal prejudice waxes and wanes, more single mothers enter the workforce, and public opinion about such programs shifts (Ludwig & Phillips, 2007). Given this ever-changing milieu, program effects are more difficult to tease out. We examine some of the newest research next, but the Head Start program will probably always fluctuate from site to site, forever have its critics, be subject to research biases, and continue to transform as federal and state policies, the political climate, and funding change.

Many authors claim that Head Start demonstrates that the program provides benefits for children (Love, Tarullo, Raikes, & Chazan-Cohen, 2006; Ludwig & Phillips, 2007; Administration for Children and Families, 2005). Some studies do show short-term gains for the children. For example, a major research study (3,200 children in 40 programs) concluded that Head Start narrows the gap between disadvantaged children and all other children in vocabulary and writing skills. Another study (Administration for Children and Families, 2006) also resulted in findings that showed Head Start children over time improved social skills and that Head Start led to better word knowledge, letter recognition, and math and writing skills compared to nonprogram children when they reached kindergarten. The same study also showed that Head Start children experienced modest gains in health status as well as improved parenting (e.g., use of more educational materials and less physical discipline).

But what about long-term effects? In a study of some of the earliest graduates of Head Start, the researcher found that as adolescents, Head Start students appeared comparable to other adolescents in regard to the highest grade completed, their sense of personal mastery, health, and mental health (Caputo, 2004). Another way to look at long-term effects is by means of cost-effectiveness. In these terms, early intervention programs like Head Start again appear to pay their way. Cost-effectiveness is a measure of great interest to taxpayers and policy makers. Ludwig and Phillips (2007) recently reviewed the cost-benefit literature on the program. They determined, "There is now an accumulating body of evidence on Head Start's long-term impacts that seems to suggest the program probably passed a benefit-cost test for those children who participated during the program's first few decades" (p. 3).

For example, children from Head Start (as compared to nonparticipating siblings) are more likely to complete high school and more likely to attend college. Head Start also reduces the chances of being arrested and subsequently being charged with a crime. Many of these results held regardless of the child's race or ethnicity. There are also benefits to parents and society in that high-quality child care is typically provided in Head Start, special education placements are reduced, and grade retention (repeating a year) is lower. In sum, Ludwig and Phillips conclude that Head Start generated benefits in excess of program costs with the ratio possibly being as high as seven to one. Notably, Ludwig and Phillips also argue that each extra dollar of program funding a county spends easily outweighs the extra spending.

Head Start is not the only early intervention program available, but it probably is the best-known one. The High/Scope Perry Preschool program was also designed to alter the causal chain that leads from childhood poverty to school failure to subsequent adult poverty and related social problems, such as involvement with the criminal justice system. The High/Scope program incorporates into its design developmentally appropriate learning materials based on psychological principles of development, small class sizes, staff trained in early childhood development, in-service training for staff, parental involvement, and sensitivity to the noneducational needs of the child and family. What is fairly unique about this program is that it views the child as an active rather than passive, self-initiating learner. Typically, the child selects his or her own activities from among a variety of learning areas the teacher prepares—called **participatory learning** (Schweinhart, 2006; Weikart & Schweinhart, 1997).

Research on the High/Scope Perry Preschool project is impressive. In the short run the High/Scope Perry project improves educational outcomes, such as higher IQ and achievement test scores. The program also reduces the need for school remedial services (Ramey & Ramey, 2003). In the long run, evidence collected over more than two decades shows that the program results in lowered crime rates, reduced high school dropout, less need for welfare assistance, increased earnings as adults, and higher personal wealth (Schweinhart & Weikart, 1998). The wealth accrues in several ways, not the least of which is higher likelihood of employment and home ownership and fewer evictions from rental units (Schweinhart, 2007).

Nores, Belfield, Barnett, and Schweinhart (2005) claim that the High/Scope Perry Preschool program returns an amazing $5.67 to $12.90 for every dollar expended, depending on the calculations used. Savings or benefits occur in lowered welfare assistance, lower special education and justice system costs, savings to crime victims, and increased tax revenues from higher earnings by the participants (Nores et al., 2005; Parks, 2000). This research again illustrates that the participants, their parents, the public, and the adult graduates of early interventions programs all benefit from such programs.

THE PUBLIC SCHOOLS

Although education laws vary by state, at the age of five or six, most children in the United States attend public schools: elementary first, then middle school, and then high school. Many students breeze through the school system without difficulty. Others experience difficulties on entering school, and some develop problems later in their academic careers. For example, the transition from early childhood—whether the child is reared at home or provided day care or preschool—can be difficult for some children. Transition from middle school to high school can also be troublesome. Such times of transition or milestones help psychologists predict who might be at risk for developing school-related problems (Koizumi, 2000; Warren-Sohlberg, Jason, Orosan-Weine, Lantz, & Reyes, 1998).

In addition, schools are remarkable social institutions shaped by political and social events, such as the civil rights movement, the introduction of computers into schools, and the changing demographic trends, such as the increase in our Hispanic population. One event of major importance—the desegregation of schools—is reviewed first.

Desegregation, Ethnicity, and Prejudice in the Schools

Because Roberto, the young man in the opening vignette, is now about 22 years old, he benefited from the civil rights movement of the 1950s and 1960s. Or has he? It is necessary to examine the complex effects of societal prejudice as well as public policy changes designed to confront prejudice, discrimination, and segregation—in particular, on children and schools. Seymour Sarason (1997), a leading expert on U.S. schools, called the nation's schools our Achilles' heel. He argued that the nearly total failure of the education reform movement has had and will continue to have consequences beyond the educational arena, one of these being racism. Has anything improved in over a decade since Sarason made these comments?

The Historical Context. Despite the fact that amendments to the U.S. Constitution long ago gave equal protection under the laws and the right to vote to all citizens, it was not until the 1950s that events took place that have had a lasting and sweeping effect on our schools. In 1954, the Supreme Court of the United States decided the case of *Brown v. Board of Education of Topeka, Kansas*. In fashioning their decision, the Supreme Court justices heard major testimony from social scientists about the detrimental effects of segregation on African American pupils (see, for example, Clark & Clark, 1947). In the official unanimous rendering, the judges cited social science research as being influential in their deliberations (Levine & Perkins, 1997). The consequence of the decision was that there would no longer be a place for segregation in schools, not even for separate but equal educational facilities. Interestingly, the judges were not initially concerned with implementing their decision, nor in the precise effects of desegregation on children once it was instituted. Despite school desegregation, the ruling did little to alter a society that remained segregated in housing and other social institutions, such as places of worship (Well, Holme, Atanda, & Revilla, 2005).

Some school authorities scrambled to come into compliance with the ruling. The chosen method for desegregation was often "one-way busing" (Oskamp, 1984), where inner-city children were bused to the suburbs and all-White districts. Some school systems dragged their heels, and some openly defied the ruling; subsequent court-ordered desegregation plans were imposed on them. Public policy changed some discriminatory behaviors, voluntarily or involuntarily, but an important question is, Did it change all related behaviors? An equally important matter was whether the children were really better off with this policy. Social scientists quickly became concerned with these and other issues of desegregation (Maruyama, 2003).

Prejudice and Its Companions. In the opening vignette, Roberto revealed that he thought the other children believed he was dumb. Is this a form of prejudice? If yes, how did the children form this impression?

Prejudice is an unjustified attitude (usually negative) toward the members of some group, based solely on their group membership. If Roberto's classmates thought he was dumb because he was Hispanic, they were indeed prejudiced. A companion to prejudice is discrimination. **Discrimination** involves prejudiced actions toward particular groups based almost exclusively on group membership. If Roberto's classmates refused to play with him on the playground because of his ethnic background, they would have been discriminating against him. Interestingly, studies in social psychology have demonstrated that people can be prejudiced without discrimination or can discriminate without harboring prejudices (e.g., La Piere, 1934). **Stereotypes,** a related concept, are beliefs that all members of certain groups share the same or common traits or characteristics. In keeping with the same example, if Roberto's classmates classified all Hispanics as dumb, then they would have held a stereotype.

Important historical research on stereotyping in classrooms was conducted by Rosenthal and Jacobson (1968). In their study, teachers were told that perfectly normal children were either "bloomers" or "normal." Teachers were *not* told to treat these two groups differently. By the end of the study, the so-called bloomers showed dramatic improvements in classroom performance and IQ scores, probably because they had been the beneficiaries of positive prejudice. It is important to remember that all children were randomly assigned to the conditions of normal or bloomer. This study demonstrates that teachers' labels and their stereotypes of children somehow fulfill the teachers' prophecies. This phenomenon, where a labeled individual fulfills someone else's forecast, is called the **self-fulfilling prophecy.** Studies have shown that teachers' expectations in a variety of classroom settings *do* influence student achievement and motivation (Weinstein et al., 1991).

Research on contemporary society indicates that people's prejudices and labels may be quite different from those of the cohort groups previous to the civil rights movement (Hitlan, Camillo, Zárate, & Aikman, 2007). Before 1950, **traditional racism** was more *overt* (Dovidio, Gaertner, Nier, Kawakami, & Hodson, 2004) with open name calling, different laws for certain groups ("Negroes ride in the back of the bus"), and, in fact, mob actions against as well as lynchings of certain groups. In **modern prejudice** (Dovidio & Gaertner, 1998; Duffy, Olczak, & Grosch, 1993), sometimes called **aversive racism** (Dovidio et al., 2004), people's attitudes are more *covert* and subtle. These subtle forms of prejudice and discrimination allow their users to conceal the hidden, negative views they really hold.

Pettigrew and Meertens (1995) offered an interesting demonstration of the existence of blatant as well as more contemporary forms of prejudice. They administered prejudice scales to participants and found individuals who were high in blatant (overt) prejudice, high in subtle (modern) prejudice, or low on both types of prejudice. As predicted, participants' attitudes toward immigrants could be forecast by their scores on the prejudice scales. Those high in blatant or old-fashioned prejudice wanted to send immigrants back to their own countries. Those low in all types of prejudice wanted to take actions that would help immigrants remain in their new country and improve their rights. Most interestingly, those who scored high on the modern racism scale tended to reject immigrants in subtle and covert ways—for example, they were not willing to do anything to improve either immigrant rights or their own relations with the immigrants.

Prejudice, then, has not disappeared simply because the courts have ruled that desegregation and equal opportunity must prevail. It has simply taken on a different appearance—a more subtle form. Given that prejudice still pervades society and that more diverse groups (e.g., Hispanics and Asians) are being added to the United States (American Psychological Association, 2005), we should devote some attention to immigrant experiences.

Until recently, the United States boasted of its heritage of immigrants (Mahalingam, 2006). Indeed, today, we are still a nation of immigrants (Deaux, 2006). Much of our population is first-, second-, or third-generation immigrants. Census data tell us since 1970, the number of immigrants living in the United States has tripled, and during the 1990s, the immigrant population grew by more than 50 percent (Silka, 2007). Census data also reveal that large cities are made up of multiple immigrant populations. New York City's population, for example, was comprised of 28 percent immigrants in 1990; today immigrants make up 40 percent of New York's population (Deaux, 2006). What census data do *not* tell us is that arriving immigrants face different cultural traditions and values, different languages, and different religions. They also face different business customs, health care practices, art forms, and schools (Silka, 2007). Immigrants also face much prejudice, marginalization, and discrimination that cause myriad adjustment problems for them (Mahalingam, 2006). Immigration undeniably is a "hot button" issue today (Deaux, 2006). Witness the large role immigration played in the candidates' remarks leading up to the presidential election in 2008.

Immigrants of color face the most prejudice (Mahalingam, 2006). Historically, biases against various immigrant groups have waxed and waned; Japanese citizens, for instance, faced high levels of prejudice before, during, and after World War II. More recently, Arab and Mexican immigrants have faced immense prejudice (Hitlan et al., 2007). "Americans" who perceive themselves as "American" often manifest the most prejudice (Hitlan et al., 2007), especially those high in social dominance (Danso, Sedlovskaya, & Suanda, 2007). They do so by over-including strangers in immigrant out-groups (this concept is covered shortly) (Kosic & Phalet, 2006) and by dehumanizing immigrants—not seeing them in personalized ways (Danso et al., 2007)—or isolating them (Silka, 2007).

The actions that people take toward immigrants occur, for the most part, at the community level (Silka, 2007). For this chapter, then, an important question is, When children from all of these different backgrounds are intermingled in classrooms, do they experience prejudice? Discrimination? Stereotyping? If yes—and you already know the answer is yes—what can we do to lessen the effects of any prejudices they bring from home? Given that children begin to develop ethnic attitudes by age three and systematic racial prejudices between five and seven years of age (Houlette et al., 2004), most intervention efforts are directed at young children. Psychologists have some interesting and innovative programs to address this issue.

Fostering Acceptance of Diversity in the Classroom. In a famous demonstration with children called "The Eye of the Storm," teacher Jane Elliot told the dark-eyed children that they were inferior to the light-eyed children. In fact, she said they were so inferior that the light-eyed children were not to play or have contact with the dark-eyed children. The light-eyed children soon segregated, taunted, and mistreated the dark-eyed children. Elliot then reversed the roles; the light-eyed children were now the inferior ones. When she debriefed the children and they discussed their feelings, the children talked about how horrible it felt to be the victims of such intense prejudice. This demonstration reveals just one means by which children in schools can be familiarized with what prejudice feels like. What other techniques are in the psychological arsenal for fostering acceptance of diversity in classrooms?

One other approach to reduce prejudice is to *actively* involve children with one another. **Intergroup contact** is when two conflicting groups come together, and the contact enables them to better understand and appreciate one another (Brewer, 1999; Kawakami, Phills, Steele, & Dovidio, 2007; Molina & Wittig, 2006; Paluk, 2006; Zirkel & Cantor, 2004). Research demonstrates that only certain intergroup contacts enhance people's understanding and acceptance of each other (Kawakami et al., 2007; Marcus-Newhall & Heindl, 1998; Molina & Wittig, 2006).

Stuart Cook has been a leading proponent of the contact hypothesis for reducing prejudice. The **contact hypothesis** states that personal contact between people from disliked groups works to decrease the negative attitudes *but only under certain conditions*. The five conditions are:

1. The groups or individuals must be of equal status.
2. The attributes of the disliked group that become apparent during the contact must be such as to disconfirm the prevailing stereotyped beliefs about the group.
3. The contact situation must encourage, or perhaps require, a mutually independent relationship or cooperation to achieve a joint goal.
4. The contact situation must promote association of the sort that will reveal enough details about members of the disliked group to encourage seeing them as individuals rather than as persons with stereotyped group characteristics.
5. The social norms of contact must favor the concept of group equality and egalitarian intergroup association (Allport, 1954/1979; Cook, 1985).

Of all of these, interdependence appears to be very important (Molina & Wittig, 2006). Molina and Wittig would also add that respected authority figures need to support such intergroup efforts if they are to decrease bias, for example, in the schools. They also acknowledge that knowing which contact conditions are optimal for what outcomes and for which groups will improve success in intergroup contact programs. In other words, one size does not fit all.

Several quasi-experimental and laboratory experimental studies of the intergroup contact hypothesis have been conducted and support the hypothesis (Pettigrew, 1998). Only one set of studies are reviewed here. Wright, Aron, McLaughlin-Volpe, and Ropp (1997) examined the hypothesis that if it is known that an in-group member has a close relationship with an out-group member, more positive intergroup attitudes will result. The **in-group** is the group with which one identifies, whereas the **out-group** is the group one perceives as being different from one's own group, as in racial groups to which one does *not* belong (Duffy & Atwater, 2008).

In one study, Wright and colleagues (1997) found that participants who knew an in-group member who had a friendship with an out-group member held less negative attitudes toward the out-group. In another study, competition and conflict were induced to create in- and out-groups. When in-group members discovered that their own group members had cross-group friendships (that in-group members were friends with some members of the out-group), negative attitudes toward the out-group were reduced.

In line with these studies, other authors have found that intergroup contact reduces prejudice or creates a greater appreciation for diverse groups at a variety of grade levels—college, for example (Gunn, Ratnesh, Nagda, & Lopez, 2004; Hurtado, 2005; Lopez, 2004). Molina and Wittig (2006) recently found that in schools, the opportunity for individualized interactions with members of diverse groups helps reduce prejudice. Kawakami et al. (2007) found that merely approaching members of a certain group can lead to more favorable attitudes toward that group.

Kawakami and colleagues warn, though, that their research addresses only a basic and limited mechanism—approach behavior. In the world at large, their research does not speak to the more general questions related to the impact of contact in everyday settings and over extended periods of time. Research on intergroup contact needs to continue. Undoubtedly, many schools, workplaces, and other organizations promote diversity or provide some form of diversity or cultural sensitivity training (Paluk, 2006). However, because these programs are not always grounded in sound theory—such as intergroup contact theory—and research, they do not always work (Paluk, 2006).

Elliot Aronson (2004) and his colleagues pioneered another technique called the **jigsaw classroom.** In this type of classroom, students initially work on a project in mastery groups. In this first type of group, students all learn the same general material, but each group learns different details about that material. The mastery groups then break into jigsaw groups such that one student from each mastery group comprises the jigsaw group. For example, if students were learning about prejudice, one mastery group would learn the definitions and examples for *prejudice, discrimination,* and *stereotypes.* A second mastery group would learn about the detrimental effects of prejudice. A third might learn about ways to reduce prejudice, and so on. In the jigsaw groups, one student from the definition group, one student from the detrimental effects group, and one from the how-to-reduce-prejudice group would come together and teach the others the appropriate module. In this way, isolated students become more central to the group, and competitive students learn to cooperate. Without everyone's interdependence and cooperation in the jigsaw group, the group cannot achieve its learning goals. Students who trip over English words are prompted and assisted by the other children; otherwise, no one can learn (Aronson, Blaney, Stephan, Sikes, & Snapp, 1978; Walker & Crogan, 1998).

In one of the first major experiments on the jigsaw technique, Blaney, Stephan, Rosenfield, Aronson, and Sikes (1977) found that attitudes toward classmates and the school, self-esteem, cooperative learning, and school performance all improved over control students' in standard classrooms. Of course, competitiveness also declined. Other research has documented that peer teaching, as used in the jigsaw method, improves peer liking, learning, and perceptions of the classroom climate (Slavin, 1985; Wright & Cowen, 1985). Exciting news is that positive results from cooperative strategies such as peer teaching seem to generalize to children not in the immediate school environment (Miller, Brewer, & Edwards, 1985), for example, to all members of a minority group. Some authors have even suggested that the jigsaw classroom will work with older students, including college students (Williams, 2004).

Since the jigsaw technique was introduced, other similar cooperative learning techniques have been developed (e.g., Houlette et al., 2004; Slavin, 1996). What is important is that the positive results of these forms of cooperative learning have been replicated in thousands of classrooms, thus making cooperative learning "a major force within the field of public education. . . . [Cooperative learning] is generally accepted as one of the most effective ways of improving race relations and instruction in desegregated schools" (Aronson, Wilson, & Akert, 1999, p. 544).

Some states have experimented with **magnet schools** to reduce prejudice, where students from a variety of school districts attend a certain school because it specializes in a particular discipline, such as music or foreign languages. Interested students are thus attracted to the schools like steel to a magnet. These schools create a natural experiment on intergroup contact because students of many backgrounds attend. Rossell (1988) compared the effectiveness of voluntary plans at magnet schools to mandatory reassignment desegregation plans. She found that magnet schools produce greater long-term interracial exposure than mandatory reassignment, probably because of what she and others have called "White flight" from the reassigned districts. In line with this, Fauth, Leventhal, and Brooks-Gunn (2007) recently reported that even court-ordered moving of disadvantaged, minority students and their families to higher income neighborhoods (and schools) can have deleterious effects not only on the youths but on their parents and their parenting styles. Forced desegregation does not appear to be working as well as some of the programs described here.

We can conclude that once classrooms are desegregated, by court order or by voluntary design, there are some good, empirically tested means by which children can become more accepting and helpful to one another. But what happens to the academic and social performance of these students? If the courts determined that separate education was not only unequal but inferior for many economically disadvantaged students, does desegregation in any form accelerate the upward path of the targeted children?

Effects of Desegregation. One noted authority (Pettigrew, 2004) reviewed research on the effects of desegregation and concluded that desegregation does work as supported by research but *only when the research controls for social class*. As you may have learned in Chapter 7, socioeconomic class is intricately intertwined with race and ethnic inequities (Hochschild, 2003), so it needs to be carefully scrutinized alongside desegregation. In specific, Pettigrew's review concluded that compared to Black children in segregated schools, Black children from desegregated schools are more likely to:

- attend and finish college, even White-dominated colleges,
- work with White co-workers and have better jobs,
- live in interracial neighborhoods,
- earn higher incomes,
- have more White friends and more positive attitudes toward Whites.

Pettigrew laments, however, that the historic upward trajectory toward equal education for Blacks and Whites was slow and circuitous, whereas the retreat from it has been swift and direct, with much of the backpedaling blamed on court decisions. In fact, some courts have even lifted desegregation orders, for example, in Nashville, Tennessee (Goldring, Cohen-Vogel, Smrekar, & Taylor, 2006). In many of these instances, students returned to neighborhood schools that were closer to their homes. What has been the result of this latest trend? Once again, social scientists have some interesting perspectives and answers.

Goldring and colleagues studied schooling closer to home and found that geographic proximity to school does not necessarily translate into supportive community contexts for children. Black children, they found, were more likely to be reassigned to schools in higher risk (high poverty and crime rates) neighborhoods than were White children. Another noted expert on desegregation, John Diamond (2006) explains that even in integrated (wealthier?) suburbs, the playing field still is not level at school. For one thing, suburban Blacks often teeter on the fence between privilege and peril, as he calls it, because of the difference between "wealth" and "assets." Blacks in suburbs still do not have as many assets (e.g., own their homes) as Whites. Daniel (2004) adds that the new emphasis on "accountability" and "achievement" has undermined the movement toward desegregation by distracting attention away from it. Furthermore, Davis (2004) suggests that segregation issues have also become less urgent because Americans are now focused more on school safety issues. Arias (2005) also bemoans that fact that the *Brown v. Board of Education* was designed to assist African Americans, and to date we have little information about whether desegregation and other related strategies are appropriate for Latinos and other ethnic or racial minorities. There is still much to be done to research and overcome these and other educational issues (King, 2004).

The Schools and Adolescents

Despite nationwide efforts to desegregate U.S. schools, and despite the best-laid plans to provide early intervention programs for targeted children, it remains true that many children isolated in the inner city continue to be economically disadvantaged and receive poor-quality education. These children are usually from a racial or ethnic minority, yet they have never benefited from any of the mentioned programs; thus, inner-city children mature to adolescence still trapped in poverty. Psychologists consider inner-city adolescents most at risk for academic failure, dropping out of school, teen pregnancy, drug use, and myriad other problems that interfere with obtaining an education necessary to break the cycle of poverty (Caputo, 2003; Magnuson & Waidfugel, 2005; Stipek & Hakuta, 2007; Webster-Stratton & Reid, 2007). Eventually, as adults, they are more likely to experience life's stresses and strains (Golding, Potts, & Aneshensel, 1991; Rank, 2005).

In the interest of space, two relevant issues will be examined here: dropping out of school and school violence. First, however, will be a discussion of the role of the school itself in creating some of the problems found within it (Branson, 1998).

The School Climate.   It is not just inner-city and minority children who have problems in school. There are multitudes of reasons middle-class students drop out, get pregnant, fail, or underachieve in school. Some of the reasons are the same as for the inner-city students. Remember also that not all minorities live in the inner city, so they need to be tapped for research purposes, as well (Milburn, Gary, Booth, & Brown, 1991). It would be easy to blame students for being alienated or for having some personality flaw that makes them restless and unmotivated (Legault, Green-Demers, & Pelletier, 2006), but research shows that even gifted children become bored with, disinterested in, or bullied at school (Feldheusen, 1989; Meade, 1991). An important, relevant construct for us is **alienation from school.** According to Bronfenbrenner (1986), *alienation* means lacking a sense of belonging, feeling cut off. *School alienation* means lacking a sense of belonging in school. This phenomenon has received much attention in the community psychology literature, but community psychologists focus on the circumstances in which the alienated child finds him- or herself rather than just on the child.

In 1983, Seymour Sarason authored *Schooling in America: Scapegoat and Salvation*, in which he suggested that schools are relatively uninteresting places for both children and teachers. Sarason contended that children often exhibit more intellectual curiosity and learn faster outside of school (Sarason, 1983; Weinstein, 1990). Bronfenbrenner (1986) added that children under stress at home can easily feel distracted and alienated at school. Some 20 years later, Aronson (2004) issued a rather harsh invective against American schools, particularly our high schools, in his analysis of the Columbine (Colorado) school tragedy in which a teacher and 14 students were killed. He stated that

> the rampage killings are just the pathological tip of an enormous iceberg: The poisonous social atmosphere prevalent at most high schools in this country—an atmosphere characterized by exclusion, rejection, taunting and humiliation. In high school there is an iron-clad hierarchy of cliques. . . . At the bottom are kids who are too fat, too thin, too short, too tall, who wear the wrong clothes or simply don't fit in. . . . My interviews with high school students indicate that almost all of them know the rank ordering of the hierarchy and are well aware of their own place in that hierarchy. (p. 355)

My own (Duffy) in-class research with students in two community psychology classes reveals another interesting feature of schools. I asked two different classes of students six years apart to record their most memorable experience—the one that stands out most in their minds—from public school. Out of 40 students, only 1 reported a positive academic experience, 4 reported positive nonacademic experiences (e.g., athletic championships), and 34 reported negative nonacademic experiences. The students mostly remembered sad or frightening incidents involving fights between students or between students and teachers, fires, bombs, child abuse, and other unfortunate events. In other words, at least retrospectively, the salient features of schools seem to be negative and unrelated to learning. Some of the students' experiences are revealed in Case in Point 8.1. What is your most salient memory of school thus far?

Contemporary authors have identified some of the ecological components of schools or, loosely, of the **school climate**—which encompasses the entire culture of the school and not just educational methods and goals (Van Houtte, 2005)—that contribute to school alienation. Teacher, administrative, and peer support (Gregory et al., 2007) as well as clarity and consistency of school rules and regulations are some of the features contributing to a school's climate (Way, Reddy, & Rhodes, 2007). Safety in the physical facility, student autonomy, and teacher/administrator abuse of power, among others, are also characteristics that contribute to school climate (Langhout, 2004). Loukes, Suzuki, and Horton (2006) also mention cohesiveness between, friction with, and competition against other students as components of school climate. These and other aspects of school climate are related to student problems such as violence and school dropout.

CASE IN POINT 8.1
STUDENTS' MEMORIES OF PUBLIC SCHOOL

As described, I (Duffy) asked students in my community psychology classes to record their most memorable experience in school. No other instructions were given. For example, I did not tell them to think of a positive or negative experience. Most incidents recalled by the students were negative, and almost all pertained to nonacademic events, such as fights, disagreements between teachers and students, bombs, and so on. Here are some randomly selected ones.

> In 10th grade I had a chemistry teacher who enjoyed belittling students. One girl was the brunt of almost every joke. She was overweight, and he called her a whale and would make comments like "Nuke the whales!" Not surprisingly, she dropped out of the class, but the joking didn't stop. One day, disgusted with my teacher, I raised my hand in the middle of one of his rampages. When he called on me, I proceeded to tell him that I thought he was the most immature, cruel, vindictive, and irresponsible teacher I'd ever met. . . . He told me that since I felt I had to come to [this overweight girl's] rescue that he'd just pick on me. From then on, his teasing of me became nastier than it had been before.

> Four honor students planted a bomb in my high school one night, attempting to blow up the school. They were all caught, tried, and sentenced. One culprit would have probably been salutatorian. The administration hush-hushed the incident, so I don't know why they did it or how long their sentences were.

> It was the last day of school and my teacher was in the process of distributing our report cards. After he had done about three-fourths of the class, he announced that anyone he hadn't given one to had to line up at his desk and get their birthday spanking from him before they got the report card (their birthdays were in the summer, so everyone else had gotten their [spanking] during the course of the school year). . . . Three years later my teacher was convicted of over 100 counts of child molestation involving his stepdaughter. I guess these spankings meant a lot more to him than we could have ever known.

> I had a [Black] friend who got into an argument with a White kid. The White kid called [him] a nigger at one point (big mistake). [My friend] punched the kid once, square in the nose. The kid wobbled around for a second or two before he fell unconscious on the floor. His nose had a metal plate on it for about a month. [My friend] had to pay medical expenses. . . . A day without a physical fight was very rare.

Schools are indeed places of learning but not just of reading, writing, and arithmetic. The whole school environment is a learning experience that can sometimes place the students at risk.

As you can see, the nature of schools is complex, so responses require an array of options that should have their foundations in research (Freiberg & Lapoint, 2006). One sample response to poor school climate and subsequent school alienation is **alternative education**. Alternative education, or alternate schools, have components that differ from traditional schools. For example, in traditional schools, the curriculum and requirements are designed by teachers and administrators. In alternative settings, the students and perhaps their parents in consultation with teachers design the curriculum or select classes in which the student will enroll or help set up rules (Vieno, Perkins, Smith, & Santinello, 2005). Students generally express a desire to have some autonomy, independence, and choice in school (Langhout, 2004). This more democratic type of school environment is reminiscent of the High/Scope Perry Preschool discussed previously and has been identified for being responsible for creating a greater sense of community in the school (Vieno et al., 2005). In addition, in alternative schools, the classes might also be smaller (Boyd-Zaharias, 1999; Muir, 2000–2001), and learning can occur outside a traditional classroom setting (Coffee & Pestridge, 2001).

Solomon, Watson, Battisch, Schaps, and Delucchi (1996) designed an alternative program to provide students with the environment and experiences essential to the development of a sense of community in their schools. Students in the alternative program were compared to nonparticipating students to evaluate the program. Specifically, the program included cooperative rather than individual learning, interpersonal helping and other prosocial activities, active promotion of discussions about prosocial values (such as fairness), and empathy and interpersonal understanding. Results indicated that the program was successful in heightening the sense of community in the classrooms. Moreover, sense of community related positively to a number of student outcomes, such as ability to manage conflicts with and likelihood of helping others. Further studies indicate that alternative education is successful in creating higher student and teacher satisfaction with the schools and better student achievement (Arnold et al., 1999; Catterall & Stern, 1986; Coffee & Pestridge, 2001; Gray & Chanoff, 1986; Trickett, McConahay, Phillips, & Ginter, 1985).

Just what are the mechanisms by which alternative education creates these effects? Studies have identified the elements of student participation, self-direction, and empowerment (Gray & Chanoff, 1986; Matthews, 1991); innovative and relaxed atmospheres (Fraser, Williamson, & Tobin, 1987; Matthews, 1991); and empathetic teachers (Taylor, 1986–1987). All of these factors are *outside* the student; they are not personality attributes of the students in the alternate settings but factors related to the ecology of the alternate setting, which is in line with principles of community psychology.

One other promising intervention currently receiving attention in the literature is the use of mentors to assist children with their social, interpersonal, and other skills both inside and outside the school (Cassinerio & Lane-Garon, 2006; Novotney, Mertinko, Lange, & Baker, 2000; Phillip & Hendry, 2000). A **mentor** is a caregiver or other adult who develops a close bond with the child. Mentors often make a positive and lasting impression on a child. Cassinerio and Lane-Garon, for example, assigned university-level students to urban middle school children learning to become mediators or neutral conflict managers for their schools. Analysis of results of the mentoring program reveals that at year's end the school climate was rated more positively, and there were fewer reports of violence in the school compared to the previous year. The study is notable because the school enrolled not only White students but many Asians, Hispanics, and African Americans—a situation ripe for student conflicts.

Other Factors Related to School Success or Failure. The school climate is not the only school-related risk factor affecting children. Students who transfer from one school to another and those who are moving from elementary to junior high or junior high to high school (Compas, Wagner, Slavin, & Vannatta, 1986; Koizumi, 2000; Reyes, Gillock, Kobus, & Sanchez, 2000; Reyes & Jason, 1991) are also considered at risk for problems. These and a host of other factors require attention from educators if children are to adjust to schools. Also important is the finding that poor marks in school, absence of positive coping behaviors, and presence of negative coping behavior in the early grades predict mental health problems some 15 years later (Ialongo et al., 1999; Spivack & Marcus, 1987).

One of the most promising approaches to ensure healthy adjustment—not just in school but throughout life—is **cognitive problem solving** (Cowen, 1980) or other programs that teach social skills (Magee Quinn, Kavale, Mathur, Rutherford, & Forness, 1999). Cognitive problem solving involves generating alternative strategies to reach one's goal as well as consideration of the consequences of each alternative. Cognitive problem solving also generally includes developing specific ideas for carrying out one's chosen solution (Elias et al., 1986).

Cognitive problem solving can be used for interpersonal problems, such as racial and teacher–student conflicts, school-related problems, and many other areas of concern. When used for interpersonal problems, it is called **interpersonal cognitive problem solving** (Rixon & Erwin, 1999; Shure, 1997, 1999; Shure & Spivack, 1988). Research has uncovered the fact that a significant difference between well-adjusted and less well-adjusted children is that the latter group fails to generate and evaluate a variety of solutions for coping with a personal problem. Although this method is not without controversy (Gillespie, Durlak, & Sherman, 1982; Rickel & Burgio, 1982), training in cognitive problem solving has been used successfully as an intervention to assist children with coping with stressors and reducing student conflict (Edwards, Hunt, Meyers, Grogg, & Jarrett, 2005). Both teachers and parents can be trained to teach children cognitive problem solving.

Using a pre-post design, Elias and colleagues (1986) taught elementary children interpersonal cognitive problem-solving skills and compared them to a no-treatment group on entry into middle school. The intervention group's curriculum included training in interpersonal sensitivity, generating alternative methods to reach goals, discovering obstacles for solving problems, and creating in the children expectancies that their initiatives could result in positive resolution of their problems. The training was significantly related to reductions in the severity of a variety of middle-school stressors, such as finding one's way around a new school, establishing new peer relations, and resisting pressure to engage in certain negative behaviors (e.g., smoking). Work and Olsen's (1990) research also demonstrated that training in problem solving improves adjustment in children and is probably effective because of increases in empathy in the trained children. Elias and associates (1986) suggested that the reason some studies show equivocal results for cognitive problem-solving training is that they are conducted simultaneously in too many different and varied settings.

There have been well over 50 child and adolescent interventions conducted based on the premise that cognitive problem-solving skills mediate adjustment (Denham & Almeida, 1987; Shure, 1999) and improve interpersonal skills (i.e., reduce conflict) (Edwards et al., 2005; Erwin, Purves, & Johannes, 2005). Although many of the studies support this strategy as competency enhancing, cognitive problem solving is not without its critics. Durlak (1983), for example, advocates task-specific rather than generic problem-solving training.

Dropping Out of School. In the opening vignette, Roberto wisely chose to stay in school despite his early feelings of frustration and alienation. Some students, however, do not choose to stay in school; they drop out. Over 500,000 public school students drop out of grades 9–12 each year (National Center on Education Statistics, 2007). This translates into one in eight students never graduating from high school, and one student dropping out of high school every nine seconds (Christenson & Thurlow, 2004).

TABLE 8.1 Percent of High School Dropouts among Persons 16 Years and Older by Race/Ethnicity and Historic Timeframe

YEAR	PERCENT OF TOTAL NUMBER OF STUDENTS	WHITE	BLACK	HISPANIC
1985	12.6%	10.4%	15.2%	27.6%
1995	12.0%	8.6%	12.1%	30.0%
2005	9.4%	6.0%	10.4%	22.4%

Source: National Center for Education Statistics (accessed February 18, 2008).

Demographic differences exist, just as we might expect. Dropout rates for males are higher than for females, except for Hispanic students (Kaplan, Turner, & Badger, 2007), in particular Mexicans (Olatunji, 2005). The dropout rate varies by race and ethnicity, as Table 8.1 illustrates. Notice that dropout rates have diminished only slightly over time, and Hispanics have the highest dropout rates of the groups covered in the table. Inner-city youth, especially those living in poverty (Orthner & Randolph, 1999; Pong & Ju, 2000; Roscigno, Tomaskovic-Devey, & Crowley, 2006), students who are chronically absent (Sheldon & Epstein, 2004), students who repeat a grade (Entwisle, Alexander, & Olson, 2005; Stearns, Moller, Blau, & Potochnick, 2007), those who attend large urban schools (Christenson & Thurlow, 2004), and adolescents who switch schools multiple times (South, Haynie, & Bose, 2007) are at particular risk for dropping out. Family factors, such as English as a second language and the absence of learning materials in the home, have been implicated as well. Students who have friends who drop out are also likely to drop out. Some young people drop out because they would rather work or need to earn money (Entwisle, Alexander, & Olson, 2004; Olatunji, 2005). Finally, personality variables, such as low self-esteem and loss of sense of control (Reyes & Jason, 1991) and shyness (Ialongo et al., 1999) predict dropping out. Dropout rates are worrisome not only in the United States but around the world, making it a vexing and perplexing issue almost everywhere (Smyth & McInerney, 2007).

The costs of dropping out of school are immense. High school dropouts experience more unemployment during their work careers, have lower earnings when employed, are more likely to be on public assistance, and are more likely to use illegal substances or commit crimes than those who complete high school or college (Christenson & Thurlow, 2004; Christie, Jolivette, & Nelson, 2007). Young women who drop out of school are more likely to become pregnant at young ages and more likely to become single parents living in poverty (Cantelon & LeBoeuf, 1997). The costs to the youths, then, are enormous, but so are the costs to society in terms of unemployment, lost revenues, welfare costs, crime prevention programs, and prosecution and incarceration costs, which run into billions of dollars (Christenson & Thurlow, 2004). Thus, finding preventions and interventions for those at risk of dropping out are extremely important.

What can be done about the dropout problem in the United States? Early efforts were focused on the individual student and included counseling (Baker, 1991; Downing & Harrison,

1990; Rose-Gold, 1992) or improvement of self-image or self-esteem (Muha & Cole, 1990). Because there are *multiple causes* of dropping out (Christie et al., 2007; Christenson & Thurlow, 2002; Ialongo et al., 1999; Lee & Breen, 2007; McNeal, 1997; Svec, 1987), a more ecological approach is desirable (Oxley, 2000). An ecological approach would take into account situational or contextual factors, for example, characteristics of the schools, including the same topics mentioned under school alienation (Christie et al., 2007; Patrikakou & Weissberg, 2000). Community and neighborhood variables (Leventhal & Brooks-Gunn, 2004), such as social isolation (Vartonian & Gleason, 1999), poverty (Christie et al., 2007), and adult involvement with the student (e.g., community mentors) (Sheldon & Epstein, 2004), would also be considered ecological factors that affect students' decisions to stay or leave school.

One of the more successful, better-known prevention programs for students at risk for dropping out is one designed by Felner (Felner, 2000a; Felner, Ginter, & Primavera, 1982). Today the program is known as the STEP Program or the School Transitional Environment Program. STEP was designed to address multiple issues, and it is discussed here as a model program to address school dropouts. Felner and associates understood that transitions in school are risk factors for children, for example, the transition from junior high to high school, especially when the high school population is comprised of students from multiple feeder schools or who have other risk factors, such as low socioeconomic class, minority group membership, simultaneous life transitions, or low levels of family support (American Youth Policy Forum, 2008).

There are two major components to STEP. The first is reducing the degree of flux and complexity in the new high school (e.g., participants or cohorts are in classes together in only one wing or section of the school), so that in essence a smaller school is created within a larger one (Felner, Seitsinger, Brand, Burns, & Bolton, 2007). The second component involves restructuring the roles of the homeroom teachers (e.g., more informal and individualized meetings with the students). Notably, the homerooms were also comprised solely of program participants (American Youth Policy Forum, 2008). The teachers, who undergo two-day training, use meetings to discuss students' personal problems, help select classes and schedules, and clarify understanding of school rules and expectations. Teachers also maintain contact with the students' families as well as with other STEP teachers within the school.

The beauty of STEP is that it takes precious little time away from instruction, costs very little, does not change instructional methods or content, and lasts only one year, the transitional year. With these simple ecological changes and short intervention, program participants compared to nonparticipants show better attendance, higher grade-point averages, more stable self-concepts, and lower transition stress (Felner, 2008; National Center on Secondary Education and Transition, 2008). Important to this discussion is the lower dropout rate for STEP participants. Positive fallout for the teachers includes higher job satisfaction and higher comfort levels in the school (American Youth Policy Forum, 2008).

School Violence. School violence is a difficult and complex issue and an important one because of its escalation in the past decade. The National School Safety and Security Services (2008) reports that for the 2006–2007 school year there were 32 school-associated deaths in the United States with another 171 additional nondeath but high-profile incidents, including shootings, stabbings, and riots.

The costs to victims are enormous, not the least of which are emotional, social, behavioral, and academic problems. The costs to society are large, too. In tracking 227 truly troubled youths who were removed from school and placed in special behavioral units, researchers found that the cost of these units to society was over $10 million. This figure did *not* include ancillary costs, such as police work, court appearances, property damage, detention and housing costs, professionals' time spent with the youths (e.g., psychologists and social workers), and treatment programs (Eisenbraun, 2007).

The U.S. Department of Education (1998), out of concern for this epidemic of violence, issued *A Guide for Safe Schools*. Other authors have echoed similar concerns (e.g., Garbarino, 2001). The guide offers warning signs for parents and teachers of potentially violent students: social withdrawal, excessive feelings of isolation and rejection, low school interest and poor performance, a history of discipline problems including aggressive behavior, intolerance for differences and prejudicial attitudes, and access to drugs, alcohol, and/or firearms.

Many of these warning signs appear to blame the individual student and do not address issues of student–school fit or of school climate (Reid, Peterson, Hughey, & Garcia-Reid, 2006), which may inadvertently present challenges to violence-prone children (Baker, 1998). In addition, these warning signs do not directly address prevention—a key concept for community psychologists. Just what can be done in the schools to reduce or prevent violence and aggression among students? Are the schools waiting for violence to occur, or are the schools working with younger children (students not yet in middle or high schools) to prevent violence altogether?

First, research on crime in schools shows that many situational crime prevention techniques in schools (e.g., installing video cameras or metal detectors) are not working (O'Neill & McGloin, 2007). Second, national data seem to demonstrate that we are waiting too long to introduce nonviolent methods into the schools. Adolescence may be too late, because it is clear that the incidence of aggressive behavior problems in young children is also escalating (Webster-Stratton & Reid, 2007). Until recently, at best, many high schools offered counseling after a particularly violent incident or harsh discipline or increased security as a response to school violence (Klein, 2005).

Clearly, we need to dip earlier into children's academic careers to abate this epidemic of violence (Howard, Flora, & Griffin, 1999). We also need to continue to find ways to improve school climates (Khoury-Kassabri, Benbenishty, Astor, & Zeira, 2004). In particular, violence prevention programs need to take into account family and community characteristics, not just youth or school characteristics (Laracuenta & Denmark, 2005) during program design, because school violence appears to be a multilevel and ecologically nested issue (Eisenbraun, 2007; Farver, Xu, Eppe, Fernandez, & Schwartz, 2005). Poverty, discrimination, lack of opportunities for education and employment, and paltry social capital (as defined elsewhere in the book) are also community risk factors for interpersonal violence (Farver et al., 2005).

Research is demonstrating that school-based programs that are comprehensive (that is, address a variety of problem behaviors with a variety of curricula), holistic (address the whole child), and well integrated with parents and the community are the most successful (Flay & Alfred, 2003). Programs that are also research-based, where program participants or schools are compared to nonparticipants over time, are most effective (Scheckner, Rollin, Kaiser-Ulrey, & Wagner, 2004). We examine one sample program here—the Positive Action (PA) program (Flay & Alfred, 2003)—but there are others.

The PA program was developed by Carol Alfred, a schoolteacher, and researched by Brian Flay. The program is comprehensive in that it includes the entire school, staff, teachers, administrators, families, and students. Another component is that students making positive and healthy choices will develop a higher sense of self-worth, which in turn, will result in better outcomes for the student and the school (Flay & Alfred, 2003). Starting in the early school years, students are exposed to over 100 15- to 20-minute lessons designed to focus on multiple behaviors. For example, there is a unit on getting along with others (topics covered include respect, fairness, and empathy among others), a unit on being honest (e.g., not blaming others, finding one's weaknesses as well as strengths), and a unit on the need to seek continual improvement (e.g., better problem solving, the courage to try new things). Working with school personnel, PA attempts to change the school climate to one that focuses on positive actions rather than negative ones (such as violence and alienation). The program also extends itself in that families receive some training in PA and are encouraged to become involved with the school and the program. A program kit is available to the community so that the students, their families, the schools, and the community align seamlessly in their efforts toward promoting student well-being.

One of the positive results of the program, based on well-designed research, is that PA schools, as compared to control schools, experience a dramatic drop in school violence, specifically, 68 percent fewer violent incidents per 100 students. There are also other behavioral changes, for example, far fewer school suspensions, fewer students absent for multiple days, fewer other problem behaviors (such as substance use), and lower dropout rates. Academically, program participants are far more likely to graduate and continue their education, probably in part due to the fact that academic scores rise (Flay & Alfred, 2003; Office of Juvenile Justice and Delinquency Programs, 2008a). What is interesting about this program is that many positive effects of PA endured from primary school through to middle school and high school (Flay & Alfred, 2003).

Two other programs designed to reduce school violence that you might want to research further include Safe Harbor (Nadel, Spellmann, Alvarez-Canino, Lausell-Bryant, & Landsberg, 1996; Office of Juvenile Justice and Delinquency Programs, 2008a) and PeaceBuilders (Embry, Flannery, Vazsonyi, Powell, & Atha, 1996; Office of Juvenile Justice and Delinquency Programs 2008a).

Other ideas for reducing school violence and victimization are appearing in the literature. For example, the violence surrounding children in their own neighborhoods (Raviv et al., 2001) and in the media (Jason, Kennedy, & Brackshaw, 1999) needs to be reduced, perhaps by public policy or otherwise. Likewise, when teachers make salient to their students that there are norms against aggression, aggressive behavior diminishes (Henry et al., 2000; Khoury-Kasssabri et al., 2004). Programs need to be designed for after school as well (Bilchik, 1999; Danish & Gullotta, 2000; Taulé-Lunblad, Galbavy, & Dowrick, 2000), because this is a time when violence escalates. Attempts to control Internet bullying, which is on the rise (Williams & Guerra, 2007), might also prove useful.

There are, of course, many other school problems that we could discuss, such as peer pressure to engage in sex or try illicit drugs. Due to limited space, we include only one other, one that affects a large number of children. Case in Point 8.2 discusses the high divorce rate in the United States and its effects on children even as they cross the threshold of the school's door.

CASE IN POINT 8.2
CHILDREN OF DIVORCE

One million children each year experience the stress of parental divorce (Pedro-Carroll, 2005a), which suggests that cumulatively, by age 18, 40 percent of American children will have experienced parental divorce (Greene, Anderson, Doyle, & Riedelbach, 2006). Divorce and subsequent life in a single-parent family have become reality for a large number of children. Children's reactions to divorce include (but, of course, are not limited to) anxiety, behavior problems at home and at school, and somatic symptoms (Pedro-Carrolla, 2005a).

Studies of divorce have indicated that in the child's natural environment are several factors that can moderate the effects of stress from divorce, such as the availability of support from other family members (Farber, Felner, & Primavera, 1985) and peer support (Lustig, Wolchik, & Braver, 1992). In fact, there is a consistent and fairly strong negative correlation between the child's adjustment to divorce and the availability of social support.

Some interventionists prefer not to take a passive role—waiting to see whether there are tools available in the child's natural environment that can help him or her cope. The schools can build and participate in interventions for children of divorce. Cowen (1996) and his colleagues at the Primary Mental Health Project, a comprehensive school-based program that promotes overall mental health in children, did just that. One aspect of the multifaceted project is the Children of Divorce Intervention Program (CODIP). CODIP is based on the premise that timely preventive intervention for children of divorce can offer both important short- and long-term benefits. CODIP's goals, simply stated, are to provide social support and to teach coping skills to children of divorce (Pedro-Carroll, 2005a).

The program was initially designed for fourth- to sixth-graders. Newer versions have been tailored to younger and older children, each with its own unique techniques matched to the developmental needs of the particular age group (Pedro-Carroll, 2005a). Older children, for example, are plagued by loyalty conflicts and anger, whereas younger children experience intense sadness, confusion, and guilt (over having caused the marital break-up). CODIP is conducted in age-matched groups because children who have gone through common stressful experiences are more credible to peers than those who have not had these experiences or, alternatively, authoritative-sounding adults. Developmental factors shape the group size as well as the methods used (e.g., puppets, role-plays, books, discussion, games, etc.). For example, younger children have shorter attention spans and are more prone to want concrete activities than are older children.

In a typical group, both a man and woman (selected from school personnel) act as leaders. They are selected because they are interested, skilled, and sensitive to the needs of the children of divorce and are trained in the CODIP program techniques. Modules for a typical fourth- to sixth-grade group might include the following:

- Fostering a supportive group environment (e.g., the importance of confidentiality),
- Understanding changes in the family (e.g., a group discussion that stimulates children to express their feelings about changes),
- Coping with change (e.g., discussing adaptive ways to cope with divorce rather than losing one's temper),
- Introducing a six-step procedure for solving interpersonal problems (similar to interpersonal cognitive problem-solving, discussed earlier),
- Understanding and dealing with anger (e.g., how to use I statements),
- Focusing on families (e.g., understanding that there are diverse family forms).

Results of program evaluations of CODIP demonstrate that the program results in gains for children's school-related competencies and their ability to ask for help when needed. Likewise, the program appears to decrease school-related problem behaviors in children of divorce. Parents also report positive

(continued)

CASE IN POINT 8.2   CONTINUED

improvements in their children's home adjustment; for example, they report that the children are less moody and anxious (Cowen et al., 1996; Pedro-Carroll, 1997, 2005a). Follow-up research on early program participants also demonstrates that program effects endure. Program children report less anxiety, more positive feelings, and more confidence about themselves and their families compared with children of divorce who do not participate. Amazingly, teachers "blind" to whether the children have participated in the program or not and report fewer school problems and more competencies than a comparison group of children of divorce. CODIP and other programs like it (e.g., Children's Support Group) provide evidence that early and systematic intervention—empirically documented—with children of divorce has promising preventive potential (Pedro-Carroll, 2005a). The next steps for these programs may well be concurrent parent programs and/or collaborative partnerships between courts, researchers, and community organizations (Pedro-Carroll, 2005a, 2005b).

SUMMARY

The world of schools, children, families, and communities is fascinating and complex. Some children enter school at risk for a variety of problems, but innovative programs are available to intercede with the children, their families, and their communities. Traditional interventions have focused mostly on deficits of the child or the family, but the more effective programs usually take into account the setting, such as the school climate or the neighborhood, as well as the actors in it.

Psychologists recognize how important the early childhood environment is. Children who are advantaged economically or otherwise in early childhood often have fewer problems in later life than disadvantaged children. Intervention programs for young children at risk include quality day care and enrichment education programs. Research has demonstrated that children of working mothers may not be disadvantaged; nonetheless, if they are to stay employed, these mothers need day care for their children. On the other hand, inner-city and some minority children are at risk for a variety of problems day care alone cannot adequately address. Programs designed to give them the early push they need to later succeed in school are often successful. Project Head Start is one such example. Head Start programs are all-encompassing programs; for example, they include parental involvement, health care, academic pursuits, and so on. Studies demonstrate that children who have attended Head Start have an easier transition into elementary school, academically achieve at higher levels, and have had their health problems attended to, as compared with children who do not enroll in such programs. Longitudinal studies are now demonstrating some of Head Start's positive long-term effects.

Desegregation has had an interesting effect on U.S. schools. Desegregation touches children of all ages and races. When the courts ordered the schools to desegregate, the Supreme Court justices did not envision the effects of desegregation on children, nor did they formulate methods for fostering acceptance of diversity in schools. Those jobs fell to psychologists and school staff, who have demonstrated that desegregation often has positive effects for minority as well as White children. Various active methods for decreasing prejudice include intergroup contact—for example, the jigsaw classroom. The more passive programs, such as mere exposure to diverse others, are more likely to fail.

Young children are not the only ones facing problems in this country. Adolescents often use drugs, drop out of school, or become pregnant. Most of the programs that are successful in preventing school dropout do not try to change only the at-risk individual but also make adjustments in the school environment or the community to better accommodate the individual student.

School violence is another concern because it is escalating in the United States. Again, appropriate programs and student involvement can enhance school safety and decrease violence. Children of divorce are often considered at risk for a variety of school-related as well as other problems. Once again, intervention programs for children of divorce have proven successful when they provide for appropriate changes and needed social support.

CHAPTER 9

LAW, CRIME, AND THE COMMUNITY

THE TRADITIONAL JUSTICE SYSTEM
  Introduction
  Crime and Criminals
  ■ **CASE IN POINT 9.1** Neighborhood Youth Services
  The Prisons
  Victims and Fear of Being Victimized
  Enforcement Agencies

ADDRESSING JUSTICE SYSTEM ISSUES WITH COMMUNITY PSYCHOLOGY
  Primary Prevention
    Prevention with At-Risk Individuals
  ■ **CASE IN POINT 9.2** Working with At-Risk Youth
    Designing the Environment to Prevent Crime

  Secondary Prevention
    Early Assistance for Crime Victims
    Crisis Intervention for Victims
    Restorative Justice Programs
    Reintegration Programs for Incarcerated Individuals

SUMMARY

Two men look out through the same bars; one sees the mud, and one the stars.
—Frederick Langbridge

Mike was only four months old when he was adopted by a middle-class, older couple, Edna and Walt Farnsworth, who had always wanted children but were unable to bear their own. Mike's childhood was uneventful, although his father, Walt, felt that his wife "doted on the boy a bit too much."

During his childhood, Mike was an average student in school. By junior high school, he seemed more interested in sports and cars than in his studies. When Mike reached puberty, he grew quickly, and by the time he was 16, he soared to 6 feet

2 inches, 210 pounds. His imposing size and apparent boredom with school inspired consternation in his teachers, who weren't quite sure how to manage him.

It was at this point that trouble came to the Farnsworth home. Mike realized that his father, who was a slender man of small frame, was intimidated by him. Mike would yell at his mother and disrespect his father. Mike called his father "old man" as often as he could to embarrass Walt. He reasoned that his parents were older than his friends' parents so why not call them old.

When Mike could finally drive a car, he wanted nothing but to take his parents' car after school and drive around his small town, showing off to his friends or assessing what "action was going down" on Main Street. The town had few organized activities for its youth. He and his father argued often about the car, Mike's coming home late, and his school grades. His mother, Edna, felt torn between the son and the husband she loved.

One night, Mike had been drinking beer despite knowing that he was under the legal age. His father was particularly angry when he smelled his son's breath. When Walt yelled, "You could have killed somebody with *my* car!" Mike struck out at his father. Walt went crashing through the drywall of their small home. Mike fled into the night, which left Edna with immense worry as to what he would do next and great sorrow that her husband had been injured in the fracas.

This scenario was repeated again and again between Mike and Walt, who raged at both his wife and his son that he "didn't want this kid around anymore." Edna tried to referee these fights but to no avail. As the conflicts escalated, Mike asserted his size and independence more.

Taking matters into his own hands and without consulting Edna, Walt went to the local police department to have his son arrested for "anything you can arrest him for—just get him out of my house." The police were used to such domestic squabbles and didn't feel an arrest was in order. Instead, they referred Walt to the probation department so that he could have Mike declared a PINS (Person in Need of Supervision). The Probation Department was not surprised to see Walt; they had interviewed many parents just like him, all making the same request.

Was Mike really headed for a life of crime? Was the family at fault for the turmoil in their home? Were any community systems to blame? For example, was the school environment so alienating that Mike's disenchantment with school was displaced onto his family? How better could the justice system manage this family conflict?

This chapter examines crime and community in the United States. We not only examine the traditional system and how it manages those individuals who interact with it, we also address some alternative and innovative programs designed to humanize this same system that are more in line with community psychology. Of course, as community psychologists, we also examine how the environment or context contributes to crime, fear of victimization, and other justice system issues.

THE TRADITIONAL JUSTICE SYSTEM

Introduction

Pick up any newspaper from a major city in the United States, and you see splashed across its pages reports of crime—crime in the streets, conflict in homes, corruption in business and government, Internet fraud, identity theft—crime just about everywhere. Compared to Japan (Henderson, 2006) and Korea (Yoon & Joo, 2005), for example, with their exceptionally low crime rates, the United States has the largest prison population of any developed country in the world (Bonhomme, Stephens, & Braithwaite, 2006). Although crime rates have generally fallen over the past decade or so (Thomas, 2008), statistics still give us all pause to shudder. In 2006 alone, U.S. citizens aged 12 years old or over experienced 25 million crimes. The violent crime (e.g., assault or homicide) rate in that same year was 24.6 per 1,000 households, and the property crime rate (e.g., vandalism or theft) was 159.5 per 1,000 households. In addition, almost eight youngsters a day are killed in gun violence in the United States (Office of Justice Programs, 2007).

These statistics are based on the compilations of reported crimes of local law enforcement agencies, such as city police and county sheriff departments throughout the nation. The data, however, include only crimes *known* to the police. There is often little correspondence between the crimes that are committed in a community and the crimes that are reported. Research suggests that often the committed crimes, especially violent ones, are about twice the reported nonviolent crimes (e.g., property crimes) in number. An example of an unreported crime would be a storekeeper who catches his neighbor's son shoplifting but admonishes the boy not to shoplift rather than face the boy's parents with the news that their son is a thief who will be prosecuted. A more extreme and unfortunate example is the case of rape; slightly more than half of all rapes go unreported (Bureau of Justice Statistics, 1993). On the other hand, homicide is almost always reported to the police.

Community psychologists share the average citizen's concern about "the grim reality" (Thompson & Norris, 1992) of interpersonal violence and crime in our communities. Citizens and psychologists want to know what can be done to prevent crime and how to manage criminals so they will not commit more crimes. Community psychologists also share the concern that victims be assisted in their recovery from crime. In a special edition of the *American Journal of Community Psychology* years ago, Roesch (1988) called for increased involvement by community psychologists in criminal justice issues by going beyond the individual level of analysis to the examination of situational and environmental factors that contribute to criminal behavior. He called for community psychologists to help predict problematic behavior and adopt preventive measures for at-risk individuals. Yet today, there is still little involvement by community psychologists in or research on the justice system in our journals. In fact, Biglan and Taylor (2000) argued that we have made more progress on reducing tobacco use than we have on reducing violent crime. We lack both a clear, cogent, empirically based analysis and a set of organizations that effectively advocate policies and programs with regard to crime. Melton (2000) added to this emphasis by suggesting that law should be a major focus of study for those who wish to understand community life. At the time of this writing, there remains a paucity of information on crime and victimization in the community psychology literature, although more research and commentary is slowly appearing on at-risk youth and domestic violence.

The justice and enforcement systems in our country are multilayered and complex. They involve the various courts (municipal, state and federal, civil and criminal, and higher and lower) as well as the judges, juries, lawyers, plaintiffs, and defendants; the prisons, jails, and corrections officers; the police, sheriffs, and other enforcement agencies; the departments of parole and probation; and the multitude of ancillary services, such as legal aid societies and neighborhood justice centers. We turn our attention to some of the actors in this system.

Crime and Criminals

Did Mike commit a crime because he hit his father? Some would argue he did. Others would suggest that he was simply a confused or frustrated adolescent—a person in need of some counseling but certainly not a criminal.

Just what is a crime, and who exactly are criminals? It is beyond the scope of this book to argue about definitions of the term *crime*. Just as laws are never perfect, definitions are never perfect. Laws that determine and therefore define crime change from society to society and from one historical era to the next (Hess et al., 1991), making the definition of the term difficult. Nonetheless, a rudimentary definition of crime might assist you in understanding its complexity. A **crime** is an intentional act that violates the prescriptions or proscriptions of the criminal law under conditions in which no legal excuse applies and where there is a state with power to codify such laws and to enforce penalties in response to their breach.

The uninformed public might well blame Mike for being "a bad kid" or his parents for being "bad parents." Psychologists, sociologists, and criminologists might view the situation in a completely different way. Rather than examining what's "wrong" with Mike or his family, they also would turn to ecological or contextual explanations for crime and violence, including Mike's.

One of the first factors to capture the attention of psychologists was the availability of guns in the United States. Gun violence represents a major threat to the health and safety of all Americans. Every day in the United States, more than 90 people die from gunshot wounds, and another 240 sustain gunshot injuries. Incredibly, a teenager in the United States is more likely to die of a gunshot wound than from the total of all *natural* causes of death. Young African American males have the most elevated homicide victimization rate of any racial group.

Often, in a particular country, other methods of committing homicide (e.g., with a knife) are higher, yet no one would say that high rates of knife ownership caused the killing (Kleck, 1991). We would need to know more about a nation's cultural and ethnic background, history of racial conflict, rigidity and obedience to authority, subjective sense of unjust deprivation, and so on before we could make claims that gun control within a nation causes fewer handgun deaths (Kleck, 1991; Spitzer, 1999). Guns alone do not cause crime. What else is responsible for the high crime and incarceration rates in the United States?

Another historically well-researched factor is childhood exposure to violence as portrayed in the media, especially on television. Mike was a fan of crime shows and boxing matches and also loved to play violent video games. Extensive research over the years has demonstrated that media violence causes violent behavior. Recently, Graber, Nichols, Lynne, Brooks-Gunn, and Botvin (2006) as well as Patchin, Huebner, McCluskey, Varano, and Bynum (2006) reconfirmed this connection among the group most at-risk for crime and violence—urban minority youth. Representatives of the American Psychological Association (APA) have also testified before Congress on the impact of media violence on children (McIntyre, 2007). Specifically, the APA warns that repeated exposure to media violence places children at risk for:

- Increased aggression,
- Desensitization to acts of violence,
- Unrealistic fears of becoming a victim of violence.

Exposure to media violence, then, is something that could be monitored, prohibited, or limited by parents or legislation as a preventive measure. Media violence alone, however, does not account for all crime and violence, so simply limiting it will not prevent all crimes. What else do we know about causes?

Parental monitoring was just mentioned. Studies suggest that when parents know where their adolescents are and with whom they are spending time, risks for actual violence and crime as well as exposure to community violence are reduced. This is not to say that "bad" parenting causes crime and violence, although there is a strong link to child maltreatment and later crime activity (Schuck & Widom, 2005). Rather, good parenting (i.e., monitoring of youth) offsets risk trajectories and promotes forms of competence among adolescents (Graber et al., 2006). Essentially, poor parental monitoring increases a youth's opportunity to associate with delinquent peers or be victimized or witness others committing violence (Lambert, Ialongo, Boyd, & Cooley, 2005). Campaigns such as "Do you know where your child is tonight?" and parenting classes where monitoring issues are discussed might go a long way toward preventing youth crime and violence.

As just inferred, witnessing community violence often leads to delinquency, crime, and more violence (Lambert et al., 2005; Youngstrom, Weist, & Albus, 2003), but this factor is more complicated than it would appear at first blush (Bolland, Lian, & Formichella, 2005). In the psychological literature, it is now quite well known that decaying, disordered, unstable, and disorganized communities can contribute to delinquency and crime (Patchin et al., 2006). This alone may significantly explain why urban minority youths are more prone to crime and violence than other youths. Beyond these community factors, though, are the pockets of extreme poverty found in some communities. Poverty and economic disadvantage are highly related to neighborhood decay and are highly predictive of crime and violence as identified in research by Strom and MacDonald (2007), Krueger, Bond Huie, Rogers, and Hummer (2004), Hannon (2005), and Eitle, D'Alessio, and Stolzenberg (2006). It is not surprising, then, that unemployment also corresponds with increased levels of crime and violence, even in relatively crime-free places like Korea (Yoon & Joo, 2005). Interestingly, globalization is also identified as a cause of increased crime in the United States. The migration of job opportunities to other countries has probably resulted in the increase of low-income Americans and youth participating in the underground economy and the drug trade (Cross, 2006).

What else in communities besides disintegration and economic disadvantage contribute to crime and violence? For one thing, in disorganized and decaying neighborhoods, there may be a paucity of supportive community institutions (e.g., religious, social service, and neighborhood organizations) and deprivation of other resources (e.g., recreational programs to provide youths after-school activities) to help buffer the deleterious effects of economic disadvantage (Hannon, 2005). Thus, an already at-risk individual (e.g., someone maltreated as a child) may be more crime-prone in this type of neighborhood (Schuck & Widom, 2005). Likewise, a poor overall quality of life may lead to more substance abuse and mental health problems (and perhaps criminal activity) (Gabbidon & Peterson, 2006). These environments also contribute to a sense of hopelessness and the fear or perception that one is not in control of one's life (Bolland et al., 2005). Any expectation of reducing such hopelessness would probably require a restructuring of American society—a seemingly difficult task. Fortunately, research by Bolland, Lian, and Formichella indicates that only half of their research participants expressed strong feelings of hopelessness. Undoubtedly, there are protective factors at work somewhere. We will identify some of them in a later section in this chapter. Crime, then, is not just a police or victim problem but a problem belonging to the community as well. Case in Point 9.1 offers an example of what one community did about its high incidence of crime.

CASE IN POINT 9.1
NEIGHBORHOOD YOUTH SERVICES

Neighborhood Youth Services (NYS) is an award-winning, community-based program for so-called at-risk youth in Duluth, Minnesota. At the outset, a cadre of youth care workers at NYS decided not to use the label "at risk," primarily because they see all of the youngsters as having great potential. The program was established in a neighborhood with the distinction of having one of the highest crime rates in all of northern Minnesota, so it is primarily designed to intervene with and prevent children from becoming involved in the juvenile justice system. The neighborhood is also exceptionally diverse, so program staff is representative of this diversity.

Staff members work daily to:

- break down stereotypes that each racial or ethnic group holds of each other,
- identify children's strengths,
- teach children new ways to engage in society,
- discover the children's hidden potential,
- encourage the children to express themselves freely and in safe ways,
- explore new ways of relating to others.

In the NYS youth center, which was planned to feel home-like, the children involve themselves in art, reading, poetry, and other projects designed to allow free expression. This after-school program also offers tutoring services, computers, and athletic activities. The children and staff exhibit mutual respect for each other. As with some other programs (e.g., Head Start), parents are encouraged to become involved, too.

NYS is housed in a building with other community services, so referrals to additional resources are easily provided and readily available to families. The program is funded by individual donations, state prevention funds, and grants, so it is free and voluntary for all community children and families. The program lives by the adage that money spent up front (in early intervention) pays important dividends to communities willing to invest. NYS is just one example of the burgeoning programs spawned by mounting attention to prevention and intervention—one of the cardinal principles of community psychology.

Adapted from: Quigley (2005).

At least three other community-level factors are undoubtedly at work contributing to crime (Caldwell, Kohn-Wood, Schmeelk-Cone, Chavous, & Zimmerman, 2004)—racial/ethnic prejudice, discrimination, and segregation. Most of these terms are defined in the chapter on schools. In review, prejudice is an *attitude* toward members of some group; discrimination involves prejudiced *actions* against a particular group; segregation means *isolation* of a group from others in the community. Racial discrimination leads to fewer opportunities (i.e., jobs) and less social support from others and thus may lead to crime or violence (Caldwell et al., 2004). Being Black is not causal to violence; being subjected to high levels of discrimination and prejudice may be and therefore explains some of the high rates of crime and violence for African American youths. With the increase in America's Hispanic-Latino population, data are now showing that social isolation (à la discrimination and segregation) may also be contributing to their homicide rates (Burton, 2004).

Although this review is not exhaustive, by now you should understand that there exist multiple factors that contribute to violence and crime. Many risk factors are contextual rather than individual, so it does little good to blame Mike or any other person for criminal behavior. Sadly, individuals who experience more than one of these risk factors are more exponentially likely to become involved in crime or violence. Again, however, there is evidence that certain individuals casting about in these environments *do* escape the cycle of crime and violence that such settings can engender (Farmer, Price, O'Neal, & Man-Chi, 2004). We'll explore these factors shortly.

The Prisons

Once an individual commits a crime or act of violence, it may be too late for prevention. Apparently, prevention efforts are few and far between given the number of Americans locked up in jails and prisons. Let's look first at traditional means of and some statistics for addressing such individuals. Traditional means include arrest, prosecution, conviction, and imprisonment or **incarceration** of the guilty individual. When Walt Farnsworth approached his local police department in the opening vignette, he had this process in mind. He wanted his son arrested, taken out of the home, and removed from him and the rest of society.

The philosophy behind incarceration is generally retribution, not rehabilitation. **Retribution** in the legal system is supposed to mean repayment for the crime, but it translates in reality to punishment for the crime. If anyone is repaid, it is usually not the victim. Indeed, the victim is the only person who has no official role in the process so is the "forgotten" participant (Wemmers & Cyr, 2005). Amazingly, the victim need not even appear at the trial. The state is the entity that administers the punishment and receives the remuneration, if any. For instance, if an individual is found guilty and is fined, the fine does not go to the victim but to the state. If the guilty party is sent to prison, the state decides the sentence and the type of prison. In the past, the victim rarely got to speak out about any of these issues.

Does this retributional approach work? Is the convicted person reformed or corrected in correctional facilities? Or does he or she **recidivate** (return to a life of crime)? In 2006, 2,258,983 individuals were incarcerated in federal or state prisons or local jails. Many of the inmates were of minority status, with Blacks being by far the most likely to be incarcerated, as illustrated in Figure 9.1. The number of women in prison increased 4.5 percent and of

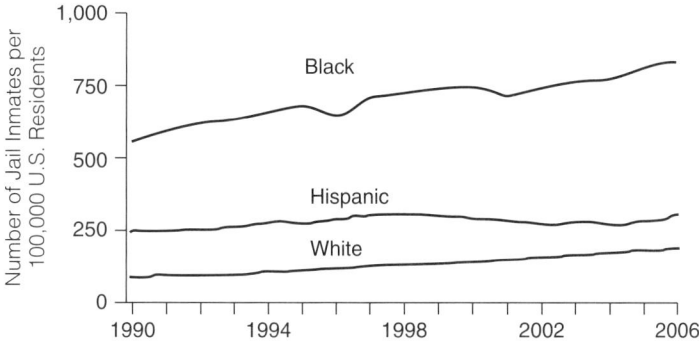

FIGURE 9.1 Blacks Are More Likely To Be in Jail: Jail Incarceration Rates by Race and Ethnicity, 1990–2006

Note: U.S. resident population estimates for race and Hispanic origin were made using a U.S. Census Bureau Internet release with adjustments for census undercount. Estimates for 2000–2006 are based on the 2000 Census and then estimated for July 1 each year.

Source: Bureau of Justice Statistics Correctional Surveys (The Annual Survey of Jails and Census of Jail Inmates) as presented in Correctional Populations in the United States, 1997, and Prison and Jail Inmates at Midyear series, 1998–2006.

men increased 2.7 percent from the previous year (Bureau of Justice Statistics, 2008). Apparently, fear of incarceration did not deter them from committing crimes. Additionally, at year's end in 2006, over 5 million individuals were being supervised by federal or state authorities (on probation and parole) for crimes committed. This statistic represents a 1.8 percent increase from the year before (Bureau of Justice Statistics, 2008). Once again, fear of having freedoms restricted does not seem to reduce crime rates. Based on these data, we can say that the retributive and punitive form of crime management does not work.

A classic study in psychology highlights what occurs in prisons that makes inmate reform unlikely. Philip Zimbardo and colleagues (Haney, Banks, & Zimbardo, 1973) obtained volunteers to act either as prisoners or guards in a mock prison. Subjects were all mentally healthy before the study began and were randomly assigned to their roles. The researchers told the guards to "do only what was necessary to keep order." The prisoners were all "arrested" unexpectedly at their homes and driven to the mock prison by real police officers. The prisoners were stripped, searched, dressed in hospital-style gowns, and given identification numbers by the guards. Within a few days of assuming their roles, the guards became abusive of the prisoners. They harassed the prisoners, forced them into crowded cells, awakened them in the night, forced them into frequent countdowns, and subjected them to hard labor and solitary confinement. Conditions in the mock prison became so brutal, the prisoners so depressed, and the guards so involved in their roles that Zimbardo and his colleagues prematurely ended the study. The prison experience, even for these "normal" men, proved overwhelming.

Inmates today often live in overcrowded conditions (Lösel, 2007). This overcrowding has led to more and more individuals living under community supervision, which may be unsettling to community citizens. Additionally, HIV is present in our prisons, and the rates of transmission of this virus and hepatitis are growing rapidly (Myers, Catalano, Sanchez, & Ross, 2006). Furthermore, inmate-to-inmate violence and a prison culture not conducive to successful and productive return to mainstream society are problems with the prison and jail system (Lahm, 2008). On top of these issues, substance abuse among inmates is increasing (Office of Justice Programs, 2006) and allegations of sexual violence are on the rise in prisons (Bureau of Justice Statistics, 2007). Incarceration is also demonstrated to have negative effects on intergenerational relations (e.g., between children and incarcerated parents) and to create family instability (Bonhomme et al., 2006). In fact, one set of justice system experts claimed that local jails serve only to brutalize and embitter individuals, further preventing them from returning to a useful role in society (Allen & Simonsen, 1992). Had Walter Farnsworth known the realities of the corrections system, perhaps he would not have jumped so quickly at the notion of having his son arrested. Not surprisingly, Ortmann (2000), based on his own longitudinal research, contended that prisons are extremely unfavorable places for the positive correction of people.

Courts have ruled that the prison system must be restructured (*Ruiz v. Estelle*), but this restructuring has sometimes escalated inmate–inmate and inmate–guard violence. Inmate lawsuits over the crowded conditions in prisons have led to early release for many, which sometimes results in higher recidivism rates and subsequent return to the crowded prisons (Kelly & Ekland-Olson, 1991). Although legal decrees to change prisons do exist, there is concern that the decrees do not translate readily into *real* change. In the meantime, the growth in the number of inmates continues to exceed the growth in prison space, which leads to more overcrowding. There must be a better way than to incarcerate individuals. We examine some prevention programs designed to do just that shortly.

Mounting evidence suggests that alternative forms of punishment outside of the traditional prison system are not good alternatives either. Several studies have demonstrated that shock incarceration camps or **boot camps** that are run by corrections personnel but resemble intensive army training camps fall short of their goals (MacKenzie, Wilson, Armstrong, & Gover, 2001; Palmer & Wedge, 1989). A report of work by the Office of Juvenile Justice and Delinquency Prevention (U.S. Department of Justice, 1997) revealed that "reoffending youth in the experimental groups (boot camps) committed new offenses more quickly—that is, had shorter survival periods—than reoffending youth in the control group" (p. 23). In programs described in the report, youth in some of the boot camps actually recidivated at rates higher than those youth not in boot camps (control groups).

Victims and Fear of Being Victimized

Recall that in 2006, U.S. citizens experienced 25 million crimes. The number of violent victimizations alone is about 26 per thousand for men and 23 per thousand for women (Bureau of Justice Statistics, 2006). These numbers are staggering, especially given that many crimes are never reported to authorities, so the true number is likely to be higher. DeFrances and Smith (1998) surveyed households that had been victimized and found that 44 percent said the crime problem was so objectionable that they wished they could move out of the neighborhood. Rader, May, and Goodrum (2007) more recently revealed that one in three residents in the United States are afraid to walk alone where they live.

Community psychologists, sociologists, and criminologists are interested both in fear of crime and its relationship to actual victimization (Chadee, Austen, & Ditton, 2007; Kruger et al., 2007; Thompson & Norris, 1992). Those who are the most fearful are sometimes the least likely to be victimized—a phenomenon called the **fear-victimization paradox.** Not all research supports the inverse relationship between fear and actual victimization (Mawby, 1986; Sutton & Farrall, 2005; Taylor & Shumaker, 1990; Thompson & Norris, 1992), but it is an interesting phenomenon. One reason may be that the concept of fear of crime is complex, and individual risk perceptions are based on interpretations that are far removed from reality (Chadee et al., 2007; Rader et al., 2007). Discussed here are data that support the paradox.

Men (compared to women) are more likely to be victimized yet the least afraid of violent crime (Schafer, Huebner, & Bynum, 2006). Young urban men are especially likely to be crime victims but are not very fearful of crime compared to young women (Bayley & Andersen, 2006; Perkins, 1997; Roll & Habemeier, 1991). Of course, the elderly are more afraid of crime even though their victimization rate is much lower than they actually perceive (Beaulieu, Dubé, Beron, & Cousineau, 2007; Schuller, 2006). Specifically, elderly women are most fearful yet least likely to be victimized of any group (Bayley & Anderson, 2006; Mawby, 1986; Perkins & Taylor, 1996; Rountree, 1998). Even though Black-on-Black crime is frequent, young Black men are less likely to fear crime than are Whites or Hispanics (Bayley & Anderson, 2006).

Whether or not an individual is actually victimized, the cost of fear and suffering to potential or real victims is enormous. Thompson and Norris (1992) and others (e.g., Youngstrom et al., 2003) found that victims of violent crimes, especially those of low economic status, suffer pervasive consequences of the crime, including alienation, fear of crime, avoidance, and other behaviors. Additional studies have demonstrated that neighborhood deterioration, which can also signal unsafe conditions (i.e., potential victimization), is related to stress and depression (Kruger et al., 2007). Some authors even claim that fear of crime may extend to America's obesity epidemic (Loukaitou-Sideris & Eck, 2007), because fear of victimization reduces the likelihood of walking around one's neighborhood or using other forms of active and healthy living.

Why do some individuals fear crime even if they are not likely to be victimized? For one, people often perceive environments, especially urban ones, as dangerous (Glaberson, 1990; Wandersman & Nation, 1998). City residents with the greatest fear are usually dissatisfied with their neighborhoods or mistrust other residents (Ferguson & Mindel, 2007; Schafer et al., 2006). When an area contains symbols of disintegration and disorganization such as abandoned buildings, vandalism, graffiti, litter, unkempt lawns, and other signs of "incivilities" (Brown, Perkins, & Brown, 2004; Kruger et al., 2007; Taylor & Shumaker, 1990), its residents are more fearful because these signs suggest neighborhood deterioration (Kruger et al., 2007) and social disorder (Ross & Jang, 2000), both of which they identify with their personal safety. Other research demonstrates that adverse neighborhood conditions, such as poverty, also increase the risk of children's emotional and behavioral problems above and beyond genetic predispositions (Caspi et al., 2000). The perception of crime level and risks of victimization also undermines an individual's confidence in the effectiveness of the government, for example, in elected officials and in enforcement agencies (Williamson, Ashby, & Webber, 2006).

Fortunately, there are factors that reduce fear of crime and actual crimes, such as attachment to one's neighborhood and social cohesiveness in a community (Brown et al., 2004). Availability of social support networks (e.g., nearby family and friends) and various types of police presence (Ferguson & Mindel, 2007) also enhance perceptions of safety. Similarly, high levels of social capital contribute to reduced fear of crime (Williamson et al., 2006). Social capital as defined elsewhere in this book includes trust, reciprocity, cooperation, and supportive interaction within families, between neighborhoods, and among community organizations.

Aside from fear of crime, there are other concerns about victims. Victims often do not know their rights; because of this, many victims' assistance programs have flourished in the United States. There are over 3,000 such organizations today, but only a fraction of crime victims receive much-needed services (Turman, 2001). Victim assistance can include crisis intervention, counseling, emergency transportation to court, and support and advocacy during the justice process. Because of fairly new public policy, victims in most states now have the right of notification of all court proceedings; the right to participate in proceedings; the right to be reasonably protected from the accused; the right to have input at sentencing; and the right to information about the conviction, imprisonment, and release of the offender.

Enforcement Agencies

Some see the police as peace officers, keeping communities harmonious and free of crime. Perhaps this attitude led Walt Farnsworth to the police when the conflict with his son escalated. Others see enforcement officers or the police as dishonest, unethical, prejudiced, and prone to misconduct (Ackerman et al., 2001; Dowler & Zawilski, 2007; Ross, 2006; Weitzer & Tuch, 2005). This is particularly true of America's racial and ethnic minorities, with Blacks and Hispanics holding far more negative attitudes toward the police than do Whites.

Regardless of one's views of the police, interesting research has demonstrated how difficult the job of policing communities can be. In fact, there is mounting interest in police burnout and stress (Anshel, 2000; Goodman, 1990). Why is the career of an enforcement officer so difficult? One reason is that the police force and community citizens hold different views of the role of the officers. New police recruits often maintain a serve-and-protect orientation toward the community, but after training, their attitudes often shift toward one of remoteness. In fact, police officers increasingly see themselves as hampered by community attitudes and constraints (Ellis, 1991) and as holding differing views from the community as to what police actually do (Salmi, Voeten, & Keskinen, 2005).

The police force and citizens also hold different views as to which community incidents ought to involve the police. Police are often called by citizens for public nuisance offenses (e.g., loud noise or drunkenness), traffic accidents, illegally parked vehicles, and investigation of suspicious persons—not very glamorous tasks and surely not the exciting roles portrayed in televised, fictional dramas about the police. In fact, heavy users of the media are more likely to believe that police use unpopular methods (such as racial profiling) and participate in misconduct than low-level users (Dowler & Zawilski, 2007; Weitzer & Tuch, 2005). The police are also likely to be called to intervene in family conflicts—a role for which they need more training—which can sometimes lead to assault on the officer if managed ineffectively. Another frequent role of the police is to intervene in mental health crises; that is, the police are asked to intercede in an incident involving someone with a mental disorder, then make a quick evaluation, and promptly decide whether to use placement in a hospital or a jail based on whether the person is a danger to self or others. Police officers do not relish this job and are often required to make such decisions without much training in mental health issues (Borum, 2000; Cordner, 2000).

A primary question about policing is whether *active* enforcement and a police presence in a community affect its actual crime rate and the fear of crime as well as residents' perceptions of their community. Community policing emerged in the early 1980s as a response to criticism regarding the stiff and professional style of policing used at the time (Roh & Oliver, 2005). **Community policing** involves the formation of partnerships or collaboration between police and community citizens. A major tenet of community policing is to identify problems based on the needs of the particular community and then deal with those problems with the cooperation and participation of the residents and related agencies (Zhong & Broadhurst, 2007). For example, the police might casually drop in on businesses to see how things are going, stop and talk to citizens on the street even when no crime has been reported, or provide talks to school children in an effort to gather knowledge about the community in general and crime in specific.

Salmi, Voeten, and Keskinen (2000) found that seeing police on foot patrol around the neighborhood (rather than in patrol cars) increases police visibility and improves the relationship between the police and the public. Later, these same researchers demonstrated that many citizens respond more positively to the police simply because of community policing (Salmi et al., 2005). Community policing also appears to reduce fear of crime, but it seems to do so in indirect ways. Specifically, community policing apparently reduces the perception of "incivilities," as mentioned before (Roh & Oliver, 2005). In fact, reducing dissatisfaction with one's community and one's quality of life (Roh & Oliver, 2005) as well as decreasing neighborhood disorder and disintegration (Wells, 2007) accounts more for positive views of the police than does an individual's race. Police presence, particularly in the form of community policing, is sometimes effective in reducing crime and fear of crime as well as raising residents' esteem for their communities. Interestingly, some research has demonstrated that in the highest crime neighborhoods, citizens are least likely to become involved in crime prevention strategies such as community policing (Pattavina, Byrne, & Garcia, 2006). A cogent question, however, is, "Is this the only way or the best way to accomplish all of this?"

Community psychologists, of course, believe that crime prevention is better than police patrols, citizen arrest, prosecution, and possible incarceration after a crime has been committed. In the following section, we examine programs designed by community psychologists and other prevention experts interested in tackling the diverse needs of the citizens, victims, offenders, and relevant professionals involved in the criminal justice system.

ADDRESSING JUSTICE SYSTEM ISSUES WITH COMMUNITY PSYCHOLOGY

Was there anything in Mike Farnsworth's background that would have helped someone predict he would turn into an irascible and difficult adolescent? Perhaps his adoption, being placed with older parents, his large size, school alienation, and other factors contributed to his family difficulties. Maybe there were community-level factors that would have helped us predict he would eventually turn aggressive toward his father, such as befriending delinquent peers.

In the foregoing units, we have already examined some of the predictors of criminal and violent behavior; knowing of them, we might be able to intercede better with prevention programs. In review, some of the factors alluded to include access to guns, lack of parental monitoring, family instability, child maltreatment, exposure to violence in the community or in the media, prejudice and its horrific companions (discrimination and segregation), and especially poverty and neighborhood disorder. What can be done about these issues so as to prevent crime or to improve a community to make it safer?

Primary Prevention

Prevention with At-Risk Individuals. Given the list of risk factors just mentioned, you can probably guess some of the suggested methods for reducing risk for violence and crime. Removing violence from the media might go a long way toward changing the cultural norms for violence. Similarly, the nurse home visitation program developed by David Olds and colleagues (see Chapter 7) is also helpful. These programs align with the principles of community psychology, but first we examine what has traditionally taken place with adjudicated or delinquent youth.

You probably already know there are juvenile "correctional" facilities dotted around every state—each meant to "reform" juvenile "offenders." In large part, these facilities do *not* work. Some states report that recidivism rates for youth emerging back into the community are as high as 55 percent (Woodward, 2008). Research also demonstrates that many youth in these facilities are uncertain about their ability to change their behavior, and they think their incarceration will not deter future delinquent activity. In addition most youth, when interviewed, articulate that there is a major disconnect between what they learned on the "inside" and the reality of life on the "outside" (Abrams, 2006). Upon the youth's release from these facilities, families are considered critical to interrupting the pattern of delinquent and criminal behavior, but other research shows that follow-up, face-to-face family visits by youth service workers are few and far between (Ryan & Yang, 2005). Youth service workers and community psychologists—indeed, anyone working with such youth—can have a difficult time interacting with these individuals, not just because of their backgrounds and their sense of hopelessness, but also because of the subculture that they live in. Case in Point 9.2 offers some insight into how difficult it is to work with at-risk youth.

On the other hand, although a positive adult role model cannot single-handedly change families or whole communities (Broussard, Mosley-Howard, & Roychoudhury, 2006), research with at-risk youth who are involved with a caring, consistent adult suggests that such youths are more likely to withstand a range of negative influences, such as poverty, family conflict, impoverished neighborhoods, and so on (Rhodes, Spencer, Keller, Liang, & Noam, 2006; Southwick, Morgan, Vythilingam, & Charney, 2006). Positive adult role models are considered preventive in that they contribute to the completion of future important milestones, such as high school graduation or employment (Broussard et al., 2006). In general, positive adult role models are considered to enhance a young person's development by influencing resiliency. **Resiliency** can be defined as the capacity

CASE IN POINT 9.2
WORKING WITH AT-RISK YOUTH

Working with youths at risk for delinquency, running away from home, and dropping out of school can be extremely challenging. They live in a rather closed subculture where "squealing" is not only looked down on but can be downright dangerous. Community psychologists and other professionals are learning how to work better and smarter with such street youth who can be resistant to the most well-intentioned efforts.

In an interesting project, Hackerman (1996) recognized that just as a country has its own language, so do street youth. Street gangs in particular, such as the Crips and the Bloods, use their own symbols and words to communicate. Psychologists and others (such as ministers, school officials, and youth probation officers) need to be able to speak the unique street language of these young people if they are to work with and design programs for them. In essence, they need to become cultural anthropologists in addition to their other training if they hope to be able to even begin to understand the youths. Over a two-year period, Hackerman put together a much-needed glossary of terms for individuals working with this target group. She noted that not all terms were used by all youth. Hispanic youth in Los Angeles often speak a language different from African American youth in New York City. Hackerman's work demonstrates the importance of ethnography in community psychology. Some of the terms from her glossary are at the top of the next column. Cover the right side and see how many terms on the left side you know. Based on your awareness of terminology, how successful do you think you would be working with street youth?

STREET TERMINOLOGY	MEANING OF TERM TO YOUTH
Blue light	Order someone killed
Bo	A marijuana cigarette, a joint
Flying colors	Wearing gang colors
Jack up	Rob someone
Strap	A gun
Jankin'	Teasing

More recently, Taylor and Taylor (2007) have identified hip hop as an important, evolving youth subculture with its own language. Because hip hop has gone somewhat mainstream, it is essential that community psychologists and other adults (parents, social workers) understand the lingo. Much of the language used in the hip hop movement expresses what young people encounter in their struggle to find meaning in home communities that too often leave them feeling hopeless (Taylor & Taylor, 2007). Here are some examples of this new language. See if you know any just from listening to hip hop music or by walking around your community.

STREET TERMINOLOGY	MEANING OF TERM TO YOUTH
Running a train	Multiple men engaging in sex with one woman
Blazing	Violence
Hurting someone	Gun violence
Ho	Whore
Bitch	Woman
Punks	Adults

What do you think the effects are on young people of hearing such terms over and over again?

of those who are at risk to overcome those risks and avoid long-term negative outcomes (Bilchik, 1998). Specifically as related to this chapter, a close bond with a supportive caregiver or other adult—in other words, a **mentor**—might help prevent a young person from entering a life of delinquency and crime. A mentor, as defined in the chapter on schools, is a caring and responsible adult role model who can make a positive and lasting impression on a child.

Mentoring can be informal, such as when a neighbor has frequent, unstructured contacts with a child over a period of time, or it can be formalized, as in a community mentoring program. Informal mentoring occurs spontaneously in the form of attentive and caring athletic coaches, teachers, neighbors, or clergy. Research reveals that informal mentoring can and does occur quite naturally (Hamilton et al., 2006; Helping America's Youth, 2008) when an extended family member (e.g., an uncle) or even a shopkeeper or municipal worker (Basso, Graham, Pelech, DeYoung, & Cardy, 2004) watches over a particular child's safety and well-being when the parents aren't around. In fact, some studies indicate that over 50 percent of youth report having a natural mentor (Helping America's Youth, 2008). For children who do not have a naturally occurring mentoring network, a formal mentor can supply the extra attention, affection, supervision, and prosocial role modeling that is not always available in other environments (Bilchik, 1998). Formal mentors tend to come from youth development, service-learning, or faith-based organizations (Hamilton et al., 2006).

Mentors, formal or informal, play various roles, such as providing tutoring for school subjects, attending or participating in recreational activities with the child, and talking to the child about various personal issues. On a more psychological level, mentors appear to help children escape from daily stresses (such as parental discord), provide positive interpersonal relationships that may generalize to the child's other relationships (peers and parents), assist in modeling better emotional regulation (e.g., when and why not to lose one's temper), and bolster the child's self-esteem (Rhodes et al., 2006).

There are now an estimated 3 million young people who have an adult, volunteer mentor (Rhodes, 2008). One of the best-known and oldest formal mentoring programs is Big Brothers/Big Sisters. This program primarily connects middle-class adults with disadvantaged youths or a fatherless boy with an adult male or a motherless girl with an adult female. Another federally sponsored program is JUMP (Juvenile Mentoring Program). In both programs, mentors are selected, trained, and matched to children (often by race and/or gender). The mission of such mentoring programs is usually to prevent delinquency and/or improve school performance by providing a caring adult role model. JUMP also involves coordination among community resources (referrals to human service agencies in the community), the schools, and the families, although there is variation from program to program (Bilchik, 1998).

Although there is still scanty research and theory on mentoring (Keller, 2007), the early data are promising. Tierney, Grossman, and Resch (1995) compared data from mentored youths in the Big Brothers/Big Sisters Program to youths on a waiting list. At the end of the 18-month study period, several positive results were documented for the mentored youths. Mentored youth were less likely to use or initiate use of drugs and alcohol, more likely to attend school (missing half as many days as the wait-list group), and less likely to report hitting someone. Subsequent research has illustrated that the program does have beneficial effects in other areas, such as reduced emotional problems and social anxiety as well as better self-control (De Wit et al., 2007). Alternatively, research also confirms that a mentor's inconsistent presence might be detrimental to the children (e.g., lower the child's self-esteem) (Helping America's Youth, 2008) and in fact do more harm than good (Karcher, 2005). Before assigning "Bigs" and "Littles," careful screening should occur for this and many other reasons.

Some preliminary data are also available for JUMP (Bilchik, 1998). Both youths and mentors responded positively on a survey about the mentoring experience with youths being more positive than their mentors. When mentors and youths were asked whether mentoring improved or prevented problems, they generally responded "yes" to varying degrees. Adults and children reported that the mentored child was getting better grades; attending classes; staying away from alcohol, drugs, gangs, knives, or guns; avoiding friends who start trouble; and getting along better with their families. Mentoring, then, holds great promise for reducing the risk of delinquent behavior, so community psychologists are continuing their efforts to sort out the literature and continue researching the best practices for youth mentoring programs (Rhodes, 2008).

Mentoring is not the only solution to delinquency prevention. A much newer program is Safe Start. In 2000, the Office of Juvenile Justice and Delinquency Prevention of the federal government launched Safe Start to address the needs of children exposed to community violence. Recall that witnessing community violence often leads to delinquency, crime, and more violence (Lambert et al., 2005; Youngstrom et al., 2003). Safe Start is designed to reduce the negative consequences of exposure to violence and create conditions that enhance the well-being of all children and adolescents through prevention interventions. Safe Start's definition of exposure to violence includes direct exposure (such as child maltreatment) and indirect exposure (such as witnessing family or community violence). The Safe Start Initiative envisions federal, state, and local governments working together (Office of Juvenile Justice and Delinquency Prevention, 2008b). Some local programs have been established in early child-care centers so as to reach children as early as possible (Hampton, Epstein, Johnson, & Reixach, 2004). Safe Start sometimes engages classroom teachers who have been mentored by a trained professional to model appropriate strategies for children's socioemotional development. Other programs use social workers who arrive on the scene of violence to which young children are witnesses, and other programs establish groups of parents of children who have been exposed to violence that are facilitated by a trained leader. Each program depends greatly on the community and its unique issues with crime and violence as well as local agencies available to participate. Programs like Big Brothers/Big Sisters and Safe Start show great promise as crime prevention programs because they address multiple and complex risk factors and target appropriate subgroups of children and adolescents (Case & Haines, 2007).

Designing the Environment to Prevent Crime. The issue of how the environment contributes to whether an individual is likely to fear crime or be an actual victim needs to be examined here. **Environmental psychologists**—those who study the effect of the environment on behavior—have much to offer community psychologists in terms of recommendations for arranging the environment so that crime is less likely to occur.

Do characteristics of the environment influence crime? Research suggests the answer is yes (Robinson, 2000). Traditional approaches to crime deterrence in various environments include installing burglar alarms, motion sensors, and other devices designed to prevent or catch someone in the act of breaking the law. Schools have made a particularly concerted effort to reduce crime by widening corridors, limiting the number of entrances to the building, using landscaping to define campus boundaries, and keeping up the facility to deter vandalism and crime (Kennedy, 2006). However, some of the solutions to altering the built environment (e.g., gated communities) are purchased at the cost of loss of movement and even higher fear of crimes (Zhong & Broadhurst, 2007). Many of these techniques simply do not completely prevent crime, whereas others prevent one type of crime but not others (Farrington, Gill, Waples, & Argomaniz, 2007). Short of creating the perception of a community or building as a fortress (Davey, Wootton, Cooper, & Press, 2005), there must be other aspects of environments and communities that can be altered to help reduce crime and fear of crime. Happily, there are!

When citizens and residents feel a lack of social solidarity and attachment to the community, traditional approaches to altering the built environment simply create indifference, suspicion or even outright hostility. Furthermore, such approaches isolate prevention activities from the surrounding social context—such as citizen diversity—and fail to take into account community needs, priorities, and capacities. In addition, Kelly, Caputo, and Jamieson (2005) suggest that merely altering the physical environment by means of better lighting or redesign doesn't work because such projects reflect top-down decision making where outsiders bring prevention projects to the community or building.

Many community psychologists and criminologists echo what you have already read—that citizens need to feel an attachment to (Brown, Perkins, & Brown, 2003) and ownership of their communities to prevent crime. The actual research on the effects of crime on citizen participation or empowerment are ambiguous at present, with some studies indicating that crime has a chilling effect on participation and others demonstrating that it has an energizing effect (Dupéré & Perkins, 2007; Saegert & Winkel, 2004). However, several authors suggest that citizens can become more interested in and empowered to do something about crime in their particular building or their own community (e.g., Dupéré & Perkins, 2007). One approach is to empower citizens to design their *own* programs so that the response becomes enmeshed in the social fabric of the community (Kelly et al., 2005). One means for empowering and involving citizens is to take advantage of or build social capital of community citizens. Social capital helps groups achieve both individual and collective goals. Once social capital is developed, a sense of shared obligation, shared norms, trustworthiness, and information flow are created (Dupéré & Perkins, 2007). Let's examine two ways to build social capital—one at the building level and one at the community level.

An example of a building-level intervention (which could also be used at the community level) designed to increase social capital is the development of **neighborhood crime watches** (National Crime Prevention Council, 1989). In neighborhood crime watches, neighbors are on active alert for suspicious activity or actual break-ins to each other's homes (Bennett, 1989). Certain environmental factors also predict who will and will not join neighborhood watches (Perkins et al., 1990; Sampson, Raudenbush, & Earls, 1997). Crime watches as collaborative activities among neighbors help build a sense of community (Levine, 1986). A sense of community is one of the most important variables related to lower fear of crime (Schweitzer, Kim, & Mackin, 1999).

Here is a second sample program at the community level. The discrepancies between police attitudes and community citizens' attitudes about how the police should serve their communities were already reviewed. Programs that reduce these differences might give citizens more confidence in their police and allow the police to better service each individual community. Walker and Walker (1990) have described a **Community Police Station Program** in which citizens play a major role in the determination, design, and delivery of crime-prevention programs. Citizens from the community see to the daily operation of the station and to the delivery of specific programs, such as Seniors Calling Seniors, a program designed to give shut-in or isolated seniors a sense of contact with others as well as a sense of safety. The program also includes a citizens' advisory board that helps identify the crime-prevention needs of each area of the city and sees that programs are developed to address those needs. In the Community Police Station Program, the police and citizens collaborate to make police services more acceptable and effective. In other communities, citizens and community members have been used to help recruit and select new police officers, again allowing collaboration and building a sense of community among citizens and enforcement personnel.

Secondary Prevention

This section explores exemplary measures designed to intercede as early as possible after a crime. Primary prevention at this point is too late. The strategy thus becomes secondary prevention. In the case of the Farnsworths from the opening vignette, when Mike first argued with his father, stayed out beyond the agreed-on curfew, or missed school, someone should have or could have intervened before the situation deteriorated. As it was, Mike struck his father and, in so doing, committed a crime. Primary prevention was too late.

Early Assistance for Crime Victims. Victims need their concerns addressed as early as possible after the victimization. They may experience a wide variety of emotions, ranging from fright, rage, a sense of violation, and vengefulness to sorrow, depression, despair, and shock. Victims can also experience an array of health consequences after the crime, for example, HIV infection after a rape (Britt, 2000). As mentioned earlier, the justice system does little for the victim, who does not even have an official role to play in the trial, if there is one (Wemmers & Cyr, 2005). The National Victims Resource Center is a national clearinghouse that provides victims with educational materials, funds victim-related studies, makes referrals to assistance programs, and provides information on compensation programs. Some state governments have also developed victim assistance programs (Woolpert, 1991) where victims are compensated for their injuries or awarded money from the offender's selling his or her story to the media or where victims can participate in decisions on their offender's parole (Educational Conference on Psychiatry, Psychology and the Law, 1990). (**Parole** means supervision in the community after incarceration.) However, victim compensation programs are rare because an offender in prison does not earn much money that could be used for restitution.

Financial compensation alone, though, cannot take away the psychological pain of being victimized nor can it assist the victim in reducing vengeful or angry thoughts about being victimized. Even with a trial, victims may have to wait months or years before their side of the story is aired in court. There are at least two types of programs available to victims that afford early and substantially successful interventions. The programs are crisis intervention and neighborhood justice centers.

Crisis Intervention for Victims. One program available to victims is **crisis intervention,** which is a set of procedures used by a trained individual to help others recover from the effects of temporary or time-limited but extreme stress. Early efforts at crisis intervention were focused on potential suicides, victims of violence, unpredictable or dangerous situations, and natural disasters. Since its early days, crisis intervention has expanded to assistance of victims of major school incidents (Blom, 1986; Eaves, 2001; Weinberg, 1990), military disasters (McCaughey, 1987), sexual assaults (Kitchen, 1991), individuals with chronic mental disorders (Dobmeyer, McKee, Miller, & Westcott, 1990; Holcomb & Ahr, 1986), students in a disciplinary crisis (Hagborg, 1988), and even victims of international terrorism (Everly, Phillips, Kane, & Feldman, 2006). Every year, millions of individuals are confronted with crisis-producing events that they are unable to resolve on their own, so they frequently seek help from crisis intervention specialists. Crisis intervention has become the most widely used, time-limited treatment in the world. Although its potential uses seem limitless, not all situations are appropriate for it (Roberts & Everly, 2006).

Crisis intervention is usually a face-to-face or phone (hot line) intervention that uses *immediate* intercession in the form of social support and focused problem solving to assist a person in a state of elevated crisis or trauma. Its immediate purpose is to avert catastrophe and quell distress, so in this way it is a sort of psychological first aid (Everly et al., 2006). Crisis intervention centers can be staffed by professionals or trained volunteers and are often open 24 hours a day. Note, though, that crisis intervention is not designed to be a stand-alone intervention; usually it is the beginning of a continuum of future interventions for the same individual. For example, many individuals witnessed the September 11, 2001, terrorist bombings or lost loved ones in the collapse of the World Trade Center towers. Others were traumatized when they visited the devastated site or witnessed news reports over and over again. While crisis intervention teams were available to many affected individuals and helped them in about 90 percent of the cases (Jackson, Covell, Shear, & Zhu, 2006), some required ongoing therapy or other interventions.

A pertinent question about crisis intervention is whether it is an effective means of providing help at the onset of the crisis and thus of preventing future problems. Mishara (1997) examined the effects of different telephone styles used with suicidal callers. Using calls from 617 callers, nearly 70,000 responses by crisis counselors were categorized and then evaluated for success of the crisis intervention. Mishara found that Rogerian or nondirective (rather than directive) interaction with the caller resulted in better outcomes—that is, it resulted in decreased depressive mood and in contractual behavior as to how to manage the crisis. Crisis counseling is even being conducted electronically (Wilson & Lester, 1998), but whether this is as effective as phone contact remains to be determined. Campfield and Hills (2001) found that the closer the crisis intervention occurs in time to an actual crime, the lower the number and severity of symptoms for the victim in the long run.

Because of the maturation of the crisis intervention field and proliferating research on it, Roberts and Everly (2006) recently were able to conduct a statistical literature review (meta-analysis) of well-designed crisis intervention studies to determine whether it is superior to psychiatric hospitalization and other long-term interventions. The 36 studies they examined all had pre-post designs or an experimental and control group matched on multiple variables. The researchers concluded that "adults in acute crisis or with trauma symptoms and abusive families in acute crisis can be helped with intensive intervention [crisis intervention] . . . in a large number of cases" (p. 10).

Restorative Justice Programs. You have already learned that recidivism rates for inmates of correctional facilities (juvenile detention centers, prisons, and jails) are quite high. Once these individuals are released, they often return to a life of crime. What can be done to reduce recidivism? This question speaks to the issue of secondary prevention. Although community psychologists much prefer primary prevention, secondary prevention becomes an important issue in this chapter because of the likelihood of recidivism, especially when the person is released into the same environment and the same peer group that may have cued crime in the first place.

Recidivism remains just one of the problems when crime-prone individuals emerge from any of the traditional forms of justice (e.g., incarceration). The traditional system is designed to administer **retribution** or punishment. You read earlier that incarceration generally does not deter a person from committing a subsequent crime. In fact, some studies find that very few persons who experience retribution or punish from the traditional system are deterred from crime, so the rate of recidivism may be as high as 90 percent (Bradshaw & Roseborough, 2005). What the traditional system offers in the form of secondary prevention is supervision in the community, such as parole. Less frequently, **rehabilitation services** might be offered to the juvenile delinquent or adult offender and are designed to reform or change the individual away from crime-proneness, such as using illegal drugs.

Neighborhood justice centers or community mediation centers, on the other hand, comprise a category of secondary intervention for both the offender *and* their victims where a third type of justice is offered—**restorative justice,** a method for making right the wrong that was done (Wemmers & Cyr, 2005). Restorative justice can involve victim compensation, but in this case, restoration also includes repairing the psychological harm done by the crime. The process aims to benefit the victim, the offender, and the community. Victims are able to express their feelings, emotionally heal, get questions answered regarding the crime, and have input into a reparation plan. The offender is held personally accountable for the crime (Rodriguez, 2005) by providing restitution as well as details about the crime and his or her plans to reintegrate into the community. **Neighborhood justice centers** are almost always linked to courts where judges or intake workers refer cases away from adjudication and to mediation. **Community mediation centers** are often nonprofits that use volunteer mediators to facilitate discussion among individuals involved in conflicts. Both types of centers are established in the local community and are designed to handle cases from criminal, juvenile, family, and civil courts or from other community agencies, such as community mental health centers and religious organizations (Hedeen, 2004). Although the exact number of such programs is elusive, estimates range from between 500 and 1,000 centers in the United States that manage a remarkable 100,000 cases a year (Hedeen, 2004).

At these centers, in a special type of mediation or restorative justice when crimes have been committed **victim-offender mediation** can occur. In this type of mediation, a trained person hears the case as presented by both the victim and the offender. This neutral person, the **mediator,** assists the two parties in understanding their involvement and fashioning a resolution that is satisfactory to each. Mediators use a variety of strategies to facilitate discussion and guide the parties toward restoration (Carnevale & Pruitt, 1992; Heisterkamp, 2006; Ostermeyer, 1991). Mediators are supposed to use reality testing (a process in which one person is asked to "get in the other person's shoes"), a futuristic (rather than retrospective) orientation, turn taking, compromise, reciprocity in concession making, and active listening, among other skills. Analysis of the process of mediation demonstrates that mediators generally do remain neutral and use unbiased paraphrasing as well as invitations to take the other person's perspective. In some respects, mediation and psychotherapy are parallel processes, but mediation focuses more on problems and issues rather than emotions or relationships (Forlenza, 1991; Milne, 1985; Weaver, 1986). The resolutions in most programs are legally binding, do not require decisions about guilt or innocence (thus can "clear" an arrest record), and must be mutually agreeable (Duffy, 1991).

The centers and the process of mediation embody many of the values of community psychology, too. The centers are generally available to the parties in or near their own communities. The centers provide an alternative to the sometimes oppressive, bureaucratic, and almost always adversarial court system (Duffy, 1991). Mediation empowers the parties to play a major and active role in determining their own solutions. Research on compliance with the contracts suggests that they usually prevent conflicts and crimes from recurring in the future (Duffy, 1991). Similarly, the centers are generally available to every community citizen regardless of income, race, or creed (Crosson & Christian, 1990; Duffy, 1991; Harrington, 1985), and the mediators are trained to *respect the unique perspective* and *diversity* of the parties (Duffy, 1991). Empirical research has demonstrated that mediation is a humanistic process because it enhances the functioning of both participants as measured by Maslow's hierarchy of needs (Duffy & Thompson, 1992).

These centers hold several advantages over more traditional forms of seeking justice. For one thing, the centers dispense with cases in a more timely fashion than is provided by the court system (Duffy et al., 1991; Hedeen, 2004). One state reports a 15-day turnaround time from intake to resolution at its mediation centers (Crosson & Christian, 1990; Duffy, 1991) so in essence they offer early intervention. Second, victims no longer have to play a passive role in the justice system; in mediation, the victim plays an active role (Smith, 2006). Third, some studies have shown that victims demonstrate very little knowledge about the justice system and services available for them (Sims, Yost, & Abbott, 2005), so referral to mediation, where subsequent referrals to helping services can be made, educates victims about their rights and about other available supports. Furthermore, other research has found that victims are very dissatisfied with more traditional forms of justice (such as trials). They often are not told the full facts of the case and frequently have difficulty trying to recover personal property or even a loved one's remains because the police view these items as evidence (Goodrum, 2007). Additionally, many crime victims can achieve emotional repair, even forgiveness, in the mediation process (Armour & Umbreit, 2006; Strang, Sherman, Angel, & Woods, 2006). Charkoudian (2005) found that community mediation reduces repeat police calls for the same or continuing problem. Importantly, recent studies have found that those offenders who take part in restorative justice programs such as victim-offender mediation are far less likely to recidivate (Bradshaw & Roseborough, 2005; de Beus & Rodriguez, 2007; Rodriguez, 2007). One study followed parties in victim-offender mediation for three years and found that restorative justice programs are significantly related to better outcomes (e.g., less recidivism) than are traditional programs (e.g., parole).

Most victims are highly satisfied with the process of mediation (Bazemore, Elis, & Green, 2007; Carnevale & Pruitt, 1992; Duffy, 1991; Hedeen, 2004; McGillis, 1997; Wemmers & Cyr, 2005) because they get to tell their version of the story soon after their victimization. They are also allowed to vent their emotions (something usually prohibited in court) and they are availed of the opportunity to address the person they believe caused their distress. Respondents or offenders appreciate the process because they typically do not come out of it with a guilty verdict or an additional criminal record. Likewise, they are afforded the opportunity to provide evidence that the other party sometimes plays a role in the "crime" (as in harassment, where both parties have actually harassed each other).

The end result in about 85 to 90 percent of the cases is an agreement or contract between the parties (Duffy, 1991; Hedeen, 2004; McGillis, 1997). What is equally important is that 80 to 90 percent of victims and defendants emerge from the process satisfied (Duffy, 1991; Hedeen, 2004; McGillis, 1997). The agreements can contain anything from restitution and apologies to guidelines as to how the parties will interact in the future. Just about anything that both parties agree to that is legal can be part of the mediated settlement. Mediation has been successfully used in landlord–tenant and consumer–merchant disputes; neighborhood conflicts; crimes such as assault, harassment, and larceny; family dysfunction; racial conflict; environmental disputes; school conflict; and a host of other areas where individuals disagree or infract on each other's rights.

In fact, the opening vignette of Mike Farnsworth is a true story; Mike and his parents were referred to a mediation center by the probation department. Although the hearing was long, Mike and his parents eventually agreed on rules (e.g., curfews) and a reward system (which had been missing before the mediation). A punishment system had long been in place. The reward system would be used when Mike's grades were good or when his behavior was positive. During the hearing, Mike and his father finally listened to one another (rather than bellowed) and began to better understand each other's perspective. Mike's mother, Edna, learned some valuable skills from the mediator, such as compromise and reciprocity of concessions, for use in refereeing future disagreements between Mike and his father, should they arise. The Farnsworths (whose name we changed to protect their anonymity) have lived much more harmoniously since mediation.

Neighborhood justice centers have experienced tremendous growth in the past three decades (Duffy, 1991; Emery & Wyer, 1987; Meehan, 1986) but are not without their critics (e.g., Greatbatch & Dingwall, 1989; Presser & Hamilton, 2006; Rodriguez, 2005; Vidmar, 1992). Some critics argue that mediators hold too much control over the process and the parties and fail to challenge attitudes conducive to crime (Presser & Hamilton, 2006). Others explain that Hispanic/Latino and Black juveniles are less likely than Whites to be referred to restorative justice programs (Rodriguez, 2005). Finally, Latimer, Dowden, and Muise (2005) argue that some of the research on restorative justice is poorly designed, and because it is often voluntary—even for the offender—there is an important self-selection bias in the research. The foregoing information, then, needs to be tempered by these criticisms.

Reintegration Programs for Incarcerated Individuals. You know now that Mike Farnsworth's story had a fairly happy ending. Imagine, though, how Mike would feel if he had been imprisoned because of his repeated assaults on his father and then released after five years. He would have learned much in prison, most of it counterproductive. He may have learned how to fashion weapons out of ordinary household implements, such as mirrors and pens. He may have learned how to intimidate others merely by staring at them in a certain way, and he may have learned how to commit more heinous crimes than the assault on his father. Even though prison might have hardened Mike, he might also have felt intimidated about his reentry into society and insecure about his newly acquired freedom. Where would he find a job? How would he feel about going to see his parole officer? Would his parents allow him to come home? What would the neighbors and his friends think?

Each year, thousands of individuals are released from prisons and jails to communities (Byrne & Taxman, 2004; Mellow & Dickinson, 2006). The increase in number of parolees over the past few years is indicated in Figure 9.2. Although crime rates are declining somewhat, inmate numbers continue to rise because many are serving longer sentences or sentences that are now mandatory rather than discretionary on the part of a judge or jury (Bracey, 2006). For most inmates, returning to the community is problematic. First, their lives and decision making are totally controlled by the correctional staff while they are incarcerated. Thus, day-to-day prison life runs counter to the day-to-day life inmates will face outside of prison (Taxman, 2004). Furthermore, inmates probably lack skills to obtain employment. They may emerge from incarceration with some of the same problems (i.e., substance abuse) that got them there in the first place. Some inmates reappear in the community with health problems they did not have on entry to the prison (i.e., HIV/AIDS). Some of them have learned negative institutional behaviors (e.g., gang behavior), have lost contact with family members and friends, and will be stigmatized by community members and potential employers so that they cannot find housing or employment (Byrne & Taxman, 2004). Heap on top of these issues the stigma of having lost personal rights such as voting and parental rights, compounded by not being able to run for elective office and being unable to sit on juries, and the parolee can experience a profound sense of disconnection to the same community in which the crime was committed (Bazemore & Stinchcomb, 2004). Predictably, the longer the individual remains incarcerated, the more likely there will be changes in the family, peers, and neighborhood dynamics (Byrne & Taxman, 2004), too. It should not be unexpected, then, that recidivism occurs. Criminologists project that over two-thirds of all parolees will eventually be rearrested, and 40 percent of them will likely return to jail (Byrne & Taxman, 2004).

As already mentioned, the typical program for those being released from incarceration is parole. Some previously incarcerated persons are also court-ordered to treatment

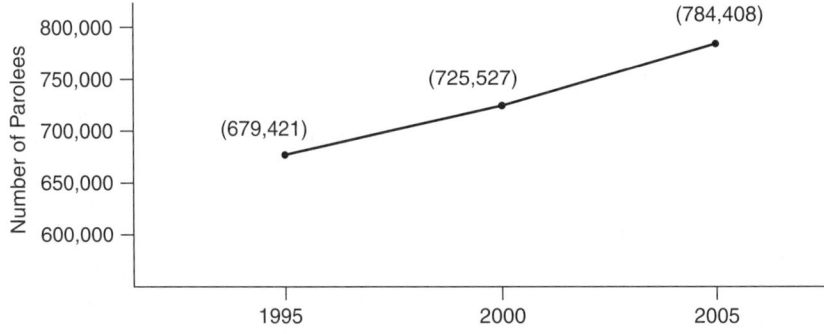

FIGURE 9.2 Number of Individuals on Parole in the Community

Source: Bureau of Justice Statistics (2003). One in every 32 adults now on probation, parole, or incarcerated. Retrieved from www.ojp.usdoj.gov/bjs/pub/press/ppus02pr.htm.

programs, but data reveal that they are unlikely to attend. Correctional personnel have known for decades that the high rate of recidivism is largely related to ineffective transition programs (e.g., parole) for inmates released back to the community (Bonhomme et al., 2006). Better pre- and postrelease programs are necessary. Research clearly shows that getting started right immediately on return to the community is extremely important (Bullis, Yovanoff, & Havel, 2001) if recidivism is to be reduced and the former inmate is to become a successful community member (Baltodano, Platt, & Roberts, 2005).

As for prerelease programs, we know little about them empirically (Byrne, 2004). Many prisons and jails now offer mental health counseling and substance abuse rehabilitation, as well as educational programs to inmates. It is well known that the prison population is less well educated than the general population. There are, however, limited data on how well schooling programs work or how much education actually takes place. What we do know is that such programs are quite variable (Byrne & Taxman, 2004), depending on the state, the community, and available funding. Some states don't offer educational programs. The existing studies, however, do indicate that prison-based education programs have positive effects on reducing recidivism (Vacca, 2004). Unfortunately, however, the number of prison staff dedicated to inmate education has declined over the years (Bracey, 2006).

Another well-known factor that enhances positive reintegration to the community is family and social support. Formerly incarcerated individuals who return home or live with relatives have a lower probability of rearrest and reincarceration than those who don't (Baltodano et al., 2005; Bahr, Armstrong, Gibbs, Harris, & Fisher, 2005). Of course, having stable housing and being employed also reduce the likelihood of running into trouble with the law. Practical prerelease programs designed to help former inmates secure housing and jobs *before they are released* would be advantageous because most inmates enter the community with no money, a poor work history (Barr et al., 2005; Shivy, Wu, Mann, & Eacho, 2007), and no housing options because they are expected to make all such arrangements while they are still in prison (Taxman, 2004).

One promising program designed to address all these needs and to reduce recidivism is the **restorative circle.** These circles empower the inmate to choose how he or she will live on the outside—which may create higher compliance with such programs (Taxman, 2004). Circle programs were originally developed in Hawaii for foster children aging out of the foster care system. In prison, the restorative circle is a group planning process for inmates, their families, significant others, and prison staff. In restorative circles, the professional facilitators do not tell inmates and their families how they should deal with problems but instead ask appropriate questions so that the involved parties can find solutions themselves. In many instances, family members or other emotionally supportive individuals reach out with suggestions for the inmate in developing the plan (Walker, Sakai, & Brady, 2006).

Circles can occur when the individual is first incarcerated and detail who will visit the inmate, how often, and so forth. On the other hand, a community reentry circle might include where the inmate will live, how much interaction he or she will have with the family, where a job or job skills training will be sought, and what the inmate will do to remain crime-free and drug-free once in the community. In both cases (on admission or on release) circle plans can also describe how the inmate will restore justice (e.g., write a letter to the victim, return stolen items, etc.). Identifying strengths of the inmate is also a key feature of this solution-focused approach. For example, if the inmate is identified as being highly intelligent, family members might encourage him or her to include an education component in the plan while in prison or after release. The program eventually results in a written plan (Walker et al., 2006). A recircle meeting is also planned for a later time where the written plan is reviewed to tweak its various components. Restorative circle programs certainly feature many of community psychology's tenets (such as empowerment and social support), but the programs are so new, we await sufficient literature on their efficacy (Walker et al., 2006).

In conclusion, criminal justice is a complex system comprised of many different players with a variety of motives and functions. Community psychologists are collaborating with individuals involved in the justice system, and together they are making headway on preventing crime and assisting those involved in the crime once it occurs. Better yet, community psychologists and others hope to keep the community and its members "whole" before, during, and after the crime.

SUMMARY

The traditional justice system includes enforcement agencies such as the police, the courts, the prisons, and related programs. Such programs allow only a small role, if any, for the victim and tend to seek retribution or punishment for the offender.

Psychologists who have tried to parcel out the causes of crime know that guns, gun control, and related factors are not the only predictors of crime. Certain ecological settings and certain groups of individuals are likely to be involved in crime. Young African American men are most likely to be victimized by crime and most likely to be convicted of and incarcerated for crime. Societal prejudice and the history of African Americans in the United States may in part be what underlies some of the statistics. Poverty and community disorder are other good predictors of crime rates.

Prisons are bleak, overcrowded institutions often fraught with problems such as violence, AIDS, and illegal substances. Prisons do not tend to rehabilitate nor treat offenders. Thus, recidivism rates remain high.

Victims and those who fear crime have been neglected populations in the traditional criminal justice system. An interesting phenomenon, the crime-victimization paradox, which has tempered support in the literature, suggests that those who fear crime the most are often least likely to be victimized. An example would be an elderly woman who fears crime but is very unlikely to be a victim.

Police are asked to play a variety of roles in a community. Some are roles for which they are ill prepared, such as intervention in domestic disputes and mental health issues. Police officers often report that they feel alienated from the communities they serve and feel that their superiors offer little understanding for street life.

Community psychologists believe that criminal behavior can be predicted. Some studies have successfully predicted delinquent behavior in at-risk youths. Environments can also be altered to reduce the probability of crime. An example is removing violent cues from the media, which tend to bias reports of crime.

Community programs, such as neighborhood crime watches, are successfully reducing the fear of crime. Other innovative programs involve citizens in collaborative efforts with officers at enforcement agencies.

In terms of secondary prevention, community-based programs show much promise for intervening in the cycle of delinquency and recidivism. There also exist programs for early assistance to actual crime victims. Two such programs include crisis intervention and neighborhood justice centers or community mediation centers.

Victims, for example, may need follow-up services long after the crime. One new and interesting program is the victim-offender mediation program in which the victim and offender meet face to face and discuss their impact on one another as well as plans for restitution to the victim.

Programs comparing incarceration to alternative community services are difficult to assess with research due to confounding issues, but many community programs offer hope that even chronic offenders can be assisted. An especially important type of program is one that is designed to ease adjustment of an incarcerated person into the community, such as a restorative circle program.

CHAPTER 10

THE HEALTH CARE SYSTEM

THE AMERICAN HEALTH CARE SYSTEM
   National Health Indicators
   Observations on the System
      Cost and Access
      Adherence and Compliance
COMMUNITY PSYCHOLOGY AND THE HEALTH CARE SYSTEM
   Prevention over Remediation
   Shifting Focus from Individuals to Groups, Neighborhoods, and Systems

   Building Systems
   Increasing Accessibility
      Timely Interventions
   ■ **CASE IN POINT 10.1**   Teen Pregnancy Prevention
      Dealing with Diverse Communities
      Rural Health
   Social Support and Health
SUMMARY

The speaker was a famous Black American figure. He was being honored by the association for his work and accomplishments. The band played, and the audience came to its feet. The speaker spoke in stentorian tones about the honor and his life. But before he did so, he dedicated the time there and his comments to his recently departed uncle. Dearly remembered, the uncle had been a friend and a grounding force in the famous person's life.

    As the story unfolded, it became apparent why this uncle was the point of dedication. It turned out that he had had health problems for a while. However, like many, he put off going in to see a doctor. It was too expensive. It seemed a needless cost when times were difficult economically, or at least it did not seem worth the extra expense. By the time the uncle made it to the doctor's office, the cancer had progressed to the point of irreversibility. Then it was just a matter of time. The family came together. People said their goodbyes. The uncle died. The speaker had nearly canceled his engagement with the award ceremony. He was grieving. Yet he decided to come and to speak about his uncle. He hoped to point out the example this presented for us all. Was the delay in seeking health care necessary? Was it a function of poor habits? Was it a pattern of behavior that was culturally established long ago? Were the concerns about money justified? What was the cost in the end? These are the questions he put to the audience that evening. These were the challenges the speaker wanted to present to those who honored him. Where are the answers? Would they come from those to whom he spoke that night? What could we, would we contribute to solving this problem, made personal by his uncle, but otherwise found in data collected every year in the United States?

A second story completes our picture of a health care system looking for answers. In this story, we find a successful clinical psychologist, working in a large metropolitan area. Going for a check-up for symptoms she could not explain, her physician discovered over the course of several days and many tests that she had a rare form of cancer that was quite virulent. For her to receive the cutting-edge treatment, which would have provided her with the best chance of survival, she needed to go to where the treatment was being tested. Unfortunately, the medical center where this treatment occurred was in another state, several hundred miles away. At first she was able to travel between her home and the other site. However, besides the travel expenses, her medical expenses mounted quickly. Soon, she discovered that the regimen of therapies cost in the hundreds of thousands of dollars. While her insurance decided if she qualified, and if her treatment qualified, she had to bear the cost herself. Eventually, the determination was that the insurance did not believe they were responsible for her treatments. Meanwhile, the psychologist had to close down her practice because she was not able to adequately care for her patients. Soon she had run through her savings and was looking at the choices of death or going further into debt. She also had to decide whether to stay in her home city with her circle of friends or move to a strange city where she knew no one.

So what, then, of our health care system? What could community psychology contribute to making it better? That is what we explore in this chapter.

THE AMERICAN HEALTH CARE SYSTEM

National Health Indicators

The World Health Organization reports on global health indicators. Among them are life expectancy and neonate mortality rates. The 2008 World Health Statistics state that for those born in 2006 in the United States, life expectancy is slightly lower than many European countries, Japan, and Canada, or rather, is comparable to Cuba. However, these numbers still look much better when compared to global life expectancies (World Health Organization, 2008a). Neonate mortality rates per 1,000 follow a similar pattern. See Table 10.1.

In the 2007 annual report on health within the United States, life expectancy was at an all-time high. Life expectancy for children born in 2004 was three years greater for males and one year greater for females than in 1990. Given the 2003 figures, the United States ranks 26th in the world for life expectancy (Japan and Hong Kong are 1st and 2nd, respectively). Infant mortality is also low at 6.8 infants per 1,000 or 4.5 neonates per 1,000, making us 29th in world rankings (Singapore and Hong Kong are 1st and 2nd). However, these health status indicators were not uniformly found throughout the U.S. population, with ethnic minority groups faring less well. In particular, Black or African American figures had more than

TABLE 10.1 Comparative World Health Status Statistics: Mortality Measures, 2006

	LIFE EXPECTANCY (AGE IN YEARS)		NEONATE MORTALITY (NUMBER WHO DIE PER 1,000, BIRTH TO 28 DAYS OF AGE)
	MALE	FEMALE	BOTH SEXES
Canada	78	83	3
Cuba	76	80	4
France	77	84	2
Germany	77	82	3
Ireland	77	82	4
Japan	79	86	1
Mexico	72	77	11
Spain	78	84	2
Switzerland	79	84	3
United Kingdom	77	81	3
United States	75	80	4
Global	65	69	28

Source: World Health Organization, "Global Health Indicators," *World Health Indicators,* 2008.

double the norm for both infant and neonate deaths. Black or African Americans also had lower life expectancies than their white counterparts by approximately 5 years (White males—75 years, Black males—69 years, White females—80 years, Black females—76 years) (National Center for Health Statistics, 2007b, p. 4). Also cited in the report were concerns over the problems of rural health. The U.S. 2007 health status report described increasing sophistication in health treatments that could help in physical illnesses. Yet the access to health care professionals and the attendant treatments were more easily attained in urban centers. For example, we see in Figure 10.1 that in the specialty area of obstetrics and gynecology, there were large (mostly rural) sectors of the nation without any identified physicians with this specialty. The report cautioned that such shortages meant that patients had to travel far to obtain services and these services, in turn were placed under extraordinary demands to meet the health needs of the wider geographic area (p. 5).

One final observation gathered from this report was the overall concern over unhealthy lifestyles, which included diet, exercise, risky behaviors, and alcohol- and drug-related habits. The combination of these lifestyle risk factors contributed to a formidable portion of health-related concerns. For example, it was estimated that in 2006, approximately 39 percent of the population over 18 years of age were inactive during their leisure time (p. 286). Among those 18 years and older who drank, more than a third reported consuming more than five alcoholic drinks in one day during the past year (p. 9).

Given these health statistics, we understand that the United States does well in health care, though it is not the best, and there are national behavior patterns that place us at risk. As well, the benefits of living in the United States are not evenly distributed, with health advantages going to the White ethnic majority. Risk factors include poverty and lack of health insurance. Other advantages accrue to those in cities, who have a larger supply of

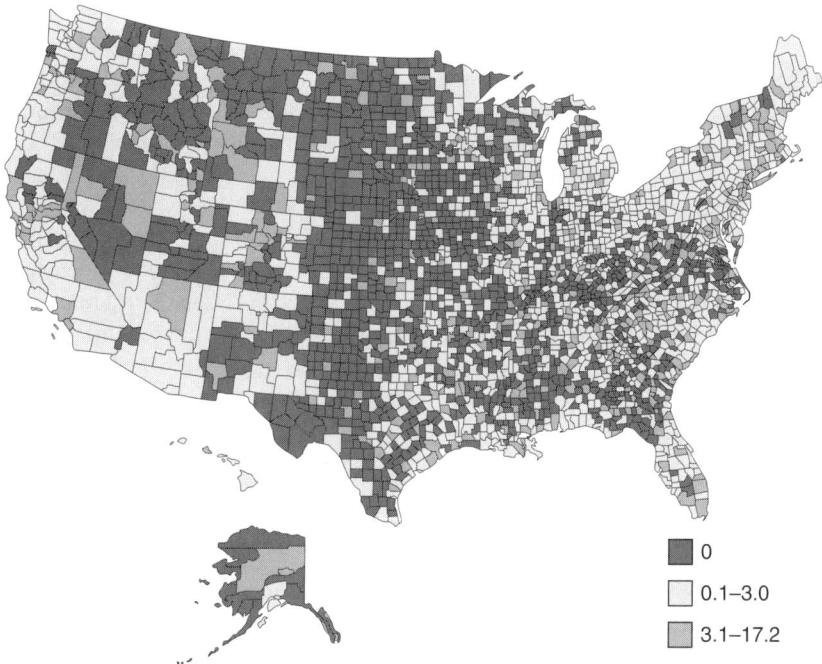

FIGURE 10.1 OB/GYNs per 10,000 Female Population Age 15+, by County (2004)

Sources: Centers for Disease Control and Prevention; National Center for Health Statistics (2007b), Fig. 23. Data from the Area Resource File.

doctors. According to this latest report, urban areas as a whole have access to more health resources. The report singles out a particular challenge for the country in the unhealthy lifestyle choices made by many. These choices lead to problems that come with the lack of exercise and excess weight to which we tend.

Observations on the System

Given these numbers, what of the existing health system? In the not too distant past, access to health care more or less depended on one's ability to pay for it. The establishment of federally funded programs, such as Medicaid and Medicare, in the 1960s, as well as the institutionalization of employment-based health care, has been a significant step forward for a healthy nation. However, health maintenace organizations (HMOs) place restrictions on doctor–patient discourse.

This overly simplistic description points to at least four sets of interrelated, multifaceted elements and players. If we as a country are to engage in a meaningful discourse on health care reform, they need to be addressed. The first element is financing the mechanism; the second is legislation; the third is the health care providers; and the fourth is the consumers or patients. So far, virtually all proposed efforts tend to focus on one or two elements. The first and second ones certainly have the most exposure in people's daily life. Often, the first, the economics of the situation, dictates ability to access health care. Until this barrier is removed, there will always be less than optimal health among some segments of the population.

The United States is first in the world with regards to medical expenditures, with $2 trillion spent in 2005 (National Center for Health Statistics, 2007b). This is a 7 percent increase from 2004, at a time when Social Security only granted a 2.7 percent increase in its payments for a cost of living adjustment (COLA) (http://www.ssa.gov/cola/colafacts2005.htm). It would be easier to work off an assumption that more money buys more and better care, but the United States ranks 26th in life expectancy and 29th in neonate mortality. The correlation is not as one might expect. Nonetheless, the issue of cost remains.

The United States found itself in a state of flux over the past few decades, struggling to contend with the expenses of health care and the manner in which patients can pay for it. In 2005, 36 percent of costs have been paid by private insurance, 34 percent by the federal government, and 11 percent as "out of pocket" expenditures. There are a variety of proposals on who should pay for health care. The coming decade may provide us with clearer direction because health care and its costs were on the agenda for the presidential contest of 2008 and are of growing concern to business interests and consumers alike.

Cost and Access. The issues of access and cost are among the leading concerns in health care today (National Center for Health Statistics, 2007b, pp. 56–58). Ross, Bradley and Busch (2006) see a relationship between ability to pay and other "access problems." They note that lack of health insurance places none-too-subtle pressure on the potential patient to be frugal with health care usage. Without insurance, there is less health care usage, regardless of income level for the patient. The threshold for seeking help may be set at a higher standard due to the drain on resources that occurs when a person seeks medical help. Especially when insurance is lacking, the individual or her or his family must decide as to the allocation of funds to treatments that can reach into the thousands or tens of thousands of dollars. The fear of this potential cost alone would place a psychological barrier to medical attention. This appears to be present for those in higher income brackets such as the psychologist with cancer as well as those in lower income brackets, as long as there is no insurance. "However, uninsured people are not significantly less likely than insured people to have undiagnosed . . . 'medical conditions' (authors' phrase)" (National Center for Health Statistics, 2007b, p. 6). The findings that on average over 45 million Americans were uninsured between 2000 and 2004, and that over the next year, there were 6 million more uninsured, was all the more sobering (Holahan & Cook, 2005).

Research by Maloy, Darnell, Nolan, Kenney, and Cyprien (2000) argued that the ability to access health care is a necessary but not sufficient condition to promote healthy lifestyles. People's willingness to access is important for engagement and retention in care. This speaks to the traditional domain of doctor–patient discourse—that is, that your doctor "understands" you, and you in turn want to seek her or his advice. The feeling of being informed as to medical information and where to get it illustrates consumer or patient empowerment. This empowerment is not uniformly felt.

There are health disparities between ethnic minority groups in comparison to the U.S. norms (National Center for Health Care Statistics, 2007b). Although some of these disparities may be due to language and to geographic distance from facilities, other factors are also at work. Given that colorectal cancer is the second leading cause of cancer-related death in America, the importance of regular exams among high-risk populations seems clear. Cancer is best diagnosed early. Early discovery and treatment leads to higher rates of treatment success. Therefore, it is important to do regular check-ups once individuals pass the age of 50 (U.S. Preventive Services Task Force, 2002). Despite these recommendations, check-ups for colorectal cancer follow the same pattern of low rates among the ethnic minority elderly (National Center for Health Care Statistics, 2007b). Shih, Zhao, and Elting (2006) studied various possible causes for these low rates. They find that the access issues of language, lack of health information on this topic and culturally based perceptions of the screening procedures stand as barriers to these examinations.

In both of our opening stories, we find concerns about access and cost. The perception of the cost of regular medical check-ups holds back the individual in the first vignette from going until his ailment progressed to an untreatable stage. The lack of knowledge relating to the health issues played an important role in both cases. They did not know the symptoms. The psychologist discovers that medical treatment can be expensive, is not available near her home where she needs it, and her insurance coverage is inadequate. She is in private practice, and therefore is a small business, which brings expensive insurance costs and lower benefits. Once her insurance runs out or is denied, she is left with no coverage. This is inevitably a bad set of scenarios.

Adherence and Compliance. Beyond cost and access, there is the issue of the patient/consumer doing as instructed. This is called adherence or compliance. Haynes, McDonald, and Garg (2002) note that typical adherence runs about 50 percent for medication regimens. Lower rates of adherence are reported for prescriptions of changes in lifestyle, for example, changes in diet and exercise. Following a review of research on adherence, McDonald, Garg, and Haynes (2002) report that short-term compliance (less than 2 weeks) can be increased with patient instruction, but long-term compliance takes a combination of instruction, social support, emphasis of the importance of the prescription, provision for positive feedback on compliance, and regular reminders as to the regimen. This represents change in the patient's context or his or her social environment.

Given new technologies, like the Internet, psychology might inform the manner in which compliance or adherence is measured and its effects on program success. Such an example of this is presented by Manwaring, Bryson, and Goldschmidt (2008). Using adherence measures, the number of weeks in an Internet-based treatment program, the number of pages read over the Internet, the number of times engaged in online discussions, and the use of a computer-based booster program, Manwaring et al. (2008) looked at the effectiveness of an eating disorder program on problematic eating behaviors and attitudes. They found these to be a good way to measure compliance.

Studies of who complies with instructions for physical exercise may help in determining at-risk populations. Butcher, Sallis, and Mayer (2008) identified older adolescent girls and lower income youth as segments of the targeted youth group who were less likely to follow up on exercise regimens. Using a 100-city sample, they found that these two groups did not adhere to physical activity guidelines as presented. Though not providing explanations for this finding, the demographic variables were predictive of behavior tendencies.

DiMatteo (2004) conducted a meta-analysis of studies examining medical adherence and the role of social support. Studies dealing with psychiatric populations and alcohol- and drug-related issues were not included so as to look at situations uncomplicated by those factors. The examination of the group of studies on social support and adherence suggested functional social support (people giving help directly to the individual) to be more beneficial than structural social support factors (group membership, such as marital status, living alone or with others). Of the ways in which functional support was provided, practical social support (instrumental—providing information, lending a hand) was the best predictor of medical adherence. These patterns were instructive as to the risks of nonadherence with medical prescriptions and were helpful in devising interventions to increase following of medical instructions. The usefulness of the stress model and its components was helpful in explaining these findings.

In an earlier study of how physician characteristics related to patient adherence, DiMatteo et al. (1993) found that the physician's ratings of overall job satisfaction, the number of patients seen by the physician in a week and the doctor's willingness to answer questions were all significantly predictive of patient follow-through on medical prescriptions. Though the specifics in isolation seem curious, the holistic impression for adherence was of a physician who liked what he or she was doing, was thoroughly engaged in the work, and communicated with patients.

Note that embedded within these descriptions was the importance of the supportive relationships and a broader network of support for healthy behaviors. It was more than the correct technique or adequate technology; it was the ability of the medical system to reach out to the consumers/clients, connect with them, and then make a meaningful impact on the larger social context within which the consumers/clients reside. Given these findings, it is not so strange to think in terms of a community psychology contributing to the health care system.

COMMUNITY PSYCHOLOGY AND THE HEALTH CARE SYSTEM

Revenson and Schiaffino (2000) argued that the cost versus benefit of our health care system indicated things were not working. They proposed that a focus on preventive health services needed to be further developed and the emphasis on hospitals and emergency rooms as primary sites for receiving medical care needed to be reexamined. Because many of the physical illnesses that presently concern modern American medicine were related to lifestyle choices and habits, community psychology could help in changing these from unhealthy to healthy tendencies. They suggested that community intervention programs should contend with sociocultural contexts, build off of community strengths, emphasize the adaptation of healthy behavior styles, seek change at the community level, and target communities for intervention, rather than individuals. Among the intervention strategies they list are mass media campaigns, community organizing, use of existing community institutions such as schools and churches, and social policy changes. We examine how community psychology and community psychologists have contributed to these concepts.

Prevention over Remediation

The Stanford Heart Disease Prevention Project served as an excellent example of a program aimed at public education of a targeted population regarding factors contributing to heart disease. The Three Community Project reported on use of media (newspapers, radio, TV, printed matter) aimed at identified at-risk groups of two California coastal communities. The targeted communities showed significant improvement in heart disease–related factors in comparison to the one control community without the educational program (Maccoby & Altman, 1988). A second study on five cities produced similar findings in the two program targeted urban sites compared to three reference-control cities (Farquhar et al., 1985; Flora, Jatilus, & Jackson, 1993). A follow-up study three years later showed these effects to have lasted (Winkleby, Taylor, Jatilus, & Fortmann, 1996). The intervention phase lasted for six years. Working with a multidisciplinary team, the Stanford Project showed the effectiveness of a preventive, universal population, targeted multimedia program that included radio and TV spots, flyers, and classes. The Stanford Project was similar to two other community-based disease prevention programs of that era: the Minnesota Heart Health Program (Luepker et al., 1994) and the Pawtucket Heart Health Program (Carleton, Lasater, Assaf, Feldman, & McKinlay, 1995). All of these programs attempted to change how individuals behaved within their community settings. They were multidisciplinary in nature and involved the targeted communities in organizing and implementing programs.

Other population-focused prevention programs have been developed and run successfully. They used media along with multiple interventions within the community. These programs worked to ensure community involvement in project development. This involvement has helped establish and maintain new norms for behavior and new values to sustain healthy choices (DuRant, Wolfson, LaFrance, Balkrishnan, & Altman, 2006; Jason, 1998). When the ownership of the projects is clearly community-based, ecological factors dictate greater acceptance and identification with the changes.

Shifting Focus from Individuals to Groups, Neighborhoods, and Systems

Whereas large community interventions are clearly the focus of public health initiatives, the focus on groups, neighborhoods, and community systems has also been of interest to community psychology. Further discussion of the public health perspective occurs in the next chapter. The point here is that the traditional health focus is on treatment of the individual. Broadening the focus of interventions from the individual to the community or neighborhood is a strength of the community psychology tradition. The public health model of studying the patterns of illness and health and the factors that contribute to those patterns also contribute to a community research methodology. The previous section on prevention demonstrates the effectiveness of such interventions.

Stephens (2007) discussed the shift to health promotion efforts using community concepts. We earlier provided descriptions of the debates in how to define community, that is, whether it should be a matter of place or of identity (Campbell & Murray, 2004). Beyond these basic considerations, what community psychology has added to this model has been the definition of what variables contribute to the psychological awareness of neighborhood and community and how this has been used to advance the efforts to influencing entire groups. What were the natural boundaries to communities, who were the agents of change within those groups, how was the message effectively communicated, and how was the community awareness and motivation to be healthy aroused (Altman, & Wandersman, 1987; Imm, Kehres, Wandersman, & Chinman, 2006; Manzo & Perkins, 2006; Nicotera, 2007; Perkins et al., 1990; Shinn & Toohey, 2003)? There has been an extensive body of literature addressing these issues. The work of Wandersman and his colleagues has been previously cited in earlier chapters. Indicators of social cohesion versus social disorganization, defined by existence of local friendship networks, and participation in community organizations, as well as other neighborhood characteristics, have been shown to be associated with physical health indicators (Caughy, O'Campus, & Brodsky, 1999; Shinn & Toohey, 2003). **Goodness of fit** between individual and social environment—as defined by (1) similarities between the individual and the social environment, (2) the individual's needs and the environment's resources, and (3) the agreement of environmental features and individual preferences—has been linked to well-being (Shinn & Rapkin, 2000). Following a review of the community context variables studied in psychology, Shinn and Toohey (2003) caution against "context minimalization error," or a tendency to focus on the individual and to ignore the community/context that brings about behaviors and health outcomes. Community psychology has brought a focus on the larger picture. It has also helped conceptualize, develop, and evaluate systems addressing health issues.

Snowden (2005) wrote of "population thinking," or consideration of given groups of people, how well they do in their environment, and the variables affecting that status. The focus was on the social mechanisms and how they work. What brought about and what maintained the population's health or illnesses? In Snowden's discussion, he cited the work done on poor communities as a good example of what these analyses yielded. Poverty placed communities at risk, but there have been poor communities where residents do well, that is, were resilient. Studies of these resilient communities found them to have people who feel *responsible* for what happens and who *actively help* their communities maintain a positive orientation. Poverty was not what brings about the higher risks, it was that poverty made this positive orientation harder to hold.

Bolland and colleagues (2005) found measures of social disruption and social connectedness to predict levels of hopelessness in poor inner-city youth. It was not the poverty per se but the exposure to violence, worry, and trauma (**social disruption**) and the sense of community, warmth toward mother, and religiosity (**social connectedness**) that influenced the hopelessness, with disruption increasing and connectedness decreasing despair. Bolland (2003) had earlier found hopelessness to be related to risky behaviors. Therefore, any work on hopelessness was really work on risky behaviors. The community psychology orientation yielded social variables that have been demonstrated to have a link to a community's health. Treat the social connections and social disruptions and intervene in hopelessness and thus lower risky behaviors.

Building Systems

Community psychologists have had interests in the creation of systems and settings (Sarason, 1972/1999). Emshoff et al. (2007) described a program of collaboration building among community agencies that aimed to change systems of health care in Georgia. Lasker, Weiss, and Miller (2001) have defined collaboration as "a process that enables independent individuals and organizations to combine their human and material resources so they can accomplish objectives they are unable to bring about alone" (p. 183). Roussos and Fawcett's (2000) review of collaboratives led them to the conclusion that the collaboration in itself brought about changes to the system. By its nature, the collaboration should result in greater sharing of information, an increase in efficiencies since duplication of services is reduced, and the overall functioning of the health system for an area is improved. Emshoff et al. (2007) believed systems-level changes were produced through building collaboration efforts. They found that changes in service delivery did occur in the first few years, that the activity levels of the collaborative (number of meetings) related to more changes, and that the longer term collaborative chair helped bring about greater systems' changes. The overall impression of the collaborative was that the successful ones could do more and could do it better. This would fit with Lasker et al.'s (2001) belief that when collaboration was best realized and created the opportunity for synergy among the elements, the result was more than the sum of its parts. This realization of greater potential would help explain Roussos and Fawcett's (2000) note about the rapid growth of these partnerships. The health community has come to realize that "most objectives . . . cannot be achieved by any single person, organization or sector working alone" (Lasker et al., 2001, p. 179). Notably, Allen's (2005) study of coordinating councils found that the ones that work best were inclusive of their members and had an active and diverse membership.

This study of new systems to provide services and the effects of these ways on service provision have been within the purview of community psychology. This included how pooling of resources could be successfully accomplished. These collaborative systems may represent the wave of the future for health care with its attendant demands on cost and the need for a variety of expertise and equipment.

Increasing Accessibility

Timely Interventions. There are several ways to consider accessibility problems. There is the most obvious variable of accessibility: the cost of services. As described earlier, the costs of sophisticated treatments are formidable. Yet timely interventions, early in the development of disorders, from a secondary prevention point of view, are one of the answers to the cost containment issue. As noted earlier, some of the costs of health care are related to lifestyle choices. These choices can and have been modified by psychological interventions at the community level.

Among the array of such programs is an early one on reduction of a risky behavior: not using seatbelts for securing children in cars (Fawcett, Seekins, & Jason, 1987). Through collection of behavioral data on seatbelt usage and social opinion data on acceptability of requiring use, followed by strategic use of this information with legislatures, community psychologists were able to help in the passage of child seatbelt laws in the states of Kansas and Illinois. This program was successful before use of seatbelts came to national attention. These laws helped pave the way for the seatbelt laws found throughout the United States today. Presently, most people would consider the use of seatbelts to be a normal behavior.

More recently, community psychology has provided research and programs in tobacco use, alcohol use, and safe sexual practices. These efforts are described and discussed in the next chapter. These are all health system interventions in that they are directly aimed at health concerns. Accessibility in these terms are with regard to a broader conceptualization of what health interventions are. Pregnancy prevention is a topic covered earlier in the text, within the chapter on social and health services. As noted there, infants of teen mothers have lower birth weight and higher mortality rates. Case in Point 10.1 takes a second look at pregnancy prevention and community perspectives on what can help.

Accessibility can also be defined as willingness to take part in regular health visits and in increasing one's **health literacy** (knowledge of health-related issues). Having an annual

CASE IN POINT 10.1
TEEN PREGNANCY PREVENTION

The U.S. teen pregnancy rate is the second highest among industrialized nations (Darrouch, Frost, & Singh, 2001; Kirby, 2007). In a study of five developed Western countries, Darrouch et al. (2001) found sexual activity in females before age 20 to be nearly equivalent (see Table 10.2), yet the pregnancy rates for the United States were notably higher (see Table 10.3). Among the reasons cited for this difference was the lack of pregnancy prevention measures taken.

TABLE 10.2 Percentage of Women Aged 20–24 Who Had First Intercourse before Age 20

- Sweden: 86%
- France: 83%
- Canada: 75%
- Great Britain: 85%
- United States: 81%

TABLE 10.3 Teenage Birth Rate per 1,000 Births

- Sweden: 7
- France: 9
- Canada: 20
- Great Britain: 31
- United States: 49

Kirby's (2007) review of pregnancy prevention programs examined which ones had been successful. He considered only those programs that were examined using experimental or quasi-experimental designs (see Chapter 2) and had an adequate sample size for meaningful statistical analyses. He found that comprehensive prevention programs that taught contraceptive procedures as well as encouraging abstinence could be effective. However, abstinence-only programs did not demonstrate positive effects to the level his review required. Programs that focused on nonsexual protective factors, such as plans for the future, school performance, connections to family, and religion, were successful. Also, participation in service learning programs, such as volunteering in the community with discussion and writing about the service, proved to significantly decrease teen pregnancy rates. From program evaluations of a variety of teen pregnancy programs, a clear picture emerges. Some programs have demonstrated positive effects, and some do not have evidentiary support.

Beyond the evaluation of the specific programs, the importance of context to these programs was demonstrated in the implementation of a comprehensive, school- and community-based teen pregnancy prevention program in Kansas (Paine-Andrews et al., 2002). This study found that the prevention program success varied as a function of the amount of community change that came about due to the program. In the area that produced more system and program changes, the pregnancy rates dropped. In the area where fewer system and program changes occurred, the pregnancy rates did not drop.

Pursuing the goal of providing the appropriate contexts and capacities for implementation of effective teen pregnancy prevention programs, Rolleri, Wilson, Paluzzi, and Sedivy (2008) described their work at the national level with Healthy Teen Network and Education Training and Research Associates. Using a training model, they taught practitioners in the use of a logical process for defining interventions through the Behavior, Determinant, Intervention Logic model. This model called for a four-step process: goal definition, identifying behaviors to achieve the goal, identifying determinants to those behaviors, and identifying interventions to affect the determinants. Follow-up evaluations and future work with the members of the practitioner systems have continued to build their understanding of the program and evaluation/research processes. The authors' work has helped in the implementation of prevention programs at the state level and built programs' capacities to do more science-based work.

---

check-up and a willingness to visit a physician when detecting symptoms of disorder means that a person is willing to possibly hear bad news regarding one's health (Rothman & Salovey, 1997). These perceptions of risk and ability to respond are constructed by social knowledge of procedures, cost, and the likelihood of treatment success. In addition, there are expectations and assumptions regarding the resources that one has to call on, if there is need for treatment. Reluctance to go to the doctor delayed the diagnosis found in this chapter's first story. Delaying the inevitable only places the potential patient at higher risk and is typical of many ethnic minority community members' behavior patterns (Agency for Healthcare Research and Quality, 2006). Unfortunately, in the case presented in the story, waiting was fatal. So how can these disparities be addressed?

Dealing with Diverse Communities. Snowden (2006) studied the variety of clinic program variables believed to affect minority client use of mental health services in California. Looking at Medi-Cal (California's Medicare program) patients, Snowden found that **outreach** (where clinic staff would go out into the community to meet people and, when needs were discovered, bring patients in to the clinic) helped increase Latino and Native American use of mental health services. For Asian Americans, having **bilingual** (speaking English and an Asian language) or **bicultural** (being familiar with American and Asian cultures) staff was associated with better care usage rates. In an interesting turn to this data, having bilingual and bicultural receptionists led to decreases in Asian Americans receiving services. For all groups, including Whites, increased numbers of mental health providers led to increased use rates. These findings are highly suggestive of ways for programs to increase health usage.

In an outreach and education program for New York state on breast cancer, Rapkin et al. (2006) used a partnership model between the state Department of Health and community-based organizations (CBOs). This program, called ACCESS, brought discussions of health information needs to specific community sites. From these discussions, interventions were developed for that particular site. Learning from the CBOs about the targeted communities, the program could devise information tailored for the population to be found in each given context. These site discussions resulted in more effective interventions and in building better relationships with the community organizations. At the end of the project, the CBOs requested more information and more opportunities to work with the program. The community program worked to bring about partnerships between the medical education center and the various sites (e.g., churches, youth groups, schools), which extended the reach of the program out into the neighborhoods. The program served as an entry point into these settings. The working relationships that had developed appeared to be useful for future efforts at extending medical information beyond the traditional office or hospital settings. What was described was a program that was ecologically formulated to promote growth. This would be the ideal goal for any program, much less one that dealt with diversity in its many forms.

Rural Health. Making treatment relevant to the community is especially important. The ACCESS plan described in the last section was a good example of working to make the interventions fit the settings where they resided. These cancer education programs were in a variety of communities throughout New York, which includes both rural and urban settings. The respect for the specific context of each setting applies to rural health programs as well. In other programs directed to the growth of rural health services, the inclusion of the community in determining needs and services has had good results. Such empowerment of the community is very much in the tradition of community psychology.

Two separate programs servicing different parts of the country described similar approaches to community inclusion in definition of problems and in decision making. In North Dakota, meetings with organizations working in rural settings and in Native American communities attempted to define the health care barriers and to ask how the rural health center could help (Moulton, Miller, & Offutt, 2007). From these conversations, strategic plans were devised and groups formed to address the problems identified. The engagement of the community in participating has resulted in more useful interventions for the targeted groups.

A second study in a similar vein used a participation model (Hoshin) for engaging community members in the definition of goals, strategies, objectives, and action plans for health programs in rural Hawaii. What they found was a great deal of involvement and agreement within the participant groups. Among the common community needs identified were economic factors within the community (poverty, unemployment, insurance, ability to pay), drug use, lack of leadership, lack of health services or access to such services, lack of healthy activities for youth, and poor public education. We would observe that these concerns are broadly defined and demonstrate an ecological perspective to the problems. All this emerges from community discussions. The concerns of rural health are more than a lack of medical doctors. These results suggested the need for multilevel interventions for multideterminant problems, and a comprehension of these needs within the rural community contexts. Among the issues raised are those that might be characterized as social support and network resources. We examine some of the work on the importance of social support next; keep in mind that these considerations might be guided by models of stress, coping, and resilience described earlier.

Social Support and Health

The study of the health benefits of a good social support system has been a part of the literature for several decades (Wallston, Alagna, & DeVellis, 1983). In their early review of the existent work on social support and health benefits, Wallston and colleagues did not find much of significance. Few studies clearly demonstrated the advantages of social support on overall health. However, there was research indicating such support was helpful in health recovery.

Over a decade later, a review of the literature by Uchin et al. (1996) found studies suggesting social support to be beneficial to cardiovascular, endocrine, and immune system health. The precise physiological mechanisms that affected these relationships were unclear. Models of the manner in which social support might play a role in the process of health and illness were beginning to emerge. Social support was seen to influence both behavioral and psychological processes, which then, in turn, influenced physiological reactions bringing better or worse health (Berkman, Glass, Brissette, & Seeman, 2000; Uchino, 2004). Findings are starting to more clearly demonstrate the physiological pathways from social support to the cardiovascular, endocrine, and immune systems (Uchino, 2004, 2006). Social support is a community variable. Interventions to improve social support may become a regular part of treatment prescription. Experimental studies are examining the impact of programs to improve the social connections of patients contending with medical conditions. If such treatments prove successful, new systems for treatment would need to be implemented for dealing with health promotion and health remediation.

SUMMARY

The health care system would appear to be a natural place for the application of community psychology principles. Although there are a variety of health care systems in the world, the United States served as our focal point. In this national example, we found a sophisticated and modern set of personnel and facilities, with vast amounts of money expended for care. Among the world's best technological and research capacities, and with vast amounts of money in play, the outcomes still leave the United States ranking 26th in the world for longevity.

In analyzing areas of concern that contribute to this ranking, several topics arise. Among the more conspicuous issues are those of access and cost. Access can be defined in terms of timely medical information and the means to gain and use that information. Cost of course has to do with how much the individual and his or her family has to pay for this access. There are clearly defined populations within the United States who are at risk due to access and cost problems. These include those in rural settings, particular ethnic minority groups, and those without health insurance. A second identified area of concern regarding health care may have to do with compliance issues. Of course, compliance may be influenced by cost and access, but there are socially driven ways to increase compliance.

In response to these concerns, community psychology contributes the argument for the advantages of prevention rather than reparative treatment, the focus on the efficiencies and benefits of a community, neighborhood, or group focus for intervention, certain knowledge and technologies for building systems of care, ways to increase accessibility, and the knowledge of the healthy effects of social support. Community psychology may have historically had issues with the medical model, but community psychology has always been an advocate for the health model and the holistic approach. The challenge and the opportunity is to realize the potential for community psychology applied to health systems (Minden & Jason, 2002; Revenson & Schiaffino, 2000).

CHAPTER 11

COMMUNITY HEALTH AND PREVENTIVE MEDICINE

TOBACCO
  Extent of the Problem
  Antitobacco Efforts
  Community-Based Approaches

ALCOHOL
  Extent of the Problem
  Alcohol Safety Laws
  A Community Psychology Approach

ILLICIT DRUGS
  Extent of the Problem
  Possible Solutions and Challenges
  ■ CASE IN POINT 11.1   Prescription Drug Misuse: Risk Factors for Problem Users

SEXUALLY TRANSMITTED DISEASES
  Extent of the Problem
  Possible Solutions and Challenges

HIV AND AIDS
  Overview
  Extent of the Problem
  Complexities and Controversies
  Possible Solutions: Community-Based Approaches
  ■ CASE IN POINT 11.2   Evaluation and Implementation of STD/HIV Community Intervention Program in Lima, Peru
  ■ CASE IN POINT 11.3   The Bilingual Peer Advocate (BPA) Program

SUMMARY

All human actions have one or more of these seven causes: chance, nature, compulsion, habit, reason, passion, and desire.

—Aristotle, c. 384–322 BCE

Elizabeth is a freshman in college at a large state school. She considers herself similar to many of her peers—she drinks on the weekends and has occasionally blacked out. Elizabeth likes to have a good time, but she definitely thinks she doesn't have a problem. On homecoming weekend, she spent the day tailgating and pregaming. In the evening, she attends several parties, where she takes multiple shots of vodka and plays various drinking games. At one of the parties, she runs into Jake from her chemistry class, who proceeds to flirt with her all evening. When Jake suggests that she come back to his place, Elizabeth eagerly joins him; he is cute, and she reminds herself that this is what college is all about. They end up having drunken sex, and in the morning Elizabeth realizes that in their inebriated state they did not use a condom. Her mind races: She is not taking birth control, what if she gets pregnant? Jake is a nice guy, but people say he gets around; what if he has an STD? Where could she go for help?

Biological and natural sciences have gained tremendous progress in the past several decades, ranging from the first open heart surgery to the cloned sheep named Dolly to the morning after pill and the so-called miracle drug Viagra (sildenafil). Yet there exist great health disparities: Americans and people living in the industrialized world are dying from noncommunicable and often preventable diseases, whereas in the developing world people are dying of communicable diseases and easily treatable infections (Centers for Disease Control and Prevention, 2000). Although the overall health status in America has improved greatly, there still exist great public health challenges. In 2006, over 16,000 people were killed in the United States in alcohol-related traffic accidents, representing 32 percent of traffic fatalities for that year (National Highway Traffic Safety Administration, 2008). Infectious diseases (including STDs) are at an all-time high, coupled with the emergence of drug-resistant bacteria and viruses (Morbidity and Mortality Weekly Report [MMWR], 1998a). Globally, 40 million people are living with HIV (UNAIDS, 2002). Collectively, these scenarios speak to the importance of community health and preventive medicine as integral components of a healthy lifestyle. With education and prevention campaigns, Elizabeth would have recognized her risky behavior and been able to access available resources.

To that end, this chapter examines five health issues from the perspectives of community psychology and preventive medicine; policy-based prevention targeting society in general or a single community will also be discussed. These health issues were chosen for two main reasons. First, they have each received enormous attention in the media. Second, each is highly preventable if certain activities are practiced. Additionally, a large number of people are affected or have the potential to be affected by these issues if prevention efforts do not occur.

Statistics used to describe each of the health issues are drawn from various agencies in the U.S. Department of Health and Human Services (DHHS) (e.g., the CDC) and other federal (e.g., National Highway Traffic Safety Administration), state (e.g., Massachusetts Department of Public Health), national (e.g., American Public Health Association), and local (e.g., Asian and Pacific Islander Coalition on HIV/AIDS) as well as international (e.g., the United Nations Programme on HIV/AIDS) entities. Each agency or source has its own approach and method in estimating the extent of a health issue (e.g., substance abuse). For example, the Substance Abuse and Mental Health Services Administration (SAMHSA), an agency within the DHHS whose mission is provision of substance-abuse treatment and services, conducts the National Household Survey on Drug Abuse targeting noninstitutionalized individuals age 12 and older nationwide. Another DHHS agency, the Centers for Diseases Control (CDC), whose mission is public health epidemiology and

TABLE 11.1   Some Resources for Health-Related Statistics and Information

AGENCY	SOURCE	WEB ADDRESS
American Psychological Association	APA Monitor (June 2001, special issue on substance abuse)	www.apa.org
American Public Health Association	The Nation's Health	www.apha.org
Asian and Pacific Islander Coalition on HIV/AIDS		www.apicha.org
Asian and Pacific Islander Wellness Center		www.apiwellness.org
Centers for Disease Control and Prevention (including National Center for Health Statistics, Office on Smoking and Health)	Morbidity and Mortality Weekly Report Behavior Risk Factor Surveillance (adults only) Youth Risk Behavior Surveillance System	www.cdc.gov
Food and Drug Administration		www.fda.gov
Legacy Foundation		www.americanlegacy.org
National Institutes of Health (including National Cancer Institute, National Institute on Drug Abuse)		www.nih.gov
Office of National Drug Control Policy		www.whitehousedrugpolicy.gov
Substance Abuse and Mental Health Services Administration	National Household Survey on Drug Abuse	www.samhsa.gov
United Nations Programme on HIV/AIDS	AIDS epidemic update Declaration of Commitment on HIV/AIDS	www.unaids.org

surveillance, conducts the **Youth Risk Behavior Surveillance System (YRBSS)**—a school-based survey—and also yields estimates of alcohol use. Given this variability and the lag time in reporting the latest findings, you are encouraged to check these various resources for their methodologies and updated information (see Table 11.1 for some examples).

TOBACCO

Extent of the Problem

According to the World Health Organization (2008), globally, tobacco use is the cause of more than 5 million deaths each year. In the United States alone, tobacco use (including smoking) is the number one preventable cause of death (Office on Smoking and Health,

FIGURE 11.1 Some Ingredients in Smokeless Tobacco

Acetaldehyde (irritant)
Benzopyrene (cancer-causing agent)
Cadmium (used in car batteries)
Formaldehyde (embalming fluid)
Lead (nerve poison)
Nicotine (addictive drug)
N-nitrosamines (cancer-causing agents)
Polonium-210 (radioactive element found in nuclear waste)
Uranium-235 (radioactive element used in nuclear weapons)

2001). Each year, tobacco use causes more deaths than HIV, illegal drug use, alcohol use, motor vehicle injuries, suicides, and murders combined (McGinnis & Foege, 1993; MMWR, 2005). Tobacco use and smoking are often used interchangeably; note, however, that tobacco use also includes smokeless tobacco (see Figure 11.1), which is linked to various oral cancers. Regular tobacco use increases the risk for developing a number of serious diseases, including chronic bronchitis, heart and blood problems, emphysema, and lung cancer, just to name a few.

The **National Household Survey on Drug Use & Health (NSDUH)** is the primary source of information on the prevalence, patterns, and consequences of drug and alcohol use and abuse in the general U.S. civilian noninstitutionalized population (including shelters, rooming houses, dormitories, and civilians living in military bases) aged 12 and older. With regard to tobacco, results from the 2006 NSDUH survey indicated that 72.9 million Americans aged 12 or older were current tobacco product users, representing 29.6 percent of the population in that age range. Additionally, young adults between the ages of 18 and 25 had the highest rate of current tobacco product use, comprising 43.9 percent of users. In terms of gender, the 2006 survey found that current use of a tobacco product was reported by a higher percentage of males (36.5 percent) among persons aged 12 or older than females (23.3 percent). In women aged 15 to 44, combined 2005 and 2006 data indicated that the rate of cigarette use in the past month was lower among pregnant woman (16.5 percent) than among women who were not pregnant (29.5 percent). However, when isolating the women aged 15 to 17, the rate of cigarette smoking for pregnant women (23.1 percent) was significantly higher than for nonpregnant women (17.1 percent). The NSDUH also analyzes tobacco product use across several other determinants, including education, employment, and geographic area (SAMHSA, 2007).

The YRBSS is a nationwide survey funded by the CDC that monitors priority health-risk behaviors among youth and young adults, including 40 state surveys and 21 local surveys among students in grades 9 through 12 (MMWR, 2006). Findings indicated that, in 2005, 23.0 percent of students had smoked cigarettes on at least one day in the preceding 30 days ("current cigarette use"). White and Hispanic students were more likely (25.9 percent and 22.0 percent, respectively) than Black students (19.2 percent) to report current smoking. Overall, cigarette use in general was higher among male (55.9 percent) than female students (53.7 percent). In terms of age, older students were more likely to smoke than younger students. In 2006, 58.3 percent of 12th-grade females reported current cigarette use, as compared to 48.7 percent of 9th-grade females. The same was true for males: 62.2 percent of 12th-grade males reported being current smokers, as compared to 49.8 percent of 9th-grade males.

Among women, cigarette smoking increases the grave risk for infertility, preterm delivery, stillbirth, sudden infant death syndrome (SIDS), and low birth weight (U.S. Department of Health and Human Services, 2001b). Birth weight is directly correlated with chances of child survival. Smoking also strongly contributes to ectopic pregnancy and spontaneous abortion (U.S. Department of Health and Human Services, 2004). Nevertheless, 13 to 17 percent of pregnant women continue to smoke throughout their pregnancies (U.S. Department of Health and Human Services, 2004).

Another way to appreciate the negative consequences of smoking is to calculate or estimate the money needed to provide medical and health-related services to people who are suffering or dying from smoking-related diseases or illnesses. These services include but are not limited to ambulatory care, prescription drugs, hospital care, home health services, and nursing home care. These services are used to calculate **state medical expenditures**—the financial cost to the state in providing medical and health-related services to people suffering from smoking-attributable diseases or illnesses (CDC, 1996).

In a comprehensive analysis, Miller, Zhang, Rice, and Max (1998) found that in 1993, "the estimated proportion of total medical expenditures attributable to smoking for the United States as a whole was 11.8%. . . . Total U.S. medical expenditures attributable to smoking amounted to an estimated $72.7 billion in 1993" (p. 447). In short, these dollar figures are staggering! Another study, which cited Miller et al., reported that although previous research has shown an increase in health care cost among people who quit smoking, smoking cessation did not result in sustained cost increases among former smokers (Fishman, Thompson, Merikle, & Curry, 2006). In other words, it certainly pays to quit smoking in the long run.

Even nonsmokers are not safe from tobacco-related health issues. **Secondhand smoke,** formally called **environmental tobacco smoke (ETS),** is classified as a Group A (known human) carcinogen by the U.S. Environmental Protection Agency. In fact, more than 50 individual carcinogens have been identified in secondhand smoke (U.S. Department of Health and Human Services, 2006). Exposure to secondhand smoke alone causes approximately 38,000 deaths each year (MMWR, 2005). Although there has been a decline in exposure of nonsmokers to secondhand smoke since 1986, secondhand smoke remains a major cause of premature death and disease among both children and adults (U.S. Department of Health and Human Services, 2006). Despite efforts to control tobacco in public areas, millions of American nonsmokers, children and adults alike, are still exposed to secondhand smoke, especially in their homes and workplaces (U.S. Department of Health and Human Services, 2006).

Antitobacco Efforts

Since the establishment of the connection between tobacco, smoking, lung cancer, and several other health issues, antitobacco efforts have taken place at many levels, spanning from elementary school awareness programs to state-enforced smoking bans in restaurants. Based on the connection between smoking and lung cancer, the **National Cancer Institute (NCI),** as part of the U.S. National Institutes of Health, funds a number of smoking awareness and prevention programs. One program was the America Stop Smoking Intervention Study (ASSIST). The study, which took place from 1991 to 1999, is one of the largest government-funded demonstration projects to help states develop effective smoking reduction strategies. ASSIST provided funding for 17 states and found a noticeable decrease in per capita cigarette consumption among the states that experienced improvement in tobacco control policies. The study also sheds light on the latest evidence available with regard to state tobacco control programs: investing in state tobacco control programs that focus on strict policies and regulation is an important and effective strategy for reducing tobacco use (National Cancer Institute, 2004).

The American Legacy Foundation, "dedicated to building a world where young people reject tobacco and anyone can quit," is a foundation that has developed a number of programs to combat tobacco and cigarette smoking (American Legacy Foundation, 2008a). The foundation has been involved in antitobacco efforts from the national Truth youth smoking prevention campaign to research initiatives aimed at tobacco reduction and outreach programs that target smoking cessation among priority populations (American Legacy Foundation, 2008b). Among one of the foundation's most recent campaigns is the Smoke Free Movies Campaign. With the motivation of eliminating the deep smoking impressions left by Hollywood on youth, the campaign aims to make any new movie with smoking in it rated R, end brand appearances on the screen, and include antismoking ads prior to movies that contain tobacco of any sort (American Legacy Foundation, 2008a).

At the global level, the World Health Organization (2008) has created a new landmark report that represents "the first in a series of WHO reports that will track the status of the tobacco epidemic and the impact of interventions implemented to stop it." The report outlines six policies as part of the WHO's MPOWER package that will serve to "counter the tobacco epidemic and reduce its deadly toll." The components of the MPOWER package consist of the following:

- Monitor tobacco use and prevention policies,
- Protect people from tobacco smoke,
- Offer help to quit tobacco use,
- Warn about the dangers of tobacco,
- Enforce bans on tobacco advertising, promotion, and sponsorship,
- Raise taxes on tobacco.

In her introduction to the report, Dr. Margaret Chan, director-general of the World Health Organization, emphasized that "the global consensus that we must fight the tobacco epidemic has already been established by the more than 150 Parties to the WHO Framework Convention on Tobacco Control." Now, governments and organizations around the world must implement the policies necessary to curb the dire health effects of tobacco.

Despite a variety of antitobacco efforts, every year the tobacco industry spends millions of dollars in advertising and promoting tobacco (e.g., free coupons, leather jackets with logos of the product, etc.). According to the *Federal Trade Commission Cigarette Report for 2003* (issued in 2005), 2003 tobacco industry spending on advertising and promotions was as high as $41.5 million a day. In addition, the industry is quick to use image-based propaganda, which has been demonstrated to be effective with youth as well as the less educated. For instance, DiFranza and colleagues (1991) found that Joe Camel (a cartoon character smoking a Camel cigarette) was more readily recognized by children than Mickey Mouse. In other words, those who engage in antitobacco efforts (including the NCI and the WHO) are facing a Herculean task as the tobacco industry is far from admitting defeat and submitting to antitobacco and antismoking public health efforts.

Community-Based Approaches

The fact that 48.5 percent of youth in a nationwide school-based survey (2005 Youth Risk Behavior Surveillance) were able to purchase cigarettes without proof of age (MMWR, 2006) suggests that health-related legal policy (e.g., "no sale to minors") is just the first step in the fight for a smoke-free environment (Jason, Berk, Schnopp-Wyatt, & Talbot, 1999). Biglan and associates (1996) argued that

> many law enforcement officers feel that there are more important crimes to deal with and that judges will be annoyed if such cases are brought before them. In addition, if the value of reducing such sales has not been adequately publicized, there is a risk that enforcement will produce a backlash against tobacco control efforts. (p. 626)

Implicit in these words are that members in a community must have a sense of ownership, including how they view and implement health-related legal policy. To test this premise, Biglan and colleagues designed a five-component intervention program to reduce youth access to tobacco products in two small Oregon communities. The outcome of interest was the proportion of tobacco outlets in the community that were willing to sell tobacco products to youth.

Using a quasi-experimental design, Biglan and colleagues (1996) conducted their intervention in the two selected Oregon communities; two other similar communities did not receive the intervention. Specifically, activities of *mobilization of community support* included a letter and signature campaign sought from members of various community sectors (e.g., school district, health care providers, and civic organizations) to produce a proclamation of no sale of tobacco to youth. *Merchant education* involved visits and distribution of the proclamation to all tobacco outlets. A modified sting operation was employed to *change consequences to clerks* for selling or not selling tobacco to those under age 18. That is, those who complied with the law were rewarded each time with a gift certificate worth $2 for use in a local business. Those who violated the law were given a reminder of the law and the community proclamation of no sale of tobacco to youth. These activities were described in public media (e.g., newspapers) as part of the *publicity intervention strategy*. Finally, *owners of tobacco outlets were personally informed* about these activities (identity of clerks were masked). In brief, the five components represented a range of macro level (e.g., mobilization of community) to micro level (e.g., feedback to store owners) comprehensive community intervention strategies. Results indicated that tobacco outlets' willingness to sell tobacco products to youth was significantly lower in the intervention group than those in the control group.

The research by Biglan and colleagues (1996) speaks to the importance of community-based involvement in augmenting health-related legal policy. On the flip side, the general populace may not realize that their community as a whole may have an impact on issues such as tobacco access among youth. To explore the adult attitudes and beliefs surrounding the issue of restricting youth access to tobacco, Siegel and Alvaro (2003) conducted a study in two Arizona counties. According to their findings, an overwhelming majority of adults believed that it was easy for minors to get access to tobacco and that the parents of the youth purchasing tobacco were most responsible for the problem. Furthermore, most adults responded that "there is nothing that they or the community can do to stop minors who wish to purchase tobacco." In turn, although there are proven cases in which the community at large can play a significant and important role in improving the status of a health-related issue, there is also a sense that individual community members do not understand their role as part of the fabric of the community.

ALCOHOL

Extent of the Problem

In addition to cigarettes, **alcohol** is a gateway drug to other drug use and abuse. According to the 2005 YRBSS data (MMWR, 2006), 74.3 percent of all students had had at least one drink of alcohol during their lifetimes. Furthermore, approximately one-quarter (25.6 percent) of students had drunk more than a few sips of alcohol for the first time prior to the age of 13 years. Gender, age, and racial/ethnic differences served to further define the profile of students who drank before age of 13 years. For example, a higher percentage of males (29.2 percent) drank before the age of 13 than did females (22.0 percent).

Nationwide, 43.3 percent of students were current alcohol users (or had least one drink of alcohol in the past 30 days). Current alcohol use also varied across gender, age, and racial/ethnic differences. For example, current alcohol use was more prevalent among White and Hispanic females (45.9 percent and 44.8 percent, respectively) than Black females (32.5 percent). Furthermore, 25.5 percent of all students had participated in episodic heavy drinking (at least five drinks of alcohol in a row within a couple of hours on more than one of the 30 days preceding the survey). Prevalence of episodic heavy drinking was higher among male (27.5 percent) than female (23.5 percent) students. Additionally, White students (29.9 percent) were more likely to have taken part in episodic heavy drinking than Black (11.1 percent) and Hispanic (25.3 percent) students.

Alcohol use before or during sex is a major risk for unprotected sex (Leigh & Stall, 1993), which might result in unwanted pregnancy and acquisition of STDs (including HIV). According to the 2005 YRBSS data, nearly one-fourth (23.3 percent) of all students had used alcohol or drugs before their most recent sexual intercourse. (Overall, 33.9 percent of students were sexually active at the time of the survey.) Prevalence of drinking alcohol or using drugs before the last sexual intercourse was much higher among male (27.6 percent) than female (19.0 percent) students. In terms of racial/ethnic differences, White and Hispanic students (25.0 percent and 25.6 percent, respectively) were more likely to engage in this behavior than Black students (14.1 percent). Note, however, that a higher percentage of Black students (47.4 percent) reported being currently sexually active (had sexual intercourse with at least one person during the three months preceding the survey) than White and Hispanic students (32.0 percent and 35.0 percent, respectively).

Finally, **binge drinking** is a major issue associated with alcohol use and abuse that spans from college campuses to entire societies across the globe. The National Institute of Alcohol Abuse and Alcoholism (2004) defines binge drinking as "a pattern of drinking that brings a person's blood alcohol concentration (BAC) to 0.08 percent or above," a level that is usually reached by men after consuming five or more drinks and by women after consuming four or more drinks in a time span of approximately two hours. According to the CDC, binge drinking is associated with a slew of health problems, from unintentional injuries and neurological damage to sexual dysfunction and liver disease (U.S. Department of Health and Human Services, CDC, 2008). In the United States, binge drinking makes up a large part of alcohol consumption. In fact, approximately 90 percent of alcohol consumed by youth under 21 years of age is in the form of binge drinks (Pacific Institute for Research and Evaluation, 2005). Additionally, about 92 percent of adults who drink excessively report binge drinking within the past 30 days (Town et al., 2008).

For Russians, who have been found by several sources to drink less frequently but consume large amounts of alcohol per occasion, binge drinking is a specific feature of alcohol consumption (Bobak et al., 2004; Jukkala, Makinen, Kislitsyna, Ferlander, & Vagero, 2008; Leinsalu, 2004; Simpura, Levin, & Mustonen, 1997). In their 2008 study, Jukkala et al. explained binge drinking as an important factor in Russia's mortality crisis and found binge drinking patterns to be related to an individual's "economic situations and social relations." Furthermore, gender was found to be an important factor in whether an individual would participate in binge drinking. Some of the key findings were as follows.

- Men with economic problems drink heavily, whereas women with economic problems drink less.
- Married men binge drink as much as their nonmarried friends, while married women binge drink much less than their nonmarried friends.
- Women's drinking is concentrated in the context of friends, whereas men's occurs elsewhere.
- Drinking patterns indicate that women and young people of both genders seem to be drinking more than they were previously.

Although the study sheds light on issues that provide justified worries with regard to the future of Russia's alcohol-related problems, it also links important connections between individual health and the community with regard to binge drinking. Because binge drinking is a possible contributor to the "extremely large gender gap in Russian mortality statistics," these connections can potentially serve as important points of emphasis in a community health approach to solving important public health issues (Jukkala et al., 2008). When addressing preventive health issues across the globe, it is necessary to assess the community in terms of its own unique cultural phenomena.

Alcohol Safety Laws

In the United States, motor vehicle crashes are the leading cause of death for Americans between the ages of 2 and 34 years, and 41 percent of these fatal crashes involve alcohol

(National Highway Traffic Safety Administration, 2008). Approximately one-third of driving while intoxicated (DWI) or driving under the influence (DUI) arrests each year involve individuals who were previously convicted of DWI or DUI (National Highway Traffic Safety Administration, 2008). Furthermore, impaired driving is the most frequently committed crime in the United States (National Highway Traffic Safety Administration, 2008).

Despite these grim statistics, alcohol-related deaths have been more controlled today than they were before the 1990s, due in part to a series of laws that have sought to limit and discourage alcohol-related driving incidents. In one study Voas, Tippetts, and Fell (2000) evaluated the effect of three major alcohol safety laws, including administrative license revocation laws, 0.10 illegal per se laws, and 0.08 illegal per se laws. The results of the study indicated that each of the three types of laws had a significant relationship to the downward trend in alcohol-related fatal crashes in the United States between 1982 and 1997. The study also pointed out that the significant decline in alcohol-related fatal crashes could not be attributed to one single law, but to the combined effect of several laws over time. Other factors, such as the media's attention to drinking-and-driving issues and increased use of sobriety checkpoints, were also identified as possibilities not tested in the model but that may also have contributed to the decline. The many contributors to increased alcohol safety on the road show the importance of implementing a comprehensive community approach when addressing preventive health issues like limiting the number of deaths or injuries as a result of traffic accidents.

A Community Psychology Approach

As argued earlier, health-related legal policy is most appreciated or effective when people feel they are empowered to make informed choices and decisions, including why they should heed health advice by experts or government officials. A key component in this equation is that empowerment (and its effect on decision making) often begins at home (e.g., parents talk to their children about the good and bad of drinking, premarital sex, etc.) and at school (e.g., peers for prosocial behaviors). In other words, values and skills learned or derived from the two Oregon communities are thought to be instrumental in health-related decision-making processes. Thus, next is a brief review of a study using parent–child involvement as a strategy to address alcohol use among youth.

Spoth, Redmond, Hockaday, and Yoo (1996) identified (1) affectional relationship with parents, (2) affiliation with prosocial peers, and (3) mastery esteem (being in control of the forces affecting one's destiny) as three key protective factors to reduce the risk of substance use among youth in an intervention study (Preparing Drug Free Years [PDFY]) using a wait-list design. The basic format of PDFY consisted of a total of five two-hour sessions involving at least one parent and the child. Each session was a mixture of family-focused competency training and skills building. It was hypothesized that positive parental involvement would increase the youth's tendency to select peers who have similar values as those of the youth's parents. This prosocial peer relationship would in turn lead to mastery esteem. Overall, results supported the claim of the protective effects of the three factors on self-reported behavioral tendency toward alcohol abstinence. That is, such effects were significantly more pronounced in the intervention group than in the control group.

In a more recent review, Velleman, Templeton, and Copello (2005) found a plethora of "highly sound research" that "suggests strongly that the family can have a central role in preventing substance use and later misuse amongst young people." In another review, Vimpani (2005) states, however, that "much remains to be done to enable the promise of effective universal and targeted early intervention to be translated into policies, programs and practices." Thus, although many relationships between early alcohol intervention, the family, and the community have been established, existing programs that serve to take advantage of these important connections are still lacking.

ILLICIT DRUGS

Extent of the Problem

Use of illicit drugs is a problem across the globe. According to the World Health Organization (2008), there are at least 15.3 million people in the world who have drug use disorders. Drug use not only causes adverse personal and community health consequences, it is also the source of a huge economic and financial burden in terms of treatment for drug users in the short and long term. As a result, investing in drug treatment early on can limit future health and social costs. In fact, for every $1 invested in drug treatment, approximately $7 are saved in health and social costs (World Health Organization, 2008).

In the United States, among other countries, youth drug use is a serious issue. According to the YRBSS survey (MMWR, 2006), "ever used" of (1) **marijuana,** (2) **cocaine** (including powder, crack, and freebase), (3) illegal **injection drugs,** (4) illegal **steroids,** (5) **inhalants,** (6) **hallucinogenic drugs** (including LSD [lysergic acid diethylamide], acid, PCP [phencyclidine], angel dust, mescaline, and mushrooms), (7) **heroin,** (8) **methamphetamine** (also known as "speed," "crystal," "crank," and "ice"), and (9) **ecstasy** (methylenedioxymethamphetamine, MDMA), were reported by 38.4 percent, 7.6 percent, 2.1 percent, 4.0 percent, 12.4 percent, 8.5 percent, 2.4 percent, 6.2 percent, and 6.3 percent, respectively, of all students. Slightly less than 1 in 10 of all students (8.7 percent) had tried marijuana before 13 years of age. There were gender, grade, and racial/ethnic differences in this behavior. For example, male students (11.0 percent) were significantly more likely than female students (6.3 percent) to have tried marijuana before age 13.

For marijuana, state prevalence rates (current behaviors) ranged from 7.6 to 26.2 percent (median 18.9 percent); local prevalence rates ranged from 12.3 to 24.0 percent (median 18.6 percent). For cocaine, state prevalence rates ranged from 2.0 to 7.9 percent (median 3.3 percent); local prevalence rates ranged from 0.9 to 4.9 percent (median 3.0 percent). For illegal injection drugs, state lifetime (i.e., ever used) rates ranged from 0.9 to 4.3 percent (median 2.3 percent); local lifetime rates ranged from 1.0 to 5.9 percent (median 2.0 percent). For illegal steroids, state lifetime rates ranged from 2.0 to 6.5 percent (median 3.9 percent); local lifetime rates ranged from 1.6 to 7.7 percent (median 3.0 percent). For inhalants, state lifetime rates ranged from 8.6 to 17.1 percent (median 12.2 percent); local lifetime rates ranged from 5.5 to 17.9 percent (median 9.7 percent). For heroin, state lifetime rates ranged from 1.3 to 5.3 percent (median 2.7 percent); local lifetime rates ranged from 0.8 to 7.4 percent (median 2.2 percent). For methamphetamine, state lifetime rates ranged from 2.6 to 11.7 percent (median 5.9 percent); local lifetime rates ranged from 1.0 to 11.0 percent (median 3.7 percent). Finally, for ecstasy, state prevalence of lifetime use ranged from 3.3 to

9.2 percent (median 6.1 percent); local lifetime prevalence rates ranged from 3.3 to 9.1 percent (median 5.6 percent). (Note: State and local prevalence ranges for hallucinogenic drugs were not available in the MMWR 2006 report.)

Marijuana was the most popular choice of drug—20.2 percent of all students had used marijuana one or more times during the 30 days preceding the survey. However, there is a great deal of variability in illegal drug use depending on such factors as gender, grade, and race/ethnicity. For example, male students were more likely than female students to have ever used marijuana (40.5 versus 35.9 percent) and illegal steroids (4.8 versus 3.2 percent), whereas females were more likely than males to have ever used inhalants (13.5 versus 11.3 percent). Additionally, White and Hispanic students (7.7 and 12.2 percent, respectively) were more likely to report having ever used cocaine than Black students (2.3 percent).

Because most illicit drugs are not regulated for content, it is impossible for users to monitor exactly what they are consuming from a given drug. Marijuana, for example, may be more dangerous for users today than it was 30 years ago. At the time of this writing, levels of THC, the psychoactive ingredient in marijuana, are at the highest recorded amount since scientific analysis of marijuana began at the end of the 1970s (Office National Drug Control Policy, 2008). The outcome of the analysis of THC levels from the University of Mississippi's Potency Monitoring Project, released by the Office of National Drug Control Policy (ONDCP) and the National Institute on Drug Abuse (NIDA), is cause for authorities to be concerned. In the ONDCP press release on increased marijuana potency, John Walters, director of National Drug Control Policy and President Bush's "drug czar," expressed his concern with the finding:

> Baby boomer parents who still think marijuana is a harmless substance need to look at the facts. Marijuana potency has grown steeply over the past decade, with serious implications in particular for young people, who may be not only at increased risk for various psychological conditions, cognitive deficits, and respiratory problems, but are also at significantly higher risk for developing dependency on other drugs, such as cocaine and heroin than are non-smokers.

Finally, there are many dire consequences due to illicit drug use, including but not limited to crime, domestic violence, illnesses, loss in productivity, and increases in STDs, including HIV/AIDS. For instance, of the 136 countries that reported injecting drug use, 93 reported HIV infection among the same population (World Health Organization, 2008). This is just one statistic among many that demonstrates the fact that the effects of illicit drugs are far-reaching, penetrating societies far beyond the users themselves.

Possible Solutions and Challenges

The **National Drug Control Strategy 2008 Annual Report** of the ONDCP outlines several characteristics of the drug problem in the United States and the programs and interventions proposed or in place to combat the issues at hand. The report recognizes the progress that the United States has made, stating that approximately 860,000 fewer young people are using drugs as of 2008 than in 2001 and that programs have expanded to many sectors of society, from public health settings to the criminal justice system. Additionally, the report speaks to the necessity of "pursuing a balanced strategy that addresses the epidemiology of drug use and the economic of drug availability" to "reduce drug use in America." The report is broken down into three chapters, which permeate from the George W. Bush administration's national drug control strategy, which sought to combat the rebound of drug use in the United States since its decline throughout the 1980s and early 1990s. The three chapters include:

1. Stopping Drug Use Before It Starts
2. Intervening and Healing America's Drug Users
3. Disrupting the Market for Illegal Drugs

The first chapter discusses programs aimed at several aspects of drug use, from changing existing attitudes in society through youth medical campaigns to encouraging a drug-free workplace. The second chapter illustrates the many aspects involved in combating addiction, including the importance of screening tools for detecting drug use early on and interventions with regard to prescription drug abuse (see Case in Point 11.1). Finally, the third chapter addresses the many sources of illicit drugs in the United States (including illegal domestic production and cross-border drug trade) and provides discussions on how to improve both intelligence and international relations to work at both national and international levels to reduce drug use across the globe. Since the rebound in drug use in the United States, the National Drug Control Strategy 2008 Annual Report acknowledges a present decline in youth drug use and points toward an improved understanding of the trends that surround use to combat the issues at hand. For example, given the knowledge that adolescence is a critical period in determining the risk of an individual to be drug-dependent later in life, additional resources can be focused to target important at-risk groups among youth. As researchers and authorities further their understanding of the many factors that contribute to the illicit drug use problem, policies and programs can be put in place to improve the drug use status of the population at home and abroad.

CASE IN POINT 11.1
PRESCRIPTION DRUG MISUSE: RISK FACTORS FOR PROBLEM USERS

Prompted by data that documented that 10 million individuals, or 7 percent of the U.S. population, reported nonmedical use of prescription drugs (Substance Abuse and Mental Health Services Administration, 2000), Simoni-Wastila and Strickler (2004) set out to identify the risk factors associated with problem use of prescription drugs. Nonmedical prescription drug use encompasses a vast range of behaviors, from simple noncompliance to recreational use and serious abuse (Wesson, Smith, Ling, & Seymour, 1997).

Simoni-Wastila and Strickler first estimated the prevalence of problem use of prescription drugs using the National Household Survey on Drug Abuse. "Problem users" were identified based on meeting one of the following criteria for dependency/heavy use, including:

1. Inability to cut down,
2. Getting less work done,
3. Using substance in past month and being depressed, argumentative, anxious, or upset, feeling isolated, and/or having health problems and/or difficulty thinking clearly,
4. Needing larger amounts,
5. Experiencing withdrawal symptoms.

In the study, identified problem users were analyzed based on race, age, gender, marital status, urbanicity, education, work status, health insurance, income, and general health status. The results showed that more than 8.2 million individuals, or 4 percent of the U.S. population, report some sort of past year nonmedical use of prescription drugs annually. Furthermore, of these 8.2 million, 1.3 million individuals were categorized as "problem users of prescription drugs." Discovered risk factors for problem use included being female, being in poor or fair health, and drinking alcohol daily. Conversely, being young (under the age of 25 years) and employed full-time were found to protect against problem use. Additionally, other factors, such as marital status, education, employment status, and income, were found to be uniquely associated with individual therapeutic classes of drugs. For example, being an unmarried female above the age of 35 was found to increase an individual's likeliness of being a problem user of narcotic analgesics.

Simoni-Wastila and Strickler point out that their study, the first to estimate the prevalence of problem use of prescription drugs, illustrates a possible need for further risk factor identification and treatment for problem users of prescription drugs in the future. This case study shows that prescription drugs, although regulated and legal, can easily fall into the same category as illicit drugs in terms of their far-reaching effects and consequences for a population and may require the same community health measures necessary to address illicit drug problems in the United States and abroad.

SEXUALLY TRANSMITTED DISEASES

Susan Chandle debated whether to vaccinate her 12-year-old daughter, Alexandra, with the human papillomavirus (HPV) vaccine. It seemed odd to vaccinate against a sexually transmitted virus before her daughter became sexually active. She had barely spoken to Alexandra about sex and was uncomfortable even mentioning the premise of the vaccine. But Susan considered herself a vigilant mother and wanted to protect her daughter from the possibility of developing cervical cancer. She spoke to the doctor and weighed the pros and cons of the vaccine. The vaccine, known as Gardasil, was recently approved by the Food and Drug Administration (FDA) to provide complete immunity from the four most predominate strains of HPV. However, there are hundreds of strains of HPV, thus it is possible to have the vaccine and not be protected from all types of HPV or all forms of cervical cancer. Also, Susan was concerned this vaccine would embolden her daughter to believe she was protected against all STDs and thus engage in more sexual activity. Additionally, the vaccine was costly; it required three doses at $120 per dose over a seven-month period and was not yet covered under the family's insurance plan. The vaccine was still relatively new, and the side effects and long-term health risk was unknown.

When she finally decided to vaccinate her daughter, she told her daughter that she was getting a vaccine to protect against cancer. Susan made no mention that HPV was sexually transmitted and decided to wait until Alexandra was taught about sex at school.

Extent of the Problem

Sexually transmitted diseases (STDs) have long been considered a hidden epidemic of tremendous health and economic consequences. Many Americans are reluctant to address sexual health topics openly due to both the biological and social characteristics of these diseases. Although progress has been made in the treatment, diagnosis, and prevention of

TABLE 11.2 Overview of Symptoms, Prevalence, and Modes of Transmission of STDs

NAME	SYMPTOMS	TRANSMISSION	TREATMENT	PREVALENCE
Chlamydia, *Chlamydia trachomatis*	Known as the "silent" disease, as many infected people show no symptoms In women, symptoms may be abnormal vaginal discharge or burning sensation while urinating In men, discharge from penis or burning sensation when urinating If untreated, women can develop pelvic inflammatory disease	Transmitted during vaginal, anal, or oral sex Infected mother to her baby during vaginal childbirth	Can be easily treated and cured with antibiotics	Over 1 million infections in 2006
Genital herpes Herpes simplex virus, either type 1 (HSV-1) or type 2 (HSV-2)	Outbreak occurs within two weeks after initial infection Primary episode includes blisters around the genitals or rectum that gradually give way to sores (ulcers) Other outbreaks can appear weeks or months later, usually four to five outbreaks within a year, decreasing frequency over the years Most people with HSV-2 infection never have sores or have unrecognizable signs	Virus released from the sores, but can also be released from skin that does not appear to have sores HSV-1 causes "fever blisters" of the mouth and lips and can cause an infection of the genitals by oral–genital or genital–genital contact	No treatment to cure herpes but antiviral medications shorten or prevent outbreaks Daily suppressive therapy for symptomatic herpes to prevent transmission	45 million people ages 12 and older have genital herpes One out of five adolescents and adults have genital HSV More common in women
Syphilis Caused by bacterium *Treponema pallidum*	Many people do not have any symptoms for years but are at risk for later complications Primary stage is the appearance of a single sore; if not treated, infection progresses to secondary stage Secondary stage is characterized by skin rashes and mucous membrane lesion Late and latent stages cause damage to the internal organs and difficulty coordinating muscle movements	Passed through direct contact with syphilis sore, sores occur commonly on external genitals and lips and mouth Transmission during vaginal, anal, oral sex	Easy to cure in the early stages Treated with injection of penicillin	Most syphilis cases occur in people aged 20–39 years Between 2005–2005, syphilis cases increased by 11.8% 64% of cases were among men who have sex with men in 2006

Gonorrhea Caused by bacterium *Neisseria gonorrhoea*	In men, symptoms include burning sensation while urinating or white, yellow, or green discharge from penis Gonorrhea can cause epidymistis and lead to infertility if not treated Women often experience mild or no symptoms and often symptoms mistaken for bladder or vaginal infections If untreated, can cause pelvic inflammatory disease	Spread through contact with penis, vagina, mouth, or anus Can be transmitted from mother to baby during delivery	Several antibiotics are used to treat gonorrhea but the increasing number of drug-resistant strains is a cause of concern	In 2006, the rate of reported infections was 120.9 per 100,00 people CDC estimates over 700,00 new cases each year

Source: CDC (2006). Reproduced by kind permission of UNAIDS, www.unaids.org.

STDs, 19 million new infections occur each year (CDC, 2006). Moreover, the United States has one of the highest rates of STDs in the industrialized world. Additionally, adolescents (10–19-year-olds) and young adults (20–24-year-olds) are at the highest risk of contracting an STD. Table 11.2 is an overview of symptoms, prevalence, and modes of transmission of prevalent STDs.

The nature and impact of STDs are multifaceted. They pose a substantial economic burden; the direct medical costs associated with STDs are estimated up to US$14.7 billion annually. In 2000, there were 9 million new cases of STDs among 15–24-year-olds, and the direct economic burden of STDs was estimated to be $6.5 billion. Costs differ depending on specific the disease, with HPV having the highest direct medical cost ($2.9 billion) and syphilis the least ($3.6 million) (Chesson et al., 2004). Although many people experience few or no symptoms (and thus are never treated), diseases can still cause a great impact on personal health. For example, chlamydia, whether or not it is detected, may be the cause of a woman's infertility. Moreover, rates of STDs tend to be higher among drug users (both intravenous and nonintravenous [including alcohol] drug users). Epidemiological studies consistently demonstrate that concurrent STDs increase the transmission probability for HIV infection. The mutually reinforcing nature of these infectious processes has been called **epidemiological synergy** (MMWR, 1998a).

Possible Solutions and Challenges

The Advisory Committee for HIV and STD Prevention made the following recommendations.

1. Assess and ensure timely access to high-quality STD clinical care for persons seeking medical services for symptoms of STDs in private and public medical-care setting.
2. Screen for asymptomatic or recognized STD infection in medical-care settings according to current guidelines, and expand screening as needed based on prevalence of infections detected in pilot screening efforts.
3. Establish or expand STD screening in nonmedical settings where persons at high risk for HIV infection and curable STDs are encouraged and can be treated efficiently,

including jails and other correctional facilities, substance abuse treatment centers, and hospital emergency departments.
4. Provide cross-training to program and management staff including HIV prevention community planning groups, on the role of STD detection and treatment in HIV prevention. (MMWR, 1998a, p. 11)

These recommendations are derived from an extensive review of the scientific and empirical literature on STD prevention and intervention. Another point of interest is the use of Internet-based prevention programs. As the Internet has become the predominate medium of communication, public health officials are harnessing it to stage public health interventions. The National Coalition of STD Directors (NCSD) developed guidelines for nongovernmental organizations and health departments to use the Internet to focus on three distinct online activities: partner services, outreach, and health communication. Internet-based partner services (IPS) is a useful process to notify a person via the Internet of their potential exposure to an infectious disease. Key to the IPS program is the concept of partner services, rather than just partner notification; this notification not only informs partners of possible exposure but offers available services. Internet-based outreach guidelines give tips on creating online identity, how to observe online community and culture, and specific elements to be included programs. The last facet in the guidelines is the online integration of health communication. This includes ensuring that all STD/HIV-related health communications have a Web site; this is especially important for passive health seekers to gain information without talking to medical personnel (NCSD, 2008). The use of the Internet in public health interventions acknowledges the necessity of programs to be both relevant and dynamic to shifting times.

In addition to access to care and early detection and screenings, implicit in the recommendations is that sex education as part of a healthy lifestyle must be integral to the community-focused or community-based prevention and intervention programs, which are echoed in the recent report the Surgeon General's Call to Action to Promote Sexual Health and Responsible Sexual Behavior, by the U.S. Surgeon General, Dr. David Satcher (2001). The challenge for U.S. community-based researchers is how to integrate sex education into such programs without coming across as promoting certain sexual practices or lifestyles (e.g., bisexual, homosexual) that a major segment of the society finds unacceptable. A review of studies published in the *American Journal of Community Psychology* and the *Journal of Community Psychology* from 1990 to 2001 presumes that community psychologists have done little or no work on STD (excluding HIV and AIDS) prevention and intervention. A second review of studies in these journals from 2001 to 2008 found five articles over the eight years. What are the reasons for the paucity or lack of research? Is it because sex is a taboo or an uncomfortable topic for discussion?

Additionally, sexual behaviors have changed, especially among adolescents. The Kaiser Family Foundation reports a decline in percentage of high school students engaging in sexual intercourse and an increase of contraceptive use among sexually active teens in the last decade. These both have contributed to a decreased pregnancy rate; however "about a third (34%) of young women become pregnant at least once before they reach the age of 20" (Kaiser Family Foundation, 2005a). These developments show that community-based public health programs have been effective in targeting youth. However, there still exist many barriers for adolescents to receive comprehensive reproductive care and services. These factors include state laws regarding parental consent, cost of care, few youth-friendly service delivery systems, and general ignorance of services available.

In the story that began this section, Susan decided to vaccinate her daughter despite her reluctances. By doing so, she is aiding in the fight to eliminate HPV. Currently HPV is the most common STD, and at least 50 percent of sexually active men and women will contract genital HPV at some point in their life (CDC, 2004). This scenario represents the discrepancies between culture, medical technology, and basic epidemiology. HPV poses a serious health risk that cannot be overlooked. The new technology offers a way of combating HPV, but it is by no means a cure. Multiple approaches in treatment and prevention are needed to address STDs. Additionally, there needs to be a concerted effort by public health officials, schools, and parents in the realm of adolescent sexual health. Susan assumed that Alexandra's school would talk to her daughter, but conversations about sex must occur early and often.

HIV AND AIDS

AIDS vaccine: possible solution? An AIDS vaccine is considered the safest, most inexpensive, effective, globally accessible, and practical means of controlling and ending the HIV/AIDS pandemic. HIV presents unique challenges for vaccine development because it does not have many of the viral features that vaccinologists have used to develop successful vaccines (Berkeley & Koff, 2007). In September 2007, the most promising vaccine failed in a large international human trial, and further development was halted. The HIV Vaccine Trail Network, a Merck, National Institute of Allergy and Infectious Disease (NIAID), and academic consortium, used a new approach to develop immune response by generating T cell response to limit viral load and disease progression (Sekaly, 2008). The STEP Trial, as it was known, consisted of immunizing close to 3,000 healthy HIV-negative participants. The vaccine was designed to produce visible cellular immunity, but it demonstrated no protection against infection. More alarmingly, the vaccine may have increased the risk of HIV transmission in some study participants (Altman, 2008).

In addition to scientific difficulties of vaccine development, progress is dependent on commercial and political support. Small, innovative biotechnological companies do not have sufficient financial incentives to investigate AIDS vaccines, largely due to high scientific uncertainty and risky financial returns (Berkeley & Koff, 2007). Despite these setbacks, the AIDS vaccine research needs to be integrated in AIDS prevention public health priorities. Progress can be made with interdisciplinary research and novel innovative approaches (Cohen, 2007).

The failure of the vaccine thus far demonstrates that the HIV/AIDS epidemic involves a complex infectious disease that a vaccine won't instantly cure. Not only does HIV pose an immunological challenge, it requires international cooperation by the medical community, governments, and other community leaders. Currently the HIV/AIDS epidemic is one of the greatest challenges in public health.

Overview

By the end of 2007, over 33 million people were living with HIV worldwide. AIDS remains one of the top 10 causes of death globally and the primary cause of death in Sub-Saharan

FIGURE 11.2 Characteristics of People with HIV or AIDS

Brain lesions (advanced stage of AIDS)
Frequent diarrhea
Loss of appetite
Low-grade fever that will not go away
Low T cell count (below 400; T cells are involved in fighting infection)
Oral thrush (e.g., fungus inside the mouth)
Pneumonia
Skin lesions (e.g., Kaposi's sarcoma)
Swollen glands
Weight loss

Africa. Although 2007 marked a significant revision of global estimates of the AIDS epidemic due in part to better surveillance programs, AIDS remains a global crisis. Every day more than 6,800 people become infected with HIV, and slightly fewer than 6,000 people die from AIDS (UNAIDS, 2007). It is important to note that HIV is not the cause of AIDS. Rather, being HIV-positive weakens one's immune system, thus opening the door for opportunistic infections that lead to AIDS (see Figure 11.2). Although there is a small group of dissenting scientists who do not believe HIV is responsible for AIDS, the mainstream scientific community generally ignores them.

In the late 1970s and early 1980s, the medical community in the United States began to notice a strange disease, mostly infecting homosexual men and IV drug users. Very soon after, terms such as HIV, AIDS, and ARC (AIDS-related complex) became household words. Although HIV and AIDS were first recognized in homosexual men in this country, the disease has now been shown to infect all men, including heterosexual men, and women (see Table 11.3). Scientists and laypeople alike speculate about the origin of HIV and AIDS; theories range from the "green monkey theory" (a species of African monkey that is thought to be the genesis of the incurable disease) to biological warfare conducted by the U.S. Central Intelligence Agency. Still others (Eigen, 1993) have argued that HIV has been present in human beings for more than 120 years, just waiting for the right circumstances to attack the human immune system. Figure 11.3 on page 262 presents some statements about AIDs to test your knowledge about this disease.

Encouraging developments have been made to combat the AIDS epidemic, including improving prevention programs and increasing access to effective treatment. However, the number of people living with HIV continues to rise yearly. In many of the global regions, new HIV infections are concentrated among young people (15–24 years old). Sub-Saharan Africa bears most of the burden of disease—roughly two-thirds of all adults and children with HIV live in Sub-Saharan Africa (UNAIDS, 2006).

Extent of the Problem

In the United States, AIDS cases have been reported in all 50 states, however, 10 states/areas make up 71 percent of all reported cases. AIDS cases in the United States are concentrated in

TABLE 11.3 Regional HIV Statistics and Features, End of 2007

REGION	EPIDEMIC STARTED	ADULTS & CHILDREN LIVING WITH HIV/AIDS	ADULT PREVALENCE (AGE 15-49)	ADULT AND CHILD DEATHS DUE TO AIDS
Sub-Saharan Africa	Late 1970s–early 1980s	22.5 million	5.0%	1.6 million
North Africa and Middle East	Late 1980s	380,000	0.3%	25,000
South and Southeast Asia	Late 1980s	4.0 million	0.3%	270,000
East Asia and Pacific	Late 1980s	800,000	0.1%	32,000
Latin America	Late 1970s–early 1980s	1.6 million	0.5%	58,000
Caribbean	Late 1970s–early 1980s	230,000	0.1%	11,000
Eastern Europe and Central Asia	Early 1990s	1.6 million	0.9%	55,000
Western and Central Europe	Late 1970s–early 1980s	760,000	0.3%	12,000
North America	Late 1970s–early 1980s	1.3 million	0.6%	21,000
Oceania	Late 1970s–early 1980s	75,000	0.4%	12,000
Total		**33.2 million**	**0.8%**	2.1 million

Source: UNAIDS (2007).

urban and Southern areas, with the District of Columbia having the highest case rate in the nation. Additionally, AIDS has exceedingly affected racial and ethnic minorities, predominately Blacks and Latinos. More alarming is the demographical comparison of AIDS diagnoses and the U.S. population. For instance, whereas Blacks make up 12 percent of the population, they account for 49 percent of the AIDS cases. In 2004, HIV was the fourth leading cause of death for Black men and the third for Black women aged 25–44 (Kaiser Family Fund, 2008b). The impact of HIV and AIDS among the various racial/ethnic minority communities can be gleaned and understood from at least three interrelated perspectives: (1) **knowledge, attitudes, beliefs, and behaviors (KABBs)**, (2) **HIV testing,** and (3) **linkage to care.**

Although research on HIV/AIDS prevention and intervention indicates that KABBs alone are not sufficient for safer behavioral maintenance (staying HIV-negative or practicing safer behaviors among HIV-positive individuals) or changes for safer behaviors (Choi & Coates, 1994), misconception or less than optimal KABBs are likely to place people at risk. Researchers report the African American community consistently underestimates their risk of contracting HIV. The CDC found that many sexually active Black women in

FIGURE 11.3 Test Your Knowledge of AIDS

Determine whether the following statements are true (T) or false (F):
1. Most infants born to mothers infected with HIV will test negative after 18 months.
2. The *window period* refers to the time between infection and the detection of antibodies in the blood.
3. Once you have tested positive for HIV, it is certain that you will develop AIDS.
4. *Confidential testing* means that you do not have to give your name when you get tested.
5. Latex condoms are an effective barrier to HIV.
6. You cannot get HIV if you are having sex with only one partner.
7. Oil-based lubricants should be used with latex condoms to prevent HIV.
8. In 2001, complications from AIDS was the leading cause of death for all Americans, ages 25 to 44.

Answers: 1. F; 2. T; 3. T; 4. F; 5. T; 6. F; 7. F; 8. T

North Carolina engaged in high-risk sexual behaviors. The reasons for involvement in these behaviors reported were:

> 1) financial dependence on male partners, 2) feeling invincible, 3) low self-esteem coupled with a need to feel loved by a male figure, and 4) alcohol and drug use. In addition, participant's proposed strategies for reducing HIV transmission among black women in North Carolina included 1) introducing HIV and STD educational activities in elementary and middle schools, 2) increasing condom availability and usage, and 3) integrating targeted HIV-education and -prevention messages into church and community activities, as well as into media and popular culture. (MMWR, 2005)

One barrier to combating the AIDS epidemic is HIV testing, which serves as a critical entry point to ensure linkage to care. By the mid-1990s, over one-third of adults in the United States had been tested for HIV. Including blood donation, the proportion increased from 16 percent in 1987 to 40 percent in 1995 (Anderson, Carey, & Taveras, 2000). In the three national surveys of household-based probability samples on which these figures are based, rates of testing were much higher for persons at increased risk (e.g., multiple sexual partners, IV drug use) for HIV. Twice as many people received HIV tests in private locations (medical offices, hospitals and emergency rooms, employee clinics, nursing home, and at home via home testing kits) as in public locations (health departments, community clinics, HIV counseling and testing sites, family planning clinics, military and immigration sites, and STD clinics). Of those at increased risk for HIV, 70 percent had been tested for it. These patterns of findings suggest that there are at least two aspects to HIV testing: ability to access services and willingness to access services. Just because service is available does not mean that people (especially disenfranchised populations, including immigrants and refugees as well as those with limited English-speaking ability and some segments of racial/ethnic and cultural groups) will use it. In fact, available data indicate disparity in HIV testing among certain racial/ethnic and cultural groups. For example, Asians and Pacific Islanders have one of the lowest testing rates. However, little is known about why people are unwilling to access HIV testing. Meanwhile, although the overall rates of HIV testing are high, more than half of the persons tested in public programs did not report that a health professional talked to them about HIV-related issues (KABBs) when they were tested, indicating that many are either not receiving counseling or are not recognizing their interaction with staff as counseling. The rate of counseling is even lower in private settings. These findings further underscore the complex relationship of KABBs, HIV testing, linkage to care, and most of all, their less than optimal effect in the fight against HIV. One theory, for example, acknowledges the relationship between an individual's sense of optimism and pessimism and HIV screening. A study of pregnant women in Ghana found that those who were most optimistic were not tested for HIV before pregnancy and had the least knowledge of HIV. This raises the question as to whether optimism translates into a denial or ignorance of potential risk. On the other hand, are pessimists better suited when it comes to HIV testing because they may be prepared for the worst (Moyer et al., 2008)? These findings acknowledge that psychosomatic issues and emotional difficulties are involved in electing to test for HIV.

Prevention and testing alone cannot combat HIV. Treatment of HIV-positive individuals with **antiretrovirals (ARTs)** can extend their lives and increase quality of life. However, some argue that ARTs are expensive and the lack of health infrastructure in developing countries is a serious impediment to the delivery of treatment. However, Paul Farmer of Partners in Health created a successful HIV treatment program in rural Haiti, demonstrating that community-based approaches to HIV treatment in resource-poor settings are possible. Partners in Health provided directly observed therapy combined with **highly active antiretroviral therapy (HAART).** Each patient had an "accompagnateur" or health advocate (often a community health worker) who observed the ingestion of pills and provided emotional, moral, and social support. Additionally, monthly meetings were offered to discuss illness and other concerns. The initial cohort responded extremely well to medicine, was less likely to be hospitalized, and reported higher morale. Farmer advocates that the success of the HAART program in the poorest country in the Western hemisphere shows it can be implemented anywhere (Farmer et al., 2001).

Complexities and Controversies

In 2003, President George W. Bush committed $15 billion over five years as the U.S. government's initiative to combat the HIV/AIDS epidemic. The plan is known as **PEPFAR,** or **President's Emergency Plan for AIDS Relief.** Congress divided the sum in 55 percent for treatment of HIV-positive individuals, 15 percent for **palliative care** (end of life care) of individuals with HIV/AIDS, 20 percent for HIV/AIDS prevention, and 10 percent for AIDS orphans and vulnerable children. Additionally, of the money devoted to prevention, at least 33 percent is allocated to **abstinence until marriage programs** (Avert, 2008). PEPFAR has garnered a considerable amount of criticism and disagreement with regard to funds distribution. Midcourse evaluation by a panel of experts praised PEPFAR on the grounds that it was able to rapidly scale up AIDS services as it recommended a shift from emergency relief to capacity building. The largest criticism was that only a small percentage of money went toward preventing the spread of HIV, what some argue was the most necessary element in the long-term fight against the disease. Another criticism was that PEPFAR restricts the money given to needle-sharing programs that give clean needles to injecting drug users (*New York Times* Editorial Board, 2007). Overall, the program has great potential but is severely limited by restrictions.

AIDS education raises many controversial questions. As part of education, should condoms be distributed in schools to prevent the spread of AIDS? If so, at what grade level? Such controversy has almost torn apart school systems across the nation. People with AIDS are growing impatient with the FDA in the regulation of experimental drugs and treatment criteria. To be treated, people must have more than 20 symptoms as defined by the CDC, a federal agency that oversees most HIV and AIDS surveillance. However, it took a lot of political lobbying before the CDC added to its list symptoms specific to women with AIDS (e.g., cervical cancer). Meanwhile, many people with AIDS have died from taking illegal treatments (usually smuggled into this country). The American Foundation for AIDS Research (Honorable Chairperson Elizabeth Taylor) publishes a listing of all drugs for treating AIDS, including those that do not have FDA approval. The list is available free of charge.

On one hand, the pandemic has decreased in the United States and other industrialized countries due in large part to public health efforts and antiretroviral drugs. Yet in Sub-Saharan Africa, AIDS continues to have devastating social, economic, political, and demographic consequences. Some argue that prevention and control in Africa has been based on earlier public models that were based on policies from industrialized countries that did not take into account the nature of the epidemic (generalized rather than in specific risk groups) and African culture. Additionally, a uniform global approach may not be suited to such extreme political and epidemiological diversity of the pandemic. Questions have arisen as to how to best tackle the epidemic in Africa. Should health officials require mandatory testing? How should limited funds be allocated within a country, on prevention or treatment? How do you combat stigma, discrimination, and depression seen in HIV-positive individuals? What should be done when ARTs are available but there is not enough medical staff to administer them? Who should pay for treatment and testing? Should policies be made by local governments or international governing bodies like World Health Organization or the World Bank?

Morality and politics aside, community psychologists and public health advocates have learned to use the public health model to slow down the spread of AIDS. After two decades of fighting the epidemic, it has been widely recognized that behavioral changes are paramount in preventing the transmission of HIV (National Commission on AIDS, 1993). Moreover, attitudinal variables are often viewed as determinants of compliance with HIV prevention recommendations (Fisher & Fisher, 1992). According to the Health Belief Model (Becker, 1974; Rosentock, 1986), readiness to perform health-related behaviors is seen as a function of perceived vulnerability, perceived severity of disease, perceived barriers to health-protective action, and feelings of self-efficacy concerning ability to protect oneself from disease. This meta-model has since been adapted or modified to meet the challenges and needs of the specific populations participating in HIV prevention programs.

Possible Solutions: Community-Based Approaches

The preceding issues only scratch the surface of a very complex—and often volatile—problem. The virus is more than a biological epidemic; it has political and social valences, as well. It is beyond the scope of this chapter to review all solutions; however, a heuristic approach is to conceptualize solutions (with an emphasis on the principles of community psychology) along three interrelated dimensions: (1) prevention (KABBs), (2) HIV testing (see Case in Point 11.2), and (3) linkage to care (including psychosocial support; see Case in Point 11.3). The term *prevention* is used here in an inclusive sense to capture the overlap of primary, secondary, and tertiary modalities that occur in the AIDS literature and in the implementation of the clinical programs.

CASE IN POINT 11.2
EVALUATION AND IMPLEMENTATION OF STD/HIV COMMUNITY INTERVENTION PROGRAM IN LIMA, PERU

Community programs focus on affecting the entire community to create widespread change in behavioral norms. The U.S. National Institute of Mental Health (NIMH) developed a collaborative model of community-level prevention focusing on mobilizing and training **community popular opinion leaders (CPOLs)** to promote healthy sexual behavior. NIMH is in the process of testing implications and effects of this intervention in Lima, Peru, in three different populations: men who identify as homosexual, women with multiple partners, and heterosexually identified men. This study looks at midterm evaluation of programs and how to best implement STD prevention programs in low-income communities.

The program is based on Jeff Kelley and colleagues' Popular Opinion Leader model and adapts the four core elements (1) visible target population, (2) identification of CPOLs (criteria often include how popular, trusted, or respected they are among their peers), (3) training CPOLs over multiple sessions on theory-based prevention methods, and (4) goal setting with CPOLs.

The intervention in Peru is called *Qué te Cuentas* (What's up) and targets the young, urban, poor population where the HIV/STD epidemic is largely concentrated. Qué te Cuentas uses an innovative training approach and gives CPOLs information on sexuality, HIV and STDs, effective communication, and how to deliver nonthreatening, brief, and informal prevention messages. Researchers found the program to be overwhelmingly successful. CPOLs felt empowered by their position and ability to effect change in the community. Many CPOLs were surprised that conversations flowed easily at social spaces, including bars, soccer games, and homes. The intervention seems to be well accepted by the community, and a sense of ownership has developed among neighbors who perceive the intervention as a positive asset for the community.

Further evaluation of the program found that using CPOLs to disseminate STD prevention information created more culturally appropriate messages. Given the context of poverty and societal exclusion, CPOLs were given a chance to feel useful and a part of something. Initial findings also demonstrated that the intervention has directly changed CPOLs' knowledge, attitudes, and sexual risk behavior. Additionally, the community has greater knowledge of how to prevent STDs and HIV (Maiorana et al., 2007). (See Community-Based Approaches for more information on this diffusion model.)

CASE IN POINT 11.3
THE BILINGUAL PEER ADVOCATE (BPA) PROGRAM

Nationwide, a majority of the AIDS/HIV cases among Asian and Pacific Islanders (APIs) are foreign-born individuals. In New York City, AIDS cases among APIs account for 95 percent of adult AIDS cases among APIs in the state and 13 percent of adult cases among APIs in the United States (Sy, Chng, Choi, & Wong, 1998).

Although they represent an expanding population (e.g., the highest growth rate from 1980 to 1990 in New York City) with increasing needs for HIV-related services, APIs are prevented from adequately accessing such services because of a number of barriers, including the following:

- Lack of culturally competent, linguistically accessible, and HIV-sensitive providers,
- Lack of health insurance,
- Distrust of institutions,
- Stigma in API communities surrounding sex, substance use, homosexuality, illness, and death,
- Lack of coordinated primary care and case-management services.

Ideally, any API immigrant living with AIDS/HIV in New York City would be able to access any needed HIV-related service in the language that he or she speaks. In this ideal situation, the service would also be provided in a way that recognizes the cultural practices and attitudes of the client or patient. But given a tight funding environment, a lack of prioritization of API issues, and the numerous API languages, national, and cultural groups that exist, such an ideal is difficult to achieve. As part of a five-year national demonstration study (Chin & Wong, 2003), the Bilingual Peer Advocate (BPA) program, with its reliance on part-time peer workers, was designed to allow the Asian and Pacific Islander Coalition on HIV/AIDS (APICHA) to hire a large team of workers to meet the diverse language and cultural needs of APIs living with AIDS while also remaining within realistic cost parameters.

The program trains and maintains a corps of paid, part-time BPAs to act as language interpreters, cultural guides, and advocates for clients as they negotiate New York City's service system. In addition to helping service providers understand the clients' culture, BPAs are able to explain the culture of the health and social services to clients. BPAs are provided clinical supervision by three full-time case managers, one speaking Mandarin Chinese and two more speaking Japanese.

BPAs are paid because they commit more time to work and training than volunteers do. These individuals start with a three-day intensive training program and then receive a two- to three-hour follow-up training each month after. They are expected to be available on a regular basis; some are on call and carry beepers. BPAs work only part-time to retain a level of flexibility that full-time staff do not have and, more important, to allow APICHA to hire a broader range of individuals to represent more cultures and languages.

Currently, APICHA maintains a corps of 15 BPAs. Among them, they speak the following major languages: Bengali, Cantonese, English, Gujarati, Hindi, Japanese, Korean, Mandarin, Tagalog, Toisanese, and Urdu. Of APICHA's current 70-plus HIV-positive clients receiving comprehensive case management, 24 are being served by BPAs. Each month, BPAs spend about 8 to 12 hours working directly with clients, 3 to 5 hours conducting client outreach, 10 hours in travel, and 2 hours in training.

SUMMARY

This chapter has reviewed five health issues: tobacco, alcohol, illicit drugs, STDs, and HIV/AIDS. These issues were examined from the perspectives of community psychology and preventive medicine; policy-based prevention (targeting a community) was also discussed (see Table 11.4). These issues were chosen for two main reasons: (1) They have

TABLE 11.4 Five Issues of Community Health and Preventive Medicine: A Snapshot

ISSUE	EXTENT OF THE PROBLEM	CONSEQUENCE	POSSIBLE SOLUTION
Tobacco	■ 23.0% of all adolescents smoked a cigarette at least once in past 30 days	■ Smoking is a strong contributor to ectopic pregnancy and spontaneous abortion ■ An estimated $72.7 billion tobacco-related medical expenditures in 1993	■ America Stop Smoking Intervention Study (ASSIST) ■ Smoke Free Movies campaign
Alcohol	■ 74.3% of all students have had at least one drink of alcohol during their lifetimes ■ 25.6% of all students have used alcohol before age 13	■ 41% of fatal motor vehicle crashes involve alcohol ■ Risk for contraction of HIV is increased	■ Parent–child skill building (Spoth et al., 1996) ■ Early intervention that involves the family and community
Illicit Drugs	■ Marijuana—38.4% of students ever used ■ Cocaine—7.6% of students ever used ■ Injection drugs—2.1% of students ever used ■ Steroids—4.0% of students ever used ■ Inhalants—12.4% of students ever used ■ Hallucinogenics—8.5% of students ever used ■ Heroin—2.4% of students ever used ■ Methamphetamine—6.2% of students ever used ■ Ecstasy—6.3 percent of students ever used	■ Users are consuming drugs without knowledge of unmonitored content and potential adverse health effects (rising THC levels in marijuana) ■ HIV cases are directly linked to injection drug use worldwide ■ Nonmedical use of prescription drugs is becoming just as high risk as "traditional" narcotics	■ National Drug Control Strategy, 2008 (Office of National Drug Control Policy, 2008): early preventive programs, intervention and healing of current drug users, combating the market of illegal drugs
STDs	■ In 2000, there were 9 million new cases of STDs among 15–24-year-olds	■ Risk for contraction of HIV is increased ■ New infections in mostly young people ■ Direct economic burden of STDs is estimated to be $6.5 billion yearly	■ Advisory Committee for HIV and STD Prevention (MMWR, 1998a) ■ Community intervention (e.g., Peru)
HIV/AIDS	■ In 2004, HIV was the fourth leading cause of death for Black men and third for Black women aged 25–44. ■ HIV deaths seen predominately in Africa	■ Incurable disease with a long incubation period ■ Resource allocation ■ Stigma	■ KABBs prevention and intervention ■ HAART ■ HIV testing

each received enormous attention in the media, and (2) each is highly preventable if certain activities are practiced. In addition, a large number of people are affected or have the potential to be affected if prevention does not occur.

Internationally, tobacco is the cause of more than 5 million deaths each year (WHO, 2008). In the United States alone, tobacco use (including smoking) is the number one preventable cause of death (U.S. DHHS, 2001b). Each year, tobacco use causes more deaths than HIV, illegal drug use, alcohol use, motor vehicle injuries, suicides, and murders combined (CDC, 2005; McGinnis & Foege, 1993). The American Legacy program has been effective in its antismoking efforts as seen its Truth youth smoking prevention and Smoke Free Movie campaigns. Biglan and colleagues illustrated the use of information and public policy to change behavior (cigarette sales to minors) for the good of the community. Biglan's research also demonstrated how various community services such as the police, elected officials, merchants, and psychologists can collaborate on programs for the community.

In addition to cigarette smoking, alcohol is a gateway drug to other drug use and abuse. More American students are consuming alcohol with 43.3 percent of students current alcohol users (or had least one drink of alcohol in the past 30 days) (MMWR, 2005). Binge drinking is a major issue associated with alcohol use and abuse that spans from college campuses to entire societies across the globe. Research has shown that family largely influences substance use and later misuse in young people. Other health policy–related research suggests that alcohol warning labels and signs may be a useful way to inform women of child-bearing age about the danger of alcohol use during pregnancy.

Overall, illicit drug use has remained stable in this country. Globally, there are at least 15.3 million people in the world who have drug use disorders (WHO, 2008). Yet certain drugs continue to be used by some segments of the population. For example, marijuana is the most popular drug used among youth and young adults. Consequences of illicit drugs include crimes, domestic violence, and other problems (e.g., increased HIV transmission). Proportionately, this country spends more money on law enforcement–related activities than on drug prevention, intervention, and treatment. Research has demonstrated the contribution of community psychology in preventing drug use; yet community psychologists need to take a more proactive role in advocating for more resources in prevention activities (i.e., other than law enforcement–related activities).

The United States has one of the highest rates of STDs in the industrialized world. Furthermore, epidemiological studies consistently demonstrate that concurrent STDs increase the transmission probability for HIV infection. Unfortunately, community psychologists have done little or no work in this area. It is recommended that the field of community psychology take a proactive role in heeding the recommendations of the Advisory Committee for HIV and STD Prevention, including promoting sexuality as a healthy lifestyle.

In the absence of a cure or vaccine, prevention and information dissemination and behavioral intervention (e.g., the diffusion model) appear to be the only hope to slow the spread of HIV. Given that HIV/AIDS is also a political and social disease, coupled with the advent of medical technology, prevention takes on added dimensions and meanings beyond the traditional definition used in community health and community medicine.

CHAPTER 12

COMMUNITY/ORGANIZATIONAL PSYCHOLOGY

WHAT DO ORGANIZATIONAL AND
COMMUNITY PSYCHOLOGY SHARE?
- CASE IN POINT 12.1 Smart Car Sales Personnel

EVERYDAY ORGANIZATIONAL ISSUES
  Stress
  Burnout
  Organizational Culture
  Other Ecological Conditions
- CASE IN POINT 12.2 Dealing with a Diverse Workforce

TRADITIONAL TECHNIQUES FOR MANAGING ORGANIZATIONS
  Compensation Packages
  Rules and Regulations

OVERVIEW OF ORGANIZATIONAL CHANGE
  Reasons for Change
  Issues Related to Organizational Change

CHANGING THE ORGANIZATION
  Leadership
  Reorganization
  Quality of Work Life Programs
  Team Building

HELPING INDIVIDUALS CHANGE WITHIN THE ORGANIZATION
  Burnout and Stress
  Health Maintenance Issues: Smoking Cessation

SUMMARY

A business that makes nothing but business is a poor kind of business.
—Henry Ford

As Sarah Anderson walked out the door of Harmony House, she glanced back at the building that had been her home away from home for the past eight months. She felt a sense of relief and a paradoxical sense of sadness as she exited for the last time. "What went wrong?" she wondered. "How could my job have become such a sore point in my life when only a few short months ago I had accepted it so enthusiastically?"

Harmony House was run by a private nonprofit corporation that managed eight group homes for at-risk adolescents in Sarah's city. The adolescents were sent to the homes, including Harmony House, by judges, probation officers, schools, and parents. The group homes boasted the ability to "turn kids around"—that is, get them off drugs, raise their school grades, and make them productive citizens again, in about six months.

A psychology major with a human services minor from a small liberal arts college, Sarah had been actively recruited by Harmony House after summer volunteer work there. Her grades were very good, and the combination of training in college and volunteer work plus her winning personality during interviews made her eagerly sought after by several community organizations. She had always wanted to be a case manager for one of them. Harmony House won her over because they offered the best salary, had an excellent training program, and had a good reputation. Harmony House seemed to be on the leading edge of innovations in treatment, which Sarah thought would give her the upper hand when she sought to move on to bigger and better agencies.

The idealistic and perhaps naive Sarah approached her first few days at Harmony House with immense enthusiasm. Her supervisor, Jan Hayes, mentored and coached her for the first few months. Sarah felt she was getting plenty of attention and good training under Jan. She was slowly developing a sense of confidence in handling each new difficult youth as he or she entered Harmony House.

Six months into her service, Sarah's career took a downturn that mirrored the changes occurring at corporate headquarters. Jan was moved from Harmony House to headquarters to become the chief trainer, and Sarah received a new supervisor who cared much less about mentoring her and more about keeping costs low. Sarah explained to her supervisor that she was fairly new to the job so would like to be mentored, but the new supervisor told her to stop complaining and start performing.

As the weeks passed, Sarah realized that not only was she without the tutelage and attention afforded her by Jan but that the budget cuts at the group home were taking their toll on the clients. The television broke, which left the youths with more free time than they needed. The furniture was in need of replacement, and the menu each day was much less appetizing. There were fewer field trips and fewer group therapy sessions, too. All these changes and others made the youths more discontented and harder to work with.

Sarah approached her supervisor and commented on these negative changes. His response was, "These are tough times; I have to make these cuts and changes. I suggest that if you think things are better elsewhere, you find another job." Sarah worked another two months before she resigned. She did not have any active job prospects, but she was so utterly dismayed with the changes at Harmony House, she felt she had to quit.

Sarah's story is told to introduce this chapter on organizations, which, in a community psychology book, could be controversial. However, the authors and others (Keys & Frank, 1987; Klein & D'Aunno, 1986; Shinn & Perkins, 2000) feel that there is much community psychologists can learn from organizational psychologists and just as much that organizational psychologists can learn from community psychologists.

WHAT DO ORGANIZATIONAL AND COMMUNITY PSYCHOLOGY SHARE?

As you now know, community psychology examines the effects of social and environmental factors on behavior as it occurs in various levels in communities, including the organizational level, to produce beneficial change. To understand the effects of environmental factors or settings on individuals, one must understand something about the setting—in this case, organizations, whether they are private sector businesses, mental health clinics, prisons, or any other community organization. In fact, it is futile to attempt to understand individuals apart from the settings to which they belong (Keys & Frank, 1987). This chapter looks at the effects of the organization on the individual and the effects of the individual on the organization with an eye toward the goals of community psychology. Specifically, discussions attend to ways that organizations adversely affect their members, both staff and clients, and means by which organizations can be improved to better serve their members and the community.

Organizational behavior and organizational psychology, which are the study of how groups and individuals interface with the organizations they are in, have much to offer community psychology. **Organizational psychology** approaches the examination of organizations from the perspective of the individual, whereas **organizational behavior** approaches the study of organizations from a systems perspective, or as if organizations are systems (Smither, 1998).

It is obvious what organizational psychology and organizational behavior have in common, but what do they share with community psychology? First, organizational specialists have developed paradigms, or models, as well as constructs and measurement techniques that go beyond the individual level of analysis (Riger, 1990; Shinn & Perkins, 2000). This is a goal of community psychology. For instance, from the study of organizations comes **organizational development (OD).** OD is a set of social science techniques designed to plan and implement long-term change in organizational settings for purposes of improving the effectiveness of organizational functioning and enhancing the individuals within the organizations (Baron & Greenberg, 1990; French & Bell, 1990). In other words, concern for the organization and the individual in the organization should be equal (Beer & Walton, 1990).

Another aspect of organizational psychology important to community psychology is the understanding that individuals and organizations have a dynamic relationship—that is, an ever-changing, transactional relationship over time (Keys & Frank, 1987; Maton, 2008). For instance, at one point, an individual might be highly motivated to stay in an organization, while at another time, he or she may be motivated to leave, as did Sarah. However, just when the disgruntled individual wants to leave the organization, the organization most needs that person. The cycle then continues. The study of such dynamic relationships is the domain of both community psychology and organizational psychology.

Organizational scientists, as do community psychologists, have a long tradition of conducting research from an ecological perspective as well as a systems perspective (Foster-Fishman, Newell, & Yang, 2007; Shinn & Perkins, 2000). They know how to include all organizational participants (e.g., managers and employees) as well as coordinating mechanisms and processes in their research endeavors as they attempt to study and change the overall organization. It is this multilevel or holistic type of research that community psychologists hope to achieve, rather than endeavors focused merely on the individual. Cascio's (1995) challenge to industrial and organization psychology is to examine the impact of the shifts in how work and the effects of technology, globalization, and the definitions of worth are changing the nature of organizations and the definitions of leadership and management. He believes the worth of the worker to be shifting, based on the fundamental assumptions. Such a consideration of paradigm shifts, of the implications for systems, and the call to examine how workers and their work environments need to evolve is very much in the nature of a community psychology.

Another aspect of similarity between organizational psychology and community psychology is that for most individuals, work is part of their self-concepts. Therefore, work has consequences for well-being (Blustein, 2008), the promotion of which is a goal of community psychology (Price, 1985). Furthermore, there is spillover between work organizations and communities. Work influences how people feel; hence, if people emotionally withdraw from work, they might also feel alienated from their families and their communities. Likewise, feelings about community also spill into the work world. Working mothers, for example, probably experience more work stress than any other employee because they experience the most stress at home (Price, 1985). The importance of work to well-being has been discussed by several authors (Blustein, 2008; Fassinger, 2008; Fouad & Bynner, 2008); Blustein presents policy implications arising from such assumptions. Three personal needs derive from his psychology-of-work perspective: the need for survival, the need for relatedness, and the need for self-determination. The parallel of these needs to community psychology principles is not surprising.

Interestingly, there is a serious point at which the study of organizations and community psychology part company (Riger, 1990; Shinn & Perkins, 2000). In the field of

---

CASE IN POINT 12.1
SMART CAR SALES PERSONNEL

Cascio (1995) mentions a case of worker empowerment in which the individual worker is seen to have direct control over productivity and therefore his or her value to the company. Beyond this, value is redefined as service provision rather than product movement in sales. An example is the car dealer Smart, which offers fuel-efficient two-seaters designed by Mercedes Benz and built in France. Smart has U.S. showroom personnel on salary, with provisions for bonuses based not on the number of cars sold or the amount of money negotiated per car unit but on customer satisfaction. The car price is set. How the customer feels about the helpfulness of the sales personnel determines what the salesperson makes. Shifts in control and shifts in criteria bring about changes in behaviors. The sales personnel were very helpful and informative. They sought to answer all questions and be candid regarding the product. There was no feeling of being manipulated or being sold. The car sold itself. They were there to help. Paradigms shifted in regard to what is valued and expected, what is rewarded, and how something is sold. The system changes result in behavior changes in personnel and management of those personnel.

organizational behavior, most efforts are aimed at improving organizational efficiency and profits, sometimes at the expense of the individuals in the organizations. If the organizational effort benefits individuals, it is often only incidental to the main task of improving the organization (Lavee & Ben-Ari, 2008; Riger, 1990). For instance, if Sarah's new supervisor had taken into consideration her concerns about the budget cuts, he probably would have done so only if it affected Harmony House and not because it would have made Sarah happier. More specifically, suppose Sarah knew of a dangerous circumstance that might have resulted in Harmony House being sued, such as an elevator that was in disrepair. Her new supervisor might likely have listened to her but not to please her. Rather, he would have been concerned about the financial well-being of the organization.

On the other hand, the primary aim in community psychology is usually to enhance the functioning of individuals in organizations (Shinn & Perkins, 2000). The intent is to empower individuals within organizations to create innovative solutions to the problems facing them, ensure that the innovations and changes are humanistic, and promote a sense of community within the organization (Peterson & Zimmerman, 2004). From these values, organizational specialists can also learn. For instance, community psychologists feel that creating a sense of community within an organization or a sense of belonging to the organization can enhance human functioning. Organizational psychologists focusing less on the organization and more on the sense of community or cohesiveness are beginning to understand that work group cohesiveness goes hand in hand with other factors, such as job satisfaction (Burroughs & Eby, 1998) and turnover (Moynihan & Pandey, 2008). In fact, some research has found that an organization develops its own unique sense of community (Hughey, Speer, & Peterson, 1999).

Organizational psychology and community psychology may be linked in the use of organizational theories in community interventions and in the community research and perspectives that may inform organizational change (Keys, 2007). Though this relationship has some strong historical ties (e.g., Michigan State University's Ecological Psychology Program and University of Illinois at Chicago Circle's Organizational-Community Psychology Program's evolution into the Community and Prevention Research Program), Keys (2007) notes that these linkages are sometimes ignored or less evident in community psychologists' considerations. That is not the intention of this text, because many of the topics covered in social change are indeed organizationally informed, and the return to organizational topics for full chapter consideration is a conscious decision on our part.

EVERYDAY ORGANIZATIONAL ISSUES

Why this interest in organizations? People spend a great deal of their adult lives in organizations, particularly in their place of employment but also in volunteer, recreational, educational, and other groups. One's organizational affiliations often bring economic well-being, emotional security, happiness, a sense of self-esteem and status, as well as the social rewards of belonging to a group and a sense of accomplishment (Schultz & Schultz, 1998). On the other hand, organizations can also frustrate and alienate people and cause much stress (Rubin & Brody, 2005). With that in mind, we turn to a sampling of the problems of today's organizations.

Stress

Stress was discussed at length in Chapter 3 as a possible guiding model for community psychology studies or community psychologist interventions. The workplace is one of the central and defining contexts to an individual's identity, so it may be expected to provide a source of both pride and stress (Blustein, 2008). Receiving a promotion can be as stressful as being fired. Remember, these situations are construed as stressful *only* if the individual perceives them as taxing or exceeding his or her resources and endangering well-being (Lazarus & Folkman, 1984). Major readjustments, such as a new job (Holmes & Rahe, 1967), as well as everyday work hassles (Kanner et al., 1981) like rising prices, too many things to do, and being late for work, can be stressful. Zohar (1999) found that work hassles are correlated to negative mood and later fatigue. A link between everyday job stress and alcohol and drug abuse has also been shown to exist (Frone, 2008). When Frone examined the stress–substance abuse relationships, he found that general alcohol and substance use is not related to work stress (e.g., How frequently do you have a drink?). However, when the question was placed within a certain context (i.e., the time of day) then the work stress and substance abuse relationship appeared (e.g., How many drinks do you have at the end of a given [identified] day?). In these findings, Frone (2008) believed he demonstrated the stress dampening effect of substance abuse. So in answer to the question, "Why are drugs and alcohol such a problem in the United States?" we might say that part of the answer lies in the stressfulness of the workplace.

Stress can occur in any facet of people's lives, but the concern here is with causes of stress in organizations. Organizational causes of stress are varied and sometimes complex (Rubin & Brody, 2005). Organizational members can be too busy *or* too bored, both of which can cause stress. Interpersonal conflicts between coworkers may exist, or the individual may not feel competent or sufficiently trained to do the work. Likewise, the individual may have a dangerous job, such as working on a ward with violent individuals, or be in a demanding environment where noise, fumes, poor lighting, or other environmental conditions produce stress. The person might also have a supervisor with whom he or she does not get along. There may be too many or too few rules or too much or too little structure. Or the individual might have problems at home that he or she brings to work or feel deprived when work detracts from family activities. Zohar (1997) proposed three categories of work hassles to test his model of work stress: **role conflict** (when there are conflicting work expectations), **role ambiguity** (what one is expected to do is unclear), and **role overload** (there is just too much to do).

Burnout

A concept related to but slightly different from stress is burnout. **Burnout** is a feeling of overall exhaustion that is the result of too much pressure and not enough sources of satisfaction (Maslach, Schaufeli, & Leiter, 2000; Moss, 1981). Burnout has three components:

1. The feeling of being drained or exhausted,
2. Depersonalization or insensitivity to others, including clients, and a kind of cynicism,
3. A sense of low personal accomplishment or the feeling that one's efforts are futile (Jackson, Schwab, & Schuler, 1986; Leiter & Maslach, 2005).

Symptoms of burnout include loss of interest in one's job, apathy, depression, irritability, and finding fault with others. The quality of the individual's work also deteriorates, and the person often blindly and superficially follows rules and procedures (Schultz & Schultz, 1998), topics soon discussed in this chapter.

Burnout is most likely to affect those organizational members who are initially eager, motivated, and perhaps idealistic (Van Fleet, 1991). Research has demonstrated that many individuals in community service organizations—including police officers, Social Security employees, social workers, teachers, and nurses—indeed suffer from burnout (Adams, Boscarino, & Figley, 2006; Pines & Guendelman, 1995). In fact, you may have realized that many of these occupations are primarily filled by women. While an earlier study suggests that women suffer more from burnout than men (Pretty, McCarthy, & Catano, 1992), we have come to understand that there are no gender differences in burnout, but women's health may be more susceptible to work stressors (Toker, Shirom, Shapira, Berliner, & Melamed, 2005). Perhaps this was part of Sarah's problem; she was simply too burned out and was beginning to feel unhealthy, so she resigned. Poor fit between the person and the organization can also result in burnout (Maslach & Goldberg, 1998). For example, Xie and Johns (1995) examined the roles of **job scope** or job-related activities performed by the employee and burnout. They found that individuals who perceived a misfit between their abilities and the demands or scope of the job experienced higher burnout and stress.

Six organizational factors have been identified as contributing to burnout (Leiter & Maslach, 2004, 2005). They are:

1. **Workload:** Overload of duties and responsibilities,
2. **Control:** Lack of participation in decision making,
3. **Reward:** Inadequate social, institutional, and/or monetary recognition,
4. **Community:** Social support is wanting and lack of social integration,
5. **Fairness:** Do not feel just or equitable environment, lack of reciprocity,
6. **Values:** Incongruency of meaning and goals between individual and environment.

Maslach and Leiter (2008) find that they can identify those who are at high risk for burnout by looking at the worker's perception of site fairness and earlier reports of exhaustion or cynicism. When the individual's expectations of fairness do not match those of the work site, the tendency to move toward exhaustion and cynicism increases. However, when work site fairness expectations are met, the individual seems to become more engaged (as opposed to burned out) with his or her work. These findings highlight both burnout and engagement tendencies as playing a role in burnout. Leiter and Maslach's (1998) earlier suggestion is supported, that studies ought to identify those who can stay energetic, involved, and feeling effective (i.e., engaged) as well as those who burn out. This finding can contribute to prevention efforts to retain personnel and maintain job effectiveness over time. This is really a study of resilience in the face of job adversity.

Organizational Culture

Why is it that as individuals come and go from organizations, much as Sarah did, organizations do not seem to change much, even though their members do? The answer is organizational culture (Baron & Greenberg, 1990). Earlier in the history of its study, and as a narrower concept, organizational culture was referred to as *organizational climate*. Just as Type A personality (e.g., hostile, competitive) is related to an individual's style, organizational culture is related to the personality of the organization. **Organizational culture** consists of the beliefs, attitudes, values, and expectations shared by most members of the organization (Schein, 1985, 1990). Once these beliefs and values are established, they tend to persist over time as the organization shapes and molds its members in its image. For example, can you recall how different all of the freshmen looked in appearance and dress your first week of classes? By senior year, many of these same students looked more similar because other students pressured them to conform to the organization's image. Those students who most deviated from the norm of the campus often left rather than change.

Besides influencing conformity, the prevailing organizational culture guides the organization's structure. How decisions are made in the organization relates to its structure. For instance, whether decisions originate from the bottom, as when average organizational citizens participate in decisions, or from the top, when a centralized management makes the decisions, is part of the organization's structure.

The organizational structure, including the decision-making system, also determines social class distinctions within organizations, such as status differences between executives and middle managers. The distribution of power is also likely to be affected by the organization's culture. If lower-level members make decisions, they will have more power than if they are not allowed to participate in decision making. Finally, organizational culture affects the ideology of the organization. If the organization views human nature as good, it will tend to allow subordinate participation (Tosi, Rizzo, & Carroll, 1986). If the culture emphasizes the development of human potential, then the members are more likely to be allowed to develop and create new ideas without much interference from the organization.

An **open culture,** one appreciative of human dignity and one that enhances human growth, is preferred by most organizational members and by most community psychologists. Open cultures foster a sense of community, better communication, and more empowerment, which can exist in an organization just as in neighborhoods (Detert & Edmondson, 2007; Klein & D'Aunno, 1986; Pretty & McCarthy, 1991). Such organizational cultures tend to foster employee commitment (Shadur, Kienzile, & Rodwell, 1999), among their other positive effects. However, when the culture is **repressive** in that it inhibits human growth or when there are huge gaps in what the organization professes to be and what it actually is (e.g., professing to have a positive culture that is negative in reality), high levels of member cynicism develop, performance deteriorates (Baron & Greenberg, 1990), and cohesiveness drops. Perhaps this is what happened to Sarah as she felt the disregard of her new supervisor flood over her.

Community psychologists are studying a phenomenon related to organizational culture: the sense of community within an organization. Chapter 1 discussed sense of community in some detail. *Sense of community* pertains to an individual's feeling that he or she is similar to others and that he or she and the other individuals in the setting belong there. There is a sense of "we-ness" and belonging coinciding with a sense of community.

Pretty and McCarthy (1991) explored the sense of community in men and women in corporations. They found that for different employees, the sense of community was predicted by different features of the organization. For instance, men and women differed, as did managers and nonmanagers, in the characteristics that determined a sense of community for them. Male managers' sense of community was predicted best by their perceptions of peer cohesion and involvement, whereas female managers' sense of community was predicted by their perceptions of supervisor support, involvement, and amount of work pressure.

Another aspect of organizational culture is the extent to which staff in the organization perceive a sense of empowerment; in fact, organizational culture provides an excellent framework for understanding and assessing the person–environment fit needed if empowerment is to succeed in organizations (Ambrose, Arnaud, & Schminke, 2008; Foster-Fishman & Keys, 1997). Empowerment in organizations has been found to be directly related to employee effectiveness (Spreitzer, 1995). Pereira and Osburn (2008) report in their review of quality circle research that work effectiveness is improved but employee attitudes toward work are not. What are those organizational characteristics that inspire empowerment? Using the case study method, Maton and Salem (1995) found at least four:

- A belief system that inspires growth, is strengths-based, and focuses beyond the individual,
- An opportunity structure that is highly accessible,
- A support system that is encompassing, is peer-based, and provides a sense of community,
- Leadership that is inspiring, talented, shared, and committed to both the setting and the members.

Such qualities very much parallel those of an open culture.

We are reminded of Leiter and Maslach's (2004, 2005) research on organizational factors related to burnout, mentioned earlier. The six dimensions of work load, control, reward, community, fairness, and values all fit within our discussions of organizational climate. Note that the fairness dimension proves pivotal in considerations of resiliency or burnout within the worksite (Maslach & Leiter, 2008). The importance of fairness and support as contextual factors has been demonstrated in a study of women and ethnic minority police officers in New York City (Morris, Shinn, & DuMont, 1999). Their commitment to the work was significantly influenced by these elements of organizational culture. The perception of fairness is important to everyone. It may be especially so for members of historically discriminated categories, such as a given gender or ethnic minority.

Elaborating on those aspects of organizational culture that encourage diversity, Bond (1999) describes a model of connectivity in which gender, race, and class might be appreciated within a work setting. **Connectivity** would result from (1) a culture of connection where people's reliance on each other to accomplish goals is known and appreciated, and (2) a recognition of multiple realities that notes many perspectives and invites participation in the creation of the narrative of what is real. She describes the creation of an organizational culture at odds with traditional American organizations' emphasis on individuality and autonomy and the norm of sameness.

As we can see, the consideration of what makes an organizational culture and what qualities of that culture encourage or sustain the members of that culture are very much a concern of a community psychology.

Other Ecological Conditions

The size of organizations is important, too. Members of small organizations report more supportive environments, less discrimination, and more loyalty to the organization (MacDermid, Hertzog, Kensinger, & Zipp, 2001). On the other hand, large organizations often create negative conditions. For instance, Hellman, Greene, Morrison, and Abramowitz (1985) examined residential mental health treatment programs by measuring staff and client perceptions. Not surprisingly, the larger the program, the more the members experienced anxiety, held negative views of the psychosocial aspects of the organization, and perceived greater psychological distance from the organization.

However, size is just one consideration in cultural milieu. Examining the psychological sense of community (PSC) at work, Burroughs and Eby (1998) find that size of work group does not impact people's PSC. Rather, the individual's match between their personal goals and those of the organization significantly predicts PSC. In turn, the PSC relates to job satisfaction, which related to loyalty, courtesy, and willingness to help within the organization.

The growing diversity in the workplace has produced other ecological considerations for organizations. Fassinger (2008) discusses the trends toward larger proportions of the workforce being women, people of color, sexual minorities, and people with physical disabilities. The impact of such shifts in the composition of organizations can be both beneficial and challenging. Case in Point 12.2 is an excellent illustration of the way organizational psychology and applied social psychology can make contributions to the concerns of the work setting ecology and its impact on a diverse workforce.

CASE IN POINT 12.2
DEALING WITH A DIVERSE WORKFORCE

Findings on the effects of group diversity on group functioning have been mixed over the past few decades of research. Tsui, Egan, and O'Reilly (1992) found that as workers became more different from their groups, absenteeism increased and the level of job commitment declined. This finding was strongest for Whites and for males. However, Huo (2003) has found that "super-ordinate" group membership could overcome "sub-ordinate" group memberships, so if identification with a company is powerful enough, individuals would come to ignore the other differences of race, gender, or other diversity designators. Mannix and Neale (2005) summarize the studies to date on diversity in the workplace as mixed in their results. They point out the importance of organizational context to the outcomes. They cite as an example Chatman and Spataro's (2005) finding that visibly different individuals were more cooperative within a business setting when collectivist values were emphasized over individualistic values. Following their review of the research on diversity in the work place, Mannix and Neale (2005) provide three recommendations: (1) the types of tasks and goals given diverse teams should be carefully determined, because what is being asked of the team determines the dynamics within the team; (2) efforts to connect team members by establishing commonalities and similarities result in better group identity and effort; and (3) encourage the minority voice to be respected, because the pressure to conform is a normal part of group processes. Ely and Thomas (2001) encourage a shift in rationale for diversity within business settings. They argue that a "learning and effectiveness" focus for diversification efforts would highlight the advantages to seeking different perspectives and the rewards that underlie the understanding of these perspectives. Diversity is important because we live in a diverse world. An awareness of the processes whereby diverse perspectives may be of value to group products and the manner in which these contributions may best serve the group can affect the integration of diverse populations and diverse perspectives into organizations. This knowledge derived from organizational psychology is certainly applicable to communities as a whole and community psychology in particular.

TRADITIONAL TECHNIQUES FOR MANAGING ORGANIZATIONS

When Sarah left Harmony House, she was a discontented employee. She was not the only one hurt by her decision to leave, though. The organization also suffered. Harmony House would now have to recruit and select a replacement for Sarah as well as train and indoctrinate the new person. Clients might feel disoriented when they came looking for Sarah and could not find her. What do organizations traditionally do to attract and retain good members and manage poor members? Are these strategies helpful?

Compensation Packages

Many of the traditional attempts by organizations to treat employees well or terminate them focus on the individual. An age-old method of motivating employees to work hard and work well is to manipulate compensation levels. In fact, setting compensation levels is often considered the primary function of many human resources management staffs (Milkovich & Boudreau, 1991). Interestingly, organizational members rarely mention pay as the job facet most related to job satisfaction. Nonetheless, one of the common ways organizations attempt to motivate their members is by adjusting compensation and benefits packages. One study showed that raising wage and salary levels was the most common response to reducing quitting in organizations (Bureau of National Affairs, 1981). However, in reality, pay adjustments only partially increase job satisfaction (Schultz & Schultz, 1998). Interestingly, even when employees participate in their own performance reviews, which are often tied to compensation levels, satisfaction with pay remains unaffected (Morgeson, Campion, & Maertz, 2001). Unfortunately, wage disparities between men and women have not been rectified. One study reports women make 75 percent of what men make (American Association of University Women, 2007). The wage difference appears to grow over time past college graduation, from 20 percent less, 1 year postgraduation to 31 percent smaller, 10 years postgraduation while controlling for occupation, hours working, and parenthood factors. We might expect that Sarah was not making the equivalent of her male counterparts.

Rules and Regulations

Organizations also attempt to control member behavior by means of policies and regulations. Policy manuals and codes of ethics for employees have become quite common (Lewin, 1983). Some policies are specific: "No gambling on company property." Others are less so: "Employees are expected to be loyal to the company." Add to this the multitude of public policies or federal and state legislation intended to regulate organizations and the individuals in them, and the total number of regulations is overwhelming. Federal Equal Employment Opportunity Guidelines and the Occupational Safety and Health Regulations alone would create a stack of policies higher than the average person is tall!

The extent to which employees follow organizational policies is unclear, but some classic studies of employee behavior indicate that not all organizational members appreciate regulations. In the classic study of the Western Electric Plant in Hawthorne, Illinois, the men of the bank wiring room purposely worked *below* the production standard set by their supervisors. Why? They believed that if they worked up to standard, their superiors would simply raise the standard (Roethlisberger & Dickson, 1939), thereby forcing the men to work harder. It is known today that in professional bureaucracies such as hospitals, universities, and other human services agencies, professionals prefer to operate according to their *own* codes rather than the formal policies of their organizations (Cheng, 1990; Mintzberg, 1979). Most organizational members have little say in the policies or regulations of their organization; that may be the primary reason they are discontented with the guidelines and violate the rules, as is often found in studies of organizational rules. Additionally, rule violation can result in discipline, such as termination, demotion, or leave without pay. Atwater and her associates (2001) found that discipline is often perceived as unfair and that both recipients and observers consequently lose respect for the person administering the discipline as well as for the organization. Notably, the perception of fairness is seen as critical to work setting stress (Malasch & Leiter, 2008). This would appear to be a prime focus for anyone dealing with a work setting community.

In summary, then, these traditional methods of regulating individuals in organizations are typically the antithesis of what community psychologists would recommend. First, most are aimed at the individual level of the organization. They neither address nor acknowledge the role that the context or the organization itself plays in producing and influencing individual behavior. Second, most of these methods are not particularly humanizing. Community psychologists value strategies that benefit the individual and speak to the person's worthiness. On the contrary, in most of these traditional techniques, the organization benefits (if at all). Third, community psychologists emphasize prevention over treatment. In these solutions to organizational situations, the solution often comes *after* (not before) the problem has occurred. Finally, community psychologists believe that individuals should actively engage in—indeed, be empowered to—create their own environments and design the solutions to their problems. In none of these traditional approaches to organizational problems is there much room for that.

Our focus now turns to changes in organizations that encompass some of the values of community psychology. Although much of the progressive work in the fields of organizational behavior and organizational psychology has been conducted in and for industrial settings, you will see that what follows can also generally apply to most community organizations.

OVERVIEW OF ORGANIZATIONAL CHANGE

Reasons for Change

Organizations require change for a number of reasons, a few of which are mentioned briefly here. Pressures for change may be internal or external. **Internal pressures to change** come from within and include pressures from clients, staff, and supervisors. As in the case of Harmony House, internal budget pressures can force change. Organizations also sometimes change their focus or offer new or different services, which leads to further change.

Forces outside of the organization create **external pressures to change.** Government regulations, external competition, political and social trends, and other factors create the need for organizations to adapt. For example, the move to deinstitutionalize people who are mentally disabled has forced communities to provide alternative services, such as group homes. Both the availability of homes and the conditions in the institutions have been affected by this trend.

Issues Related to Organizational Change

As already mentioned in Chapters 4 and 5, change is difficult. Organizational change is no different. One reason this kind of change is complex is because many organizational members resist change. They feel threatened by changes, perhaps because they do not feel competent to handle them or they do not want to put forth the effort to adapt to them. Similarly, some organizations are more difficult to change than others—for example, public sector organizations, which are often bound by laws and civil service requirements (Shinn & Perkins, 2000).

There are other reasons change in organizations is complicated. Organizations are interdependent systems (Tosi et al., 1986). The people in the organization influence the organization, and the organization influences the people. One cannot be changed without changes occurring in the other. For example, suppose in his budget cuts, the Harmony House supervisor also decided to cut staff to save money. Fewer staff members means less attention to each youth; fewer staff members also means more work for the remaining staff. Hence, the services of the organization may start to decline; its reputation might also decline, and it would perhaps attract fewer clients and fewer qualified job applicants because of the budget cuts.

Glidewell (1987) offered a second example of the interdependence of people and organizations from the community psychology literature. Glidewell worked with a group of citizens who hoped to change a school board, which desired instead to change the citizens' attitudes. Specifically, the citizens had voted down a tax referendum three times in one year; the board hoped the citizens would pass the referendum. Glidewell tracked the changes in the citizens and the school board over several years. His data clearly showed a mutually causative, sequential, yet circular system of influence. An increase in citizen negotiation skills was followed by changes in influence on board decisions as well as changes in self-esteem of the participants. Changes in self-esteem and changes in attendance at board meetings were followed by changes in risk taking. Changes in risk taking were followed by further changes in negotiation skills. Changes in negotiation skills attracted the attention of the board; thus, the board was more likely to listen to the citizens, whose esteem was further enhanced.

Another reason organizations are difficult to change lies in the fact that the intervention or change must fit the organizational paradigm (Cheng, 1990). What does this mean? Organizations are diverse in terms of their staffing, functions, structures, and other parameters. By using two dimensions from organizational theory, Schubert and Borkman (1991) found not one but five different types of self-help groups. The two dimensions were "dependence on external funds" and "extent of internal experiential authority" (or self-determination). Therefore, even in organizations with similar purposes—in this case, self-help groups—there are diverse types of organizations varying on several dimensions. Changing organizations requires customizing the intervention or fitting the change to the organizational model (Constantine, 1991) and to the organizational constituencies.

To ensure that change is indeed needed, change should commence with *action research*. The research can also address whether the organization is ready for change. Survey-guided feedback has been suggested as a viable method for monitoring organizational change (Shinn & Perkins, 2000). **Survey-guided feedback** involves the systematic collection of data from organizational members who also receive subsequent and repeated feedback about the changes.

Both need and readiness for change are generally prompted by dissatisfaction with the organization by its members (Baron & Greenberg, 1990). The age of the organization is also important, because there exist different stages of development of community organizations (Bartunek & Betters-Reed, 1987). Some preliminary plan for change should also be in place, although a long-range plan may be better (Taber, Cooke, & Walsh, 1990). Such planning should involve staff and perhaps clients in all phases. Staff participation has a significant effect on both job satisfaction and self-esteem (Roberts, 1991; Sarata, 1984).

Change in organizations can occur at the organizational level, the group level, or the individual level. Although some community psychologists might prefer to change the whole organization—the whole community, so to speak—often it is the subparts of the organization that are easiest to change. Next is an examination of all levels of organizational change and a few techniques at each level. For a complete review of methods of organizational change, see Head and Sorenson (1988).

CHANGING THE ORGANIZATION

Leadership

Eagly, Johannesen-Schmidt, and van Egan (2003) discuss the variety of ways in which leadership styles have been defined. Early studies spoke in terms of **task-focused** versus **interpersonally focused** leaders (Bales, 1950; Fiedler, 1971; Likert, 1961). The task-focused leader is interested in getting the work done the most efficient way possible. The interpersonally focused leader is concerned for the people in the process, worrying about how people feel and seeing the importance of the social climate and interpersonal relations as end products in and of themselves. An interesting development in understanding the effectiveness of these styles is studied and summarized by Fiedler (1971), who finds that the task focus style is most effective in very favorable and unfavorable situations, whereas the interpersonal focus style is best in nonextreme situations. He called this a contingency model for leadership style.

Other researchers distinguish between **democratic/participatory** styles versus more **autocratic/directive** styles (Lewin & Lippitt, 1938). The democratic leader asks for opinions and discusses the options with those to be affected. The autocratic leader makes the decisions him- or herself and then acts. In a classic study on the effects of democracy versus autocracy leadership, Lewin, Lippitt, and White (1939) found the autocratic style to yield more aggression and frustration in a children's group and the democratic style to yield more spontaneity. These initial findings have led to the study of the leadership styles' effects on productivity and satisfaction. Gastil's (1994) meta-analysis of these studies on the two types of leadership yields mixed results. Although democratic styles bring more group satisfaction, the results are moderate at best. Neither democratic nor autocratic styles have superior productivity.

Eagly et al. (2003) examine several studies on leadership that use the newer categories of **transformational, transactional, or laissez-faire** styles. In the transformational style, the leader seeks to stimulate and inspire those they lead to become better. The transactional style is characterized by feedback on performance—positive when things are done well and negative when there are problems. A third style of leadership, called laissez-faire, is one where the leader is absent and uninvolved. Eagly and colleagues find women to be more transformational and rewarding, and men to be more transactional in their use of negative corrective feedback.

Wielkiewicz and Stelzner (2005) take exception to the direction of leadership studies. They argue that leadership is not a personal characteristic, as these studies seem to treat it. Rather, leadership "emerges" from the situation. Using James Kelly's (1968) ecological framework, Wielkiewicz and Stelzner argue that leadership is more dynamic and process-driven. Decisions are not made by the leader so much as emerge from the interaction of those involved, one of whom is designated as the leader. Given this model, what is critical are the participatory structures and the genuineness of the participation. There is usefulness to resolving this need for balance between both structure and process. It acknowledges the advantages of participation, diversity of opinion, and democracy. The belief is that with the ecological paradigm, a theory of effective leadership can be derived that is much more adaptive to the postindustrial age in which we find ourselves.

Note that the work on leadership may support community psychology principles or in the last case be derived explicitly from community psychology theory. The use of the research on leadership can also inform community interventions or the organizations that serve the public.

Reorganization

Several techniques may be employed for changing the whole organization or system; two are examined here. One change strategy is reorganization of the organization. **Reorganization** means that a structural change takes place; that is, the tasks, interpersonal relationships, reward system, or decision-making techniques are rearranged (Beer & Walton, 1990). For example, Hellman et al. (1985) studied residential mental health treatment programs and found that both staff and client perceptions of the program were more negative in the larger organizations. These researchers suggested that the change from three small homes to one large facility may have exacerbated the schizophrenic clients' fears about loss of self. Hellman and colleagues recommended careful review and related research by policy makers before commencing any other similar reorganizations.

Organizations can also be reorganized by becoming linked to, affiliated with, or networked with other organizations. Networks, enabling systems, and umbrella organizations were discussed in an earlier chapter. Suffice it to say here that these "master" organizations help ensure the survival and success of their member organizations. However, competition, lack of coordinating mechanisms, and other factors can diminish the effectiveness of such federations.

Taking the work on reciprocity and interactions into account, there is no such thing as a simple reorganization. The structural changes inherent in such changes should by definition redefine the relationships among the various components and the workers within those components. Bond's (1999) observations of forces opposed to her consultation within an agency are good examples of these kinds of difficulties. The resistance may be in the very basic value systems to which the organization or agency has adhered.

Foster-Fishman and colleagues (2007) provide a systems-based model for examining organizational and community systems. Drawing on the earlier work based on Checkland's (1981) ideas of *soft systems,* Foster-Fishman et al. (2007) gather qualitative data to understand the subjective nature of the system targeted for change and the multiplicity of perspectives that make up the perception of the system. They also use a *system dynamics* theory (Forrester, 1969; Jackson, 2003) to look at feedback and interaction within the system, causes and consequences of action, and what brings about shifts in a system. By studying these patterns, the "levers for change" might be identified. When these levers are activated, the system as a whole changes. They believe that this richer and more complex paradigm provides a true picture of a system at work and helps devise meaningful shifts in what that system is. More linear and simplistic explanatory models lead to the proposal of one component interventions for system change, which by its nature leads to failure or at best serendipitous success. Foster-Fishman argues that systems-level changes may not be always needed, but when they are, an understanding of the various components and how they interact is critical to making changes. The systems theories are helpful to study, understand, and act within this perspective.

Quality of Work Life Programs

Another change that can be made throughout an organization is to introduce **quality of work life (QWL) programs,** or programs of participatory decision making that create long-term change in organizations. Recall that these programs include **participatory decision making,** designed to encourage democracy and staff motivation, satisfaction, and commitment. Such programs also foster career development and leadership by empowering or fostering decision making in others besides the leaders or managers already designated on the organizational chart (Hollander & Offerman, 1990). In QWL programs, the staff and possibly the clients design programs and action plans that they think will be effective and are well reasoned. The programs are then implemented and perhaps funded by higher levels in the organization. Such programs have been shown to be fairly effective in improving organizational productivity as well as employee satisfaction in various settings (Baron & Greenberg, 1990), although others (Labianca, Gray, & Brass, 2000; Randolph, 2000) found that empowerment can be a particularly elusive and resisted concept in many organizations.

Managers of organizations have now come to understand that empowering those under them to participate in decision making in QWL programs is a good idea (French & Bell, 1990). One example of a QWL program is a quality circle. **Quality circles** are small groups of volunteer employees (or volunteer clients of any community service) who meet regularly to identify and solve problems related to organizational conditions. Quality circles are considered to humanize organizational environments as well as to increase participants' satisfaction with the organization (Baron & Greenberg, 1990). A meta-analysis of quality circle studies found that they have a significant though moderate effect on employee performance (Pereira & Osburn, 2007). If Sarah and other employees of Harmony House had participated in a quality circle, they might have realized that they were all discontented with the changes and developed innovative solutions to the organization's problems *before* staff turnover became high.

A second example of the use of quality circles in organizations might be useful. In a rural mental health center, volunteer clients and staff might meet as a quality circle to discuss what to do about the lack of a public transportation system for clients without cars. Together, they could develop some innovative and workable solutions so that clients could more predictably obtain services as needed. Notably, quality circles are a part of "participation and democracy" work practices discussed within the framework of empowerment theory by Klein, Ralls, Smith Major, and Douglas (2000).

Hamilton, Basseches, and Richards (1985) suggested that the number of programs in communities that promote participatory decision making is steadily increasing, but several studies suggest that simply allowing participation in community organizations is hollow and therefore not beneficial. Prestby and colleagues (1990) found that for individuals to continue to participate in block or neighborhood booster associations, benefits (such as getting to know one's neighbors better or learning a new skill like public speaking) have to exceed costs (such as feeling the association never gets anything done or having less time to spend with friends and family). Community organizations need to manage their incentive efforts so that participation by others results in satisfaction. Researchers have shown that although quality circles can improve employee satisfaction and performance, these results are sometimes short-lived. Additionally, they caution that the larger ecological context plays a critical role in the integration of organizational changes (Klein et al., 2000).

Those living with the issues best know how to address them, and quality circles and other participatory methods in organizations take advantage of this fact by empowering involved individuals to solve their own problems. Given the most recent meta-analyses, this concept is supported. Workplace effectiveness does improve (Pereira & Osburn, 2007). This is certainly incentive enough for both organizational and for community psychologists. Yet efforts to change must be considered within the larger system structure and dynamic as cautioned by the ecological considerations of Kelly (1980) and the systems concerns of Jackson (2003) representing community and organizational psychology respectively.

Team Building

One technique for improving groups in organizations is team building. **Team building** is an ongoing method in which group members are encouraged to work together in the spirit of cooperation that contributes to the group's sense of community. The purpose of team building is to *accomplish* goals and analyze tasks, member relations, and processes such as decision making in the group. In other words, the group is simultaneously the object of and a participant in the process. Teams are proving to be such a powerful force for empowerment that they form the basic building block for any intelligent organization (Pinchot & Pinchot, 1993). By means of meta-analysis, team building has been shown to be quite effective (Neuman, Edwards, & Raju, 1989; Svyantek, Goodman, Benz, & Gard, 1999).

Team building—or **team development,** as it is also known (Sundstrom, DeMeuse, & Futrell, 1990)—has been used to improve staff services to clients at mental health agencies (Bendicsen & Carlton, 1990; Cohen, Shore, & Mazda, 1991; Olson & Cohen, 1986) as well as improve the performance of both the corrections officers and staff at forensic (psychiatric) prisons (Miller, Maier, & Kaye, 1988), patients at methadone maintenance clinics (Magura, Goldsmith, Casriel, & Lipton, 1988), teachers (Thatcher & Howard, 1989), nurses at an eating disorders clinic (Sansone, Fine, & Chew, 1988), physicians (Bair & Greenspan, 1986), and staff at other types of service agencies (Davis & Luthans, 1988). Team building also has been successfully used to sensitize multiculturally staffed agencies to the needs of their diverse members (Ratiu, 1986). Some argue, however, that many employees resist teams primarily because of mistrust and low tolerance for change (Kirkman, Jones, & Shapiro, 2000).

The demand for team development consultation in business continues to grow along with research publications defining and explaining the processes (Offerman & Spiros, 2001). Surveying members of the Academy of Management's Organizational Development and Change Division, the authors find the two most often cited goals for training are goal setting and communication. The three areas with least adequate theory for practice are diversity issues, empowerment, and resource management. It is hard not to note that of these three areas, two are directly out of the community psychology lexicon. In turn, note that the issues of team building (i.e., sharing of information, developing common goals, establishment of identity) are clearly skills that come from team building/organizational management studies.

These preceding topics focus on systems-level changes and their potential impact on the larger organization and the individuals within them. They are a type of social change at the community level. Now we examine some ways the combined perspectives of organizational and community psychology might inform how the individual might better cope with the work environment.

HELPING INDIVIDUALS CHANGE WITHIN THE ORGANIZATION

It has already been stated that community psychologists prefer the ecological approach, where the whole system rather than the individual is examined and changed. However, Cowen (1985) has pointed out that a person-oriented, competency-focused approach should also find a place in community interventions. This section discusses how individuals can change, especially in coping with everyday problems instigated by their organizations. Note, however, that this particular level—the individual level—is the one most plagued by failed change efforts (Macy & Izumi, 1993; Shinn & Perkins, 2000).

Burnout and Stress

Burnout and stress are problems in contemporary organizations. Hafen, Karren, Frandsen, and Smith (1996) reported that 46 percent of U.S. workers in 1990 believed their jobs to be highly stressful, and 34 percent had considered quitting their jobs because of job-related stress. Today's organizations need to recognize that burnout and stress are related to organizational conditions rather than merely to an individual's makeup (McCulloch & O'Brien, 1986) or poor coping strategies (Shinn, Morch, Robinson, & Neuer, 1993). Some organizations, though, do little to help their staff cope with organizational stress (Shinn, Lehmann, & Wong, 1984). Organizations need to be involved in interventions, and community psychologists offer a growing literature on what can be done to alleviate these problems in organizations. Traditional organizational interventions for stress in individuals include meditation and relaxation training as well as exercise programs (Ivancevich, Matteson, Freedman, & Phillips, 1990). Such interventions treat the individual and ignore the context in which he or she works. Community psychologists have developed alternative programs, which are showcased next.

Social support from coworkers in the form of modeling various strategies for coping, showing empathy, and giving advice has been demonstrated to be useful in ameliorating the effects of stress and burnout in various community agencies (Bernier, 1998; Turnipseed, 1998). For instance, Kirmeyer and Dougherty (1988) demonstrated that social support for police dispatchers favorably reduces the officers' anxiety. Olson's (1991) research showed that appropriate support provides teachers with acculturation experiences and encourages them to make autonomous decisions. Hirsch and David (1983) and McIntosh (1991) found that social support from other nurses enables nurses to reduce general stress levels and cope better with patient death. Human services workers (Shinn et al., 1984), and more specifically social workers (Himle, Jayertne, & Thyness, 1991; Melamed, Kushnir, & Meir, 1991) also benefit from the social support of coworkers. Broman, Hamilton, and Hoffman (1990), Caplan, Vinokur, Price, and van Ryn (1989), Turner, Kessler, and House (1991), and Zippay (1990–1991) have shown that social support also alleviates the effects of unemployment for terminated employees.

Snow, Swan, and Raghavan (2003) find that a model including both coping style and social support is predictive of stress reactions in secretarial staff. Work stress and work–family conflict contribute to symptoms of stress reactions both emotionally and physically.

Active coping (dealing with the problem) leads to eventual lessening of stress symptoms (anxiety, depression, physical complaint), whereas **avoidance coping** (ignoring the problem, distracting oneself) does not. Having social support increases active coping, which in turn leads to fewer problems. We might surmise that the existence of a good social support system serves to advise the worker on how to solve the work problems. This fits with the resilience models that were described and discussed in Chapter 3.

Cautions are needed here, however. Social support often operates in complex ways in organizational settings (Schwarzer & Leppin, 1991), just as it does elsewhere; for example, group coping and support is often but not always better than individual coping strategies. In some instances, social support can actually worsen the individual's situation (Grossi & Berg, 1991). Similarly, regard must be given to each person's cultural background and what kind of support is most appropriate for that person (Jay & D'Augelli, 1991).

"Mass education" programs on stress management can help employees and community citizens cope with stress. Jason, Curran, Goodman, and Smith (1989) produced a series of television programs on stress and coping. Many viewers reported that they tried the coping methods. Measures of viewer adjustment and well-being showed significant improvement, especially among the most distressed viewers. Organizations can also provide mass education about stress and coping through newsletters, workshops, and trainings.

Quillian-Wolever and Wolever (2003) write on work stress management programs. They note that these programs are based on the extensive research done on stress and coping (see Chapter 3). They propose a framework for the program organization that addresses the multiple layers of the stress reaction: physical, cognitive, emotional, and behavioral. Among the interventions for physical and cognitive coping are exercise with its positive effects on the entire organism (Freeman & Lawlis, 2001); massage therapy, which decreases muscle tension and enhanced immune functions (Zeitlin, Keller, Shiflett, Schleifer, & Bartlett, 2000); relaxation techniques leading to positive changes in several physiological indicators of stress (Cruess, Antoni, Kumar, & Schneiderman, 2000; Freeman, 2001); and meditation with its mental focusing and attendant positive immunological and neurological shifts (Davidson et al., 2003). Many techniques have been incorporated into stress management programs. As mentioned earlier, the durability of these programs over time are more up to question. Quillian-Wolever and Wolever (2003) conceptualize the stress management programs in terms of secondary prevention (dealing with early signs of dysfunction), but describe universal prevention-educational programs for all workers. Nonetheless, the concept of prevention is critical to their model.

Nelson and Simmons (2003) propose that we might consider the eustress (positive reactions) as well as the distress (negative reactions) that come with work situations. Folkman and Moskowitz (2000) have discussed the simultaneous coexistence of positive and negative feelings during times of stress. The suggestion is that both the eustress and distress processes can co-occur and produce these two contradictory affective positions. Simmons (2000) finds that indicators of eustress were having a positive affect (happy, in a good mood) in the work situation, feeling a sense of meaning to one's work, and expressing hope that one can have a positive effect on a given situation. Eustress is believed to be facilitated by optimism, an internal locus of control, and a sense of a coherent/understandable world. Conceptions of stress may therefore better be considered a balance of eustress and distress in a given situation. Prevention of distress and promotion of eustress deal with the concept of stress more holistically according to Nelson and Simmons (2003), For example, Britt, Adler, and Bartone (2001) find that U.S. soldiers who feel there is meaning to their NATO duties in war-ravaged Bosnia are positive about their work. In another similar study of high-stress situations, hospital nurses report both distress and eustress in very demanding work situations (Simmons & Nelson, 2001). Levels of eustress are in turn related to nurses' reports of physical health. Such findings would suggest that dealing with work-related stress may involve helping individuals develop their sense of efficacy in the work situation and their sense of coherence between their self and their work demands. The challenge of interventions, therefore, would be to devise environments that foster the protective and promotive factors for its members.

Health Maintenance Issues: Smoking Cessation Example

Smoking by employees, even when not at the worksite, is troublesome for many reasons, among which are the health-related problems of the smokers, consequent health insurance costs to the organization, and complaints by others affected by secondhand smoke (Milkovich & Boudreau, 1991). In one study, psychologists hoping to reduce employee smoking enlisted participants from 43 different corporations. The smokers participated in a televised smoking cessation program combined with self-help abstinence groups. Compared to other smokers, those in the smoking cessation program reduced their smoking the most (Jason, Gruder, et al., 1987). However, in this study, **recidivism,** or return to the problem behavior—in this case, smoking—remained a dilemma. The conjectured reason for relapse was that worksites can be stressful and thus create the return to smoking.

In a second study, one group of employees received a self-help manual, another received the manual and an incentive to cease smoking, and a third group received the manual, the incentive, and social support. Social support in this study clearly had an effect on both quitting and long-term cessation (i.e., 24 months) (McMahon & Jason, 2000). Therefore, when an organization provides assistance as simple as encouraging support groups, the organization also encourages the well-being of its members. The importance of the support group to the maintenance of healthy behaviors reinforces the power of a supportive social context and the changes in the social ecology within which one functions. This emphasizes the role of community in bringing about change, even in the area of healthy behaviors. Behaviors are not solely the result of individual-based variables.

SUMMARY

Organizational and community psychology are considered by some to be siblings, with common origins in theory and application (Shinn & Perkins, 2000). Organizational psychology focuses on work place sites and community psychology on a wider array of settings. They have much to learn from each other's research literature (Keys, 2007).

Organizations are communities. Just like any community, organizations are comprised of various individuals and groups. Many of today's organizations need humanizing, as do many communities, if they are to enhance the well-being of the individuals in them.

By making today's community agencies and organizations better places in which to work for their staffs, organizations can deliver better services to their clients. The problems facing workers today include (but are not limited to) stress, burnout, repressive organizational cultures, poor environmental conditions, and human resources mismanagement.

Historically, organizations have considered individual employees' characteristics rather than anything organizational to be the root of problems. Traditional techniques for managing problem individuals have been to alter compensation packages, such as pay, or to institute rules and regulations.

Organizations need to change as their needs and those of their employees change. As a system the organization adapts to new contexts and new members. Whether that means the entire system, or subsections within the system, the environment can accommodate to the person, just as the person accommodates to the environment.

Methods for changing the whole organization include reorganization—for example, creating smaller, friendlier agencies from one large one. Another organizational strategy for change is to institute quality of work life programs. These are programs where staff members and perhaps clients participate in planning and designing the changes the organization needs.

Finally, individuals inside the organization bring with them an array of problems that can diminish the effectiveness of the organization. Burnout and stress are two examples. The use of social support from others within the organization is effective in assisting distressed individuals. Wellness programs are also useful for addressing a variety of personal problems individuals bring to work that decrease their ability to serve clients. These and other organizational development techniques have been proven effective according to recent research.

CHAPTER 13

THE FUTURE OF COMMUNITY PSYCHOLOGY

THE ESTABLISHMENT OF INSTITUTIONAL MARKERS

GROWING BEYOND NATIONAL BOUNDARIES

COMMENTARIES

ANSWERING THE PRESENT AND FUTURE NEEDS OF SOCIETY
  Appreciation for Differences and the Search for Compassion
  Environmental Concerns

  Disparities in Opportunity for Health, Education, and Economic Success
  Aging and End of Life

SUMMARY

FINAL REFLECTIONS

We are the dreams of our parents.
—Deborah Iida, Middle Son

Mary's first choice for college was Cambridge University in England. Of course, she was eight years old at the time. When she finally applied to colleges several years later, she did not include Cambridge, but decided to try the American University of Paris. She was accepted. What surprised her parents was her willingness to even consider going away from home, much less away from Wisconsin and the Midwest. She had redefined her boundaries. The normal had expanded beyond her parents' horizons.

What she found in Paris was a student body and a faculty that was equally open to global and multicultural perspectives. They were happy to read novels from around the world as readily as those from the American or British canon. She loved it. The university challenged her and her understanding of the world. She believed she was being prepared for the world in which she would live.

This story matches with other trends in colleges and universities. There have been study abroad programs for a long time, and they are now being used in record numbers. These programs have encouraged travel, exploration of global sites, and the development of an international perspective. At some U.S. colleges, over half of the student body has studied abroad before graduation. One college we know of had students on all the world's continents at one time (including Antarctica). In similar ways, community psychology has grown beyond its original boundaries and we are in areas never imagined by the original Swampscott, Massachusetts, community psychologists. In what ways have we lived the dreams of the founders of the American movement? And in what ways have we gone beyond their horizons?

THE ESTABLISHMENT OF INSTITUTIONAL MARKERS

The dream of a community psychology seems to be born in "distant mists" by now. Yet it is really just a few academic generations away from today that community psychology in the United States was formally born. From a set of ideas and concepts regarding the potential for psychology outside of the office and the laboratory, community psychology has developed a value system, an intervention focus, a skill set, and theories to direct our work in society and our research programs. There is a *Handbook of Community Psychology* (Rappaport & Seidman, 2000), and the *Annual Review of Psychology* publishes community psychology–oriented chapters with regularity (Bloom, 1980; Cowen, 1973; Gesten & Jason, 1987; Heller, 1990; Iscoe & Harris, 1984; Kelly, Snowden, & Munoz, 1977; Kessler & Albee, 1975; Levine et al., 1993; Reppucci, Woolard, & Fried, 1999; Shinn & Toohey, 2003; Sundberg, Snowden, & Reynolds, 1978).

There are research universities producing a volume of published studies in community psychology journals, for instance, the *American Journal of Community Psychology* and *Journal of Community Psychology* (Jason, Pokorny, Patka, Adams, & Morello, 2007). These universities are numbered among the best in the United States (see Table 13.1). Notable among those universities not making the top 10 list for the entire period of the survey but producing more than 1.5 articles per year in the last time period (1995–2004) were University of Maryland at Baltimore, University of Washington, Columbia University, Johns Hopkins University, and Georgia State University.

The existence of graduate programs as cited in Chapter 1 underscores the vitality of the area. If there are graduate programs, there are graduates who have studied community psychology and who identify as community psychologists. The future of community psychology appears established within the infrastructures of psychology as a field, with regard to publications, institutions of higher education, and the products of these institutions, research, and graduates.

What is not so positive regarding these accomplishments is the lack of a clearly community-oriented chapter in the *Annual Review* since 2003. There are other chapters addressing community issues, such as Mays, Cochran, and Barnes (2007) on race, discrimination, and health outcomes, but nothing that takes the community psychology perspective by itself, either as an intervention or as a research topic. In the area of graduate schools, Weinstein (2006) believes the number of identified clinical-community programs to be declining. Is this because there is no longer a need to make the distinction between clinical

TABLE 13.1   Top 15 Universities Publishing in the *American Journal of Community Psychology* and *Journal of Community Psychology*, 1973–2004

1. UCLA
2. Arizona State University
3. University of Illinois, Chicago
4. University of Michigan
5. Vanderbilt University
6. Michigan State
7. University of Rochester
8. University of Illinois, Urbana-Champaign
9. Yale University
10. University of Maryland, College Park
11. University of California, Berkeley
12. DePaul University
13. Pennsylvania State University
14. New York University
15. University of South Carolina

Source: Jason et al. (2007).

and community psychology perspectives, with clinical psychology embracing the concept of prevention and psycho-education, or because there is in fact a lessening interest in social change and the systems-level interventions that would facilitate this change? Or was this an artifact of the historical and political context of the first years of the 21st century in the United States? In this case, shifts in political and social philosophy may bring renewed and greater interests in this area of psychology. What has undoubtedly happened is that community psychology has practitioners across the globe.

GROWING BEYOND NATIONAL BOUNDARIES

Beyond the U.S. borders, community psychology appears to have continued to grow. Among the articles found in the *AJCP* and *JCP* for 2006 through 2008 were research on Italian crime (Amerio & Roccato, 2007), Colombian violence (Brook, Brook, & Whiteman, 2007), Canadian homeless youth (Kidd & Davidson, 2007), stress and the role of religion in dealing with stress in a South African township (Copeland-Linder, 2006), Australian Aboriginal sense of community (Bishop, Colquhoun, & Johnson, 2006), Israeli volunteer burnout (Kulik, 2006), Jamaican attitudes toward mental illness (Jackson & Hetherington, 2006), building support systems for HIV/AIDS management in rural South Africa (Campbell, Nair, & Maimane, 2007), and filial piety and kinship care in Hong Kong (Cheung, Kwan, & Ng, 2006). These articles are representative of the growing international body of community psychology literature. Lorian's (2007) editor's comments for the *Journal of Community Psychology* explicitly mentioned the expanded international composition of the journal's editorial board in a strategic decision to broaden perspectives beyond the United States. There is a text on *Community Psychology and Social Change: Australia and New Zealand*

Perspectives in its second edition (Thomas & Veno, 1996). The Web site for Division 27 of the American Psychological Association (Society for Community Research and Action) states among its goals the promotion of an "international field of inquiry and action" (www.scra27.org, on July 19, 2008). Besides the production of research within U.S. universities, community psychology is being studied in sites around the world. We note that this has come a long way from Swampscott, Massachusetts, where the American version of community psychology traces its birth.

One future trend for community psychology is already well on its way. The field of study and work has crossed boundaries and is well at work in Europe, Africa, Asia, and the Pacific.

The original framers of the community psychology movement in the United States did not directly mention crossing international boundaries. However, Glidewell's (1966) discussion of "social change" anticipated the implications of a "shrinking globe" and what it would mean to our challenges. As

> the population of the world moves about and one value system confronts another value system, as social systems grow in size, specialization and complexity, as the population shifts from rural to metropolitan areas, as mutual expectations become subject to much faster change, inter-personal and inter-group tensions rise. The tension may become a motivating force toward flexibility . . . or inducing emotional confusion and . . . rigidity. . . . Whether the tension provokes one or the other depends upon the capacity of the individual and the social organization to develop innovations. (p. 44).

COMMENTARIES

What would the founders say about our current status and the progress made? What would they hope for the future of community psychology, and what cautions would they provide? Luckily for us, several of the early writers, researchers, and interventionists have provided responses to the present concepts, efforts at practice and research, and the placement of community psychology within psychology as a whole.

Rappaport (2005) has cautioned against becoming too sure as to what was being studied or too set in how it was to be studied. He worries that the quest to be a "science" would lead to doctrinaire approaches of correct and incorrect. He would rather have us remember the role of the community psychologist is to provide a "critical consciousness" to the status quo. Community psychology is where innovation and change could find a home. This means that the methodologies for discovery should be flexible. Having been influenced by Kuhn's schema of scientific revolutions, community psychology by definition is looking for the anomalies in the traditional.

Sarason (2004) cautions that the intervention process is not easily captured in the research literature, and the impression of a clean and linear process can be misleading. He believes the "before-the-beginning" phase of research and intervention development is rich with critical details. Before a project begins, the discussions with colleagues and the contacts with community leaders and community systems are the context that give birth to the eventual social action or research. Kelly et al.'s (2004) description of the long personal history behind his work on community leadership in Chicago captures the kind of complexity of personal and social networks and relationship development that go into a community project. Kelly speaks of the collaborative efforts and the implications of opening conversations regarding his interests in jazz with a key community leader as pivotal to the project's development. Sarason raises the issue of person skills in the community process. He sees the need for relationships that are respectful, concerned, and open to asking questions. This can be described, but can it be trained?

Weinstein (2006) warns about the loss of community psychology's original initiatives. She challenges the field to raise our sights and work on systems-level interventions. Her top social priorities are to deal with "entrenched disparities and perceptions of the other." The disadvantaging differences are sustained because of our perceptions of others as different and by that difference judged to be outsiders and less worthy. These resulting discrepancies can be found in schooling advantages, health treatment opportunities, housing access, economic opportunities, and favoritism in the legal system. They have at their heart a perception of "us" versus the "others" in our society, and how "they" deserve what they have gotten. These structural advantages lead to advantages at the personal level. There are clear advantages to internal locus of control, a sense of efficacy with regard to our destiny, and an agentic attitude (willingness to act). These personal styles are demonstrably associated with favorable placement in a social structure. Contextual and environmental factors facilitate the development of these individual variables. For example, the problems of self-fulfilling prophecy and negative expectations within the school system have led to inequality in schooling. Weinstein therefore argues for intervention within the schools to address these negative expectations.

Fyson (1999), following over 20 years of community work in the schools of Australia, discusses community psychology's efforts to resolve the tension between the One (individual) and the Many (collective). He believes the transformational sense of community can bring together these two extreme positions. It is what Newborough (1995) called the *third position*. Between the "I" and the "they" is the "we." From what we understand of the importance of this perspective, the advantages that accumulate to the in-group, those who are perceived as a part of one's community, the "we," are substantial. The disadvantages of perception as a member of the out-group, those seen as not part of our community, the alien, the "they," are also substantial. Researchers have continued to demonstrate the subtle and blatant ways these differences in membership continue to affect us (Gaertner & Dovidio, 2005).

Snowden (2005) calls for social and community analyses at the level of populations, in what he calls population thinking. From this perspective, population parameters are the level of analysis and focus and the "underlying processes and structures of social change" (p. 3) and maintenance. He cites as an example a study by Sampson, Raudenbush, and Earls (1997), who find collective efficacy to be the variable related to reduced crime in neighborhoods. So it is efficacy and not ethnic minority composition of those neighborhoods that is the critical variable to crime. Snowden argues for the development of prosocial norms and practices as well as constructive traditions and institutions. In this manner, the disparities in our society can be more effectively addressed. The population level of thinking should lead to research uncovering the social mechanisms perpetuating these differences and policy-level solutions. For example, knowing that crime is based on collective efficacy and not on race should direct our interventions.

These are new and exciting ways to reconceptualize the problems of our society. Kelly (2002) warns of the loss of this excitement as the field matures and of the difficulties in maintaining the balance between being a respected science and being constrained by traditional design or methodology. He challenges us to be adventuresome in our research (Tolan et al., 1990, p. xvi) and look for ways we might share this heritage of challenging the status quo. While the field has succeeded in many ways, it must be careful to maintain its spirit of openness and willingness to dissent.

Watts and Serrano-Garcia (2003) present a broad challenge in their call for a "liberating community psychology" engaged in social and political power issues that underlie the community's problems. They conceptualize the typical community concerns over violence, identity, stress, and education in terms of systems of oppression. Fostering an awareness of these systems, the intervention-researchers help groups change these systems. The importance of contexts and the need to create or re-create these contexts are therefore the focus of interventions. The goal is to build systems to promote health as opposed to reacting to problems once they have arisen. De Fatima Qunital de Freitas (2000) states that among the guiding principles of a community psychology in Brazil/Latin America is the realization that "it is clearly political." From an ecological point of view, the acknowledgment of this larger exosystem (Bronfenbrenner, 1979) seems only appropriate.

Cowen (2000) believes in a shift from a risk and prevention model to promotion of growth, competency, and enhancement of life models. The community provides opportunities for successful development and the realization of potential. The focus of a community psychology might be better placed on how various community contexts may foster and develop trajectories for success. Through a better understanding of these trajectories and the factors that help bring them to fruition, our interventions may be positively focused on critical timeframes and the adaptive capacities of communities and its members. Longitudinal studies of the effects of social competence are starting to discern the relationships among childhood competencies and the development of pathology over time (Burt, Obradovic, Long, & Masten, 2008).

For community psychologists to work within the various national or ethnic communities, Sue (2006) focuses on the pragmatics of cultural competency in dealing with the diverse and various groups found within the community. In answer to those who argue that there is no such thing as cultural competency, he offers three general processes. Of the processes, "scientific mindedness" is the tendency to formulate hypotheses based on initial observations rather than conclusions based on group membership, with the hypotheses tested against further observations; "dynamic sizing" is the ability to know when to generalize based on group membership and when to individualize, recognizing the uniqueness of the person or situation; and "culture-specific skills" is the cultural knowledge base for the given group. Sue's work underscores the necessity for cultural competency in mental health settings, noting several decades ago that there are discrepancies in community mental health center use and in treatment outcomes (Sue, 1977). His 2006 article articulates the processes discovered to be necessary to correct these discrepancies.

Kloos (2005) provides fair warning that community psychology must be sure not to become too insular. By having our own journals and our own conferences, we are able to communicate more efficiently with each other, but at the same time we are not exposing our research and program findings to the broader field of psychology nor to the interdisciplinary settings that might find them useful. This is the challenge to community psychology, to continue to be relevant and continue to impact the broad range of areas that impact the health of the community we hope to serve.

This sample of observations relating to the state of the field provides a fairly diverse sampling of community psychologists. Their common challenge to us is to be more ambitious in our thinking and remember our humanity, with all its complexity. There are a variety of systems to which a community psychology can be applied. We have reviewed a number of them. Yet the tendency has been to work on person-oriented programs (Cowen, 1985). After all, there are pressing needs at the personal level, and the outcomes are more immediate. However, the community psychologist perspective requires thinking in terms of both short-term outcomes that demonstrate the usefulness of the paradigm and longer term outcomes, which may be required to bring about systemic evolution. Although there are many environmental demands for quick results, what we all hope for is lasting change. These commentaries all argue for the importance of a long-term relationship with the community. They also call for respect for the community, an understanding of similarities and differences within and between communities, an openness to learning, and a flexibility with regard to our own models and worldviews. A community member once commented that the difference between the community psychologist and others who had come to do research before is that the community psychologist attends neighborhood events and celebrates the successes and commiserates over the sorrows and losses the members experience. The psychologist becomes a part of the community in which she works. So she is not "the professor" from the university, who flies in, hands out surveys, and leaves, but demonstrates her caring, concern, and connection with her community.

Having reviewed the status of current thinking and progress in the field, we turn our attention to areas for future work for community psychologists.

ANSWERING THE PRESENT AND FUTURE NEEDS OF SOCIETY

As communities participate in the definition of what direction to take the interventions (Jason, Keys, et al., 2004), the role of the community psychologist will continue to require the use of our understanding of how communities and systems work. The goal continues to be one of helping groups implement programs and interventions that they determine to be relevant. Though the obvious problems of crime, drug and alcohol abuse, serious mental illness, and the epidemic spread of HIV/AIDS are among the immediate issues facing all communities, we would add the challenges of developing an appreciation for differences; the search for compassion; environmental concerns; disparities in opportunities in education, health, and economics; and the issues around an aging population and end-of-life care. These areas of significant concern warrant further study and possible intervention within the community psychology framework being used in the 21st century.

Christens, Hanlin, and Speer (2007) remind us that we must have a **social imagination**—we must be able to make the connection between the individual's experiences and the social systems that influence those experiences. From this ability to conceive of social systems linked to the personal, we can start to conceptualize community interventions.

Social change (social, economic, political, environmental) is personal change. We have to be able to imagine things differently before we can make things different. Boyd and Bright (2007) write of the potential in shifts of perspective from problem-focused to opportunity-focused research and intervention. Using a participatory research methodology, called the appreciative inquiry technique, they engage poor rural communities in a process of defining problems and opportunities for their area. Appreciative inquiry asks neighborhood members to imagine what a community can do with the strength of its connections to each other and beyond. This is one way of gathering the resources available to a given group. Again, the emphasis is on being able to imagine what can be.

Appreciation for Differences and the Search for Compassion

Differences can make contributions to our success. Different people bring different perspectives and different information to problem-solving situations. This diversity can come from background, experiences, or cultures. We usually associate this diversity with demographic variables, such as ethnicity, social class, geographic origin, or gender. This argument has been made with regard to educational or economic advantages (Bowen & Bok, 2000; Gurin, Nagda, & Lopez, 2004; Page, 2007). We are better informed, more open to differing opinions, and more comfortable with ideas beyond our typical range of thinking as the result of experiences with difference. In the end, this diversity can provide better decision making and more comfort with the pluralistic society found within the United States that is to be expected from expansion to global perspectives. Given that the United States is growing more diverse (U.S. Census, 2004) with projections of ethnic minorities becoming a majority by 2050, such appreciation of diversity is adaptive and far-sighted.

An appreciation of differences challenges the tendency to categorize and exclude based on superficial characteristics, such as physical appearance or demographic variables. This tendency to categorize can lead to advantages for those perceived to be in-group members. The definition of an in-group is based on establishment of shared characteristics (physical appearance, hometown, friends, tasks). Community psychology may have some beneficial perspectives on how these characteristics might be structured into social settings, establishing an appreciation of the differences and a **compassionate** attitude, that is, sharing in others' suffering and willingness to help. We have not seen empathy or compassion as dependent variables in the community literature yet; they would seem to be natural concerns. The area of resilience has a compassionate community implied. Jason and Perdoux (2004) describe compassionate qualities in their text on "havens for community healing." What structural qualities facilitate the appreciation of differences? How can we help generate compassionate communities? At what stage can this occur? In the chapter on resilience, Greenberg et al. (2007) discussed the development of resiliency and emotional intelligence. Could this be brought to bear on community efforts?

Environmental Concerns

Global warming and the waste of natural resources are urgent international issues. The United Nations Framework Convention on Climate Change was entered into on March 21,

1994. Under this convention, governments from around the world entered a joint effort to deal with the problems of greenhouse gases and carbon dioxide. The world's climate was recognized as a natural resource (see unfccc.int/essential_background/convention/items/2627.php; July 31, 2008). The reduction of greenhouse gases is the target for international strategies. What it requires is an overall consciousness regarding renewable resources to power the world.

Increases in energy costs have underscored the necessity of such concerns and brought the immediacy of this topic to prominence. Consumption practices are under discussion, and renewed efforts are being made to modify them. To the rest of the world, this realization may seem late in coming, but psychologically we know that this awareness and willingness to act are based on multiple factors. Community psychology may have some role in helping curb local community and national appetites for consumption of nonrenewable resources and learning to live in a finite world. How do members of the community become more aware? How do we change our behaviors? How are these efforts sustained in a world where we find ourselves highly distractible? Once we have these answers, how do we successfully implement these programs within communities, across a nation, and around the world? There is a lot of work that can occur in regard to placement of, attitudes toward, and practices to optimize the use of mass transit. Attitudes regarding alternative power sources, the construction of networks to support these alternatives, and the building of public will to do that are also important. Lifestyle shifts away from the five-day work week could be studied. The definition of work sites (e.g., home, away from headquarters, distant from other workers) and work times (e.g., midnight to the early morning, staggered hours) could be researched, as well as work practices to adjust to these new definitions to accommodate personal preferences, spreading the load on the transportation infrastructure or global timeframes. Dean and Bush (2007) have described environmental organization processes, identifying five in particular that are relevant to these issues. They are problem analysis, impacting decision making, working on organizational relationships, involving the community, and transferring gained knowledge beyond the organization or project. They believe the community psychology perspective can contribute to all of these processes.

Disparities in Opportunity for Health, Education, and Economic Success

Prelliltensky and Fox (2007) discussed the relationship between wellness and justice. They argued that to feel like one lives in a just society and has been treated justly contributes to one's sense of well-being. **Psychopolitical literacy** is the recognition of this relationship between societal conditions and psychological states. This is in the tradition of Freire's (1970) "pedagogy of the oppressed" mentioned in an earlier chapter.

Weinstein (2006) specifically called for the study of the disparities in our society and mounting interventions to rectify them. These differences are attributed to social, cultural, or institutional barriers to the equality of opportunity. Although the work on disparities is no small task, it is worthy of attention from a discipline that espouses justice and liberation among its principles. This goes beyond the appreciation of diversity. These disparities have historical roots, and shifts in these patterns require patient and persistent efforts at the local and policy levels. There are instances where addressing these disparities requires changes in patterns of power and reexamination of the basic assumptions regarding the social status quo. Beliefs in a just world and in the presence of equal opportunity may be among the basic assumptions to established life that need to be examined and changed. What structural obstacles exist to reduction of disparities? How are these obstacles vulnerable to influence? Community psychology may contribute to answering these questions. Is it a matter of empowerment? If so, Maton (2008) calls on community psychology to use what it has learned about empowering groups to foster these groups and their development. He presented the characteristics of successful empowered groups as having a central belief system, a clear and inspirational purpose, and an opportunity role structure. There needed to be meaningful and engaging tasks for members; core activities that reinforced self-efficacy and skill development; a caring and supportive relational environment; leadership that was inspirational, motivating, had contact with most members, and was empowered to do things; and an organization that was open to learning and had bridges to the external environment (i.e., was not isolated). How might these processes empower more people and bring about the dissolution of social disparities?

Aging and End of Life

Growing old and dying are two of the inevitabilities of life. The population in the United States is aging quickly (He, Segupta, Velkoff, & DeBarros, 2005). U.S. Census estimates reported those over 65 years of age are doubling in numbers from 2000 to 2030. This same report believed that worldwide, there were approximately 420 million people over the age of 65 in 2000. Projections were made for 974 million people over 65 years old in 2030. So the aging of the population is a global phenomenon. These demographic pressures call for attention to the issues of aging. What are the issues of aging? How does staying in a community help? How do we deal with the attendant concerns of death and dying? LaVeist, Sellers, Brown, and Nickerson (1997) reported that extreme isolation for African American women (isolation defined by living alone and not seeing family or friends for over two years) was related to higher likelihood of death within five years. This is after controlling for physical conditions. In a later study of Hong Kong elderly by Cheng, Chan, and Phillips (2004) that combined qualitative interview and quantitative survey data, four factors were found to determine quality of life for this population. These factors were: contributing to society (generativity); good relationships with family and friends; good health; and a comfortable material circumstance. In postsurvey interviews, the importance of interpersonal relationships and health was overwhelmingly endorsed. In a qualitative study of White American elderly, Farquhar (1995) found quality of life to be defined in terms of family, being active, social relationships, health, and material comfort. These community studies consistently emphasize the importance of social contact and social purpose, with noticeably greater significance than the more obvious health and material well-being factors. These studies can be helpful in guiding future programs related to aging. While the field is silent on the topic of death and dying, one wonders if these variables may play a role in the final phase of life, that is, having a good death. The topic of good aging and death and what that means seems quite appropriate for consideration in the context of a community psychology.

SUMMARY

Community psychology has established itself over the past 40 years in many of the formal ways that one expects. There are journals devoted to the topic, a division in the American Psychological Association, and regular contributions made to the *Annual Review of Psychology* and other texts.

Commentary on the present state of the field, made by community psychologists who have been involved with its development, points to the accumulation of professional gains but cautions with regard to the need for social and systems-level interventions, the focus on promotion of well-being as well as the prevention of pathology, the renewal of the spirit of change and revolution, and the reminder that the processes attendant to community change are long, complex, and personally based.

Given the move to empower communities to help in the definition of issues and problems and how research and interventions are to be conducted, the direction of the field in terms of topics is harder to define. The obvious concerns over crime, mental illness, and drug and alcohol abuse are present but tend to tertiary preventions. Potential areas for growth and development that are listed include an appreciation for diversity and the development of compassion, the conservation of our environment and the fostering of lifestyles that are sustainable and environmentally friendly, rectifying social disparities in the many domains where they are found, and the issues of aging and death. Though not exhaustive, these topics appear to have currency in today's society and bring the possibilities of prevention and promotion to our conceptions of community.

FINAL REFLECTIONS

Chapter 1 starts with a quote from *A Tale of Two Cities,* describing the paradoxes that presented themselves, of freedom and order, opportunities for life, and the problems of excess. We search for the balance of our need for individuality and freedom and for affiliation and belonging. We need the freedom to explore and the security of being grounded. Our premise is that psychological health calls for both. Our search for community is an excellent expression of this tension. We are also a science and a practice. We require the science to inform our practice. Our science is a form of practice. This final chapter's commentators recommend we attend to both.

The opening vignette to Chapter 1 presented a story emphasizing the need for community for all people. The following excerpt from the novel *Volcano* by Garrett Hongo expresses the desire for home and community. Hongo speaks of land and a mountain, but in a metaphorical sense, it captures the feeling that community psychology endeavors to create.

> Years later, I was returning to Hawai'i to spend a week.... I stepped off the plane, and when the full blast of the island's erotic and natal wind hit me, when I caught sight of Mauna Loa's[1] purple slopes disappearing into clouds, a sob of gratitude filled my chest.... What

---

[1] Mauna Loa is the largest volcano in the Hawaiian chain, situated on the biggest island in the archipelago.

radiates as knowledge from that time is that there is a beauty in belonging to this earth and to its past. . . . Every singer of every mountain of magnificence in every land knows it. I wish you knowing. I wish you a land.

The land and the mountain are our communities. When we are grounded in them, we are connected to our heritage and our sources of strength. We may wander from that community, but we know when we are back and drawing on all that it can give us. While it is a feeling, we also *know* it. The science of community psychology looks at how the community contributes to our resilience and how it has a hand in shaping us through its contexts. As we have reviewed in this text, science has made progress in discovering the variables of importance, and the psychologists have used them in intervention. There have been both successes and challenges. As we suggest in the opening of this final chapter, the dreams of our founders have been put into action and in some ways gone beyond their vision. But the work is far from complete. There are new dreams to be dreamed and realized. But that is for you, the student, to help determine.

REFERENCES

Aber, J. L., Brooks-Gunn, J., & Maynard, R. A. (1995). Effects of welfare reform on teenage parents and their children. *Critical Issues for Children and Youths, 5,* 53–71.

Abrahams, R. B., & Patterson, R. D. (1978–1979). Psychological distress among the community elderly: Prevalence, characteristics and implications for service. *International Journal of Aging and Human Development, 9,* 1–18.

Abrams, L. S. (2006). Listening to juvenile offenders: Can residential treatment prevent recidivism? *Child and Adolescent Social Work Journal, 23,* 61–85.

Ackerman, G., Anderson, B., Jensen, S., Ludwig, R., Montero, D., Plante, N., et al. (2001). Crime rates and confidence in the police: America's changing attitudes toward crime and policy, 1972–1999. *Journal of Sociology & Social Welfare Special Issues, 28,* 43–54.

Adams, R. E. (1992). Is happiness a home in the suburbs? The influence of urban versus suburban neighborhoods on psychological health. *Journal of Community Psychology, 20,* 353–371.

Adams, R. E., Boscarino, J. A., & Figley, C. R. (2006). Compassion fatigue and psychological distress among social workers: A validation study. *American Journal of Orthopsychiatry, 76,* 103–108.

Administration for Children and Families (2005). Retrieved from www.acf.hhs.gov.

Administration for Children and Families (2006). Retrieved from www.acf.hhs.gov.

Administration for Children and Families (2008). Retrieved from www.acf.hhs.gov.

Agency for Healthcare Research and Quality (2006). *National healthcare disparities report, 2006.* Rockville, MD. Retrieved on July 10, 2008, from www.ahrq.gov/qual/nhdr06/nhdr06.htm.

Alan Guttmacher Institute (2004). *Adolescent pregnancy.* Retrieved from www.nlm.nih.gov/medlineplus/ency/article/001516.

Alan Guttmacher Institute (2006). *Facts on sex education in the United States.* Retrieved from www.guttmacher.org/pubs/fb_sexEd2006.html.

Albee, G. (1982). Preventing psychopathology and promoting human potential. *American Psychologist, 37*(9), 1043–1050.

Albee, George W. (1998). The politics of primary prevention. *Journal of Primary Prevention, 19*(2), 117–127.

Albee, G. W., & Gullotta, T. (Eds.). (1997). *Primary prevention works.* Thousand Oaks, CA: Sage.

Alderson, G., & Sentman, E. (1979). *How you can influence Congress: The complete handbook for the citizen lobbyist.* New York: Dutton.

Alinsky, S. (1971). *Rules for radicals: A practical primer for realistic radicals.* New York: Random House.

Allen, H., & Simonsen, C. E. (1992). *Corrections in America: An introduction.* New York: Macmillan.

Allen, J. P., Seitz, V., & Apfel, N. H. (2007). The sexually mature teen as a whole person: New directions in prevention and intervention for teen pregnancy and parenthood. In A. J. Lawrence, S. J. Bishop-Josef, S. M. McLearn, K. Taaffe, & D. A. Phillips (Eds.), *Child development and social policy: Knowledge for action.* Washington, DC: American Psychological Association.

Allen, N. (2000). Welfare reform and women's poverty: Exploring the need for broader social change. *Community Psychologist, 33,* 11–13.

Allen, N. (2005). A multi-level analysis of community coordinating councils. *American Journal of Community Psychology, 35,* 49–63.

Allen-Meares, P., & Shore, D. A. (1986). A transactional framework for working with adolescents and their sexualities. Special issue: Adolescent sexualities: Overview and principles of intervention. *Journal of Social Work and Human Sexuality, 5,* 71–80.

Allport, G. W. (1954/1979). *The nature of prejudice.* Reading, MA: Addison-Wesley.

Altman, I. (1987). Community psychology twenty years later: Still another crisis in psychology? *American Journal of Community Psychology, 15,* 613–627.

Altman, L. (2008, March 26). Rethinking is urged on vaccine for AIDS. *New York Times.* Retrieved

March 28, 2008, from www.nytimes.com/2008/03/26/health/policy/26HIV.html?ref=research.

Altman, I., & Wandersman, A. (1987). *Neighborhood and community environments*. New York: Plenum Press.

Ambrose, M., Arnaud, A., & Schminke, M. (2008). Individual moral development and ethical climate: The influence of person–organization fit on job attitudes. *Journal of Business Ethics, 77*(3), 323–333.

American Association of University Women (2007). *Behind the pay gap*. Washington, DC: American Association of University Women, Legal Advocacy Fund.

American Legacy Foundation (2008a). *Smoking in the movies*. Retrieved June 13, 2008, from www.americanlegacy.org/70.aspx.

American Legacy Foundation (2008b). *Who we are*. Retrieved June 13, 2008, from www.americanlegacy.org/whoweare.aspx.

American Psychological Association (1985). *Standards for educational and psychological testing* (3rd ed.). Washington, DC: Author.

American Psychological Association. (2005). *Report of the task force on urban psychology: Toward an urban psychology: Research, action, and policy*. Washington, DC: Author.

American Psychological Society (1991). The importance of the citizen scientist in national science policy. *APS Observer, 4*, 10, 12, 23.

American Psychological Society (1992, February). Schooling and literacy. *APS Observer Special Issue: The Human Capital Initiative*, 17–20.

American Youth Policy Forum. (2008). *Some things do make a difference for youth*. Retrieved from Apyf.org/publications.

Amerio, P., & Roccato, M. (2007). Psychological reactions to crime in Italy: 2002–2004. *Journal of Community Psychology, 35*(1), 91–102.

Anderson, J. E., Carey, J. W., & Taveras, S. (2000). HIV testing among the general US population and persons at increased risk: Information from national surveys, 1987–1996. *American Journal of Public Health, 90*, 1089–1095.

Anderson, L., Cooper, S., Hassol, L., Klein, D., Rosenblum, G., & Bennett, C. (1966). *Community psychology: A report of the Boston Conference on the Education of Psychologists for Community Mental Health*. Boston: Boston University.

Angell, R. (April 28, 1980). The sporting scene: A learning spring. *New Yorker*, 47–96.

Ajzen, I. (1985). From intensions to actions: A theory of planned behavior. In J. Kuhl & J. Beckman (Eds.), *Action-control: From cognition to behavior* (pp. 11–39). Heidelberg, Germany: Springer.

Ajzen, I. (1991). The theory of planned behavior. *Organizational Behavior and Human Decision Processes, 50*, 179–211.

Ajzen, I., & Fishbein, M. (Eds.). (1980). *Understanding attitudes and predicting social behavior*. Englewood Cliffs, NJ: Prentice-Hall.

Annas, G. J., & Grodin, M. A. (1998). Human rights and maternal-fetal HIV transmission prevention trials in Africa. *American Journal of Public Health, 88*, 560–563.

Anshel, M. H. (2000). A conceptual model and implications for coping with stressful events in police work. *Criminal Justice & Behavior, 27*, 375–400.

Applebaum, L. D., Lennon, M. C., & Lawrence, A. J. (2006). When effort is threatening: The influence of the belief in a just world on Americans' attitudes toward antipoverty policy. *Political Psychology, 27*, 387–402.

Arias, B. M. (2005). The impact of *Brown* on Latinos: A study of transformation of policy intentions. *Teachers College Record, 107*, 1974–1998.

Armour, M. P., & Umbreit, M. S. (2006). Victim forgiveness in restorative justice dialogue. *Victims & Offenders, 1*, 123–140.

Arnold, D. A., Ortiz, C., Curry, J. C., Stowe, R. M., Goldstein, N. E., Fisher, P. H., et al. (1999). Promoting academic success and preventing disruptive behavior disorders through community partnership. *Journal of Community Psychology, 27*, 589–598.

Aronson, E. (2004). How the Columbine High School tragedy could have been prevented. *Journal of Individual Psychology, 60*, 355–560.

Aronson, E., Blaney, N., Stephan, C., Sikes, J., & Snapp, M. (1978). *The jigsaw classroom*. Beverly Hills: Sage.

Aronson, E., Wilson, T. D., & Akert, R. M. (1999). *Social psychology*. New York: Longman.

Atwater, L., Carey, J., & Waldman, D. (2001). Gender and discipline in the workplace: Wait until your father gets home. *Journal of Management, 27*(5), 537–561.

Auerbach, J. D., Wypijewska, C., & Brodie, H. K. H. (Eds.). (1994). *AIDS and behavior: An integrated approach.* Washington, DC: National Academy Press.

Avert. (2008). Retrieved from http://www.avert.org/abstinence.htm.

Ayers, T., Sandler, I., West, S., & Roosa, M. (1996). A dispositional and situational assessment of children's coping: Testing alternative models of coping. *Journal of Personality, 64,* 923–958.

Baba, Y., & Austin, D. M. (1989). Neighborhood environmental satisfaction, victimization, and social participation as determinants of perceived neighborhood safety. *Environment and Behavior, 21,* 763–780.

Bachrach, L. L. (1989). Deinstitutionalization: A semantic analysis. *Journal of Social Issues, 45,* 161–171.

Backer, T. E., Howard, E. A., & Moran, G. E. (2007). The role of effective discharge planning in preventing homelessness. *Journal of Primary Prevention, 28,* 229–243.

Bagby, W. (1981). *Contemporary American social problems.* Chicago: Nelson-Hall.

Bahr, S. J., Armstrong, A. H., Gibbs, B. G., Harris, P. E., & Fisher, J. K. (2005). The reentry process: How parolees adjust to release from prison. *Fathering, 3,* 243–265.

Bair, J. P., & Greenspan, B. K. (1986). Teamwork training for interns, residents, and nurses. *Hospital and Community Psychiatry, 37,* 633–635.

Baker, J. (1998). Are we missing the forest for the trees? Considering the social context of school violence. *Journal of School Psychology, 36,* 29–44.

Baker, R. A. (1991). Modeling the school dropout phenomenon: School policies and prevention program strategies. *High School Journal, 74,* 203–210.

Bales, R. (1950). *Interaction process analysis: A method for the study of small groups.* Cambridge, MA: Addison-Wesley.

Baltes, M. M., & Baltes, P. B. (Eds.). (1986). *The psychology of control and aging.* Hillsdale, NJ: Erlbaum.

Baltodano, H. M., Platt, D., & Roberts, C. W. (2005). Transition from secure care to the community: Significant issues for youth detention. *Journal of Correctional Education, 56,* 372–388.

Bandura, A. (1977). Self-efficacy: Toward a unifying theory of behavior change. *Psychological Review, 84,* 191–215.

Bandura, A. (1986). *Social foundations of thought and action: A social cognitive theory.* Englewood Cliffs, NJ: Prentice-Hall.

Bandura, A. (1994). Social cognitive theory and exercise of control over HIV infection. In R. J. DiClemente and J. L. Peterson (Eds.), *Preventing AIDS: Theories and methods of behavioral interventions* (pp. 25–29). New York: Plenum.

Bandura, A. (2000, June). Exercise of human agency through collective efficacy. *Current Directions in Psychological Science, 9,* 75–78.

Banyard, V., & Miller, K. (1998). The powerful potential of qualitative research for community psychology. *American Journal of Community Psychology, 26*(4), 485–505.

Banziger, G., & Foos, D. (1983). The relationship of personal financial status to the utilization of community mental health centers in rural Appalachia. *American Journal of Community Psychology, 11,* 543–552.

Barak, G. (1991). *Gimme shelter: A social history of homelessness in contemporary America.* New York: Praeger.

Barker, Roger G. (1965). Explorations in ecological psychology. *American Psychologist, 20,* 1–14.

Baron, R. A., & Greenberg, J. (1990). *Behavior in organizations* (3rd ed.). New York: Allyn & Bacon.

Barrera, M. (2000). Social support research in community psychology. In J. Rappaport & E. Seidman (Eds.), *Handbook of community psychology* (pp. 215–245). New York: Plenum.

Bartunek, J. M., & Betters-Reed, B. L. (1987). The stages of organizational creation. Special issue: Organizational perspectives in community psychology. *American Journal of Community Psychology, 15,* 287–303.

Basso, R. V. J., Graham, J., Pelech, W., De Young, T., & Cardey, R. (2004). Children's street connections in a Canadian community. *International Journal of Offender Therapy and Comparative Criminology, 48,* 189–202.

Bassuk, E. L., & Rosenberg, L. (1988). Why does family homelessness occur? A case-control study. *American Journal of Public Health, 78,* 783–788.

Batson, C. D., Batson, J., Todd, R. M., Brummett, B., Shaw, L., & Aldeguer, C. (1995). Empathy and the collective good: Caring for one of the others in a social dilemma. *Journal of Personality and Social Psychology, 68,* 619–631.

Bauman, Z. (2000). The deficiencies of community. *Responsive Community, 10,* 74–79.

Bayer, R. (1998). The debate over maternal-fetal HIV transmission prevention trials in Africa, Asia, and the Caribbean: Racist exploitation or exploitation of racism. *American Journal of Public Health, 88,* 567–570.

Bayley, B. K., & Andersen, J. D. (2006). Fear of crime among urban American youth. *Journal of Family and Consumer Sciences, 98,* 26–32.

Bazemore, G., Elis, L., & Green, D. L. (2007). The "independent variable" in restorative justice: Theory-based standards for evaluating the impact and integrity of victim sensitive process (Part II). *Victims & Offenders, 2,* 351–373.

Bazemore, G., & Stinchcomb, J. (2004). A civic engagement model of reentry: Involving community through service and restorative justice. *Federal Probation, 68,* 14–24.

Beacon Hill Institute for Public Policy Research (1997, Winter). What charitable organizations have to say about volunteers. *NewsLink,* 1. Summary found online at www.bhi.sclas.suffolk.edu/NewsLink/vln2volun.html.

Beaulieu, M., Dubé, M., Bergeron, C., & Cousineau, M. (2007). Are elderly men worried about crime? *Journal of Aging Studies, 21,* 336–346.

Becker, M. H. (1974). The health belief model and personal health behavior. *Health Education Monographs, 2,* 220–243.

Becker, M. H., & Maiman, L. A. (1980). Strategies for enhancing patient compliance. *Journal of Community Health, 6,* 113–115.

Beer, M., & Walton, E. (1990). Developing the competitive organization. *American Psychologist, 45,* 154–161.

Belcher, J. R. (1988). Are jails replacing the mental health care system for the homeless mentally ill? *Community Mental Health Journal, 24,* 185–195.

Bell, C. C. (2007). Review of Black males left behind. *International Journal of Men's Health, 6,* 167–168.

Belsky, J. (2006). Early child care and early child development: Major findings of the NICHD study of early child care. *European Journal of Developmental Psychology, 31,* 95–110.

Bendicsen, H., & Carlton, S. (1990). Clinical team building: A neglected ingredient in the therapeutic milieu. *Residential Treatment for Children and Youth, 8,* 5–21.

Benjamin, L., & Crouse, E. (2002). The American Psychological Association's response to *Brown versus the Board of Education*: The case of Kenneth B. Clark. *American Psychologist, 57,* 38–50.

Bennett, C. C., Anderson, L. S., Cooper, S., Hassol, L., Klein, D. C., & Rosenblum, G. (1966). *Community psychology: A report of the Boston Conference on the Education of Psychologists for Community Mental Health.* Boston, MA: Boston University and South Shore Mental Health Center.

Bennett, T. (1989). Factors related to participation in neighborhood watch schemes. *British Journal of Criminology, 29,* 207–218.

Benviente, G. (1989). *Mastering the politics of planning: Crafting credible plans and policies.* San Francisco: Jossey-Bass.

Berkeley, S., & Koff, W. (2007). Scientific and policy challenges to development of an AIDS vaccine. *Lancet, 370*(9581), 94–101.

Berkman, L., Glass, T., Brissette, I., and Seeman, T. (2000). From social integration to health: Durkheim in the new millennium. *Social Science and Medicine, 51,* 843–857.

Bernal, G., Trimble, J., Burlew, A. K., & Leong, F. (Eds.) (2003). *Handbook of racial and ethnic minority psychology.* Thousand Oaks, CA: Sage.

Bernier, D. (1998). A study of coping: Successful recovery from severe burnout and other reactions to severe work-related stress. *Work & Stress, 12,* 50–65.

Biegel, D. (1984). Help seeking and receiving in urban ethnic neighborhoods: Strategies for improvement. In J. Rapport, C. Swift, & R. Hess (Eds.), *Studies in empowerment: Steps toward understanding and action.* New York: Haworth.

Biglan, A., Ary, D., Koehn, V., Levings, D., Smith, S., Wright, Z., et al. (1996). Mobilizing positive reinforcement in communities to reduce youth access to tobacco. *American Journal of Community Psychology, 24,* 625–638.

Biglan, A., & Taylor, T. K. (2000). Why have we been more successful in reducing tobacco use than violent crime? *American Journal of Community Psychology, 28,* 269–302.

Bilchik, S. (1998). *1998 report to Congress: Juvenile mentoring program.* Washington, DC: Office of Juvenile Justice and Delinquency Prevention.

Bilchik, S. (1999). *Promising strategies to reduce gun violence.* Washington, DC: Office of Juvenile Justice and Delinquency Prevention.

Bishop, B., Colquhoun, S., & Johnson, G. (2006). Psychological sense of community: An Australian aboriginal experience. *Journal of Community Psychology, 34,* 1–7.

Bishop, B., & Drew, N. (1998). The community psychologist as subtle change agent in the public policy arena. *Community Psychologist, 31,* 20–23.

Blakely, C. H., Mayer, J. P., Gottschalk, R. G., Schmidt, N., Davidson, W. S., Roitman, D. B., et al. (1987). The fidelity-adaptation debate: Implications of the implementation of public sector social programs. *American Journal of Community Psychology, 15,* 253–268.

Blakemore, J. L., Washington, R. O., & McNeely, R. L. (1995). The demography of aging. In P. K. H. Kim (Ed.), *Services to the aging and aged: Public policies and programs.* New York: Garland.

Blaney, N. T., Stephan, C., Rosenfield, D., Aronson, E., & Sikes, J. (1977). Interdependence in the classroom: A field study. *Journal of Educational Psychology, 69,* 139–146.

Blom, G. E. (1986). A school disaster: Intervention and research aspects. *Journal of the American Academy of Child Psychiatry, 25,* 336–345.

Bloom, B. (1980). Social and community interventions. *Annual Review of Psychology, 31,* 111–142.

Bloom, B. L. (1984). *Community mental health: A general introduction.* Monterey, CA: Brooks/Cole.

Bloom, B. L., & Hodges, W. F. (1988). The Colorado Separation and Divorce Program: A preventive intervention program for newly separated persons. In R. Price, E. W. Cowen, R. P. Lorion, & J. Ramos-McKay (Eds.), *14 ounces of prevention.* Washington, DC: American Psychological Association.

Bloom, M. (1987). Toward a technology in primary prevention: Educational strategies and tactics. *Journal of Primary Prevention, 8,* 25–48.

Blustein, D. (2008). The role of work in psychological health and well being: A conceptual, historical and public policy perspective. *American Psychologist, 63,* 228–240.

Bobak, M., Room, R., Pikhart, H., Kubinova, R., Malyutina, S., Pajak, A., et al. (2004). Contribution of drinking patterns in rates of alcohol related problems between three urban populations. *Journal of Epidemiology and Community Health, 58*(3), 238–242.

Bogat, A., & Jason, L. (1997). Interventions in the school and community. In R. T. Ammerman & M. Hersen (Eds.), *Handbook of prevention and treatment with children and adolescents: Intervention in the real world context* (pp. 134–154). New York: Wiley.

Bogat, A., & Jason, L. (2000). Behaviorism and community psychology. In J. Rappaport & E. Seidman (Eds.), *Handbook of community psychology* (pp. 101–114). New York: Kluwer/Plenum.

Boggiano, A. K., & Katz, P. (1991). Maladaptive patterns in students: The role of teachers' controlling strategies. *Journal of Social Issues, 47,* 35–52.

Bolland, J. M., Lian, B. E., & Formichella, C. M. (2005). The origins of hopelessness among inner-city African-American adolescents. *American Journal of Community Psychology, 36,* 293–306.

Bond, G. R., Miller, L. D., & Krumweid, R. D. (1988). Assertive case management in three CMHCs: A controlled study. *Hospital Community Psychiatry, 39,* 411–417.

Bond, G. R., Witheridge, T. F., Dincin, J., & Wasmer, D. (1991). Assertive community treatment: Correcting some misconceptions. *American Journal of Community Psychology, 19,* 41–51.

Bond, G. R., Witheridge, T. F., Dincin, J., Wasmer, D., Webb, J., & DeGraaf-Kaser, R. (1990). Assertive community treatment for frequent users of psychiatric hospitals in a large city: A controlled study. *American Journal of Community Psychology, 18,* 865–891.

Bond, M. (2004). Gender, race, and class in organizational contexts. *American Journal of Community Psychology, 27*(3), 327–355.

Bond, M. A. (1990). Defining the research relationship: Maximizing participation in an unequal world. In P. Jolan, C. Keep, F. Chertok, & L. Jason (Eds.), *Research community psychology: Issues of theory and methods* (pp. 183–184). Washington, DC: American Psychological Association.

Bond, M. A. (1998). Social policy, prevention, and inter-organizational linkages. *Community Psychologist, 31,* 3–6.

Bond, M. A., & Harrell, S. (2006). Diversity challenges in community research and action: The story of a special issue of AJCP. *American Journal of Community Psychology, 37,* 157–165.

Bond, M. A., Hill, J., Mulvey, A., & Terenzio, M. (2000). Weaving feminism and community psychology: An introduction to a special issue. *American Journal of Community Psychology, 28,* 585–597.

Bonhomme, J., Stephens, T., & Braithwaite, R. (2006). African-American males in the United States prison system: Impact on family and community. *Journal of Men's Health & Gender, 3,* 223–226.

Bootzin, R. R., Shadish, W. R., & McSweeney, A. J. (1989). Longitudinal outcomes of nursing home care for severely mentally ill patients. *Journal of Social Issues, 45,* 31–48.

Borum, R. (2000). Improving high risk encounters between people with mental illness and the police. *Journal of the American Academy of Psychiatry & Law, 28,* 332–337.

Bouey, P. D., Duran, B., Henrickson, M., Wong, F. Y., Haviland, L., Sember, R. E., & Lo, W. (1997). A cultural competent model for HIV care: A conceptual framework for the collaborative evaluation of HIV services and care programs. Unpublished document (originally prepared for Ryan White CARE Act's Special Projects of National Significance, National Multi-Site Evaluation Program).

Bowen, W., & Bok, D. (2000), *The shape of the river: Long term consequences of considering race in university and college admissions.* Princeton: Princeton University Press.

Bowman, L. S., Stein, R. E. K., & Ireys, H. T. (1991). Reinventing fidelity: The transfer of social technology among settings. *American Journal of Community Psychology, 19,* 619–639.

Boyd, N., & Bright, D. (2007). Appreciative inquiry as a mode of action research for community psychology. *Journal of Community Psychology, 35*(8), 1019–1036.

Boyd-Zaharias, J. (1999, Summer). Project star. *American Educator,* 30–36.

Bracey, G. W. (2006). Locked up, locked out. *Phi Delta Kappan, 88,* 253–254.

Bradshaw, T. K. (1999). The community development society. *The Community Psychologist, 32,* 9–10.

Bradshaw, W., & Roseborough, D. (2005). Restorative justice dialogue: The impact of mediation and conferencing on juvenile recidivism. *Federal Probation, 69,* 15–21.

Branson, R. K. (1998). Teaching centered schooling has reached its upper limit: It doesn't get any better than this. *Current Directions in Psychological Science, 7,* 126–135.

Bravo, M., Rubio-Stipec, M., Canino, G. J., Woodbury, M. A., & Ribera, J. C. (1990). The psychological sequelae of disaster stress prospectively and retrospectively evaluated. *American Journal of Community Psychology, 18,* 661–680.

Breakey, W. R. (1996). *Integrated mental health services: Modern community psychiatry.* New York: Oxford University Press.

Brewer, M. B. (1999). The psychology of prejudice: Ingroup love or outgroup hate? *Journal of Social Issues Special Issue: Prejudice and Intergroup Relations, 55,* 429–444.

Brissette, I., Scheier, M., & Carver, C. (2002). The role of optimism in social network development, coping and psychological adjustment during a life transition. *Journal of Personal and Social Psychology, 82,* 102–111.

Britt, C. L. (2000). Health consequences of criminal victimization. *International Review of Victimology, 8,* 63–73.

Britt T., Adler, A., & Bartone, P. (2001). Deriving benefits from stressful events: The role of engagement in meaningful work and hardiness. *Journal of Occupational Health Psychology, 6,* 53–63.

Brodsky, A., Senuta, K., Weiss, C., Marx, C., Loomis, C., Arteaga, S., Moore, H., Benhorin, R., & Castagnera-Fletcher, A. (2004). When one plus one equals three: The role of relationships and context in community research. *American Journal of Community Psychology, 33,* 229–241.

Broman, C. L., Hamilton, V. L., & Hoffman, W. S. (1990). Unemployment and its effects on families: Evidence from a plant closing study. *American Journal of Community Psychology, 18,* 643–659.

Bronfenbrenner, U. (1977). Toward an experimental ecology of human development. *American Psychologist, 32,* 513–531.

Bronfenbrenner, U. (1979). *The ecology of human development: Experiments by nature and design.* Cambridge, MA: Harvard University Press.

Bronfenbrenner, U. (1986, February). Alienation and the four worlds of childhood. *Phi Delta Kappan,* 430–436.

Bronfenbrenner, U. (1999). Environments in developmental perspective: Theoretical and operational models. In S. L. Friedman & T. D. Wachs (Eds.), *Measuring environment across the life span:*

Emerging methods and concepts. Washington, DC: American Psychological Association.

Brook, J., Brook, D., & Whiteman, M. (2007). Growing up in a violent society: Longitudinal predictors of violence in Colombian adolescents. *American Journal of Community Psychology, 40*(1–2), 82–95.

Brooks, E. R., Zuniga, M., & Penn, N. E. (1995) The decline of public mental health in the United States. In C. V. Willie, P. P. Rieker, B. M. Kramer, & B. S. Brown (Eds.), *Mental health, racism, and sexism* (pp. 51–117). Pittsburgh, PA: University of Pittsburgh Press.

Brosnan, M. J., & Thorpe, S. J. (2006). An evaluation of two clinically-derived treatments for technophobia. *Computers in Human Behavior, 22,* 1080–1095.

Broussard, A. C., Mosley-Howard, S., & Roychoudhury, A. (2006). Using youth advocates for mentoring at-risk students in urban settings. *Children & Schools, 28,* 122–127.

Brown, B. B., Perkins, D. D., & Brown, G. (2003). Place attachment in a revitalizing neighborhood: Individual and block levels of analysis. *Journal of Environmental Psychology, 23,* 259–271.

Brown, B. B., Perkins, D. D., & Brown, G. (2004). Incivilities, place attachment, and crime: Block and individual effects. *Journal of Environmental Psychology, 24,* 359–371.

Bruce, M. L., Takeuchi, D. T., & Leaf, P. J. (1991). Poverty and psychiatric status: Longitudinal evidence from the New Haven Epidemiologic Catchment Area Study. *Archives of General Psychiatry, 48,* 470–474.

Bruce, M., & Thornton, M. (2004). It's my world? Exploring Black and White perceptions of personal control. *Sociological Quarterly, 45,* 597–612.

Buckner, J. C. (1988). The development of an instrument to measure neighborhood cohesion. *American Journal of Community Psychology, 16,* 771–791.

Bullis, M., Yovanoff, P., & Havel, E. (2001). The importance of getting started right: Further examination of the facility-to-community transition of formerly incarcerated youth. *The Journal of Special Education, 38,* 80–94.

Bureau of Justice Statistics. (1993). *Highlights from 20 years of surveying crime victims.* Washington, DC: U.S. Department of Justice.

Bureau of Justice Statistics (2006). *Criminal victimization.* Retrieved from www.ojp.usdoj.gov/bjs/abstract/cv06.htm.

Bureau of Justice Statistics (2007). *Correctional authorities reported more than 6,000 allegations of sexual violence in prisons and jails during 2006.* Retrieved from www.ojp.usdoj.gov/bjs/pub/press/svrca06pr.htm.

Bureau of Justice Statistics (2008). *Probation and parole statistics.* Retrieved from www.ojp.usdoj.gov/bjs/pandp.htm.

Bureau of Labor Statistics (2007). *Employment characteristics of families summary.* Retrieved from www.bls.gov/news.release/famee.nr0.htm.

Bureau of National Affairs (1981). Job absence and turnover control. *Personnel Forum Survey no. 132.* Washington, DC: Author.

Burroughs, S. M., & Eby, L. T. (1998). Psychological sense of community at work: A measurement system and exploratory framework. *Journal of Community Psychology, 26,* 509–532.

Burt, K., Obradovic, J., Long, J., & Masten, A. (2008). The interplay of social competence and psychopathology over 20 years: Testing transactional and cascade models. *Child Development, 79*(2), 359–374.

Burt, M. R., Pearson, C., & Montgomery, A. E. (2007). Community-wide strategies for preventing homelessness: Recent evidence. *Journal of Primary Prevention, 23,* 213–228.

Burton, C. E. (2004). Segregation and Latino homicide victimization. *American Journal of Criminal Justice, 29,* 21–36.

Butcher, K., Sallis, J., & Mayer, J. (2008). Correlates of physical activity guideline compliance for adolescents in 100 U.S. cities. *Journal of Adolescent Health, 42,* 360–368.

Byrne, J. M. (2004). Introduction: Reentry—the emperor's new clothes. *Federal Probation, 69,* 1–2.

Byrne, J. M., & Taxman, F. S. (2004). Targeting for reentry: Inclusion/exclusion criteria across eight model programs. *Federal Probation, 68,* 53–61.

Cadena, B., Danziger, S., & Seefeldt, K. (2006). Measuring state welfare policy changes: Why don't they explain caseload and employment outcomes? *Social Science Quarterly, 87,* 798–807.

Caldwell, C. H., Kohn-Wood, L. P., Schmeelk-Cone, K. H., Chavous, T. M., & Zimmerman, M. A. (2004). Racial discrimination and racial identity as risk or protective factors for violent behaviors in African American young adults. *American Journal of Community Psychology, 33,* 91–105.

Campaign for Our Children. (2001). *About Campaign for Our Children*. Retrieved from www.cfoc.org.

Campbell, C., & Murray, M. (2004). Community health psychology: Promoting health analysis and action for social change. *Journal of Health Psychology, 9,* 187–195.

Campbell, C., Nair, Y., & Maimane, S. (2007). Building contexts that support effective community responses to HIV/AIDS: A South African case study. *American Journal of Community Psychology, 39,* 347–363.

Campbell, D., & Stanley, J. (1963). *Experimental and quasi-experimental designs for research.* Chicago: Rand McNally.

Campbell, R., Baker, C. K., & Mazurek, T. L. (1998). Remaining radical? Organizational predictors of rape crisis centers' social change initiatives. *American Journal of Community Psychology, 26,* 457–483.

Campbell, R. & Wasco, S. (2000). Feminist approaches to social science: Epistemological and Methodological tenets. *American Journal of Community Psychology, 28*(6), 773–791.

Campfield, K. M., & Hills, A. M. (2001). Effect of timing of critical incident stress debriefing on post-traumatic symptoms. *Journal of Posttraumatic Stress Special Issue, 14,* 327–340.

Cantelon, S., & LeBoeuf, D. (1997, June). Keeping young people in school. Community programs that work. *Juvenile Justice Bulletin,* 1–9.

Caplan, G. (1964). *Principles of preventive psychiatry.* New York: Basic Books.

Caplan, G. (1989). Recent developments in crisis intervention and the promotion of support service. *Journal of Primary Prevention, 10,* 3–25.

Caplan, N., Morrison, A., & Stambaugh, R. J. (1975). *The use of social science knowledge in policy decisions at the national level: A report to respondents.* Ann Arbor: Institute for Social Research, University of Michigan.

Caplan, R. D., Vinokur, A. D., Price, R. H., & van Ryn, M. (1989). Job seeking, reemployment, and mental health. *Journal of Applied Psychology, 74,* 759–769.

Caputo, R. K. (2003). Head Start, other preschool programs, and life success in a youth cohort. *Journal of Sociology & Social Welfare, 30,* 105–126.

Caputo, R. K. (2004). The impact of intergenerational Head Start participation on success measures among adolescent children. *Journal of Family and Economic Issues, 25,* 199–223.

Carbonell, J. (2003). *Baby boomers at the gate: Enhancing independence through innovation and technology.* U.S. Department of Health and Human Services. Retrieved January 10, 2006, from www.hhs.gov.asl.testify/t030520.html.

Carleton, R., Lasater, T., Assaf, A., Feldman, H., & McKinlay, S. (1995). The Pawtucket Heart Health Program: Community changes in cardiovascular risk factors and projected disease risk. *American Journal of Public Health, 85,* 777–785.

Carmony, T., Lock, T., Crabtree, A., Keller, J., Yanasak, B., & Moritsugu, J. (2000). Teaching community psychology: A brief review of undergraduate courses. *Teaching of Psychology, 27,* 214–215.

Carnevale, P. J., & Pruitt, D. G. (1992). Negotiation and mediation. *Annual Review of Psychology, 43,* 531–582.

Carver, C. S., Scheier, M. F., & Weintraub, J. K. (1989). Assessing coping strategies: A theoretically based approach. *Journal of Personality and Social Psychology, 56*(2), 267–283.

Cascio, W. (1995). Whither industrial and organizational psychology in a changing world of work? *American Psychologist, 50,* 928–939.

Case, S., & Haines, L. (2007). Offending by young people: A further risk factor analysis. *Security Journal, 20,* 96–110.

Caspi, A., Taylor, A., Moffitt, T. E., & Plomin, R. (2000). Neighborhood deprivation affects children's mental health: Environmental risks identified in a genetic design. *Psychological Science, 11,* 338–342.

Cassinerio, C., & Lane-Garon, P. S. (2006). Changing school climate one mediator at a time: Year-one analysis of a school-based mediation program. *Conflict Resolution Quarterly, 23,* 447–460.

Casswell, S. (2000). A decade of community action research. *Substance Use & Misuse Special Issue: Community Action and the Prevention of Alcohol-Related Problems at the Local Level, 35,* 55–74.

Catterall, J. S., & Stern, D. (1986). The effects of alternative school programs on high school completions and labor market outcomes. *Educational Evaluation and Policy Analysis, 8,* 77–86.

Cauce, A. (1990). A cautionary note about adventuresome research: Musings of a junior researcher. In P. Tolan, C. Keys, F. Chertok, & L. Jason (Eds.), *Researching community psychology: Issues of theory and methods* (p. 205). Washington, DC: American Psychological Association.

Caughy, M., O'Campus, P., & Brodsky, A. (1999). Neighborhoods, families and children: Implications for policy and practice. *Journal of Community Psychology, 27,* 615–633.

Center on Philanthropy (2001, April 18). *Report on the December 2000 Philanthropic Giving Index.* Retrieved from www.philanthropy.IUPUI.edu.

Centers for Disease Control and Prevention (1996). *State behavioral risk factor surveillance system, 1993* [data tape]. Atlanta, GA: Author.

Centers for Disease Control and Prevention (1999). *Teen pregnancy.* Retrieved from www.cdc.gov/nccdphp/teen.htm.

Centers for Disease Control and Prevention (2000). *CDC fact book 2000/2001.* Atlanta, GA: Author.

Centers for Disease Control and Prevention (2004). *HIV/AIDS surveillance report.* Vol. 16. Atlanta, Georgia: US Department of Health and Human Services, CDC; 2005. Retrieved from http://www.cdc.gov/hiv/topics/surveillance/resources/reports/2004report/default.htm.

Centers for Disease Control and Prevention (2004). *Report to Congress: Prevention of genital human papillomavirus infection.* Atlanta, GA: Author.

Centers for Disease Control and Prevention (2006). Epidemiology of HIV/AIDS United States, 1981–2004, *MMWR Weekly,* June 2, 2006 / 55(21); 589–592. Retrieved from cdc.gov/mmwr/preview/mmwrhtml/mm5521a2.htm.

Centers for Disease Control and Prevention (2006). *HIV/AIDS Surveillance Report,* vol. 18. Atlanta, GA: Department of Health and Human Services.

Centers for Disease Control and Prevention (2007a). *Adolescent reproductive health: Teen pregnancy.* Retrieved from www.cdc.gov/reproductivehealth/adolescentreprohealth.

Centers for Disease Control and Prevention (2007b). *CDC fact sheet: The role of STD prevention and treatment in HIV prevention.* Atlanta, GA: Department of Health and Human Services.

Centers for Disease Control and Prevention (2007c, Summer). Child maltreatment. *Facts at a Glance,* 1.

Chadee, D., Austen, L., & Ditton, J. (2007). The relationship between likelihood and fear of criminal victimization: Evaluating risk sensitivity as a mediating concept. *British Journal of Criminology, 47,* 133–153.

Chaffin, M. (2004). Is it time to rethink Healthy Start/Healthy Families? *Child Abuse & Neglect, 28,* 589–595.

Chan, C. K. (2004). Placing dignity at the center of welfare policy. *International Journal of Social Work, 47,* 227–239.

Chanley, V. A., Rudolph, T. J., & Rahn, W. M. (2000). The origins and consequences of public trust in government. *Public Opinion Quarterly, 54,* 239–256.

Chapman, J., & Ferrari, J. (1999). An introduction to community based service learning. In J. Ferrari & J. Chapman (Eds.), *Educating students to make a difference: Community based service learning* (pp. 1–3). New York: Haworth Press.

Chapman, L. (2007). Closing thoughts. *American Journal of Health Promotion, 21,* 8.

Charkoudian, L. (2005). A quantitative analysis of the effectiveness of community mediation in decreasing repeat police calls for service. *Conflict Resolution Quarterly, 23,* 87–98.

Chatman, J., & Spataro, S. (2005). Using self-categorization theory to understand relational demographic based variations in people's responsiveness to organizational culture. *Academy of Management Journal, 48,* 321–331.

Chavis, D. M. (1993). A future for community psychology practice. *American Journal of Community Psychology, 21,* 171–183.

Chavis, D. M., Florin, P., & Felix, M. R. J. (1992). Nurturing grass roots initiatives for community development: The role of enabling systems. In T. Mizrahi & J. Morrison (Eds.), *Community organization and social administration: Advances, trends, and emerging principles.* Binghamton, NY: Haworth.

Chavis, D. M., Stucky, P. E., & Wandersman, A. (1983). Returning research to the community: A relationship between scientist and citizen. *American Psychologist, 38,* 424–434.

Chavis, D. M., & Wandersman, A. W. (1990). Sense of community in the urban environment: A catalyst for participation and community development. *American Journal of Community Psychology, 18,* 55–82.

Checkland, P. (1981). *Systems thinking: Systems practice.* Wiley: Chichester.

Cheng, S. (1990). Change processes in the professional bureaucracy. *Journal of Community Psychology, 18,* 183–193.

Cheng, S., Chan, A., & Phillips, D. (2004). Quality of life in old age: An investigation of well older persons in Hong Kong. *Journal of Community Psychology, 32*(3), 309–326.

Cherniss, C. (1999). Training in cultural competence: A survey of graduate programs in community research and action. *Community Psychologist, 32,* 22–23.

Chesson, H., Gift, T. L., & Pulver, A. L. S. (2004). The economic value of reductions in gonorrhea and syphilis incidence in the United States, 1990–2003. *Preventive Medicine, 43,* 411–415.

Cheung, C., Kwan, A., & Ng, S. (2006). Impacts of filial piety on preference for kinship versus public care. *Journal of Community Psychology, 34,* 617–634.

Cheung, F. M. C. (1986). Psychopathology among Chinese people. In M. H. Bond (Ed.), *The psychology of the Chinese people.* New York: Oxford University Press.

Cheung, F. M. (1988). Surveys of community attitudes toward mental health facilities: Reflections or provocations? *American Journal of Community Psychology, 16,* 877–882.

Child Welfare Information Gateway. (2006). *Child abuse and neglect fatalities: Statistics and interventions.* Retrieved from www.childwelfare.gov/pubs/factsheets/fatality.cfm.

Children's Aid Society. (2008). *The Carrera Program.* Retrieved from www.childrensaidsociety.org/youthdevelopment/carrera/components.

Chin, J. J., & Wong, F. Y. (2003). Improving access to care for cultural, linguistic and racial minorities: The Bilingual Peer Advocate Program of the Asian & Pacific Islander Coalition on HIV/AIDS. In J. Erwin, D. Smith, & B. S. Petersee (Eds.), *Ethnicity and HIV.* International Medical Press.

Chipperfield, J. (1993). Perceived barriers in coping with health problems: A twelve-year longitudinal study of survival among elderly individuals. *Journal of Aging and Health, 5,* 123–139.

Choi K-H., & Coates, T. J. (1994). Prevention of infection. *AIDS, 8,* 1371–1389.

Choi, N. G., & Wodarski, J. S. (1996). The relationship between social support and health status of elderly people: Does social support slow down physical and functional deterioration? *Social Work Research, 20,* 52–63.

Christens, B., Hanlin, C., & Speer, P. (2007). Getting the social organism thinking: Strategy for systems change. *American Journal of Community Psychology, 39*(3-4), 229–238.

Christensen, J. A., & Robinson, J. W. (1989). *Community development in perspective.* Ames: Iowa State University Press.

Christensen, L. (1988). Deception in psychological research. *Personality and Social Psychology Bulletin, 14,* 664–675.

Christenson, S. L., & Thurlow, M. L. (2004). School dropouts: Prevention considerations, interventions, and challenges. *Current Directions in Psychological Science, 13,* 36–39.

Christian, T. F. (1986). A resource for all seasons: A state-wide network of community dispute resolution centers. In J. Palenski & H. Launer (Eds.), *Mediation: Contexts and challenges.* Springfield, IL: Thomas.

Christie, C. A., Jolivette, K., & Nelson, M. (2007). School characteristics related to high school dropout rates. *Remedial and Special Education, 28,* 325–339.

Cicchetti, D. (2007). Intervention and policy implications of research on neurobiological functioning in maltreated children. In L. J. Aber, S. J. Bishop-Josef, S. M. Jones, K. Taffe, & D. A. Phillips (Eds.), *Child development and social policy: Knowledge for action.* Washington, DC: American Psychological Association.

Cicchetti, D., Toth, S. C., & Rogosch, F. A. (2000). The development of psychological wellness in maltreated children. In D. Cicchetti & J. Rappaport (Eds.), *The promotion of wellness in maltreated children and adolescents.* Washington, DC: Child Welfare League of America.

Cicchetti, D., & Valentino, K. (2006). An ecological-transactional perspective on child maltreatment: Failure of the average expectable environment and its influence on child development. In D. Cichetti & D. J. Cohen (Eds.), *Developmental psychopathology.* Hoboken, NJ: Wiley.

Clark, K. B., & Clark, M. P. (1947). Racial identification and preference in Negro children. In T. M. Newcomb & E. L. Hartley (Eds.), *Readings in social psychology.* New York: Holt.

Clark, R., Anderson, N., Clark, V., & Williams, D. (1999). Racism as a stressor for African Americans: A biopsychosocial model. *American Psychologist, 54,* 805–816.

Clary, E. G., & Snyder, M. (1999). The motivations to volunteer: Theoretical and practical considerations.

Current Directions in Psychological Science, 8, 156–160.

Cock, K., Mbori-Ngacha, D., & Marum, E. (2002). Shadow on the continent: Public health and HIV/AIDS in Africa in the 21st century. *Lancet, 360,* 67–72.

Coffee, J. N., & Pestridge, S. (2001, May). The career academy concept. *OJDP Fact Sheet,* 1–2.

Cohen, J. (2007). AIDS research: Promising AIDS vaccine's failure leaves field reeling. *Science, 318*(5847), 28–29.

Cohen, M. D., Shore, M. F., & Mazda, N. A. (1991). Development of a management training program for state mental health program directors. Special issue: Education in mental health administration. *Administration and Policy in Mental Health, 18,* 247–256.

Cohen, S., & Wills, T. (1985). Stress, social support and the buffering hypothesis. *Psychological Bulletin, 98,* 310–357.

Coleman, J. (1999). Social capital in the creation of human capital. In P. Dasgupta & I. Serageldin (Eds.), *Social capital: A multifaceted perspective* (pp. 13–39). Washington, DC: World Bank.

Coleman, R., & Widon, C. (2004). Childhood abuse and neglect and adult intimate relationships: A prospective study. *Child Abuse and Neglect, 28,* 1133–1151.

Coley, R. L., & Chase-Lansdale, P. L. (1998). Adolescent pregnancy and parenthood. *American Psychologist, 53,* 152–166.

Coley, R. L., Kuta, A., & Chase-Lansdale, P. L. (2000). An insider view: Knowledge and opinions of welfare from African American girls in poverty. *Journal of Social Issues Special Issue: The Impact of Welfare Reform, 56,* 707–726.

Coley, R. L., Lohman, B. J., Votruba-Drzal, E., Pittman, L. D., & Chase-Lansdale, P. L. (2007). Maternal functioning, time and money: The world of work and welfare. *Children and Youth Services Review, 29,* 721–741.

Colman, R., & Widom, C. (2004). Childhood abuse and neglect and adult intimate relationships: A prospective study. *Child Abuse & Neglect, 28,* 1133–1151.

Compas, B. (2006). Psychobiological processes of stress and coping: Implications for resilience in children and adolescents—comments. *Annals of the New York Academy of Sciences, 1094,* 226–234.

Compas, B. E., Connor-Smith, J. K., Saltzman, H., Thomsen, A. H., & Wadsworth, M. (2001). Coping with stress during childhood and adolescence: Progress, problems, and potential. *Psychological Bulletin, 127,* 87–127.

Compas, B. E., Wagner, B. M., Slavin, L. A., & Vannatta, K. (1986). A prospective study of life events, social support, and psychological symptomatology during the transition from high school to college. *American Journal of Community Psychology, 14,* 241–257.

Connors, M. M., & McGrath, J. W. (1997). The known, unknown, and unknowable in AIDS research in anthropology. *Anthropology Newsletter, 38,* 1–5.

Cook, S. W. (1985). Experimenting on social issues: The case of school desegregation. *American Psychologist, 47,* 452–460.

Cook, T.D., & Shadish, W. R. (1986). Program evaluation: The worldly science. *Annual Review of Psychology, 37,* 193–232.

Cook, T. D., & Shadish, W. R. (1994). Social experiments: Some developments over the past fifteen years. In L. W. Porter & M. R. Rosenzweig (Eds.), *Annual review of psychology.* Palo Alto, CA: Annual Reviews.

Cooper, J. (2006). The digital divide: The special case of gender. *Journal of Computer Assisted Learning, 22,* 320–334.

Copeland-Linder, N. (2006). Stress among black women in a south African township: The protective role of religion. *Journal of Community Psychology, 34*(5), 577–599.

Corcoran, J., & Pillai, V. K. (2007). Effectiveness of secondary pregnancy prevention programs: A meta-analysis. *Research on Social Work Practice, 17,* 5–18.

Cordner, G. W. (2000). A community policing approach to persons with mental illness. *Journal of the American Academy of Psychiatry & the Law, 28,* 326–331.

Coulton, C. J., Korbin, J. E., & Su, M. (1996). Measuring neighborhood context for young children in an urban area. *American Journal of Community Psychology, 24,* 5–32.

Coulton, C. J., Korbin, J., & Su, M. (1999). Neighborhoods and child maltreatment: A multi-level study. *Child Abuse & Neglect, 23,* 1019–1040.

Cowen, E. (1973). Social and community interventions. *Annual Review of Psychology, 24,* 423–472.

Cowen, E. L. (1980). The wooing of primary prevention. *American Journal of Community Psychology, 8,* 258–284.

Cowen, E. L. (1985). Person-centered approaches to primary prevention in mental health: Situation-focused and competence-enhancement. *American Journal of Community Psychology, 13*(1), 31–48.

Cowen, E. (1991). In pursuit of wellness. *American Psychologist. 46,* 404–408.

Cowen, E. L. (1996). The ontogenesis of primary prevention: Lengthy strides and stubbed toes. *American Journal of Community Psychology, 24,* 235–249.

Cowen, E. L. (1997a). The coming of age of primary prevention research: Comments on Durlak and Wells's meta-analysis. *American Journal of Community Psychology, 25,* 153–167.

Cowen, E. L. (1997b). On the semantics and operations of primary prevention and wellness enhancement (or will the real primary prevention please stand up?). *American Journal of Community Psychology, 25,* 245–255.

Cowen, E. (2000). Community psychology and routes to psychological wellness. In J. Rappaport and E. Seidman (Eds.), *Handbook of community psychology* (pp. 79–99). New York: Kluwer/Plenum.

Cowen, E. L., Hightower, A. D., Pedro-Carroll, J. L., Work, W. C., Wyman, P. A., & Haffey, W. G. (1996). *School-based prevention for children at risk.* Washington, DC: American Psychological Association.

Crockett, L., Iturbide, M., Torres-Stone, R., McGinley, M., Raffaelli, M., & Carlo, G. (2007). Acculturative stress, social support and coping: Relations to psychological adjustment among Mexican American college students. *Cultural Diversity and Ethnic Minority Psychology, 13,* 347–355.

Cromartie, S. P. (2007, July/August). Labor force status of families: A visual essay. *Monthly Labor Review, 130*(7), 35–41.

Crosby, R. A., & Holtgrave, D. R. (2005). The protective value of social capital against teen pregnancy: A state-level analysis. *Journal of Adolescent Health, 7,* 245–252.

Cross, W. (2006). Globalism, America's ghettos, and Black youth development. In C. Daiute, Z. Beykont, C. Higson-Smith, & L. Nucci (Eds.), *International perspectives on youth conflict and development* (pp. 269–288). New York: Oxford University Press.

Crosson, M. T., & Christian, T. F. (1990). *The Community Dispute Resolution Centers Program annual report.* Albany, NY: Office of Court Administration.

Cruess, D., Antoni, M., Kumar, M., & Schneiderman, N. (2000). Reductions in salivary cortisol are associated with mood improvement during relaxation training among HIV-seropositive men. *Journal of Behavioral Medicine, 23,* 107–122.

Cuddy, A. J. C., Norton, M. I., & Fiske, S. T. (2005). This old stereotype: The pervasiveness and persistence of the elderly stereotype. *Journal of Social Issues, 61,* 267–285.

Currie, J. M. (2006). *The invisible safety net: Protecting the nation's poor children and families.* Princeton, NJ: Princeton University Press.

Cutrona, C. E., Russell, D. W., Hessling, R. M., Brown, P. A., & Murry, V. (2000). Direct and moderating effects of community context on the psychological well-being of African American women. *Journal of Personality & Social Psychology, 79,* 1088–1101.

Dandeneau, S., Baldwin, M., Baccus, J., Sakellaropoulo, M., & Pruessner, J. (2007). Cutting stress off at the pass: Reducing vigilance and responsiveness to social threat by manipulating attention. *Journal of Personality and Social Psychology, 93,* 651–666.

Daniel, P. T. K. (2004). Accountability and desegregation: *Brown* and its legacy. *Journal of Negro Education, 73,* 255–267.

Danish, S. J. (1983). Musings about personal competence: The contributions of sport, health, and fitness. *American Journal of Community Psychology, 11,* 221–240.

Danish, S. J., & Gullotta, T. P. (2000). *Developing competent youth and strong communities through after-school programming.* Washington, DC: Child Welfare League of America.

Danso, H. A., Sedlovskaya, A., & Suanda, S. H. (2007). Perceptions of immigrants: Modifying the attitudes of individuals higher in social dominance orientation. *Personality and Social Psychology Bulletin, 33,* 1113–1123.

Dapp, U., Anderson, J., von Rentein-Kruse, W., & Meier-Baumgartner, H. P. (2005). Active health promotion in old age: Methodology of a preventive intervention programme provided by an interdisciplinary health advisory team for independent old people. *Journal of Public Health, 13,* 122–127.

Darling, N., Bogat, A., Cavell, T., Murphy, S., & Sánchez, B. (2006). Gender, ethnicity, development, and risk: Mentoring and the consideration of individual differences. *Journal of Community Psychology, 34*(6), 765–779.

Darrouch J., Frost, J., & Singh, S. (2001). Differences in teenage pregnancy rates among five developed countries: The roles of sexual activity and contraceptive use. *Family Planning Perspectives, 33*(Nov.–Dec.), 244–250 and 281.

Davey, C. L., Wootton, A. B., Cooper, R., & Press, M. (2005). Design against crime: Extending the reach of crime prevention through environmental design. *Security Journal, 18,* 39–51.

Davidson, R., Kabat Zinn, J., Schumacher, J., Rosenkranz, M., Muller, D., Santorelli, S., et al. (2003). Alterations in brain and immune function produced by mindfulness meditation. *Psychosomatic Medicine, 65,* 564–570.

Davidson, W. B., & Cotter, P. R. (1991). The relationship between sense of community and subjective well-being: A first look. *Journal of Community Psychology, 19,* 246–253.

Davis, D. M. (2004). Merry-go-round: A return to segregation and the implications for creating democratic schools. *Urban Education. Special Issue: De Jure, De Facto: Defining Quality Education 50 Years Beyond Brown, 39,* 394–407.

Davis, M. K., & Gidycz, C. A. (2000). Child sexual abuse prevention programs: A meta-analysis. *Journal of Clinical Child Psychology, 29,* 257–265.

Davis, P., & Cummings, E. (2006). Interparental discord, family process and developmental psychopathology. In D. Cicchetti & D. Cohen (Eds.), *Developmental psychopathology: Vol. 3 Risk, disorder and adaptation* (2nd ed.) (pp. 86–128). New York: Wiley.

Davis, P., Sturge-Apple, M., Cicchetti, D., & Cummings, E. (2007). The role of child adrenocortical functioning in pathways between interparental conflict and child maladjustment. *Developmental Psychology, 43,* 918–930.

Davis, T. R., & Luthans, F. (1988). Service OD: Techniques for improving the delivery of quality service. *Organization Development Journal, 6,* 76–80.

Dean, A., & Lin, N. (1977). The stress-buffering role of social support. *Journal of Nervous and Mental Disease, 165,* 403–417.

Dean, J., & Bush, R. (2007). A community psychology view of environmental organization processes. *American Journal of Community Psychology, 40,* 146–166.

Deaux, K. (2006). A nation of immigrants: Living our legacy. *Journal of Social Issues, 62,* 633–651.

De Beus, K., & Rodriguez, N. (2007). Restorative justice practice: An examination of program completion and recidivism. *Journal of Criminal Justice, 35*(3), 337–347.

de Fatima Qunital de Freitas, M. (2000). Voices from the south: The construction of Brazilian community social psychology. *Journal of Community and Applied Social Psychology, 10,* 315–326.

DeFrances, C., & Smith, S. (1998). *Perceptions of neighborhood crime.* Bureau of Justice Statistics Special Report NCI 165811. Washington, DC: Department of Justice.

Delgado, G. (1986). *Organizing the movement: The roots and growth of ACORN.* Philadelphia: Temple University Press.

Delongis, A., Coyne, J., Dakof, G., Folkman, S., & Lazarus, R. (1982). The relationship of daily hassles, uplifts and major life events to health status. *Health Psychology, 1,* 119–136.

Denham, S. A., & Almeida, M. C. (1987). Children's social problem-solving skills, behavioral adjustment, and interventions: A meta-analysis evaluating theory and practice. *Journal of Applied Developmental Psychology, 8,* 391–409.

D'Ercole, A., Skodol, A. E., Struening, E., Curtis, J., & Millman, J. (1991). Diagnosis of physical illness in psychiatric patients using Axis III and a standardized medical history. *Hospital and Community Psychiatry, 42,* 395–400.

Derogatis, L., & Coons, H. (1993). Self-report measures of stress. In L. Goldberger and S. Breznitz (Eds.), *Handbook of stress: Theoretical and clinical aspects* (2nd ed.). New York: Free Press.

De Schipper, J. C., Van IJzendoorn, M. H., & Tavecchio, L. W. C. (2004). Stability in center day care: Relations with children's well-being and problem behavior in day care. *Social Development, 13,* 531–550.

Detert, J. R., & Edmondson, A. C. (2007). Why employees are afraid to speak. *Harvard Business Review, 85,* 23–30.

Deutsch, M., & Hornstein, H. A. (Eds.). (1975). *Applying social psychology: Implications for research, practice, and training.* Hillsdale, NJ: Erlbaum.

Devine, P. (1989). Prejudice and stereotypes: Their automatic and controlled components. *Journal of Personality and Social Psychology, 56,* 5–18.

Devine, P. (2005). Breaking the prejudice habit: Allport's inner conflict revisited. In J. Dovidio, P. Glick, & L. Budman (Eds.), *On the nature of prejudice: Fifty years after Allport* (pp. 327–342). Malden, MA: Blackwell.

DeVita, C. J. (1997). *Viewing nonprofits across the states: Changing civil society.* Retrieved from www.urban.org/periodcl/cnp_1.htm.

De Wit, D. J., Lipman, E., Manzano-Munguia, M., Bisanza, J., Graham, K., Offord, D. R., et al. (2007). Feasibility of a randomized controlled trial for evaluating Big Brothers Big Sisters community match program at the national level. *Children and Youth Services Review, 29,* 383–404.

Diamond, J. B. (2006). Still separate and unequal: Examining race, opportunity, and school achievement in "integrated" suburbs. *Journal of Negro Education, 75,* 495–505.

Diamond, P. M., & Schnee, S. B. (1990, August). *Tracking the costs of chronicity: Towards a redirection of resources.* Presented to the Annual Meeting of the American Psychological Association, Boston, MA.

Dickerson, S., & Kemeny, M. (2004). Acute stressors and cortisol responses: A theoretical integration and synthesis of laboratory research. *Psychological Bulletin, 130,* 355–391.

DiClemente, R. J., & Peterson, J. L. (Eds.). (1994). *Preventing AIDS: Theories and methods of behavioral interventions.* New York: Plenum.

DiFranza, J. R., et al. (1991). RJR Nabisco's cartoon camel promotes Camel cigarettes to children. *Journal of the American Medical Association, 266,* 3149–3154.

DiMatteo, D., Sherbourne, C., Hays, R., Ordway, L., Kravitz, R., McGlynn, E., et al. (1993). Physicians' characteristics influence patients' adherence to medical treatment: Results from the Medical Outcomes Study. *Health Psychology, 12,* 93–102.

DiMatteo, M. R. (2004). Social support and patient adherence to medical treatment: A meta-analysis. *Health Psychology, 23,* 207–218.

Dobmeyer, T. W., McKee, P. A., Miller, R. D., & Wescott, J. S. (1990). The effect of enrollment in a prepaid health plan on utilization of a community crisis intervention center by chronically mentally ill individuals. *Community Mental Health Journal, 26,* 129–137.

Doherty, G., Forer, B., Lero, D. S., Goelman, H., & LaGrange, A. (2006) Predictors of quality family child care. *Early Childhood Research Quarterly, 21,* 296–312.

Dohrenwend, B. S. (1978). Social stress and community psychology. *American Journal of Community Psychology, 6,* 1–14.

Dovidio, J. F., & Gaertner, S. L. (1998). On the nature of contemporary prejudice: The causes, consequences, and challenges of divisive racism. In J. L. Eberhardt & S. T. Fiske (Eds.), *Confronting racism: The problem and the response.* Thousand Oaks, CA: Sage.

Dovidio, J. F., & Gaertner, S. L. (2004). Aversive racism. In Mark Zanna (Ed.), *Advances in experimental social psychology,* Vol. 36 (pp. 1–52). San Diego, CA, US: Elsevier Academic Press.

Dovidio, J., Gaertner, S., & Kawakami, K. (2002). Implicit and explicit prejudice and interracial interaction. *Journal of Personality and Social Psychology, 82,* 62–68.

Dovidio, J., Gaertner, S. L., Nier, J. A., Kawakami, K., & Hodson, G. (2004). Contemporary racial bias: When good people do bad things. In A. G. Miller (Ed.), *The social psychology of good and evil.* New York: Guilford.

Dovidio, J., Glick, P., & Budman, L. (Eds.). (2005). *On the nature of prejudice: Fifty years after Allport.* Malden, MA: Blackwell.

Dowell, D. A., & Farmer, G. (1992). Community response to homelessness: Social change and constraint in local intervention. *Journal of Community Psychology, 20,* 72–83.

Dowler, K., & Zawilski, V. (2007). Public perceptions of police misconduct and discrimination: Examining the impact of media consumption. *Journal of Criminal Justice, 35,* 193–203.

Downing, J., & Harrison, T. C. (1990). Dropout prevention: A practical approach. *School Counselor, 38,* 67–74.

Duffy, K. G. (1991). Introduction to community mediation programs: Past, present and future. In K. G. Duffy, J. W. Grosch, & P. V. Olczak (Eds.), *Community mediation: A handbook for practitioners and researchers*. New York: Guilford.

Duffy, K. G., & Atwater, E. (2008). *Psychology for living*. Upper Saddle River, NJ: Prentice-Hall.

Duffy, K. G., Grosch, J. W., & Olczak, P. V. (1991). *Community mediation: A handbook for practitioners and researchers*. New York: Guilford.

Duffy, K. G., Olczak, P. V., & Grosch, J. W. (1993). *The influence of minority status on mediation outcome*. Paper presented to the International Association for Conflict Management, Henglehoef, Belgium.

Duffy, K. G., & Thompson, J. (1992). Community mediation centers: Humanistic alternatives to the court system, a pilot study. *Journal of Humanistic Psychology, 32*, 101–114.

Dumas, J. E., Rollock, D., Prinz, R. J., Hops, H., & Blechman, E. A. (1999). Cultural sensitivity: Problems and solutions in applied and preventive intervention. *Applied & Preventive Psychology, 8*, 175–196.

Dumont, M. P. (1982). Review of *Private lives/public spaces*, by E. Baxter & K. Hopper, and *Shopping bag ladies*, by A. M. Rousseau. *American Journal of Orthopsychiatry, 52*, 367–369.

Dupéré, V., & Perkins, D. D. (2007). Community types and mental health: A multilevel study of local environmental stress and coping. *American Journal of Community Psychology, 39*, 107–119.

DuRant, R. H., Wolfson, M., LaFrance, B., Balkrishnan, R., & Altman, D. (2006, March). An evaluation of a mass media campaign to encourage parents of adolescents to talk to their children about sex. *Journal of Adolescent Health, 38*(3).

Durlak, J. A. (1983). Social problem-solving as a primary prevention strategy. In R. D. Felner, L. A. Jason, J. N. Moritsugu, & S. S. Farber (Eds.), *Prevention psychology: Theory, research, and practice*. New York: Pergamon.

Durlak, J. A. (1995). *School-based prevention programs for children and adolescents*. Thousand Oaks, CA: Sage.

Durlak, J. A., & Wells, A. M. (1997). Primary prevention mental health programs for children and adolescents: A meta-analytic review. *American Journal of Community Psychology, 25*, 115–152.

Eagly, A., Johannesen-Schmidt, M., & van Engen, M. (2003). Transformational, transactional, and laissez-faire leadership styles: A meta-analysis comparing women and men. *Psychological Bulletin, 129*(4), 569–591.

Earls, M., & Nelson, G. (1988). The relationship between long-term psychiatric clients' psychological well-being and their perceptions of housing and social support. *American Journal of Community Psychology, 16*, 279–293.

Eaves, C. (2001). The development and implementation of a crisis response team in a school setting. *International Journal of Emergency Mental Health Special Issue, 3*, 35–46.

Ebata, A. T., & Moos, R. H. (1991). Coping and adjustment in distressed and healthy adolescents. *Journal of Applied Developmental Psychology, 12*(1), 33–54.

Ebert-Flattau, P. (1980). *A legislative guide*. Washington, DC: Association for the Advancement of Psychology.

Eckenrode, J., Ganzel, B., Henderson, C. R., Smith, E., Olds, D. L., Powers, J., et al. (2000). Preventing child abuse and neglect with a program of nurse home visitation: The limiting effects of domestic violence. *Journal of the American Medical Association, 284*, 1385–1391.

Educational Conference on Psychiatry, Psychology and the Law (1990). Dangerousness and discharge. *American Journal of Forensic Psychology, 8*, 19–58.

Edwards, D., Hunt, M. H., Meyers, J., Grogg, K. R., & Jarrett, O. (2005). Acceptability and student outcomes of a violence prevention curriculum. *Journal of Primary Prevention, 26*, 401–418.

Edwards, R. W., Jumper-Thurman, P., Plested, B. A., Oetting, E. R., & Swanson, L. (2001). Community readiness. Research to practice. *Journal of Community Psychology, 28*, 291–307.

Eigen, M. (1993). Viral quasispecies. *Scientific American, 269*, 42–49.

Eisenbraun, K. D. (2007). Violence in schools: Prevalence, prediction, and prevention. *Aggression and Violent Behavior, 12*, 459–469.

Eitle, D., D'Alessio, S. J., & Stolzenberg, L. (2006). Economic segregation, race, and homicide. *Social Science Quarterly, 87*, 638–657.

Elder, G. (1974). *Children of the Great Depression*. Chicago: University of Chicago.

Elias, M. J., Gara, M., Ubriaco, M., Rothbaum, P. A., Clabby, J. F., & Schuyler, T. (1986). Impact of a preventative social problem solving intervention on children's coping with middle-school stressors. *American Journal of Community Psychology, 14,* 259–275.

Ellam, G., & Shamir, B. (2005). Organizational change and self concept. *Journal of Applied Behavioral Science, 41,* 399–421.

Elliott, K., & Urquiza, A. (2006). Ethnicity, culture, and child maltreatment. *Journal of Social Issues, 62,* 787–808.

Ellis, R. T. (1991). Perceptions, attitudes and beliefs of police recruits. *Canadian Police College Journal, 15,* 95–117.

Elvin, J. (2000, July 21). Is mental illness all in your head? *Insight on the News, 16,* 35.

Ely, R., & Thomas, D. (2001). Cultural diversity at work: The effects of diversity perspectives on work group processes and outcomes. *Administrative Science Quarterly, 46* (2), 229–273.

Embry, D. D., Flannery, D. J., Vazsonyi, A. T., Powell, K. E., & Atha, J. (1996). PeaceBuilders: A theoretically driven school based model for early violence prevention. *American Journal of Preventive Medicine, 12,* 91–100.

Emery, R. E., & Wyer, M. M. (1987). Divorce mediation. *American Psychologist, 42,* 472–480.

Emshoff, J., Darnell, A., Darnell, D., Erickson, S., Schneider, S., & Hudgins, R. (2007). Systems change as an outcome and a process in the work of community collaborative for health. *American Journal of Community Psychology, 39,* 255–267.

Entwisle, D. R., Alexander, K. L., & Olson, L. S. (2004). Temporary as compared to permanent high school dropout. *Social Forces, 82,* 1181–1205.

Entwisle, D. R., Alexander, K. L., & Olson, L. S. (2005). Urban teenagers: Work and dropout. *Youth & Society, 37,* 3–32.

Epel, E., Blackburn, E., Lin, J., Dhabhar, F., Adler, N., Morrow, J., et al. (2004, December 7). Accelerated telomere shortening in response to life stress. *Proceedings of the National Academy of Sciences, 101*(49), 17323–17324.

Erwin, P. G., Purvee, D., & Johannes, C. K. (2005). Involvement and outcomes in short-term interpersonal cognitive problem solving groups. *Counseling Psychology Quarterly, 18,* 41–46.

Evans, G. W. (2004). The environment of childhood poverty. *American Psychologist, 59,* 77–92.

Everly, G. S., Phillips, S. B., Kane, D., & Feldman, D. (2006). Introduction to and overview of group psychological first aid. *Brief Treatment and Crisis Intervention, 6,* 130–136.

Eysenck, H. J. (1952). The effects of psychotherapy: An evaluation. *Journal of Consulting Psychology, 16,* 319–324.

Eysenck, H. J. (1961). The effects of psychotherapy. In H. J. Eysenck (Ed.), *Handbook of abnormal psychology.* New York: Basic Books.

Fairweather, G. W. (1980). *The Fairweather lodge: A twenty-five year retrospective.* San Francisco: Jossey-Bass.

Fairweather, G. W. (1986). The need for uniqueness. *American Journal of Community Psychology, 14,* 128–137.

Fairweather, G. W., & Davidson, W. S. (1986). *An introduction to community experimentation.* New York: McGraw-Hill.

Fairweather, G., & Fergus, E. O. (1993). *Empowering the mentally ill: Theory and application.* Manchester, NH: Morgan Press.

Fairweather, G. W., Sanders, D. H., Maynard, H., & Cressler, D. L. (1969). *Community life for the mentally ill.* Chicago: Aldine.

Fairweather, G. W., & Tornatzky, L. G. (1977). *Experimental methods for social policy research.* New York: Pergamon.

Faith, M. S., Wong, F. Y., & Carpenter, K. M. (1995). Group sensitivity training: Update, meta-analysis, and recommendations. *Journal of Counseling Psychology, 42,* 390–399.

Farber, S. S., Felner, R. D., & Primavera, J. (1985). Parental separation/divorce and adolescents: An examination of factors mediating adaptation. *American Journal of Community Psychology, 13,* 171–186.

Farmer, P., Leandre, F., Mukherjee, J., Claude, M.S., Nevil, P., Smith-Fawzi, M., et al. (2001). Community-based approaches to HIV treatment in resource-poor settings. *Lancet, 345,* 404–409.

Farmer, T. W., Price, L. N., O'Neal, K. K., & Man-Chi, L. (2004). Exploring risk in early adolescent African-American youth. *American Journal of Community Psychology, 33,* 51–59.

Farquhar, M. (1995). Elderly people's definitions of quality of life. *Social Science and Medicine, 41,* 1439–1446.

Farquhar, J., Fortmann, S., Maccoby, N., Haskell, W., Williams, P., Flora, J., et al. (1985). The Stanford

Five-City Project: Design and methods. *American Journal of Epidemiology, 122,* 323–334.

Farrington, D. P., Gill, M., Waples, S. J., & Argomaniz, J. (2007). The effects of closed-circuit television on crime: Meta-analysis of an English national quasi multi-site evaluation. *Journal of Experimental Criminology, 3,* 21–38.

Farver, J. M., Xu, Y., Eppe, S., Fernandez, A., & Schwartz, D. (2005). Community violence, family conflict, and preschoolers' socioemotional functioning. *Developmental Psychology, 41,* 160–170.

Fassinger, R. (2008). Workplace diversity and public policy: Challenges, and opportunities for psychology. *American Psychologist, 63,* 252–268.

Fauth, R. C., Leventhal, T., & Brooks-Gunn, J. (2007). Welcome to the neighborhood? Long-term impacts of moving to low-poverty neighborhoods on poor children's and adolescents' outcomes. *Journal of Research on Adolescence, 17,* 249–282.

Fawcett, S. B. (1990). Some emerging standards for community research and action: Aid from a behavioral perspective. In P. Tolan, C. Kelp, F. Chertak, & L. Jason (Eds.), *Researching community psychology: Issues of theory and methods* (pp. 64–75). Washington, DC: American Psychology Association.

Fawcett, S. B., Seekins, T., & Jason, L. A. (1987). Policy research and child passenger safety legislation: A case study and experimental evaluation. *Journal of Social Issues, 43*(2), 133–148.

Federal Register (2008). 2008 poverty guidelines. *Federal Register, 73,* 3971–3972.

Federal Trade Commission (2005). *Federal Trade Commission Cigarette Report for 2003.* Washington, DC: Author.

Feldheusen, J. F. (1989, March). Synthesis of research on gifted youth. *Educational Leadership,* 6–11.

Felitte, V., Anda, R., Nordenberg, D., Williamson, D., Spitz, A., & Edwards, V. (1998). Relationship of childhood abuse and household dysfunction to many of the leading causes of death in adults. *American Journal of Preventive Medicine, 14,* 245–258.

Felner, R. D., Jason, L., Moritsugu, J., & Riger, S. (1983). *Preventive psychology: Theory, research and practice.* New York: Pergamon Press.

Felner, R. D. (2000a). Educational reform as ecologically-based prevention and promotion. The project on high performance learning communities. In D. Cicchetti & J. Rappaport (Eds.), *The promotion of wellness in children and adolescents.* Washington, DC: Child Welfare League of America.

Felner, R. (2000b). Prevention in mental health and social intervention. In J. Rappaport & E. Seidman (Eds.), *Handbook of community psychology* (pp. 9–42). New York: Kluwer/Plenum.

Felner, R. (2008). *School transitional environment project (STEP).* Retrieved from www.personal.psy.edu/dept/prevention/STEP.htm.

Felner, R. D., Ginter, M., & Primavera, J. (1982). Primary prevention during school transitions: Social support and environmental structure. *American Journal of Community Psychology, 10,* 277–290.

Felner, R. D., Seitsinger, A. M., Brand, S., Burns, A., & Bolton, N. (2007). Creating small learning communities: Lessons from the project on high-performing learning communities about "what works" in creating productive, developmentally enhancing, learning contexts. *Educational Psychologist. Special Issue: Promoting Motivation at School: Interventions that Work, 42,* 209–221.

Felton, B. (2005). Defining location in the mental health system: A case study of a consumer-run agency. *American Journal of Community Psychology, 36,* 373–386.

Ferguson, K. M., & Mindel, C. H. (2007). Modeling fear of crime in Dallas neighborhoods: A test of social capital theory. *Crime & Delinquency, 53,* 322–349.

Ferrari, J., Billows, W., Jason, L., & Grill, G. (1997). Matching the needs of the homeless with those of the disabled: Empowerment through caregiving. *Journal of Prevention and Intervention in the Community, 15,* 83–93.

Ferrari, J. R., & Jason, L. A. (1996). Integrating research and community service: Incorporating research skills into service learning experiences. *College Student Journal, 30,* 444–451.

Fiedler, F. (1971). Validation and extension of the contingency model of leadership effectiveness: A review of empirical findings. *Psychological Bulletin, 76,* 128–148.

Finkelhor, S., & Jones, L. (2006). Why have child maltreatment and child victimization declined? *Journal of Social Issues, 62,* 685–716.

Firdion, J., & Marpsat, M. (2007). A research program on homelessness in France. *Journal of Social Issues, 63,* 567–587.

Fischer, C. S., Jackson, R. M., Stueve, C. A., Gerson, G., & McAllister-Jones, L. (1977). *Networks and places.* New York: Free Press.

Fisher, J. D., & Fisher, W. A. (1992). Changing AIDS-risk behavior. *Psychological Bulletin, 111,* 455–474.

Fishman, P. A., Thompson, E. E., Merikle, E., & Curry, S. J. (2006). Changes in health care costs before and after smoking cessation. *Nicotine & Tobacco Research, 8,* 393–401.

Fiske, S. T., Bersoff, D. N., Borgida, E., Deaux, K., & Heilman, M. E. (1991). Social science research on trial: Use of sex stereotyping research in *Price Waterhouse v. Hopkins. American Psychologist, 46,* 1049–1060.

Flay, B. R., & Alfred, C. G. (2003). Long-term effects of the Positive Action program. *American Journal of Health Behavior, 27,* 6–21.

Flay, B. R., & Petraitis, J. (1991). Methodological issues in drug use prevention research: Theoretical foundation. In C. G. Leukefeld & W. J. Buoski (Eds.), *Drug abuse prevention intervention research methodology.* National Institute on Drug Abuse Research Monograph 107. DHHS publication number (ADM) pp. 91–1761. Washington, DC: Superintendent of Documents, U.S. Government Printing Office.

Flick, U. (2007). Homelessness and health: Challenges for health psychology. *Journal of Health Psychology, 12,* 691–695.

Flora, J., Jatilus, D., & Jackson, C. (1993). The Stanford Five-City Heart Disease Prevention Project. In T. E. Backer & E. M. Rogers (Eds.), *Organizational aspects of health communication campaigns: What works?* (pp. 101–128). Thousand Oaks, CA: Sage.

Florin, P. (1989). *Nurturing the grassroots: Neighborhood volunteer organizations and American cities.* New York: Citizen's Committee for New York City.

Florin, P., & Wandersman, A. (1990). An introduction to citizen participation, voluntary organizations, and community development: Insights for improvement through research. *American Journal of Community Psychology, 18,* 41–54.

Flowers-Coulson, P. A., Kushner, M. A., & Bankowski, S. (2000). The information is out there, but is anyone getting it? Adolescent misconceptions about sexuality education and reproductive health and the use of the internet to get answers. *Journal of Sex Education & Therapy, 25,* 178–188.

Folkman, S., & Lazarus, R.S. (1980). An analysis of coping in a middle-aged community sample. *Journal of Health and Social Behavior, 21,* 219–239.

Folkman, S., & Moskowitz, J. (2000). Positive affect and the other side of coping. *American Psychologist, 55,* 647–654.

Ford, J. D., Ford, L. W., & D'Amelio, A. (2008). Resistance to change: The rest of the story. *Academy of Management Review, 33,* 362.

Forlenza, S. G. (1991). Mediation and psychotherapy: Parallel processes. In K. G. Duffy, T. W. Grosch, & P. V. Olczak (Eds.), *Community mediation: A handbook for practitioners and researchers.* New York: Guilford.

Forrester, J. (1969). *Principles of system.* Cambridge, MA: Wright-Allen.

Foster, H. W., Greene, L. W., & Smith, M. S. (1990). A model for increasing access: Teenage pregnancy prevention. *Journal of Health Care for the Poor and Underserved, 1,* 136–146.

Foster-Fishman, P., & Behrens, T. (2007). Systems change reborn: Rethinking our theories, methods, and efforts in human services reform and community-based change. *American Journal of Community Psychology, 39*(3–4), 191–196.

Foster-Fishman, P. G., & Keys, C. B. (1997). The person/environment dynamics of employee empowerment: An organizational culture analysis. *American Journal of Community Psychology, 25,* 345–369.

Foster-Fishman, P., Newell, B., & Yang, H. (2007). Putting the system back into system change: A framework for understanding and changing organizational and community systems. *American Journal of Community Psychology, 39,* 197–215.

Foster-Fishman, P. G., Salem, D. A., Chibnall, S., Legler, R., & Yapchai, C. (1998). Empirical support for the critical assumptions of empowerment theory. *American Journal of Community Psychology, 26,* 507–536.

Fouad, N., & Bynner, J. (2008). Work transitions. *American Psychologist, 63,* 241–251.

Foundation Center. (2008). *Foundation giving grows across all program areas, Foundation Center Reports.* Retrieved from www.foundationcenter.org/media/news/pr_0802b.html.

4parents.gov. (2007). *Teen pregnancy.* Washington, DC: U.S. Department of Health and Human Services.

Fozard, J. L., & Kearns, W. D. (2007). Technology, aging, and communication. In G. Lesnoff-Caravaglia (Ed.), *Gerontechnology: Growing old in a technological society.* Springfield, IL: Charles C. Thomas.

Frank, J. D. (1983). Galloping technology, a new social disease. *Journal of Social Issues, 39,* 193–206.

Franklin, C., Grant, D., Corcoran, J., Miller, P. O., & Bultan, L. (1997). Effectiveness of prevention programs for adolescent pregnancy: A meta-analysis. *Journal of Marriage & the Family, 59,* 551–567.

Fraser, B. J., Williamson, J. C., & Tobin, K. G. (1987). Use of classroom and school climate scales in evaluating alternative high schools. *Teaching and Teacher Education,* 219–231.

Freedman, A. M. (1989). Mental health programs in the United States: Idiosyncratic roots. *International Journal of Mental Health, 18,* 81–98.

Freeman, L. (2001). Relaxation therapy. In L. Freeman & G. Lawlis (Eds.), *Mosby's complementary and alternative medicine: A research-based approach* (pp. 138–165). St. Louis: Mosby.

Freeman, L., & Lawlis, G. (2001). Exercise as an alternative therapy. In L. Freeman & G. Lawlis (Eds.), *Mosby's complementary and alternative medicine: A research-based approach* (pp. 424–454). St. Louis: Mosby.

Freeman, R. J., & Roesch, R. (1989). Mental disorder and the criminal justice system. *International Journal of Law and Psychiatry, 12,* 105–115.

Freiberg, J. H., & Lapoint, J. M. (2006). Research-based programs for preventing and solving discipline problems. In C. M. Evertson & C. S. Weinstein (Eds.), *Handbook of classroom management: Research, practice, and contemporary issues.* Mahwah, NJ: Erlbaum.

Freire, P. (1970). *Pedagogy of the oppressed.* New York: Continuum.

Freire, P. (1994). *Pedagogy of hope.* New York: Continuum.

Freisthler, B., Bruce, E., & Needell, B. (2007). Understanding geospatial relationship of neighborhood characteristics and rates of maltreatment for Black, Hispanic, and White children. *Social Work, 52,* 7–16.

French, W. L., & Bell, C. H. (1990). *Organizational development: Behavioral science interventions for organization improvement.* Englewood Cliffs, NJ: Prentice Hall.

Friedman, S. M., Neagius, A., Jose, B., Curtis, R., Goldstein, M., Ildefonso, G., et al. (1997). Network and sociohistorical approaches to the HIV epidemic among drug injectors. In L. Sherr, J. Catalan, & B. Hedge (Eds.), *The impacts of AIDS: Epidemiological and social aspects of HIV infection.* Chur, Switzerland: Harwood.

Frone, M. (2008). Are work stressors related to employee substance use? The importance of temporal context in assessments of alcohol and illicit drug use. *Journal of Applied Psychology, 93,* 199–206.

Frumkin, P. (2000). The face of the new philanthropy. *Responsive Community, 10,* 41–48.

Fyson, S. (1999). Developing and applying concepts about community: Reflections from the field. *Journal of Community Psychology, 27*(3), 347–365.

Gabbidon, S. L., & Peterson, S. A. (2006). Living while Black: A state-level analysis of the influence of select social stressors on the quality of life among Black Americans. *Journal of Black Studies, 37,* 83–102.

Gaertner, S., & Dovidio, J. (2005). Understanding and addressing contemporary racism: From aversive racism to the common in-group identity model. *Journal of Social Issues, 61,* 615–639.

Gallagher, S., Phillips, A., Ferraro, A., Drayson, M., & Carroll, D. (2008) Social support is positively associated with the immunoglobulin M response to vaccination with pneumococcal polysaccharides. *Biological Psychology, 78*(2), 211–215.

Garbarino, J. (2001). *Making sense of school violence: Why do kids kill?* Washington, DC: American Psychiatric Press.

Garbarino, J., & Kostelny, K. (1992). Child maltreatment as a community problem. *Child Abuse and Neglect, 16,* 455–464.

Garbarino, J., & Kostelny, L. (1994). Neighborhood-based programs. In G. B. Melton & F. D. Barry (Eds.), *Protecting children from abuse and neglect: Foundations for a new strategy.* New York: Guilford.

Garces, E., Thomas, D., & Currie, J. (2000, December). Longer term effects of Head Start. Retrieved June 1, 2008, from www.rand.org/labor/DRU/DRU2439.pdf.

Garmezy, N. (1974). Children at risk. The search for the antecedents of schizophrenia: II. Ongoing research programs, issues and intervention. *Schizophrenia Bulletin, 9,* 55–125.

Garmezy, N., Masten, A. S., & Tellegen, A. (1984). The study of stress and competence in children: A building block for developmental psychopathology. *Child Development, 55,* 97–111.

Garmezy, N., & Streitman, S. (1974). Children at risk. The search for the antecedents of schizophrenia: I. Conceptual models and research methods. *Schizophrenia Bulletin, 8,* 14–90.

Gastil, J. (1994). A meta-analytic review of the productivity and satisfaction of democratic and autocratic leadership. *Small Group Research, 25,* 384–410.

Geen, R., Fender, L., Leos-Urbel, J., & Markowitz, T. (2001). *Welfare reform's effect on child welfare caseloads.* Washington, DC: Urban Institute. Assessing the New Federalism Discussion Paper 01-04.

Gesten, E., & Jason, L. (1987). Social and community interventions. *Annual Review of Psychology, 38,* 427–460.

Gewirtz, A. H. (2007). Promoting children's mental health in family supportive housing: A community-university partnership for formerly homeless children and families. *Journal of Primary Prevention, 28,* 359–374.

Gignac, M. A. M., Kelloway, E. K., & Gottlieb, B. H. (1996). The impact of caregiving on employment: A mediational model of work-family conflict. *Canadian Journal of Aging, 15,* 525–542.

Gillespie, D. F., & Murty, S. A. (1994). Cracks in a postdisaster service delivery network. *American Journal of Community Psychology, 22,* 639–660.

Gillespie, J. F., Durlak, J., & Sherman, D. (1982). Relationship between kindergarten children's interpersonal problem solving skills and other indices of school adjustment: A cautionary note. *American Journal of Community Psychology, 10,* 149–153.

Gilliam, M. L. (2007). The role of parents and partners in the pregnancy behaviors of young Latinas. *Hispanic Journal of Behavioral Sciences, 29,* 50–67.

Ginexi, E. M., Weihs, K., Simmens, S. J., & Hoyt, D. R. (2000). Natural disaster and depression: A prospective investigation of reactions to the 1993 Midwest floods. *American Journal of Community Psychology, 28,* 495–515.

Glaberson, W. (1990, February 19). Mean streets teach New Yorkers to just walk on by. *New York Times,* pp. B1–B2.

Glenwick, D. S., & Jason, L. A. (Eds.). (1980). *Behavioral community psychology: Progress and prospects.* New York: Praeger.

Glidewell, J. (1966). Perspectives in community health. In C. Bennett, L. Anderson, S. Cooper, L. Hassol, D. Klein, & G. Rosenblum (Eds.), *Community psychology: A report of the Boston Conference on the Education of Psychologists for Community Mental Health* (pp. 33–49). Boston, MA: Boston University and South Shore Mental Health Center.

Glidewell, J. (1987). Induced change and stability in psychological and social systems. *American Journal of Community Psychology, 15*(6), 741–772.

Glidewell, J. C. (1976). A theory of induced social change. *American Journal of Community Psychology, 4,* 227–239.

Golding, J. M., Potts, M. K., & Aneshensel, C. S. (1991). Stress exposure among Mexican Americans and non-Hispanic whites. *Journal of Community Psychology, 19,* 37–59.

Goldring, E., Cohen-Vogel, L., Smrekar, C., & Taylor, C. (2006). Schooling closer to home: Desegregation policy and neighborhood contexts. *American Journal of Education, 112,* 335–362.

Gomby, D. S. (2000). Promise and limitations of home visitation. *Journal of the American Medical Association, 284,* 1430–1431.

Goodman, A. M. (1990). A model for police officer burnout. *Journal of Business and Psychology, 5,* 85–99.

Goodrum, S. (2007). Victims' rights, victims' expectations, and law enforcement workers' constrains in cases of murder. *Law & Social Inquiry, 32,* 725–757.

Goodstein, L. D., & Sandler, I. (1978). Using psychology to promote human welfare: A conceptual analysis of the role of community psychology. *American Psychologist, 33,* 882–892.

Gore, A. (1990). Public policy and the homeless. *American Psychologist, 45,* 960–962.

Gottlieb, B. H. (1981). Social networks and social support in community mental health. In B. H. Gottlieb (Ed.), *Social networks and social support.* Beverly Hills: Sage.

Gottlieb, B. (1997). Conceptual and measurement issues in the study of chronic stress. In B. Gottlieb (Ed.), *Coping with chronic stress* (pp. 3–37). New York: Plenum.

Gottschalk, B., & Gottschalk, P. (1988). The Reagan retrenchment in historical context. In M. K.

Brown (Ed.), *Remaking the welfare state: Retrenchment and social policy in America and Europe*. Philadelphia: Temple University Press.

Graber, J. A., Nichols, T., Lynne, S. D., Brooks-Gunn, J., & Botvin, G. J. (2006). A longitudinal examination of family, friend, and media influences on competent versus problem behaviors among urban minority youth. *Applied Developmental Science, 10,* 75–85.

Granovetter, M. (1973). The strength of weak ties. *American Journal of Sociology, 78,* 1360–80.

Granovetter, M. (1983*)*. The strength of weak ties: A network theory revisited. *Sociological Theory, 1,* 201–233.

Gray, P., & Chanoff, D. (1986). Democratic schooling: What happens to young people who have charge of their own education? *American Journal of Community Psychology, 94,* 182–213.

Gray, S., Sheeder, J., O'Brien, R., & Stevens-Simon, C. (2006). Having the best intentions is necessary but not sufficient: What would increase the efficacy of home visiting for preventing second teen pregnancies? *Prevention Science, 7,* 389–395.

Greatbatch, D., & Dingwall, R. (1989). Selective facilitation: Some preliminary observations on a strategy used by divorce mediators. *Law and Society Review, 23,* 613–641.

Greenberg, A. (1999). Defending the "American people." *Responsive Community, 9,* 52–58.

Greenberg, M., Riggs, N., & Blair, C. (2007). The role of preventive interventions in enhancing neurocognitive functioning and promoting competence in adolescence. In D. Romer & E. Walker (Eds.), *Adolescent psychopathology and the developing brain: Integrating brain and prevention science*. New York: Oxford.

Greene, S. M., Anderson, E. R., Doyle, E. A., & Riedelbach, H. (2006). Divorce. In G. G. Bear & K. M. Minke (Eds.), *Children's needs III: Development, prevention, and intervention*. Washington, DC: National Association of School Psychologists.

Greenglass, E., Fiksenbaum, L., & Eaton, J. (2006). The relationship between coping, social support, functional disability and depression in the elderly. *Anxiety, Stress & Coping: An International Journal, 19,* 15–31.

Greenhouse, L. (July 1, 2007). In steps big and small, Supreme Court moved right. *New York Times.* Retrieved from http://www.nytimes.com/2007/07/01/washington/01scotus.html?scp=1&sq=%20July%201,%202007,%20in%20steps%20big%20and%20small%20the%20supreme%20court%20moves%20right&st=cse.

Gregory, A., Henry, D. B., & Schoeny, M. E. (2007). School climate and implementation of a preventive intervention. *American Journal of Community Psychology, 40,* 250–260.

Grob, G. N. (1991). *From asylum to community: Mental health policy in modern America*. Princeton, NJ: Princeton University Press.

Grogan-Kaylor, A. (2005). Review of *One nation, underprivileged: Why American poverty affects us all*. *Children and Youth Services Review, 27,* 687–689.

Grossi, E. L., & Berg, B. L. (1991). Stress and job dissatisfaction among correctional officers: An unexpected finding. *International Journal of Offender Therapy and Comparative Criminology, 35,* 73–81.

Gunn, P., Ratnesh, B., Nagda, A., & Lopez, G. E. (2004). The benefits of diversity in education for democratic citizenship. *Journal of Social Issues, 60,* 17–34.

Gurin, G., Veroff, J., & Feld, S. (1960). *Americans view their mental health: A nationwide interview survey*. New York: Basic Books.

Gurin, P., Nagda, B. A., & Lopez, G. (2004). The benefits of diversity in education for democratic citizenship. *Journal of Social Issues, 60*(1), 17–34.

Gutierrez, P., & Silk, K. (1980). Prescription privileges for psychologists: A review of the psychological literature. *Professional Psychology: Research and Practice, 29,* 213–222.

Haber, M., Cohen, J., Lucas, T., & Baltes, B. (2007). The relationship between self-reported received and perceived social support: A meta-analytic review. *American Journal of Community Psychology, 39*(1–2), 133–144.

Hackerman, A. E. (1996). Intervening with the adolescent gang member: Understanding the spoken language. *Community Psychologist, 29,* 17–21.

Hadley-Ives, E., Stiffman, A. R., Elze, D., Johnson, S. D., & Dore, P. (2000). Measuring neighborhood and school environments: Perceptual and aggregate approaches. *Journal of Human Behavior in the Social Environment, 3,* 1–28.

Hagborg, W. J. (1988). A study of the intensity and frequency of crisis intervention for students enrolled in a school for the severely emotionally disturbed. *Adolescence, 23,* 825–836.

Hagestad, G. O., & Uhlenberg, P. (2005). The social separation of old and young: A root of ageism. *Journal of Social Issues, 61,* 343–358.

Halpern, D., & Nazroo, J. (2000). The ethnic density effect: Result from a national community survey of England and Wales. *International Journal of Social Psychiatry, 46,* 34–46.

Hamid, P. N., Yue, X. D., & Leung, C. M. (2003, Spring). Adolescent coping in different Chinese family environments. *Adolescence, 38,* 111–130.

Hamilton, S. F., Basseches, M., & Richards, F. A. (1985). Participatory-democratic work and adolescents' mental health. *American Journal of Community Psychology, 13,* 467–496.

Hamilton, S. F., Hamilton, M. A., Hirsch, B. J., Hughes, B. J., Hughes, J., King, J., et al. (2006). Community contexts for mentoring. *Journal of Community Psychology, 34,* 727–746.

Hampton, C. V., Epstein, M. J., Johnson, D. B., & Reixach, K. A. (2004). Rochester, NY: Early childhood education intervention. *Community Psychologist, 37,* 42–47.

Handel, G. (1982). *Social welfare in Western society.* New York: Random House.

Haney, C., Banks, C., & Zimbardo, P. (1973). Interpersonal dynamics in a simulated prison. *International Journal of Criminology and Penology, 1,* 69–97.

Hannon, L. E. (2005). Extremely poor neighborhoods and homicide. *Social Science Quarterly. Special Issues: Income, Poverty, and Opportunity, 86,* 1418–1434.

Harcourt, B. (2007, January 15). The mentally ill, behind bars. *New York Times.* Retrieved from www.nytimes.com/2007/01/15/opinion/15harcourt.html.

Hardin, E., & Khan-Hudson, A. (2005). Elder abuse—"society's dilemma." *Journal of the National Medical Association, 97,* 91–94.

Harrington, C. (1985). *Shadow justice: The ideology and institutionalization of alternatives to court.* Westport, CT: Greenwood Press.

Haskins, R. (2005). Child development and child-care policy: Modest impacts. In D. B. Pilllemer & S. H. White (Eds.), *Developmental psychology and social change: Research, history and policy.* New York: Cambridge University Press.

Hatfield, A. B. (1997, September/October). Elderly individuals with mental illnesses: The overlooked and underserved generation. *NAMI Advocate,* pp. 13–18.

Haynes, R. B., McDonald, H. P., & Garg, A. X. (2002). Helping patients follow prescribed treatment. *Journal of the American Medical Association, 288,* 2880–2883.

Head, T. C., & Sorenson, P. F. (1988). Contemporary trends in OD. *Organizational Development Journal, 7,* 13–24.

He, W., Sengupta, M., Velkoff, V. & DeBarros, K. (December, 2005). *65+ in the United States: 2005.* Washington, D.C.: U.S. Department of Health and Human Services, National Institute on Aging and the U.S. Census Bureau. Retrieved from http://www.census.gov/PressRelease/www/releases/archives/aging_population/006544.html.

Hedeen, T. (2004). The evolution and evaluation of community mediation: Limited research suggests unlimited progress. *Conflict Resolution Quarterly, 22,* 101–133.

Hedegaard, M. (1996). The zone of proximal development as basis for instruction. In H. Daniels (Ed.), *An introduction to Vygotsky* (pp. 171–195). New York: Routledge.

Heisterkamp, B. L. (2006). Conversational displays of mediator neutrality in a court-based program. *Journal of Pragmatics, 38,* 2051–2064.

Helgeson, V., & Cohen, S. (1996). Social support and adjustment to cancer: Reconciling descriptive, correlational and intervention research. *Journal of Health Psychology, 15,* 135–148.

Helping America's Youth. (2008). *The impact of caring adults in communities.* Retrieved from www.helpingamericasyouth.gov/facts.cfm.

Heller, K. (1989). Ethical dilemmas in community intervention. *American Journal of Community Psychology, 17,* 367–378.

Heller, K. (1989). The return to community. *American Journal of Community Psychology, 17*(1), 1–15.

Heller, K. (1990). Social and community intervention. In L. W. Porter & M. R. Rosenzweig (Eds.), *Annual review of psychology.* Palo Alto, CA: Annual Reviews.

Heller, K., Jenkins, R., Steffen, A., & Swindle, R. W. (2000). Prospects for a viable community mental health system: Reconciling ideology, professional traditions, and political reality. In

J. Rappaport & E. Seidman (Eds.), *Handbook of community psychology* (pp. 445–470). New York: Plenum.

Heller, K., Price, R. H., Reinharz, S., Riger, S., & Wandersman, A. (1984). *Psychology and community change.* Homewood, IL: Dorsey.

Heller, K., Thompson, M. G., Trueba, P. E., Hogg, J. R., & Vlachos-Weber, I. (1991). Peer support telephone dyads for elderly women: Was this the wrong intervention? *American Journal of Community Psychology, 19,* 53–74.

Heller, K., Wyman, M. F., & Allen, S. M. (2000). Future directions for prevention science: From research to adoption. In C. R. Snyder & R. E. Ingram (Eds.), *Handbook of psychological change: Psychotherapy processes and practices for the 21st century.* New York: Wiley.

Hellman, I. D., Greene, L. R., Morrison, T. L., & Abramowitz, S. I. (1985). Organizational size and perceptions in a residential treatment program. *American Journal of Community Psychology, 13,* 99–110.

Henderson, C. (2006). Review of Japan as a low-crime nation. *Journal of Forensic Psychiatry & Psychology, 17,* 356–358.

Henry, D., Guerra, N., Huesmann, R., Tolan, P., VanAcker, R., & Eron, L. (2000). Normative influences on aggression in urban elementary school classrooms. *American Journal of Community Psychology, 28,* 59–81.

Heppner, P. P., Heppner, M. J., Lee, D.-G., Wang, Y.-W., Park, H.-J., & Wang, L.-F. (2006). Development and validation of a collectivist coping styles inventory. *Journal of Counselling Psychology, 53,* 107–125.

Hersch, C. (1969). From mental health to social action: Clinical psychology in historical perspective. *American Psychologist, 24,* 906–916.

Hess, B. B., Markson, E. W., & Stein, P. J. (1991). *Sociology.* New York: Macmillan.

Hill, J., Bond, M. A., Mulvey, A., & Terenzio, M. (2000). Methodological issues and challenges for a feminist community psychology: An introduction to a special issue. *American Journal of Community Psychology, 28,* 759–772.

Himle, D. P., Jayertne, S., & Thyness, P. (1991). Buffering effects of four social support types on burnout among social workers. *Social Work Research and Abstracts, 27,* 22–27.

Hingson, R., Heeren, T., & Winter, M. (1998). Effects of Maine's 0.05% legal blood alcohol level for drivers with DWI convictions. *Public Health Report, 113,* 440–446.

Hirsch, B. J., & David, T. G. (1983). Social networks and work/nonwork life: Action research with nurse managers. *American Journal of Community Psychology, 11,* 493–508.

Hitlan, R. T., Camillo, K., Zárate, M. A., & Aikman, S. N. (2007). Attitudes toward immigrant groups and the September 11 terrorist attacks. *Peace and Conflict: Journal of Peace Psychology, 13,* 135–152.

Hladikova, A., & Hradecky, I. (2007). Homelessness in the Czech Republic. *Journal of Social Issues, 63*(3), 607–622.

Hobfoil, S. E. (1998). Ecology, community, and AIDS prevention. *American Journal of Community Health, 26,* 133–144.

Hobfoil, S., & Vaux, A. (1993). Social support: Social resources and social context. In L. Goldberg & S. Breznitz (Eds.), *Handbook of stress: Theoretical and clinical aspects* (pp. 685–705). New York: Free Press.

Hochschild, A. R. (2003). *The second shift.* New York: Penguin.

Hofen, B., Karren, K., Frandsen, K., Smith, N. (1996). *Mind/body health: The effects of attitudes, emotions, and relationships.* Toronto, ON: Allyn & Bacon.

Hofferth, S. L. (1991). Programs for high risk adolescents: What works? Special issue: Service to teenage parents. *Evaluation and Program Planning, 14,* 3–16.

Holahan, C., Moos, R., & Bonin, L. (1997). Social support, coping, and psychological adjustment: A resources model. In G. Pierce, B. Lakey, I. Sarason, & B. Sarason (Eds.), *Sourcebook of social support and personality* (pp. 169–186). New York: Plenum.

Holahan, J., & Cook, A. (2005). Changes in economic conditions and health insurance coverage, 2000–2004. *Health Affairs,* 498–508.

Holcomb, W. B., & Ahr, P. R. (1986). Clinicians' assessments of the service needs of young adult patients in public mental health care. *Hospital and Community Psychiatry, 37,* 908–913.

Hollander, E. P., & Offerman, L. (1990). Power and leadership in organizations. *American Psychologist, 45,* 179–189.

Hollingshead, A., & Redlich, C. (1958). *Social class and mental illness*. New York: Wiley.

Holmes, T. H., & Rahe, R. H. (1967). The social readjustment rating scale. *Journal of Psychosomatic Research, 11,* 213–218.

Houlette, M. A., Gaertner, S. L., Johnson, Kelly, M., Banker, B. S., Riek, B. M., et al. (2004). Developing a more inclusive social identity: An elementary school intervention. *Journal of Social Issues, 60,* 35–55.

House, J., Landis, K., & Umberson, D. (1988). Social relationships and health. *Science, 241,* 540–545.

Howard, J. (2003). Service-learning research: Foundational issues. In S. Billig & A. Waterman (Eds.), *Studying service-learning: Innovations in research methodology* (pp. 1–12). Mahwah, NJ: Erlbaum.

Howard, K. A., Flora, J., & Griffin, M. (1999). Violence-prevention programs in schools: State of the science and implications for future research. *Applied & Preventive Psychology, 8,* 197–215.

Hudiburg, R., & Necessary, J. (1996). Coping with computer stress. *Journal of Educational Computing Research, 15*(2), 113–124.

Hudiburg, R. (1990). *Comparing computer-related stress to computerphobia*. Eric ED 318986. Retrieved from http://eric.ed.gov:80/ERICDocs/data/ericdocs2sql/content_storage_01/0000019b/80/20/4d/aa.pdf.

Hughey, J., Speer, P., & Peterson, N. A. (1999). Sense of community in community organizations: Structure and evidence of validity. *Journal of Community Psychology, 27,* 97–113.

Hunter, A., & Riger, S. (1986). The meaning of community in community mental health. *Journal of Community Psychology, 14,* 55–71.

Huo, Y. (2003). Procedural justice and social regulation across group boundaries: Does subgroup identification undermine relationship-based governance. *Personality and Social Psychology Bulletin, 29,* 336–348.

Hurtado, S. (2005). The next generation of diversity and intergroup relations reseatch. *Journal of Social Issues, 61,* 595–567.

Ialongo, N. S., Rogosch, F., Cicchetti, D., Toth, S., Buckley, J., Petras, H., et al. (2006). A developmental psychopathology approach to the prevention of mental health disorder. In D. Cicchetti & D. Cohen (Eds.), *Developmental psychopathology: Vol. 1. Theory and method* (2nd ed., pp. 968–1018). Hoboken, NJ: Wiley.

Ialongo, N. S., Werthamer, L., Kellam, S. G., Brown, C. H., Wang, S., & Lin, Y. (1999). Proximal impact of two first-grade preventive interventions on early risk behaviors for later substance abuse, depression, and antisocial behavior. *American Journal of Community Psychology, 27,* 599–642.

Imm, P., Kehres, R., Wandersman, A., & Chinman, M. (2006). Mobilizing communities for positive youth development: Lessons learned from neighborhood groups and community coalitions. In C. Gil & J. Rhodes (Eds.), *Mobilizing adults for positive youth development: Strategies for closing the gap between beliefs and behaviors* (pp. 137–157). New York: Springer Science + Business Media.

Independent Sector (2006). *Facts and figures about charitable organizations*. Retrieved from www.indepedentsector.org.

Iscoe, I. (1987). From Boston to Austin and points beyond: The tenacity of community psychology. *American Journal of Community Psychology, 15,* 587–590.

Iscoe, I. (1994). The early years of community psychology. *Community Psychologist, 28,* 22–23.

Iscoe, I., & Harris, L. (1984). Social and community interventions. *Annual Review of Psychology, 35,* 333–360.

Ivancevich, J., Matteson, M., Freedman, S., & Phillips, J. (1990). Worksite stress management interventions. *American Psychologist, 45*(2), 252–261.

Jackson, C. T., Covell, N. H., Shear, K. M., & Zhu, C. (2006). The road back: Predictors of regaining preattack functioning among project liberty clients. *Psychiatric Services, 57,* 1283–1290.

Jackson, M. (2003). *Systems thinking*. Chichester: Wiley.

Jackson, D., & Hetherington, L. (2006). Young Jamaicans' attitudes toward mental illness: Experimental and demographic factors associated with social distance and stigmatizing opinions. *Journal of Community Psychology, 34,* 563–576.

Jackson, S. E., Schwab, R. L., & Schuler, R. S. (1986). Toward an understanding of the burnout phenomenon. *Journal of Applied Psychology, 71,* 630–640.

Jacobs, J. B. (1980). The prisoners' rights movement and its impacts, 1960–1980. In N. Morris & M. Tonry (Eds.), *Crime and justice: An annual review of research*. Chicago: University of Chicago Press.

James, D., & Glaze, L. (2006). *Mental health problems of prison and jail inmates* (Bureau of Justice Statistics Special Report). Washington, DC: U.S. Department of Justice, Office of Justice Programs.

Janz, N. K., & Becker, M. H. (1984). The health belief model: A decade later. *Health Education Quarterly, 11*, 1–47.

Jason, L. A. (1991). Participation in social change: A fundamental value of our discipline. *American Journal of Community Psychology, 19*, 1–16.

Jason, L. A. (1998). Tobacco, drug, and HIV preventive media. *American Journal of Community Psychology, 26*, 151–187.

Jason, L. A., Berk, M., Schnopp-Wyatt, D. L., & Talbot, B. (1999). Effects of enforcement of youth access laws on smoking prevalence. *American Journal of Community Health, 27*, 143–160.

Jason, L. A., Curran, T., Goodman, D., & Smith, M. (1989). A media-based stress management intervention. *Journal of Community Psychology, 17*, 155–165.

Jason, L. A., Davis, M., Suarez-Balcazar, Y., Keys, C., Taylor, R., Holtz Isenberg, D., et al. (2004). Conclusion. In L. Jason, K. Keys, Y. Suarez-Balcazar, R. Taylor, & M. Davis (Eds.), *Participatory community research*. Washington, DC: American Psychological Association.

Jason, L., & Glenwick, D. (Eds.). (2002). *Innovative strategies for promoting health and mental health across the life span*. New York: Springer.

Jason, L. A., Gruder, C. L., Martins, S., Flay, B. R., Warnecke, R., & Thomas, N. (1987). Work site group meeting and the effectiveness of a televised smoking cessation intervention. *American Journal of Community Psychology, 15*, 57–72.

Jason, L., Hess, R., Felner, R., & Moritsugu, J. (1987). Toward a multidisciplinary approach to prevention. *Prevention in Human Services, 5*(2), 1–10.

Jason, L. A., Kennedy, H. L., & Brackshaw, E. (1999). Television violence and children: Problems and solutions. In T. P. Gulotta & S. J. McElhaney (Eds.), *Violence in homes and communities: Prevention, intervention, and treatment*. Thousand Oaks, CA: Sage.

Jason, L. A., Keys, K., Suarez-Balcazar, Y., Taylor, R., & Davis, M. (Eds.). (2004). *Participatory community research*. Washington, D.C.: American Psychological Association.

Jason, L. A., La Pointe, P., & Bellingham, S. (1986). The media and self-help: A preventive community intervention. *Journal of Primary Prevention, 6*, 156–167.

Jason, L., & Perdoux, M. (2004). *Havens: Stories of true community healing*. Westport, CT: Praeger Publishers/Greenwood Publishing Group.

Jason, L., Pokorny, S., Parka, M., Adams, M., & Morello, T. (2007). Ranking institutional settings based on publications in community psychology journals. *Journal of Community Psychology, 35*(8), 967–979.

Jay, G. M., & D'Augelli, A. R. (1991). Social support and adjustment to university life: A comparison of African-American and White freshman. *Journal of Community Psychology, 19*, 95–100.

Jemelka, R., Trupin, E., & Chiles, J. A. (1989). The mentally ill in prisons: A review. *Hospital and Community Psychiatry, 40*, 481–491.

Jemmott, J. B., & Jemmott, L. S. (1994). Intervention for adolescents in community settings. In R. J. DiClemente and J. L. Peterson (Eds.), *Preventing AIDS: Theories and methods of behavioral interventions* (pp. 141–174). New York: Plenum.

Johnson, D. (1991). Psychology in Washington: Why should government support science now that the Russians aren't competing? *Psychological Science, 2*, 133–134.

Johnston, D. F. (1980). *The handbook of social indicators: Success, characteristics, and analysis*. New York: Garland STPM.

Johnston, L. D., O'Malley, P. M., & Bachman, J. G. (1993). *National survey results on drug use from monitoring the future study, 1975–1992*. Rockville, MD: National Institute on Drug Abuse.

Jones, E. E., & Nisbett, R. E. (1971). *The actor and the observer: Divergent perceptors of the causes of behavior*. Morristown, NJ: General Learning Press.

Jones, J. (1997). *Prejudice and racism* (2nd ed.). New York: McGraw-Hill.

Jones, J. (2003). TRIOS: A psychological theory of African legacy in American culture. *Journal of Social Issues, 59*, 217–242.

Joseph, M., & Ogletree, R. (1998). Community organizing and comprehensive community initiative. *Journal of Sociology and Social Welfare, 25*, 71–79.

Jukkala, T., Makinen, I. H., Kislitsyna, O., Ferlander, S., & Vagero, D. (2008). Economic strain, social relations, gender, and binge drinking in Moscow. *Social Science & Medicine, 66*, 663–674.

Kaiser Family Foundation. (2005a). *U.S. teen sexual activity*. Menlo Park, CA: Author.

Kaiser Family Foundation. (2005b). *HIV/AIDS epidemic fact sheet*. Menlo Park, CA: Author.

Kamradt, B. (2000). Wraparound Milwaukee: Aiding youth with mental health needs. *Juvenile Justice, 7*, 14–23.

Kanabus, A., & Noble, R. (2008). President's emergency plan for AIDS relief. AVERT.org Retrieved May 31, 2008, from avert.org/pepfar.htm.

Kanner, A. D., Coyne, J. C., Schaefer, C., & Lazarus, R. S. (1981). Comparison of two models of stress management: Daily hassles and uplifts versus major life events. *Journal of Behavioral Medicine, 4*, 1–39.

Kaplan, C. P., Turner, S. G., & Badger, L. W. (2007). Hispanic adolescent girls' attitudes toward school. *Child & Adolescent Social Work Journal, 24*, 173–193.

Kaplan, G. (1994). Reflections on present and future research on bio-behavioral risk factors. In S. Blumenthal, K. Matthews, & S. Weiss (Eds.), *New research frontiers in behavioral medicine: Proceedings of the national conference*. Washington, DC: NIH Publications.

Karavidas, M., Lim, N. K., & Katsikas, S. L. (2005). The effects of computers on older adult users. *Computers in Human Behavior, 21*, 697–711.

Karcher, M. J. (2005). The effects of developmental mentoring and high school mentors' attendance on their younger mentees' self-esteem, social skills, and connectedness. *Psychology in the Schools, 42*, 65–77.

Karim, Q. A., Karim, S. S. A., Coovadia, H. M., & Susser, M. (1998). Informed consent for HIV testing in a South African Hospital: Is it truly informed and truly voluntary? *American Journal of Public Health, 88*, 637–640.

Katz, D. (1983). Factors affecting social change: A social psychological interpretation. *Journal of Social Issues, 39*, 25–44.

Kaufman, J. S., Crusto, C. A., Quan, M., Ross, E., Friedman, S. R., O'Reilly, K., et al. (2006). Utilizing program evaluation as a strategy to promote community change: Evaluation of a comprehensive community-based family violence initiative. *American Journal of Community Psychology, 38*(3–4), 191–200.

Kaufman, J. S., Ross, E., Quan, M. A., O'Reilly, K., & Crusto, C. A. (2004). Building the evaluation capacity of community-based organizations: The Bridgeport Safe Start Initiative. *Community Psychologist, 37*(4), 45–47.

Kaufman, K., Gregory, W. L., & Stephan, W. (1990). Maladjustment in statistical minorities within ethnically unbalanced classrooms. *American Journal of Community Psychology, 18*, 757–765.

Kawakami, K., Phills, C. E., Steele, J. R., & Dovidio, J. F. (2007). Distance makes the heart grow fonder: Improving implicit racial attitudes and interracial interactions through approach behaviors. *Journal of Personality and Social Psychology, 92*, 957–971.

Kazden, A. E. (1980). *Research design in community psychology*. New York: Harper and Row.

Keinan, G. (1997). Social support, stress, and personality: Do all women benefit from their husband's presence during childbirth? In G. Pierce, B. Lakey, I. Sarason, & B. Sarason (Eds.), *Sourcebook of social support and personality* (pp. 409–427). New York: Plenum.

Kellam, S. G., Koretz, D., & Moscicki, E. K. (Eds.). (1999a). Special issue: Prevention science, Part I. *American Journal of Community Psychology, 27*, 461–595.

Kellam, S. G., Koretz, D., & Moscicki, E. K. (Eds.). (1999b). Special issue: Prevention science, Part II. *American Journal of Community Psychology, 27*, 697–731.

Keller, T. E. (2007). Youth mentoring: Theoretical and methodological issues. In T. D. Allen & L. T. Eby (Eds.), *The Blackwell handbook of mentoring: A multiple perspectives approach*. Malden, MA: Blackwell.

Kelly, C., & Breinlinger, S. (1996). *The social psychology of collective action: Identity, injustice, and gender*. Washington, DC: Taylor & Francis.

Kelly, G. W. R., & Ekland-Olson, S. (1991). The response of the criminal justice system to prison overcrowding: Recidivism patterns among four successive parolee courts. *Law and Society Review, 25*, 601–620.

Kelly, H. H. (1973). The process of causal attribution. *American Psychologist, 28*, 107–128.

Kelly, J. (1966). Ecological constraints on mental health services. *American Psychologist, 21*, 535–539.

Kelly, J. (1968). Toward an ecological conception of preventive interventions. In J. Carter (Ed.),

Research contributions from psychology to community mental health (pp. 75–99). New York: Behavioral Publications.

Kelly, J. (May, 6, 1980). *On the conservation of community leadership: An ecological view.* Invited Address at the Western Psychological Association meetings, Honolulu, Hawaii.

Kelly, J. G. (1986a). An ecological paradigm: Defining mental health consultation as a preventative service. *Prevention in the Human Services, 4,* 1–36.

Kelly, J. G. (1986b). Context and process: An ecological view of the interdependence of practice and research. *American Journal of Community Psychology, 14,* 581–589.

Kelly, J. G. (1990). Changing contexts and the field of community psychology. *American Journal of Community Psychology, 18,* 769–792.

Kelly, J. G. (1999). Contexts and community leadership: Inquiry as an ecological expedition. *American Psychologist, 54*(11), 953–961.

Kelly, J. (2002). The Seymour Sarason Award address: The spirit of community psychology. *American Journal of Community Psychology, 30,* 43–63.

Kelly, J. G. (2006). *Becoming ecological: An expedition into community psychology.* New York: Oxford University Press.

Kelly, J., Azelton, L., Lardon, C., Mock, L., Tandon, S., & Thomas, M. (2004). On community leadership: Stories about collaboration in action research. *American Journal of Community Psychology, 33*(3–4), 205–216.

Kelly, J., Dassoff, N., Levin, I., & Schreckengost, J. (1988). A guide to conducting prevention research in the community: First steps. *Prevention in Human Services, 6*(1), 174.

Kelly, J., Snowden, L., & Munoz, R. (1977). Social and community interventions. *Annual Review of Psychology, 28,* 323–361.

Kelly, K. D., Caputo, T., & Jamieson, W. (2005). Reconsidering sustainability: Some implications for community-based crime prevention. *Critical Social Policy, 25,* 306–324.

Kelsey, J. L., Thompson, W. D., & Evans, A. S. (1986). *Methods in observational epidemiology.* New York: Oxford University.

Kennedy, C. (1989). Community integration and well-being: Toward the goals of community care. *Journal of Social Issues, 45,* 65–78.

Kennedy, M. (2006). On your guard. *American School & University, 78,* 40–48.

Keppel, B. (2002). Kenneth B. Clark in the patterns of American culture. *American Psychologist, 57*(1), 29–37.

Kerlinger, F. N. (1973). *Foundations of behavioral research.* New York: Holt, Rinehart & Winston.

Kessler, M., & Albee, G. (1975). Primary prevention. *Annual Review of Psychology, 26,* 557–591.

Kessler, R. C., Chiu, W., Demler, O., & Walters, E. (2005). Prevalence, severity, and comorbidity of 12-month DSM-IV disorders in the national comorbidity survey replication. *Archives of General Psychiatry, 62,* 617–627.

Kessler, R. C., McGonagle, K. A., Zhao, S., Nelson, C. B., Hughes, M., Eshleman, S., et al. (1994). Lifetime and 12-month prevalence of DSM-III-R psychiatric disorders in the United States: Results from the national comorbidity survey. *Archives of General Psychiatry, 51,* 8–19.

Kettner, P. M., Daley, J. M., & Nichols, A. W. (1985). *Initiating change in organizations of communities: A macro practice model.* Monterey, CA: Brooks Cole.

Key, J. D., O'Rourke, K., Judy, N., & McKinnon, S. A. (2005–2006). Efficacy of a secondary adolescent pregnancy prevention: An ecological study before, during and after implementation of the second chance club. *International Quarterly of Community Health Education, 24,* 231–240.

Keys, C. (2007). Forward to the special issue: Exploring the intersection of organization studies and community psychology. *Journal of Community Psychology, 35,* 277–280.

Keys, C. B., & Frank, S. (1987). Organizational perspectives in community psychology (special issue). *American Journal of Community Psychology, 15.*

Khoury-Kassabri, M., Benbenishty, R., Astor, R. A., & Zeira, A. (2004). The contributions of community, family, and school variables to student victimization. *American Journal of Community Psychology, 34,* 187–204.

Kidd, S., & Davidson, L. (2007). 'You have to adapt because you have no other choice': The stories of strength and resilience of 208 homeless youth in New York City and Toronto. *Journal of Community Psychology, 35*(2), 219–238.

Kidd, S. & Kral, M. (2005). Practicing participatory action research. *Journal of Counseling Psychology, 52*(2), 187–195.

Kiernan, M., Toro, P. A., Rappaport, J., & Seidman, E. (1989). Economic predictors of mental health

service utilization: A time-series analysis. *American Journal of Community Psychology, 17,* 801–820.
Kiesler, C. A. (1980). Mental health policy as a field of inquiry for psychology. *American Psychologist, 35,* 1066–1080.
Kiesler, C. A. (1992). Mental health policy: Doomed to fail. *American Psychologist, 47,* 1077–1082.
Kim, M. M., & Ford, J. D. (2006). Trauma and post-traumatic stress among homeless men: A review of current research. *Journal of Aggression, Maltreatment, & Trauma, 13,* 1–22.
Kimbro, R. T., Bzostek, S., Goldman, N., & Rodríguez, G. (2008). Race, ethnicity, and education gradient in health. *Health Affairs, 27,* 361–372.
King, R. H. (2004). *The Brown decade. Patterns of Prejudice, 38,* 333–353.
Kirby, D. (2007). Emerging answers 2007: New research findings on programs to reduce teen pregnancy. Report of The National Campaign to Prevent Teen and Unplanned Pregnancy. Retrieved from http://www.thenationalcampaign.org/resources/reports.aspx.
Kirkman, B. L., Jones, R. G., & Shapiro, D. L. (2000). Why do employees resist teams? Examining the "resistance barrier" to work team effectiveness. *International Journal of Conflict Management, 11,* 74–92.
Kirmeyer, S. L., & Dougherty, T. W. (1988). Workload, tension, and coping: Moderating effects of supervisor support. *Personnel Psychology, 41,* 125–139.
Kitchen, C. D. (1991). Crisis intervention using reality therapy for adult sexual abuse victims. *Journal of Reality Therapy, 10,* 34–39.
Kite, M. E., Stockdale, G. D., Whitley, B. E., & Johnson, B. T. (2005). Attitudes toward younger and older adults: An updated meta-analytic review. *Journal of Social Issues, 61,* 241–266.
Kleck, G. (1991). *Point blank: Guns and violence in America.* New York: De Gruyter.
Klein, D. (1987). The context and times at Swampscott: My story. *American Journal of Community Psychology, 12,* 515–517.
Klein, J. (2005). America is from Mars, Europe from Venus: How the United States can learn from Europe's social work response to school shootings. *School Social Work Journal, 30,* 1–24.
Klein, K. J., & D'Aunno, T. A. (1986). Psychological sense of community in the workplace. *Journal of Community Psychology, 14,* 365–377.
Klein, K. J., Ralls, R. S., Smith Major, V., & Douglas, C. (2000). Power and participation in the workplace: Implications for empowerment theory, research, and practice. In J. Rappaport & E. Seidman (Eds.), *Handbook of community psychology.* New York: Plenum.
Kleinman, J. C., & Madanas, J. H. (1985). The effects of maternal smoking, physical stature, and educational attainment on the incidence of low birthweight. *American Journal of Epidemiology, 121,* 843–855.
Kling, R. (2000). Learning about information technologies and social change: The contribution of social informatics. *Information Society, 16,* 217–232.
Kloos, B. (2005). Community science: Creating an alternative place to stand? *American Journal of Community Psychology, 35,* 259–267.
Knitzer, J. (2007). Putting knowledge into policy: Toward an infant-toddler policy agenda. *Infant Mental Health Journal: Special Issue: Infant Mental Health in Early Head Start, 28,* 237–245.
Koch, T., & Kralik, D. (2006). *Participatory action research in health care.* Oxford: Blackwell.
Koch, W. (January 1, 2006). Poll: Washington scandals eating away public trust. *USA Today.* Retrieved from http://www.usatoday.com/news/washington/2006-12-11-ethics_x.htm.
Koegel, P., Burnam, M. A., & Farr, R. K. (1990). Substance adaptation among homeless adults in the inner city of Los Angeles. *Journal of Social Issues, 46,* 83–107.
Kofkin-Radkin, J. (2003). *Community psychology* (pp. 171–173). New York: Prentice Hall.
Kohlberg, L. (1984). *Essays on moral development (vol. 2). The nature and validity of moral stages.* San Francisco: Harper & Row.
Koizumi, R. (2000). Anchor points in transitions to a new school environment. *Journal of Primary Prevention, 20,* 175–187.
Korbin, J. E., & Coulton, C. J. (1996). The role of neighbors and the government in neighborhood-based child protection. *Journal of Social Issues, 52,* 163–176.
Kosic, A., & Phalet, K. (2006). Ethnic categorization of immigrants: The role of prejudice, perceived acculturation strategies, and group size. *International Journal of Intercultural Relations, 30,* 769–782.

Kotch, J., Blakely, C., Brown, S., & Wong, F. (1992). *A pound of prevention: The case for university maternity care in the US*. Washington, DC: American Public Health Association.

Kranz, D. H. (1998). Predictors of homelessness among families in New York City: From shelter request to housing stability. *American Journal of Public Health, 88,* 1651–1657.

Kreisler, A., Snider, A. B., & Kiernan, N. E. (1997). Using distance education to educate and empower community coalitions: A case study. *International Quarterly of Community Health Education, 17,* 161–178.

Krueger, P. M., Bond Huie, S. A., Rogers, R. G., & Hummer, R. A. (2004). Neighbourhoods and homicide mortality: An analysis of race/ethnic differences. *Journal of Epidemiology & Community Health, 58,* 223–230.

Kruger, D. J., Reischl, T. M., & Gee, G. C. (2007). Neighborhood social conditions mediate the association between physical deterioration and mental health. *American Journal of Community Psychology, 40,* 261–271.

Kuhn, T. (1962/1996). *The structure of scientific revolutions*. Chicago: University of Chicago Press.

Kulik, L. (2006). Burnout among volunteers in the social services: The impact of gender and employment status. *Journal of Community Psychology, 34,* 541–561.

Kuo, F. E., Sullivan, W. C., Coley, R. L., & Brunson, L. (1998). Fertile ground for community: Inner-city neighborhood common spaces. *American Journal of Community Psychology, 26,* 823–852.

Labianca, G., Gray, B., & Brass, D. J. (2000). A grounded model of organizational schema change during empowerment. *Organization Science, 11,* 235–257.

Laguna, K., & Babcock, R. L. (1997). Computer anxiety in young and older adults: Implications for human-computer interactions in older populations. *Computers in Human Behavior, 13,* 317–326.

Lahm, K. F. (2008). Inmate-on-inmate assault. *Criminal Justice and Behavior, 35,* 120–137.

Lal, S. (2002). Giving children security: Mamie Phipps Clark and the racialization of child psychology. *American Psychologist, 57*(1), 20–28.

Lamb, M. E., & Ahnert, L. (2006). Nonparental child care: Context, concepts, correlations, and consequences. In K. A. Renninger, I. E. Sigel, W. Damon, & R. M. Lerner (Eds.), *Handbook of child psychology: Volume 4: Child psychology in practice*. Hoboken, NJ: Wiley.

Lambert, E. Y. (Ed.). (1990). The collection and interpretation of data from hidden populations. *NIDA Monograph 98*. Rockville, MD: NIDA.

Lambert, M. J., & Barley, D. E. (2001). Research summary on the therapeutic relationship and psychotherapy outcome. *Psychotherapy: Theory, Research, Practice, Training, 38,* 357–361.

Lambert, S. F., Ialongo, N. S., Boyd, R. C., & Cooley, M. R. (2005). Risk factors for community violence exposure in adolescence. *American Journal of Community Psychology, 36,* 29–48.

Landers, S. (1989). Homeless children lose childhood. *APA Monitor, 20* (12), 1, 33.

Langer, L. J., & Rodin, J. (1976). The effects of choice and enhanced personal responsibility for the aged: A field experiment in an institutional setting. *Journal of Personality and Social Psychology, 34,* 191–198.

Langhout, R. D. (2004). Facilitators and inhibitors of positive school feelings: An exploratory study. *American Journal of Community Psychology, 34,* 111–127.

La Piere, R. T. (1934). Attitudes and actions. *Social Forces, 13,* 230–237.

Laracuenta, M., & Denmark, F. L. (2005). What can we do about school violence? In F. L. Denmark, H. H. Krause, R. W. Wesner, E. Midlarsky, E. Gielen, & P. Uwe (Eds.), *Violence in schools: Cross-national and cross-cultural perspectives*. New York: Springer.

Lasker, R., Weiss, E., & Miller, R. (2001). Partnership synergy: A practical framework for studying and strengthening the collaborative advantage. *Milbank Quarterly, 79*(2), 179–205.

Latimer, J., Dowden, C., & Muise, D. (2005). The effectiveness of restorative justice practices: A meta-analysis. *Prison Journal, 85,* 127–144.

Latkin, C. A., Mandell, W., Vlahov, D., Oziemkowska, M., & Celentano, D. (1996). The long-term outcome of a personal network-oriented HIV prevention intervention for injection drug users: The SAFE study. *American Journal of Community Psychology, 24,* 341–364.

Lavee, Y., & Ben-Ari, A. (2008). The association between daily hassles and uplifts with family and life satisfaction: Does cultural orientation make a difference? *American Journal of Community Psychology, 1–2,* 89-98.

LaVeist, T., Sellers, R., Brown, K., & Nickerson, K. (1997). Extreme social isolation, use of community-based senior support services, and mortality among African American elderly women. *American Journal of Community Psychology, 25*(5), 721–732

Lavoie, K. L., & Barone, S. (2006). Prescription privileges for psychologists: A comprehensive review and critical analysis of current issues and controversies. *CNS Drugs, 20*(1), 51–66.

Lawson, A., & Rhode, D. L. (1993). *The politics of pregnancy: Adolescent sexuality and public policy.* New Haven, CT: Yale University Press.

Lazarus, R. (1999). *Stress and emotion: A new synthesis.* New York: Springer.

Lazarus, R. S., & Folkman, S. (1984). *Stress, appraisal, and coping.* New York: Springer-Verlag.

Lee, T., & Breen, L. (2007). Young people's perceptions and experiences of leaving school early: An exploration. *Journal of Community & Applied Social Psychology, 17,* 329–346.

Legault, L., Green-Demers, I., & Pelletier, L. (2006). Why do high school students lack motivation in the classroom? Toward an understanding of academic motivation and the role of social support. *Journal of Educational Psychology, 98,* 567–582.

Lehr, U., Seiler, E., & Thomae, H. (2000). Aging in cross-cultural perspective. In L. Comunian & U. P. Gielen (Eds.), *International perspectives on human development.* Lengerich, Germany: Pabst Science.

Leigh, B. C., & Stall, R. (1993). Substance abuse and risky behavior for exposure to HIV: Issues in methodology, interpretation, and prevention. *American Psychologist, 48,* 1035–1045.

Leinsalu, M. (2004). *Troubled transitions: Social variation and long-term trends in health and mortality in Estonia.* Stockholm: Almqvist & Wiksell.

Leiter, M., & Maslach, C. (1998). Burnout. In H. Friedman (Ed.), *Encyclopedia of Mental Health.* San Diego: Academic Press.

Leiter, M. P., & Maslach, C. (2004). Areas of work life: A structured approach to organizational predictors of job burnout. In P. Perrewe & D. Ganster (Eds.), *Research in occupational stress and well being* (vol. 3, pp. 91–134). Oxford: Elsevier.

Leiter, M. P., & Maslach, C. (2005). A mediation model of job burnout. In A. Antoniou & C. Cooper (Eds.), *Research companion to organizational health psychology* (pp. 544–564). Cheltenham: Edward Elger.

Lempert, R., & Sanders, J. (1986). *An invitation to law and social science.* New York: Longman.

Leonard, P. A., Dolbeare, C. N., & Lazere, E. B. (1989). *A place to call home: The crisis in housing for the poor.* Washington, DC: Center on Budget and Policy Priorities and Low Income Housing Information Service.

Lesesne, C. A., Lewis, K. M., White, C. P., & Green, D. C. (2008). Promoting science-based approaches to teen pregnancy prevention: Proactively engaging the three systems of interactive systems framework. *American Journal of Community Psychology, 41,* 379–393.

Lettieri, D. J., Sayers, M., & Pearson, H. W. (Eds.). (1984). *Theories on drug abuse: Selected contemporary perspectives.* National Institute on Drug Abuse Research Monograph 30. Washington, DC: Superintendent of Documents, U.S. Government Printing Office.

Leventhal, T., & Brooks-Gunn, J. (2004). A randomized study of neighborhood effects on low income children's educational outcomes. *Developmental Psychology, 40,* 488–507.

Levi, Y., & Litwin, H. (1986). *Communities and cooperatives in participatory development.* Brookfield, VT: Gower Press.

Levine, I. S., & Huebner, R. D. (1991). Homeless persons with alcohol, drug, and mental disorders. *American Psychologist, 46,* 1113–1114.

Levine, M. D. (1986). Working it out: A community re-creation approach to crime prevention. *Journal of Community Psychology, 14,* 378–390.

Levine, M. (1988). An analysis of mutual assistance. *American Journal of Community Psychology, 16,* 167–188.

Levine, M. (1998). Prevention and community. *American Journal of Community Psychology, 26,* 189–206.

Levine, M. (1999, Spring). Prevention and progress. *Community Psychologist, 32,* 11–14.

Levine, M., & Perkins, D. V. (1997). *Principles of community psychology: Perspectives and applications.* New York: Oxford University Press.

Levine, M., & Perkins, D. (2004) *Principles of community psychology. Perspectives and applications,* Third Edition. New York: Oxford Press.

Levine, M., Toro, P. A., & Perkins, D. V. (1993). Social and community interventions. In L. W. Porter & M. R. Rosenzweig (Eds.), *Annual review of psychology*. Palo Alto, CA: Annual Reviews.

Leviton, L. C. (1989). Theoretical foundations of AIDS prevention programs. In R. O. Valdiserri (Ed.), *Preventing AIDS: The design of effective programs* (pp. 42–90). New Brunswick, NJ: Rutgers University Press.

Levy, L. H. (2000). Self-help groups. In J. Rappaport & E. Seidman (Eds.), *Handbook of community psychology*. New York: Plenum.

Lewin, K. (1936). *Principles of topological psychology.* New York: McGraw-Hill.

Lewin, K. (1946). Action research and minority problems. *Journal of Social Issues, 2*(4), 34–46.

Lewin, K. (1948). *Resolving social conflict.* New York: Harper.

Lewin, K. (1951). *Field theory in social science.* New York: Harper & Row.

Lewin, K., & Lippett, R. (1938) An experimental approach to the study of autocracy and democracy. A preliminary note. *Sociometry, 1,* 292–300.

Lewin, K., Lippett, R., & White, R. (1939) Patterns of aggressive behavior in experimentally created "social climates." *Journal of Social Psychology 10,* 271–299.

Lichtenstein E., Lopez, K., Glasgow, R. E., Gilbert-McRae, S., & Hall, R. (1996). Effectiveness of a consultation intervention to promote tobacco control policies in northwest Indian tribes: Integrating experimental evaluation and services delivery. *American Journal of Community Psychology, 24,* 639–655.

Light, D., & Keller, S. (1985). *Sociology.* New York: Knopf.

Likert, R. (1961). *New patterns of management.* New York: McGraw-Hill.

Lin, N., Simonre, R., Ensel, W., & Kuo, W. (1979). Social support, stressful life events, and illness: A model and an empirical test. *Journal of Health and Social Behavior, 20,* 108–119.

Linney, J. A. (1990). Community psychology into the 1990's: Capitalizing opportunity and promoting innovation. *American Journal of Community Psychology, 18,* 1–17.

Linney, J. (2005). Might we practice what we've preached? Thoughts on the special issue papers. *American Journal of Community Psychology, 35,* 253–258.

Lippett, R., Watson, J., & Westley, B. (1958). *The dynamics of planned change.* New York: Harcourt, Brace, & World.

Lohr, S. (October 31, 2006). Computing 2016, what won't be possible? *New York Times.* Retrieved from http://www.nytimes.com/2006/10/31/science/31essa.html?_r=1&oref=slogin

Long, D., & Perkins, D. (2003). Confirmatory factor analysis of the Sense of Community Index and development of a brief SCI. *Journal of Community Psychology, 31,* 279–296.

Loo, C., Fong, K. T., & Iwamasca, G. (1988). Ethnicity and cultural diversity: An analysis of work published in community psychology journals, 1965–1985. *Journal of Community Psychology, 16,* 332–349.

Lopez, G. E. (2004). Interethnic contact, curriculum, and attitudes in the first year of college. *Journal of Social Issues, 60,* 75–94.

Lorion, R. P. (1983). Evaluating preventive interventions: Guidelines for the serious social change agent. In R. Felner, L. Jason, J. Moritsugu, & S. Farber (Eds.), *Preventive psychology: Theory, research and practice* (pp. 251–268). New York: Pergamon.

Lorion, R. P. (1991). Targeting preventive interventions: Enhancing risk estimates through theory. *American Journal of Community Psychology, 19,* 859–865.

Lorion, R. (2007). From the editor. *Journal of Community Psychology, 35*(1), 1–2.

Lösel, F. (2007). Counterblast: The prison overcrowding crisis and some constructive perspectives for crime policy. *Howard Journal of Criminal Justice, 46,* 512–519.

Loukaitou-Sideris, A., & Eck, J. E. (2007). Crime prevention and active living. *American Journal of Health Promotion. Special Issue: Active Living Research, 21,* 380–389.

Loukes, A., Suzuki, R., & Horton, K. D. (2006). Examining social connectedness as a mediator of school climate effects. *Journal of Research on Adolescence, 16,* 491–502.

Lounsbury, J. W., Leader, D. S., Meares, E. P., & Cook, M. P. (1980). An analytic review of research in community psychology. *American Journal of Community Psychology, 8,* 415–441.

Love, J. M., Tarullo, L. B., Raikes, H., & Chazan-Cohen, R. (2006). Head Start: What do we know about its effectiveness? What do we need to know? In K. McCartney & D. Malden (Eds.), *Blackwell handbook of early childhood development*. Malden, MA: Blackwell.

Lovell, A. M. (1990). Managed cases, drop-ins, dropouts, and other by-products of mental health care. *American Journal of Community Psychology, 18*, 917–921.

Lowenthal, M. F., & Haven, C. (1968). Interaction and adaptation: Intimacy as a cultural variable. *American Sociological Review, 33*, 20–30.

Ludwig, J., & Phillips, D. (2007). The benefits and costs of Head Start. *Social Policy Report, 21*, 1–20.

Luepker, R., Murray, D., Jacobs, D., Mittelmark, M., Bracht, N., Carlaw, R., et al. (1994). Community education for cardiovascular disease prevention: risk factor changes in the Minnesota Heart Health Program. *American Journal of Public Health, 84*, 1383–1393.

Lustig, J. L., Wolchik, S. A., & Braver, S. L. (1992). Social support in chumships and adjustment in children of divorce. *American Journal of Community Psychology, 20*, 391–393.

Lynch, M. (2006). Children exposed to community violence. In M. M. Feerick & G. B. Silverman (Eds.), *Children exposed to violence*. Baltimore, MD: Brookes.

Maccoby, N., & Altman, D. (1988). Disease prevention in communities: The Stanford Heart Disease Prevention Program. In R. Price, E. Cowen, R. Lorion, & J. Ramos-McKay (Eds.), *Fourteen ounces of prevention: A casebook for practitioners* (pp. 165–174). Washington, DC: American Psychological Association.

MacDermid, S. M., Hertzog, J. L., Kensinger, K. B., & Zipp, J. F. (2001). The role of organizational size and industry in job quality and work-family relationships. *Journal of Family & Economic Issues Special Issue, 22*, 119–126.

MacKenzie, D. L., Wilson, D. B., Armstrong, G. S., & Gover, A. R. (2001). The impact of boot camps and traditional institutions on juvenile residents: Perceptions, adjustment, and change. *Journal of Research in Crime & Delinquency Special Issue, 38*, 279–313.

Macy, B. A., & Izumi, H. (1993). Organizational change, design, and work innovation: A meta-analysis of 131 North American field studies—1961–1991. In R. W. Woodman & W. A. Pasmore (Eds.), *Research in organizational change and development*, vol. 7. Greenwich, CT: JAI.

Madera, E. J. (1986). A comprehensive approach to promoting mutual AIDS self-help groups: The New Jersey Self-Help Clearinghouse model. *Journal of Voluntary Action Research, 15*, 57–63.

Magee Quinn, M., Kavale, K. A., Mathur, S. R., Rutherford, R. B., & Forness, S. R. (1999). A meta-analysis of social skill interventions for students with emotional or behavioral disorders. *Journal of Emotional & Behavioral Disorders, 7*, 54–64.

Magnuson, K. A., & Waidfugel, J. (2005). Early childhood care and education: Effects on ethnic and racial gaps in school readiness. *Future of Children, 15*, 169–196.

Magura, S., Goldsmith, D. S., Casriel, C., & Lipton, D. S. (1988). Patient-staff governance in methadone maintenance treatment: A study in participative decision making. *Narcotic and Drug Research, 23*, 253–278.

Mahalingam, R. (2006). *Cultural psychology of immigrants*. Mahwah, NJ: Erlbaum.

Maiorana, A., Kegeles, S., Fernandez, P., et al. (2007). Implementation and evaluation of an HIV/STD intervention in Peru. *Evaluation and Program Planning, 30*, 82–93.

Maloy, K. A., Darnell, J., Nolan, L., Kenney, K., & Cyprien, S. (2000). *Effect of the 1996 welfare and immigration reform laws on immigrants' ability and willingness to access Medicaid and health care services: Findings from four metropolitan sites* (vol. 1). Washington, DC: Center for Health Services Research and Policy, George Washington University School of Public Health and Health Services.

Mann, J., Tarantola, D., & Netter, T. (1992). *AIDS in the world*. Cambridge, MA: Harvard University Press.

Mannix, E., & Neale, M. (2005). What differences make a difference? *Psychological Science in the Public Interest, 6*, 31–55.

Manwaring, J., Bryson, S., & Goldschmidt, A. (2008). Do adherence variables predict outcome in an online program for the prevention of eating disorders? *Journal of Consulting and Clinical Psychology, 76*, 341–346.

Manzo, L., & Perkins, D. (2006). Finding common ground: The importance of place attachment to community participation and planning. *Journal of Planning Literature, 20*, 335–350.

Marchel, C., & Owens, S. (2007). Qualitative research in psychology: Could William James get a job? *History of Psychology, 10*(4), 301–324.

Marcus-Newhall, A., & Heindl, T. R. (1998). Coping with interracial stress in ethnically diverse classrooms: How important are Allport's contact conditions? *Journal of Social Issues Special Issue: Understanding and Resolving National and International Group Conflict, 54,* 813–830.

Marin, G. (1993). Defining culturally appropriate community interventions: Hispanics as a case study. *Journal of Community Psychology, 21,* 149–161.

Marlatt, G. A., & Gordon, J. R. (1985). *Relapse prevention: Maintenance strategies in the treatment of addictive behaviors.* New York: Guilford.

Marlowe, L. (1971). *Social psychology: An interdisciplinary approach to human behavior.* Oxford, England: Holbrook, 1971.

Martin, J., & Hall, G. N. (1992). Thinking Black, thinking internal, thinking feminist. *Journal of Counseling Psychology, 39,* 509–514.

Martin, P., Lounsbury, D., & Davidson II, W. (2004). AJCP as a vehicle for improving community life: An historic-analytic review of the journal's contents. *American Journal of Community Psychology, 34,* 163–173.

Maruyama, G. (2003). Disparities in educational opportunities and outcomes: What do we know and what can we do? *Journal of Social Issues, 59,* 653–676.

Marx, J. D., & Hopper, F. (2005). Faith-based versus fact-based social policy: The case of teenage pregnancy prevention. *Social Work, 50,* 280–282.

Maslach, C., & Goldberg, J. (1998). Prevention of burnout: New perspectives. *Applied and Preventive Psychology, 7,* 63–74.

Maslach, C., & Jackson, D. (1981). *Maslach burnout inventory manual.* Palo Alto, CA: Consulting Psychologist Press.

Maslach, C., & Leiter, M. P. (2008). Early predictors of job burnout and engagement. *Journal of Applied Psychology, 93,* 498–512.

Maslach, C., Schaufeli, W. B., & Leiter, M. P. (2000). Job burnout. *Annual Review of Psychology, 52,* 397–422.

Massachusetts Department of Public Health. (1991). *Handbook on smoking laws and regulations for Massachusetts Communities.* Boston: Author.

Masten, A. (2001). Ordinary magic: Resilience processes in development. *American Psychologist, 56,* 227–238.

Masten, A., & Coatsworth, J. (1998). The development of competence in favorable and unfavorable environments. *American Psychologist, 53*(2), 205–220.

Masten, A., & Obradovic, J. (2006). Competence and resilience in development. *Annals of the New York Academy of Sciences, 1094,* 13–27.

Maton, K. I. (1988). Social support, organizational characteristics, psychological well being, and group appraisal in three self-help group populations. *American Journal of Community Psychology, 16,* 53–78.

Maton, K. (2000). Making a difference: The social ecology of social transformation. *American Journal of Community Psychology, 28,* 25–57.

Maton, K. (2008). Empowering community settings: Agents of individual development, community betterment, and positive social change. *American Journal of Community Psychology, 41*(1–2), 4–21.

Maton, K. I., Levanthal, G. S., Madera, E. J., & Julien, M. (1989). Factors affecting the birth and death of mutual help groups: The role of national affiliation, professional involvement, and member focal point. *American Journal of Community Psychology, 17,* 643–671.

Maton, K. I., Meissen, G. J., & O'Conner, P. (1993). The varying faces of graduate education in community psychology: Comparisons by program type and program level. *Community Psychologist, 26,* 19–21.

Maton, K. I., Perkins, D. D., Altman, D. G., Guitierrez, L., Kelly, J. G., Rappaport, J., et al. (2006). Community-based interdisciplinary research: Introduction to the special issue. *American Journal of Community Psychology, 38,* 1–8.

Maton, K. I., Perkins, D. D., & Saegert, S. (2006). Community psychology at the crossroads: Prospects for interdisciplinary research. *American Journal of Community Psychology, 38,* 9–21.

Maton, K. I., & Salem, D. A. (1995). Organizational characteristics of empowering community settings: A multiple case approach. *American Journal of Community Psychology, 23,* 631–656.

Matthews, D. B. (1991). The effects of school environment on intrinsic motivation of middle-school children. *Journal of Humanistic Education and Development, 30,* 30–38.

Mawby, R. (1986). Fear of crime and concern over the crime problem among the elderly. *Journal of Community Psychology, 14,* 300–306.

Mayer, J. P., & Davidson, W. S. (2000). Dissemination of innovation as social change. In J. Rappaport & E. Seidman (Eds.), *Handbook of community psychology.* New York: Plenum.

Mays, V., Cochran, S., & Barnes, N. (2007). Race, race-based discrimination, and health outcomes among African Americans. *Annual Review of Psychology, 58,* 201–225.

McAlister, A. (2000). Action-oriented mass communication. In J. Rappaport & E. Seidman (Eds.), *Handbook of community psychology.* New York: Plenum.

McBride, T. D., Calsyn, R. J., Morse, G. A., Klinkenberg, W. D., & Allen, G. A. (1998). Duration of homeless spells among severely mentally ill individuals: A survival analysis. *Journal of Community Psychology, 26,* 473–490.

McCaughey, B. G. (1987). U.S. Navy special psychiatric rapid and intervention team (SPRINT). *Military Medicine, 152,* 133–135.

McCave, E. L. (2007). Comprehensive sexuality education vs. abstinence-only sexuality education: The need for evidence-based research and practice. *School Social Work Journal, 32,* 14–28.

McConnell, A., Rydell, R., & Strain, L. (2008). Forming implicit and explicit attitudes toward individuals: Social group association cues. *Journal of Personality and Social Psychology, 94*(5), 792–807.

McCulloch, A., & O'Brien, L. (1986). The organizational determinants of worker burnout. *Children and Youth Services Review, 8,* 175–190.

McDonald, H. P., Garg, A. X., Haynes, R. B. (2002). Interventions to enhance patient adherence to medication prescriptions: scientific review. *Journal of the American Medical Association, 288,* 2868–2879.

McGillis, D. (1997). *Community mediation programs: Developments and challenges.* Washington, DC: U.S. Department of Justice.

McGinnis, J., & Foege, W. H. (1993). Actual causes of death in the United States. *Journal of American Medical Association, 270,* 2207–2212.

McGrath, J. E. (1983). Looking ahead by looking backwards: Some recurrent themes about social change. *Journal of Social Issues, 39,* 225–239.

McIntosh, N. J. (1991). Identification of properties of social support. *Journal of Organizational Behavior, 12,* 201–217.

McIntyre, J. J. (2007). Impact of media violence on children. Testimony before the U.S. Senate Committee on Commerce, Science, and Transportation. Washington, DC: Public Policy Office of the American Psychological Association.

McMahon, S. D., & Jason, L. A. (2000). Social support in a worksite smoking intervention: A test of theoretical modes. *Behavior Modification, 24,* 184–201.

McMillan, D. W., & Chavis, D. M. (1986). Sense of community: A definition and theory. *Journal of Community Psychology, 14*(1), 6–23.

McNeal, R. B. (1997). High school dropouts: A closer examination of school effects. *Social Science Quarterly, 78,* 209–222.

Meade, J. (1991). Turning on the bright lights. *Teacher Magazine,* 36–42.

Medway, F. J., & Updyke, J. F. (1985). Meta-analysis of consultation outcome studies. *American Journal of Community Psychology, 13,* 489–505.

Meehan, T. (1986). Alternatives to lawsuits. *Alternatives to Legal Reform, 6,* 9–12.

Meehl, P. E. (1954). *Clinical versus statistical prediction.* Minneapolis: University of Minnesota Press.

Meehl, P. E. (1960). The cognitive activity of the clinician. *American Psychologist, 15,* 19–27.

Melamed, S., Kushnir, T., & Meir, E. I. (1991). Attenuating the impact of job demands: Addictive and interactive effects of perceived control and social support. *Journal of Vocational Behavior, 39,* 40–53.

Mellow, J., & Dickinson, J. M. (2006). The role of pre-release handbooks for prisoner reentry. *Federal Probation, 70,* 70–76.

Melton, G. B. (2000). Community change, community stasis, and the law. In J. Rappaport & E. Seidman (Eds.), *Handbook of community psychology.* New York: Plenum.

Méndez-Negrete, J., Saldaña, L. P., & Vega, A. (2006). Can a culturally informed after-school curriculum make a difference in teen pregnancy prevention? Preliminary evidence in the case of San Antonio's escuelitas. *Families in Society, 87,* 95–104.

Milburn, N. G., Gary, L. E., Booth, J. A., & Brown, D. R. (1991). Conducting research in a minority community: Methodological considerations. *Journal of Community Psychology, 19,* 3–12.

Milkovich, G. T., & Boudreau, J. W. (1991). *Human resource management.* Homewood, IL: Irwin.

Miller, L. S., Zhang, X., Rice, D., & Max, W. (1998). State estimates of total medical expenditures attributable to cigarette smoking, 1993. *Public Health Report, 113,* 447–458.

Miller, N., Brewer, M. B., & Edwards, K. (1985). Cooperative interaction in desegregated settings: A laboratory analogue. *Journal of Social Issues, 41,* 63–79.

Miller, R. D., Maier, G. J., & Kaye, M. S. (1988). Orienting the staff of a new maximum security forensic facility. *Hospital and Community Psychiatry, 39,* 780–781.

Milne, A. (1985). Mediation or therapy—which is it? In S. C. Grebe (Ed.), *Divorce and family mediation.* Rockville, MD: Aspen.

Minden, J., & Jason, L. (2002). Preventing chronic health problems. In L. Jason & D. Glenwick (Eds.), *Innovative strategies for promoting health and mental health across the life span* (pp. 227–243). New York: Springer.

Mintzberg, H. (1979). *The structuring of organizations.* Englewood Cliffs, NJ: Prentice Hall.

Mischel, W. (1968). *Personality and assessment.* Mahwah, NJ: Erlbaum.

Mishara, B. L. (1997). Effects of different telephone intervention styles with suicidal callers at two suicide prevention centers: An empirical investigation. *American Journal of Community Psychology, 25,* 861–885.

Mitchell, R. E. (1982). Social networks and psychiatric clients: The personal and environmental context. *American Journal of Community Psychology, 10,* 387–402.

Moffitt, T. (1993). Adolescence-limited and life-course-persistent antisocial behavior: A developmental taxonomy. *Psychological Review, 100*(4), 674–701.

Molina, L. E., & Wittig, M. A. (2006). Relative importance of contact conditions in explaining prejudice reduction in a classroom context: Separate and equal? *Journal of Social Issues, 62,* 489–509.

Molnar, J. (1988). *Home is where the heart is: The crisis of homeless children and families in New York City.* New York: Bank Street College of Education.

Molnar, J. M., Rath, W. R., & Klein, T. P. (1990). Constantly compromised: The impact of homelessness on children. *Journal of Social Issues, 46,* 109–124.

Moos, R. (1973). Conceptualizations of human environments. *American Psychologist, 28*(8), 652–665.

Moos, R. H. (1994). *Work environment scale manual: Development, applications, research,* Third Edition. Palo Alto, CA: Consulting Psychologists Press, Inc.

Moos, R. (2003). Social contexts: Transcending their power and their fragility. *American Journal of Community Psychology, 31*(1–2), 1.

Morbidity and Mortality Weekly Report (1997). *State-specific prevalence of cigarette smoking among adults, and children's and adolescents' exposure to environmental tobacco smoke—United States, 1996, 46,* 1038–1043. Atlanta, GA: Author.

Morbidity and Mortality Weekly Report (1998a, September 11). *Preventing emerging infectious diseases: A strategy for the 21st century, 47* (no. RR-15). Atlanta, GA: Author.

Morbidity and Mortality Weekly Report (1998b, October 9). *Incidence of initiation of cigarette smoking—United States, 47* (no. 39), 837–840. Atlanta, GA: Author.

Morbidity and Mortality Weekly Report (1998c, August 14). *Youth Risk Behavior Surveillance—United States, 1997, 47* (no. SS-3). Atlanta, GA: Author.

Morbidity and Mortality Weekly Report (2005). *Annual smoking-attributable mortality, year of potential life lost, and productivity losses—United States, 1997–2001, 54,* 625–628. Atlanta, GA: Author.

Morbidity and Mortality Weekly Report (2006, June 9). *Youth risk behavior surveillance—United States, 2005, 47* (no. SS-5), 1–108. Atlanta, GA: Author.

Morgeson, F. P., Campion, M. A., & Maertz, C. P. (2001). Understanding pay satisfaction: The limits of a compensation system implementation. *Journal of Business & Psychology Special Issue, 16,* 133–149.

Moritsugu, J., & Sue, S. (1983). Minority status as a stressor. In R. Felner, L. Jason, J. Moritsugu, & S. Farber (Eds.), *Preventive psychology.* New York: Pergamon.

Morris, A., Shinn, M., & DuMont, K. (1999). Contextual factors affecting the organizational commitment of diverse police officers: A levels of analysis perspective. *American Journal of Community Psychology, 27,* 75–105.

Moses, D. J., Kresky-Wolff, M., Bassuk, E. L., & Brounstein, P. (2007). Guest editorial: The promise of homelessness prevention. *Journal of Primary Prevention, 28,* 191–197.

Moss, L. (1981). *Management stress.* Reading, MA: Addison-Wesley.

Moulton, P., Miller, M., & Offutt, S. (2007). Identifying rural health care needs using community conversations. *Journal of Rural Health, 23*(1), 92–96.

Mowbray, C. T. (1979). A study of patients treated as incompetent to stand trial. *Social Psychiatry, 14,* 31–39.

Mowbray, C. T. (1990). Community treatment for the seriously mentally ill: Is this community psychology? *American Journal of Community Psychology, 18,* 893–902.

Mowbray, C. T., Herman, S. E., & Hazel, K. (1992). Subgroups and differential treatment needs of young adults with long-term severe mental illness. *Psychosocial Rehabilitation Journal, 16,* 45–62.

Moyer, C., et al. (2008). Quality of life, optimism/pessimism, and knowledge and attitudes toward HIV screening among pregnant women in Ghana. *Women's Health Issues,* x, 1–9.

Moynihan, D. R., & Pandey, S. K. (2008). The ties that bind: Social networks, person-organization value fit, and turnover intention. *Journal of Public Administration Research and Theory, 18,* 205–227.

Mrazek, P., & Haggerty, R. (1994). Reducing risks for mental disorders: Frontiers for preventive intervention research. *National Academy of Sciences, Institute of Medicine, Division of Biobehavioral Sciences & Mental Disorders, Committee on Prevention of Mental Disorders* (p. 605). Washington, DC: National Academies Press.

Muenchow, S., & Marsland, K. W. (2007). Beyond baby steps: Promoting the growth and development of U.S. child-care policy. In J. L. Aber, S. J. Bishop-Josef, S. M. Jones, K. T. McLearn, & D. Phillips (Eds.), *Child development and social policy: Knowledge for action.* Washington, DC: American Psychological Association.

Muha, D. G., & Cole, C. (1990). Dropout prevention and group counseling: A review of the literature. *High School Journal, 74,* 76–80.

Muir, E. (Winter 2000–2001). Smaller schools. *American Educator,* 40–46.

Muñoz, M., Panadero, S., Santos, E. P., & Quiroga, M. A. (2005). Role of stressful life events in homelessness: An intragroup analysis. *American Journal of Community Psychology, 35,* 35–46.

Murphy, S. E., & Halpern, D. (2006). Vison for the future of work and family interaction. In D. F. Halpern & S. E. Murphy (Eds.). *From work-family balance to work-family interaction.* Mahwah, NJ: Erlbaum.

Myers, W. C., Catalano, G., Sanchez, D. L., & Ross, M. M. (2006). HIV/AIDS among prisoners. In F. Fernandez & P. Ruiz (Eds.), *Psychiatric aspects of HIV/AIDS.* Philadelphia: Lippincott Williams & Wilkins.

Nadel, H., Spellmann, M., Alvarez-Canino, T., Lausell-Bryant, L., & Landsberg, G. (1996). The cycle of violence and victimization: A study of the school-based intervention of multidisciplinary youth violence-prevention program. *American Journal of Preventive Medicine, 12,* 109–119.

Naisbett, J., & Aburdene, P. (1990). *Megatrends 2000.* New York: William Morrow.

National Campaign to Prevent Teen and Unwanted Pregnancy (2008). *Teen pregnancy prevention.* Retrieved from www.teenpregnancy.org/data/genlfact.asp.

National Cancer Institute (2004, June 16). *American Stop Smoking Intervention Study (ASSIST) evaluation: Questions and answers.* Retrieved June 13, 2008, from www.cancer.gov/cancertopics/factsheet/assistqa.

National Center for Education Statistics (2007). *Numbers and rates of public high school dropouts: School year 2004–2005.* Washington, DC: Author.

National Center for Education Statistics (2008). *What are the dropout rates of high school students?* Retrieved on February 18, 2008, from www.Nces.ed.gov/fastfacts/display.asp?id=16.

National Center for Health Statistics (2007a). *Teen birth rate rises for first time in 15 years.* Retrieved from www.cdc.gov/nchs/pressroom/07newsreleases/teenbirth.htm.

National Center for Health Statistics (2007b). *Health, United States, 2007.* Washington, D.C.: U.S. Government Printing Office. Retrieved on July 5, 2008, from www.cdc.gov/nchs/hus.htm.

National Center on Secondary Education and Transition (2008). *Increasing rates of school completion: Moving from policy and research to practice: A manual for policymakers, administrators, and educators*. Retrieved on February 18, 2008, from www.ncset.org/publications/essentialtools/dropout/part3.3.09.asp.

National Coalition for the Homeless (1999). *NCH Fact Sheets 1–3*. Retrieved from www.nationalhomeless.org.

National Coalition for the Homeless (2006). *A dream denied: The criminalization of homelessness in U.S. cities*. Washington, DC: Author.

National Coalition for the Homeless (2007a). *How many people experience homelessness? NCH Fact Sheet #2*. Washington, DC: Author.

National Coalition for the Homeless (2007b). *Who is homeless? NCH Fact Sheet #3*. Washington, DC: Author.

National Coalition of STD Directors (2008). *National guidelines for Internet-based STD/HIV prevention*. Washington, DC: US. Government Printing Office.

National Commission on AIDS. (1993). *Behavioral and Social Sciences and the HIV/AIDS Epidemic.* Washington, D.C. (1990).

National Crime Prevention Council (1989). The success of community crime prevention. *Canadian Journal of Criminology, 31,* 487–506.

National Drug Control Strategy 2008 Annual Report (Rep.) (2008). Washington, DC: White House.

National Highway Traffic Safety Administration (1995, February). *Repeat DWI offenders in the United States.* NHTSA Technology Series no. 85. Washington, DC: Author.

National Highway Traffic Safety Administration (1996). *Traffic safety facts 1995: Alcohol.* Washington, DC: Author.

National Highway Traffic Safety Administration (1997). *Setting limits, saving lives: The case for .08% BAC laws.* Pub. no. DOT HS 808 524. Washington, DC: Author.

National Highway Traffic Safety Administration (2008, January). Repeat intoxicated driver laws. *Traffic Safety Facts Laws.*

National Institute of Alcohol Abuse and Alcoholism (2004). NIAAA council approves definition of binge drinking. *NIAAA Newsletter, 3,* 3.

National Institute of Child and Human Development (2006). *Study of early child care and youth development.* Washington, DC: U.S. Government Printing Office.

National Institute of Child and Human Development, Early Child Care Research Network (2001). Nonmaternal care and family factors in early development: An overview of the NICHD Study of Early Child Care. *Journal of Applied Developmental Psychology, 22,* 457–492.

National School Safety and Security Services (2008). *School violence facts & figures.* Retrieved from www.schoolsecurity.org/trends/school-violence.html.

National Science Foundation (2003). *Science and technology: Public attitudes and public understanding.* Retrieved from www.nsf.gov/sbe/srs/seind02/c7/c7h.htm.

Nation's Health (1998, October). *DWI deaths reach historic low: Proportion falls below 40 percent of first time on record,*. Washington, DC: Author.

Nation's Health (2001, August). *Arizona smoking rates decline.* Washington, DC: Author.

Nelson, D., & Simmons, B. (2003). Health psychology and work stress: A more positive approach. In J. Quick & L. Tetrick (Eds.), *Handbook of occupational health psychology* (pp. 97–119). Washington, DC: American Psychological Association.

Nelson, G., Aubrey, T., & Lafrance, A. (2007). A review of the literature on the effectiveness of housing and support, assertive community treatment, and intensive case management interventions for persons with mental illness who have been homeless. *American Journal of Orthopsychiatry, 77*(3), 350–361.

Nelson, G., Ochocka, J., Griffin, K., & Lord, J. (1998). "Nothing about me, without me." Participatory action research with self-help/mutual aid organizations for psychiatric consumer survivors. *American Journal of Community Psychology, 26,* 881–912.

Nemoto, T., Wong, F. Y., Ching, A., Chng, C. L., Bouey, P., Hendrickson, M., et al. (1998). HIV seroprevalence, risk behaviors, and cognitive factors among Asian and Pacific Islander American men who have sex with men: A summary and critique of empirical studies and methodological studies. *AIDS Education and Prevention, 10* (Supplement A), 31–47.

Neuman, G. A., Edwards, J. E., & Raju, N. S. (1989). Organizational development interventions: A meta-analysis of their effects on satisfaction and other attitudes. *Personnel Psychology, 42,* 461–489.

Newborough, J. (1992). Toward community: A third position. *American Journal of Community Psychology, 23*(1), 9–37.

Newbrough, J. R., & Chavis, D. M. (Eds.). (1986). Psychological sense of community, I: Forward. *American Journal of Community Psychology, 14,* 3–5.

New York Times Editorial Board. (2007, April 4). Shackles on the AIDS Program. *New York Times.* Retrieved May 25, 2008, from www.nytimes.com/2007/04/04/opinion/04weds3.html?scp=1&sq=PEPFAR&st=nyt.

Nicotera, N. (2007). Measuring neighborhood: A conundrum for human service researchers and practitioners. *American Journal of Community Psychology, 40,* 26–51.

Nikelly, A. G. (1990). *Political activism: A new dimension for community psychology.* Paper presented to the Annual Convention of the American Psychological Association, Boston, MA.

Nores, M., Belfield, C. R., Barnett, S. W., & Schweinhart, L. (2005). Updating the economic impacts of the High/Scope Perry Preschool Program. *Educational Evaluation and Policy Analysis, 27,* 245–261.

Novotney, L. C., Mertinko, E., Lange, J., & Baker, T. K. (2000, September). Juvenile mentoring program: A progress review. *Juvenile Justice Bulletin,* 1–8.

O'Connell, J. J. (2007). The need for homelessness prevention: A doctor's view of life and death on the streets. *Journal of Primary Prevention, 28,* 199–203.

O'Donnell, C. (2006). Beyond diversity: Toward a cultural community psychology. *American Journal of Community Psychology, 37*(1–2), 1–7.

O'Donnell, C., & Ferrari, J. (2000). Employment in community psychology: The diversity of opportunity. *Journal of Prevention and Intervention in the Community, 19*(2).

Offerman, L., & Spiros, R. (2001). The science and practice of team development: Improving the link. *Academy of Management Journal, 44,* 376–392.

Office of Head Start (2007). *Statistical fact sheet fiscal year 2007.* Washington, DC: Administration for Children and Families.

Office of Justice Programs (2006). *Methamphetamine use increasing among state and federal prisoners.* Washington, DC: Department of Justice.

Office of Justice Programs (2007). *Urban and suburban crime rates stable from 2005 to 2006* (Press release). Washington, DC: Department of Justice.

Office of Juvenile Justice and Delinquency Programs (2008a). *Model programs.* Retrieved from www.dsgonline.com/mpg2.5/TitleV_MPG_Table_Ind_Rec.asp?ed=390.

Office of Juvenile Justice and Delinquency Prevention (2008b). *Safe Start: Promising approaches for communities.* Retrieved from www.safestartcenter.org.

Office of National Drug Control Policy (1998). *The national drug control strategy, 1998. A ten-year plan.* Washington, DC: Author.

Office of National Drug Control Policy (2008, June 12). New report finds highest-ever levels of THC. *Office of National Drug Control Policy Press Release.* Retrieved June 12, 2008, from www.whitehousedrugpolicy.gov/news/press08/061208.html.

Office of Smoking and Health (2001). *Women and smoking: A report of the Surgeon General.* Atlanta, GA: U.S. Department of Health and Human Services, Public Health Service, CDC.

Okamato, Y. (2007). A comparative study of homelessness in the United Kingdom and Japan. *Journal of Social Issues, 63,* 525–542.

Olatunji, A. N. (2005). Dropping out of high school among Mexican-origin youths: Is early work experience a factor? *Harvard Educational Review, 75,* 286–306.

Olds, D. (1997). The prenatal early infancy project: Preventing child abuse and neglect in the context of promoting maternal and child health. In D. A. Wolfe, R. J. McMahon, & R. D. Peters (Eds.), *Child abuse: New directions in prevention and treatment across the lifespan.* Thousand Oaks, CA: Sage.

Olds, D. L. (2005). The nurse-family partnership: Foundations in attachment theory and epidemiology. In L. J. Berlin, Y. Ziv, L. Amaya-Jackson, & M. T. Greenberg (Eds.), *Enhancing early attachments: Theory, research, intervention and policy. Duke series in child development and public policy.* New York: Guilford.

Olds, D. L. (2006). The nurse-family partnership: An evidence-based prevention intervention. *Infant Mental Health Journal. Special Issue: Early Preventive Intervention and Home Visiting, 27,* 5–25.

Olds, D. L. (2007). Preventing crime with prenatal and infancy support of parents: The nurse-family partnership. *Victims & Offenders: Special Issue on Early Intervention, 2,* 205–225.

Olds, D. L., Eckenrode, J., & Kitzman, H. (2005). Clarifying the impact of the nurse-family partnership on child maltreatment: Response to Chaffin (2004). *Child Abuse & Neglect, 29,* 229–233.

Olds, D., Henderson, C., Chamberlin, R., & Tetelbaum, R. (1986). Preventing child abuse and neglect: A randomized trial of nurse home visitation. *Pediatrics, 78,* 65–78.

Olds, D., Hill, P., & Rumsey, E. (1998, November). Prenatal and early childhood nurse home visitation. *Juvenile Delinquency Bulletin,* 1–7.

Olfson, M. (1990). Assertive community treatment. An evaluation of experimental evidence. *Hospital Community Psychiatry, 41,* 631–641.

Olson, M. R. (1991). Supportive growth experiences of beginning teachers. *Alberta Journal of Educational Research, 37,* 19–30.

Olson, M., & Cohen, A. A. (1986). An alternative approach to the training of residential treatment. *Residential Group Care and Treatment, 3,* 65–88.

O'Neill, L., & McGloin, J. M. (2007). Considering the efficacy of situation crime prevention in schools. *Journal of Criminal Justice, 35,* 511–523.

O'Neill, P. (1989). Responsible to whom? Responsible to what? Some ethical issues in community intervention. *American Journal of Community Psychology, 17*(3), 323–341.

O'Neill, P., Duffy, C., Enman, M., Blackman, E., & Goodwin, J. (1988). Cognition and citizen participation in social action. *Journal of Applied Sociology, 18,* 1067–1083.

Opulente, M., & Mattaini, M. A. (1997). Toward welfare that works. *Research on Social Work Practice, 7,* 115–135.

Orthner, D. K., & Randolph, K. A. (1999). Welfare reform and high school dropout patterns for children. *Children and Youth Services Review, 21,* 881–900.

Ortmann, R. (2000). The effectiveness of social therapy in prison—A randomized experiment. *Crime & Delinquency Special Issue: Advising Criminal Justice Policy through Experimental Evaluations: International Views, 46,* 214–232.

Oskamp, S. (1984). *Applied social psychology.* Englewood Cliffs, NJ: Prentice Hall.

Ostermeyer, M. (1991). Conducting the mediation. In K. G. Duffy, J. W. Grosch, & P. V. Olizcak (Eds.), *Community mediation: A handbook for practitioners and researchers.* New York: Guilford.

Oxley, D. (2000). The school reform movement. In J. Rappaport & E. Seidman (Eds.), *Handbook of community psychology.* New York: Plenum.

Pacific Institute for Research and Evaluation in Support of the Office of Juvenile Justice and Delinquency Prevention Enforcing the Underage Drinking Laws Program (2005). *Drinking in America: Myths, realities, and prevention policy* [brochure]. Washington, DC: Author.

Padilla, A., Ruiz, R., & Alvarez, R. (1975). Community mental health services for the Spanish-speaking/surnamed. *American Psychologist, 9,* 892–905.

Page, S. (2007). *The Difference: How the Power of Diversity Creates Better Groups, Firms, Schools, and Societies.* Princeton: Princeton University Press.

Paine-Andrews, A., Fisher, J., Patton, J., Fawcett, S., Williams, E., Lewis, R., et al. (2002). Analyzing the contribution of community change to population health outcomes in an adolescent pregnancy prevention initiative. *Health Education & Behavior, 29,* 183–193.

Palmer, T., & Wedge, R. (1989). California's juvenile probation camps: Findings and implications. *Crime and Delinquency, 35,* 234–253.

Paluk, E. L. (2006). Diversity training and intergroup contact: A call to action research. *Journal of Social Issues, 62,* 577–595.

Pargament, K. I. (1986). Refining fit: Conceptual and methodological challenges. *American Journal of Community Psychology, 14,* 677–684.

Parks, G. (October 2000). The High/Scope Perry Preschool Project. *Juvenile Justice Bulletin,* 1–8.

Patchin, J. W., Huebner, B. M., McCluskey, J. D., Varano, S. P., & Bynum, T. S. (2006). Exposure to community violence and childhood delinquency. *Crime & Delinquency, 52,* 307–332.

Patrikakou, E., & Weissberg, R. P. (2000). Parents' perceptions of teacher outreach and parent involvement in children's education. *Journal of Prevention & Intervention in the Community, 20,* 103–119.

Pattavina, A., Byrne, J. M., & Garcia, L. (2006). An examination of citizen involvement in crime prevention in high-risk versus low-to-moderate risk neighborhoods. *Crime & Delinquency, 52,* 203–231.

Patterson, D. (1990). Gaining access to community resources: Breaking the cycle of adolescent pregnancy. *Journal of Health Care for the Poor and Undeserved, 1,* 147–149.

Patton, M. (1997). *Utilization-focused evaluation: The new century text* (3rd ed.). Thousand Oaks, CA: Sage.

Pedersen, P. (2008). Ethics, competence, and professional issues in cross-cultural counselling. In P. Pedersen, J. Draguns, W. Lonner, & J. Trimble, (Eds.), *Counselling Across Cultures* (6th ed., pp. 5–20). Los Angeles: Sage.

Pedersen, P., Draguns, J., Lonner, W., & Trimble, J. (Eds.). (2008). *Counselling across cultures* (6th ed). Los Angeles: Sage.

Pedro-Carroll, J. (1997). The children of divorce intervention program: Fostering resilient outcomes for school-aged children. In G. W. Albee & T. P. Gullotta (Eds.), *Primary prevention works*. Thousand Oaks, CA: Sage.

Pedro-Carroll, J. L. (2005a). Fostering resilience in the aftermath of divorce: The role of evidence-based programs for children. *Family Court Review: Special Issue on Prevention: Research, Policy, and Evidence-based Practice, 43*, 52–64.

Pedro-Carroll, J. L. (2005b). Special issue on prevention: Research, policy, and evidence based practice. *Family Court Review: Special Issue on Prevention: Research, Policy, and Evidence-based Practice, 43*, 18–21.

Pentz, M. A. (2000). Institutionalizing community-based prevention through policy change. *Journal of Community Psychology, 28*, 257–270.

Pereira, G., & Osburn, H. (2007). Effects of participation on performance and employee attitudes: A quality circles meta-analysis. *Journal of Business and Psychology, 22*, 145–153.

Perkins, C. A. (1997). *Special report: Age patterns of victims of serious violent crimes*. Washington, DC: Bureau of Justice Statistics.

Perkins, D. D. (1988). The use of social science in public interest litigation: A role for community psychologists. *American Journal of Community Psychology, 16*, 465–485.

Perkins, D. D., Brown, B. B., & Taylor, R. B. (1996). The ecology of empowerment: Predicting participation in community organizations. *Journal of Social Issues, 52*, 85–110.

Perkins, D. D., Florin, P., Rich, R. C., Wandersman, A., & Chavis, D. M. (1990). Participation and the social and physical environment of residential blocks: Crime and community context. *American Journal of Community Psychology, 18*, 83–115.

Perkins, D. D., & Taylor, R. B. (1996). Ecological assessments of community disorder: Their relationship to fear of crime and theoretical implications. *American Journal of Community Psychology, 24*, 63–107.

Perkins, D. D., & Zimmerman, M. A. (1995). Empowerment theory, research, and application. *American Journal of Community Psychology, 23*, 569–579.

Peterson, J. L. (1998). Introduction to the special issue: HIV/AIDS prevention through community psychology. *American Journal of Community Psychology, 26*, 1–5.

Peterson, N. A., Speer, P., & Hughey, J. (2006). Measuring sense of community: A methodological interpretation of a factor structure debate. *Journal of Community Psychology, 34*, 453–469.

Peterson, N. A., Speer, P., & McMillan, D. (2008). Validation of a Brief Sense of Community Scale: Confirmation of a principle theory of "sense of community." *Journal of Community Psychology, 36*, 61–73.

Peterson, N. A., & Zimmerman, M. A. (2004). Beyond the individual: Toward anomological network of organizational empowerment. *American Journal of Community Psychology, 1–2*, 129–141.

Pettigrew, T. F. (1998). Intergroup contact theory. *Annual Review of Psychology, 49*, 65–85.

Pettigrew, T. F. (2004). Justice deferred a half century after Brown v. Board of Education. *American Psychologist, 59*, 521–529.

Pettigrew, T., & Meertens, R. W. (1995). Subtle and blatant prejudice in Western Europe. *European Journal of Social Psychology, 25*, 57–75.

Phares, J. E. (1991). *Introduction to personality*. New York: HarperCollins.

Phares, J. E., & Chaplin, W. F. (1997). *Introduction to personality*. New York: Longman.

Philliber, S., Kaye, J., & Herrling, S. (2001) *The national evaluation of the Children's Aid Society Carrera-Model Program to prevent teen pregnancy*. Accord, NY: Philliber Research Associates.

Phillip, K., & Hendry, L. B. (2000). Making sense of mentoring or mentoring making sense? Reflections on the mentoring process by adult mentors with young people. *Journal of Community & Applied Social Psychology, 10*, 211–223.

Phillips, D. A. (2000). Social policy and community psychology. In J. Rappaport & E. Seidman (Eds.),

Handbook of community psychology. New York: Plenum.

Phillips, D. A., Howes, C., & Whitebook, M. (1992). The social policy context of child care: Effects on quality. *Journal of Community Psychology, 20,* 25–50.

Pinchot, G., & Pinchot, E. (1993). *The end of bureaucracy and the rise of the intelligent organization.* San Francisco: Berrett-Koehler.

Pickren, W., & Tomes, H. (2002). The legacy of Kenneth B. Clark to the APA: The Board of Social and Ethical Responsibility for Psychology. *American Psychologist, 57*(1), 51–59.

Pines, A., & Guendelman, S. (1995). Exploring the relevance of burnout to Mexican blue-collar women. *Journal of Vocational Behavior, 47,* 1–20.

Piven, F. F., & Cloward, R. A. (1996). Welfare reform and the new class war. In M. B. Lykes, A. Banuazizi, R. Liem, & M. Morris (Eds.), *Myths about the powerless: Contesting social inequalities.* Philadelphia: Temple University Press.

Plante, T. (2005). *Contemporary clinical psychology* (2nd ed.). Hoboken, NJ: Wiley.

Pogrebin, M. R., & Poole, E. D. (1987). Deinstitutionalization and increased arrest rates among the mentally disordered. *Journal of Psychiatry and Law, 15,* 117–127.

Pogrebin, M. R., & Regoli, R. M. (1985). Editorial. Mentally disordered persons in jail. *Journal of Community Psychology, 13,* 409–412.

Pong, S. L., & Ju, D. B. (2000). The effects of change in family structure and income on dropping out of middle and high school. *Journal of Family Issues, 21,* 147–169.

Popper, K. R. (1957/1990). Philosophy of science: A personal report. In C. A. Mace (Ed.), *British philosophy in the mid-century.* London: Allen & Unwin.

Popper, K. R. (1968). *The logic of scientific discovery.* New York: Harper Torchbooks.

Popovich, P. M., Gullekson, N., Morris, S., & Morse, B. (2008). Comparing attitudes towards computer usage by undergraduates from 1986 to 2005. *Computers in Human Behavior, 24,* 986–992.

Porter, B. E. (2001). Empowerment-based interventions are not useful. *Community Psychologist, 34,* 22–23.

Presser, L., & Hamilton, C. A. (2006). The micropolitics of victim-offender mediation. *Sociological Inquiry, 76,* 316–342.

Prestby, J., & Wandersman, A. (1985). An empirical exploration of a framework of organizational viability: Maintaining block organization. *Journal of Applied Behavioral Sciences, 21,* 287–305.

Prestby, J., Wandersman, A., Florin, P., Rich, R., & Chavis, D. (1990). Benefits, costs, incentive management and participation in volunteer organizations: A means to understanding and promoting empowerment. *American Journal of Community Psychology, 18,* 117–150.

Pretty, G. M., & McCarthy, M. (1991). Exploring the psychological sense of community among women and men of the corporation. *Journal of Community Psychology, 19,* 351–361.

Pretty, G. M., McCarthy, M. E., & Catano, V. M. (1992). Psychological environments and burnout: Gender considerations within the corporation. *Journal of Organizational Behavior, 13,* 701–711.

Prezza, M., Amici, M., Tiziana, R., & Tedeschi, G. (2001). Sense of community referred to the whole town: Its relations with neighboring, loneliness, life satisfaction, and area of residence. *Journal of Community Psychology, 29,* 29–52.

Price, R. (1983). The education of a prevention psychologist. In R. Felner, L. Jason, J. Moritsugu, & S. Farber (Eds.), *Preventive psychology: Theory, research and practice* (pp. 290–296). New York: Pergamon.

Price, R. H. (1985). Work and community. *American Journal of Community Psychology, 13,* 1–12.

Price, R. H. (1990). Whither participation and empowerment? *American Journal of Community Psychology, 18,* 163–167.

Price, R. H., Cowen, E. L., Lorion, R. P., & Ramos-McKay, J. (1988). *14 ounces of prevention.* Washington, DC: American Psychological Association.

Prilleltensky, I., & Fox, D. (2007). Psychopolitical literacy for wellness and justice. *Journal of Community Psychology, 35*(6), 793–805.

Primavera, J. (1999). The unintended consequences of volunteerism: Positive outcomes for those who serve. *Journal of Prevention & Intervention in the Community, 18,* 125–140.

Primavera, J., & Brodsky, A. (2004). Introduction to the special issue on the process of community research and action. *American Journal of Community Psychology, 33,* 177–180.

Prince-Embury, S., & Rooney, J. F. (1995). Psychological adaptation among residents following restart of Three Mile Island. *Journal of Traumatic Stress, 8,* 47–59.

PsychInfo. (2002). Database at American Psychological Association. Washington, DC.

Public Health Service. (1980). *Toward a national plan for the chronic mentally ill.* Washington, DC: U.S. Department of Health and Human Services.

Quigley, R. (2005). Building strengths in the neighborhood. *Reclaiming Children and Youth, 14,* 104–106.

Quillian-Wolever, R., & Wolever, M. (2003). Stress management at work. In J. Quick & L. Tetrick (Eds.), *Handbook of occupational health psychology* (pp. 355–375). Washington, DC: American Psychological Association.

Quintana, S., Vogel, M., & Ybarra, V. (1991). Meta-analysis of Latino students' adjustment in higher education. *Hispanic Journal of Behavioral Sciences, 13*(2), 155–168.

Rader, N. E., May, D. C., & Goodrum, S. (2007). An empirical assessment of the "threat of victimization": Considering fear of crime, perceived risk, avoidance, and defensive behaviors. *Sociological Spectrum, 27,* 475–505.

Rafferty, Y. (1990). *Testimony on behalf of Advocates for Children of New York and the American Psychological Association to the oversight hearings on homelessness.* House of Representatives, Washington, DC.

Rafferty, Y., & Shinn, M. (1991). The impact of homelessness on children. *American Psychologist, 46,* 1170–1179.

Rahe, R., Meyers, M., Smith, M., Kjaer, G., & Holmes, T. (1964). Social stress and illness onset. *Journal of Psychosomatic Research, 8,* 35–44.

Raikes, J. A., Raikes, H. H., & Wilcox, B. (2005). Regulation, subsidy receipt and provider characteristics: What predicts quality in child care homes? *Early Childhood Research Quarterly, 20,* 164–184.

Ramey, S. L., & Ramey, C. T. (2003). Understanding efficacy of early educational programs: Critical design, practice, and policy issues. In A. J. Reynolds, M. C. Wang, & H. J. Wallberg (Eds.), *Early childhood programs for a new century.* Washington, DC: Child Welfare League of America.

Randolph, W. A. (2000). Re-thinking empowerment: Why is it so hard to achieve? *Organizational Dynamics, 29,* 94–107.

Rank, M. R. (2005). *One nation, underprivileged: Why American poverty affects us all.* New York: Oxford University Press.

Rapkin, B. D., Massie, M. J., Janskym, E. J., Lounsbury, D. W., Murphy, P. D., & Powell, S. (2006). Developing a partnership model for cancer screening with community-based organizations: The ACCESS Breast Cancer Education and Outreach Project. *American Journal of Community Psychology, 38*(3–4):153–164.

Rappaport, J. (1977). *Community psychology: Values, research, and action.* New York: Holt, Rinehart & Winston.

Rappaport, J. (1981). In praise of paradox: A social policy of empowerment over prevention. *American Journal of Community Psychology, 9,* 1–25.

Rappaport, J. (1987). Terms of empowerment/exemplars of prevention: Toward a theory for community psychology. *American Journal of Community Psychology, 15,* 121–148.

Rappaport, J. (1990). Research methods and the empowerment social agenda. In P. Tolan, C. Keys, F. Chertok, & L. Jason (Eds.), *Researching community psychology: Issues of theory and methods.* Washington, DC: American Psychological Association.

Rappaport, J. (2000). Community narratives: Tales of terror and joy. *American Journal of Community Psychology, 28*(1), 1–24.

Rappaport, J. (2005). Community psychology is (thank god) more than science. *American Journal of Community Psychology, 35,* (3–4), 231–238.

Rappaport, J., & Seidman, E. (Eds.). (2000). *Handbook of community psychology.* New York: Kluwer/Plenum.

Rappaport, J., Seidman, E., Toro, P., McFadden, L. S., Reischl, T. M., Roberts, L. J., et al. (1985). Collaborative research of a mutual help organization. *Social Policy, 15,* 12–24.

Rappaport, J., Swift, C., & Hess, P. (Eds.). (1984). *Studies in empowerment: Steps toward understanding and action.* New York: Haworth.

Ratiu, I. S. (1986). A workshop on managing in a multicultural environment. Special issue: International management and development. *Management Education and Development, 17,* 252–256.

Raviv, A., Erel, O., Fox, N. A., Leavitt, L. A., Raviv, A., Dar, I., et al. (2001). Individual measurement of exposure to everyday violence among elementary schoolchildren across various settings. *Journal of Community Psychology, 29,* 117–140.

Redeinstitutionalization. (1986, August 25). *New York Times,* p. A18.

Reich, J. W., & Zautra, A. J. (1991). Experimental and measurement approaches to internal control in at-risk older adults. *Journal of Social Issues, 47,* 143–158.

Reid, R. J., Peterson, N. A., Hughey, J., & Garcia-Reid, P. (2006). School climate and adolescent drug use: Mediation effects of violence victimization in the urban high school context. *Journal of Primary Prevention, 27,* 281–292.

Rein, M., & Schon, D. A. (1977). Problem setting in policy research. In C. H. Weiss (Ed.), *Using social research in public policy making.* Lexington, MA: Lexington Books.

Reppucci, N. D. (1987). Prevention and ecology: Teen-age pregnancy, child sexual abuse, and organized youth sports. *American Journal of Community Psychology, 15,* 1–22.

Reppucci, N., Woolard, J., & Fried, C. (1999). Social, community, and preventive interventions. *Annual Review of Psychology, 50,* 387–418.

Revenson, T., D'Augelli, A., French, S., Hughes, D., Livert, D., Seidman, E., Shinn, M., & Yoshikawa, H. (2002). *Ecological research to promote social change: Methodological advances from community psychology.* New York: Kluwer Academic/Plenum.

Revenson, T., & Schiaffino, K. (2000). Community-based health interventions. In J. Rappaport & E. Seidman (Eds.), *Handbook of community psychology* (pp. 471–493). New York: Kluwer/Academic/Plenum.

Reyes, O., Gillock, K. L., Kobus, K., & Sanchez, B. (2000). A longitudinal examination of the transition into senior high school for adolescents from urban, low-income status, and predominantly minority backgrounds. *American Journal of Community Psychology, 28,* 519–544.

Reyes, O., & Jason, L. (1991). An evaluation of a high school dropout prevention program. *Journal of Community Psychology, 19*(3), 221–230.

Rhodes, J. E. (2008). Improving youth mentoring interventions through research-based practice. *American Journal of Community Psychology, 41,* 35–42.

Rhodes, J. E., Spencer, R., Keller, T. E., Liang, B., & Noam, G. (2006). A model for the influence of mentoring relationships on youth development. *Journal of Community Psychology, 34,* 691–707.

Richmond, C., Ross, N., & Egeland, G. (2007). Social support and thriving health: A new approach to understanding the health of indigenous Canadians. *American Journal of Public Health, 97,* 1827–1833.

Rickel, A. U., & Burgio, J. C. (1982). Assessing social competencies in lower income preschool children. *American Journal of Community Psychology, 10,* 635–647.

Riger, S. (1989). The politics of community intervention. *American Journal of Community Psychology, 17,* 379–383.

Riger, S. (1990). Ways of knowing and organizational approaches to community psychology. In P. Tolan, C. Keys, F. Chertak, & L. Jason (Eds.), *Researching community psychology.* Washington, DC: American Psychological Association.

Riger, S. (1993). What's wrong with empowerment. *American Journal of Community Psychology, 21,* 279–292.

Riley, D. A., Roach, M. A., Adams, D., & Edie, D. (2005). Section III—policy affecting and evaluation of quality: From research to policy: In search of an affordable statewide system for rating child care quality. *Early Education and Development: Special Issue: Early Childhood Program Quality, 16,* 493–504.

Rixon, R., & Erwin, P. G. (1999). Measure of effectiveness in a short-term interpersonal cognitive problem-solving programme. *Counseling Psychology Quarterly, 12,* 87–93.

Roak, K. S. (1991). Facilitating friendship formation in late life: Puzzles and challenges. *American Journal of Community Psychology, 19,* 103–110.

Roberts, A. R., & Everly, G. S. (2006). A meta-analysis of 36 crisis intervention studies. *Brief Treatment and Crisis Intervention, 6,* 10–21.

Roberts, D. G. (1991). I don't get no respect. *Organization Development Journal, 9,* 55–60.

Robins, L. N., et al. (1984). Lifetime prevalence rates of DIS/DSM-III disorders. *Archives of General Psychiatry, 41,* 952–958.

Robinson, M. B. (2000). From research to policy: Preventing residential burglary through a systems approach. *American Journal of Criminal Justice, 24,* 169–179.

Robinson, W. L. (1990). Data feedback and communication to the host setting. In P. Tolan, C. Keys, F.

Chertak, & L. Jason (Eds.), *Researching community psychology: Issues of theory and methods.* Washington, DC: American Psychological Association.

Rodin, J., & Langer, E. J. (1977). Long-term effects of a control-relevant intervention with the institutionalized aged. *Journal of Personality and Social Psychology, 35,* 897–902.

Rodin, J., Timko, C., & Harris, S. (1986). The construct of control: Biological and psychological correlates. In C. Eisdorfer, M. P. Lawson, & G. I. Maddoy (Eds.), *Annual review of gerontology and geriatrics.* New York: Springer.

Rodriguez, N. (2005). Restorative justice, communities, and delinquency: Whom do we reintegrate? *Criminology & Public Policy, 4,* 103–130.

Rodriguez, N. (2007). Restorative justice at work: Examining the impact of restorative justice resolutions on juvenile recidivism. *Crime and Delinquency, 53,* 355–379.

Roesch, R. (1988). Community psychology and the law. *American Journal of Community Psychology, 14,* 451–463.

Roethlisberger, F. J., & Dickson, W. J. (1939). *Management and the worker: An account of a research program conducted by the Western Electric Company, Chicago.* Cambridge, MA: Harvard University Press.

Rogers, E. M. (1982). *Diffusion of innovations.* New York: Free Press.

Roh, S., & Oliver, W. M. (2005). Effects of community policing upon fear of crime: Understanding the causal linkage. *Policing, 28,* 640–683.

Rokeach, M. (1960). *The open and closed mind.* New York: Basic Books.

Roll, J. M., & Habemeier, W. (1991, April). *Gender differences in coping with potential victimization.* Paper presented at the Annual Meeting of the Eastern Psychological Association, New York.

Rolleri, L., Wilson, M., Paluzzi, P., & Sedivy, V. (2008). Building capacity of state adolescent pregnancy prevention coalitions to implement science-based approaches. *American Journal of Community Psychology, 41*(3–4), 225–234.

Romeo, R., & McEwan, B. (2006). Stress and the adolescent brain. *Annals of the New York Academy of Sciences, 1094,* 202–214.

Roscigno, V. J., Tomaskovic-Devey, D., & Crowley, M. (2006). Education and the inequalities of place. *Social Forces, 84,* 2121–2145.

Rose-Gold, M. S. (1992). Intervention strategies for counseling at-risk adolescents in rural school districts. *School Counselor, 39,* 122–126.

Rosenberg, Y. (2006). Talking 'bout our generation. *Fortune, 153,* 106.

Rosenfeld, S. (1991). Homelessness and rehospitalization: The importance of housing for the chronic mentally ill. *Journal of Community Psychology, 19,* 60–69.

Rosenhack, R., Kasprow, W., Frisman, L., & Liu-Mares, W. (2003). Cost-effectiveness of supported housing for homeless persons with mental illness. *Archives of General Psychiatry, 60,* 940–951.

Rosenhan, D. L. (1973). On being sane in insane places. *Science, 179,* 250–258.

Rosenthal, R., & Jacobson, L. V. (1968). *Pygmalion in the classroom: Teacher expectation and pupils' intellectual development.* New York: Holt.

Rosentock, I. M. (1986). Why people use health services. *Milburn Memorial Fund Quarterly, 44,* 94–127.

Ross, C. E., & Jang, S. J. (2000). Neighborhood disorder, fear, and mistrust: The buffering role of social ties with neighbors. *American Journal of Community Psychology, 28,* 401–420.

Ross, J., Bradley, E., & Busch, S. (2006). Use of health care services by lower-income and higher-income uninsured adults. *Journal of the American Medical Association, 295,* 2027–2036.

Ross, L. (2006). Where do we belong? Urban adolescents' struggle for place and voice. *American Journal of Community Psychology, 37,* 293–301.

Ross, R. R., Altmaier, E. M., & Russell, D. W. (1989). Job stress, social support, and burnout among counseling center staff. *Journal of Counseling Psychology, 36,* 464–470.

Rossell, C. H. (1988). How effective are voluntary plans with magnet schools? *Educational Evaluation and Policy Analysis, 10,* 325–342.

Rossi, P. H. (1989). *Down and out in America: The origins of homelessness.* Chicago: University of Chicago Press.

Rossi, P. H. (1990). The old homeless and the new homelessness in historical perspective. *American Psychologist, 45,* 954–959.

Rothman, A., & Salovey, P. (1997). Shaping perceptions to motivate healthy behavior: The role of message framing. *Psychological Bulletin, 121,* 3–19.

Rothman, J. (1974). Three models of community organization practice. In F. Cox, J. Erlich, J.

Rothman, & J. Tropman (Eds.), *Strategies of community organization: A book of readings* (2nd ed.). Itasca, IL: Peacock.

Rountree, P. W. (1998). A reexamination of the crime-fear linkage. *Journal of Research in Crime and Delinquency, 35,* 341–372.

Roussos, S. T. & Fawcett, S. (2000). A review of collaborative relationships as a strategy for improving community health. *Annual Review of Public Health, 21,* 369–402.

Rubin, B. A., & Brody, C. J. (2005). Contradictions of commitment in the new economy: Insecurity, time, and technology. *Social Science Research, 34,* 843–851.

Ruggiero, K., & Taylor, D. (1997). Why minority group members perceive or do not perceive the discrimination that confronts them: The role of self-esteem and perceived control. *Journal of Personality and Social Psychology, 72*(2), 373–389.

Runyan, D., Wattam, C., Ikeda, R., Hassan, F., & Ramiro, L. (2002). Child abuse and neglect by parents and caregivers. In E. Krug, L. I. Dahlberg, J. A. Mercy, A. B. Zwi, & R. Lozano (Eds.), *World report on violence and health*. Geneva: World Health Organization.

Rutter, M. (1981). The city and the child. *American Journal of Orthopsychiatry, 51,* 610–625.

Rutter, M. (1985). Resilience in the face of adversity: Protective factors and resistance to psychiatric disorder. *British Journal of Psychiatry, 147,* 598–611.

Rutter, M. (1987). Psychosocial resilience and protective mechanisms. *American Journal of Orthopsychiatry, 57,* 316–331.

Rutter, M. (2006). Implications of resiliency concepts for scientific understanding. *Annals of the New York Academy of Sciences, 1094,* 1–12.

Ryan, W. (1971). *Blaming the victim*. New York: Pantheon.

Ryan, J. P., & Yang, H. (2005). Family contact and recidivism: A longitudinal study of adjudicated delinquents in residential care. *Social Work Research, 29,* 31–39.

Saegert, S., & Winkel, G. (2004). Crime, social capital, and community participation. *American Journal of Community Psychology, 34,* 219–233.

Salazar, J. M. (1988, August). *Psychology and social change in Latin America.* Paper presented to the Annual Convention of the American Psychological Association, Atlanta, GA.

Salem, D. A. (1990). Community-based services and resources: The significance of choice and diversity. *American Journal of Community Psychology, 18,* 909–915.

Salmi, S., Voeten, M. J. M., & Keskinen, E. (2000). Relation between police image and police visibility. *Journal of Community and Applied Social Psychology, 10,* 433–447.

Salmi, S., Voeten, M., & Keskinen, E. (2005). What citizens think about the police: Assessing actual and wished-for frequency of police activities in one's neighbourhood. *Journal of Community & Applied Social Psychology. Special Issue: Community Policing, 15,* 1888–2002.

Sammons, M. T., & Brown, A. (1997). The department of defense psychopharmacology demonstration project: An evolving program for postdoctoral education in psychology. *Professional Psychology: Research and Practice, 28,* 107–112.

Sammons, M. T., Gorny, S. W., Zinner, E. S., & Allen, R. P. (2000). Prescriptive authority for psychologists: A consensus of support. *Professional Psychology: Research & Practice, 31,* 604–609.

Sampson, R., & Groves, W. (1989). Community structure and crime: Testing social-disorganization theory. *American Journal of Sociology, 94*(4) 774.

Sampson, R., & Raudenbush, S. (1999). Systematic social observation of public spaces: A new look at disorder in urban neighborhoods. *American Journal of Sociology, 105*(3), 603–651.

Sampson, R. J., Raudenbush, S. W., & Earls, F. (1997). Neighborhoods and violent crime: A multilevel study of collective efficacy. *Science, 277,* 918–924.

Sandler, I. (1980). Social support resources, stress, and maladjustment of poor children. *American Journal of Community Psychology, 8,* 41–52.

Sandler, I., Braver, S., & Gensheimer, L. (2000) Stress. In J. Rappaport & E. Seidman (Eds.), *Handbook of community psychology*. New York: Kluwer/Plenum.

Sandler, I. N., & Keller, P. A. (1984). Trends observed in community psychology training descriptions. *American Journal of Community Psychology, 12,* 157–164.

Sansone, R. A., Fine, M. A., & Chew, R. (1988). A longitudinal analysis of the experiences of nursing staff on an inpatient eating disorder unit. *International Journal of Eating Disorders, 7,* 125–131.

Sarason, S. B. (1972/1999). *The creation of settings & the future societies.* San Francisco: Jossey-Bass.

Sarason, S. B. (1974). *The psychological sense of community: Prospects for a community psychology.* San Francisco: Jossey-Bass.

Sarason, S. B. (1976a). Community psychology and the anarchist insight. *American Journal of Community Psychology, 4,* 246–259.

Sarason, S. B. (1976b). Community psychology, networks, and Mr. Everyman. *American Journal of Community Psychology, 18,* 317–328.

Sarason, S. B. (1978). The nature of problem solving in social action. *American Psychologist, 33,* 370–380.

Sarason, S. B. (1983). *Schooling in America: Scapegoat and salvation.* New York: Free Press.

Sarason, S. (2004). What we need to know about intervention and interventionists. *American Journal of Community Psychology, 33*(3–4), 275–277.

Sarason, S. (1984). Community psychology and public policy: Missed opportunity. *American Journal of Community Psychology, 12*(2), 199–207.

Sarason, S. B. (1997). The public schools: America's Achilles heel. *American Journal of Community Psychology, 25,* 771–786.

Sarason, S. B., Carroll, C. F., Maton, K., Cohen, S., & Lorentz, E. (1977). *Human services and resource networks.* San Francisco: Jossey-Bass.

Sarata, B. P. V. (1984). Changes in staff satisfactions after increases in pay, autonomy, and participation. *American Journal of Community Psychology, 12,* 431–445.

Scales, P. (1990). Developing capable young people: An alternative strategy for prevention programs. *American Journal of Community Psychology, 10,* 420–438.

Scarr, S., & Eisenberg, M. (1993). Child care research: Issues, perspectives, and results. *Annual Review of Psychology, 44,* 613–644.

Schafer, J. A., Huebner, B. M., & Bynum, T. G. (2006). Fear of crime and criminal victimization: Gender-based contrasts. *Journal of Criminal Justice, 34,* 285–301.

Scheckner, S., Rollin, S. A., Kaiser-Ulrey, C., & Wagner, R. (2004). School violence in children and adolescents: A meta-analysis of the effectiveness of current interventions. In E. R. Gerler (Ed.), *Handbook of school violence.* New York: Haworth.

Schein, E. H. (1985). How culture forms, develops and changes. In R. H. Kilmann, M. J. Saxton, & R. Serpa (Eds.), *Gaining control of the corporate culture.* San Francisco: Jossey-Bass.

Schein, E. H. (1990). Organizational culture. *American Psychologist, 45,* 109–119.

Schiaffino, K. M. (1991). Fine-tuning theory to the needs of the world: Responding to Heller et al. *American Journal of Community Psychology, 19,* 99–102.

Schinke, S. P. (1998). Preventing teenage pregnancy: Translating research knowledge. *Journal of Human Behavior in the Social Environment, 1,* 53–66.

Schmolling, P. Jr., Youkeles, M., & Burger, W. R. (1989). *Human services in contemporary America.* Pacific Grove, CA: Brooks Cole.

Schubert, M., & Borkman, T. (1991). An organizational typology for self-help groups. *American Journal of Community Psychology, 19,* 769–787.

Schuck, A. M., & Widom, C. S. (2005). Understanding the role of neighborhood context in the long-term criminal consequences of child maltreatment. *American Journal of Community Psychology, 36,* 207–222.

Schuller, N. (2006). Older people, crime and justice. *Community Safety Journal, 5,* 37–43.

Schultz, D., & Schultz, S. (1990). *Psychology and industry today.* New York: Macmillan.

Schultz, D., & Schultz, S. E. (1998). *Psychology and work today.* Upper Saddle River, NJ: Prentice Hall.

Schulz, R., & Heckhausen, J. (1996). A life span model of successful aging. *American Psychologist, 51,* 702–714.

Schur, L. A., & Kruse, D. L. (2000). What determines voter turnout? Lessons from citizens with disabilities. *Social Science Quarterly, 81,* 571–587.

Schwarzer, R., & Leppin, A. (1991). Social support and health: A theoretical and empirical overview. *Journal of Social and Personal Relations, 8,* 99–127.

Schweinhart, L. J. (2006). The High/Scope approach: Evidence that participatory learning in early childhood contributes to human development. In N. F. Watt, C. Ayoub, R. H. Bradley, J. E. Puma, & W. A. LeBoeuf (Eds.), *The crisis in youth mental health: Critical issues and effective programs, Vol. 4: Early intervention programs and policies. Child psychology and mental health.* Westport, CT: Praeger.

Schweinhart, L. J. (2007). Crime prevention by the High/Scope Perry Preschool Program. *Victims & Offenders. Special Issue on Early Intervention, 2*, 141–160.

Schweinhart, L. J., & Weikart, D. (1998). High/Scope Perry Preschool Program effects at age twenty-seven. In J. Crane (Ed.), *Social programs that work*. New York: Sage.

Schweitzer, J. H., Kim, J. W., & Mackin, J. R. (1999). The impact of the built environment on crime and fear of crime in urban neighborhoods. *Journal of Urban Technology, 6*, 59–74.

Scileppi, J. A., Teed, E. L., & Torres, R. D. (2000). *Community psychology: A common sense approach to mental health*. Upper Saddle River, NJ: Prentice Hall.

Scott, E. K., London, A. S., & Edin, K. (2000). Looking to the future: Welfare-reliant women talk about their job aspirations in the context of welfare reform. *Journal of Social Issues Special Issue: The Impact of Welfare Reform, 56*, 727–746.

Scully, J., Tosi, H., & Banning, K. (2000). Life event checklists: Revisiting the social readjustment rating scale after 30 years. *Educational and Psychological Measurement, 60*(6), 864–876.

Searight, H. R., Oliver, J. M., & Grisso, J. T. (1986). The community competence scale in the placement of the deinstitutionalized mentally ill. *American Journal of Community Psychology, 14*, 291–301.

Seekins, T., & Fawcett, S. B. (1987). Effects of a poverty-clients agenda on resource allocations by community decision-makers. *American Journal of Community Psychology, 15*, 305–322.

Seidman, E. (1983). Unexamined premises of social problem solving. In E. Seidman (Ed.), *Handbook of social intervention*. Beverly Hills: Sage.

Seidman, E. (1990). Pursuing the meaning and utility of social regularities for community psychology. In P. Tolan, C. Keys, F. Chertak, & L. Jason (Eds.), *Researching community psychology: Issues of theory and methods*. Washington, DC: American Psychological Association.

Seidman, E., & Rappaport, J. (1974). You have got to have a dream, but it's not enough. *American Psychologist, 29*(7), 569–570.

Seidman, E., & Rappaport, J. (1986). *Redefining Social Problems*. New York: Springer.

Seitz, V., Apfel, N., & Efron, C. (1977). *Long-term effects of early intervention: A longitudinal investigation*. Paper presented at the Annual Meeting of the American Association for the Advancement of Science. Denver, CO.

Seitz, V., Apfel, N., & Rosenbaum, L. (1991). Effects of an intervention program for pregnant adolescents: Educational outcomes at two years post partum. *American Journal of Community Psychology, 19*(6):9 11–30.

Sekaly, R. (2008). The failed HIV Merck vaccine study: A step back or a launching point for future vaccine development? *Journal of Experimental Medicine, 205*(1), 7–12.

Seligman, M. E. P. (1975). *Helplessness: On depression, development, and death*. San Francisco: Freeman.

Selye, H. (1936). A syndrome produced by diverse nocuous stimuli. *Journal of Neuropsychiatry and Clinical Neurosciences, 138*, 32.

Selye, H. (1956). *The stress of life*. New York: McGraw-Hill.

Selye, H. (1974). *Stress without distress*. Philadelphia: Lippincott.

Selznick, P. (2000). Reflections on responsibility: More than just following the rules. *Responsive Community, 10*, 57–61.

Sennett, R. (2003). *Respect: The formation of character in an age of inequality*. London: Allen Lane.

Serrano-Garcia, I. (1990). Implementing research: Putting our values to work. In P. Tolan, C. Keys, F. Chertak, & L. Jason (Eds.), *Researching community psychology: Issues of theory and methods*. Washington, DC: American Psychological Association.

Serrano-Garcia, I. (1994). The ethics of the powerful and the power of ethics. *American Journal of Community Psychology, 22*, 1–20.

Serrano-Garcia, I., Lopez, M. M., & Rivera-Medena, E. (1987). Toward a social-community psychology. *Journal of Community Psychology, 15*, 431–446.

Seyfried, S. F. (1998). Academic achievement of African American preadolescents: The influence of teacher perceptions. *American Journal of Community Psychology, 26*, 381–402.

Shadish, W. R. (1990). Defining excellence criteria in community research. In P. Tolan, C. Keys, F. Chertak, & L. Jason (Eds.), *Researching community psychology: Issues of theory and methods*.

Washington, DC: American Psychological Association.

Shadish, W., Cook, T., & Campbell, D. (2002). *Experimental and quasi-experimental designs for generalized causal inference.* Boston: Houghton Mifflin.

Shadish, W. R., Cook, T. D., & Leviton, L. C. (1991). *Foundations of program evaluation: Theories of practice.* Newbury Park, CA: Sage.

Shadish, W. R., Lurigio, S. J., & Lewis, D. A. (1989). After deinstitutionalization: The present and future of mental health long-term care policy. *Journal of Social Issues, 45,* 1–15.

Shadish, W. R., Thomas, S., & Bootzin, R. R. (1982). Criteria for success in deinstitutionalization: Perceptions of nursing homes by different interest groups. *American Journal of Community Psychology, 10,* 553–566.

Shadur, M. A., Kienzie, R., & Rodwell, J. J. (1999). The relationship between organizational climate and employee perceptions of involvement: The importance of support. *Group & Organization Management, 24,* 479–503.

Shaheen, G., & Rio, J. (2007). Recognizing work as a priority in preventing or ending homelessness. *Journal of Primary Prevention, 28,* 341–358.

Shapira, N., Barak, A., & Gal, I. (2007). Promoting older adults' well-being through Internet training and use. *Aging & Mental Health, 11,* 477–484.

Sharstein, S. (2000). Whatever happened to community mental health? *Psychiatric Services, 51,* 612–620.

Sheldon, S. B., & Epstein, J. L. (2004). Getting students to school: Using family and community involvement to reduce chronic absenteeism. *School Community Journal, 14,* 39–56.

Shepherd, M. D., Schoenberg, M., Slavich, S., Wituk, S., Warren, M., & Meissen, G. (1999). Continuum of professional involvement in self-help groups. *Journal of Community Psychology, 27,* 39–53.

Shih, Y., Zhao, L., & Elting, L. (2006). Does Medicare coverage of colonoscopy reduce racial/ethnic disparities in cancer screening among the elderly? *Health Affairs, 25,* 1153–1162.

Shinn, M. (1992). Homelessness: What is a psychologist to do? *American Journal of Community Psychology, 20,* 1–24.

Shinn, M. (1997). Family homelessness: State or trait. *American Journal of Community Psychology, 25,* 755–769.

Shinn, M. (2007). International homelessness: Policy, socio-cultural, and individual perspectives. *Journal of Social Issues, 63,* 657–677.

Shinn, M., & Gillespie, C. (1993). *Structural vs. individual explanation for homelessness: Implications for intervention.* Paper presented at the ninth annual Northeast Community Psychology Conference, New York.

Shinn, M., Gottlieb, J., Wett, J. L., Bahl, A., Cohen, A., & Ellis, D. B. (2007). Predictors of homelessness among older adults in New York City: Disability, economic, human and social capital and stressful events. *Journal of Health Psychology, 12,* 696–708.

Shinn, M., Lehmann, S., & Wong, N. W. (1984). Social interaction and social support. *American Journal of Community Psychology, 40,* 55–76.

Shinn, M., Morch, H., Robinson, P. E., & Neuer, R. A. (1993). Individual, group, and agency strategies for coping with job stressors in residential child care programmes. *Journal of Community and Applied Social Psychology, 3,* 313–324.

Shinn, M., & Perkins, D. N. T. (2000). Contributions from organizational psychology. In J. Rappaport & E. Seidman (Eds.), *Handbook of community psychology.* New York: Plenum.

Shinn, M., & Rapkin, B. (2000). Cross-level analysis without cross-ups. In J. Rappaport & E. Seidman, (Eds.), *Handbook of community psychology* (pp. 669–695). New York: Kluwer Academic/Plenum.

Shinn, M., & Toohey, S. (2003). Community contexts of human welfare. *Annual Review of Psychology, 54,* 427–259.

Shinn, M., & Tsemberis, S. (1998). Is housing the cure for homelessness? In X. Arriaga & S. Oskamp (Eds.), *Addressing community problems: Psychological research and interventions.* Thousand Oaks, CA: Sage.

Shinn, M., & Weitzman, B. C. (1990). Research on homelessness: An introduction. *Journal of Social Issues, 46,* 1–11.

Shinn, M., Weitzman, B. C., Strojanovic, D., Knickman, J. R., Jimenez, L., Duchon, L., James, S., & Kranz, D. H. (1998). Predictors of homelessness among families in New York City: From shelter request to housing stability. *American Journal of Public Health, 88,* 1651–1657.

Shivy, V. A., Wu, J. J., Moon, A. E., Mann, S. C., & Eacho, C. (2007). Ex-offenders reentering the workforce. *Journal of Counseling Psychology, 54*, 466–473.

Shpungin, E., & Lyubansky, M. (2006). Navigating social class roles in community research. *American Journal of Community Psychology, 37*, 227–235.

Shumaker, S. A., & Brownell, A. (1984). Toward a theory of social support: Closing conceptual gaps. *Journal of Social Issues, 40*, 11–36.

Shumaker, S. A., & Brownell, A. (1985). Introduction: Social support interventions. *Journal of Social Issues, 41*, 1–4.

Shure, M. B. (1997). Interpersonal cognitive problem-solving: Primary prevention of high-risk behaviors in the preschool and primary years. In G. W. Albee & T. P. Gullotta (Eds.), *Primary prevention works*. Thousand Oaks, CA: Sage.

Shure, M. B. (1999, April). Preventing violence the problem-solving way. *Juvenile Justice Bulletin*, 1–10.

Shure, M. B., & Spivack, G. (1988). Interpersonal cognitive problem solving. In R. H. Price, E. L. Cowan, R. P. Lorion, & J. Ramos-McKay (Eds.), *14 ounces of prevention: A casebook for practitioners*. Washington, DC: American Psychological Association.

SIECUS National Guidelines Task Force (2004). *Guidelines for comprehensive sexuality education* (3rd ed.). Washington, DC: Sexuality Information and Education Council of the United States.

Siegel, J. T., & Alvaro, E. M. (2003). Youth tobacco access: Adult attitudes, awareness, and perceived self-efficacy in two Arizona counties. *Journal of Community Health, 28*, 439–449.

Siegel, J., & Kuykendall, D. A. (1990). Loss, widowhood, and psychological distress among the elderly. *Journal of Consulting and Clinical Psychology, 58*, 519–524.

Silka, L. (2007). Immigrants in the community: New opportunities, new struggles. *Analysis of Social Issues and Public Policy, 7*, 75–91.

Simmons, B. (2000). *Eustress at work: Accentuating the positive*. Unpublished doctoral dissertation, Oklahoma State University.

Simmons, B., & Nelson, D. (2001). Eustress at work: The relationship between hope and health in hospital nurses. *Health Care Management Review, 26*, 7–18.

Simoni-Wastila, L., & Strickler, G. (2004). Risk factors associated with problem use of prescription drugs. *American Journal of Public Health, 94*, 266–268.

Simpura, J., Levin, B. M., & Mustonen, H. (1997). Russian drinking in the 1990s: Patterns and trends in international comparison. In J. Simpura & B. M. Levin (Eds.), *Demystifying Russian drinking. Comparative studies from the 1990s* (pp. 79–107). Helsinki: STAKES.

Sims, B., Yost, B., & Abbott, C. (2005). Use and nonuse of victim services programs: Implications from a statewide survey of crime victims. *Criminology & Public Policy, 4*, 361–383.

Singer, M. (1994a). AIDS and the health crisis of the US urban poor: The perspective of critical medical anthropology. *Social Science and Medicine, 39*, 931–948.

Singer, M. (1994b). Implementing a community-based AIDS prevention program for ethnic minorities: The Comunidad y Responsibilidad Project. In J. P. Van Vugt (Ed.), *AIDS prevention and services: Community based research* (pp. 59–92). Westport, CT: Gergin and Garvey.

Singer, M., & Borrero, M. (1984). Indigenous treatment for alcoholism: The evidence for Puerto Rican spiritism. *Medical Anthropology, 8*, 246–273.

Singer, M., Flores, C., Davison, L., Burke, G., Castillo, Z., Scaon, K., & Rivera, M. (1990). SIDA: The economic, social, and cultural context of AIDS among Latinos. *Medical Anthropology Quarterly, 4*, 73–117.

Singer, M., & Weeks, M. R. (1996). Preventing AIDS in communities of color: Anthropology and social prevention. *Human Organization, 55*, 488–492.

Singleton, J. (2000). Women caring for elderly family members: Shaping non-traditional work and family initiatives. *Journal of Comparative Family Studies, 31*, 367–375.

Siska, D. (1998, March/April). Boom time. *Foundation News and Commentary*. Retrieved from www.cof.org/fnc/28growth.htm#Growth.

Skinner, B. F. (1974). *About behaviorism*. New York: Vintage.

Skinner, E., Edge, K., Altman, J., & Sherwood, H. (2003). Searching for the structure of coping: A review and critique of category systems for classifying ways of coping. *Psychological Bulletin, 129*(2), 216–269.

Slavin, R. E. (1985). Cooperative learning: Applying contact theory in desegregated schools. *Journal of Social Issues, 41*, 45–62.

Slavin, R. (1996). Research on cooperative learning and achievement: What we know, what we need to know. *Contemporary Educational Psychology, 21,* 43–69.

Smart Growth (2008). *Private foundations.* Retrieved from www.epa.gov/smartgrowth/topics/private_foundations.htm.

Smith, H. P. (2006). Violent crime and victim compensation: Implications for social justice. *Violence and Victims, 21,* 307–322.

Smith, S. J., Easterlow, D., Munro, M., & Turner, K. M. (2003). Housing as health capital: How health trajectories and housing paths are linked. *Journal of Social Issues, 59,* 501–546.

Smither, R. D. (1998). *The psychology of work and human performance.* New York: Longman.

Smyth, J., & McInerney, P. (2007). Living on the edge: A case of school reform working for disadvantages adolescents. *Teachers College Record, 109,* 1123–1170.

Snow, D., Swan, S., & Raghavan, C. (2003).The relationship of work stressors, coping and social support to psychological symptoms among female secretarial employees. *Work & Stress, 17,* 241–263.

Snowden, L. R. (1987). The peculiar successes of community psychology: Service delivery to ethnic minorities and the poor. *American Journal of Community Psychology, 15,* 575–586.

Snowden, L. R. (1992). Community psychology and the "severely mentally ill." *Community Psychologist, 25,* 3.

Snowden, L. (2005). Racial, cultural and ethnic disparities in health and mental health: Toward theory and research at community levels. *American Journal of Community Psychology, 35,* 1–8.

Snowden, L. (2006). Strategies to improve minority access to public mental health services in California: Description and preliminary evaluation. *Journal of Community Psychology, 34,* 225–235.

Snowden, L. R., Martinez, M., & Morris, A. (2000). Community psychology and ethnic minority populations. In J. Rappaport & E. Seidman (Eds.), *Handbook of community psychology.* New York: Plenum.

Social Security Online (2005). *Cost of living adjustments for 2005.* Retrieved on July 5, 2008, from www.ssa.gov/cola/colafacts2005.htm.

Society for Community Research and Action (1994). *Final report of the task force on homeless women, children, and families.* Washington, DC: American Psychological Association.

Society for Community Research and Action (2007) *Practice Task Force report.* Washington, DC: American Psychological Association.

Solarz, A., & Bogat, G. A. (1990). When social support fails: The homeless. *Journal of Community Psychology, 18,* 79–96.

Solomon, D., Watson, M., Battisch, V., Schaps, E., & Delucchi, K. (1996). Creating classrooms that students experience as communities. *American Journal of Community Psychology, 24,* 719–748.

Sosin, M., Piliavin, I., & Westerfelt, H. (1990). Toward a longitudinal analysis of homelessness. *Journal of Social Issues, 46,* 157–174.

South, S. J., Haynie, D. L., & Bose, S. (2007). Student mobility and school dropout. *Social Science Research, 36,* 68–94.

Southwick, S. M., Morgan, C. A., Vythilingam, M., & Charney, D. (2006). Mentors enhance resilience in at-risk children and adolescents. *Psychoanalytic Inquiry, 26,* 577–584.

Speer, P., Dey, A., Griggs, P., Gibson, C., Lubin, B., & Hughey, J. (1992). In search of community: An analysis of community psychology research from 1984–1988. *American Journal of Community Psychology, 20,* 195–209.

Speer, P., & Hughey, J. (1995). Community organizing: An ecological route to empowerment and power. *American Journal of Community Psychology, 23,* 729–748.

Speigel, H. (1987). Coproduction in the context of neighborhood development. *Journal of Voluntary Research, 16,* 54–61.

Spillman, B. C., & Pezzin, L. E. (2000). Potential and active family caregivers: Changing networks and the "sandwich generation." *Millbank Quarterly, 78,* 347–374.

Spitzer, R. J. (1999, Summer). The gun dispute. *American Educator,* 10–17.

Spivack, G., & Marcus, J. (1987). Marks and classroom adjustment as early indicators of mental health at age twenty. *American Journal of Community Psychology, 15,* 35–56.

Spoth, R. (1997). Challenges in defining and developing the field of rural mental disorder preventive intervention research. *American Journal of Community Psychology, 25,* 425–448.

Spoth, R., Redmond, C., Hockaday, C., & Yoo, S. (1996). Protective factors and young adolescent tendency to abstain from alcohol use: A model using two waves of intervention study data. *American Journal of Community Psychology, 24,* 749–770.

Sprague, J., & Hayes, J. (2000). Self-determination and empowerment: A feminist standpoint analysis of talk about disability. *American Journal of Community Psychology, 28,* 671–695.

Spreitzer, G. M. (1995). An empirical test of a comprehensive model of intrapersonal empowerment in the workplace. *American Journal of Community Psychology, 23,* 601–629.

Stack, L. C., Lannon, P. B., & Miley, A. D. (1983). Accuracy of clinicians' expectancies for psychiatric rehospitalization. *American Journal of Community Psychology, 11,* 99–113.

Stanton, A., Kirk, S., Cameron, C., & Danoff-Burg, S. (2000). Coping through emotional approach: Scale construction and validation. *Journal of Personality and Social Psychology, 78,* 1150–1169.

Stearns, E., Moller, S., Blau, J., & Potochnick, S. (2007). Staying back and dropping out: The relationship between grade retention and school dropout. *Sociology of Education, 80,* 210–240.

Steffen, A. M. (1996). Community psychology's response to the promises and problems of aging. *The Community Psychologist, 29,* 19–21.

Stein, C., & Mankowski, E. (2004). Asking, witnessing, interpreting, knowing: Conducting qualitative research in community psychology. *American Journal of Community Psychology, 33*(1–2), 21–35.

Stein, L., & Test, M. A. (1985). The training in community living model: A decade of experience. In *New Directions for Mental Health Services* (Vol. 26). San Francisco: Jossey-Bass.

Stein, L. I., & Test, M. A. (1980). An alternative to mental hospital treatment. I: Conceptual model, treatment program, and clinical evaluation. *Archives of General Psychiatry, 37,* 392–397.

Stephens, C. (2007). Community as practice: Social representations of community and their implications for health promotion. *Journal of Community and Applied Social Psychology, 17,* 103–114.

Sternberg, L. (2004). Risk-taking in adolescence. *Annals of the New York Academy of Science, 1021,* 108.

Stipek, D., & Hakuta, K. (2007). Strategies to ensure that no child starts from behind. In L. J. Aber, S. J. Bishop-Josef, S. M. Jones, K. Taffe, & D. A. Phillips (Eds.), *Child development and social policy: Knowledge for action.* Washington, DC: American Psychological Association.

Stoiber, K. C., & McIntyre, J. (2006). Adolescent pregnancy and parenting. In G. G. Bear & K. M. Minke (Eds.), *Children's needs III: Development, prevention, and intervention.* Washington, DC: National Association of School Psychologists.

Storch, M., Gaab, J., Küttel, Y., Stüssi, A.-C., & Fend, H. (2007). Psychoneuroendocrine effects of resource-activating stress management training. *Health Psychology, 26*(4), 456–463.

Strange, J., Sherman, L., Angel, C. M., & Woods, D. J. (2006). Victim evaluations of face-to-face restorative justice conferences: A quasi-experimental analysis. *Journal of Social Issues, 62,* 281–306.

Strom, K., & MacDonald, J. (2007). The influence of social and economic disadvantage on racial patterns in youth homicide over time. *Homicide Studies, 11,* 50–69.

Strother, C. R. (1987). Reflections on the Stanford Conference and subsequent events. *American Journal of Community Psychology, 15,* 519–522.

Struening, E. L., & Padgett, D. K. (1990). Physical health status, substance use and abuse, and mental disorders among homeless adults. *Journal of Social Issues, 46,* 65–81.

Strumer, S., Snyder, M., & Omoto, A. (2005). Prosocial emotions and helping: The moderating role of group membership. *Journal of Personality and Social Psychology, 88,* 532–546.

Suarez-Balcazar, Y., Davis, M., Ferrari, J., Nyden, P., Olsen, B., Alverez, A., et al. (2004). University-community partnerships: A framework and an exemplar. In L. Jason, C. Keys, Y. Suarez-Balcazar, R. Taylor, & M. Davis (Eds.), *Participatory community research: Theories and methods in action* (pp. 105–120). Washington, DC: American Psychological Association.

Suarez-Balcazar, Y., Durlak, J. A., & Smith, C. (1994). Multicultural training practices in community psychology programs. *American Journal of Community Psychology, 22,* 785–798.

Substance Abuse and Mental Health Services Administration (2000). *Summary of findings from the 1999 National Household Survey on Drug Abuse* (Publication no. 00-3466). Rockville, MD: U.S. Department of Health and Human Service, Substance Abuse and Mental Health Services Administration.

Substance Abuse and Mental Health Services Administration (2007). *Results from the 2006 National Survey on Drug Use and Health: National findings.* Rockville, MD: SAMHSA Office of Applied Studies.

Sue, D. W., Bingham, R. P., Porché-Burke, L., & Vasquez, M. (1999). The diversification of psychology: A multicultural revolution. *American Psychologist, 54,* 1061–1069.

Sue, D., Bucceri, J., Lin, A., Nadal, & Torino, G. (2007). Racial microaggressions and the Asian American experience. *Cultural Diversity and Ethnic Minority Psychology, 13,* 72–81.

Sue, S. (1977). Community mental health services: Some optimism, some pessimism. *American Psychologist, 32,* 616–624.

Sue, S. (1999). Science, ethnicity, and bias: Where have we gone wrong? *American Psychologist, 54*(12), 1070–1077.

Sue, S. (2003). In defense of cultural competency in psychotherapy and treatment. *American Psychologist, 58,* 964–970.

Sue, S. (2006). Cultural competency: From philosophy to research and practice. *Journal of Community Psychology, 34,* 273–245.

Sundberg, N. D. (1985). The use of future studies in training for prevention and promotion in mental health. *Journal of Primary Prevention, 6,* 98–114.

Sundberg, N., Snowden, L., & Reynolds, W. (1978). Toward assessment of personal competence and incompetence in life situations. *Annual Review of Psychology, 29,* 179–221.

Sundstrom, E., DeMeuse, K. P., & Futrell, D. (1990). Work teams. *American Psychologist, 45,* 120–133.

Surgeon General's Call to Action to Promote Sexual Health and Responsible Sexual Behavior. (2001). Retrieved from http://www.surgeongeneral.gov/library/sexualhealth/call.htm.

Susser, E., Moore, R., & Link, B. (1993). Risk factors for homelessness. In H. K. Armenian, L. Gordis, J. L. Kelsey, M. Levine, & S. B. Thacker (Eds.), *Epidemiologic reviews* (vol. 15). Baltimore, MD: Johns Hopkins University School of Hygiene and Public Health.

Susser, E., Valencia, E., & Conover, S. (1993). Prevalence of HIV infection among psychiatric patients in a New York City men's shelter. *American Journal of Public Health, 83,* 55–57.

Sutton, R. M., & Farrall, S. (2005). Gender, socially desirable responding and the fear of crime: Are women really more anxious about crime? *British Journal of Criminology, 45,* 212–224.

Svec, H. (1987). Youth advocacy and high school dropout. *High School Journal, 70,* 185–192.

Svyantek, D. J., Goodman, S. A., Benz, L. L., & Gard, J. (1999). The relationship between organizational characteristics and team building success. *Journal of Business & Psychology, 14,* 265–283.

Swift, C., & Levin, G. (1987). Empowerment: An emerging mental health technology. *Journal of Primary Prevention, 8,* 71–94.

Sy, F. S., Chang, C. L., Choi, S. T., & Wong, F. Y. (1998). Epidemiology of HIV and AIDS among Asians and Pacific Islander Americans. *AIDS Education and Prevention,* 10 (Supplement A), 4–18.

Szasz, T. S. (1961). *The myth of mental illness.* New York: Dell.

Taber, T. D., Cooke, R. A., & Walsh, J. T. (1990). A joint business-community approach to improve problem solving by workers displaced in a plant shutdown. *Journal of Community Psychology, 18,* 19–33.

Talbott, J. A. (1975). Current clichés and platitudes in vogue in psychiatric vocabularies. *Hospital and Community Psychiatry, 26,* 530.

Tartaglia, S. (2006). A preliminary study for a new model of sense of community. *Journal of Community Psychology, 34,* 25–36.

Taulé-Lunblad, J., Galbavy, R., & Dowrick, P. (2000). Putting the cool into after school: Responsive after-school community learning centers. *Community Psychologist, 33,* 33–34.

Tausig, M. (1987). Detecting "cracks" in mental health service systems: Application of network analytic techniques. *American Journal of Community Psychology, 15,* 337–351.

Taxman, F. S. (2004). The offender and reentry: Supporting active participation in reintegration. *Federal Probation, 68,* 31–35.

Taylor, C., & Taylor, V. (2007). Hip hop is now: An evolving youth culture. *Reclaiming Children and Youth, 15,* 210–213.

Taylor, R. B., & Shumaker, S. A. (1990). Local crime as a natural disaster: Implications for understanding the relationship between disorder and fear of crime. *American Journal of Community Psychology, 18,* 619–641.

Taylor, S. E. (1986–1987). The impact of an alternative high school program on students labeled "deviant." *Educational Research Quarterly, 11,* 8–12.

Taylor, S. E., Helgeson, V. S., Reed, G. M., & Skokan, L. A. (1991). Self-generated feelings of control and adjustment to physical illness. *Journal of Social Issues, 47,* 91–110.

Thatcher, J., & Howard, M. (1989). Enhancing professional effectiveness: Management training for the head teacher. *Educational and Child Psychology, 6,* 45–50.

Thoits, P. (1984). Explaining distributions of psychological vulnerability: Lack of social support in the face of life stress. *Social Forces, 63*(2), 453–481.

Thoits, P. (1985). Social support and psychological well being: Theoretical possibilities. In I. Sarason & B. Sarason (Eds.), *Social support: Theory, research and application* (pp. 51–72). Netherlands: Martinus Nijhoff.

Thoits, P. (1986). Social support as coping assistance. *Journal of Consulting and Clinical Psychology, 54,* 416–423.

Thomas, D., & Veno, A. (Eds.) *Community Psychology and Social Change:Australian and New Zealand Perspectives* (2nd Ed.). Palmerston North, New Zealand: Dunmore Press.

Thomas, E., Rickel, A. U., Butler, C., & Montgomery, E. (1990). Adolescent pregnancy and parenting. *Journal of Primary Prevention, 10,* 195–206.

Thomas, J. (2008). *Crime Rates in the United States remain at 30-year lows.* Retrieved from www.america.gov/st/washfile-english/%202005/September/200509281446271.

Thompson, M. P., & Norris, F. H. (1992). Crime, social status and alienation. *American Journal of Community Psychology, 20,* 97–119.

Thompson, S. C., & Spacespan, S. (1991). Perceptions of control in vulnerable populations. *Journal of Social Issues, 47,* 1–21.

Thorpe, S. J., & Brosnan, M. J. (2007). Does computer anxiety reach levels which conform to DSM IV criteria for specific phobia? *Computers in Human Behavior, 23,* 1258–1272.

Tice, C. H. (1991). Developing informal networks of caring through intergenerational connections in school settings. *Marriage and Family Review, 16,* 377–389.

Tierney, J. P. Grossman, J. B., & Resch, N. (1995). *Making a difference: An impact study of Big Brother/Big Sister.* Philadelphia: Public/Private Ventures.

Timothy, T. (2004). *Clinical Psychology.* Florence, Kentucky: Wadsworth Publishing.

Tobler, N. S., Ronna, M., Ochshorn, P., Marshall, D. G., Streke, A., & Stackpole, K. M. (2000). School-based adolescent drug prevention programs: 1998 meta-analysis. *Journal of Primary Prevention, 20,* 275–336.

Toker, S., Shirom, A., Shapira, I., Berliner, S., & Melamed, S. (2005). The association between burnout, depression, anxiety, and inflammation biomarkers: C-reactive protein and fibrinogen in men and women. *Journal of Occupational Health Psychology, 10,* 344–362.

Tolan, P., Keys, C., Chertak, F., & Jason, L. (1990). *Researching community psychology.* Washington, DC: American Psychological Association.

Tompsett, C. J., Toro, P. A., Guzicki, M., Manrique, M., & Zatakia, J. (2006). Homelessness in the United States: Assessing changes in prevalence and public opinion, 1993–2001. *American Journal of Community Psychology, 37,* 47–61.

Toro, P. A. (1990). Evaluating professionally operated and self-help programs for the seriously mentally ill. *American Journal of Community Psychology, 18,* 903–907.

Toro, P. (2005). Community psychology: Where do we go from here? *American Journal of Community Psychology, 35*(1–2), 9–16.

Toro, P. A. (2007). Toward an international understanding of homelessness. *Journal of Social Issues, 63,* 461–481.

Torrey, E. F. (1997, June). The release of the mentally ill from institutions: A well-intentioned disaster. *Chronicle of Higher Education,* B4–B5.

Tosi, H. L., Rizzo, J. R., & Carroll, S. J. (1986). *Managing organizational behavior.* Marshfield, MA: Pitman.

Town, M., Naimi, T. S., Mokdad, A. H., & Brewer, R. D. (2006). Health care access among U.S. adults who drink alcohol excessively: missed opportunities for prevention. *Preventing Chronic Disease, 3,* A53.

Traynor, M. P., Begay, M. E., & Glantz, S. A. (1993). New tobacco industry strategy to prevent local tobacco control. *Journal of the American Medical Association, 270,* 479–486.

Trickett, E. (1996). A future for community psychology: The contexts of diversity and the diversity of contexts. *American Journal of Community Psychology, 24,* 209–234.

Trickett, E. J., McConahay, J. B., Phillips, D., & Ginter, M. A. (1985). Natural experiments and the educational context: The environment and effects of an alternative inner-city public school on adolescents. *American Journal of Community Psychology, 13,* 617–643.

Trotter, R. T. (1995). Drug use, AIDS, and ethnography: Advanced ethnographic research methods exploring the HIV epidemic. In R. H. Needle, S. G. Gesner, & R. T. Trotter (Eds.), *Social networks, drug abuse, and HIV transmission* (pp. 38–53). Rockville, MD: National Institute on Drug Abuse.

Tseng, V., & Seidman, E. (2007). A systems framework for understanding social settings. *American Journal of Community Psychology, 39*(3–4), 217–228.

Tsui, A., Egan, T., & O'Reilly, C. (1992) Being different: Relational demography and organizational attachment. *Administrative Science Quarterly, 37,* 549–579.

Turman, K. M. (2001, January/February). Crime victims. *National Criminal Justice Reference Service Catalog,* p14.

Turner, J. B., Kessler, R. C., & House, J. S. (1991). Factors facilitating adjustment to unemployment: Implications for intervention. *American Journal of Community Psychology, 19,* 521–524.

Turnipseed, D. L. (1998). Anxiety and burnout in the health care work environment. *Psychological Reports, 82,* 627–642.

Uchino, B. (2004). *Social support and physical health: Understanding the health consequences of relationships.* New Haven, CT: Yale University Press.

Uchino, B. (2006). Social support and health: A review of physiological processes potentially underlying links to disease outcomes. *Journal of Behavioral Medicine, 29,* 377–387.

Uchino, B., Cacioppo, J., & Kiecolt-Glaser, J. (1996). The relationship between social support and physiological processes: A review with emphasis on underlying mechanisms and implications for health. *Psychological Bulletin, 119*(3), 488–531.

UNAIDS. (2006). *AIDS Epidemic Update.* Geneva, Switzerland: WHO Library Cataloguing. World Health Organization (2008a, b)

Unger, D. G., & Wandersman, A. (1985). The importance of neighbors: The social, cognitive and affective components of neighboring. *American Journal of Community Psychology, 13,* 139–170.

Unger, D. G., & Wandersman, L. P. (1985b). Social support and adolescent mothers: Action research contributions to theory and application. *American Journal of Community Psychology, 41,* 29–45.

U.S. Census Bureau (2004). *U.S. Interim projections by age, sex, race, and Hispanic origin.* Retrieved from (http://www.census.gov/ipc//www/interimproj/).

U.S. Department of Education (1998). *Guide to safe schools.* Washington, DC: Author.

U.S. Department of Health and Human Services (2000). *Healthy people 2000: National health promotion and disease prevention objectives.* DHHS publication no. (PHS) 91–50212. Washington, DC: Superintendent of Documents, U.S. Government Printing Office.

U.S. Department of Health and Human Services (1998). *Profile of homelessness.* Retrieved from www.aspe.os.dhhs.gov/progsys/homeless/profile.htm.

U.S. Department of Health and Human Services (2001a). *Head Start factsheet 2001.* Retrieved from www.acf.dhhs.gov/programs/hsb/about/fact2001.htm.

U.S. Department of Health and Human Services (2001b). *Women and smoking: A report of the Surgeon General.* Atlanta, GA: U.S. Department of Health and Human Services, Centers for Disease Control and Prevention, National Center for Chronic Disease Prevention and Health Promotion, Office on Smoking and Health.

U.S. Department of Health and Human Resources (2003). *STD in adolescents and young adults: Special focus profiles.* Washington, DC: U.S. Government Printing Office.

U.S. Department of Health and Human Services (2004). *The health consequences of smoking: A report of the Surgeon General.* Atlanta, GA: U.S. Department of Health and Human Services, Centers for Disease Control and Prevention, National Center for Chronic Disease Prevention and Health Promotion, Office on Smoking and Health.

U.S. Department of Health and Human Resources (2006). *STD surveillance national profile.* Washington, DC: U.S. Government Printing Offices.

U.S. Department of Health and Human Services, CDC (2008, April 2). *Alcohol and public health—binge drinking*. Retrieved June 13, 2008, from www.cdc.gov/alcohol.quickstats/binge_drinking.htm

U.S. Department of Justice (1997). *What you can do if you are a victim of crime*. Washington, DC: Author.

U.S. Department of Labor, Bureau of Labor Statistics (2006). *Futurework: Trends and challenges for work in the 21st century*. Retrieved from www.dol.gov/oasam/programs/history/herman/reports/futurework/report/chapter4/main.htm.

U.S. Preventive Services Task Force (November, 2002). Screening for colorectal cancer: U.S. Preventive Services Task Force recommendation statement, *Annals of Internal Medicine, 149*(9). Retrieved from http://www.annals.org/cgi/content/full/0000605-200811040-00243v1.

U.S. Surgeon General (1999). *Mental health: A report of the U.S. Surgeon General*. Retrieved July 1, 2008, from www.surgeongeneral.gov/library/mentalhealth/home.html.

Vacca, J. S. (2004). Educated prisoners are less likely to return to prison. *Journal of Correctional Education, 55,* 297–315.

Valdiserri, R. O., West, G., Moore, M., Darrow, W. W., & Hinman, A. R. (1992). Structuring HIV prevention services delivery systems on the basis of social science theory. *Journal of Community Health, 17,* 259–269.

Valentiner, D., Holohan, C., & Moos, R. (1994). Social support, appraisals of event controllability, and coping: An integrative model. *Journal of Personality and Social Psychology, 66,* 1094–1102.

Van Fleet, D. D. (1991). *Behavior in organizations*. Boston: Houghton Mifflin.

Van Houtte, M. (2005). Climate or culture? A plea for conceptual clarity in school effectiveness research. *School Effectiveness and School Improvement, 16,* 71–89.

Varmus, H., & Satcher, D. (1997). Ethical complexities of conducting research in developing countries. *New England Journal of Medicine, 337,* 1003–1005.

Vartonian, T. P., & Gleason, P. M. (1999). Do neighborhood conditions affect high school dropout and college graduation rates? *Journal of Socio-Economics, 28,* 21–41.

Vaux, A. (1991). Let's hang up and try again: Lessons learned from a social support intervention. *American Journal of Community Psychology, 19,* 85–90.

Velleman, R. B., Templeton, L. J., & Copello, A. G. (2005). The role of the family in preventing and intervening with substance use and misuse: A comprehensive review of family interventions, with a focus on young people. *Drug and Alcohol Review, 24,* 93–109.

Vidal, A. P. C., Howitt, A. M., & Foster, K. P. (1986). *Stimulating community report? An assessment of the local initiative support corporation*. Cambridge, MA: John F. Kennedy School of Government.

Vidmar, N. (1992). Procedural justice and alternative dispute resolution. *Psychological Science, 3,* 224–228.

Vieno, A., Perkins, D. D., Smith, T. M., & Santinello, M. (2005). Democratic school climate and a sense of community in school: A multilevel analysis. *American Journal of Community Psychology, 36,* 327–341.

Vimpani, G. (2005). Getting the mix right: Family, community and social policy interventions to improve outcomes for young people at risk of substance misuse. *Drug and Alcohol Review, 24,* 111–125.

Vincent, T. A. (1990). A view from the hill: The human element in policy making on Capitol Hill. *American Psychologist, 45,* 61–64.

Vitaliano, P., DeWolfe, D., Maiuro, R., Russo, J., & Katon, W. (1990). Appraised changeability of a stressor as a modifier of the relationship between coping and depression: A test of the hypothesis of fit. *Journal of Personality and Social Psychology, 59,* 582–592.

Voas, R. B., Tippetts, A. S., & Fell, J. (2000). The relationship of alcohol safety laws to drinking drivers in fatal crashes. *Accident Analysis and Prevention, 32,* 483–492.

Vogelman, L. (1990). Psychology, mental health care and the future: Is appropriate transformation in post-apartheid South Africa possible? *Social Science and Medicine, 31,* 501–505.

Wagner, B., Compas, B., & Howell, D. (1988). Daily and major life events: A test of an integrative model of psychosocial stress. *American Journal of Community Psychology, 16*(2), 189–205.

Walfish, S., Polifka, J. A., & Stenmark, D. E. (1986). The job search in community psychology: A survey of recent graduates. *American Journal of Community Psychology, 14,* 237–240.

Walker, C. R., & Walker, S. G. (1990). The citizen and the police: A partnership in crime prevention. *Canadian Journal of Criminology, 32,* 125–135.

Walker, I., & Crogan, M. (1998). Academic performance, prejudice, and the jigsaw classroom: New pieces to the puzzle. *Journal of Community & Applied Social Psychology, 8,* 381–393.

Walker, L., Sakai, T., & Brady, K. (2006). Restorative circles—a reentry planning process for Hawaii inmates. *Federal Probation, 70,* 33–38.

Wallerstein, N., & Bernstein, S. (1988). Empowerment education: Freire's idea adapted to health education. *Health Education Quarterly, 15,* 379–394.

Wallston, B., Alagna, S., & DeVellis, B. (1983). Social support and physical health. *Health Psychology, 2,* 367–391.

Walsh, M. E., & Jackson, J. H. (2005). Psychological services for children and families who are homeless. In R. G. Steele & M. C. Roberts (Eds.), *Handbook of mental health services for children, adolescents, and families.* New York: Kluwer.

Walsh, R. T. (1987). A social historical note on the formal emergence of community psychology. *American Journal of Community Psychology, 15,* 523–529.

Wandersman, A., & Florin, P. (2000). Citizen participation and community organizations. In J. Rappaport & E. Seidman (Eds.), *Handbook of community psychology.* New York: Plenum.

Wandersman, A., Florin, P., Friedman, R., & Meier, R. (1987). Who participates, who does not and why? An analysis of voluntary neighborhood organizations in the United States and Israel. *Sociological Forum, 2,* 534–555.

Wandersman, A., Hallman, W., & Berman, S. (1989). How residents cope with living near a hazardous waste landfill: An example of substantive theorizing. *American Journal of Community Psychology, 17,* 575–584.

Wandersman, A., Kloos, B., Linney, J., & Shinn, M. (2005). Science and community psychology: Enhancing the vitality of community research and action. *American Journal of Community Psychology, 35,* 105–106.

Wandersman, A., Morrissey, E., Davino, K., Seybolt, D., Crusto, C., Nation, M., et al. (1998). Comprehensive quality programming and accountability: Eight essential strategies for implementing successful prevention programs. *Journal of Primary Prevention, 19,* 3–30.

Wandersman, A., & Nation, M. (1998). Urban neighborhoods and mental health: Psychological contributions to understanding toxicity, resilience, and interventions. *American Psychologist, 53,* 647–656.

Wardlaw, D. M. (2000). Persistent themes in the history of community psychology: A preliminary analysis of *The Community Psychologist* or do we have an identity after all? *Community Psychologist, 33,* 15–18.

Warner, R. (1989). Deinstitutionalization: How did we get where we are? *Journal of Social Issues, 45,* 17–30.

Warren-Sohlberg, L., Jason, L. A., Orosan-Weine, A. M., Lantz, G. D., & Reyes, O. (1998). Implementing and evaluating preventive programs for high-risk transfer students. *Journal of Educational & Psychological Consultation, 9,* 309–324.

Wasik, B. H., Ramey, C. T., Bryant, D. M., & Sparling, J. J. (1990). A longitudinal study of two early intervention strategies: Project CARE. *Child Development, 61,* 1682–1696.

Watters, J., & Biernacki, P. (1989). Targeted sampling options for the study of hidden populations. *Social Problems, 36,* 416–430.

Watts, R. J. (1992). Elements of a psychology of human diversity. *Journal of Community Psychology, 20,* 116–131.

Watts, R., & Serrano-Garcia, I. (2003). The quest for a liberating community psychology: An overview. *American Journal of Community Psychology, 31,* 73–78.

Watts-English, T., Fortson, B. L., Gibler, N., Hooper, S. R., & De Bellis, M. D. (2006). The psychobiology of maltreatment in childhood. *Journal of Social Issues, 62,* 717–736.

Watzlawick, P., Weakland, J., & Fisch, R. (1974). *Change: Principles of problem formation and problem resolution.* New York: Norton.

Way, M., Reddy, R., & Rhodes, J. (2007). Students' perceptions of school climate during the middle school years: Associations with trajectories of psychological and behavioral adjustment. *American Journal of Community Psychology, 40,* 194–213.

Weaver, J. (1986). Therapeutic implications of divorce mediation. *Mediation Quarterly, 12,* 75–90.

Webb, D. H. (1989). PBB: An environment contaminant in Michigan. *Journal of Community Psychology, 17,* 30–46.

Webster-Stratton, C., & Reid, M. J. (2007). Incredible years parents and teachers training series: A Head Start partnership to promote social competence and prevent conduct problems. In P. Tolan, J. Szapocznik, & S. Sambrano (Eds.), *Preventing youth substance abuse: Science-based programs for children and adolescents.* Washington, DC: American Psychological Association.

Wechsler, H., Dowdall, G. W., Maenner, G., Gledhill-Hoyt, L., & Lee, H. (1998). Changes in binge drinking and related problems among American college students between 1993 and 1997: Results of the Harvard School of Public Health College Alcohol Study. *American College Health, 47,* 51–55.

Weed, D. S. (1990, August). *Providing consultation to primary prevention programs: Applying the technology of community psychology.* Paper presented to the Annual Convention of the American Psychological Association, Boston, MA.

Weeks, M. R. (1990). *Community outreach prevention effort: Designs in culturally appropriate AIDS intervention.* Hartford, CT: Institute for Community Research.

Weeks, M. R., Schensul, J. J., Williams, S. S., Singer M., & Grier, M. (1995). AIDS prevention for African-American and Latina women: Building culturally and gender-appropriate intervention. *AIDS Education and Prevention, 7,* 251–263.

Weeks, M. R., Singer, M., Grier, M., Hunte-Marrow, J., & Haughton, C. (1991). *Project COPE: Preventing AIDS among injection drug users and their sex partners.* Hartford, CT: Institute for Community Research.

Weikart, D. P., & Schweinhart, L. J. (1997). High/Scope Perry Preschool Program. In G. W. Albee & T. P. Gullotta (Eds.), *Primary prevention works.* Thousand Oaks, CA: Sage.

Weinberg, R. B. (1990). Serving large numbers of adolescent victim-survivors: Group interventions following trauma at school. *Professional Psychology Research and Practice, 21,* 271–278.

Weinstein, R. S. (1990). The universe of alternatives in schooling: The contributions of Seymour B. Sarason to education. *American Journal of Community Psychology, 18,* 359–369.

Weinstein, R. (2006). Reaching higher in community psychology: Social problems, social settings, and social change. *American Journal of Community Psychology, 37,* (1–2), 9–20

Weinstein, R. S., Soule, C. R., Collins, F., Cone, J., Mehlhorn, M., & Simontacchi, K. (1991). Expectations and high school change: Teacher-researcher collaboration to prevent school failure. *American Journal of Community Psychology, 19,* 333–362.

Weissberg, R., Kumpfer, K., & Seligman, M. (2003). Prevention that works for children and youth: An introduction. *American Psychologist, 58*(6–7), 425–432.

Weitzer, R., & Tuch, S. A. (2005). Racially biased policing: Determinants of citizen perceptions. *Social Forces, 83,* 1009–1030.

Weitzman, B. C., Knickman, J. R., & Shinn, M. (1990). Pathways to homelessness among New York City families. *Journal of Social Issues, 46*(4), 125–140.

Well, S. S., Holme, J. J., Atanda, A. K., & Revilla, A. T. (2005). Tackling racial segregation one policy at a time: Why school desegregation only went so far. *Teachers College Record, 107,* 2141–2177.

Wells, W. (2007). Type of contact and evaluations of police officers: The effects of procedural justice across three types of police-citizen contact. *Journal of Criminal Justice, 35,* 612–621.

Wemmers, J., & Cyr, K. (2005). Can mediation be therapeutic for crime victims? An evaluation of victims' experiences in mediation with young offenders. *Canadian Journal of Criminology and Criminal Justice, 47,* 527–554.

Werner, E., & Smith, R. (2001). *Journeys from childhood to midlife: Risk, resilience, and recovery.* Ithaca, NY: Cornell University Press.

Wesson, D. R., Smith, D. E., Ling, W., & Seymour, R. B. (1997). *Sedative-hypnotics and tricyclics.* In J. H. Lowinson, Substance abuse a comprehensive textbook (3rd ed.). Baltimore: Williams & Wilkins.

Western Regional Advocacy Project (2006). *Without housing: Decades of federal housing cutbacks, massive homelessness and policy failures.* San Francisco: Author.

Wheaton, B. (1997). The nature of chronic stress. In B. Gottlieb (Ed.), *Coping with chronic stress* (pp. 43–103). New York: Plenum.

White, R. W. (1959). Motivation reconsidered: The concept of competence. *Psychological Review, 66,* 297–333.

WHO Report on the Global Tobacco Epidemic, 2008: The MPOWER package (2008). Geneva: World Health Organization.

Widom, C., DuMont, K., & Czaja, S. (2007). A prospective investigation of major depressive disorder and comorbidity in abused and neglected children grown up. *Archives of General Psychiatry, 64,* 49–56.

Widom, C., Marmorstein, N., & White, H. (2006). Childhood victimization and illicit drug use in middle adulthood. *Psychology of Addictive Behaviors, 20,* 394–403.

Wielkiewicz, R., & Stelzner, S. (2005). An ecological perspective on leadership theory, research and practice. *Review of General Psychology, 9,* 326–341.

Wilcox, B. (1981). Social support, life stress, and psychological adjustment: A test of the buffering hypothesis. *American Journal of Community Psychology, 9*(4), 371–386.

Wilcox, B. L., Robbennolt, J. K., O'Keeffe, J. E., & Pynchon, M. E. (1996). Teen nonmarital childbearing and welfare: The gap between research and political discourse. *Journal of Social Issues, 52,* 71–90.

Wilczenski, F. L., & Coomey, S. M. (2007). *A practical guide to service learning: Strategies for positive development in schools.* New York: Springer Science.

Wilkinson, D. (2007). The multidimensional nature of social cohesion: Psychological sense of community, attraction, and neighboring. *American Journal of Community Psychology, 40,* 214–229.

Wilkinson-Lee, A. M., Russell, S. T., & Lee, F. C. H. (2006). Practitioners' perspectives on cultural sensitivity in Latina/o teen pregnancy prevention. *Family Relations, 55,* 376–389.

Williams, D. (2004). Improving race relations in higher education: The jigsaw classroom as a missing piece to the puzzle. *Urban Education, 39,* 316–344.

Williams, K. R., & Guerra, N. G. (2007). Prevalence and predictors of Internet bullying. *Journal of Adolescent Health, 41,* S41–S21.

Williamson, T., Ashby, D., & Webber, R. (2006). Classifying neighbourhoods for reassurance policing. *Policing & Society, 16*(2), 189–218.

Willis, T. A. (1991). Comments on Heller, Thompson, Trueba, Hogg and Vlachos-Weber: Peer support telephone dyads for elderly women. *American Journal of Community Psychology, 19,* 75–83.

Willowbrook plan worked. (1982, September 4). *New York Times,* p. 20.

Wilson, G., & Lester, D. (1998). Suicide prevention by e-mail. *Crisis Intervention and Time-Limited Treatment, 4,* 81–87.

Wilson, G. T., O'Leary, K. D., & Nathan, P. (1992). *Abnormal psychology.* Englewood Cliffs, NJ: Prentice Hall.

Wilson, J. B., Ellwood, D. T., & Brooks-Gunn, J. (1996). Welfare-to-work through the eyes of children. In P. L. Chase-Lansdale & J. Brooks-Gunn (Eds.), *Escape from poverty: What makes a difference for children?* New York: Cambridge University Press.

Winkleby, M., Taylor, C., Jatulis, D., & Fortmann, S. (1996). The long-term effects of a cardiovascular disease prevention trial: The Stanford Five City Project. *American Journal of Public Health, 86,* 1773–1779.

Withy, K., Andaya, J., Mikami, J., & Yamada, S. (2007). Assessing health disparities in rural Hawaii using the Hoshin facilitation method. *Journal of Rural Health, 23*(1), 84–88.

Wittig, M. A., & Schmitz, J. (1996). Electronic grassroots organizing. *Journal of Social Issues, 52,* 53–69.

Wolff, T. (1987). Community psychology and empowerment: An activist's insights. *American Journal of Community Psychology, 15,* 151–166.

Wollert, R., & The Self-Help Research Team (1987). The self-help clearinghouse concept: An evaluation of one program and its implications for policy and practice. *American Journal of Community Psychology, 15,* 491–508.

Wong, F. Y., Blakely, C. H., & Worsham, S. L. (1991). Techniques and pitfalls of applied behavioral science research: The case of community mediation. In K. G. Duffy, J. W. Grosch, & P. V. Olczak (Eds.), *Community mediation: A handbook for practitioners and researchers* (pp. 35–41). New York: Guilford.

Wong, F. Y., & Bouey, P. D. (2001). *Substance use/HIV health among urban Native Indians.* Unpublished manuscript. Washington, DC: George Washington University School of Public Health and Health Services.

Woodward, T. G. (2008). Using protective factors to change the future of corrections. *Corrections Today, 70,* 76–77.

Woolpert, S. (1991). Victim-offender reconciliation programs. In K. G. Duffy, J. W. Grosch, & P. V. Olczak (Eds.), *Community mediation: A handbook for practitioners and researchers.* New York: Guilford.

Worchel, S., Cooper, J., & Goethals, G. R. (1991). *Understanding social psychology.* Pacific Grove, CA: Brooks/Cole.

Worchel, S., & Lundgren, S. (1991). The nature of conflict and conflict resolution. In K. G. Duffy, J. W. Grosch, & P. V. Olczak (Eds.), *Community mediation: A handbook for practitioners and researchers.* New York: Guilford.

Work, W. C., Cowen, E., Parker, G. R., & Wyman, P. A. (1990). Stress resilient children in an urban setting. *Journal of Primary Prevention, 11,* 3–17.

Work, W. C., & Olsen, K. H. (1990). Evaluation of a revised fourth grade social problem solving curriculum: Empathy as a moderator of adjustive gain. *Journal of Primary Prevention, 11,* 143–157.

World Health Organization (2004). *Managing child abuse: A handbook for medical officers.* New Delhi: Author.

World Health Organization (2008a). *Global health indicators, World health statistics 2008* (pp. 36–46). Retrieved on July 5, 2008, from www.who.int/whosis/whostat/2008/en/index.html.

World Health Organization (2008b). *WHO facts and figures.* Retrieved on June 13, 2008, from www.who.int/substance_abuse/facts/en.

Wright, S. C., Aron, A., McLaughlin-Volpe, T., & Ropp, S. A. (1997). The extended contact effect: Knowledge of cross-group friendships and prejudice. *Journal of Personality and Social Psychology, 73,* 73–90.

Wright, S., & Cowen, E. L. (1985). The effects of peer teaching on student perceptions of class environment, adjustment, and academic performance. *American Journal of Community Psychology, 13,* 417–432.

Wrosch, C., Dunne, E., Scheier, M. F., & Schulz, R. (2006). Self-regulation of common age-related challenges: Benefits for older adults' psychological and physical health. *Journal of Behavioral Medicine, 29,* 299–306.

Xie, J. L., & Johns, G. (1995). Job scope and stress: Can job scope be too high? *Academy of Management Journal, 38,* 1288–1309.

Yates, M., & Youniss, J. (1998). Community service and political identity development in adolescence. *Journal of Social Issues Special Issue: Political Development: Youth Growing Up in a Global Community, 54,* 495–512.

Yang, P., & Barrett, N. (2006). Understanding public attitudes towards Social Security. *International Journal of Social Welfare, 15,* 95–109.

Yoon, O., & Joo, H. (2005). A contextual analysis of crime rates: The Korean case. *Crime, Law and Social Change, 43,* 31–55.

Youngstrom, E., Weist, M., & Albus, K. E. (2003). Exploring violence exposure, stress, protective factors and behavioral problems among inner-city youth. *American Journal of Community Psychology, 32,* 115–129.

Yunus, M. (1999, November). The Grameen Bank. *Scientific American,* 114–119.

Yunus, M. (2007). *Grameen bank at a glance.* Retrieved from www.grameen-info.org/bank/GBGlance.htm.

Zarit, S. H., Pearlin, L., & Schaie, K. W. (2003). Personal control in social and life course contexts. In S. H. Zarit, L. Pearlin, & K. W. Schaie (Eds.), *Social impact on aging.* New York: Springer.

Zeitlin, D., Keller, S., Shiflett, S., Schleifer, S., & Bartlett, J. (2000). Immunological effects of massage therapy during acute academic stress. *Psychosomatic Medicine, 62,* 83–84.

Zhong, L. Y., & Broadhurst, R. G. (2007). Building little safe and civilized communities: Community crime prevention with Chinese characteristics? *International Journal of Offender Therapy and Comparative Criminology, 51,* 52–67.

Zigler, E. (1990). Shaping child care policies and programs in America. *American Journal of Community Psychology, 18,* 183–216.

Zigler, E. (1994). Reshaping early childhood intervention to be a more effective weapon against poverty. *American Journal of Community Psychology, 22,* 37–48.

Zigler, E. F., & Muenchow, S. (1992). *Head Start: The inside story of America's most successful educational experiment.* New York: Basic Books.

Zigler, E. F., & Gilman, E. D. (1998). Day care and early childhood settings: Fostering mental health in young children. *Child and Adolescent Psychiatric Clinics of North America, 7,* 483–498.

Zigler, E. F., & Goodman, J. (1982). The battle for day care in America: A view from the trenches. In

E. F. Zigler & E. W. Gordon (Eds.), *Day care: Scientific and social policy issues*. Boston: Auburn House.

Zigler, E., & Lang, M. (1991). *Childcare choices*. New York: Free Press.

Zimmerman, M. (1995). Psychological empowerment: Issues and illustrations. *American Journal of Community Psychology, 23*(5), 581–599.

Zimmerman, M. A., Ramírez-Valles, J., & Maton, K. L. (1999). Resilience among urban African American male adolescents: A study of the protective effects of sociopolitical control on their mental health. *American Journal of Community Psychology, 27*, 733–751.

Zimmerman, M. A., & Rappaport, J. (1988). Citizen participation, perceived control, and empowerment. *American Journal of Community Psychology, 16*, 725–750.

Zippay, A. (1990–1991). The limits of intimates: Social networks and economic status among industrial workers. *Special issue: Applications of social support and social network interventions in direct practice. Journal of Applied Social Sciences, 15*, 75–95.

Zirkel, S., & Cantor, N. (2004). 50 years after *Brown v. Board of Education*: The promise and challenge of multicultural education. *Journal of Social Issues, 60*, 1–14.

Zlotnick, C., Robertson, M. J., & Lahiff, M. (1999). Getting off the streets: Economic resources and residential exits from homelessness. *Journal of Community Psychology, 27*, 209–224.

Zohar, D. (1997). Predicting burnout with a hassle based measure of role demands. *Journal of Occupational Behavior, 101*–115.

Zohar, D. (1999). When things go wrong: The effect of daily work hassles on effort, exertion and negative mood. *Journal of Occupational and Organizational Psychology, 72*, 265–283.

Zugazaga, C. (2004). Stressful life event experiences of homeless adults: A comparison of single men, single women, and women with children. *Journal of Community Psychology, 32*, 643–654.

NAME INDEX

A
Abbott, C, 222
Aber, J. L., 151
Abrahams, R. B., 165
Abramowitz, S. I., 278
Abrams, L. S., 214
Aburdene, P., 86
Ackerman, G., 212
Adams, D., 180
Adams, M., 292
Adams, R. E., 23, 275
Adler, A., 288
Administration for Children and Families, 152, 181, 182
Agency for Healthcare Research and Quality, 239
Ahnert, L., 176, 180, 182
Ahr, P. R., 220
Aikman, S. N., 185
Ajzen, I., 39
Akert, R. M., 189
Alagna, S., 240
Alan Guttmacher Institute, 158, 159, 160
Albee, G. W., 17, 60, 143, 292
Albus, K. E., 206
Alderson, G., 115
Alexander, K. L., 195
Alfred, C. G., 197, 198
Alinsky, S., 92, 97
Allen, G. A., 169
Allen, H., 210
Allen, J. P., 160
Allen, N., 149, 237
Allen, R. P., 3
Allen, S. M., 17, 18
Allen-Meares, P., 158
Allport, G. W., 85, 91, 134, 187
Almeida, M. C., 194
Altmaier, E. M., 102
Altman, D., 235
Altman, I., 236
Altman, J., 66
Altman, L., 21
Alvarez, R., 9
Alvarez-Canino, T., 198
Alvaro, E. M., 249
Ambrose, M., 277
American Association of University Women, 279
American Cancer Society, 80
American Legacy Foundation, 247
American Psychological Association, 167, 171, 172, 186
American Psychological Society, 115
American Youth Policy Forum, 196
Amerio, P., 293
Amici, M., 23
Anders, J., 164
Anderson, E. R., 199
Anderson, J. D., 211
Anderson, J. E., 262
Anderson, L., 33
Anderson, N., 63
Aneshensel, C. S., 190
Angel, C. M., 222
Angell, R., 13
Annas, G., 54
Anshel, M. H., 212
Antoni, M., 288
Apfel, N. H., 110, 160
Applebaum, L. D., 148
Argomaniz, J., 218
Arias, B., 190
Armour, M. P., 222
Armstrong, A. H., 225
Armstrong, G. S., 210
Arnaud, A., 277
Arnold, D. A., 193
Aron, A., 187
Aronson, E., 188, 189, 191
Ashby, D., 211
Assaf, A., 235
Astor, R. A., 197
Atanda, A. K., 184
Atha, J., 198
Atwater, E., 78, 81, 87, 165, 187
Atwater, L., 86, 280
Aubrey, T., 138
Auerbach, J. D., 37
Austen, L., 210
Austin, D. M., 87
Avert, 263
Ayers, T., 65

B
Baba, Y., 87
Babcock, R. L., 81
Baccus, J., 64
Bachrach, L. L., 130, 131
Backer, T. E., 169
Badger, L. W., 195
Bagby, W., 90
Bahr, S. J., 225
Bair, J. P., 286
Baker, C. K., 113
Baker, J., 197
Baker, R. A., 195
Baker, T. K., 193
Baldwin, M., 64
Bales, R., 282
Balkrishnan, R., 235
Baltes, M. M., 68, 165
Baltes, P. B., 165
Baltodano, H. M., 225
Bandura, A., 39
Bankowski, S., 159
Banks, C., 209
Banning, K., 62
Banyard, V., 45
Banziger, G., 132
Barak, A., 165
Barak, G., 172
Barerra, M., 68
Barker, R., 10
Barley, D. E., 121
Barnes, N., 63, 292

363

Barnett, S. W., 183
Baron, R. A., 271, 275, 276, 282, 285
Barone, S., 125
Barrera, M., 98, 102
Barrett, N., 147
Bartlett, J., 288
Bartone, P., 288
Bartunek, J. M., 282
Basseches, M., 285
Basso, R. V. J., 216
Bassuk, E. L., 167, 171
Batson, C. D., 91
Battisch, V., 193
Bauman, Z., 89
Bayer, R., 55
Bayley, B. K., 211
Bazemore, G., 222, 224
Beacon Hill Institute for Public Policy Research, 102
Beaulieu, M., 211
Becker, M. H., 39
Beer, M., 271, 283
Beernal, G., 110
Behrens, T., 91
Belcher, J. R., 134
Belfield, C. R., 183
Bell, C. C., 149
Bell, C. H., 271, 285
Belsky, J., 177
Benbenishty, R., 197
Bendicsen, H., 286
Benjamin, L., 76
Bennett, C. C., 7, 20
Bennett, T., 218
Benviente, G., 57, 90
Benz, L. L., 286
Berg, B. L., 288
Bergeron, C., 211
Berk, M., 248
Berkeley, S., 259
Berkman, L., 241
Berliner, S., 275
Berman, S., 77
Bernier, D., 287
Bernstein, S., 39
Bersoff, D. N., 116
Betters-Reed, B. L., 282
Biernacki, P., 38

Biglan, A., 204, 248, 249
Bilchik, S., 198, 215, 216, 217
Billows, W., 27
Bingham, R. P., 110
Bishop, B., 107, 293
Blair, C., 72
Blakely, C., 158
Blakely, C. H., 109
Blakemore, J. L., 163
Blaney, N., 188
Blau, J., 195
Blechman, E. A., 9
Blom, G. E., 220
Bloom, B. L., 17, 108, 134, 292
Blustein, D., 272, 274
Bobak, M., 249
Bogat, A., 11, 22, 110, 124
Boggiano, A. K., 87
Bok, D., 298
Bolland, J. M., 206, 207, 236
Bolton, N., 196
Bond, G. R., 138, 159, 277, 284
Bond, M. A., 10, 20, 89, 139
Bond Huie, S. A., 206
Bonhomme, J., 204, 210, 225
Bonin, L., 65
Booth, J. A., 190
Bootzin, R. R., 135, 136
Borgida, E., 116
Borkman, T., 282
Borrero, M., 39
Borum, R., 213
Boscarino, J. A., 275
Bose, S., 195
Botvin, G. J., 205
Boudreau, J. W., 279, 289
Bouey, P. D., 37, 39, 40, 42, 44, 50
Bowen, W., 298
Bowman, L. S., 109
Boyd, N., 298
Boyd, R. C., 206
Boyd-Zaharias, J., 193
Bracey, G. W., 225
Brackshaw, E., 198
Bradley, E., 232
Bradshaw, T. K., 98
Bradshaw, W., 221, 222
Brady, K., 225
Braithwaite, R., 204

Brand, S., 196
Branson, R. K., 190
Brass, D. J., 285
Braver, S. L., 65, 199
Bravo, M., 86
Breakey, W. R., 142
Breen, L., 196
Breinlinger, S., 100
Brewer, M. B., 187, 188
Bright, D., 298
Brissette, I., 69, 241
Britt, C. L., 219
Britt, T., 288
Broadhurst, R. G., 213, 218
Brodie, H. K. H., 37
Brodsky, A., 45, 58, 93, 236
Brody, C. J., 273, 274
Broman, C. L., 287
Bronfenbrenner, U., 12, 13, 143, 175, 191, 296
Brook, D., 293
Brook, J., 293
Brooks, E. R., 132, 137
Brooks-Gunn, J., 151, 189, 196, 205
Brosnan, M. J., 81
Brounstein, P., 171
Broussard, A. C., 214
Brown, A., 125
Brown, B. B., 100, 211, 218
Brown, D. R., 190
Brown, G., 211, 218
Brown, K., 300
Brown, P. A., 23
Brown, S., 158
Brownell, A., 98
Bruce, E., 155
Bruce, M. L., 87, 132
Brunson, L., 14
Bryant, D. M., 179
Bryson, S., 233
Bucceri, J., 63
Buckner, J. C., 25
Budman, L., 85
Bullis, M., 225
Bullotta, T. P., 198
Bureau of Justice Statistics, 204, 209, 210
Bureau of National Affairs, 279

NAME INDEX

Burger, W. R., 115
Burgio, J. C., 194
Burlew, A. K., 110
Burnam, M. A., 169
Burns, A., 196
Burroughs, S. M., 273, 278
Burt, K., 296
Burt, M. R., 167, 169, 171
Burton, C. E., 208
Busch, S., 232
Bush, R., 299
Butcher, K., 233
Butler, C., 162
Bynner, J., 272
Bynum, T. G., 211
Bynum, T. S., 206
Byrne, J. M., 213, 224

C

Cacioppo, J., 68
Cadena, B., 148, 149
Caldwell, C. H., 208
Calsyn, R. J., 169
Cameron, C., 66
Camillo, M. A., 185
Camp, K. M., 220
Campaign for Our Children, 159
Campbell, C., 235, 293
Campbell, D., 43, 44
Campbell, R., 45, 113
Campfield, K. M., 220
Campion, M. A., 279
Canino, G. J., 86
Cantelon, S., 195
Caplan, G., 16
Caplan, N., 115
Caplan, R. D., 287
Caputo, R. K., 183, 190
Caputo, T., 218
Carbonell, J., 86
Cardey, R., 216
Carey, J. W., 262
Carleton, R., 235
Carlton, S., 286
Carmony, T., 26
Carnevale, P. J., 221, 222
Carpenter, K. M., 124
Carroll, C. F., 103
Carroll, D., 68

Carroll, S. J., 276
Carver, C. S., 65, 69
Cascio, W., 272
Case, S., 217
Caspi, A., 23, 211
Casriel, C., 286
Cassinerio, C., 193
Casswell, S., 25
Catalano, G., 209
Catano, V. M., 275
Catterall, J. S., 193
Cauce, A., 45
Caughy, M., 236
Cavell, T., 110
Centers for Disease Control and Prevention, 152, 158, 243, 246, 268
Chadee, D., 210, 211
Chaffin, M., 155
Chamberlin, R., 155
Chan, A., 300
Chang, C. L., 265
Chanley, V. A., 115
Chanoff, D., 193
Chaplin, W. F., 82
Chapman, J., 28
Chapman, L., 163
Charkoudian, L., 222
Charney, D., 214
Chase-Lansdale, P. L., 148, 149, 157, 162
Chatman, J., 278
Chavis, D. M., 23, 24, 78, 89, 100, 101, 102, 103, 114, 115
Chavous, T. M., 208
Chazan-Cohen, R., 182
Cheng, S., 280, 282, 300
Cherniss, C., 9
Chertak, F., 33
Chesson, H., 257
Cheung, C., 293
Cheung, F. M., 132, 133
Chew, R., 286
Chibnall, S., 12
Children's Aid Society, 160, 161
Chiles, J. A., 133
Chin, J. J., 266
Chinman, M., 236
Chipperfield, J., 164

Chiu, W., 121
Choi, K-H., 261
Choi, N. G., 165
Choi, S. T., 265
Christens, B., 297
Christensen, J. A., 57, 76, 82, 89, 97, 102, 105
Christensen, L., 53
Christenson, S. L., 194, 196
Christian, T. F., 83, 222
Christie, C. A., 195, 196
Cicchetti, D., 72, 153, 154
Clark, K. B., 184
Clark, M. P., 76, 184
Clark, R., 63
Clark, V., 63
Clary, E. G., 27
Cloward, R. A., 151
Coates, T. J., 261
Coatsworth, J., 71
Cochran, S., 63, 292
Coffee, J. N., 193
Cohen, A. A., 286
Cohen, C. D., 286
Cohen, J., 68, 259
Cohen, S., 33, 68, 69, 103
Cohen-Vogel, L., 190
Cole, C., 196
Coleman, J., 103
Coley, R. L., 14, 148, 149, 157, 162
Colman, R., 153
Colquhoun, S., 293
Compas, B. E., 62, 65, 193
Connors, M. M., 37, 38
Connor-Smith, J. K., 65
Conover, S., 130
Constantine, L. L., 282
Cook, A., 232
Cook, M. P., 25
Cook, S. W., 187
Cook, T. D., 43, 44, 49, 96
Cooke, R. A., 282
Cooley, M. R., 206
Coomey, S. M., 28
Coons, H., 62
Cooper, J., 81, 82, 102
Cooper, R., 218
Coovadia, H. M., 53

365

Copeland-Linder, N., 293
Copello, A. G., 251
Corcoran, J., 162
Cordner, G. W., 213
Cosson, M. T., 222
Cotter, R. B., 23
Coulton, C. J., 24, 154
Cousineau, M., 211
Covell, N. H., 220
Cowen, E. L., 17, 18, 19, 23, 61, 188, 200, 287, 292, 296, 297
Coyne, J. C., 62
Cressler, D. L., 138
Crockett, L., 69
Crogan, M., 188
Cromartie, S. P., 86
Crosby, R. A., 158
Cross, W., 206
Crouse, E., 76
Crowley, M., 195
Cruess, D., 288
Crusto, C. A., 51
Cuddy, A. J. C., 164
Cummings, E., 72
Curran, T., 288
Currie, J. M., 114, 181
Curtis, J., 142
Cutrona, C. E., 23
Cyprien, S., 232
Cyr, K., 208, 219, 221, 222
Czaja, S., 153

D

Dakof, G., 62
D'Alessio, S. J., 206
Daley, J. M., 77
D'Amelio, A., 88, 89, 90, 91, 92
Dandeneau, S., 64
Daniel, P. T. K., 190
Danish, S. J., 198
Danoff-Burg, S., 66
Danso, H. A., 186
Danziger, S., 148
Dapp, U., 164
Darling, N., 110
Darnell, J., 232
Darrouch, J., 238
Darrow, W. W., 37

D'Augelli, A. R., 288
D'Aunno, T. A., 270, 276
Davey, C. L., 218
David, T. G., 287
Davidson, L., 37, 293
Davidson, R., 288
Davidson, W., II, 9
Davidson, W. S., 78, 89, 90, 93, 109, 110, 116
Davis, D. M., 190
Davis, M. K., 52, 93, 157
Davis, P., 72
Davis, T. R., 286
Davison, W. B., 23
Dean, A., 68
Dean, J., 299
Deaux, K., 116, 186
DeBarros, K., 300
De Bellis, M. D., 153
De Beus, K., 222
de Fatima Quintal de Freitas, M., 296
Delgado, G., 78, 79, 105
Delucchi, K., 193
DeMeuse, K. P., 286
Demler, O., 121
Denham, S. A., 194
Denmark, F. L., 197
D'Ercole, A., 142
Derogatis, L., 62
De Schipper, J. C., 179
Detert, J. R., 276
DeVellis, B., 240
Devine, P., 64, 85
DeVita, C. J., 80
De Wit, D. J., 216
DeWolfe, D., 65
DeYoung, S. F., 216
Diamond, J. B., 190
Diamond, P. M., 133, 134
Dickerson, S., 64
Dickinson, J. M., 224
Dickson, W. J., 280
DiClemente, R. J., 37
DiFranza, J. R., 248
DiMatteo, M. R., 234
Dincin, J., 138
Dingwall, R., 223
Ditton, J., 210

Dobmeyer, T. W., 220
Doherty, G., 180
Dohrenwend, B., 60
Dolbeare, C. N., 22
Dore, P., 23
Dougherty, T. W., 287
Douglas, C., 285
Dovidio, J. F., 63, 64, 84, 85, 185, 187, 295
Dowden, C., 223
Dowell, D. A., 166
Dowler, K., 212
Downing, J., 195
Dowrick, P., 198
Doyle, E. A., 199
Draguns, P., 110
Drayson, M., 68
Drew, N., 107
Dubé, M., 211
Duchon, L., 170
Duffy, K. G., 78, 81, 83, 86, 87, 102, 165, 185, 187, 222, 223
Dumas, J. E., 9
DuMont, K., 153, 277
Dumont, M., 130
Dunne, E., 166
Dupéré, V., 218
Duran, B., 37
DuRant, R. H., 235
Durlak, J. A., 9, 19, 143, 176, 194

E

Eacho, C., 225
Eagly, A., 282, 283
Earls, F., 218, 295
Earls, M., 132, 133
Easterlow, D., 167
Eaton, J., 165
Eaves, C., 220
Ebata, A. T., 65
Ebert-Flattau, P., 115
Eby, L. T., 273, 278
Eck, J. E., 211
Eckenrode, J., 155, 157
Edge, K., 66
Edie, D., 180
Edin, K., 149
Edmondson, A. C., 276
Edwards, D., 194

Edwards, J. E., 286
Edwards, K., 188
Edwards, R. W., 106
Egan, T., 278
Egeland, G., 69
Eigen, M., 260
Eisenberg, M., 177, 178, 180
Eisenbraun, K. D., 197
Eitle, D., 206
Ekland-Olson, S., 210
Elder, G., 72
Elias, M. J., 194
Elis, L., 222
Ellam, G., 90
Elliott, K., 152
Ellis, R. T., 212
Ellwood, D. T., 151
Elting, L., 233
Elvin, J., 5
Ely, R., 279
Elze, D., 23
Embry, D. D., 198
Emery, R. E., 223
Emshoff, J., 236
Ensel, W., 68
Entwisle, D. R., 195
Epel, E., 62
Eppe, S., 197
Epstein, J. L., 196
Epstein, M. J., 217
Erwin, P. G., 194
Evans, A. S., 47
Evans, G. W., 151
Everly, G. S., 220
Eysenck, H. J., 5, 121

F

Fairweather, G. W., 78, 82, 89, 90, 93, 109, 110, 116, 138
Faith, M. S., 124
Farber, S. S., 199
Farmer, G., 166
Farmer, P., 263
Farmer, T. W., 208
Farquhar, J., 235, 300
Farr, R. K., 169
Farrall, S., 211
Farrington, D. P., 218
Farver, J. M., 197

Fassinger, R., 272, 278
Fauth, R. C., 189
Fawcett, S. B., 11, 89, 105, 237
Feld, S., 121
Feldheusen, J. F., 191
Feldman, D., 220
Feldman, H., 235
Felitte, V., 153
Felix, J. R. J., 78
Fell, J., 251
Felner, R. D., 18, 21, 143, 196, 199
Felton, B., 46
Fend, H., 64
Fender, L., 151
Fergus, E., 138
Ferguson, K. M., 211, 212
Ferlander, S., 249
Fernandez, A., 197
Ferrari, J., 27, 28
Ferraro, A., 68
Fiedler, F., 282
Figley, C. R., 275
Fiksenbaum, L., 165
Fine, M. A., 286
Finkelhor, S., 152
Firdion, J., 170
Fisch, R., 76
Fischer, C. S., 103
Fishbein, M., 39
Fisher, J. D., 264
Fisher, J. K., 225
Fisher, W. A., 264
Fiske, S. T., 116, 164
Flannery, D. J., 198
Flay, B. R., 37, 197, 198
Flick, U., 167
Flora, J., 197, 235
Flores, C., 37
Florin, P., 78, 89, 97, 100, 101, 103
Flowers-Coulson, P. A., 159
Foege, W. H., 245, 268
Folkman, S., 62, 63, 64, 65, 66, 67, 274, 288
Fong, K. T., 9
Foos, D., 132
Ford, J. D., 88, 89, 90, 91, 92, 168
Ford, L. W., 88, 89, 90, 91, 92
Forer, B., 180
Forlenza, S. G., 222

Formichella, C. M., 206
Forness, S. R., 194
Forrester, J., 284
Fortmann, S., 235
Fortson, B. L., 153
Foster, H. W., 158
Foster, K. P., 104
Foster-Fishman, P. G., 12, 91, 271, 277, 284
Fouad, N., 272
Foundation Center, 79
Fox, D., 299
Fozard, J. L., 165
Frandsen, K., 287
Frank, J. D., 81
Frank, S., 57, 96, 270, 271
Fraser, B. J., 193
Freedman, A. M., 77
Freedman, S., 287
Freeman, L., 288
Freeman, R. J., 134
Freiberg, J. H., 192
Freire, P., 91, 114, 299
Freisthler, B., 155
French, W. L., 271, 285
Fried, C., 292
Friedman, R., 100
Friedman, S. M., 46
Frisman, L., 139
Frone, M., 274
Frost, J., 238
Frumkin, P., 79
Futrell, D., 286
Fyson, S., 295

G

Gaab, J., 64
Gabbidon, S. L., 207
Gaertner, S. L., 63, 64, 84, 185, 295
Gal, I., 165
Galbavy, R., 198
Gallagher, S., 68
Garbarino, J., 154, 197
Garces, E., 114
Garcia, L., 213
Garcia-Reid, P., 197
Gard, J., 286
Garg, A. X., 233
Garmezy, N., 70, 71

Gary, L. E., 190
Gastil, J., 283
Gee, G. C., 87
Geen, R. R., 151
Gensheimer, L., 65
Gerson, G., 103
Gesten, E., 292
Gewirtz, A. H., 167
Gibbs, B. G., 225
Gibler, N., 153
Gidycz, C. A., 157
Gignac, M. A. M., 164
Gill, M., 218
Gillespie, C., 22
Gillespie, D. F., 47
Gillespie, J. F., 194
Gilliam, M. L., 161
Gillock, K. L., 193
Gilman, E. D., 179, 254
Ginexi, E. M., 85
Ginter, M. A., 193, 196
Glaberson, W., 211
Glass, T., 241
Glaze, L., 133, 134
Gleason, P. M., 196
Glenwick, D. S., 11, 110
Glick, P., 85
Glidewell, J. C., 88, 89, 90, 281, 294
Goelman, H., 180
Goethals, G. R., 102
Goldberg, J., 275
Golding, J. M., 190
Goldring, E., 190
Goldschmidt, A., 233
Goldsmith, D. S., 286
Goodman, A. M., 212
Goodman, D., 288
Goodman, J., 115
Goodman, S. A., 286
Goodrum, S., 210, 222
Goodstein, L. D., 76
Gore, A., 171
Gorny, S. W., 3
Gottlieb, B. H., 62, 136, 164
Gottschalk, B., 3
Gottschalk, P., 3
Gover, A. R., 210
Graber, J. A., 205, 206

Graham, J., 216
Granovetter, M., 103, 105
Gray, B., 285
Gray, P., 193
Gray, S., 163
Greatbatch, D., 223
Green, D. C., 162
Green, D. L., 222
Greenberg, A., 114
Greenberg, J., 271, 275, 276, 282
Greenberg, M., 72, 73, 298
Green-Demers, I., 190
Greene, L. R., 278
Greene, L. W., 158
Greene, S. M., 199
Greenglass, E., 165
Greenspan, B. K., 286
Gregory, A., 90, 191
Gregory, W. L., 63
Grier, M., 38, 39
Griffin, K., 20
Griffin, M., 197
Grill, G., 27
Grisso, J. T., 137
Grob, G. N., 128, 130
Grodin, M., 54
Grogan-Kaylor, A., 147
Grogg, K. R., 194
Grosch, J. W., 83, 185
Grossi, E. L., 288
Grossman, J. B., 216
Gruder, C. L., 289
Guendelman, S., 275
Guerra, N. G., 198
Gullekson, N., 82
Gullotta, T., 143
Gunn, P., 188
Gurin, G., 298
Gurin, P., 121
Gutierrez, P., 125
Guzicki, M., 166

H

Habemeier, W., 211
Haber, M., 68
Hackerman, A. E., 215
Hadley-Ives, E., 23
Hagestad, G. O., 164
Haggerty, R., 18, 19

Haines, L., 217
Hakuta, K., 181, 190
Hall, G. N., 87
Hallman, W., 77
Halpern, D., 63, 180
Hamid, P. N., 66
Hamilton, C. A., 223
Hamilton, S. F., 216, 285
Hamilton, V. L., 287
Hampton, C. V., 217
Handel, G., 148, 149
Haney, C., 209
Hanlin, C., 297
Hannon, L. E., 206, 207
Harcourt, B., 133
Hardin, E., 164
Harrell, S., 10
Harris, L., 292
Harris, P. E., 225
Harris, S., 87
Harrison, T. C., 195
Haskins, R., 176, 180
Hassan, F., 152
Hatfield, A. B., 142
Haughton, C., 39
Havel, E., 225
Haven, C., 165
Hayes, J., 12
Haynes, R. B., 233
Haynie, D. L., 195
Hazel, K., 132
He, W., 300
Head, T. C., 282
Heckhausen, J., 166
Hedeen, T., 221, 222, 223
Hedegaard, M., 92
Heilman, M. E., 116
Heindl, T. R., 187
Helgeson, V. S., 68, 87
Heller, K., 6, 7, 16, 17, 18, 23, 24, 45, 57, 77, 89, 102, 108, 134, 135, 143, 165, 292
Hellman, I. D., 278, 283
Helping America's Youth, 216, 217
Henderson, C., 155, 204
Hendrickson, M., 37
Hendry, L. B., 193
Henry, D. B., 90, 198
Heppner, P. P., 66

Herman, S. E., 132
Herrling, S., 161
Hersch, C., 7
Hertzog, J. L., 278
Hess, B. B., 117
Hess, P., 97
Hess, R., 21
Hessling, R. M., 23
Hetherington, L., 293
Hill, J., 10, 20, 45
Hill, P., 153
Hills, A. M., 220
Himle, D. P., 287
Hirsch, M. R., 287
Hitlan, R. T., 185, 186
Hladikova, A., 168
Hobfoil, S. E., 66, 69
Hochschild, A. R., 147, 189
Hockaday, C., 251
Hodges, W. F., 17
Hodson, G., 185
Hofen, B., 287
Hofferth, S. L., 158
Hoffman, W. S., 287
Hogg, J., 165
Holahan, C., 65, 68
Holahan, J., 232
Holcomb, W. B., 220
Hollander, E. P., 284
Hollingshead, A., 6
Holme, J. J., 184
Holmes, T. H., 62, 274
Holtgrave, D. R., 158
Hooper, S. R., 153
Hopper, F., 159
Hops, H., 9
Horton, K. D., 191
Houlette, M. A., 186, 189
House, J. S., 68, 287
Howard, E. A., 169
Howard, J., 28
Howard, K. A., 37, 197
Howard, M., 286
Howes, C., 180
Howitt, A. M., 104
Hoyt, D., 85
Hradecky, I., 168
Hudiburg, R., 81
Huebner, B. M., 205, 211

Huebner, R. D., 133, 142
Hughes, C., 74
Hughey, J., 101, 197, 273
Hummer, R. A., 206
Hunt, M. H., 194
Hunte-Marrow, J., 39
Hunter, A., 143
Huo, Y., 278
Hurtado, S., 188

I
Ialongo, N. S., 193, 195, 196, 206
Ikeda, R., 152
Imm, P., 236
Independent Sector, 79
Ireys, H. T., 109
Iscoe, I., 7, 292
Ivancevich, J., 287
Iwamasa, G., 9
Izumi, H., 287

J
Jackson, C. T., 220, 235
Jackson, D., 102, 293
Jackson, J. H., 167
Jackson, M., 284, 286
Jackson, R. M., 103
Jackson, S. E., 274
Jacobs, J. B., 116
Jacobson, L. V., 185
James, D., 133, 134
James, S., 170
Jamieson, W., 218
Jang, S. J., 23, 87, 211
Janz, N. K., 39
Jarrett, O., 194
Jason, L. A., 11, 21, 27, 33, 52, 76, 93, 96, 110, 124, 143, 184, 193, 195, 198, 235, 237, 241, 248, 288, 289, 292, 297, 298
Jatilus, D., 235
Jay, G. M., 288
Jayertne, S., 287
Jemelka, R., 133
Jemmott, J. B., 39
Jemmott, L. S., 39
Jenkins, R., 134, 143
Jimenez, L., 170
Johannes, C. K., 194

Johannesen-Schmidt, M., 282
Johns, G., 275
Johnson, B. T., 164
Johnson, D., 114, 217
Johnson, G., 293
Johnson, S., 23
Johnston, D. F., 87
Jolivette, K., 195
Jones, E. E., 22
Jones, J., 63, 85
Jones, L., 152
Jones, R. G., 286
Joo, H., 204, 206
Joseph, M., 97
Ju, D. B., 195
Judy, N., 163
Jukkala, T., 249
Julien, M., 105
Jumper-Thurman, P., 106

K
Kaiser Family Foundation, 258, 261
Kaiser-Ulrey, C., 197
Kamradt, B., 140, 141
Kane, D., 220
Kanner, A. D., 62, 274
Kaplan, C. P., 195
Karavidas, M., 81
Karcher, M. J., 217
Karim, Q. A., 53
Karim, S. S. A., 53
Karren, 287
Kasprow, W., 139
Katon, W., 65
Katsikas, S. L., 81
Katz, D., 86
Katz, P., 87
Kaufman, J. S., 51, 57
Kaufman, K., 63
Kavale, K. A., 194
Kawakami, K., 64, 185, 187, 188
Kaye, J., 161
Kaye, M. S., 286
Kazden, A. E., 57
Kearns, W. D., 165
Kehres, R., 236
Kellam, S. G., 87
Keller, P. A., 28

Keller, S., 78, 90, 288
Keller, T. E., 214, 216
Kelloway, E. K., 164
Kelly, C., 100
Kelly, G. W. R., 210
Kelly, H. H., 22
Kelly, J. G., 6, 7, 13, 16, 21, 25, 51, 52, 57, 89, 101, 108, 143, 283, 286, 294, 296
Kelly, K. D., 218
Kelsey, J. L., 47
Kemeny, M., 64
Kennedy, C., 135
Kennedy, H. L., 198
Kennedy, M., 218
Kenney, K., 232
Kensinger, K. B., 278
Keppel, B., 76
Kerlinger, F. N., 34
Keskinen, E., 212, 213
Kessler, M., 292
Kessler, R. C., 120, 287
Kettner, P. M., 77, 78, 88, 89, 91, 92
Key, J. D., 163
Keys, C. B., 33, 52, 57, 96, 270, 271, 277, 289, 297
Keys, K., 93
Khan-Hudson, A., 164
Khoury-Kassabri, M., 197, 198
Kidd, S., 52, 293
Kiecolt-Glaser, J., 68
Kienzile, R., 276
Kiernan, M., 132
Kiernan, N. E., 82, 109
Kiesler, C. A., 130, 135
Kim, J. W., 218
Kim, M. M., 168
King, R. H., 190
Kirby, D., 17, 238
Kirk, S., 66
Kirkman, B. L., 286
Kirmeyer, S. L., 287
Kislitsyna, O., 249
Kitchen, C. D., 220
Kite, M. E., 164
Kitzman, H., 155
Kjaer, G., 62
Kleck, G., 205

Klein, D., 7
Klein, J., 197
Klein, K. J., 270, 276, 285
Klein, T. P., 167
Kling, R., 81
Klinkenberg, W. D., 169
Kloos, B., 296
Knickman, J. R., 169, 170
Knitzer, J., 179, 180, 181
Kobus, K., 193
Koch, W., 115
Koegel, P., 169
Koff, W., 259
Kofkin-Radkin, J., 16, 117
Kohlberg, L., 116
Kohn-Wood, L. P., 208
Koizumi, R., 184, 193
Korbin, J. E., 24, 154
Koretz, D., 87
Kosic, A., 186
Kostelny, K., 154
Kotch, J., 158
Kral, M., 52
Kranz, D. H., 170
Kreisler, A., 82, 109
Kresky-Wolff, M., 171
Krueger, P. M., 206
Kruger, D. J., 87, 210, 211
Krumweid, R. D., 138
Kruse, D. L., 78
Kuhn, T. S., 34, 35, 36, 91
Kulik, L., 293
Kumar, M., 288
Kumpfer, K., 18
Kuo, F. E., 14
Kuo, W., 68
Kushner, M. A., 159
Kushnir, T., 287
Kuta, A., 148
Kuttel, Y., 64
Kuykendall, D. A., 164
Kwan, A., 293

L
Labianca, G., 285
Lafrance, A., 138
LaFrance, B., 235
LaGrange, A., 180
Laguna, K., 81

Lahiff, M., 170
Lahm, K. F., 210
Lal, S., 76
Lamb, M. E., 176, 180, 182
Lambert, E. Y., 38
Lambert, M. J., 121
Lambert, S. F., 206, 217
Landers, S., 23
Landis, K., 68
Landsberg, G., 198
Lane-Garon, P. S., 193
Lang, M., 179
Lange, J., 193
Langer, L. J., 165, 166
Langhout, R. D., 191, 192
Lannon, P. B., 136
Lantz, G. D., 184
La Piere, R. T., 185
Lapoint, J. M., 192
Laracuenta, M., 197
Lasater, T., 235
Lasker, R., 236, 237
Latimer, J., 223
Lausell-Bryant, L., 198
LaVeist, T., 300
Lavoie, K. L., 125
Lawlis, G., 288
Lawrence, A. J., 148
Lawson, A., 159
Lazarus, R. S., 62, 63, 64, 65, 66, 67, 274
Lazere, E. B., 22
Leader, D. S., 25
Leaf, P. J., 132
LeBoeuf, D., 195
Lee, T., 196
Legault, L., 190
Legler, R., 12
Lehmann, S., 287
Lehr, U., 164
Leigh, B. C., 249
Leinsalu, M., 249
Leiter, M. P., 274, 275, 277, 280
Lempert, R., 116
Lennon, M. C., 148
Leonard, P. A., 22
Leong, F., 110
Leos-Urbel, J., 151
Leppin, A., 288

Lero, D. S., 180
Lesesne, C. A., 162
Lester, D., 220
Lettieri, D. J., 37
Leung, C. M., 66
Levanthal, G. S., 105
Levanthal, H., 196
Leventhal, T., 189
Levi, Y., 97, 101, 102
Levin, B. M., 249
Levin, G., 12
Levine, I. S., 133, 142
Levine, M. D., 17, 78, 89, 90, 98, 109, 112, 137, 138, 184, 218, 292
Leviton, L. C., 37, 49
Levy, L. H., 98
Lewin, K., 7, 10, 51, 101, 280, 283
Lewis, D. A., 128
Lewis, K. M., 162
Lian, B. E., 206
Liang, B., 214
Light, D., 78, 90
Likert, R., 282
Lim, N. K., 81
Lin, A., 63
Lin, N., 68
Ling, W., 254
Linney, J. A., 21, 25, 97, 109
Lippett, R., 88, 283
Lipton, D., 286
Litwin, H., 97, 101, 102
Liu-Mares, W., 139
Lohman, B. J., 149
Lohr, S., 46
London, A. A., 149
Long, D., 24
Long, J., 296
Lonner, W., 110
Loo, C., 9
Lopez, G. E., 188, 298
Lopez, M. M., 22
Lord, J., 20
Lorentz, E., 103
Lorian, R. P., 18, 33, 88, 293
Lösel, F., 209
Loukaitou-Sideris, A., 211
Loukes, A., 191
Lounsbury, D., 9

Lounsbury, J. W., 25
Love, J. M., 182
Lovell, A. M., 132
Lowenthal, M. F., 165
Lucas, T., 68
Ludwig, J., 180, 181, 182, 183
Luepker, R., 235
Lundgren, S., 82
Lurigio, S. J., 128
Lustig, J. L., 199
Luthans, F., 286
Lynne, S. D., 205
Lyubansky, M., 114

M

Maccoby, N., 235
MacDermid, S. M., 278
MacDonald, J., 206
MacKenzie, D. L., 210
Mackin, J. R., 218
Macy, B. A., 287
Madera, E. J., 105
Maertz, C. P., 279
Magee Quinn, M., 194
Magnuson, K. A., 181, 190
Magura, S., 286
Mahalingam, R., 186
Maier, G. J., 286
Maiman, L. A., 39
Maimane, S., 293
Maiorana, A., 265
Makinen, I. H., 249
Maloy, K. A., 232
Man-Chi, L., 208
Mankowski, E., 45
Mann, J., 38, 54
Mann, S. C., 225
Mannix, E., 278
Manrique, M., 166
Manwaring, J., 233
Manzo, L., 236
Marcus, J., 193
Marcus-Newhall, A., 187
Markowitz, T., 151
Markson, E. W., 117
Marlowe, L., 76
Marmorstein, N., 153
Marpsat, M., 170
Marsland, K. W., 176, 179, 180

Martin, J., 87
Martin, P., 9, 25
Maruyama, G., 185
Marx, J. D., 159
Maslach, C., 102, 274, 275, 277, 280
Masten, A. S., 70, 71, 72, 74, 296
Mathur, S. R., 194
Maton, K. I., 21, 28, 76, 77, 78, 82, 89, 96, 98, 99, 103, 105, 108, 271, 277, 300
Mattaini, M. A., 151
Matteson, M., 287
Matthews, D. B., 193
Mauiuro, R., 65
Mawby, R., 211
Max, W., 246
May, D. C., 210
Mayer, J. P., 109, 110, 233
Maynard, H., 138
Maynard, R. A., 151
Mays, V., 63, 292
Mazda, N. A., 286
Mazurek, T. L., 113
McAlister, A., 111
McAllister-Jones, L., 103
McBride, T. D., 169
McCarthy, M. E., 275, 276
McCaughey, B. G., 220
McCave, E. L., 157, 159, 160
McConahay, J. B., 193
McConnell, A., 134
McCulloch, A., 287
McDonald, H. P., 233
McEwan, B., 62
McGillis, D., 83, 222, 223
McGinnis, J., 245, 268
McGloin, J. M., 197
McGrath, J. E., 88
McGrath, J. W., 37, 38
McInerney, P., 195
McIntosh, N. J., 287
McIntyre, J., 161
McKee, P. A., 220
McKinlay, S., 235
McKinnon, S. A., 163
McLaughlin-Volpe, T., 187
McMahon, S. D., 289
McMillan, D. W., 24

McNeal, R. B., 196
McNeely, R., 163
McSweeney, A. J., 135
Meade, J., 191
Meares, E. P., 25
Medway, F. J., 107
Meehan, T., 223
Meehl, P. E., 5
Meertens, R. W., 185
Meier, R., 100
Meier-Baumgartner, H. P., 164
Meir, E. I., 287
Meissen, G. J., 28
Melamed, S., 275, 287
Mellow, J., 224
Melton, G. B., 204
Méndez-Negrete, J., 162
Mertinko, E., 193
Meyer, M., 62
Meyers, J., 194
Milburn, N. G., 190
Miley, A. D., 136
Milkovich, G. T., 279, 289
Miller, K., 45
Miller, L. D., 138
Miller, L. S., 237, 246
Miller, M., 240
Miller, R. D., 220, 286
Millman, J., 142
Milne, A., 222
Mindel, C. H., 211, 212
Minden, J., 241
Mintzberg, H., 280
Mischel, W., 11
Mishara, B. L., 220
Mitchell, R. E., 136
Moffin, T., 73
Moffitt, T. E., 23
Molina, L. E., 187, 188
Moller, S., 195
Molnar, J. M., 167
Montgomery, A. E., 167
Montgomery, E., 162
Moore, M., 37
Moos, R. H., 14, 46, 65, 68
Moran, G. E., 169
Morbidity and Mortality Weekly Report, 243, 245, 246, 249, 253, 257, 258, 268

Morch, H., 287
Morello, T., 292
Morgan, C. A., 214
Morgeson, F. P., 279
Moritsugu, J., 21, 63
Morris, A., 277
Morris, S., 82
Morrison, A., 115
Morrison, T. L., 278
Morse, B., 82
Morse, G. A., 169
Moscicki, E. K., 87
Moses, D. J., 171
Moskowitz, J., 288
Mosley-Howard, S., 214
Moss, L., 274
Moulton, P., 240
Mowbray, C. T., 56, 106, 132, 133, 139
Moynihan, D. R., 273
Mrazek, P., 18, 19
Muenchow, S., 176, 179, 180, 181, 182
Muha, D. G., 196
Muir, E., 193
Muise, D., 223
Mulvey, A., 10, 20
Munoz, E., 292
Muñoz, M., 167
Munro, M., 167
Murphy, S., 110
Murphy, S. E., 180
Murray, M., 235
Murry, V., 23
Murty, S. A., 47
Mustonen, H., 249
Myers, W. C., 209

N
Nadel, H., 63, 198
Nagda, A., 188
Nagda, B. A., 298
Nair, Y., 293
Naisbett, J., 86
Nathan, P., 123
Nation, M., 211
National Campaign to Prevent Teen and Unwanted Pregnancy, 157
National Cancer Institute, 247

National Center for Education Statistics, 194
National Center for Health Statistics, 157, 230, 232, 233
National Center on Secondary Education and Transition, 196
National Center on Shaken Baby Syndrome, 153
National Coalition for the Homeless, 166, 167, 169, 170
National Crime Prevention Council, 218
National Highway Traffic Safety Administration, 243, 251
National Institute of Alcohol Abuse and Alcoholism, 249
National Institute of Child and Human Development, 176, 179
National School Safety and Security Services, 196
National Science Foundation, 81–82
Nazroo, J., 63
Neale, M., 278
Needell, N., 155
Nelson, D., 288, 289
Nelson, G., 20, 132, 133, 138, 139
Nelson, M., 195
Nemoto, T., 37
Netter, T., 38
Neuer, R. A., 287
Neuman, G. A., 286
Newborough, J. R., 23, 295
Newell, B., 271
New York Times Editorial Board, 263
Ng, S., 293
Nichols, A. W., 77
Nichols, T., 205
Nickerson, K., 300
Nicotera, N., 236
Nier, J. A., 185
Nikelly, A. G., 112, 116
Nisbett, R. E., 22
Noam, G., 214
Nolan, L., 232
Nores, M., 183
Norris, F. H., 204, 210, 211

NAME INDEX

Norton, M. I., 164
Novotney, L. C., 193

O

Obradovic, J., 70, 72, 296
O'Brien, L., 287
O'Brien, R., 163
O'Campus, P., 236
Ochocka, J., 20
O'Connell, J. J., 167
O'Conner, P., 28
O'Donnell, C., 9, 28
Oetting, E. R., 106
Offerman, L., 284, 286
Office of Head Start, 181
Office of Justice Programs, 204, 210
Office of Juvenile Justice and Delinquency Prevention, 217
Office of Juvenile Justice and Delinquency Programs, 198
Office of National Drug Control Policy, 253
Office on Smoking and Health, 244
Offutt, S., 240
Ogletree, R., 97
Okamato, Y., 168
O'Keefe, J. E., 158
Olatunji, A. N., 195
Olczak, P. V., 83, 185
Olds, D., 153, 155, 156, 157, 214
O'Leary, K. D., 123
Oliver, J. M., 137
Oliver, W. M., 213
Olsen, K. H., 194
Olson, L. S., 195
Olson, M. R., 286
Oman, D., 165
Omoto, A., 91
O'Neal, K. K., 208
O'Neill, L., 197
O'Neill, P., 57, 99
Opulente, M., 151
O'Reilly, C., 278
O'Reilly, K., 51
Orosan-Weine, A. M., 184
O'Rourke, K., 163
Orthner, D. K., 195
Osburn, H., 277, 285

Oskamp, S., 89, 92, 102, 113, 115, 184
Ostermeyer, M., 84, 221
Owens, S., 45

P

Pacific Institute for Research and Evaluation, 249
Padgett, D. K., 132, 133
Padilla, A., 9
Page, S., 298
Paine-Andrews, A., 238
Palmer, T., 210
Paluk, E. L., 188
Paluzzi, P., 239
Panadero, S., 167
Pandey, S. K., 273
Pargament, K. I., 14
Parker, G. R., 23
Parks, G., 183
Patchin, J. W., 205, 206
Patka, M., 292
Patrikakou, E., 196
Pattavina, A., 213
Patterson, D., 158
Patterson, R. D., 165
Pearlin, L., 165
Pearson, C., 167
Pearson, H. W., 37
Pedersen, J., 110
Pedro-Carroll, J. L., 199, 200
Pelech, W., 216
Pelletier, L., 190
Penn, N. E., 132
Perdoux, M., 298
Pereira, G., 277, 285
Perins, D. D., 100
Perkins, D. D., 12, 24, 100, 109, 113, 116, 192, 211, 218, 236
Perkins, D. N. T., 270, 271, 272, 281, 282, 287, 289
Perkins, D. V., 78, 89, 90, 98, 112, 137, 184
Pestridge, S., 193
Peterson, J. L., 37
Peterson, N. A., 24, 197, 273
Peterson, S. A., 207
Petraitis, J., 37
Pettigrew, T. F., 185, 189

Pezzin, L. E., 86
Phalet, K., 186
Phares, J. E., 82, 116
Philliber, S., 161
Phillip, K., 193
Phillips, A., 68
Phillips, D. A., 114, 180, 181, 182, 183, 193, 300
Phillips, J., 287
Phillips, S. B., 220
Phills, C. E., 187
Pickren, W., 76
Piliavin, I., 169
Pillai, V. K., 162
Pinchot, E., 286
Pinchot, G., 286
Pines, A., 275
Pittman, L. D., 149
Piven, F. F., 151
Plante, T., 15
Platt, D., 225
Plested, B. A., 106
Plomin, R., 23
Pogrebin, M. R., 133, 134
Pokorny, S., 292
Polifka, J. A., 28
Pong, S. L., 195
Poole, E. D., 133
Popovich, P. M., 82
Popper, K. R., 36
Porché-Burke, L., 110
Porter, B. E., 12
Potochnick, S., 195
Potts, M. K., 190
Powell, K. E., 198
Prelliltensky, I., 299
Press, M., 218
Presser, L., 223
Prestby, J., 89, 101, 103, 285
Pretty, G. M., 275, 276
Prezza, M., 23, 24
Price, L. N., 208
Price, R. H., 6, 18, 33, 93, 101, 151, 272, 287
Primavera, J., 27, 93, 196, 199
Prinz, R. J., 9
Pruessner, J., 64
Pruitt, D. G., 221, 222
Public Health Service, 135

NAME INDEX

Purves, D., 194
Pynchon, M. E., 158

Q
Quillian-Wolever, R., 288
Quintana, S., 69
Quiroga, M., 167

R
Rader, N. E., 210, 211
Rafferty, Y., 23, 167
Raghavan, C., 287
Rahe, R. H., 62, 274
Rahn, W. M., 115
Raikes, H. H., 180, 182
Raikes, J. A., 180
Raju, N. S., 286
Ralls, R. S., 285
Ramey, C. T., 179, 183
Ramey, S. L., 183
Ramiro, L., 152
Ramos-McKay, J., 18
Ram'rez-Valles, J., 99
Randolph, W. A., 195
Rank, M. R., 147, 190
Rapkin, B., 236
Rapkin, B. D., 239
Rappaport, J., 3, 4, 7, 11, 14, 16, 20, 61, 76, 89, 97, 132, 134, 294
Ratcliffe, A., 117
Rath, W. R., 167
Ratiu, I. S., 286
Ratnesh, B., 188
Raudenbush, S. W., 218, 295
Reddy, R., 191
Redlich, C., 6
Redmond, C., 251
Reed, G. M., 87
Regoli, R. M., 133, 134
Reich, J. W., 165
Reid, M. J., 181, 190
Reid, R. J., 197
Rein, M., 130, 137
Reinharz, S., 6
Reischl, T. M., 87
Reixach, K. A., 217
Reppucci, N. D., 159, 292
Resch, N., 216

Revenson, T., 20, 234, 241
Revilla, A. T., 184
Reyes, O., 184, 193, 195
Rhode, D. L., 159
Rhodes, J. E., 191, 214, 216, 217
Rhodes, W., 7
Ribera, J. C., 86
Rice, D., 246
Rich, R. C., 100, 101
Richards, F. A., 285
Richmond, C., 69
Rickel, A. U., 162, 194
Riedelbach, H., 199
Riger, S., 6, 12, 103, 143, 271, 272
Riggs, N., 72
Riley, D. A., 180
Rivera-Medena, E., 22
Rixon, R., 194
Rizzo, J. R., 276
Roach, M. A., 180
Roak, K. S., 165
Robbennolt, J. K., 158
Roberts, A. R., 220
Roberts, C. W., 225
Roberts, D. G., 282
Robertson, M. J., 170
Robinson, J. W., 57, 76, 82, 89, 97, 102, 105
Robinson, M. B., 217
Robinson, P. E., 287
Robinson, W. L., 114, 117
Roccato, M., 293
Rodin, J., 87, 165, 166
Rodriguez, N., 221, 222, 223
Rodwell, J. J., 276
Roesch, R., 134, 204
Roethlisberger, F. J., 280
Rogers, E. M., 110
Rogers, R. G., 206
Rogosch, F. A., 154
Roh, S., 213
Rokeach, M., 91, 110
Roll, J. M., 211
Rolleri, L., 239
Rollin, S. A., 197
Rollock, D., 9
Romeo, R., 62
Roosa, M., 65
Ropp, S. A., 187

Roscigno, V. J., 195
Roseborough, D., 221, 222
Rose-Gold, M. S., 196
Rosenbaum, L., 110
Rosenberg, L., 167
Rosenberg, Y., 86
Rosenfeld, S., 169
Rosenfield, D., 188
Rosenhack, R., 139
Rosenhan, D. L., 129
Rosenstock, I. M., 264
Rosenthal, R., 185
Ross, C. E., 23, 87, 211
Ross, E., 51
Ross, J., 212, 232
Ross, M. M., 209
Ross, N., 69
Ross, R. R., 102
Rossell, C. H., 189
Rossi, P. H., 22, 167
Rothman, A., 239
Rothman, J., 98
Rotter, J. B., 99
Roussos, S. T., 237
Roychoudhury, A., 214
Rubin, B. A., 273, 274
Rubio-Stipec, M., 86
Rudolph, T. J., 115
Ruggiero, K., 87
Ruiz, R., 9
Rumsey, E., 153
Runyan, D., 152, 153
Russell, D. W., 23, 102
Russo, J., 65
Rutherford, R. B., 194
Rutter, M., 70, 71, 72
Ryan, J. P., 214
Ryan, W., 20, 22
Rydell, R., 134

S
Saegert, S., 104, 218
Sakai, T., 225
Sakellaropoulo, M., 64
Saldaña, L. P., 162
Salem, D. A., 12, 139, 277
Sallis, J., 233
Salmi, S., 212, 213
Salovey, P., 239

Saltzman, H., 65
Salzar, J. M., 77
Sammons, M. T., 3, 125
Sampson, R. J., 100, 218, 295
Sánchez, B., 110, 193
Sanchez, D. L., 209
Sanders, D. H., 138
Sanders, J., 116
Sandler, I. N., 28, 65, 70, 76
Sansone, R. A., 286
Santinello, M., 192
Santos, E. P., 167
Sarason, S. B., 23, 24, 78, 96, 105, 106, 108, 113, 184, 191, 236, 294
Sarata, B. P. V., 282
Satcher, D., 54, 258
Sayers, M., 37
Scales, P., 158
Scarr, S., 177, 178, 180
Schafer, J. A., 211
Schaie, K. W., 165
Schaps, E., 193
Schaufeli, W. B., 274
Scheckner, S., 197
Scheier, M. F., 65, 69, 166
Schein, E. H., 276
Schensul, J. J., 38
Schiaffino, K. M., 165, 234, 241
Schleifer, S., 288
Schmeelk-Cone, K. H., 208
Schminke, M., 277
Schmitz, J., 82
Schmolling, P., Jr., 115
Schnee, S. B., 133, 134
Schneiderman, N., 288
Schnopp-Wyatt, D. L., 248
Schoeny, M. E., 90
Schon, D. A., 130, 137
Schubert, M., 282
Schuck, A. M., 206, 207
Schuler, R. S., 274
Schuller, N., 211
Schultz, D., 102, 273, 275, 279
Schultz, R., 166
Schultz, S. E., 102, 273, 275, 279
Schur, L. A., 78
Schwab, R. L., 274
Schwartz, D., 197

Schwarzer, R., 288
Schweinhart, L. J., 183
Schweitzer, J. H., 218
Scileppi, J. A., 17, 18
Scott, E. K., 149
SCRA Practice Task Force, 117
Scully, J., 62
Searight, H. R., 137
Sedivy, V., 239
Sedlovskaya, A., 186
Seefeldt, K., 148
Seekins, T., 105, 237
Seeman, T., 241
Segupta, M., 300
Seidman, E., 14, 20, 77, 89, 132, 134
Seiler, E., 164
Seitsinger, A. M., 196
Seitz, V., 110, 160
Sekaly, R., 259
Seligman, M., 18, 124
Sellers, R., 300
Selye, H., 61
Sentman, E., 115
Serrano-Garcia, I., 22, 89, 107, 296
Seyfried, S. F., 176
Seymour, R., 254
Shadish, W. R., 43, 49, 89, 96, 115, 128, 130, 133, 135, 136
Shadur, M. A., 276
Shaefer, C., 62
Shamir, B., 90
Shapira, L., 275
Shapira, N., 165
Shapiro, D. L., 286
Sharstein, S., 142
Shear, K. M., 220
Sheeder, J., 163
Sheldon, S. B., 196
Sherman, D., 194
Sherman, L., 222
Sherwood, H., 66
Shiflett, S., 288
Shih, Y., 233
Shinn, M., 22, 23, 166, 168, 169, 170, 270, 271, 272, 277, 281, 282, 287, 289, 292
Shirom, A., 275

Shivy, V. A., 225
Shore, D. A., 158
Shore, M. F., 286
Shpungin, E., 114
Shumaker, S. A., 86, 87, 98, 211
Shure, M. B., 194
SIECUS National Guidelines Task Force, 158, 160
Siegel, J. T., 164, 249
Sikes, J., 188
Silk, K., 125
Silka, L., 186
Simmens, S. J., 85
Simmons, B., 288, 289
Simoni-Wastila, L., 254
Simonre, R., 68
Simonsen, C. E., 210
Simpura, J., 249
Sims, B., 222
Singer, M., 37, 38, 39
Singh, S., 238
Singleton, J., 164
Skinner, E., 66, 67
Skodol, A. E., 142
Skokan, L. A., 87
Slavin, L. A., 193
Slavin, R. E., 188, 189
Smart Growth, 79
Smith, C., 9
Smith, D. E., 254
Smith, H. P., 222
Smith, M. S., 62, 158, 287, 288
Smith, R., 71
Smith, S. J., 167
Smith, T. M., 192
Smither, R. D., 271
Smith Major, V., 285
Smrekar, C., 190
Smyth, J., 195
Snapp, M., 188
Snider, A. B., 82, 109
Snow, D., 287
Snowden, L. R., 9, 138, 236, 239, 292, 295
Snyder, M., 27, 91
Solarz, A., 22
Solomon, D., 193
Sorenson, P. F., 282
Sosin, M., 169

South, S. J., 195
Southwick, J. M., 214
Spacespan, S., 165
Sparling, J. J., 179
Spataro, S., 278
Speer, P., 24, 25, 45, 55, 101, 273, 297
Spellmann, M., 198
Spencer, R., 214
Spiegel, H., 104
Spillman, B. C., 86
Spiros, R., 286
Spitzer, R. J., 205
Spivack, G., 193, 194
Spoth, R., 251
Sprague, J., 12
Spreitzer, G. M., 277
Stack, L. C., 136
Stall, R., 249
Stambaugh, R. J., 115
Stanley, J., 43, 44
Stanton, A., 66
Stearns, E., 195
Steele, J. R., 187
Steffan, A. M., 163
Steffen, A., 134
Stein, C., 45
Stein, L., 139
Stein, P. J., 117
Stein, R. E. K., 109
Stelzner, S., 283
Stenmark, D. E., 28
Stephan, C., 188
Stephan, W., 63
Stephens, C., 235
Stephens, T., 204
Stern, D., 193
Stevens-Simon, C., 163
Stiffman, A. R., 23
Stinchcomb, J., 224
Stipek, D., 181, 190
Stockdale, G. D., 164
Stoiber, K. C., 161
Stolzenberg, L., 206
Storch, M., 64
Strain, L., 134
Strang, J., 222
Streitman, S., 70
Strickler, G., 254

Strojanovic, D., 170
Strom, K., 206
Strother, C. R., 4, 21
Struening, E. L., 132, 133, 142
Strumer, S., 91
Stucky, P. E., 114
Stueve, C. A., 103
Sturge-Apple, M., 72
Stüssi, A.-C., 64
Su, M., 24
Suanda, S. H., 186
Suarez-Balcazar, Y., 9, 52, 108
Substance Abuse and Mental Health Services Administration, 245
Sue, D. W., 63, 110
Sue, S., 9, 296
Sullivan, W. C., 14
Sundberg, N. D., 88
Sundstrom, E., 286
Susser, E., 130, 133, 142
Susser, M., 53
Sutton, R. M., 211
Suzuki, R., 191
Svec, H., 196
Svyantek, D. J., 286
Swan, S., 287
Swanson, L., 106
Swift, C., 12, 97
Swindle, R. W., 134
Sy, F. S., 265
Szasz, T. S., 5, 131

T
Taber, T. D., 282
Takeuchi, D. T., 132
Talbot, B., 248
Tarantola, D., 38
Tartaglia, S., 24
Tarullo, L. B., 182
Tatelbaum, R., 155
Taulé-Lunblad, J., 198
Tausig, M., 105
Tavecchio, L. W. C., 179
Taveras, S., 262
Taxman, F. S., 224
Taylor, A., 23
Taylor, C., 190, 235
Taylor, R. B., 52, 86, 87, 100, 211

Taylor, S. E., 87, 193
Taylor, T. K., 204
Tedeschi, G., 23
Teed, E. L., 17, 18
Tellegen, A., 70
Templeton, L. J., 251
Terenzio, M., 10, 20
Test, M. A., 139
Thatcher, J., 286
Thoits, P., 68
Thomae, H., 164
Thomas, D., 114, 279, 293
Thomas, E., 162
Thomas, J., 204
Thomas, S., 136
Thompson, J., 222
Thompson, M. G., 165
Thompson, M. P., 204, 210, 211
Thompson, S. C., 165
Thompson, W. D., 47
Thomsen, A. H., 65
Thoresen, C. E., 165
Thornton, M., 87
Thorpe, S. J., 81
Thurlow, M. L., 194, 195, 196
Thyness, P., 287
Tierney, J. P., 216
Timko, C., 87
Tippetts, A. S., 251
Tiziana, R., 23
Tobin, K. G., 193
Toker, S., 275
Tolan, P., 33, 93, 296
Tomaskovic-Devey, D., 195
Tomes, H., 76
Tompsett, C. J., 166
Toohey, S., 292
Torino, G., 63
Tornatzky, L. G., 82
Toro, P. A., 9, 26, 132, 137, 166
Torres, R. D., 17, 18
Torrey, E. F., 131, 132, 142
Tosi, H. L., 62, 276, 281
Toth, S. C., 154
Trickett, E. J., 9, 193
Trimble, J., 110
Trotter, R. T., 39
Trueba, P. E., 165
Trull, 15

Trupin, E., 133
Tsemberis, S., 170
Tseng, V., 20
Tsui, A., 278
Tuch, S. A., 212
Turman, K. M., 212
Turner, J. B., 287
Turner, K., 167
Turner, S. G., 195
Turnipseed, D. L., 287

U

Uchino, B., 68, 241
Uhlenberg, P., 164
Umberson, D., 68
Umbreit, J., 222
UNAIDS, 243, 260
Unger, D. G., 24
Updyke, J. F., 107
Urquiza, A., 152
U.S. Census Bureau, 298
U.S. Department of Education, 197
U.S. Department of Health and Human Services, 82, 153, 166, 246, 249, 268
U.S. Department of Justice, 210
U.S. Department of Labor, 77
U.S. Preventive Services Task Force, 233

V

Vacca, J. S., 225
Vagero, D., 249
Valdiserri, R. O., 37
Valencia, E., 130, 142
Valentiner, D., 68
Valentino, K., 153, 154
van Egan, M., 282
Van Fleet, D. D., 275
Van Houtte, M., 191
Van IJzendoorn, M. H., 179
Vannatta, K., 193
van Ryn, M., 287
Varano, S. P., 205
Varmus, H., 54
Vartonian, T. P., 196
Vasquez, M., 110
Vaux, A., 69, 165
Vazsonyi, A. T., 198

Vega, A., 162
Velkoff, V., 300
Velleman, R. B., 251
Veno, A., 293
Verof, J., 121
Vidal, A. P. C., 104
Vidmar, N., 223
Vieno, A., 192
Vimpani, G., 252
Vincent, T., 115
Vinokur, A. D., 287
Vitaliano, P., 65
Vlachos-Weber, I., 165
Vlencia, E., 133
Voas, R. B., 251
Voeten, M. J. M., 212, 213
Vogel, M., 69
Vogelman, L., 114
von Rentein-Kruse, W., 164
Votruba-Drzal, E., 149
Vythilingam, M., 214

W

Wadsworth, M., 65
Wagner, B. M., 193
Wagner, R., 197
Waidfugel, J., 181, 190
Walfish, S., 28
Walker, C. R., 219
Walker, L., 188, 225, 226
Walker, S. G., 219
Wallerstein, N., 39
Wallston, B., 240
Walsh, J. T., 282
Walsh, M. E., 167
Walsh, R. T., 3, 6
Walters, E., 121
Walton, E., 271, 283
Wandersman, A., 6, 50, 51, 77, 89, 96, 97, 100, 101, 102, 103, 114, 211, 236
Wandersman, L. P., 24
Waples, S. J., 218
Wardlaw, D. M., 21
Warner, R., 130, 132
Warren-Sohlberg, L., 184
Wasco, S., 45
Washington, R. O., 163
Wasik, B. H., 179

Wasmer, D., 138
Watson, J., 88
Watson, M., 193
Wattam, C., 152
Watters, J., 38
Watts, B., 296
Watts, R. J., 9
Watts-English, T., 153
Watzlawick, P., 76, 91
Way, M., 191
Weakland, J., 76
Weaver, J., 222
Webb, D. H., 82
Webster-Stratton, C., 181, 190, 197
Wedge, R., 210
Weed, D. S., 106, 107
Weeks, M. R., 38, 39
Weihs, K., 85
Weikart, D. P., 183
Weinberg, R. B., 220
Weinstein, R. S., 185, 191, 292, 295, 299
Weintraub, J. K., 65
Weiss, 236
Weissberg, R., 18
Weissberg, R. P., 196
Weist, M., 206
Weitzer, R., 212
Weitzman, B. C., 169, 170
Well, S. S., 184
Wells, A. M., 19, 143
Wells, W., 213
Wemmers, J., 208, 219, 221, 222
Werner, E., 71
Wesson, D. R., 254
West, G., 37
West, S., 65
Westcott, J. S., 220
Westerfelt, H., 169
Western Regional Advocacy Project, 170
Westley, B., 88
Wheaton, B., 62
White, C. P., 162
White, H., 153
White, R. W., 18, 283
Whitebook, M., 180
Whiteman, M., 293
Whitley, B. E., 164

Widom, C. S., 153, 206, 207
Wielkiewicz, R., 283
Wilcox, B., 68, 158, 180
Wilczenski, F. L., 28
Wilkinson, D., 25
Wilkinson-Lee, A. M., 161
Williams, D., 63, 189
Williams, K. R., 198
Williams, S. S., 38
Williamson, J. C., 193
Williamson, K. R., 211
Willis, T. A., 165
Wills, T., 69
Wilson, D. B., 210
Wilson, G. T., 123, 220
Wilson, J. B., 151
Wilson, M., 239
Wilson, T. D., 189
Winkel, G., 104, 218
Winkleby, M., 235
Witheridge, T. F., 138
Wittig, M. A., 82, 187, 188
Wodarski, J. S., 165
Wolchik, S. A., 199
Wolever, M., 288
Wolff, T., 92, 105
Wolfson, M., 235
Wollert, R., 105
Wong, F. Y., 37, 39, 40, 42, 44, 50, 124, 158, 265, 266
Wong, N. W., 287

Woodbury, M. A., 86
Woods, D. J., 222
Woodward, T. G., 214
Woolard, J., 292
Woolpert, S., 219
Wootton, A. B., 218
Worchel, S., 82, 102
Work, W. C., 23, 194
World Health Organization, 229, 244, 247, 252, 253, 268
Wright, S. C., 187, 188
Wrosch, C., 166
Wu, J. J., 225
Wyer, M. M., 223
Wyman, M. F., 17, 18
Wyman, P., 23
Wypijewska, C., 37

X

Xie, J. L., 275
Xu, Y., 197

Y

Yang, H., 214, 271
Yang, P., 147
Yapchai, C., 12
Yates, M., 101
Ybarra, V., 69
Yoo, S., 251
Yoon, O., 204, 206

Yost, B., 222
Youkeles, M., 115
Youngstrom, E., 206, 217
Youniss, J., 101
Yovanoff, P., 225
Yue, X. D., 66

Z

Zárate, M. A., 185
Zarit, S. H., 165
Zatakia, J., 166
Zautra, A. J., 165
Zawilski, V., 212
Zeira, A., 197
Zeitlin, D., 288
Zhang, X., 246
Zhao, L., 233
Zhong, L. Y., 213, 218
Zhu, C., 220
Zigler, E. F., 114, 115, 179, 181, 182
Zimbardo, P., 209
Zimmerman, M. A., 11, 12, 97, 99, 100, 208, 273
Zinner, E. S., 3
Zipp, J. F., 278
Zippay, A., 287
Zlotnick, C., 170
Zohar, D., 274
Zugazaga, C., 167
Zuniga, M., 132

SUBJECT INDEX

A

Abstinence until marriage programs, 263
Abused children and social services, 151–157
Accountability and social change, 80–81, 93
Acquired immunodeficiency syndrome (AIDS), 54, 259–265, 267
 drug use and, 253
 immigrants with, 32
Action research, definition of, 20
Active coping, 65, 287
Active-passive coping, 66
Activity, 50
Acupuncture as anesthetic, 127
Acute *vs.* chronic stress, 62 (*see also* Stress)
Adaptive capacity, 14
Adaptive processes, 67
Additive effects of social support, 68–69
Adherence with medical recommendations, 233
Adolescents and schools:
 climate of, 190–193
 dropping out, 194–196
 violence, 196–198
African Americans, mental health care and, 136
Agenda setting, 115
Aging and end of life, 300
Alcohol safety laws, 250–251
Alcohol use, 249–251, 267
Alienation from school, 191
Alternative education, 192
American Journal of Community Psychology, top 15 universities publishing in, 293
America Stop Smoking Intervention Study (ASSIST), 247
Amicus curiae, 116

Antiretrovirals (ARTs), 263
Antitobacco efforts, 246–248 (*see also* Smoking)
Asian Americans, microaggressions and, 63
Assertive community treatment (ACT) of mentally ill, 138–139
Asylums, 127
At-risk behavior, 214–217
Attribution theory, 22
Autocratic/directive style of leadership, 283
Aversive racism, 185
Avoidance coping, 65, 288

B

Baby boomers and social movements, 6
Behavioral model, 124
Behavioral model of mental health, 123–124
Behavior and environment, 11
Big Brother/Big Sister mentoring program, 215
Bilingual or bicultural health staff, in mental health clinics, 239
Bilingual peer advocate (BPA) program, 265–266
Binge drinking, 250
Black-on-black violence, 208
Blacks:
 and incarceration, 208–209
 life expectancy and, 229–230
Block associations, characteristics of, 102
Board-and-care homes for mentally ill, 135
Boot camps, 210
Brown v. the Board of Education of Topeka, Kansas, 5, 76, 78, 84, 85

Buffering effects of social support, 68–69
Burnout in organizations, 274–275, 287–289

C

Change agents, 88, 90
Charity/philanthropy, 148
Child care:
 defined, 176
 effects of, 177–179
 necessity for, 177
 plans for, 179–180
Childhood environment, 175–183
 day care, 176–180
 early, 175–183
 enrichment education and early intervention, 180–183
 and school (*see* Public schools as social institutions)
Child maltreatment and social services, 151–157
Children of divorce, 199–200
 Children of Divorce Intervention Program (CODIP), 199–200
Chlamydia, 256
Chronic *vs.* acute stress, 62 (*see also* Stress)
Citizen participation, 97–103
 advantages and disadvantages of, 101–103
 defined, 97
 examples of, 99
Civil rights movement, 5–6
Classical conditioning, 123
Clearinghouse, 105
Client-centered therapy, 124
Clients, 56, 106
Clinical psychologists, 4, 125
Clinical psychology:
 community psychology *vs.,* 15–16
 definition of, 4

379

Cocaine, 252
Cognitive misers, 91
Cognitive problem solving, 194
Collaboration with other
  disciplines, 21
Collaborative problem solving, 89
Collectivist coping, 66
Combination drug therapy for
  HIV, 263
Community:
  definition of, 23
  health promotion efforts shifted
    to, 235–236
  psychological sense of, 23–25
  sense of, 23–24, 276
Community-based organizations
  (CBOs), 239
Community conflict and social
  change, 82, 83, 94
Community development
  corporations, 104
Community Development Society
  (CDS), 97–98
Community health and preventive
  medicine, 267
Community intervention strategies,
  95–118
  and citizen participation, 97–103
  consultation about, 106–112
  creating planned change, 96–97
  and networking, 103–106
  and public policy, 112–117
Community mediation, 83
Community mediation centers, 221
Community Mental Health Centers
  Act of 1963, 6, 137
Community/organizational
  psychology:
  changing individuals, 287–289
  changing organizations,
    281–284
  managing organizations,
    279–280
  problems in, 273–278
  redefining jobs, 284–286
Community Police Station
  Program, 219
Community policing, 213

Community popular opinion
  leaders (CPOLs), 265
Community programs, Bloom's
  principles on, 108
Community psychiatry, 128
Community psychologists, 7
Community psychology:
  birthdate of, 7
  clinical psychology vs., 15–16
  commentaries, 294–297
  current status of, 25
  definition of, 7
  fundamental principles, 8–16
  future of, 291–302
  graduate programs in,
    28–30, 292
  and health care system, 234–241
  historical background, 3–7
  information dissemination or
    education in, 109
  interdisciplinary perspectives, 21
  and the justice system (see
    Justice system)
  and organizational psychology,
    271–273
  and preventive medicine,
    251–252
  principles and substance abuse,
    HIV/STDs, 37–39
  research, 25–26
  stress model and definition of,
    60–61
  undergraduate education, 26–28
  urgency of research in, 52–58
Community research and action,
  guiding principles of, 8
Community researchers, as
  consultants, 56–58
Compassionate attitude, 298
Compensation, 40
Compensation packages, 279
Compensatory education, 181
Competence, concept of, 18–19
Competency enhancement
  approaches, 61
Compliance with medical
  recommendations, 233
Compressed workweeks, 299

Computer anxiety, 81
Computerphobia, 81
Conceptual purpose, 115
Conditioned response, 123
Conditioned stimulus, 123
Confounding effects, definition
  of, 40
Connectivity, 277
Constituent validity, 57
Consultants, 106–109
  advantages and disadvantages of,
    107–109
  definition of, 56
  issues related to, 107
  and research, 56–58
Consultees, 56, 106
Consumer run agency, 46
Context and environment,
  importance of, 10–11
Contraceptive use by teens,
  158–159
Control groups, in research, 25
Convenience sample, 41
Coping:
  dimensions of, 66
  schema for, 66
  with stress, 65–67, 287–288
Coping families, 67
Correlational research, 42, 43
Cost effectiveness, 80, 94
Cracks, defined, 105
Crime:
  and criminals, 205–208 (see also
    Criminal justice system)
  definitions of, 205
  reducing fear of, 211–212
Crime prevention and environment,
  217–219
Criminal justice system (see also
  Justice system):
  enforcement agencies, 212–213
  prisons, 208–210
  victims and victimization,
    210–212
Crisis intervention for victims, 220
Cultural sensitivity in research,
  55–56
Cycling of resources, 13

D

Day care, 176–180
Deinstitutionalization, 130–134
  alternatives, 137–141
  definition of, 130
  measurement of success, 135–137
  social context to, 131–134
Dementia, 128
Dementia praecox, 128
Democratic/participatory style of leadership, 283
Dependent variable, 43
Desegregation in schools, 189–190
Desensitization, 124
Design, definition of, 41
Development, 175
Diagnostic and Statistical Manual of Mental Disorders (DSM), 122
Diffusion of treatment, 40
Digital divide, 81
Direct way of coping, 66
Discrimination, definition of, 185
Discriminative stimulus, 11
Dissatisfaction with traditional services and social change, 82–83
Diversity:
  in the classroom, 186–189
  in community psychology, 298
  in health care, 239–240
  respect for, 8–10
  social change and, 77–78, 93
  in work place, 278–279
Divorce, children of, 199–200
Dogmatic individuals, 91, 110
Donor, of charity/philanthropy, 148
Dropping out of school, 194–196
Drug therapy for HIV/AIDS, 259, 263
Drug use, 252–255, 267
Drunk driving, 250–251

E

Ecological conditions in organizations, 278
Ecological perspective, 12–15
Ecological setting, 175
Economic success, disparities in opportunity for, 299–300
Ecstasy, 252
Education:
  disparities in opportunity for, 299–300
  life expectancy at age 65 by, 111
  as social change mechanism, 109
Educational change, advantages and disadvantages of, 111–112
Egocentric methodology, 47
Elderly people and social services, 163–166
Electroconvulsive therapy, 129
Emotional approach coping, 66
Emotion-focused coping, 65
Empiricism, 33
Empowerment:
  by consultants, 107
  definition of, 11–12
Endorphins, 127
Enforcement agencies, 212–213
Enrichment education, 181
Environment:
  and behavior, 11
  and crime prevention, 217–219
Environmental concerns, 298–299
Environmental psychologists, 217
Environmental tobacco smoke (ETS), 246
Epidemiological synergy, 257
Epidemiologic Catchment Area Study (ECA), 120
Epidemiology, 47–48
Equal rights, 6
Equivalency trials, 54
Ethics and research, 53–55
Ethnic minority issues, online networks for, 104
Ethnography, 44–46
Etiology of mental illness, 128
Eustress, 288
Exosystem, 13
Experimental mortality, definition of, 40
Experimental research, 42

Experiments, 25
External locus of control, 99
External pressures to change, 281
External validity of research, 40

F

Falsifiability, example of, 36
Families:
  coping, 67
  work patterns of, 86
Familismo, 161
Family Life and Sexuality Education (FLSE), 160
Fear-victimization paradox, 211
Females:
  alcohol use among, 249
  drug use and, 252
  tobacco use among, 245
Field studies, 25
First order change, 76
Fundamental attribution error, definition of, 22
Funding dilemmas for nonprofit organizations, 79–80

G

Gatekeepers, 109
Gender:
  and alcohol use, 249
  and drug use, 252
  and life expectancy, 111, 230
  and tobacco use, 245
  and victimization, 211
General adaptation syndrome (GAS), 61
Genital herpes, 256
Germ theory, 128
Globalization, and crime, 206
Global warming, 298
Goals, 49
Gonorrhea, 257
Goodness of fit, 236
Graduate programs in community psychology, 28–30
Grameen Bank model, 150
Grassroots activism, 97
Great Depression, 4
Gun violence, 205

H

Hallucinogenic drugs, 252
Hassles and stress, 62
Head Start, 7, 181–183
Health, disparities in opportunity for, 299–300
Health care:
    accessibility to, 232, 237–239
    adherence and compliance, 233–234
    and cost, 232–233
    and diversity, 239–240
    focus on groups, neighborhoods, and systems, 235–236
    national health indicators, 229–234
    prevention over remediation, 235
    rural health, 240
    social support in, 240–241
Health insurance, 232–233
Health literacy, 238
Helplessness, 99
Heroin, 252
Highly active antiretroviral therapy (HAART), 263
Homelessness, 22–23
    causes of, 169–170
    and cultural differences, 168–169
    and mental illness, 130, 135
    and poverty, 167
    and social services, 166–172
Human immunodeficiency virus (HIV):
    characteristics, 260
    community-based approaches, 264–265
    complexities and controversies, 263–264
    drug use and, 253
    immigrants with, 32
    and incarceration, 209
    prevalence, 260–263
    prevention, 267
    regional statistics, 261
    testing, 261
Humanism, 127
Humanistic model of mental health, 124–125
Human papillomavirus (HPV) vaccine, 255
Humors, 127
Hypothesis testing, 41

I

Incarceration, 208–210
    alternatives, 221–226
Incidence, 48
Independent variable (IV), 42–43
Indicated prevention programs, 18
Indirect way of coping, 66
Induced change, 88
Information dissemination and education, 109–112
Informed consent in research, 53
In-group, 91, 187
Inhalants, 252
Injection drugs, 252
Inpatient treatment for mental illness, 129
Institutionalization, alternatives to, 135
Institutional markers, establishment of, 292
Institutional review board, 53
Instrumental purpose, 115
Intensive case management (ICM), 138, 139
Interdependence, 13
Intergroup contact, 187
Internal locus of control, 99
Internal pressures to change, 281
Internal validity of research, 40
International Code of Diagnosis (ICD), 122
Interpersonal cognitive problem solving, 194
Interpersonally focused leaders, task-focused leaders *vs.*, 282
Intervention efforts in health care, 237–239
Introspection, 123

J

Jigsaw classroom, 188
Job scope, 275
Journal of Community Psychology, top 15 universities publishing in, 293
Justice system:
    at-risk behavior, 214–217
    crime and criminals, 205–208
    preventive environment, 217–219
    primary prevention, 214–217
    prisons, 208–210
    secondary prevention, 219–226
Juvenile Mentoring Program (JUMP), 215

K

Knowledge, attitudes, beliefs, and behaviors (KABBs), 261, 263, 264

L

Labeling, 124
Laissez-faire style of leadership, 283
Latino college students, and acculturation stress, social support, coping, 69
Leadership in organization, 282–283
Learned helplessness, 124
Life expectancy, by education, race, and gender, 111
Linkage to care, 261
Lobby, definition of, 115
Lobotomy, 129
Lodge Societies for mentally ill, 137–138

M

Macrosystem, 13
Magnet schools, 189
Males:
    and alcohol use, 249
    and drug use, 252
    and tobacco use, 246
Marijuana, 252, 253
Maturation, 41
Mediation:
    and crime, 221
    for victims, 221

Mediators, 83, 221
Medical model of mental health, 121–122
Mental disorders:
　famous individuals with, 136
　history of, 126–130
　model programs, 137–138
Mental health, models of, 122–125
Mental health care:
　brief history of, 126–130
　for diverse communities, 239–240
　education about, 125–126
Mental Health Parity Act, 126
Mental illness:
　epidemiological estimates of, 120–121
　and pharmacologic agents, 5
Mentor, definition of, 193, 215
Mentoring at-risk individuals, 215–217
Meridians, 127
Mesosystems, 13
Meta-analyses, definition of, 19
Methamphetamine, 252
Microaggressions, 63
Microassault, 63
Microinsult, 63
Microinvalidation, 63
Microsystem, 12
Midtown Manhattan Study of psychopathology, 121
Milestone, 50
Minority groups:
　and health disparities, 232
　and incarceration, 208–209
　and life expectancy, 229–230
Model, definition of, 35
Modern prejudice, 185
Mortality measures, world health status, 230
Multidoor approach, 84
Multiple measures in research, 55
Multiple methods, 55
Mutual assistance groups, 98

N

National Alliance for the Mentally Ill (NAMI), 141

National Association for the Advancement of Colored People (NAACP), 78
National boundaries, growing beyond, 293–294
National Cancer Institute, 246
National Drug Control Strategy 2008 Annual Report, 253
National Household Survey on Drug Use & Health (NSDUH), 245
National Institute of Mental Health (NIMH), 4, 7, 120, 141
National Mental Health Act, 4
National Training Laboratories (NTL), 7
National Victims Resource Center, 219
Needs assessment, 48–49
Neighborhood associations, 104
Neighborhood crime watches, 218
Neighborhood justice centers, 221
Neighborhoods, definition of, 24
Neighborhood Youth Services (NYS), 207
Neighboring, concept of, 24
Network analysis, methods of, 46–47
Networking, 103–106
　advantages and disadvantages of, 105–106
　issues related to, 105
Networks:
　defined, 103
　online, 104
New Deal era, 4
New homeless, 167
Nine dot problem, 77
Nomenclatures, 128
Nonequivalent pretest-posttest control design, 44
Nonprofit organizations, funding dilemmas for, 79–80

O

Ob/gyns and female population in U.S., 231
Objective, 50
Old homeless, 167

Open culture in organizations, 276
Operant conditioning, 124
Optimism, 69
Organizational behavior, definition of, 271
Organizational change, 281–282
Organizational culture, 275–277
Organizational development (OD), 271
Organizational psychology, definition of, 271
Organizational psychology and community psychology, 271–273
Outcome evaluation, 49
Outcome measures, 57
Out-group, 91, 187
Outpatient treatment for mental illness, 129
Outreach, 239
Overmanning, 10

P

Palliative care, 263
Paradigm, definition of, 35
Paradigm shift, 36
Parole, 219, 224
Participant observation, 45
Participatory decision making, 89, 284
Participatory learning, 183
Participatory research, 51–52
Patients, 124
Peace Corps, 6
Pearson correlation coefficient, 42
Personalismo, 161
Personal psychological characteristics, 60
Person and environment fit, 14
Persuasive function, 115
Pharmacologic agents, 5
Planned change, creating, 96–97
Planned social change:
　definition, 88, 94
　issues related to, 88–90
Plessy v. Ferguson, 76
Policy science, 112
Politics and science, relationship of, 52–53

Population, definition of, 41
Poverty:
    in America, 147–148
    and crime, 206
    and homelessness, 167
    and unemployment, 4
Predictive function, 115
Pregnant teens, 157–163
Prejudice:
    definition of, 185
    implicit and explicit, 64
Prescription drug misuse, 254–255
President's Emergency Plan for
    AIDS Relief (PEPFAR), 263
Pretest-posttest control group
    design, 43
Prevalence of disease or health-
    related condition, 48
Prevention:
    with at-risk individuals, 214–217
    treatment vs., 16–18
Prevention programs:
    child maltreatment, 155–157
    for the elderly, 164–166
    health care, 235
    homelessness, 170–172
    teen pregnancy, 158–162,
        238–239
Preventive medicine:
    AIDS, 264–265, 267
    alcohol, 251–252, 267
    and community health, 267
    HIV, 264–265, 267
    illicit drugs, 253–254, 267
    sexually transmitted diseases,
        257–259, 267
    tobacco, 246–249, 267
Primary appraisal, 64
Primary prevention, 19, 214–217
    definition of, 17
Prisons, 208–210
Problem solving-focused coping, 65
Process evaluation, 49
Process measures, 57
Professional change agent, 106
Program evaluation, 49
Promoting Alternative Thinking
    Strategies (PATHS), 73
Prosocial-antisocial coping, 66

Psychiatrists, 4, 125
Psychiatry, 4
Psychoanalysis (Freudian), 3,
    122–123
Psychological mediators, 60
Psychological sense of community
    (PSC), 23–25, 278
Psychopolitical literacy, 299
Psychotropic drugs, 129
Public assistance, 149
Public policy:
    advantages and disadvantages
        with, 116–117
    definition of, 112
    as means of social change,
        112–116
Public schools as social
        institutions, 184–198
    and adolescents, 190–193
    desegregation, 189–190
    diversity in, 186–189
    dropping out, 194–196
    historical context, 184
    prejudice, 185–186
    students' memories, 192
    violence, 196–198
Public welfare, definition of, 148
Purposive sample, 41

Q
Qualitative information, 45
Quality circles, 285
Quality of work life (QWL)
    programs, 284–286
Quantitative data, 45
Quasi-experimental research,
    43, 44

R
Race:
    and alcohol use, 249
    and drug use, 252
    and incarceration, 208–209
    and life expectancy, 111,
        229–230
    and mental health care, 136
Racism, 185
    implicit and explicit prejudice, 64
    and stress, 63

Radicals, rules for, 92
Random samples, 41, 43
Rape crisis centers, 113
Recidivism:
    and crime, 208
    in juvenile delinquents, 210
    in mentally ill, 136, 141
    and smoking, 289
Recidivism rates:
    of delinquents, 210
    of incarcerated, 210
Recipient, of charity/philanthropy,
    148
Rehabilitation services, 221
Reinforced behavior, 124
Reintegration programs for
    incarcerated individuals,
    223–226
Reliability of research, 39–40
Reorganizing organizations,
    283–284
Repressive culture in organizations,
    276
Research:
    methods of (see Scientific
        research methods)
    reliability, 39–40
    urgency, 52–58
Residential treatments for mentally
    ill, 138
Resilience research, four waves of,
    72–73
Resiliency, 70–73, 214
    and emotional intelligence, 298
    Kauai longitudinal studies on, 71
    useful model on, 71–72
Resources and social change, 78–79
Respecto (respect), 161
Restorative circles, 225–226
Restorative justice, definition, 221
Retribution, 208, 221
Retrospective design, 48
Role ambiguity, 274
Role conflict, 274
Role overload, 274
Rough sleepers, 168
Rules and regulations of
    organizations, 280
Rural health, 240

S

Safe Start, 217
Sample, definition of, 41
Sandwich generation, definition of, 86
Schizophrenia, 128
Schools. (*see* Public schools as social institutions)
Science and politics, relationship of, 52–53
Scientific research, process of, 34
Scientific research methods:
   characteristics of scientific research designs, 43
   correlational research, 42
   epidemiology, 47–48
   essence of, 32–37
   ethnography, 44–47
   experimental research, 42–44
   fidelity of, 39–41
   needs assessment, 48–49
   participatory research, 51–52
   population and sampling, 41–42
   program evaluation, 49–51
   quasi-experimental research, 44
   traditional, 41–44
   urgency of research, 52–58
Scientific revolutions, 36–37
Scientist-practitioner model, 126
Seatbelt use, 237
Secondary appraisal, 64
Secondary prevention, 219–226
   definition of, 18
   teen pregnancy, 162–163
Secondhand smoke, 246
Second order change, 76
Selection bias, 40
Selective prevention program, 18
Self-control, 165
Self-fulfilling prophecy, 185
Self-help groups, 98
Setting control, 11
Severely mentally ill (SMI), 137, 139
Sexually transmitted diseases (STDs), 253, 255–259, 267
   intervention program in Lima, Peru, 265
   prevalence, 255–257

   solutions and challenges, 257–259
Situational characteristics, 60
Situational mediators, 60
Situation-approaches, 61
Sliding scale fees, 79
Smart car sales personnel, 272
Smoke Free Movies Campaign, 247
Smokeless tobacco ingredients, 245
Smoking, 244–249, 289
Social activism, results of research on, 100
Social capital, 103, 158
Social change:
   and accountability, 80–81, 93
   and action research, 20–21
   and community conflict, 82, 83, 94
   and declining resources, 78–79, 93
   and desire for diversity of solutions, 83–85
   and dissatisfaction with traditional services, 82–83
   and diverse populations, 77–78, 93
   failure of, 90–93
   planned, 88–90
   reasons for and examples of, 84
   spontaneous or unplanned, 85–88
   and technological change, 81–82, 93
   types of, 85–90
Social connectedness, 236
Social disruption, 236
Social imagination, 297
Social indicators, definition of, 87
Social insurance, 149
Social integration, 136
Social interest (Adlerian), 123
Social psychologists, definition of, 22
Social Readjustment Rating Scale (SRRS), 62
Social Security system, 4

Social services:
   and child maltreatment, 151–157
   goal of, 148–149
Social support, 67–70, 98
   from coworkers, 287, 288
   effects of, 68–70
   and health, 240–241
   types of, 68
Social welfare, definition of, 148
Social workers, definition of, 126
Society for Community Research and Action, 7, 8, 9, 58
Sociometric methodology, 47
Sociopolitical control, 101
Solutions, desire for diversity of, 83–85
Spontaneous social change, definition of, 85
Spurious associations, 42
Statistics, sources for health-related, 244
Stereotypes, definition of, 185
Stigmatization of mentally ill, 129, 141
Stratified sample, 41
Strengths of individuals, enhancing, 19
Stress:
   acute *vs.* chronic, 62–63
   coping with, 65–67, 287–288
   defined, 61
   life events as sources, 62
   in organizations, 274, 287–289
   as a process, 63–64
   racism and minority status, 63
   reaction, 61–62
Stress model, and definition of community psychology, 60–61
Stressor, 61
Stress process, 61
Substance abuse and HIV/STDs, principles of community psychology, 37–39
Succession, 14
Sudden infant death syndrome (SIDS), 246
Survey-guided feedback, 282

Swampscott Conference, and birthdate of community psychology, 7
Syphilis, 256

T

Task-focused leaders, interpersonally focused leaders vs., 282
Team building in organizations, 286
Technological change and social change, 81–82, 93
Technophobia, 81
Teen pregnancy and social services, 157–163
Teen pregnancy prevention programs, 238–239
Tertiary prevention, definition of, 18
Theory, definition of, 34–35
Therapist, definition of, 126
Tobacco use, 244–249, 267
Traditional racism, 185
Transactional nature of social support, 68–69
Transactional style of leadership, 283
Transformational style of leadership, 283
Transinstitutionalization, 130. (see also Deinstitutionalization)
Treatment vs. prevention, 16–18
Triangulation, 46

U

Umbrella organizations, 104
Unconditioned stimulus, 123
Undermanning, 11
Unemployment, and crime, 206
Universal prevention program, 18
Unobtrusive measure, 55
Unplanned social change, definition of, 85, 94
Urgency of research, 52–58

V

Validity of research, 40
Victim blaming, 22
Victim-offender mediation (VOM), 221
Victims:
  assistance for, 219
  and fear of being victimized, 210–212
  interventions for, 220
Vietnam War, 6
Violence:
  media, children at risk and, 206
  in prisons, 209–210
  in schools, 196–198
  and victimization, 210–211
Volunteering, 26, 27

W

Welfare, history of, 148–151
We-ness, sense of, 295
Women:
  tobacco use among, 245
  in World War II era labor force, 4–5
Working at home, 299
Work patterns of families, 86
Workplace diversity, 278–279
Work schedule adaptations, 299
Wraparound Milwaukee, 140–141

Y

Yin and Yang and mental disorders, 127
Youth Risk Behavior Surveillance System (YRBSS), 244
Youths at risk, 214, 215

Z

Zeitgeist and mental health, 129